COBUILD
POCKET
DICTIONARY

THE UNIVERSITY
OF BIRMINGHAM

COLLINS
COBUILD

first published in this edition 1996
second edition 2000

© HarperCollins Publishers 1996, 2000

ISBN 0-00-710023-X

www.cobuild.collins.co.uk

Editorial Director
Michela Clari

Lexicographers
Bob Grossmith
with
Ian Brookes, Mary O'Neill
Maree Airlie

Project Coordinator
Joyce Littlejohn

Computing Staff
Stewart C Russell

Series Editor
Lorna Sinclair Knight

A catalogue record for this book is available from the British Library

*Based on The COBUILD Series, developed in collaboration
with the University of Birmingham*

Typeset by Stewart C Russell and Carol MacLeod

*Printed and bound by
Thomson Press (India) Ltd*

The **Collins Pocket Cobuild English Dictionary** is a completely
new concept in small dictionaries. Based on the highly popular
Cobuild Series, it is a welcome addition to the best-selling range of
Collins Pocket dictionaries.

Specially written for learners of English, this dictionary contains the
most important words in English, all defined in clear and simple
language, and in colour for ease of reference. Every meaning of
every word is illustrated by a phrase or sentence from the Bank of
English to help the learner use natural English with total confidence.

When a word has more than one meaning, each definition is
introduced by a number. When definitions contain important
expressions or phrases, these have been shown in darker print to
help you identify them. All these expressions are illustrated by
examples:

> **2** If you **look for** someone or
> something, you try to find them.
> EG *I'm looking for my keys.*

Usage notes provide clear help with common problems encountered when learning English and help you avoid making mistakes:

> ☑ The usual plural of 'person' is
> *people. Persons* is only used in very
> formal English.

Special entries clearly explain basic English grammatical concepts:

> When people talk about the **object**
> of a verb or of a sentence, they
> mean the person or thing that is
> affected by the action, rather than
> the person or thing that does it.
> EG *The cat chased **a mouse**.*

continued ⅢⅢ➡

At the top of most entries you will see other forms of the word. These are given to help you to find the correct form of a noun, verb or adjective:

NOUNS

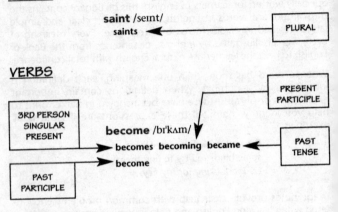

saint /seɪnt/
saints ← PLURAL

VERBS

3RD PERSON SINGULAR PRESENT

PRESENT PARTICIPLE

become /bɪˈkʌm/
becomes becoming became
become

PAST TENSE

PAST PARTICIPLE

ADJECTIVES

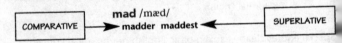

COMPARATIVE →
mad /mæd/
madder maddest ← SUPERLATIVE

The clear and attractive layout will guide you quickly to the relevant entry. There is also a set of tables at the back of the book to help you with numbers and irregular verbs.

The **Collins Pocket Cobuild English Dictionary** is an essential communication tool for learners of English all over the world.

Aa

a /ə/

ARTICLE

The word 'a' is called the 'indefinite article'. You use it before a singular noun or to avoid saying precisely which person or thing you mean.

EG *A waiter entered with a tray.*

☑ The word 'an' is used instead of 'a' when the next word begins with a vowel sound (*a, e, i, o, u*): *an elephant; an aeroplane.*

abandon /əˈbændən/
abandons abandoning abandoned

VERB

If you abandon someone or something, you leave them or give them up for good.

EG *His parents had abandoned him.*

abbreviation /əbriːvɪˈeɪʃən/
abbreviations

NOUN

a short form of a word or phrase

EG *EU is an abbreviation of European Union.*

ability /əˈbɪlɪtɪ/
abilities

NOUN

the intelligence or skill needed to do something

EG *... his ability to do the job*

EG *... children of mixed abilities*

able /ˈeɪbl/

ADJECTIVE

If you are **able to do** something, you can do it.

EG *The frog is able to jump 3 metres.*

aboard /əˈbɔːd/

PREPOSITION OR ADVERB

on a ship or plane

EG *She invited 750 people aboard the luxury yacht.*

EG *The plane crashed, killing all 271 aboard.*

abortion /əˈbɔːʃən/
abortions

NOUN

If a woman has an abortion, the pregnancy is ended deliberately.

EG *She's had two abortions.*

about /əˈbaʊt/

PREPOSITION

1 of or concerning

EG *... a book about London*

2 approximately and not exactly

EG *... about 2 o'clock*

ADVERB OR PREPOSITION

3 in different directions

EG *The kids ran about in the garden.*

EG *There were bottles scattered about the room.*

ADJECTIVE

4 present or in a place

EG *Is Carol about?*

5 If you are **about to do** something, you are just going to do it.

EG *He was about to leave.*

above /əˈbʌv/

PREPOSITION OR ADVERB

1 directly over or higher than something

EG *... above the clouds*

EG *... as seen from above*

2 greater than a level or amount

EG *The temperature didn't rise above freezing point.*

EG *... children of 12 and above*

abroad /əˈbrɔːd/

ADVERB

in a foreign country
EG *He's abroad at the moment.*

absence /'æbsəns/
absences

NOUN

Someone's or something's absence from a place is the fact that they are not there.
EG *Jane looked after the children during my absence.*

absent /'æbsənt/

ADJECTIVE

Someone or something that is absent is not present in a place or situation.
EG *He has been absent from his desk for two weeks.*

absolute /'æbsəlu:t/

ADJECTIVE

total and complete
EG *... absolute honesty*

absolutely /æbsə'lu:tlɪ/

ADVERB

totally and completely
EG *She is absolutely right.*

absorb /əb'zɔ:b/
absorbs absorbing absorbed

VERB

If something absorbs liquid or gas, it soaks it up.
EG *Plants absorb moisture from the soil.*

abstract /'æbstrækt/

ADJECTIVE

Abstract things are based on thoughts and ideas rather than physical objects or events.
EG *... starting with a few abstract principles*

absurd /əb'sɜ:d/

ADJECTIVE

ridiculous and stupid

EG *That's absurd.*

abuse /ə'bju:s/
abuses abusing abused

NOUN

1 Abuse is cruel treatment of someone.
EG *... child abuse*

2 Abuse is rude and unkind remarks directed towards someone.
EG *... a torrent of abuse*

3 The abuse of something is the use of it in the wrong way.
EG *... alcohol abuse*

VERB : /ə'bju:z/

☑ Note that you pronounce the verb differently from the noun.

4 If someone abuses someone else, they treat them cruelly.
EG *She had been sexually abused by her father since she was 11.*

5 If you abuse someone, you speak insultingly to them.
EG *They abused the workmen in the foulest language.*

6 If you abuse something, you use it wrongly or for a bad purpose.
EG *It is important not to abuse your position.*

academic /ækə'dɛmɪk/

ADJECTIVE

Academic work is work done in a school, college, or university.
EG *Their academic standards are high.*

accelerator /æk'sɛləreɪtəʳ/
accelerators

NOUN

the pedal in a vehicle which you press to make it go faster
EG *He took his foot off the accelerator.*

accent /'æksɛnt/
accents

NOUN

1 a way of pronouncing a language

EG *She had an Australian accent.*

2 a mark placed above or below a letter in some languages, which affects the way the letter is pronounced

EG *There's an accent missing from the "e".*

accept /ək'sɛpt/
accepts accepting accepted

VERB

1 If you accept something, you say yes to it or take it from someone.

EG *Eventually she accepted his offer of marriage.*

EG *He refused to accept any money for it.*

2 If you accept a situation, you realize that it cannot be changed.

EG *He accepts criticism as part of his job.*

3 If you accept a statement or story, you believe it is true.

EG *The board accepted his explanation.*

4 If a group accepts you, they treat you as one of the group.

EG *It was many weeks before he was accepted by the other members of the group.*

acceptable /ək'sɛptəbl/

ADJECTIVE

If something is acceptable, people approve of it or allow it to happen.

EG *It is becoming more acceptable for women to drink.*

EG *... acceptable levels of pollution*

access /'æksɛs/

NOUN

Access is the right or opportunity to use something or to enter a place.

EG *The hotel offers easy access to*

central London.

accident /'æksɪdənt/
accidents

NOUN

1 an unexpected event in which something unfortunate happens

EG *She had an accident at work and broke her arm.*

EG *... a road accident*

2 Something that happens **by accident** happens without being intended.

EG *He knocked over the jug by accident.*

accidental /æksɪ'dɛntl/

ADJECTIVE

happening by chance

EG *The fire was accidental.*

accommodation
/əkɒmə'deɪʃən/

NOUN

Accommodation is a place provided for someone to stay or live in.

EG *He found accommodation on the outskirts of the city.*

☑ The usual American word is 'accommodations': *luxury accommodations are also available.*

accompany /ə'kʌmpənɪ/
accompanies accompanying accompanied

VERB

1 If you accompany someone, you go with them.

EG *He offered to accompany me to the airport.*

2 If one thing accompanies another, the two things exist at the same time.

EG *... severe pain accompanied by fever*

accord /ə'kɔːd/

NOUN

If you do something **of your own accord**, you do it willingly and not because you have been forced to do it.
EG *He left the country of his own accord.*

according to

PREPOSITION

1 If something is true according to a particular person, that person says that it is true.
EG *He stayed at the hotel, according to his brother.*

2 If something is done according to a principle or plan, that principle or plan is used as the basis for it.
EG *If all goes according to plan, the concert will be on Tuesday.*

account /əˈkaunt/
accounts accounting accounted

NOUN

1 a written or spoken report of something
EG *There were accounts of the incident in the paper.*

2 If you have an account or a **bank account**, you can leave money in the bank and take it out when you need it.
EG *I'd like to open an account.*

3 If you **take** something **into account**, you include it in your planning.
EG *Urban planners have to take many different factors into account.*

4 on account of means because of
EG *He couldn't read the speech himself, on account of a sore throat.*

PLURAL NOUN

5 accounts are records of money spent and received by a person or business

EG *He kept detailed accounts.*

account for

VERB

1 If someone or something accounts for something, they explain it.
EG *This might account for her strange behaviour.*

2 If something accounts for a particular amount of something, it is that amount.
EG *The brain accounts for three per cent of body weight.*

accountant /əˈkauntənt/
accountants

NOUN

a person whose job is to keep or inspect financial accounts
EG *He's an accountant with a big law firm.*

accurate /ˈækjurɪt/

ADJECTIVE

completely correct or precise
EG *... an accurate description of the killer*

accuse /əˈkjuːz/
accuses accusing accused

VERB

If you **accuse** someone **of doing** something wrong, you say they have done it.
EG *He accused her of having an affair.*

ache /eɪk/
aches aching ached

VERB

1 If a part of your body aches, you feel a continuous dull pain there.
EG *My leg still aches when I sit down.*

NOUN

2 a continuous dull pain
EG *... an effective remedy for aches and pains*

achieve /ə'tʃiːv/
achieves achieving achieved

VERB

If you achieve something, you successfully do it or cause it to happen.

EG *We have achieved what we set out to do.*

achievement /ə'tʃiːvmənt/
achievements

NOUN

something which you succeed in doing, especially after a lot of effort

EG *… a celebration of women's achievements*

acid /'æsɪd/
acids

NOUN

a chemical liquid that can damage skin, cloth, and metal

EG *… sulphuric acid*

acknowledge /ək'nɒlɪdʒ/
acknowledges
acknowledging
acknowledged

VERB

1 If you acknowledge a fact or situation, you agree or admit that it is true.

EG *He acknowledged that he was a drug addict.*

2 If you acknowledge a message, you tell the person who sent it that you have received it.

EG *The army sent me a postcard acknowledging my request.*

acquaintance /ə'kweɪntəns/
acquaintances

NOUN

someone you know slightly but not well

EG *He's an old acquaintance of mine.*

acquire /ə'kwaɪəʳ/

acquires acquiring acquired

VERB

If you acquire something, you get it.

EG *I've recently acquired a new computer.*

acquit /ə'kwɪt/
acquits acquitting acquitted

VERB

If someone **is acquitted of** a crime, they have been tried in a court and found not guilty.

EG *He was acquitted of murder but found guilty of manslaughter.*

acre /'eɪkəʳ/
acres

NOUN

An acre is a unit for measuring areas of land. One acre is equal to 4840 square yards or about 4047 square metres.

EG *The property is set in two acres of land.*

across /ə'krɒs/

PREPOSITION OR ADVERB

1 If someone goes across a place, they go from one side of it to the other.

EG *He walked across Hyde Park.*

EG *… as she ran across to the window*

2 Something that is situated across a road or river is on the other side of it.

EG *… the houses across the street*

EG *… the people who live across from us*

act /ækt/
acts acting acted

VERB

1 If you act, you do something.

EG *We have to act quickly.*

2 If you act in a particular way, you behave in that way.

EG *You're acting like a lunatic.*

3 If a person or thing **acts as** something else, it has the function or does the job of that thing.
EG *She was able to act as an interpreter.*

4 If you act in a play or film, you play a role in it.
EG *She told her parents about her desire to act.*

NOUN
5 a single thing that someone does
EG *... acts of sabotage*

6 An **Act** is a law passed by the government.
EG *... the 1944 Education Act*

action /'ækʃən/
actions

NOUN
something you do for a particular purpose or on a particular occasion
EG *He had a reason for his action.*
EG *The government must take action now.*

active /'æktɪv/

ADJECTIVE
Someone who is active moves around a lot or does a lot of things.
EG *How physically active are you?*

activity /æk'tɪvɪtɪ/
activities

NOUN
1 Activity is a situation in which a lot of things are happening at the same time.
EG *... periods of high economic activity*

2 something you do for pleasure
EG *... sport and leisure activities*

actor /'æktər/
actors

NOUN
a man or woman whose job is performing in plays or films

EG *You have to be a good actor to play that part.*

actress /'æktrɪs/
actresses

NOUN
a woman whose job is performing in plays or films
EG *She's a great dramatic actress.*

actual /'æktjuəl/

ADJECTIVE
real or genuine rather than imagined or supposed
EG *That is the official figure: the actual figure is much higher.*

actually /'æktjuəlɪ/

ADVERB
1 really
EG *No one actually saw the shark.*

2 in fact
EG *She's a friend of mine actually.*

AD
You use AD to refer to a date after the year in which Jesus Christ is believed to have been born.
EG *... in 1136 AD*

ad /æd/
ads

NOUN
an advert
EG *She replied to an ad in the Times.*

adapt /ə'dæpt/
adapts adapting adapted

VERB
1 If you **adapt to** a new situation, you change so that you can deal with it successfully.
EG *... a book about change and how we adapt to it*

2 If you adapt something, you change it so that it is suitable for a new purpose or situation.
EG *The library was adapted for use as an office.*

A
B
C
D
E
F
G
H
I
J
K
L
M
N
O
P
Q
R
S
T
U
V
W
X
Y
Z

add /æd/
adds adding added

VERB

1 If you **add** something **to** a number of things, you put it with the other things.
EG *Each boy added more wood to the pile.*

2 If you **add** numbers **together** or **add** them **up**, you calculate the total.
EG *Two and three added together are five.*
EG *Add up the following figures.*

addict /ˈædɪkt/
addicts

NOUN

someone who cannot stop taking harmful drugs
EG *... a heroin addict*

addition /əˈdɪʃən/
additions

NOUN

1 something that has been added to something else
EG *... a fine addition to London's architecture*

2 You use **in addition to** to mention another item that is connected with what you are discussing.
EG *There's a postage fee in addition to the repair charge.*

additional /əˈdɪʃənl/

ADJECTIVE

extra or more
EG *They made the decision to take on additional staff.*

address /əˈdrɛs/
addresses addressing addressed

NOUN

1 the number of the house where you live, together with the name of the street and the town or village
EG *What's your address?*
EG *My address is 57 Castle Road, Whitstable.*

VERB

2 If a letter is **addressed to** you, it has your name and address written on it.
EG *... a letter addressed to Dr Jones*

3 If you address a group of people, you give a speech to them.
EG *He addressed a mass meeting in Bristol.*

adequate /ˈædɪkwɪt/

ADJECTIVE

If something is adequate, there is enough of it or it is good enough.
EG *... an amount adequate to buy another house*
EG *... an adequate diet*

adjective /ˈædʒɛktɪv/
adjectives

NOUN

An **adjective** is a word that tells you something about a noun. Adjectives may describe such things as size, colour, material, or nationality.
EG *... a **large** envelope*
EG *... **red** socks*
EG *... a **wooden** box*
EG *... my **Indian** cousin*
Adjectives usually come before nouns.

adjust /əˈdʒʌst/
adjusts adjusting adjusted

VERB

1 If you adjust something, you change its position or alter it in some other way.
EG *She adjusted the lamp so that it pointed at the ceiling.*

A
B
C
D
E
F
G
H
I
J
K
L
M
N
O
P
Q
R
S
T
U
V
W
X
Y
Z

2 If you **adjust to** a new situation, you get used to it.
EG *She has adjusted well to becoming a mother.*

administration /ədmɪnɪs'treɪʃən/
administrations

NOUN
1 Administration is the work of organizing and supervising an organization.
EG *Too much time is spent on administration.*
2 The administration is the group of people that manages an organization or a country.
EG *… the Clinton administration*

admire /əd'maɪər/
admires admiring admired

VERB
If you admire someone or something, you respect and approve of them.
EG *He admired the way she had coped with life.*

admission /əd'mɪʃən/

NOUN
Admission or an **admission fee** is the amount of money you pay to enter a place.
EG *The sign said "admission free".*

admit /əd'mɪt/
admits admitting admitted

VERB
1 If you admit something, or if you **admit to** it, you agree, often reluctantly, that it is true.
EG *The Vice President admitted to taking bribes.*
2 If you **admit** someone or something **to** a place or organization, you allow them to enter it.
EG *Journalists are rarely admitted to the region.*

adolescent /ædəʊ'lɛsnt/

ADJECTIVE
Adolescent is used to describe young people who are no longer children but who are not yet adults.
EG *… an adolescent boy*

adopt /ə'dɒpt/
adopts adopting adopted

VERB
1 If you adopt a child, you take him or her into your family as your son or daughter.
EG *There are hundreds of people desperate to adopt a child.*
2 If you adopt a particular attitude, you start to have it.
EG *Pupils should be helped to adopt a positive approach to the environment.*

adult /'ædʌlt/
adults

NOUN
a mature and fully developed person or animal
EG *Children under 14 must be accompanied by an adult.*

advance /əd'vɑːns/
advances advancing advanced

VERB
1 If someone or something advances, they move forward.
EG *Rebel forces are advancing on the capital.*

NOUN
2 An advance is progress in a particular area.
EG *… scientific advances*
3 If you do something **in advance**, you do it before something else happens.
EG *We booked the room well in advance.*

ADJECTIVE

4 Advance booking or warning is done or given before an event.
EG *The event received little advance publicity.*

advanced /əd'vɑːnst/
ADJECTIVE
An advanced student has learned the basic facts of a subject and is doing more difficult work.
EG *The course is suitable for both beginners and advanced students.*

advantage /əd'vɑːntɪdʒ/
advantages
NOUN
1 a benefit or something that puts you in a better position
EG *She explained the advantages of the new system over the old one.*
2 If you **take advantage of** someone, you treat them unfairly for your own benefit.
EG *She took advantage of him even after they were divorced.*
3 If you **take advantage of** something, you make use of it.
EG *I intend to take full advantage of this trip to buy the things we need.*

adventure /əd'ventʃər/
adventures
NOUN
an event that is unusual and exciting
EG *... my Arctic adventures*

adverb /'ædvɜːb/
adverbs
NOUN
An **adverb** is a word that tells you something about a verb. Adverbs tell you how, where, when, or how often something happens.
EG *She runs **quickly**.*
EG *I live **here**.*
EG *I arrived **yesterday**.*

EG *We **sometimes** meet for lunch.*
Most adverbs are formed by adding -ly to an adjective: *badly; carefully*. However some adverbs have the same form as adjectives: *fast; late*. Adverbs usually come after a verb, or after an object if there is one.

advert /'ædvɜːt/
adverts
NOUN
an announcement, for example in a newspaper or on television, that tells people about a product, an event, or a job
EG *... an advert for whisky*

advertise /'ædvətaɪz/
advertises advertising advertised
VERB
1 If you advertise something, you tell people about it, for example in a newspaper or on television.
EG *The house was advertised for sale at $149,000.*
2 If you advertise, you make an announcement, for example in a newspaper or on television.
EG *We advertised for staff in a local newspaper.*

advice /əd'vaɪs/
NOUN
If you give someone advice, you tell them what you think they should do.
EG *I gave him advice on how to do it.*
☑ If you want to talk about one particular thing that you advise someone, you say 'a piece of advice': *that's a good piece of advice.*

advise /əd'vaɪz/
advises advising advised
VERB

If you **advise** someone **to do** something, you tell them you think they should do it.
EG *She advised him to leave as soon as possible.*

aerial /'eəriəl/
aerials
NOUN
a piece of wire for receiving television or radio signals
EG *… a television aerial*

aeroplane /'eərəpleɪn/
aeroplanes
NOUN
a vehicle with wings and engines that enable it to fly
EG *We watched the aeroplanes landing and taking off.*

affair /ə'feər/
affairs
NOUN
1 an event or series of events
EG *The funeral was a sad affair.*
2 If two people who are not married to each other **have an affair**, they have a sexual relationship.
EG *He had an affair with his secretary.*
PLURAL NOUN
3 Your **affairs** are your private and personal life.
EG *Why had he interfered in her affairs?*

affect /ə'fekt/
affects affecting affected
VERB
When something affects someone or something, it causes them to change.
EG *… the ways in which computers affect our lives*

affection /ə'fekʃən/
NOUN

Affection is a feeling of love and fondness for someone.
EG *She had no affection for him.*

afford /ə'fɔːd/
affords affording afforded
VERB
1 If you cannot afford something, you do not have enough money to pay for it.
EG *I can't afford a new car.*
2 If you cannot afford something to happen, it would be harmful or embarrassing for you if it happened.
EG *We can't afford another scandal in the firm.*

afraid /ə'freɪd/
ADJECTIVE
1 If you are **afraid of** someone or **afraid to do** something, you are frightened because you think that something unpleasant is going to happen.
EG *I was afraid of the other boys.*
EG *She's afraid to go out alone.*
2 If you are **afraid** that something might happen, you are worried that it might happen.
EG *I was afraid that nobody would believe me.*

Africa /'æfrɪkə/
NOUN
Africa is the second largest continent and lies to the south of Europe.
EG *… a hat bought in Africa*

African /'æfrɪkən/
Africans
ADJECTIVE
1 belonging or relating to Africa
EG *… most African countries*
NOUN
2 someone who comes from Africa
EG *… a tall, quiet African*

after /'ɑːftəʳ/

PREPOSITION OR ADVERB

1 later than a particular time, date, or event

EG … *just after breakfast*

EG *Soon after, he went to work.*

PREPOSITION

2 If you come after someone or something, you are behind them and following them.

EG *They ran after her.*

3 If you are after someone or something, you are trying to find someone or get something.

EG *The police are after him.*

EG *He's after my job.*

afternoon /ˌɑːftə'nuːn/
afternoons

NOUN

the part of the day between 12 noon and about six o'clock

EG *He's arriving in the afternoon.*

afterwards /'ɑːftəwədz/

ADVERB

after an event or time

EG *He was taken to hospital but died soon afterwards.*

again /ə'gen/

ADVERB

happening one more time

EG *He looked forward to seeing her again.*

EG *I'll never go there again.*

against /ə'genst/

PREPOSITION

1 touching and leaning on

EG *He leaned against the wall.*

2 in opposition to

EG … *the match against England*

EG *He was against the war.*

age /eɪdʒ/
ages ageing or **aging aged**

NOUN

1 The age of something or

someone is the number of years they have lived or existed.

EG … *a boy ten years of age*

EG *At the age of 16 he left home.*

2 Age is the quality of being old.

EG … *a wine that improves with age*

3 a particular period in history

EG … *the Iron Age*

PLURAL NOUN

4 AN INFORMAL USE

ages means a very long time

EG *He's been talking for ages.*

VERB

5 If you age, you grow old or appear older.

EG *He seemed to have aged a lot recently.*

agency /'eɪdʒənsɪ/
agencies

NOUN

an organization or business which provides certain services

EG … *a detective agency*

agent /'eɪdʒənt/
agents

NOUN

1 someone who arranges work or business for other people, especially actors or singers

EG … *a theatrical agent*

2 someone who works for their country's secret service

EG … *an enemy agent*

aggressive /ə'gresɪv/

ADJECTIVE

hostile and violent

EG *Some children are much more aggressive than others.*

ago /ə'gəʊ/

ADVERB

in the past

EG *She bought her flat three years ago.*

☑ You only use 'ago' when you

A
B
C
D
E
F
G
H
I
J
K
L
M
N
O
P
Q
R
S
T
U
V
W
X
Y
Z

are talking about a period of time measured back from the present. If you are talking about a period measured back from some earlier time, you use 'before' or 'previously': *she had died a month before.*

agony /ˈægənɪ/

NOUN

very great physical or mental pain

EG *The blow made him scream in agony.*

agree /əˈgriː/

agrees agreeing agreed

VERB

1 If you **agree with** someone, you have the same opinion as them.

EG *I'm not sure I agree with you.*

EG *We both agreed there was a problem.*

2 If you **agree to do** something, you say you will do it.

EG *He agreed to pay me for the drawings.*

agreement /əˈgriːmənt/

agreements

NOUN

a decision that has been reached by two or more people

EG *No agreement was reached on the question of compensation.*

agriculture /ˈægrɪkʌltʃər/

NOUN

Agriculture refers to the methods used to look after crops and animals.

EG *... the importance of agriculture in the European economy*

ahead /əˈhɛd/

ADVERB

1 in front

EG *He looked ahead.*

2 If you are **ahead of** someone,

you are in front of them.

EG *I walked ahead of her into the house.*

3 If you are **ahead of** someone, you are more advanced than them.

EG *We are five years ahead of the competition.*

4 in the future

EG *I haven't had time to think far ahead.*

aid /eɪd/

aids

NOUN

1 Aid is money, equipment, or services provided for people in need.

EG *... food and medical aid*

2 Aid is help or support.

EG *... a report compiled with the aid of experts*

3 something that makes a task easier

EG *... teaching aids*

AIDS /eɪdz/

NOUN

AIDS is a disease which destroys the body's immune system.

EG *... the search for a vaccine against AIDS*

aim /eɪm/

aims aiming aimed

VERB

1 If you **aim** an object or weapon **at** someone or something, you point it at them.

EG *... a missile aimed at the arms factory*

2 If you **aim to do** something, you are planning or hoping to do it.

EG *I aim to arrive early.*

NOUN

3 Your aim is what you intend to achieve.

EG *The aim of the festival is to*

increase awareness of Hindu culture.

air /ɛəʳ/

NOUN

1 Air is the mixture of gases which we breathe and which forms the earth's atmosphere.

EG *… a blast of cold air*

2 the air is the space around things or above the ground

EG *The troops fired their guns into the air.*

3 You use 'air' to refer to travel in aircraft.

EG *I have to travel by air a great deal.*

aircraft /'ɛəkrɑːft/

☑ The plural is *aircraft*.

NOUN

any vehicle which can fly

EG *Three military aircraft were destroyed.*

airline /'ɛəlaɪn/
airlines

NOUN

a company which provides air travel

EG *… the Belgian national airline*

airmail /'ɛəmeɪl/

NOUN

the system of sending letters and parcels by air

EG *Goods are generally sent by airmail.*

airplane /'ɛəpleɪn/
airplanes

NOUN

In American English, an airplane is a vehicle with wings and engines that enable it to fly.

EG *… a passenger airplane*

☑ The usual British spelling is *aeroplane*.

airport /'ɛəpɔːt/
airports

NOUN

a place where people go to catch planes

EG *… after landing at Heathrow Airport*

aisle /aɪl/
aisles

NOUN

a long, narrow gap that people can walk along between rows of seats or shelves

EG *He chose an aisle seat.*

alarm /ə'lɑːm/
alarms alarming alarmed

NOUN

1 Alarm is a feeling of fear and worry.

EG *The cat sprang back in alarm.*

2 an automatic device that warns people of something

EG *… a car alarm*

VERB

3 If something alarms you, it makes you worried and anxious.

EG *We couldn't see what had alarmed him.*

alarm clock **alarm clocks**

NOUN

a clock that can be set to make a noise at a certain time to wake you up

EG *I set my alarm clock for 4.30.*

album /'ælbəm/
albums

NOUN

1 a CD, cassette, or record with a number of songs on it

EG *… the Beatles' final album*

2 a book in which you keep a collection of things such as photographs or stamps

EG *… a photograph album*

alcohol /'ælkəhɒl/

NOUN

Alcohol is any drink that can make people drunk.

EG *No alcohol is allowed on the premises.*

alcoholic /ælkə'hɒlɪk/
alcoholics

ADJECTIVE

1 An alcoholic drink contains alcohol.

EG *… whisky and other alcoholic beverages*

NOUN

2 someone who is addicted to alcohol

EG *He finally admitted that he was an alcoholic.*

alert /ə'lɜːt/
alerts alerting alerted

ADJECTIVE

1 Someone who is alert is paying full attention to what is happening.

EG *The criminal was spotted by an alert member of the public.*

VERB

2 If you **alert** someone **to** a problem or danger, you warn them of it.

EG *He wanted to alert people to the activities of the group.*

alien /'eɪlɪən/
aliens

ADJECTIVE

1 not part of your normal experience

EG *… a totally alien culture*

NOUN

2 In science fiction, an alien is a creature from outer space.

EG *… aliens with huge black eyes*

alike /ə'laɪk/

ADJECTIVE

1 People or things that are alike are very similar in some way.

EG *The sisters were remarkably alike in appearance.*

ADVERB

2 If people or things are treated alike, they are treated the same.

EG *The children are all treated alike.*

alive /ə'laɪv/

ADJECTIVE

Someone who is alive is living.

EG *She doesn't know if he is alive or dead.*

EG *He stayed alive by digging a hole in the snow.*

all /ɔːl/

ADJECTIVE, PRONOUN OR ADVERB

1 You use 'all' to refer to the whole of something.

EG *Why did he have to say all that?*

EG *She managed to finish it all.*

EG *It was all quiet.*

ADVERB

2 You use 'all' to indicate that the two sides in a game or contest have the same score…

EG *The final score was six points all.*

allergic /ə'lɜːdʒɪk/

ADJECTIVE

If you are **allergic to** something, you become ill when you eat it or touch it.

EG *I'm allergic to cats.*

alley /'ælɪ/
alleys

NOUN

a narrow passage between buildings

EG *There was a fight going on in the alley.*

allow /ə'laʊ/
allows allowing allowed

VERB

1 If you allow something, you say it is all right or let it happen.

EG *He allowed me to take the course.*

2 If you allow a period of time or an amount of something, you set it aside for a particular purpose.
EG *Allow four hours for the paint to dry.*

allowance /əˈlauəns/
allowances

NOUN

money that is given regularly to someone for a particular purpose
EG *She gets an allowance for looking after Lillian.*

all right

ADJECTIVE

1 If something is all right, it is satisfactory but not especially good.
EG *"Do you like the champagne?" — "It's all right"*

2 If someone is all right, they are safe and not harmed.
EG *Are you all right?*

3 You say 'all right' to agree to something.
EG *"Can you help?" — "All right"*

almost /ˈɔːlməust/

ADVERB

not completely but very nearly
EG *His salary has almost doubled.*
EG *They have been married for almost two years.*

alone /əˈləun/

ADJECTIVE OR ADVERB

1 not with other people or things
EG *He just wanted to be alone.*
EG *She lives alone.*

2

ADVERB

If one person or thing alone does something, only one person or thing is involved.
EG *He alone knew the code.*

along /əˈlɒŋ/

PREPOSITION

1 moving, happening, or situated continuously from one end of something to the other
EG *We walked along the road.*
EG *Bookcases stretched along each wall.*

ADVERB

2 moving forward
EG *We marched along.*

3 all along means from the beginning of a period of time until now
EG *You've known that all along.*

4 If you take or bring someone or something along, you take or bring them with you.
EG *Why don't you bring her along?*

alongside /əlɒŋˈsaɪd/

PREPOSITION OR ADVERB

1 next to
EG *They had a house in the park alongside the river.*
EG *He waited for a car to pull up alongside.*

PREPOSITION

2 together with
EG *He was thrilled to work alongside Robert De Niro.*

aloud /əˈlaud/

ADVERB

When you read or speak aloud, you speak loudly enough for other people to hear you.
EG *When we were children, our father read aloud to us.*

alphabet /ˈælfəbet/
alphabets

NOUN

a set of letters in a fixed order that is used in writing a language
EG *The modern Russian alphabet has 31 letters.*

already /ɔːlˈredɪ/

ADVERB

A
B
C
D
E
F
G
H
I
J
K
L
M
N
O
P
Q
R
S
T
U
V
W
X
Y
Z

If something has already happened, it has happened before the present time or earlier than expected.

EG *She has already gone to bed.*
EG *He was already rich.*

alright /ɔːlˈraɪt/
another spelling of **all right**

also /ˈɔːlsəʊ/

ADVERB
in addition to something that has just been mentioned

EG *He's a singer and also an actor.*
EG *Two other people were also injured.*

☑ 'Also' and 'too' are similar in meaning. 'Also' never comes at the end of a clause, whereas 'too' usually comes at the end: *He's a singer and an actor too.*

alter /ˈɔːltər/
alters altering altered

VERB
If something alters or if you alter it, it changes.

EG *Little had altered in the village.*
EG *This doesn't alter the fact that …*

alternative /ɔːlˈtɜːnətɪv/
alternatives

NOUN
1 something you can do or have instead of something else

EG *Are there alternatives to prison?*
EG *There was no alternative, we had to walk.*

ADJECTIVE
2 Alternative plans or actions can happen or be done instead of what is already happening or being done.

EG *There were alternative methods of travel available.*

although /ɔːlˈðəʊ/

CONJUNCTION

You use 'although' to say something that contrasts with something else you are saying.

EG *He wasn't well-known in America, although he did make a film there.*

altogether /ˌɔːltəˈɡɛðər/

ADVERB
1 entirely

EG *She wasn't altogether sorry to be leaving.*

2 in total; used of amounts

EG *I get paid 1000 pounds a month altogether.*

always /ˈɔːlweɪz/

ADVERB
1 all the time

EG *He's always late.*

2 forever

EG *I'll always love her.*

am /æm/
the first person singular, present tense of **be**

☑ *I am* is often shortened to *I'm*: *I'm twelve years old.*

a.m.
a.m. is used after a number between one and twelve to refer to times between midnight and noon

EG *I get up at 6 a.m.*

amateur /ˈæmətər/
amateurs

NOUN
someone who does something as a hobby rather than as a job

EG *He began playing football as an amateur.*

amazing /əˈmeɪzɪŋ/

ADJECTIVE
very surprising or remarkable

EG *New York is an amazing city.*

ambassador /æmˈbæsədər/

ambassadors

NOUN

a person sent to a foreign country as the representative of his or her own government

EG ... the German ambassador to Poland

ambition /æmˈbɪʃən/
ambitions

NOUN

If you have an ambition to achieve something, you want very much to achieve it.

EG Her ambition was to be a teacher.

ambitious /æmˈbɪʃəs/

ADJECTIVE

1 Someone who is ambitious has a strong desire for success, power, or wealth.

EG ... a very ambitious politician

2 An ambitious plan is a large one which requires a lot of work.

EG The project is extremely ambitious.

ambulance /ˈæmbjuləns/
ambulances

NOUN

a vehicle for taking sick and injured people to hospital

EG He was taken to hospital by ambulance.

America /əˈmɛrɪkə/

NOUN

America refers to the United States of America.

EG ... a trip to America

American /əˈmɛrɪkən/
Americans

ADJECTIVE

1 belonging or relating to the United States of America

EG ... American movies

NOUN

2 someone who comes from the United States of America

EG The prize was won by two Americans.

ammunition /æmjuˈnɪʃən/

NOUN

Ammunition is anything that can be fired from a gun or other weapon, for example bullets and shells.

EG He had only seven rounds of ammunition left.

among /əˈmʌŋ/
or **amongst** /əˈmʌŋst/

PREPOSITION

1 surrounded by

EG ... a garden set among pools and waterfalls

2 in the company of

EG He was among friends.

3 between more than two

EG The money will be divided among seven charities.

☑ If there are more than two people or things, you should use 'among'. If there are only two people or things you should use 'between'. 'Amongst' is a bit old-fashioned.

amount /əˈmaʊnt/
amounts amounting amounted

NOUN

1 An **amount** of something is how much there is of it, or how much you have or need.

EG I still do a certain amount of work for them.

EG You don't have to pay the full amount just now.

VERB

2 If something **amounts** to a particular total, all the parts of it add up to that total.

EG Her vocabulary amounted to

A
B
C
D
E
F
G
H
I
J
K
L
M
N
O
P
Q
R
S
T
U
V
W
X
Y
Z

only 50 words.

ample /'æmpl/

ADJECTIVE

If there is an ample amount of something, there is more than enough of it.
EG *There'll be ample opportunity to relax and swim.*

amusing /ə'mju:zɪŋ/

ADJECTIVE

Someone or something that is amusing makes you laugh or smile.
EG *He could be very amusing at times.*

an /æn, ən/

ARTICLE

The word 'an' is called the 'indefinite article'. It is used instead of 'a' in front of words that begin with a vowel sound (a, e, i, o, u).
EG *... an apple*

analyse /'ænəlaɪz/
analyses analysing analysed
US **analyze**

VERB

If you analyse something, you investigate it carefully in order to understand it or find out what it consists of.
EG *We haven't had time to analyse the samples yet.*

analysis /ə'næləsɪs/
analyses

NOUN

Analysis is the process of investigating something in order to understand it or find out what it consists of.
EG *... a full analysis of the problem*

analyze /'ænəlaɪz/

see **analyse**

ancestor /'ænsɪstər/
ancestors

NOUN

Your ancestors are the members of your family who lived many years ago.
EG *He could trace his ancestors back 700 years.*

ancient /'eɪnʃənt/

ADJECTIVE

1 existing or happening in the distant past
EG *... ancient Greece*
2 very old or having a very long history
EG *... an ancient monastery*

and /ænd/

CONJUNCTION

You use 'and' to link two or more words or phrases together.
EG *He's short, fat and bald.*
EG *Both her sister and her brother are in England.*

angel /'eɪndʒəl/
angels

NOUN

Angels are spiritual beings who some people believe live in heaven.
EG *She is in heaven with the angels.*

anger /'æŋgər/
angers angering angered

NOUN

1 Anger is the strong feeling you get when you feel someone has behaved in an unfair or cruel way.
EG *There was anger at the suffering caused by the bombing.*

VERB

2 If something angers you, it makes you feel angry.
EG *The decision has angered some Californians.*

angle /'æŋgl/
angles

NOUN

1 An angle is the distance between

two lines at the point where they join together. Angles are measured in degrees…
EG … *an angle of 90 degrees*
2 the direction from which you look at something
EG *He had painted the vase from all angles.*

angry /'æŋgrɪ/
angrier angriest
ADJECTIVE
very annoyed
EG *Are you angry with me?*

animal /'ænɪməl/
animals
NOUN
any living being except a plant
EG *He was attacked by wild animals.*

ankle /'æŋkl/
ankles
NOUN
the joint which connects your foot to your leg
EG *He twisted his ankle.*

anniversary /ænɪ'vɜːsərɪ/
anniversaries
NOUN
a date which is remembered because something important happened on that date in a previous year
EG … *our tenth wedding anniversary*

announce /ə'naʊns/
announces announcing announced
VERB
If you announce something, you tell people about it publicly or officially.
EG *The results were announced on Friday morning.*

nnouncement
/ə'naʊnsmənt/

announcements
NOUN
an official statement about something that has happened or that will happen
EG *I would like to make a short announcement.*

annoy /ə'nɔɪ/
annoys annoying annoyed
VERB
If someone or something annoys you, they make you angry or impatient.
EG *You're just saying that to annoy me.*
EG … *which made me very annoyed with him*

annual /'ænjʊəl/
ADJECTIVE
1 happening or done once a year
EG … *their annual conference*
2 happening or calculated over a period of one year
EG … *the annual budget for education*

anonymous /ə'nɒnɪməs/
ADJECTIVE
If something is anonymous, nobody knows who is responsible for it.
EG *The police received an anonymous phone call.*

another /ə'nʌðər/
ADJECTIVE OR PRONOUN
Another thing or person is one more thing or person.
EG *We're going to have another baby.*
EG *He poured a drink for his brother, then another for himself.*

answer /'ɑːnsər/
answers answering answered
VERB

1 If you answer someone, you reply to them in speech or writing.
EG *He paused before answering.*
EG *Just answer the question.*
EG *She didn't answer him immediately.*

NOUN
2 the reply you give when you answer someone
EG *I didn't receive an answer to my letter.*

3 a solution to a problem
EG *There is no easy answer to the problem.*

ant /ænt/
ants

NOUN
Ants are small insects that live in large groups.
EG *Ants swarmed out of the ground.*

Antarctica /ænt'ɑ:ktɪkə/

NOUN
Antarctica or **the Antarctic** is the continent around the South Pole.
EG *... a research trip to Antarctica*

anti- /'æntɪ/

PREFIX
opposed to or opposite to something
EG *... an anti-war march*
EG *... anticlockwise*

anticipate /æn'tɪsɪpeɪt/
anticipates anticipating anticipated

VERB
1 If you anticipate an event, you are expecting it and are prepared for it.
EG *It is anticipated that 100 jobs will be lost.*

2 If you anticipate a question or need, you do what is necessary before the question or need occurs.
EG *Do you expect your partner to anticipate your needs?*

antique /æn'ti:k/
antiques

NOUN
1 an object from the past that is collected because of its value or beauty
EG *He deals in antiques.*

ADJECTIVE
2 from or concerning the past
EG *... antique furniture*

anxiety /æŋ'zaɪətɪ/
anxieties

NOUN
Anxiety is nervousness or worry.
EG *... anxieties about the economy*

anxious /'æŋkʃəs/

ADJECTIVE
1 If you are anxious, you are nervous or worried.
EG *He admitted he was still anxious about the situation.*

2 If you are **anxious to do** something, you very much want to do it.
EG *She was anxious to leave early.*

any /'ɛnɪ/

ADJECTIVE OR PRONOUN
1 one, some, or several
EG *Do you have any paperclips I could borrow?*
EG *I haven't got any.*
EG *He was unable to tolerate any dairy products.*
☑ 'Any' is mainly used in questions and negative sentences. For more information about this use, see 'some'.

2 no matter what or which
EG *Take any of those books you want.*
EG *Any type of cooking oil will do.*

ADVERB

3 If something does not happen **any more** or **any longer**, it has stopped happening.
EG *I don't want to see her any more.*
EG *She couldn't hide her feelings any longer.*

anybody /'ɛnɪbɒdɪ/
PRONOUN
Anybody means the same as anyone.
EG *I won't tell anybody.*
EG *Did anybody see you?*
☑ 'Anybody' is mainly used in questions and negative sentences. For more information about this use, see 'somebody'.

anyhow /'ɛnɪhaʊ/
ADVERB
Anyhow means the same as anyway.
EG *She doesn't want children — not right now, anyhow.*

anyone /'ɛnɪwʌn/
PRONOUN
any person
EG *I won't tell anyone.*
EG *Was anyone else there?*
☑ 'Anyone' is mainly used in questions and negative sentences. For more information about this use, see 'someone'.

anything /'ɛnɪθɪŋ/
PRONOUN
any object, event, situation, or action
EG *Can you see anything?*
EG *He didn't say anything.*
☑ 'Anything' is mainly used in questions and negative sentences. For more information about this use, see 'something'.

anyway /'ɛnɪweɪ/
ADVERB
1 You use 'anyway' to correct or modify something that you have said.
EG *She doesn't want children — not right now, anyway.*

2 besides or in addition
EG *It's too late to go, and anyway I'm too tired.*

anywhere /'ɛnɪwɛəʳ/
ADVERB
in, at, or to any place
EG *Can you see him anywhere?*
EG *I haven't got anywhere to live.*
EG *Did you go anywhere last night?*
☑ 'Anywhere' is mainly used in questions and negative sentences. For more information about this use, see 'somewhere'.

apart /ə'pɑːt/
ADVERB OR ADJECTIVE
1 If two things or people are apart, there is a space or distance between them.
EG *The couple lived apart for four years.*
EG *The gliders landed about seventy metres apart.*

ADVERB
2 If you **take** something **apart**, you separate it into pieces.
EG *When the clock stopped, he took it apart and fixed it.*

3 **apart from** means except for, or in addition to
EG *The room was empty apart from one man seated beside the fire.*
EG *Apart from sport, my other interest is music.*

apartment /ə'pɑːtmənt/
apartments
NOUN
In American English, an apartment is a set of rooms for living in, usually on one floor of a building.
EG *She has an apartment in New York.*
☑ The usual British word is *flat*.

A
B
C
D
E
F
G
H
I
J
K
L
M
N
O
P
Q
R
S
T
U
V
W
X
Y
Z

apologize /əˈpɒlədʒaɪz/
**apologizes apologizing
apologized**; also spelt
apologise

VERB
If you **apologize to** someone,
you say you are sorry for
something that you have said or
done.
EG *He apologized to us for being
late.*
EG *I think you should apologize.*

apology /əˈpɒlədʒɪ/
apologies

NOUN
something you say or write to tell
someone you are sorry
EG *He made a public apology for
the team's performance.*

apostrophe /əˈpɒstrəfɪ/
apostrophes

NOUN
The **apostrophe** is the symbol '
that is used to show that someone
owns or possesses something.
EG *... Matthew's book*
EG *... my parents' house*
The apostrophe is also used to show
that a letter or letters have been left
out of a word.
EG *I don't know.*
EG *Who's there?*

appal /əˈpɔːl/
appals appalling appalled
US **appall**

VERB
If something appals you, it shocks
you because it is very bad.
EG *People were appalled by the
news.*

apparatus /æpəˈreɪtəs/

NOUN
The apparatus for a particular task
is the equipment used for it.
EG *... firemen wearing breathing
apparatus*

apparent /əˈpærənt/

ADJECTIVE
1 Something which is apparent
seems to be the case, although
you cannot be certain that it is.
EG *... the apparent failure of the
mission*

2 clear and obvious
EG *Everyone left the room for no
apparent reason.*

apparently /əˈpærəntlɪ/

ADVERB
You use 'apparently' to refer to
something that seems to be true.
EG *Apparently the party was a grea
success.*

appeal /əˈpiːl/
appeals appealing appealed

VERB
1 If you **appeal for** something,
you make an urgent request for it.
EG *The police appealed for
witnesses to come forward.*

2 If something or someone
appeals to you, you find them
attractive or interesting.
EG *The idea didn't appeal to me.*

NOUN
3 a formal or serious request
EG *... an appeal for peace*

4 The appeal of something is the
quality it has which people find
attractive or interesting.
EG *... the romantic appeal of the s*

appear /əˈpɪər/
**appears appearing
appeared**

VERB
1 When someone or something

which you could not see appears, they move so that you can see them.

EG *Two men suddenly appeared from nowhere.*

2 If something **appears to** be a certain way, it seems or looks that way.

EG *He appeared to be searching for something.*

EG *It appears that no solution can be found.*

appearance /əˈpɪərəns/
appearances

NOUN

1 The appearance of someone in a place is their arrival there, especially when it is unexpected.

EG *… the prompt appearance of the police*

2 Someone's or something's appearance is the way they look.

EG *She's very fussy about her appearance.*

appetite /ˈæpɪtaɪt/
appetites

NOUN

Your appetite is your desire to eat.

EG *I've lost my appetite.*

applaud /əˈplɔːd/
applauds applauding applauded

VERB

1 When a group of people applaud, they clap their hands in approval or praise.

EG *The audience laughed and applauded.*

2 When an action or attitude is applauded, people praise it.

EG *He should be applauded for his courage.*

applause /əˈplɔːz/

NOUN

Applause is clapping by a group of people.

EG *The audience burst into loud applause.*

EG *We gave him a round of applause.*

apple /ˈæpl/
apples

NOUN

a round fruit with smooth skin and firm white flesh

EG *… apple pie*

application /æplɪˈkeɪʃən/
applications

NOUN

1 a formal request for something, usually in writing

EG *His application to join the organization was rejected.*

EG *… an application form*

2 The application of a rule, system, or skill is the use of it in a particular situation.

EG *Do the results have any practical application?*

apply /əˈplaɪ/
applies applying applied

VERB

1 If you **apply for** something, you formally ask for it, usually by writing a letter.

EG *I'm continuing to apply for jobs.*

2 If you apply a rule or system, you put it into practice.

EG *The government seems to be applying the same principle.*

3 If something **applies to** a person or situation, it is relevant to that person or situation.

EG *The law applies only to people living in England and Wales.*

4 If you **apply** something **to** a surface, you put it on the surface or rub it into the surface.

EG *She applied lipstick to her mouth.*

A B C D E F G H I J K L M N O P Q R S T U V W X Y Z

appoint /əˈpɔɪnt/
appoints appointing appointed

VERB

If you **appoint** someone **to** a job or position, you formally choose them for it.

EG *... appointing people to positions of power*

EG *His successor has not yet been appointed.*

appointment /əˈpɔɪntmənt/
appointments

NOUN

1 an arrangement you have with someone to meet them

EG *I had an appointment at the dentist's.*

2 The appointment of a person to do a particular job is the choosing of that person to do it.

EG *Their duties include the appointment of all the staff.*

appreciate /əˈpriːʃɪeɪt/
appreciates appreciating appreciated

VERB

1 If you appreciate something, you like it because of its good qualities.

EG *He appreciates fine wines.*

2 If you appreciate a situation or problem, you understand it and know what it involves.

EG *I appreciate the reasons for your anxiety.*

3 If you appreciate something that someone has done for you, you are grateful to them for it.

EG *I really appreciate you coming to visit me.*

apprentice /əˈprɛntɪs/
apprentices

NOUN

a young person who works with someone in order to learn their skill

EG *I started off as an apprentice and worked my way up.*

approach /əˈprəʊtʃ/
approaches approaching approached

VERB

1 If you approach someone or something, you come near or nearer to them.

EG *He held the car door open for her as she approached.*

2 If you approach a situation or problem in a particular way, you think about it or deal with it in that way.

EG *The bank has approached the issue in a practical way.*

NOUN

An approach to a situation or problem is a way of thinking about it or dealing with it.

EG *He was very professional in his approach.*

appropriate /əˈprəʊprɪɪt/

ADJECTIVE

suitable or acceptable for a particular situation

EG *He didn't think jeans were appropriate for a vice-president.*

approval /əˈpruːvəl/

NOUN

1 Approval is agreement given to a plan or request.

EG *The plan will require the approval of the local authority.*

2 If someone or something has your approval, you like and admire them.

EG *She looked at James with approval.*

approve /əˈpruːv/
approves approving approved

VERB

1 If you **approve of** something or someone, you think that thing or person is acceptable or good.
EG *Not everyone approves of the festival.*

2 If someone in a position of authority approves a plan or idea, they formally agree to it.
EG *The Russian Parliament has approved the reforms.*

approximately /ə'prɒksɪmɪtlɪ/
ADVERB
close to but not exactly
EG *It takes approximately half an hour to drive there.*

April /'eɪprəl/
NOUN
April is the fourth month of the year.
EG *... the weather in April*

Arab /'ærəb/
Arabs
NOUN
a member of the major ethnic group in the Middle East and parts of North Africa
EG *... violence between Arabs and Jews*

Arabic /'ærəbɪk/
NOUN
1 Arabic is a language spoken by many people in the Middle East and North Africa.
EG *She is learning Arabic.*
ADJECTIVE
2 belonging or relating to the Arabs
EG *... Arabic music*

arch /ɑːtʃ/
arches arching arched
NOUN
1 a structure which is made when two columns join at the top in a curve
EG *... beneath the railway arches*
VERB
2 If something arches or if you arch it, it forms a curved line or shape.
EG *Don't arch your back; keep your spine straight.*

archaeology /ɑːkɪ'ɒlədʒɪ/
or **archeology**
NOUN
Archaeology is the study of the past by digging up and examining the remains of ancient buildings, tools, and other things.
EG *... a student of archaeology*

archbishop /ɑːtʃ'bɪʃəp/
archbishops
NOUN
a bishop of the highest rank in a Christian Church
EG *... the Archbishop of Canterbury*

archeology /ɑːkɪ'ɒlədʒɪ/
another spelling of **archaeology**

architect /'ɑːkɪtɛkt/
architects
NOUN
a person who designs buildings
EG *He's an architect.*

architecture /'ɑːkɪtɛktʃər/
NOUN
Architecture is the art or practice of designing buildings.
EG *... a fine example of traditional architecture*

are /ɑːr/
the plural form of the present tense of **be**
☑ *Are* is often shortened to *'re* after 'you', 'we', or 'they': *we're going to the beach.*

area /'ɛərɪə/
areas

A
B
C
D
E
F
G
H
I
J
K
L
M
N
O
P
Q
R
S
T
U
V
W
X
Y
Z

NOUN

1 a particular part of a place, country, or the world

EG ... *a built-up area of the city*

2 An area of knowledge, interest, or activity is a particular part of a subject or activity.

EG *Computers affect almost every area of our lives.*

arena /əˈriːnə/
arenas

NOUN

a place where sports and other public events take place

EG ... *the largest indoor sports arena in the world*

argue /ˈɑːgjuː/
argues arguing argued

VERB

1 If you **argue with** someone about something, you disagree with them about it, sometimes in an angry way.

EG ... *players who argue with referees*

EG *We don't often argue.*

2 If you argue that something is the case, you give reasons why you think it is so.

EG *She argued that her client had been wrongly accused.*

argument /ˈɑːgjumənt/
arguments

NOUN

1 If people have an argument, they disagree with each other, often angrily.

EG *She had a big argument with her mother.*

2 a point or a set of reasons that you use to try to convince people about something

EG *Do you accept this argument?*

arm /ɑːm/
arms arming armed

NOUN

1 Your arms are the part of your body between your shoulder and your wrist.

EG *She stretched her arms out.*

2 The arms of a chair are the parts on which you rest your arms.

EG *He placed his cup on the arm of the chair.*

PLURAL NOUN

3 arms are weapons used in a war

EG ... *extensive supplies of arms*

VERB

4 If you arm someone, you provide them with weapons.

EG *He armed his men with guns.*

armchair /ˈɑːmtʃeəʳ/
armchairs

NOUN

a large chair with a support on each side for your arms

EG *She was sitting in an armchair.*

army /ˈɑːmɪ/
armies

NOUN

a large group of soldiers who are trained to fight on land

EG *After returning from France, he joined the army.*

around /əˈraʊnd/

PREPOSITION OR ADVERB

☑ When 'around' is used as a preposition or an adverb, you can also use 'round': *around the table*; *round the table*. 'Around' is much more common in American English.

1 If something is around something else, it surrounds it.

EG *They were sitting around the kitchen table.*

EG ... *a house with a fence all around*

2 If something goes around something else, it moves in a circle with that thing at its centre.

EG *He wants to sail around the world.*

EG *The car had crashed but the wheels continued to go around.*

3 You can refer to an area near a place as the area around it.

EG *There's nothing to do around here.*

EG *The owner showed them around.*

PREPOSITION

4 If you go around a corner or obstacle, you go to the other side of it.

EG *Suddenly a car came around the corner.*

5 approximately

EG *The attacks began around noon.*

EG *... a salary of around $35,000*

ADVERB

6 If you turn or look around, you turn so that you are facing in a different direction.

EG *I called his name and he turned around.*

7 If you move things around, you move them so that they are in different places.

EG *He's always moving the furniture around.*

8 If you go around to someone's house, you visit them.

EG *He never comes around any more.*

☑ You can use 'round' instead of 'around', except when 'around' means 'approximately'. 'Around' is much more common in American English.

arrange /əˈreɪndʒ/
arranges arranging arranged

VERB

1 If you **arrange to do** something, you make plans to do it.

EG *Why don't you arrange to meet him later?*

2 If you **arrange** something **for** someone, you make it possible for them to have it or do it.

EG *The bank has arranged a loan for her.*

3 If you arrange objects, you set them out in a particular position.

EG *He started to arrange the books in piles.*

arrangement /əˈreɪndʒmənt/
arrangements

NOUN

1 an agreement that you make with someone to do something

EG *The caves can be visited only by prior arrangement.*

PLURAL NOUN

2 arrangements are plans and preparations which you make so that something will happen

EG *I'm in charge of all the travel arrangements.*

arrest /əˈrest/
arrests arresting arrested

VERB

1 If the police arrest someone, they take them to a police station because they believe they may have committed a crime.

EG *Police arrested five young men in connection with the attack.*

NOUN

2 An arrest is the act of arresting someone.

EG *... a reward for information leading to the arrest of the bombers*

arrival /əˈraɪvl/
arrivals

NOUN

the act or time of arriving

EG *He apologized for his late arrival.*

A
B
C
D
E
F
G
H
I
J
K
L
M
N
O
P
Q
R
S
T
U
V
W
X
Y
Z

A

arrive /əˈraɪv/
arrives arriving arrived

VERB

1 When you arrive somewhere, you reach it at the end of your journey.

EG *A new group of guests had arrived.*

2 When you **arrive at** an idea or decision you reach it.

EG *How did you arrive at that conclusion?*

arrogant /ˈærəgənt/

ADJECTIVE

Someone who is arrogant behaves as if they are better than other people.

EG *He's so arrogant.*

arrow /ˈærəʊ/
arrows

NOUN

a long, thin weapon with a sharp point at one end, shot from a bow

EG *... warriors armed with bows and arrows*

art /ɑːt/
arts

NOUN

1 Art is the activity of creating objects such as paintings and sculptures, which are thought to be beautiful or which express a particular idea; also used to refer to the objects themselves.

EG *I've never been any good at art.*

EG *... an exhibition of children's art*

2 An activity is called an art when it requires special skill or ability.

EG *... the art of diplomacy*

article /ˈɑːtɪkl/
articles

NOUN

1 a piece of writing in a newspaper or magazine

EG *... according to an article in today's paper*

2 a particular item

EG *... an article of clothing*

3 In grammar, 'the' is called the **definite article**, and 'a' or 'an' the **indefinite article**.

artificial /ˌɑːtɪˈfɪʃəl/

ADJECTIVE

created by people rather than occurring naturally

EG *... artificial limbs*

artist /ˈɑːtɪst/
artists

NOUN

a person who draws or paints or produces other works of art such as novels or music

EG *... the studio of a great artist*

artistic /ɑːˈtɪstɪk/

ADJECTIVE

1 able to create good paintings, sculpture, or other works of art

EG *... a very artistic child*

2 concerning or involving art or artists

EG *... artistic traditions*

as /æz, əz/

CONJUNCTION

1 at the same time that

EG *She waved at fans as she arrived for the concert.*

2 in the way that

EG *I'll behave towards him as I would to anyone else.*

3 because

EG *The first lesson is important, as it introduces all the main ideas.*

4 You use the structure **as ... as** when you are comparing things that are similar.

EG *It was as big as four football pitches.*

PREPOSITION

5 You use 'as' when you are saying

what role someone or something has.

EG *She worked as a waitress.*

6 You use **as if** or **as though** when you are giving a possible explanation for something.

EG *He looked at me as if I were mad.*

ash /æʃ/
ashes

NOUN

Ash is the grey or black powder that remains after something has been burnt.

EG *... cigarette ash*

EG *We scattered her ashes in the sea.*

ashamed /ə'ʃeɪmd/

ADJECTIVE

1 If you are ashamed, you feel embarrassed or guilty.

EG *My hair was such a mess I was ashamed to go out.*

2 If you are **ashamed of** someone or something, you feel embarrassed to be connected with them.

EG *She was so ashamed of her parents that she made them wait outside.*

ashtray /'æʃtreɪ/
ashtrays

NOUN

a small dish for ash from cigarettes and cigars

EG *A cigarette was still burning in the ashtray.*

Asia /'eɪʃə/

NOUN

Asia is the largest continent and lies to the east of Europe.

EG *... the sheer size of Asia*

Asian /'eɪʃən/
Asians

ADJECTIVE

1 belonging or relating to Asia

EG *... most Asian countries*

NOUN

2 someone who comes from Asia

EG *... shops run by Asians*

aside /ə'saɪd/

ADVERB

If you put something aside, you put it to one side.

EG *She closed the book and laid it aside.*

ask /ɑːsk/
asks asking asked

VERB

1 If you ask someone a question, you put a question to them for them to answer.

EG *She asked me if I'd enjoyed my dinner.*

2 If you **ask** someone **to do** something, you tell them that you want them to do it.

EG *We had to ask him to leave.*

3 If you **ask for** something, you say that you would like to have it.

EG *She asked for a drink of water.*

4 If you ask someone somewhere, you invite them there.

EG *Not everybody had been asked to the wedding.*

asleep /ə'sliːp/

ADJECTIVE

1 Someone who is asleep is sleeping.

EG *My 4-year-old daughter was asleep on the sofa.*

2 When you **fall asleep**, you start sleeping.

EG *He sat down and immediately fell asleep.*

aspect /'æspɛkt/
aspects

NOUN

An aspect of something is one of

its features.

EG *Exam results illustrate only one aspect of a school's success.*

assault /əˈsɔːlt/
assaults assaulting assaulted

NOUN

1 a violent attack on someone

EG *At the police station I was charged with assault.*

VERB

2 If someone assaults someone else, they attack them violently.

EG *She may have been sexually assaulted by her killer.*

assemble /əˈsɛmbl/
assembles assembling assembled

VERB

1 If people assemble, they gather together.

EG *... a convenient place for students to assemble between classes*

2 If you assemble something, you fit the parts of it together.

EG *She had been trying to assemble the bomb when it went off.*

assess /əˈsɛs/
assesses assessing assessed

VERB

If you assess something, you consider it carefully and make a judgment about it.

EG *We tried to assess the damage.*

asset /ˈæset/
assets

NOUN

1 a person or thing that is considered useful

EG *He will be a great asset to the club.*

PLURAL NOUN

2 The **assets** of a person or company are all the things they own that could be sold to raise

money.

EG *The company had assets of 3.5 million pounds.*

assist /əˈsɪst/
assists assisting assisted

VERB

If you assist someone, you help them to do something.

EG *The family decided to assist me with my chores.*

assistance /əˈsɪstəns/

NOUN

If you give someone assistance, you help them.

EG *He has been operating the shop with the assistance of volunteers.*

assistant /əˈsɪstənt/
assistants

NOUN

1 someone whose job is to help another person in their work

EG *His assistant took over while he went out.*

2 a person who works in a shop selling things to customers

EG *... a shop assistant*

associate /əˈsəʊʃɪeɪt/
associates associating associated

VERB

1 If you **associate** one thing **with** another, you connect the two things in your mind.

EG *Dignity is the quality which I associate mostly with her.*

2 If you **associate with** a group of people, you spend a lot of time with them.

EG *She spent her adolescence associating with criminals.*

NOUN : /əˈsəʊʃɪɪt/

☑ Note that you pronounce the noun differently from the verb.

3 Your associates are the people

you work with or spend a lot of time with.

EG ... the restaurant owner's business associates

association /əsəʊsɪˈeɪʃən/
associations

NOUN

1 an organization for people who have similar interests, jobs, or aims

EG ... a housing association

PLURAL NOUN

2 If something has particular **associations** for you, it is connected in your mind with a particular memory or feeling.

EG The place contained unpleasant associations for her.

assortment /əˈsɔːtmənt/
assortments

NOUN

a group of similar things that are different sizes or colours

EG ... an amazing assortment of old toys

assume /əˈsjuːm/
assumes assuming assumed

VERB

If you assume that something is true, you suppose that it is true, sometimes wrongly.

EG I assumed he would come.

assumption /əˈsʌmpʃən/
assumptions

NOUN

a belief that you have without having thought about it

EG The general assumption was that I was guilty.

assure /əˈʃʊəʳ/
assures assuring assured

VERB

1 If you assure someone that something is true, you tell them it is true.

EG I can assure you that the animals are well cared for.

2 If you **assure** someone **of** something, you make certain that they will get it.

EG Their two victories assured them of a medal.

astonishing /əˈstɒnɪʃɪŋ/

ADJECTIVE

very surprising

EG ... an astonishing display of physical strength

astrology /əˈstrɒlədʒɪ/

NOUN

Astrology is the study of the sun, moon, and stars in order to predict the future.

EG Do you believe in astrology?

astronaut /ˈæstrənɔːt/
astronauts

NOUN

a person who travels into space

EG ... the astronauts aboard the space station

astronomy /əˈstrɒnəmɪ/

NOUN

Astronomy is the scientific study of stars and planets.

EG ... new developments in astronomy

at /æt/

PREPOSITION

1 You use 'at' to say where someone or something is.

EG Bert met us at the airport.

2 You use 'at' to mention the direction something is going in.

EG He threw his plate at the wall.

3 You use 'at' to say when something happens.

EG The game starts at 3 o'clock.

4 You use 'at' to mention the rate or price of something.

EG The house was valued at

$200,000.

5 You use 'at' to describe the state or activity of someone or something.

EG *The two nations are at war.*

ate /eɪt/

past tense of **eat**

athlete /'æθliːt/

athletes

NOUN

someone who is good at sport and takes part in sporting events

EG *... an Olympic athlete*

athletics /æθ'letɪks/

NOUN

Sporting events such as running, jumping, and throwing are called athletics.

EG *... an athletics meeting*

☑ Although it looks like a plural, 'athletics' is a singular noun: *athletics is becoming a very popular sport.*

atmosphere /'ætməsfɪər/

atmospheres

NOUN

1 the air and other gases that surround a planet

EG *These gases pollute the atmosphere.*

2 the general mood of a place

EG *... a relaxed atmosphere*

atom /'ætəm/

atoms

NOUN

the smallest part of a substance that can take part in a chemical reaction

EG *... a carbon atom*

atomic /ə'tɒmɪk/

ADJECTIVE

relating to atoms or to the power released by splitting atoms

EG *... atomic energy*

attach /ə'tætʃ/

attaches attaching attached

VERB

If you **attach** something **to** something else, you join or fasten the two things together.

EG *The device can be attached to any surface.*

attack /ə'tæk/

attacks attacking attacked

VERB

1 If someone attacks you, they use violence against you so as to hurt or kill you.

EG *He attacked her with a knife.*

2 If you attack someone or their ideas, you criticize them strongly.

EG *He attacked the government's economic policies.*

3 In a game such as football or hockey, to attack means to get the ball into a position from which a goal can be scored.

EG *... Liverpool's decision to attack in the second half*

NOUN

4 An attack is a violent physical action against someone.

EG *... attacks on old people*

5 An **attack on** someone or on their ideas is a strong criticism of them.

EG *... his response to attacks on his work*

attempt /ə'tempt/

attempts attempting attempted

VERB

1 If you **attempt to do** something, you try to do it.

EG *They attempted to escape.*

NOUN

2 an act of trying to do something

EG *He made no attempt to help.*

attend /ə'tend/

attends attending attended

VERB

1 If you **attend** an event, you are present at it.

EG *Thousands of people attended the funeral.*

2 If you **attend** school, church, or hospital, you go there regularly.

EG *The school was attended almost entirely by local children.*

3 If you **attend to** something, you deal with it.

EG *We have business to attend to first.*

attendant /əˈtɛndənt/
attendants

NOUN

someone whose job is to serve people in a place such as a garage or cloakroom

EG *... a museum attendant*

attention /əˈtɛnʃən/

NOUN

1 If you give something your **attention**, you look at it, listen to it, or think about it carefully.

EG *You have my complete attention.*

2 If someone or something needs **attention**, they need to be dealt with or cared for.

EG *The woman needed medical attention.*

attic /ˈætɪk/
attics

NOUN

a room at the top of a house immediately below the roof

EG *We put all our junk in the attic.*

attitude /ˈætɪtjuːd/
attitudes

NOUN

Your **attitude** to someone or something is the way you think about them and behave towards

them.

EG *... the general change in attitude towards disabled people*

attorney /əˈtɜːnɪ/
attorneys

NOUN

In American English, an **attorney** is a person who is qualified to advise people about the law and represent them in court.

EG *... a prosecuting attorney*

☑ The usual British word is *lawyer*.

attract /əˈtrækt/
attracts attracting attracted

VERB

1 If something **attracts** people, it interests them and makes them want to go to it.

EG *The site is attracting many visitors.*

2 If you **are attracted to** someone, you like and admire them.

EG *He was attracted to her because of his lively personality.*

3 If something **attracts** support or publicity, it gets it.

EG *The women's movement has attracted a lot of publicity.*

attraction /əˈtrækʃən/
attractions

NOUN

1 Attraction is a feeling of liking someone or something very much.

EG *... our attraction to the opposite sex*

2 something that people visit for interest or pleasure

EG *... a major tourist attraction*

attractive /əˈtræktɪv/

ADJECTIVE

1 Someone who is **attractive** is pleasant to look at or be with.

EG *... an attractive woman*

A
B
C
D
E
F
G
H
I
J
K
L
M
N
O
P
Q
R
S
T
U
V
W
X
Y
Z

2 Something that is attractive is desirable.
EG ... an attractive idea

auction /ˈɔːkʃən/
auctions auctioning auctioned
NOUN
1 a public sale in which goods are sold to the person who offers the highest price
EG He bought the picture at an auction.
VERB
2 If someone auctions something, they sell it in an auction.
EG We'll auction them for charity.

audience /ˈɔːdɪəns/
audiences
NOUN
the group of people who are watching or listening to a performance
EG The entire audience broke into loud applause.
☑ You can use either a singular or a plural verb after 'audience': the audience was shocked; the audience were shocked.

August /ˈɔːgəst/
NOUN
August is the eighth month of the year.
EG We are due to meet in August.

aunt /ɑːnt/
aunts
NOUN
Your aunt is the sister of your mother or father, or the wife of your uncle.
EG ... a present from my Aunt Vera

Australia /ɒsˈtreɪlɪə/
NOUN
Australia is the smallest continent and the largest island in the world.

EG ... a holiday in Australia

Australian /ɒsˈtreɪlɪən/
Australians
ADJECTIVE
1 belonging or relating to Australia
EG He was proud to be Australian.
NOUN
2 someone who comes from Australia
EG ... a pub run by Australians

authentic /ɔːˈθentɪk/
ADJECTIVE
real and genuine
EG ... authentic Italian food

author /ˈɔːθəʳ/
authors
NOUN
The author of a book is the person who wrote it; an author is also a person whose job is writing.
EG She is Japan's best-selling author.

authorise /ˈɔːθəraɪz/
another spelling of **authorize**

authority /ɔːˈθɒrɪtɪ/
authorities
NOUN
1 Authority is the right to control other people.
EG The judge had no authority to order a second trial.
2 In Britain, an authority is a local government department.
EG ... the local health authority
3 Someone who is an **authority on** something knows a lot about it.
EG ... the world's leading authority on fashion

authorize /ˈɔːθəraɪz/
authorizes authorizing authorized; also spelt **authorise**
VERB
If someone authorizes something, they give their official permission

for it to happen.
EG *Only the President could authorize the use of the atomic bomb.*

automatic /ɔːtəˈmætɪk/
automatics

ADJECTIVE
1 An automatic machine is programmed to perform tasks without needing a person to operate it.
EG *Modern trains have automatic doors.*

NOUN
2 a car in which the gears change automatically as the car's speed changes
EG *He drives an automatic.*

automobile /ˈɔːtəməbiːl/
automobiles

NOUN
In American English, an automobile is a car.
EG *... the automobile industry*

autumn /ˈɔːtəm/
autumns

NOUN
Autumn is the season between summer and winter.
EG *The best time to visit is in autumn.*
EG *... the autumn of 1983*

auxiliary /ɔːgˈzɪljərɪ/
auxiliaries

ADJECTIVE OR NOUN
An **auxiliary verb** or an **auxiliary** is a verb that is used with a main verb to form a verb group. The auxiliary verbs 'be' and 'have' are used to form tenses.
EG *I **am** feeling tired.*
EG *They **have been** looking for you.*
See also **modal**.

available /əˈveɪləbl/

ADJECTIVE
1 Something that is available can be obtained.
EG *Artichokes are available in most supermarkets.*

2 Someone who is available is ready for work or free for people to talk to.
EG *She will no longer be available at weekends.*

avenue /ˈævənjuː/
avenues

NOUN
a street, especially one with trees along it
EG *... the most expensive stores on Park Avenue*

average /ˈævərɪdʒ/
averages

NOUN
1 a result obtained by adding several amounts together and then dividing the total by the number of different amounts
EG *Six pupils were examined in a total of 39 subjects, an average of 6.5 subjects per pupil.*

2 You say **on average** when mentioning what usually happens in a situation.
EG *Men are, on average, taller than women.*

ADJECTIVE
3 An average amount is the result you get when you add several amounts together and divide the total by the number of amounts.
EG *The average age was 63.*

4 Average means standard or normal.
EG *... the average American teenager*

avoid /əˈvɔɪd/
avoids avoiding avoided

VERB

1 If you **avoid doing** something, you make an effort not to do it.
EG *He started an argument just to avoid doing his homework.*

2 If you avoid someone, you keep away from them.
EG *She had to lock herself in the toilet just to avoid him.*

awake /əˈweɪk/

ADJECTIVE

Someone who is awake is not sleeping.
EG *Are you awake?*

award /əˈwɔːd/
awards awarding awarded

NOUN

1 a prize or certificate for doing something well
EG *The new library has won an architectural award.*

VERB

2 If you award someone something, you give it to them formally or officially.
EG *She was awarded the prize for both films.*

aware /əˈweər/

ADJECTIVE

1 If you are **aware of** something, you know about it.
EG *Smokers are well aware of the dangers to their health.*
EG *I wasn't aware that he'd arrived.*

2 If you are **aware of** something, you can see, hear, smell, or feel it.
EG *She was aware of a strange smell in the room.*

away /əˈweɪ/

ADVERB

1 moving from a place
EG *I saw them walk away.*

2 at a distance from a place or person
EG *Our nearest supermarket is 12 kilometres away.*
EG *They sat as far away from each other as possible.*

3 in its proper place
EG *He put his chequebook away.*

4 not at home, school, or work
EG *Jason was away on a business trip.*

5 continuously or repeatedly
EG *He continued to type away.*

awful /ˈɔːfəl/

ADJECTIVE

very unpleasant or very bad
EG *Isn't the weather awful?*

awkward /ˈɔːkwəd/

ADJECTIVE

1 difficult to deal with
EG *My lawyer is in an awkward situation.*

2 clumsy and uncomfortable
EG *It was heavy and awkward to carry.*

axe /æks/
axes
US **ax**

NOUN

a tool with a handle and a sharp blade, used for chopping wood
EG *He raised the axe above his head.*

baby /'beɪbɪ/
babies

NOUN
a child in the first year or two of its life
EG ... when I was just a baby

babysit /'beɪbɪsɪt/
babysits babysitting babysat

VERB
If you **babysit for** someone, you look after their children while they are out.
EG I promised to babysit for her.

back /bæk/
backs backing backed

ADVERB
1 When people or things move back, they move in the opposite direction from the one they are facing.
EG She stepped back from the door.
2 When people or things go back to a place or situation, they return to it.
EG I'll be back as soon as I can.
3 If you **get** something **back**, it is returned to you.
EG You'll get your money back.
4 If you do something back to someone, you do to them what they have done to you.
EG I smiled back at them.
5 in the past
EG It happened back in the early eighties.

NOUN
6 the rear part of your body
EG He was lying on his back looking up at the sky.
7 the part of something that is towards the rear or furthest from

the front
EG ... the back of a postcard
EG She sat at the back of the class.

ADJECTIVE
8 The back parts of something are the ones near the rear.
EG ... the back seat of the car

VERB
9 If a building **backs onto** something, its back faces in that direction.
EG The house backs onto the golf course.
10 When a car backs somewhere, it moves backwards.
EG He backed out of the driveway.
11 If you back a person or organization, you support them.
EG A spokesman said the union would be backing him.

back out

VERB
If you **back out of** something you have agreed to do, you change your mind and decide not to do it.
EG He backed out of the deal at the last minute.

back up

VERB
If someone or something backs up a claim or story, they produce evidence to show that it is true.
EG The girl denied being there, and the man backed her up.

background /'bækgraʊnd/
backgrounds

NOUN
1 the things in a picture or scene that are less noticeable than the main things
EG She could hear voices in the

background.

2 the kind of home you come from and your education and experience
EG *She came from a working-class background.*

3 the circumstances which help to explain an event or which caused it to happen
EG *... the economic background to the present crisis*

backpack /ˈbækpæk/
backpacks
NOUN
a large bag that hikers or campers carry on their backs
EG *... an orange backpack with a sleeping bag tied underneath*

backward /ˈbækwəd/
ADJECTIVE
1 Backward means directed behind you.
EG *... a backward glance*
2 A backward step is an action that makes your situation worse instead of better.
EG *This latest policy is a backward step.*

backwards /ˈbækwədz/
ADVERB
1 Backwards means behind you.
EG *Lucille looked backwards.*
2 If you do something backwards, you do it the opposite of the usual way.
EG *He told them to count backwards.*

bacon /ˈbeɪkən/
NOUN
Bacon is meat from the back or sides of a pig, which has been salted or smoked.
EG *... a breakfast of bacon and eggs*
◄ /bæd/

worse worst
ADJECTIVE
1 unpleasant or upsetting
EG *Is the pain bad?*
EG *I have some bad news.*
2 of poor quality
EG *... a really bad film*
3 evil or immoral in character or behaviour
EG *... a bad person*
4 lacking skill in something
EG *... a bad driver*
5 If something is **not bad**, it is quite good.
EG *The wine wasn't bad.*

badge /bædʒ/
badges
NOUN
a piece of plastic or metal with a design or message on it that you can pin to your clothes
EG *He wore a large badge on his lapel saying 'Jesus is Lord'.*

badminton /ˈbædmɪntən/
NOUN
Badminton is a game in which two or four players use special bats to hit a light object over a high net.
EG *We passed the time playing badminton.*

bag /bæg/
bags
NOUN
1 a container for carrying things in
EG *... a shopping bag*
PLURAL NOUN
2 AN INFORMAL USE
bags of something is a lot of it
EG *There's bags of room.*

baggage /ˈbægɪdʒ/
NOUN
Your baggage is the suitcases and bags that you take on a journey.
EG *... a fee for excess baggage*

☑ 'Baggage' refers to all of your suitcases and bags, not to an individual suitcase or bag.

bake /beɪk/
bakes baking baked

VERB
If you bake food, you cook it in an oven.
EG … baked potatoes

baker /'beɪkər/
bakers

NOUN
a person who makes and sells bread and cakes; you also refer to a shop that sells bread and cakes as a baker or a **baker's**
EG I bought a loaf at the baker's.

balance /'bæləns/
balances balancing balanced

VERB
1 When someone or something balances, they remain steady and do not fall over.
EG Balancing on one leg is an excellent exercise.

NOUN
2 Balance is the state of being upright and steady.
EG She lost her balance and fell.
3 The balance in someone's bank account is the amount of money in it.
EG I'd like to check the balance in my account, please.

balcony /'bælkənɪ/
balconies

NOUN
1 a platform on the outside of a building with a wall or railing round it
EG She stood on the tiny balcony of her flat.
2 an area of upstairs seats in a theatre or cinema

EG I was sitting in the balcony.

bald /bɔːld/
balder baldest

ADJECTIVE
A bald person has little or no hair on their head.
EG He's going bald.

ball /bɔːl/
balls

NOUN
1 a round object used in games such as cricket and soccer
EG … a tennis ball
2 a large formal social event at which people dance
EG … the Christmas Ball

ballet /'bæleɪ/

NOUN
Ballet is a type of artistic dancing based on precise steps.
EG I'm not keen on ballet.

balloon /bə'luːn/
balloons

NOUN
1 a small bag made of thin rubber that you blow into until it becomes larger and rounder
EG Balloons of different colours hung from the ceiling.
2 a large, strong bag filled with gas or hot air, which travels through the air carrying passengers in a basket underneath it
EG … a round-the-world balloon flight

ban /bæn/
bans banning banned

VERB
1 If something is banned, it is not allowed.
EG Smoking is banned in the office.
2 If you are **banned from doing** something, you are not

A B C D E F G H I J K L M N O P Q R S T U V W X Y Z

allowed to do it.
EG *He was banned from driving for three years.*

NOUN
3 If there is a **ban on** something, it is not allowed.
EG *There was no ban on smoking.*

banana /bəˈnɑːnə/
bananas

NOUN
a long curved fruit with a yellow skin
EG *... a bunch of bananas*

band /bænd/
bands

NOUN
1 a group of musicians who play jazz or pop music together
EG *He was a drummer in a rock band.*

2 a group of people who share a common purpose
EG *... a band of rebels*

3 a narrow strip of something that is used to hold things together
EG *... an elastic band*

bandage /ˈbændɪdʒ/
bandages

NOUN
a strip of cloth that is wrapped round a wound to protect it
EG *We put a bandage on his knee.*

bang /bæŋ/
bangs banging banged

VERB
1 If you bang something or if you **bang on** it, you hit it so that it makes a loud noise.
EG *I banged on the wall.*

2 If you bang a part of your body, you accidentally knock it against something.
EG *I keep banging my head against that shelf.*

3 a sudden, short, loud noise
EG *They covered their ears and waited for the bang.*

bank /bæŋk/
banks banking banked

NOUN
1 a business that looks after people's money
EG *I had £10,000 in the bank.*

2 the raised ground along the edge of a river or lake
EG *He followed the man along the river bank.*

bank on

VERB
If you bank on something happening, you expect it and rely on it.
EG *You might be able to get it altered, but don't bank on it.*

bank holiday bank holidays

NOUN
a public holiday, when banks are officially closed
EG *Next Monday is a bank holiday in England.*

bankrupt /ˈbæŋkrʌpt/

ADJECTIVE
People or organizations that **go bankrupt** do not have enough money to pay their debts.
EG *If the firm cannot sell its products, it will go bankrupt.*

bar /bɑːr/
bars barring barred

NOUN
1 a counter or room where alcoholic drinks are served
EG *I was standing at the bar.*
EG *He works in a bar.*

2 a long, straight piece of metal
EG *... a building with bars across the windows*

3 a piece of something made in a rectangular shape
EG *... a bar of soap*

VERB
4 If you **bar** someone's **way**, you stop them going somewhere by standing in front of them.
EG *One of his bodyguards barred the way.*

barbecue /'bɑ:bɪkju:/
barbecues

NOUN
a grill with a fire on which you cook food, usually outdoors; also an outdoor party where you eat food cooked on a barbecue
EG *Let's have a barbecue!*

barber /'bɑ:bəʳ/
barbers

NOUN
a man who cuts men's hair
EG *My mum took me to the barber's.*

bare /bɛəʳ/

ADJECTIVE
1 If a part of your body is bare, it is not covered by any clothing.
EG *Her feet were bare.*

2 If something is bare, it is not covered or decorated with anything.
EG *... bare wooden floors*

3 The **bare minimum** or the **bare essentials** means the very least that is needed.
EG *They were fed the bare minimum.*
EG *I took only the bare essentials.*

barely /'bɛəlɪ/

ADVERB
only just
EG *The girl was barely sixteen.*

bargain /'bɑ:gɪn/
bargains bargaining

bargained

NOUN
1 an agreement in which two people or groups discuss and agree what each will do, pay, or receive
EG *You keep your part of the bargain and I'll keep mine.*

2 something which is sold at a low price and which is good value
EG *At this price the wine is a bargain.*

VERB
3 When people **bargain with** each other, they discuss and agree terms about what each will do, pay, or receive.
EG *Trade unions bargain with employers for better conditions.*

bark /bɑ:k/
barks barking barked

VERB
1 When a dog barks, it makes a short, loud noise, once or several times.
EG *A small dog barked at a seagull.*

NOUN
2 the tough material that covers the outside of a tree
EG *He picked up a branch and stripped off the bark.*

barn /bɑ:n/
barns

NOUN
a large farm building used for storing crops or animal food
EG *He brought the hay from the barn.*

barrel /'bærəl/
barrels

NOUN
1 a container with rounded sides and flat ends
EG *... beer barrels*

2 The barrel of a gun is the long

A
B
C
D
E
F
G
H
I
J
K
L
M
N
O
P
Q
R
S
T
U
V
W
X
Y
Z

tube through which the bullet is fired.
EG *He aimed the barrel of the gun at her forehead.*

barrier /'bærɪər/
barriers

NOUN
a fence or wall that prevents people or animals getting from one area to another
EG *The demonstrators broke through the police barriers.*

barrister /'bærɪstər/
barristers

NOUN
a lawyer who is qualified to represent people in the higher courts
EG *… one of the top London barristers*

base /beɪs/
bases basing based

NOUN
1 the lowest part of something
EG *… the base of the cliffs*
2 a place which part of an army, navy, or air force works from
EG *… a military base*

VERB
3 If one thing is **based on** another thing, it is developed from it.
EG *The opera is based on a work by Pushkin.*
4 If you **are based** somewhere, you live there or work from there.
EG *I'm based in London but spend a lot of time abroad.*

baseball /'beɪsbɔːl/
baseballs

NOUN
1 Baseball is a team game that is played with a bat and a ball and that is especially popular in the USA.
EG *… a baseball player*
2 a ball used in this game
EG *… a brand-new baseball*

basement /'beɪsmənt/
basements

NOUN
a floor of a building built completely or partly below the ground
EG *… a basement flat*

basic /'beɪsɪk/

ADJECTIVE
1 The basic aspects of something are the most important or the simplest ones.
EG *The basic theme of these stories is love.*
2 Something that is basic has only the necessary features without any extras or luxuries.
EG *The accommodation is pretty basic.*

basically /'beɪsɪklɪ/

ADVERB
You use 'basically' to show that you are describing a situation in a simple, general way.
EG *Basically, you've got two choices.*

basis /'beɪsɪs/
bases

NOUN
1 The basis of something is the essential or main principle from which it can be developed.
EG *This was the basis of the final design.*
2 If something happens on a particular **basis**, it happens in that way.
EG *Most members work on a voluntary basis.*

basket /'bɑːskɪt/
baskets

NOUN

a container made of thin strips of wood or metal woven together

EG ... *a shopping basket*

basketball /'bɑːskɪtbɔːl/

NOUN

Basketball is a game in which two teams try to score points by throwing a ball through a circular net suspended at each end of the court.

EG ... *a basketball match*

bass /beɪs/

ADJECTIVE

A bass musical instrument is one that produces a very deep sound.

EG ... *a bass guitar*

bat /bæt/
bats

NOUN

1 a specially shaped piece of wood with a handle, used for hitting the ball in games such as cricket or baseball

EG ... *a cricket bat*

2 a small flying animal, active at night, that looks like a mouse with wings

EG *Bats were hanging upside down from the roof.*

bath /bɑːθ/
baths

NOUN

a long container which you fill with water and sit in to wash yourself; also the act of washing yourself in this way

EG *Andy's in the bath.*

EG *I think I'll take a bath.*

bathroom /'bɑːθrum/
bathrooms

NOUN

a room with a bath or shower, a sink, and often a toilet in it

EG *He phoned when I was in the bathroom.*

battery /'bætərɪ/
batteries

NOUN

a device for storing and producing electricity, for example in a torch or a car

EG *The shavers come complete with batteries.*

battle /'bætl/
battles

NOUN

a fight between armed forces or a struggle between two people or groups with different aims

EG ... *the Battle of Waterloo*

EG ... *a major legal battle*

bay /beɪ/
bays

NOUN

a part of a coast where the land curves in

EG ... *the Bay of Biscay*

BC

You use BC to refer to a date before the year in which Jesus Christ is believed to have been born. BC means 'before Christ'.

EG ... *in 49 BC*

be /biː/
am is are; being; was were; been

VERB

1 You use 'be' to give more information about the subject of a sentence.

EG *I am English.*

EG *Her name is Melanie.*

EG *We are married.*

2 You use 'be' with 'it' to describe something or to give your opinion of something.

EG *It's a long way.*

A B C D E F G H I J K L M N O P Q R S T U V W X Y Z

EG *It was nice to meet you.*

AUXILIARY VERB

3 You use 'be' with a present participle to form the continuous tense.

EG *Crimes of violence are increasing.*

4 You use 'be' to say that something will happen in the future.

EG *We are going to America next month.*

5 You use 'be' to make a sentence passive.

EG *He was murdered.*

beach /biːtʃ/
beaches

NOUN

an area of sand or stones beside the sea

EG *The children were playing on the beach.*

bead /biːd/
beads

NOUN

Beads are small pieces of coloured glass or wood with a hole through the middle, often used to make necklaces.

EG *... a string of beads*

beak /biːk/
beaks

NOUN

A bird's beak is the hard part of its mouth that sticks out.

EG *... a black bird with a yellow beak*

bean /biːn/
beans

NOUN

Beans are the seeds of a climbing plant or the part of the plant that contains the seeds, which are eaten as a vegetable; also used of some other seeds.

EG *... a tin of baked beans*
EG *... coffee beans*

bear /beəʳ/
bears bearing bore borne

NOUN

1 a large, strong wild animal with thick fur and sharp claws

EG *She was attacked by a bear.*

VERB

2 To bear something means to carry it or support it.

EG *The ice wasn't thick enough to bear their weight.*

3 If something bears the mark of something, it has it.

EG *The room bore all the signs of a violent struggle.*

4 If you cannot bear something difficult, you cannot accept it or deal with it.

EG *He can't bear to talk about it.*

beard /bɪəd/
beards

NOUN

the hair that grows on the lower part of a man's face

EG *I'm thinking of growing a beard.*

beast /biːst/
beasts

NOUN

AN OLD-FASHIONED WORD

a large wild animal

EG *... the beasts of the jungle*

beat /biːt/
beats beating beat beaten

VERB

1 To beat someone or something means to hit them hard and repeatedly.

EG *He threatened to beat her.*
EG *The rain was beating against the window.*

2 If you beat someone in a race or game, you defeat them or do better than them.

EG *Arsenal beat Oxford United 5-1.*

3 When your heart beats, it pumps blood with a regular rhythm.

EG *I could feel my heart beating faster.*

beat up

VERB

If someone beats a person up, they hit or kick them repeatedly.

EG *He told us he had been beaten up by the police.*

beaut /bjuːt/

ADJECTIVE

AN INFORMAL WORD

In Australian and New Zealand English, beaut means good or excellent.

EG *... a beaut house*

beautiful /ˈbjuːtɪful/

ADJECTIVE

very attractive or pleasing

EG *... a beautiful girl*

EG *... beautiful scenery*

beauty /ˈbjuːtɪ/

NOUN

1 Beauty is the quality of being beautiful.

EG *Even a stupid person can appreciate beauty.*

2 the beauty of an idea or plan is what makes it attractive or worthwhile

EG *The beauty of the fund is its simplicity.*

became /bɪˈkeɪm/

the past tense of **become**

because /bɪˈkɒz/

CONJUNCTION

1 You use 'because' with a clause that gives the reason for something.

EG *I went home because I was tired.*

2 You use **because of** with a noun that gives the reason for something.

EG *He retired last month because of illness.*

become /bɪˈkʌm/

becomes becoming became become

VERB

To become something means to start feeling or being that thing.

EG *I became very angry.*

EG *He'd become an actor.*

bed /bɛd/

beds

NOUN

1 a piece of furniture that you lie on when you sleep

EG *I'm going to bed.*

EG *He's in bed.*

2 The bed of a sea or river is the ground at the bottom of it.

EG *... on the sea bed*

bedroom /ˈbɛdrum/

bedrooms

NOUN

a room that is used for sleeping in

EG *... a two-bedroom flat*

bee /biː/

bees

NOUN

a flying insect that makes honey and lives in large groups

EG *A bee was buzzing by my ear.*

beef /biːf/

NOUN

Beef is the meat of a cow or bull.

EG *... roast beef*

been /biːn/

1 Been is the past participle of **be**

2 If you have been to a place, you have gone to it or visited it.

EG *Have you ever been to China?*

beer /bɪər/
beers

NOUN

1 Beer is an alcoholic drink made from grain.

EG *… a pint of beer.*

2 A beer is a glass of beer.

EG *Would you like a beer?*

before /bɪˈfɔːr/

PREPOSITION, CONJUNCTION OR ADVERB

1 If something happens before a time or event, it happens earlier than that time or event.

EG *… the day before yesterday*

EG *Can I see you before you go?*

EG *The war had ended only a month before.*

ADVERB

2 If you have done something before, you have done it on a previous occasion.

EG *Have you been to Greece before?*

PREPOSITION

3 A FORMAL USE

in front of

EG *They stopped before a large white villa.*

beforehand /bɪˈfɔːhænd/

ADVERB

If you do something beforehand, you do it earlier than a particular event.

EG *Make a list of your questions beforehand.*

beg /bɛg/
begs begging begged

VERB

1 When people beg, they ask for food or money, because they are very poor.

EG *I was surrounded by people begging.*

2 If you beg someone to do something, you ask them very

anxiously to do it.

EG *I begged him to leave me alone.*

began /bɪˈgæn/
the past tense of **begin**

beggar /ˈbɛgər/
beggars

NOUN

someone who lives by asking people for money or food

EG *There were beggars on the streets.*

begin /bɪˈgɪn/
begins beginning began begun

VERB

1 If you **begin to do** something or **begin doing** it, you start to do it.

EG *He stood up and began to move around the room.*

EG *She began threatening us.*

2 When something begins, it starts.

EG *My career as a journalist was about to begin.*

beginning /bɪˈgɪnɪŋ/
beginnings

NOUN

The beginning of something is the first part of it.

EG *This was the beginning of all her troubles.*

EG *She contacted me at the beginning of August.*

begun /bɪˈgʌn/
the past participle of **begin**

behalf /bɪˈhɑːf/

NOUN

If you do something **on behalf of** someone or something, you do it for their benefit or as their representative.

EG *Scientists are campaigning on behalf of local charities.*

behave /bɪˈheɪv/
behaves behaving behaved

VERB

1 If you behave in a particular way, you act in that way.
EG *He'd behaved badly.*

2 If you behave or **behave yourself** you act correctly or properly.
EG *They were expected to behave themselves while she was there.*

behaviour /bɪˈheɪvjər/
US **behavior**

NOUN

Your behaviour is the way that you behave.
EG *She was unable to explain his behaviour.*

behind /bɪˈhaɪnd/

PREPOSITION

1 If someone or something is behind another person or thing, they are facing the back of that person or thing.
EG *The moon was behind a cloud.*

2 If someone is behind you, they support and help you.
EG *The whole country was behind him.*

3 The people or events behind a situation are the people or events that caused it.
EG *... those behind the killing*

ADVERB

4 If you **stay behind**, you remain after other people have gone.
EG *Most of the women left early but their husbands stayed behind.*

5 If you **leave** something **behind**, you do not take it with you.
EG *The robbers escaped, leaving their guns behind.*

being /ˈbiːɪŋ/

beings

1 Being is the present participle of **be**

NOUN

2 If something **comes into being**, it begins to exist.
EG *The party came into being in 1923.*

3 a living creature, either real or imaginary
EG *... beings from another planet*

belief /bɪˈliːf/
beliefs

NOUN

a feeling of certainty that something exists or is true
EG *... a belief in God*

believe /bɪˈliːv/
believes believing believed

VERB

1 If you believe that something is true, you think that it is true.
EG *Experts believe there will be more floods in the area.*

2 If you believe someone, you accept that they are telling the truth.
EG *He knew I didn't believe him.*

3 If you **believe in** things such as God or miracles, you think that they exist or happen.
EG *I don't believe in ghosts.*

4 If you **believe in** an idea, you think it is good or right.
EG *I don't believe in experimenting on animals.*

bell /bel/
bells

NOUN

1 a hollow metal object with a piece hanging inside it that hits the sides and makes a sound
EG *... church bells*

2 a device that makes a ringing sound and is used to attract people's attention

EG *I've been ringing the door bell.*

belong /bɪˈlɒŋ/
belongs belonging belonged

VERB

1 If something **belongs to** you, it is yours and you own it.

EG *He had taken some valuables belonging to another person.*

2 If you **belong to** a group, you are a member of it.

EG *I used to belong to a youth club.*

3 If something belongs somewhere, that is where it should be.

EG *The judges could not decide which category it belonged in.*

belongings /bɪˈlɒŋɪŋz/

PLURAL NOUN

Your belongings are the things that you own.

EG *I collected my belongings and left.*

below /bɪˈləʊ/

PREPOSITION OR ADVERB

1 If something is below something else, it is in a lower position.

EG *The sun slipped below the horizon.*

EG *... the office two floors below*

2 If something is below a particular amount or level, it is less than it.

EG *Rainfall has been below average.*

EG *... temperatures at zero or below*

belt /bɛlt/
belts

NOUN

a strip of leather or cloth that you fasten round your waist

EG *He wore a belt with a large brass buckle.*

bench /bɛntʃ/

benches

NOUN

a long seat that two or more people can sit on

EG *He sat down on a park bench.*

bend /bɛnd/
bends bending bent

VERB

1 When you bend something, you use force to make it curved.

EG *... a tool for bending wire*

2 When you bend, you move your head and shoulders forwards and downwards.

EG *I bent over and kissed her cheek.*

NOUN

3 a curved part of something

EG *... a bend in the road*

beneath /bɪˈniːθ/

PREPOSITION OR ADVERB

Something that is beneath another thing is under it.

EG *She hid the bottle beneath her mattress.*

EG *On the shelf beneath he spotted a photo album.*

benefit /ˈbɛnɪfɪt/
benefits benefiting benefited

NOUN

1 The benefit of something is the advantage that it brings to people.

EG *... the benefits of a good education*

VERB

2 If you **benefit from** something, it helps you.

EG *He'll benefit from a few days on his own.*

bent /bɛnt/

past participle and past tense of **bend**

berry /ˈbɛrɪ/
berries

NOUN

Berries are small, round fruits that grow on bushes or trees.

EG *We spent the afternoon picking berries.*

beside /bɪ'saɪd/

PREPOSITION

If one thing is beside another thing, it is next to it.

EG *I sat down beside my wife.*

besides /bɪ'saɪdz/

PREPOSITION

1 in addition to

EG *What languages do you know besides English?*

ADVERB

2 You use 'besides' to give an additional reason for something.

EG *I don't need any help. Besides, I'm nearly finished.*

best /bɛst/

1 the superlative of **good** and **well**

EG *That was one of the best films I've ever seen.*

EG *She is best known as a painter.*

ADVERB

2 The thing that you like best is the thing that you prefer to everything else.

EG *What music do you like best?*

NOUN

3 Your best is the greatest effort or the highest achievement that you are capable of.

EG *I'll try my best.*

bet /bɛt/
bets betting bet

VERB

1 If you **bet on** the result of something such as a horse race, you give someone money which they give you back with extra money if the result is what you predicted.

EG *I told him which horse to bet on.*

2 AN INFORMAL USE

You say **I bet** to indicate that you are sure that something is true.

EG *I bet the answer is no.*

NOUN

3 the act of betting on something, or the amount of money that you agree to risk

EG *... after he placed the bet*

EG *... a £50 bet*

betray /bɪ'treɪ/
betrays betraying betrayed

VERB

If you betray someone who trusts you, you do something which harms them, such as helping their enemies.

EG *They offered me money if I would betray my associates.*

better /'bɛtər/

1 the comparative of **good** and **well**

EG *He's better than me at maths.*

EG *She has never played better.*

ADVERB

2 If you like one thing better than another, you like it more than the other thing.

EG *I always liked you better than Sandra.*

3 If you **had better do** something, you ought to do it.

EG *You'd better apologise.*

ADJECTIVE

4 If you are better after an illness, you are no longer ill.

EG *Have you still got a cold or are you better?*

between /bɪ'twiːn/

PREPOSITION OR ADVERB

1 If something is between two other things or is **in between** them, it is situated or happens in the space or time that separates

them.
EG *He had a cigarette between his lips.*
EG *He was headmaster between 1955 and 1974.*
EG *... flower beds with paths in between*

PREPOSITION
2 A relationship or difference between two people or things is one that involves them both.
EG *... the relationship between patients and doctors*
☑ If there are two people or things you should use 'between'. If there are more than two, you should use 'among'.

beware /bɪ'wɛəʳ/

VERB
If you tell someone to **beware of** something, you are warning them that it might be dangerous or harmful.
EG *'Beware of the Dog'*

beyond /bɪ'jɒnd/

PREPOSITION
1 If something is beyond a certain place, it is on the other side of it.
EG *Beyond the hills was the Sahara.*
2 If something continues beyond a particular point, it continues further than that point.
EG *... an education beyond the age of 16*

Bible /'baɪbl/
Bibles

NOUN
1 The Bible is the holy book of the Christian religion.
EG *It says so in the Bible.*
2 A Bible is a copy of the Bible.
EG *... a stack of Bibles*

bicycle /'baɪsɪkl/
bicycles

NOUN
a two-wheeled vehicle which you ride by pushing two pedals with your feet
EG *... a woman on a bicycle*

bid /bɪd/
bids bidding bid

NOUN
1 an attempt to obtain or do something
EG *... Clinton's successful bid for the presidency*
2 an offer to buy something for a certain sum of money
EG *There were no bids for the painting.*

VERB
3 If you bid for something, you offer to pay a certain sum of money for it.
EG *I can't afford to bid more than £150 for the table.*

big /bɪg/
bigger biggest

ADJECTIVE
1 large or important
EG *Australia's a big country.*
EG *The biggest problem at the moment is unemployment.*
2 Children often refer to an older brother or sister as their **big brother** or **big sister**.
EG *My big sister is at university.*

bike /baɪk/
bikes

NOUN
AN INFORMAL WORD
a bicycle or motorbike
EG *I never learned to ride a bike.*

bikini /bɪ' kiːnɪ/
bikinis

NOUN
a two-piece swimming costume worn by women

EG … *a woman in a bikini*

bill /bɪl/
bills

NOUN

1 a written statement of how much is owed for goods or services
EG *Could I have the bill please?*
EG *… the phone bill*
2 a formal statement of a proposed new law that is discussed and then voted on in Parliament
EG *… the toughest crime bill that Congress has passed in a decade*
3 In America, a bill is a piece of paper money.
EG *… a dollar bill*

billion /'bɪljən/
billions

NOUN

a thousand million
EG *… 3 billion dollars*
EG *… billions of pounds*

bin /bɪn/
bins

NOUN

a container, especially one that you put rubbish in
EG *He threw the letter in the bin.*

bind /baɪnd/
binds binding bound

VERB

1 If you bind something, you tie rope or string round it so that it is held firmly.
EG *She bound him to the bed.*
2 If something binds you to a course of action, it makes you act in that way.
EG *He was bound by that decision.*

bingo /'bɪŋgəʊ/

NOUN

Bingo is a game in which players aim to match the numbers that someone calls out with the numbers on the card that they have been given.
EG *… a bingo hall*

binoculars /bɪ'nɔkjʊləz/
PLURAL NOUN

Binoculars are an instrument with lenses for both eyes, which you look through in order to see objects far away.
EG *… a pair of binoculars*

biography /baɪ'ɔgrəfɪ/
biographies

NOUN

the history of someone's life, written by someone else
EG *… a new biography of Winston Churchill*

biology /baɪ'ɔlədʒɪ/

NOUN

Biology is the study of living things.
EG *… a biology lesson*

bird /bɜːd/
birds

NOUN

an animal with feathers and wings
EG *Birds were singing in the trees.*

birth /bɜːθ/
births

NOUN

1 When a baby is born, you refer to this event as its birth.
EG *The twins were separated at birth.*
2 When a woman **gives birth**, she produces a baby from her body.
EG *She's just given birth to a baby girl.*

birthday /'bɜːθdeɪ/
birthdays

NOUN

Your birthday is the anniversary of the date on which you were born.

A
B
C
D
E
F
G
H
I
J
K
L
M
N
O
P
Q
R
S
T
U
V
W
X
Y
Z

A
B
C
D
E
F
G
H
I
J
K
L
M
N
O
P
Q
R
S
T
U
V
W
X
Y
Z

EG *What do you want for your birthday?*
EG *Happy Birthday!*

biscuit /ˈbɪskɪt/
biscuits

NOUN
a small flat cake that is crisp and usually sweet
EG *... a packet of biscuits*

bishop /ˈbɪʃəp/
bishops

NOUN
a high-ranking clergyman in some Christian Churches
EG *... the Bishop of York*

bit /bɪt/
bits
1 Bit is the past tense of **bite**

NOUN
2 A **bit of** something is a small amount or piece of it.
EG *... a loaf of bread and a little bit of cheese*
EG *... a bit of paper*

3 AN INFORMAL USE
a bit means slightly or to a small extent
EG *That's a bit difficult.*
EG *I need a bit more time.*

bite /baɪt/
bites biting bit bitten

VERB
1 If you bite something, you use your teeth to cut into it or through it.
EG *I used to bite my nails as a child.*

2 When an animal or insect bites you, it cuts into your skin with its teeth or mouth.
EG *My sister's dog bit me.*

NOUN
3 a small amount that you bite off with your teeth
EG *She took a bite of her sandwich.*

4 the injury you get when an animal or insect bites you
EG *My face was covered with insect bites.*

bitter /ˈbɪtəʳ/
bitterest

ADJECTIVE
1 If someone is bitter, they feel angry and resentful.
EG *She is very bitter about the way she was treated.*

2 In a bitter argument or war, people argue or fight fiercely and angrily.
EG *... a bitter power struggle*

3 Something that tastes bitter has a sharp, unpleasant taste.
EG *The leaves taste rather bitter.*

black /blæk/
blacker blackest; blacks

ADJECTIVE OR NOUN
1 Black is the darkest possible colour, like the sky at night when there is no light.
EG *... a black leather coat*
EG *I wear a lot of black.*

2 Someone who is black is a member of a dark-skinned race.
EG *... black musicians*
EG *He was the first black to be elected to Congress.*

ADJECTIVE
3 Black coffee or tea has no milk or cream added to it.
EG *How do you like your coffee, black or white?*

4 Black humour involves jokes about death or suffering.
EG *... a black comedy*

blackboard /ˈblækbɔːd/
blackboards

NOUN
a dark-coloured board in a classroom, which teachers write on using chalk

EG *The new teacher wrote her name on the blackboard.*

blackmail /'blækmeɪl/
blackmails blackmailing blackmailed

VERB

1 If someone **blackmails** another person, they threaten to reveal an unpleasant secret about them unless that person gives them money or does something for them.

EG *He was trying to blackmail me into saying whatever he wanted.*

NOUN

2 **Blackmail** is the action of blackmailing people.

EG *The photos were being used for blackmail.*

blade /bleɪd/
blades

NOUN

1 The **blade** of a knife, axe or saw is the sharp part of it.

EG *Be careful, it has a sharp blade.*

2 A **blade** of grass is a single piece of it.

EG *The picture was so clear that you could see every blade of grass.*

blame /bleɪm/
blames blaming blamed

VERB

1 If someone **blames** you **for** something bad that has happened, they believe you caused it.

EG *I was blamed for the theft.*

EG *Who's to blame?*

NOUN

2 The **blame for** something bad that happens is the responsibility for letting it happen.

EG *He had to take the blame for everything.*

blank /blæŋk/

blanker blankest

ADJECTIVE

Something that is blank has nothing on it.

EG *... a blank sheet of paper*

EG *... a blank cassette*

blanket /'blæŋkɪt/
blankets

NOUN

a large piece of thick cloth that you put on a bed to keep you warm

EG *He crawled under the blankets.*

blast /blɑːst/
blasts blasting blasted

VERB

1 When someone **blasts** something or **blasts** a hole in something, they make a hole by means of an explosion.

EG *They're using dynamite to blast away rocks.*

NOUN

2 a big explosion, especially one caused by a bomb

EG *Ten people were killed in the blast.*

blaze /bleɪz/
blazes blazing blazed

NOUN

1 a large, hot fire

EG *... a blaze which swept through the tower block*

VERB

2 If something **blazes**, it burns or shines brightly.

EG *... a blazing fire*

bleed /bliːd/
bleeds bleeding bled

VERB

When you **bleed**, you lose blood as a result of an injury.

EG *My nose is bleeding.*

A
B
C
D
E
F
G
H
I
J
K
L
M
N
O
P
Q
R
S
T
U
V
W
X
Y
Z

blend /blɛnd/
blends blending blended

VERB

1 When you blend substances, you mix them together to form a single substance.
EG *Blend the butter with the sugar.*

2 When colours or sounds blend, they combine in a pleasing way.
EG *Paint the walls and ceilings the same colour so they blend together.*

bless /blɛs/
blesses blessing blessed

VERB

When a priest blesses people or things, he or she asks for God's protection for them.
EG *... when the Pope blessed the President*

blew /blu:/
past tense of **blow**

blind /blaɪnd/
blinds blinding blinded

ADJECTIVE

1 Someone who is blind cannot see.
EG *... a blind man*
EG *He went blind.*

VERB

2 If something blinds you, you become unable to see, either for a short time or permanently.
EG *The strong sunlight blinded him.*

NOUN

3 A blind is a roll of cloth or paper that you pull down over a window to keep out the light.
EG *She pulled the blind down before she undressed.*

blindfold /'blaɪndfəʊld/
blindfolds blindfolding blindfolded

NOUN

1 a strip of cloth that is tied over someone's eyes so that they

cannot see
EG *The magician wore a blindfold throughout the trick.*

VERB

2 If you blindfold someone, you cover their eyes with a strip of cloth so that they cannot see.
EG *He was blindfolded and his hands tied.*

blink /blɪŋk/
blinks blinking blinked

VERB

When you blink, you close your eyes quickly for a moment.
EG *They looked at each other without blinking.*

blister /'blɪstər/
blisters

NOUN

a small bubble on your skin containing watery liquid, caused by a burn or rubbing
EG *My feet were covered in blisters.*

block /blɒk/
blocks blocking blocked

NOUN

1 A block of flats or offices is a large building containing flats or offices.
EG *... a block of council flats*

2 In a town, a block is an area of land with streets on all its sides.
EG *He lives a few blocks down.*

3 A block of something is a large rectangular piece of it.
EG *... a block of ice*

VERB

4 To block a road or channel means to put something across it so that nothing can get through.
EG *The police blocked the entrance to Westminster Bridge.*

5 If someone blocks something, they prevent it from happening.
EG *The council blocked his plans.*

bloke /bləuk/
blokes

NOUN

AN INFORMAL WORD

a man

EG *He's a really nice bloke.*

blonde /blɒnd/
blondes

ADJECTIVE

1 Blonde hair is very light in colour…

EG *… a little girl with blonde hair*

NOUN

2 A blonde is a girl or woman with light-coloured hair.

EG *… a tall, attractive blonde*

blood /blʌd/

NOUN

Blood is the red liquid that flows inside your body.

EG *… a blood donor*

bloody /'blʌdɪ/
bloodier bloodiest

ADJECTIVE OR ADVERB

1 AN INFORMAL USE

Bloody is a common swearword, which people use to emphasize what they are saying, especially when they are angry.

EG *This bloody car!*

EG *It's a bloody good film.*

ADJECTIVE

2 A bloody event is one in which a lot of people are killed.

EG *… a bloody revolution*

blouse /blauz/
blouses

NOUN

a light shirt, worn by a girl or a woman

EG *… a woman in a blue skirt and white blouse*

blow /bləu/
blows blowing blew blown

VERB

1 When the wind blows, the air moves.

EG *A light breeze was blowing through the treetops.*

2 If something blows or is blown somewhere, the wind moves it there.

EG *A gust of wind blew snow in her face.*

3 If you blow a whistle, you make a sound by blowing into it.

EG *The referee blew his whistle again.*

4 If you blow your nose, you force air out of it through your nostrils in order to clear it.

EG *He took out a handkerchief and blew his nose.*

NOUN

5 If you receive a blow, someone or something hits you.

EG *He went to hospital after receiving a blow to the head.*

6 something that makes you very disappointed or unhappy

EG *Marc's death was a terrible blow.*

blow out

VERB

If you blow out a flame or candle, you blow at it so that it stops burning.

EG *I blew out the candle and closed my eyes.*

blow up

VERB

1 If someone blows something up, they destroy it with an explosion.

EG *He was going to blow the place up.*

2 If you blow up a balloon or a tyre, you fill it with air.

EG *I spent the afternoon blowing up balloons.*

A
B
C
D
E
F
G
H
I
J
K
L
M
N
O
P
Q
R
S
T
U
V
W
X
Y
Z

A
B
C
D
E
F
G
H
I
J
K
L
M
N
O
P
Q
R
S
T
U
V
W
X
Y
Z

blue /bluː/
bluer bluest; blues

ADJECTIVE OR NOUN

Blue is the colour of the sky on a sunny day.

EG … her pale blue eyes

EG … a woman dressed in blue

bluff /blʌf/
bluffs bluffing bluffed

NOUN

1 an attempt to make someone believe that you will do something when you do not really intend to do it

EG The letter was a bluff.

VERB

2 If you are bluffing, you are trying to make someone believe that you are in a position of strength.

EG Either side, or both, could be bluffing.

blunt /blʌnt/
blunter bluntest

ADJECTIVE

1 A blunt object has a rounded point or edge, rather than a sharp one.

EG My pencil's blunt.

2 If you are blunt, you say exactly what you think, without trying to be polite.

EG To be blunt, you are no longer needed here.

blur /blɜːr/
blurs blurring blurred

NOUN

1 a shape or area which you cannot see clearly because it has no distinct outline or because it is moving very fast

EG Her face was a blur.

VERB

2 If an image blurs or is blurred, it becomes a blur.

EG Her tears fell on the letter,

blurring his words.

blush /blʌʃ/
blushes blushing blushed

VERB

If you blush, your face becomes red, because you are embarrassed or ashamed.

EG I felt myself blush.

board /bɔːd/
boards boarding boarded

NOUN

1 a flat piece of wood, plastic or cardboard, which is used for a particular purpose

EG They put boards over the windows.

EG … a chess board

2 the group of people who control a company or organization

EG He put the suggestion to the board.

3 Board is the meals that are provided when you stay somewhere such as a hotel.

EG The price includes full board.

4 If you are **on board** a ship or aircraft, you are on it or in it.

EG There were only four people on board the aircraft.

VERB

5 If you board a ship or aircraft, you get on it or in it.

EG We joined the passengers waiting to board the ship.

boast /bəʊst/
boasts boasting boasted

VERB

If you **boast about** your possessions or achievements, you talk about them proudly.

EG Carol boasted about her costume.

boat /bəʊt/
boats

NOUN
a vehicle for travelling across water
EG My father met me off the boat.

body /'bɒdɪ/
bodies

NOUN
1 Your body is all of you, from your head to your feet.
EG My whole body hurt.
2 Your body is the main part of you, not including your head, arms or legs.
EG Gently pull your leg towards your body.
3 a person's dead body
EG Police later found a body.

bodyguard /'bɒdɪgɑːd/
bodyguards

NOUN
a person who is employed to protect someone
EG The President was surrounded by bodyguards.

boil /bɔɪl/
boils boiling boiled

VERB
1 When a hot liquid boils, or when you boil it, bubbles appear in it and it starts to give off steam.
EG Boil the water in the saucepan.
2 When you boil food, you cook it in boiling water.
EG She didn't know how to boil an egg.

bold /bəʊld/
bolder boldest

ADJECTIVE
1 brave or confident
EG He was not bold enough to ask them.
2 clear and noticeable
EG ... bold colours

bolt /bəʊlt/
bolts bolting bolted

NOUN
1 a metal object which screws into a nut and is used to fasten things together
EG The bolts are all tight enough.
VERB
2 If you **bolt** one thing **to** another, you fasten them together, using a bolt.
EG ... a wooden bench which was bolted to the floor
3 If you bolt a door or window, you slide a metal bar across in order to fasten it.
EG Don't forget to lock and bolt all windows.

bomb /bɒm/
bombs bombing bombed

NOUN
1 a container filled with material that explodes when it hits something or when it is set off by a timer
EG It's not known who planted the bomb.
VERB
2 When a place is bombed, it is attacked with bombs.
EG The premises were bombed in the War.

bond /bɒnd/
bonds

NOUN
a close relationship between people
EG ... the bond between mothers and babies

bone /bəʊn/
bones

NOUN
Bones are the hard parts that form the framework of a person's or animal's body.
EG Mary broke a bone in her back.

bonfire /'bɒnfaɪər/
bonfires

NOUN

a large fire made outdoors, often to burn rubbish
EG They lit a bonfire and let off fireworks.

bonus /'bəunəs/
bonuses

NOUN

1 an amount of money that is added to your usual pay
EG … the Christmas bonus
2 Something that is a bonus is a good thing that you get in addition to something else.
EG The view from the hotel was an added bonus.

book /buk/
books booking booked

NOUN

1 a number of pages held together inside a cover
EG … a book about witches

VERB

2 When you book something such as a room, you arrange to have it or use it at a particular time.
EG I'd like to book a table for four for tomorrow night.

boost /bu:st/
boosts boosting boosted

VERB

1 To boost something means to cause it to improve or increase.
EG The campaign had boosted sales.

NOUN

2 an improvement or increase
EG … a boost to the economy

boot /bu:t/
boots

NOUN

1 Boots are strong shoes that cover your whole foot and the lower part of your leg.
EG … a pair of walking boots
2 the covered space in a car, usually at the back, for carrying things in
EG There's no more room in the boot.

border /'bɔ:dər/
borders bordering bordered

NOUN

1 the dividing line between two countries
EG They crossed the border into Mexico.
2 a strip or band round the edge of something
EG … plain tiles with a bright border

VERB

3 If one thing borders another, it is next to it.
EG … a sandy beach bordered by palm trees

bore /bɔ:r/
bores boring bored

1 Bore is the past tense of **bear**

VERB

2 If something bores you, you find it dull and uninteresting.
EG I won't bore you with the details.
3 If you bore a hole in something, you make a hole using a tool such as a drill.
EG They had to bore a hole in the wall so he could breathe.

NOUN

4 someone or something that bores you
EG He's such a bore.

boring /'bɔ:rɪŋ/

ADJECTIVE

dull and uninteresting
EG … a boring job

born /bɔ:n/

VERB

When a baby **is born**, it comes

out of its mother's womb at the beginning of its life.
EG *I was born in London.*

borne /bɔːn/
past participle of **bear**

borough /'bʌrə/
boroughs

NOUN

a town or district that has its own council
EG *... the London borough of Hackney*

borrow /'bɒrəʊ/
borrows borrowing borrowed

VERB

If you borrow something that belongs to someone else, they let you have it for a period of time.
EG *May I borrow your car?*
EG *He borrowed £200 from his wife.*

boss /bɒs/
bosses bossing bossed

NOUN

1 Your boss is the person in charge of the place where you work.
EG *You're not the boss around here.*

VERB

2 If someone **bosses** you **around**, they keep telling you what to do.
EG *They've bossed us around enough.*

both /bəʊθ/

ADJECTIVE OR PRONOUN

1 You use 'both' to indicate that something is true about each of two people or people.
EG *Both policies make good sense.*
EG *He's fond of you both.*
☑ *Both the boys* means the same as *both of the boys*. 'Both' can be used after a pronoun, as in *I like them both*, but it must come

before a noun: *I like both the songs.*

CONJUNCTION

2 You use 'both' in front of the first of two words linked with 'and' to indicate that what you are saying applies to each of the things.
EG *These are dangers that threaten both men and women.*

bother /'bɒðər/
bothers bothering bothered

VERB

1 If you **do not bother to do** something, you do not do it because it takes too much effort or it seems unnecessary.
EG *The papers didn't even bother to report it.*

2 If something bothers you, you are worried or concerned about it.
EG *Is something bothering you?*

3 If you **are not bothered about** something, you are not concerned about it.
EG *She is not bothered about money.*

4 If you bother someone, you interrupt them when they are busy.
EG *I'm sorry to bother you.*

NOUN

5 Bother is trouble, fuss, or difficulty.
EG *We're having a bit of bother with the children.*

bottle /'bɒtl/
bottles

NOUN

a glass or plastic container for keeping liquids in; also the amount contained in a bottle
EG *... a bottle of wine*

bottom /'bɒtəm/
bottoms

NOUN

1 The bottom of something is its

lowest part.

EG *It sank to the bottom of the lake.*

2 Your bottom is the part of your body that you sit on.

EG *He fell on his bottom.*

ADJECTIVE

3 The bottom thing in a series of things is the lowest one.

EG *... the bottom drawer*

bought /bɔːt/

past tense and past participle of **buy**

bounce /bauns/
bounces bouncing bounced

VERB

1 When an object bounces or when you bounce it, it moves upwards or away after hitting something.

EG *The ball bounced five yards to my right.*

2 If a cheque bounces, the bank refuses to accept it because there is not enough money in the account.

EG *I hope his cheque doesn't bounce.*

bound /baund/
bounds

1 Bound is the past tense and past participle of **bind**

ADJECTIVE

2 If something is **bound to** happen, it is certain to happen.

EG *He's bound to find out.*

3 If a person or vehicle is **bound for** a place, they are going there.

EG *The ship is bound for Italy.*

PLURAL NOUN

4 bounds are limits which restrict or control something

EG *Their enthusiasm knew no bounds.*

bow /bau/

bows bowing bowed

VERB

When you bow, you bend your body or lower your head as a sign of respect or greeting.

EG *He turned and bowed to her.*

bow /bəu/
bows

NOUN

1 a knot with two loops and two loose ends

EG *... a ribbon tied in a bow.*

2 a long flexible piece of wood that is used for shooting arrows

EG *Some of the raiders were armed with bows and arrows.*

bowl /bəul/
bowls bowling bowled

NOUN

1 a round container with a wide uncovered top, used for holding liquid or for serving food

EG *... a bowl of soup*

2 the hollow, rounded part of something

EG *... a toilet bowl*

VERB

3 In cricket, to bowl means to throw the ball towards the man holding the bat.

EG *He bowled so well that we won both matches.*

bowling /'bəulɪŋ/

NOUN

Bowling is a game in which you roll a heavy ball down a narrow track towards a group of wooden objects called pins and try to knock them down.

EG *... a ten-pin bowling alley*

bowls /bəulz/

NOUN

Bowls is a game in which you try to roll large wooden balls as near

as possible to a small ball.
EG ... a group of pensioners playing bowls

☑ Although it looks like a plural, 'bowls' is a singular noun: bowls is his favourite game.

box /bɒks/
boxes

NOUN

1 a container with a firm base and sides and usually a lid
EG ... a box of chocolates

2 On a form, a box is a square space which you have to write something in.
EG Simply tick the appropriate box.

boxing /'bɒksɪŋ/

NOUN

Boxing is a sport in which two people wearing padded gloves fight, using their fists.
EG ... a boxing match

Boxing Day

NOUN

In Britain, Boxing Day is the 26th of December, the day after Christmas Day.
EG On Boxing Day we all went for a long walk.

box office box offices

NOUN

the place where tickets are sold in a theatre or cinema
EG The film was a huge box-office success.

boy /bɔɪ/
boys

NOUN

a male child
EG The eldest child was a boy of five.

boyfriend /'bɔɪfrend/
boyfriends

NOUN

someone's boyfriend is the man or boy with whom they are having a romantic relationship.
EG ... Brenda and her boyfriend Anthony

bra /brɑː/
bras

NOUN

a piece of underwear worn by a woman to support her breasts
EG ... a padded bra

brace /breɪs/
braces bracing braced

VERB

1 When you **brace yourself**, you make your body stiff in order to steady yourself or avoid falling.
EG The bus braked sharply and he braced himself.

NOUN

2 an object fastened to something in order to support it or make it straight
EG I used to wear a brace on my teeth.

PLURAL NOUN

3 **braces** are a pair of straps worn over the shoulders and fastened to the trousers to hold them up
EG ... a businessman in red braces

bracelet /'breɪslɪt/
bracelets

NOUN

a chain or band that you wear round your wrist
EG ... a silver bracelet

bracket /'brækɪt/
brackets

NOUN

Brackets are the symbols ( ), [ ], or { } that are placed around words that have been added to a piece of writing, but which could be removed and still leave a complete sentence.

EG *The comments in brackets are the author's.*

brain /breɪn/
brains

NOUN

Your brain is the organ inside your head that controls your body and enables you to think and feel; also used to refer to your mind and the way that you think.

EG *... a brain tumour*

EG *... a job where you have to use your brain*

brake /breɪk/
brakes braking braked

NOUN

1 a device for making a vehicle stop or slow down

EG *He slammed his foot on the brake.*

VERB

2 When a driver brakes, they make a vehicle stop or slow down by using its brakes.

EG *She braked sharply to avoid another car.*

branch /brɑːntʃ/
branches branching branched

NOUN

1 The branches of a tree are the parts that grow out from its trunk.

EG *There were no leaves on the branches.*

2 A branch of a business or organization is one of its offices or shops.

EG *... the Ipswich branch of Marks and Spencer's*

3 A branch of a subject is one of its areas of study or activity.

EG *... specialists in certain branches of medicine*

VERB

4 A road that **branches off** from another road splits off from it to lead in a different direction.

EG *After a few miles, a small road branched off to the right.*

brand /brænd/
brands

NOUN

A brand of something is a particular kind or make of it.

EG *... a popular brand of chocolate*

brand-new /'brænd'njuː/

ADJECTIVE

completely new

EG *... a brand-new car*

brandy /'brændɪ/
brandies

NOUN

a strong alcoholic drink, often drunk after a meal; also a glass of this drink

EG *... a glass of brandy*

EG *... after a couple of brandies*

brass /brɑːs/

NOUN OR ADJECTIVE

Brass is a yellow-coloured metal made from copper and zinc.

EG *It's made of brass.*

EG *... shining brass buttons*

brave /breɪv/
braver bravest; braves braving braved

ADJECTIVE

1 A brave person is willing to do dangerous things and does not show any fear.

EG *He made a brave attempt to prevent the hijack.*

VERB

2 If you brave an unpleasant or dangerous situation, you deliberately experience it in order to achieve something.

EG *His fans braved the rain to hear him sing.*

bread /brɛd/

NOUN

Bread is a food made from flour and baked in an oven.

EG *... a loaf of bread*

break /breɪk/
breaks breaking broke broken

VERB

1 When an object breaks or when you break it, it becomes damaged or separates into pieces.

EG *The plate broke.*

EG *She's broken her ankle.*

2 If you break a rule or promise, you fail to keep it.

EG *We didn't know we were breaking the law.*

3 If you **break free**, you free yourself from something or escape from it.

EG *She broke free by thrusting her elbow into his chest.*

4 If you break something such as bad news to someone, you tell it to them.

EG *Then Louise broke the news that she was leaving me.*

5 If you break a record, you do better than the previous recorded best.

EG *... after Greene broke the world record in the 100 metres*

NOUN

6 a short period during which you rest or do something different

EG *I'm taking a break, I'm tired.*

break down

VERB

If a machine or vehicle breaks down, it stops working.

EG *Their car broke down.*

break up

VERB

If something breaks up, it ends.

EG *The marriage broke up after a year.*

breakdown /ˈbreɪkdaʊn/
breakdowns

NOUN

1 The breakdown of a system, plan, or discussion is its failure.

EG *There was a serious breakdown of communication.*

2 A breakdown or a **nervous breakdown** is a form of mental illness.

EG *She had a nervous breakdown and had to stop working.*

breakfast /ˈbrɛkfəst/
breakfasts

NOUN

the first meal of the day

EG *He likes two eggs for breakfast.*

EG *I have breakfast at the same time every morning.*

breast /brɛst/
breasts

NOUN

A woman's breasts are the two soft, round pieces of flesh on her chest, which produce milk after she has had a baby.

EG *... women with small breasts*

breast-feed /ˈbrɛstfiːd/
breast-feeds breast-feeding breast-fed

VERB

If a woman breast-feeds her baby, she feeds it with milk from her breasts.

EG *Not all women can breast-feed their babies.*

breath /brɛθ/
breaths

NOUN

1 Your breath is the air that you

take into your lungs and let out again when you breathe.
EG *Smoking causes bad breath.*
EG *He took a deep breath.*

2 If you are **out of breath**, you are breathing with difficulty after doing something energetic.
EG *She was slightly out of breath from running.*

breathe /briːð/
breathes breathing breathed

VERB
When you breathe, you take air into your lungs and let it out again.
EG *He seemed to have stopped breathing.*

bred /bred/
past participle and past tense of **breed**

breed /briːd/
breeds breeding bred

NOUN
1 A breed of a species of domestic animal is a particular type of it.
EG *... rare breeds of cattle*

VERB
2 Someone who breeds animals or plants keeps them in order to produce more animals or plants with particular qualities.
EG *He used to breed dogs for the police.*

3 When animals breed, they mate and produce young.
EG *Frogs will usually breed in any convenient pond.*

breeze /briːz/
breezes

NOUN
a gentle wind
EG *I imagined a breeze blowing against my face.*

bribe /braɪb/

bribes bribing bribed

NOUN
1 a gift or money that is given to an official to persuade them to do something
EG *He was accused of accepting bribes.*

VERB
2 To bribe someone means to give them a bribe.
EG *We had to bribe the border guard to let us through.*

brick /brɪk/
bricks

NOUN
Bricks are rectangular blocks of baked clay used in building.
EG *... a brick wall*

bride /braɪd/
brides

NOUN
a woman who is getting married or who has just got married
EG *The guests had crowded around the bride and groom.*

bridegroom /ˈbraɪdgruːm/
bridegrooms

NOUN
a man who is getting married or who has just got married
EG *The bridegroom was kept waiting for 15 minutes.*

bridesmaid /ˈbraɪdzmeɪd/
bridesmaids

NOUN
a woman who helps and accompanies a bride on her wedding day
EG *The bridesmaids were dressed in pink.*

bridge /brɪdʒ/
bridges

NOUN
1 a structure built over a river,

road, or railway so that vehicles and people can cross
EG *I walked across the bridge.*
2 Bridge is a card game for four players.
EG *Who's your bridge partner for tonight?*

brief /bri:f/
briefer briefest; briefs briefing briefed

ADJECTIVE
1 Something that is brief lasts only a short time.
EG *... a brief visit*

VERB
2 When you **brief** someone **on** a subject, you give them all the necessary instructions or information about it.
EG *A spokesman briefed reporters on the latest developments.*

briefcase /'bri:fkeis/
briefcases

NOUN
a small flat case for carrying papers
EG *The documents were in his briefcase.*

bright /brait/
brighter brightest

ADJECTIVE
1 Bright lights or colours are strong and noticeable.
EG *... a bright light*
EG *... a bright red dress*
2 clever
EG *He's very bright.*
EG *... a bright idea*

brilliant /'briljənt/

ADJECTIVE
1 extremely clever
EG *She had a brilliant mind.*

2 AN INFORMAL USE
extremely good or enjoyable
EG *You must see the show, it's*

brilliant!

bring /brɪŋ/
brings bringing brought

VERB
1 If you bring something or someone with you when you go to a place, you take them with you.
EG *You can bring a friend to the party.*
EG *Bring me a glass of wine.*
2 To bring something to a particular state means to cause it to be like that.
EG *He brought the car to a stop.*
EG *Her children brought her great joy.*

bring about
VERB
If you bring something about, you cause it to happen.
EG *We must try to bring about a better world.*

bring up
VERB
To bring up children means to look after them while they grow up.
EG *She brought up her children alone.*

Britain /'brɪtən/
NOUN
Britain is the island consisting of England, Scotland and Wales.
EG *... the whole of Britain*

British /'brɪtɪʃ/
ADJECTIVE
belonging or relating to Britain
EG *... a celebration of British music*

broad /brɔːd/
broader broadest

ADJECTIVE
1 wide
EG *... a broad smile*
2 Something which is broad has

A
B
C
D
E
F
G
H
I
J
K
L
M
N
O
P
Q
R
S
T
U
V
W
X
Y
Z

many different aspects or concerns
many different people.
EG *A broad range of issues was discussed.*

broadcast /'brɔːdkɑːst/
broadcasts broadcasting broadcast

NOUN
1 a programme or announcement on radio or television
EG *He was criticized for making these broadcasts.*

VERB
2 To broadcast something means to send it out by radio waves, so that it can be seen on television or heard on radio.
EG *The concert will be broadcast live on TV.*

brochure /'brəuʃjuər/
brochures

NOUN
a small book which gives information about a product or service
EG *... travel brochures*

broke /brəuk/
past tense of **break**

broken /'brəukn/
past participle of **break**

bronze /brɒnz/

NOUN OR ADJECTIVE
Bronze is a yellowish-brown metal which is a mixture of copper and tin.
EG *... a bronze statue*

brooch /brəutʃ/
brooches

NOUN
a piece of jewellery which can be pinned to clothes
EG *... a brooch in the shape of a heart*

broom /brum/
brooms

NOUN
a brush with a long handle
EG *The caretaker stood leaning on a broom.*

brother /'brʌðər/
brothers

NOUN
Your brother is a boy or man who has the same parents as you.
EG *... my younger brother*

brother-in-law /'brʌðərɪnlɔː/
brothers-in-law

NOUN
Your brother-in-law is the brother of your husband or wife, or your sister's husband.
EG *We're brothers-in-law now.*

brought /brɔːt/
past tense and past participle of **bring**

brown /braun/
browner brownest; browns

ADJECTIVE OR NOUN
Brown is the colour of earth or wood.
EG *... her deep brown eyes*
EG *... the browns and greens of the forest*

bruise /bruːz/
bruises bruising bruised

NOUN
1 a purple mark that appears on your skin after something has hit it
EG *... just a few cuts and bruises*

VERB
2 If something bruises you, it hits you so that a bruise appears on your skin.
EG *I had only bruised my knee.*

brush /brʌʃ/
brushes brushing brushed

NOUN

1 an object with many short, thick hairs which you use for cleaning things, painting, or tidying your hair
EG ... a hair brush

VERB
2 If you brush something, you clean it or tidy it with a brush.
EG I must brush my teeth.
EG He brushed away the crumbs.

3 If you brush something, or if you **brush against** it, you touch it while passing it.
EG Her lips brushed his cheek.

brutal /'bru:tl/
ADJECTIVE
cruel and violent
EG ... the victim of a brutal murder

bubble /'bʌbl/
bubbles bubbling bubbled
NOUN
1 a ball of air in a liquid
EG ... air bubbles
2 a thin, hollow ball of soapy liquid
EG ... soap bubbles

VERB
3 When a liquid bubbles, bubbles form in it.
EG Heat the soup until it bubbles.

bucket /'bʌkɪt/
buckets
NOUN
a deep round container with an open top and a handle
EG The girls played in the sand with buckets and spades.

buckle /'bʌkl/
buckles buckling buckled
NOUN
1 a fastening on the end of a belt or strap
EG He wore a belt with a large brass buckle.

VERB

2 If you buckle a belt or strap, you fasten it.
EG He came out of the door buckling his belt.

3 If something buckles, it becomes bent because of severe heat or pressure.
EG The bridge buckled under the weight of so many lorries.

Buddhism /'budɪzəm/
NOUN
Buddhism is a religion which teaches that the way to end suffering is by overcoming your desires.
EG ... a lecture on Buddhism

budget /'bʌdʒɪt/
budgets
NOUN
the amount of money that is available for a particular purpose
EG The budget for the project is very small.

buffet /'bufeɪ/
buffets
NOUN
1 a café at a station
EG We sat in the station buffet drinking tea.

2 a meal at which people serve themselves
EG ... a cold buffet

bug /bʌg/
bugs bugging bugged
NOUN
1 an insect
EG There were tiny bugs all over the walls.

2 a small error in a computer program which means that the program will not work properly
EG There is a bug in the software.

3 AN INFORMAL USE
a virus or minor infection

A
B
C
D
E
F
G
H
I
J
K
L
M
N
O
P
Q
R
S
T
U
V
W
X
Y
Z

EG ... *a stomach bug*

VERB

4 If a place is bugged, tiny microphones are hidden there to record what people are saying.
EG *I found out my phone was bugged.*

build /bɪld/
builds building built

VERB

1 If you build something such as a house, you make it from its parts.
EG *John had built his own house.*

2 If people build something such as an organization, they develop it gradually.
EG *They want to build a fairer society.*

NOUN

3 Your build is the shape and size of your body.
EG ... *a man of medium build*

building /ˈbɪldɪŋ/
buildings

NOUN

a structure with walls and a roof
EG *People were still trapped inside the building.*

building society building societies

NOUN

a business in which some people invest their money, while others borrow from it to buy a house
EG ... *the largest building society in Britain*

built /bɪlt/

past participle and past tense of **build**

bulb /bʌlb/
bulbs

NOUN

1 the glass part of an electric lamp which gives out light

EG *The stairs were lit by a single bulb.*

2 an onion-shaped root that grows into a flower or plant
EG ... *tulip bulbs*

bull /bʊl/
bulls

NOUN

the male of some species of animals, especially cows
EG *He was chased by an angry bull.*

bullet /ˈbʊlɪt/
bullets

NOUN

a small piece of metal which is fired from a gun
EG *The bullet hit him right between the eyes.*

bully /ˈbʊlɪ/
bullies bullying bullied

NOUN

1 someone who uses their strength or power to hurt or frighten other people
EG *He was known as the school bully.*

VERB

2 If someone bullies you, they use their strength or power to hurt or frighten you.
EG *He was bullied at school.*

3 If someone **bullies** you **into doing** something, they make you do it by using force or threats.
EG *She bullied us into going.*

bump /bʌmp/
bumps bumping bumped

VERB

1 If you **bump into** something, you accidentally hit it while moving.
EG *They stopped walking and he almost bumped into them.*

NOUN

2 a soft or dull noise made by something knocking into something else
EG *The plane landed with a slight bump.*

3 a raised, uneven part of a surface
EG *He had a huge bump on his head.*

bumper /'bʌmpəʳ/
bumpers

NOUN

Bumpers are bars on the front and back of a vehicle which protect it if it bumps into something.
EG *The front bumper was badly dented.*

bun /bʌn/
buns

NOUN

a small, round cake
EG *… a currant bun*

bunch /bʌntʃ/
bunches

NOUN

1 a group of people or things
EG *The players were a great bunch.*
EG *… a bunch of flowers*

2 A bunch of bananas or grapes is a group of them growing on the same stem.
EG *… two bunches of bananas*

bundle /'bʌndl/
bundles bundling bundled

NOUN

1 a number of things that are tied together or wrapped up in a cloth
EG *… a bundle of five-pound notes*

VERB

2 If you bundle someone or something somewhere, you push them there quickly and roughly.
EG *They bundled him into the police van.*

bungalow /'bʌŋgələu/

bungalows

NOUN

a one-storey house
EG *We moved to a bungalow in the suburbs.*

burden /'bə:dn/
burdens

NOUN

If something is a **burden on** you, it causes you a lot of worry or hard work.
EG *This would relieve the burden on hospital staff.*

burglar /'bə:gləʳ/
burglars

NOUN

a thief who steals from a building
EG *Burglars broke into their home.*

burn /bə:n/
burns burning burned or **burnt**

VERB

1 If something **is burning**, it is on fire.
EG *One of the cars was still burning.*
EG *Fires were burning out of control.*

2 To burn something means to damage or destroy it with fire.
EG *Coal fell out of the fire and burned the carpet.*

3 If you **burn yourself** or a part of your body, you are injured by fire or by something hot.
EG *Take care not to burn your fingers.*

NOUN

4 an injury caused by fire or by something hot
EG *She suffered terrible burns to her back.*

burst /bə:st/
bursts bursting burst

VERB

1 When something bursts or when

you burst it, it splits open because of pressure from inside it.

EG *A tyre burst.*

2 If you burst into or through something, you go into it or through it suddenly and with force.

EG *Masked gunmen burst into the bank.*

NOUN

3 A **burst of** something is a sudden short period of it.

EG *… a burst of applause*

bury /'bɛrɪ/
buries burying buried

VERB

1 When a dead person is buried, their body is put into a grave and covered with earth.

EG *Soldiers helped to bury the dead.*

2 If you bury something, you put it in a hole in the ground and cover it up.

EG *… buried treasure*

bus /bʌs/
buses

NOUN

a large motor vehicle that carries passengers

EG *They had to travel everywhere by bus.*

bush /bʊʃ/
bushes

NOUN

1 a short, thick plant with many stems

EG *Trees and bushes grew down to the water's edge.*

2 In Australia, an uncultivated area outside of city areas is called **the bush.**

EG *… dying alone in the bush*

business /'bɪznɪs/
businesses

NOUN

1 Business is work relating to the buying and selling of goods and services.

EG *I'm here on business.*

EG *It's a pleasure doing business with you.*

2 an organization which produces or sells goods or provides a service

EG *He was short of cash after the collapse of his business.*

3 You can use 'business' to refer to any event, situation, or activity.

EG *This whole business has upset me.*

EG *It's none of your business.*

bust /bʌst/
busts busting bust or **busted**

NOUN

1 a statue of someone's head and shoulders

EG *… a bust of Beethoven*

2 A woman's bust is her chest and her breasts.

EG *She has a very large bust.*

VERB

3 AN INFORMAL USE

If you bust something, you break it.

EG *They will have to bust the door to get him out.*

busy /'bɪzɪ/
busier busiest

ADJECTIVE

1 If you are busy, you are doing something and are not free to do anything else.

EG *She was too busy to attend.*

2 A busy place is full of people doing things or moving about.

EG *… a busy seaside resort*

but /bʌt/

CONJUNCTION

1 You use 'but' to introduce an idea that contrasts with what you have just said.

EG *I don't miss teaching but I miss*

the pupils.
EG *I'd love to come, but I'm busy.*

PREPOSITION

2 except
EG *We've had nothing but trouble.*

butcher /'butʃər/
butchers

NOUN

a person who owns a shop that sells meat; you also refer to a shop that sells meat as a butcher or a **butcher's**
EG *I went to the butcher's for some sausages.*

butter /'bʌtər/

NOUN

Butter is a soft, yellowish food made from cream, which you spread on bread or use in cooking.
EG *... a slice of bread and butter*

butterfly /'bʌtəflaɪ/
butterflies

NOUN

an insect with large colourful wings and a thin body
EG *He collects butterflies.*

button /'bʌtn/
buttons buttoning buttoned

NOUN

1 Buttons are small, hard objects sewn on to clothing, which you use to fasten the clothing.
EG *A button has come off my shirt.*

2 a small object on a piece of equipment that you press to make it work
EG *The gate slid open at the push of a button.*

VERB

3 If you button a piece of clothing, you fasten it using its buttons.
EG *Sam stands up, buttoning his jacket.*

buy /baɪ/
buys buying bought

VERB

If you buy something, you obtain it by paying money for it.
EG *He could not afford to buy a house.*
EG *Let me buy you a drink.*

by /baɪ/

PREPOSITION

1 You use 'by' to indicate who or what has done something.
EG *The boys were rescued by firemen.*
EG *... a painting by Picasso*

2 You use 'by' to indicate how something is done.
EG *He frightened her by hiding behind the door.*
EG *... if you're travelling by car*

3 If you hold someone or something by a particular part of them, you hold that part.
EG *She grabbed the rabbit by its ears.*

4 next to
EG *I sat by her bed.*

5 before a particular time
EG *It should be ready by next spring.*

6 You use 'by' to indicate how much bigger one amount or quantity is than another.
EG *We won by fifty points.*

7 If you do something **by yourself**, you do it alone or without help from anyone else.
EG *He spent Christmas by himself.*
EG *She brought up four children all by herself.*

PREPOSITION OR ADVERB

8 If someone or something goes by you, they move past you without stopping.
EG *We drove by his house.*
EG *A police car passed by.*

Cc

cab /kæb/
cabs

NOUN
1 a taxi
EG *She called a cab.*
2 The cab of a lorry is the front part where the driver sits.
EG *Most nights he slept in the cab.*

cabbage /'kæbɪdʒ/
cabbages

NOUN
a large, round vegetable with green leaves
EG *... cabbage soup*

cabin /'kæbɪn/
cabins

NOUN
1 a room in a ship where a passenger sleeps
EG *... a first-class cabin*
2 a small wooden house, usually in the country
EG *... a log cabin*

cabinet /'kæbɪnɪt/
cabinets

NOUN
1 a small cupboard
EG *... a medicine cabinet*
2 **the cabinet** in a government is a group of ministers who advise the leader and decide policies
EG *... a former member of the Cabinet*

cable /'keɪbl/
cables

NOUN
a bundle of wires with a rubber covering, which carries electricity
EG *... overhead power cables*

cable television

NOUN
a television service which people can receive from underground wires carrying the signals
EG *The channel is only available on cable television.*

café /'kæfeɪ/
cafés

NOUN
a place where you can buy light meals and drinks
EG *... a waitress in a café*

caffeine /'kæfiːn/

NOUN
Caffeine is a chemical in coffee and tea which makes you more active.
EG *... too much caffeine*

cage /keɪdʒ/
cages

NOUN
a box made of wire or bars in which birds or animals are kept
EG *I hate to see animals in cages.*

cake /keɪk/
cakes

NOUN
a sweet food made by baking flour, eggs, fat, and sugar
EG *... a birthday cake*
EG *... a slice of cake*

calculate /'kælkjuleɪt/
calculates calculating calculated

VERB
If you calculate a number or amount, you work it out, for example by adding or multiplying numbers.
EG *The number of votes will then be calculated.*

calculator /'kælkjuleɪtər/
calculators

NOUN
a small electronic machine used for doing mathematical calculations
EG ... a pocket calculator

calendar /'kæləndər/
calendars

NOUN
a chart showing the date of each day in a particular year
EG There was a calendar on the wall, with March 6 circled in red.

calf /kɑːf/
calves

NOUN
1 a young cow
EG The calf was only a few hours old.
2 Your calves are the backs of your legs between your ankles and knees.
EG He had scratches down the calves of both legs.

call /kɔːl/
calls calling called

VERB
1 If someone or something is called a particular name, that is their name.
EG ... a man called Jeffrey
2 If you call a person or situation something, that is how you describe them.
EG They called me crazy.
3 If you call something or **call** it **out**, you say it loudly.
EG He called out his daughter's name.
4 If you call someone, you telephone them.
EG I'll call you tomorrow.
5 If you call somewhere, you make a short visit there.
EG A man called at the house.
6 If you call someone to a place,

you ask them to come there.
EG He called me into his office.

NOUN
7 If you get a call from someone, they telephone you.
EG Were there any calls while I was out?
8 If you get a call from someone, they visit you.
EG The doctor made three calls to sick patients.
9 a cry or shout
EG ... a call for help

call off

VERB
If you call something off, you cancel it.
EG The deal was called off.

calm /kɑːm/
calmer calmest; calms calming calmed

ADJECTIVE
1 Someone who is calm is quiet and does not show any worry or excitement.
EG Try to keep calm.
2 If the sea is calm, the water is not moving very much.
EG ... a clear blue sky and calm sea

VERB
3 If you calm someone or **calm** them **down**, you do something to make them less upset or excited.
EG A cup of tea will help to calm you down.

came /keɪm/
past tense of **come**

camera /'kæmərə/
cameras

NOUN
a piece of equipment used for taking photographs or for filming
EG I need some more film for my camera.

camp /kæmp/
camps camping camped

NOUN

1 a place where people live or stay in tents or caravans

EG ... *a summer camp*

2 a collection of buildings for a particular group of people such as soldiers or prisoners

EG ... *a prisoner-of-war camp*

VERB

3 If you camp or **go camping**, you stay in a tent.

EG *We camped near the beach.*

EG *They recently went camping in France.*

campaign /kæm'peɪn/
campaigns campaigning campaigned

NOUN

1 a set of actions that is intended to achieve a particular result

EG ... *an advertising campaign*

VERB

2 To campaign means to carry out a campaign.

EG *He has campaigned against smoking.*

can /kæn/
could

☑ 'Can' is a modal verb. There are no forms ending in -s, -ing, or -ed.

VERB

1 If you **can do** something, you have the ability to do it.

EG *I can speak Italian.*

2 If you **can do** something, you are allowed to do it.

EG *Can I go to the cinema?*

can /kæn/
cans

NOUN

a metal container, often a sealed one with food or drink inside

EG ... *empty beer cans*

canal /kə'næl/
canals

NOUN

a long, narrow, man-made stretch of water

EG ... *the canals of Venice*

cancel /'kænsəl/
cancels cancelling cancelled

VERB

If you cancel an event, service, or arrangement, you stop it from happening.

EG *My friend has cancelled his visit.*

cancer /'kænsər/

NOUN

Cancer is a serious disease in which cells which are not normal increase rapidly in a part of the body.

EG ... *lung cancer*

candidate /'kændɪdeɪt/
candidates

NOUN

a person who is being considered for a job

EG ... *a candidate for the office of Governor*

candle /'kændl/
candles

NOUN

a stick of hard wax with a piece of string, called a wick, through the middle. You light the wick so the candle produces light.

EG *The bedroom was lit by a single candle.*

candy /'kændɪ/
candies

NOUN

In American English, sweets such as chocolates are referred to as candy.

EG *She gave candy to the children.*

EG *... a piece of candy*

cannot /ˈkænɔt/ also spelt can't
VERB

Cannot and can't mean the same as can not.
EG *She cannot come home yet.*
EG *I can't help you.*

canteen /kænˈtiːn/
canteens

NOUN

the part of a factory, office, or shop where the workers can go to eat
EG *We usually have lunch in the canteen.*

cap /kæp/
caps

NOUN

a soft, flat hat, often with a peak at the front
EG *... a baseball cap*

capable /ˈkeɪpəbl/
ADJECTIVE

If you are **capable of doing** something, you are able to do it.
EG *He was barely capable of standing up.*

capacity /kəˈpæsɪtɪ/
capacities

NOUN

1 the maximum amount that something can hold or produce
EG *... a seating capacity of eleven thousand*
2 a person's power or ability to do something
EG *... his capacity for eating hamburgers*
3 If you do something in your **capacity as** a particular job or role, you do it as part of that job or role.
EG *... in his capacity as chairman*

capital /ˈkæpɪtl/

capitals
NOUN

1 The capital of a country is the city where the government meets.
EG *... Kathmandu, the capital of Nepal*
2 Capital is a sum of money that is owned or used by a business, or invested to make more money.
EG *Companies are having difficulty in raising capital.*
3 A capital or a **capital letter** is a larger letter that is used at the beginning of a sentence or name.
EG *Please write your name in capitals.*
EG *Start every sentence with a capital letter.*

capitalism /ˈkæpɪtəlɪzəm/
NOUN

Capitalism is an economic and political system where businesses and industries are owned by private individuals and not by the state.
EG *... the two opposed social systems, capitalism and socialism*

capitalist /ˈkæpɪtəlɪst/
capitalists

NOUN

1 a person who believes in capitalism
EG *... both socialists and capitalists*
ADJECTIVE
2 relating to capitalism
EG *... capitalist countries*

captain /ˈkæptɪn/
captains

NOUN

1 the officer in charge of a ship or aeroplane
EG *The captain apologized for the delay.*
2 the leader of a sports team
EG *... the captain of the cricket team*

A
B
C
D
E
F
G
H
I
J
K
L
M
N
O
P
Q
R
S
T
U
V
W
X
Y
Z

capture /'kæptʃər/
captures capturing captured

VERB

1 If someone or something is captured, they are caught or taken prisoner.
EG *The pilot was captured but managed to escape.*

2 If something captures a quality or mood, it succeeds in representing or describing it.
EG *... a menu that captures the spirit of the region*

car /kɑːr/
cars

NOUN

1 a motor vehicle with room for a small number of people
EG *There was nowhere to park the car.*
EG *They came by car.*

2 a railway carriage that is used for a particular purpose
EG *... the buffet car*

caravan /'kærəvæn/
caravans

NOUN

a vehicle which can be pulled by a car and in which people live or spend their holidays
EG *Most summers we rent a caravan in France.*

card /kɑːd/
cards

NOUN

1 a piece of stiff paper or plastic with information or a message on it
EG *... a birthday card*

2 Cards are thin pieces of cardboard decorated with numbers or pictures and used to play various games.
EG *We spent the afternoon playing cards.*

cardboard /'kɑːdbɔːd/

NOUN

thick, stiff paper
EG *... a cardboard box*

care /kɛər/
cares caring cared

VERB

1 If you **care about** someone or something, you are concerned about them or interested in them.
EG *All he cared about was birds.*

2 If you care about what happens, you think that what happens is important.
EG *I really don't care if he comes or not.*

3 If you **care for** someone, you feel affection towards them.
EG *He still cared for me.*

4 If you **care for** someone, you look after them.
EG *They hired a nurse to care for her.*

NOUN

5 Care of someone or something is treatment for them or help and support for them.
EG *... the care of the elderly*

6 Your cares are your concerns or worries.
EG *Relax in a hot bath and forget all your cares.*

7 If you do something **with care**, you do it with great attention so as to avoid mistakes.
EG *He wrote the numbers down with great care.*

8 If you **take care of** someone, you look after them.
EG *There was no one else to take care of their children.*

9 If you **take care of** something, you deal with it.
EG *Malcolm had taken care of all the arrangements.*

career /kəˈrɪəʳ/
careers

NOUN

a profession, or the part of your life
that you spend in a profession
EG ... *a career in journalism*
EG ... *the first part of his career*

careful /ˈkeəful/

ADJECTIVE

1 If you are careful, you pay
attention to what you are doing so
as to avoid mistakes.
EG *Be careful what you say to him.*
2 Something that is careful shows
a concern for detail.
EG *It needs very careful planning.*

careless /ˈkeəlɪs/

ADJECTIVE

If you are careless, you do not pay
enough attention to what you are
doing.
EG ... *careless driving*

car park **car parks**

NOUN

an area or building where people
can leave their cars
EG *The car park was full so we
parked on the street.*

carpet /ˈkɑːpɪt/
carpets

NOUN

a thick covering for a floor, usually
made of a material like wool
EG *They laid new carpets and
painted the walls.*

carriage /ˈkærɪdʒ/
carriages

NOUN

1 one of the separate sections of a
passenger train
EG *The man was disturbing her, so
she changed carriages.*
2 an old-fashioned vehicle for
carrying passengers, usually pulled

by horses
EG ... *an open carriage pulled by six
horses*

carrot /ˈkærət/
carrots

NOUN

a long, thin, orange-coloured root
vegetable
EG *Slice the tops off the carrots.*

carry /ˈkærɪ/
carries carrying carried

VERB

1 If you carry something, you hold
it and take it somewhere.
EG *He carried his suitcase into the
bedroom.*
2 If you carry something, you have
it with you.
EG *He always carried a gun.*

carry on

VERB

If you **carry on doing**
something you continue to do it.
EG *The assistant carried on talking.*

carry out

VERB

If you carry something out, you do
it and complete it.
EG *The work was carried out by a
local builder.*

cart /kɑːt/
carts

NOUN

an old-fashioned wooden vehicle,
usually pulled by an animal
EG ... *a horse-drawn cart*

cartoon /kɑːˈtuːn/
cartoons

NOUN

1 a humorous drawing in a
newspaper or magazine
EG ... *a political cartoon*
2 a film in which all the characters
and scenes are drawn

A
B
C
D
E
F
G
H
I
J
K
L
M
N
O
P
Q
R
S
T
U
V
W
X
Y
Z

EG *... a Tom and Jerry cartoon*

carve /kɑːv/
carves carving carved

VERB

1 If you carve an object, you cut it out of a substance such as stone or wood.
EG *One of the prisoners had carved a chess set out of wood.*

2 If you carve meat, you cut slices from it.
EG *Carve the beef into slices.*

case /keɪs/
cases

NOUN

1 a particular situation, event, or example
EG *This causes problems in some cases.*
EG *... a bad case of sunburn*

2 a container for something
EG *... a camera case*

3 a suitcase
EG *We carried our cases to the car.*

4 a crime, or a trial that takes place after a crime
EG *Police have re-opened the case.*
EG *... a court case*

5 In an argument, the **case for** an idea is the reasons used to support it.
EG *There's a strong case for reform.*

6 If something is **the case**, it is true.
EG *I hoped he would pay me, but that wasn't the case.*

7 You say **in case** to explain something that you do because a particular thing might happen.
EG *I didn't want to shout in case I frightened you.*

cash /kæʃ/
cashes cashing cashed

NOUN

1 Cash is money in the form of notes and coins.
EG *... two thousand pounds in cash*

VERB

2 If you **cash a cheque**, you take it to a bank and exchange it for money.
EG *The cheque must be cashed within three months.*

cassette /kæ'set/
cassettes

NOUN

a small flat container with magnetic tape inside, which is used for recording and playing back sounds
EG *... available on CD and cassette*

cast /kɑːst/
casts casting cast

NOUN

1 all the people who act in a play or film
EG *The cast was amazed by the film's success.*

☑ You can use either a singular or a plural verb after 'cast': *the cast was amazed; the cast were amazed.*

VERB

2 To cast actors is to choose them for roles in a play or film.
EG *He was cast as a college professor.*

3 When people **cast** their **votes** in an election, they vote.
EG *He was expected to obtain over half the votes cast.*

4 If you **cast doubt** or **suspicion** on something, you make people unsure about it.
EG *New evidence casts doubt on the theory.*

castle /'kɑːsl/
castles

NOUN

a large building with walls or

ditches round it to protect it from attack
EG ... a trip to Windsor Castle

casual /'kæʒjul/

ADJECTIVE

1 Something that is casual happens by chance and without planning.
EG ... a casual remark

2 If you are casual, you are relaxed and unconcerned.
EG He tried to appear casual.

3 Casual clothes are suitable for informal occasions.
EG ... a casual shirt

casualty /'kæʒjultı/
casualties

NOUN

a person who is killed or injured in an accident or war
EG Many of the casualties were office workers.

cat /kæt/
cats

NOUN

a small, furry animal with sharp claws and a tail, often kept as a pet
EG A large black cat lay by the fire.

catalogue /'kætəlɒg/
catalogues
US **catalog**

NOUN

a list of things, such as the goods you can buy from a company, the objects in a museum, or the books in a library
EG ... a mail order catalogue

catch /kætʃ/
catches catching caught

VERB

1 If you catch an object which is moving through the air, you grasp hold of it with your hands.
EG I jumped up to catch the ball.

2 If you catch a person or animal, you capture them.
EG The police are confident of catching the killer.
EG I caught ten fish.

3 If you **catch** someone **doing** something they should not be doing, you discover them doing it.
EG He caught me reading his diary.

4 If you catch a bus, train or plane, you get on it and travel somewhere.
EG I've got to catch a train to Edinburgh.

5 If you catch a cold or a disease, you become ill with it.
EG You're more likely to catch a cold if you're stressed.

6 If you **catch sight of** someone or something or **catch a glimpse of** them, you see them suddenly or briefly.
EG Then I caught sight of him in the crowd.

7 If something **catches fire**, it starts burning.
EG The aircraft caught fire soon after take-off.

NOUN

8 a hook that fastens or locks a door or window
EG He released the catch.

9 a problem or hidden complication in something
EG OK, but what's the catch?

catch up

VERB

If you **catch up with** someone in front of you, you reach them by walking faster than them.
EG I stopped and waited for her to catch up with me.

category /'kætɪgərı/
categories

NOUN

A
B
C
D
E
F
G
H
I
J
K
L
M
N
O
P
Q
R
S
T
U
V
W
X
Y
Z

a set of things with a particular characteristic in common
EG *Most jobs can be divided into four categories.*

cater /'keɪtər/
caters catering catered
VERB
To **cater for** people means to provide them with the things they need.
EG *Minorca is the sort of place that caters for families.*

cathedral /kə'θiːdrəl/
cathedrals
NOUN
an important church with a bishop in charge of it
EG *We visited Canterbury Cathedral.*

Catholic /'kæθəlɪk/
Catholics
ADJECTIVE OR NOUN
Catholic means the same as Roman Catholic.
EG *... a Catholic priest*
EG *She's a strict Catholic.*

cattle /'kætl/
PLURAL NOUN
Cattle are cows and bulls kept by farmers.
EG *... a herd of cattle*

caught /kɔːt/
past participle and past tense of **catch**

cauliflower /'kɒlɪflaʊər/
cauliflowers
NOUN
a large, round, white vegetable surrounded by green leaves
EG *... cauliflower cheese*

cause /kɔːz/
causes causing caused
NOUN
1 The cause of something is the

thing that makes it happen.
EG *Nobody knew the cause of the explosion.*
2 an aim or principle which a group of people are working for
EG *He is sympathetic to our cause.*
VERB
3 To cause something means to make it happen.
EG *This can cause delays.*
EG *He never caused me any problems.*

cautious /'kɔːʃəs/
ADJECTIVE
Someone who is cautious acts carefully in order to avoid danger or disappointment.
EG *Scientists are cautious about using the treatment on humans.*

cave /keɪv/
caves caving caved
NOUN
a large hole in the side of a cliff or under the ground
EG *The men were trapped overnight in a cave.*
cave in
VERB
If a roof caves in, it collapses.
EG *After the storms, part of the roof caved in.*

CD CDs
an abbreviation for 'compact disc'
EG *... now available on CD*

ceiling /'siːlɪŋ/
ceilings
NOUN
the top inside surface of a room
EG *The room was lined from floor to ceiling with books.*

celebrate /'selɪbreɪt/
celebrates celebrating celebrated
VERB

If you celebrate something, you do something special and enjoyable because of it.
EG ... *a party to celebrate the end of the exams*
EG *I felt like celebrating.*

celebration /sɛlɪ'breɪʃən/
celebrations
NOUN
a special event that is organized in order to celebrate something
EG ... *his birthday celebrations*

celebrity /sɪ'lɛbrɪtɪ/
celebrities
NOUN
a famous person
EG *The party was full of celebrities.*

cell /sɛl/
cells
NOUN
1 In biology, a cell is the smallest part of an animal or plant that can exist by itself. Animals and plants are made up of millions of cells...
EG ... *blood cells*
2 a small room in a prison or police station where a prisoner is locked up
EG ... *two years in a prison cell*

cellar /'sɛlər/
cellars
NOUN
a room underneath a building
EG ... *a wine cellar*

cement /sə'mɛnt/
NOUN
Cement is a grey powder which is mixed with sand and water to make concrete.
EG ... *a cement mixer*

cemetery /'sɛmɪtrɪ/
cemeteries
NOUN
an area of land where dead people are buried
EG *Every Sunday after church they visited the cemetery.*

cent /sɛnt/
cents
NOUN
a unit of money in the USA and in some other countries. There are 100 cents in a dollar.
EG ... *two dollars and fifty cents*

center /'sɛntər/
see **centre**

centimetre /'sɛntɪmiːtər/
centimetres
US **centimeter**
NOUN
a unit of length equal to ten millimetres or one hundredth of a metre
EG ... *a tiny plant only a few centimetres high*

central /'sɛntrəl/
ADJECTIVE
1 in or near the centre of an object or area
EG ... *central London*
2 main or most important
EG ... *the central idea of his work*

central heating
NOUN
Central heating is a heating system in which water or air is heated and passed round a building through pipes and radiators.
EG *All rooms have central heating.*

centre /'sɛntər/
centres
US **center**
NOUN
1 the middle of an object or area
EG ... *in the centre of the room*
2 a building where people go for activities, meetings, or help
EG ... *a health centre*

A B C D E F G H I J K L M N O P Q R S T U V W X Y Z

A
B
C
D
E
F
G
H
I
J
K
L
M
N
O
P
Q
R
S
T
U
V
W
X
Y
Z

century /'sɛntjʊrɪ/
centuries

NOUN

a period of one hundred years

EG ... the worst floods this century

EG ... the 19th century

☑ When people talk about the 19th century, they mean the years between 1800 and 1899.

cereal /'sɪːrɪəl/
cereals

NOUN

a food made from grain, often eaten with milk for breakfast

EG ... a bowl of cereal

ceremony /'sɛrɪmənɪ/
ceremonies

NOUN

a formal event such as a wedding or funeral

EG ... a private ceremony, attended only by the family

certain /'sɜːtən/

ADJECTIVE

1 definite and with no doubt at all

EG She is absolutely certain she's going to succeed.

EG The train is certain to be late.

2 You use 'certain' to refer to a specific person or thing without saying exactly who or what it is.

EG Certain aspects of the job appealed to me.

certainly /'sɜːtənlɪ/

ADVERB

1 without doubt

EG My boss was certainly interested.

2 of course

EG "Will you be there?" — "Certainly."

EG "Did you do this?" — "Certainly not."

certificate /sə'tɪfɪkɪt/
certificates

a document stating particular facts, for example facts about someone's birth or death

EG ... a birth certificate

chain /tʃeɪn/
chains chaining chained

NOUN

1 a number of metal rings connected together in a line

EG ... a bicycle chain

2 a number of things in a series

EG ... a chain of shops

EG ... a chain of events

VERB

3 If you **chain** one thing **to** another, you fasten them together with a chain.

EG They had chained themselves to the railings.

chair /tʃeəʳ/
chairs

NOUN

a seat for one person to sit on, with a back and four legs

EG He got up from his chair and walked to the window.

chairman /'tʃeəmən/
chairmen

NOUN

1 the person in charge of a meeting, who decides when each person may speak

EG The chairman declared the meeting open.

☑ If the person is a woman, you can refer to her as a 'chairwoman'. A 'chairperson' can be either a man or a woman.

2 the head of a company or committee

EG He's the chairman of a big oil company.

chalk /tʃɔːk/

NOUN
Chalk is a soft white rock. Small sticks of chalk are used for writing or drawing on a blackboard.
EG ... a stick of chalk

challenge /'tʃælɪndʒ/
challenges challenging challenged

NOUN
1 something that is new and exciting but requires a lot of effort
EG It's a new challenge for me.

2 a suggestion from someone to compete with them
EG He laid down a challenge.

3 A **challenge to** something is a questioning of whether it is correct or true.
EG ... a challenge to authority

VERB
4 If someone challenges you, they suggest that you compete with them in some way.
EG They had challenged and beaten the best teams in the world.

5 If you challenge something, you question whether it is correct or true.
EG This idea has never been challenged.

champagne /ʃæm'peɪn/
NOUN
Champagne is a sparkling white wine made in France.
EG ... a glass of champagne

champion /'tʃæmpɪən/
champions
NOUN
a person who wins a competition
EG ... the world champion

championship /'tʃæmpɪənʃɪp/
championships
NOUN
a competition to find the

champion of a sport or game
EG ... the world chess championship

chance /tʃɑːns/
chances chancing chanced
NOUN
1 The chance of something happening is how possible or likely it is.
EG I think we've got a good chance of winning.

2 an opportunity to do something
EG ... before I had a chance to reply

3 If you **take chances** or **take a chance**, you take a risk in which something dangerous or unpleasant may happen.
EG Don't take any chances, he's got a gun.

4 Something that happens **by chance** happens unexpectedly.
EG I only found out by chance.

VERB
5 If you chance something, you try it although you are taking a risk.
EG There's a risk I'll be caught, but I'm going to chance it.

chancellor /'tʃɑːnsələʳ/
chancellors
NOUN
1 the head of government in some European countries
EG ... a supporter of Chancellor Kohl

2 In Britain, the **Chancellor** or the **Chancellor of the Exchequer** is the minister responsible for finance and taxes.
EG The Chancellor could use the Budget to bring in tax reforms.

change /tʃeɪndʒ/
changes changing changed
NOUN
1 If there is a **change in** something, it becomes different.
EG Steven soon noticed a change in Penny's attitude.

EG *... a time of change*

2 A **change of** something is an act of replacing it.

EG *A change of leadership is not enough.*

3 Change is the money that you get back when you pay for something with more money than it costs.

EG *She handed him his change.*

4 Change is coins rather than notes.

EG *Have you got any change for the phone?*

VERB

5 When something changes or when you change it, it becomes different.

EG *Little has changed since then.*

EG *It changed my life.*

6 If you change something, you exchange it for something else.

EG *I'm thinking of changing my job.*

7 If you **change** your **mind**, you change a decision that you have made or an opinion that you have.

EG *I was going to vote for him, but I changed my mind.*

8 When you change buses or trains, you get off one and on to another in order to continue your journey.

EG *You'll need to change trains in Birmingham.*

9 When you change or **get changed**, you put on different clothes.

EG *I won't be a minute, I'm just going to get changed.*

10 If you change a sum of money, you exchange it for smaller coins or notes of the same total value, or you exchange it for foreign currency.

EG *Can you change a fifty-pound note?*

EG *I changed two hundred pounds into dollars.*

channel /'tʃænl/
channels channelling channelled

NOUN

1 a television station

EG *I was watching the other channel.*

2 The **Channel** or the **English Channel** is the stretch of sea between England and France.

EG *... the Channel Tunnel*

VERB

3 If you **channel** something such as money or energy **into** something, you use the money or energy for that purpose.

EG *We try and channel the children's energies into creative pastimes.*

chant /tʃɑːnt/
chants chanting chanted

NOUN

1 a group of words that is repeated over and over again

EG *Fifty thousand fans joined in the chant.*

VERB

2 If people chant something, they repeat it over and over again.

EG *The crowd chanted his name.*

chaos /'keɪɒs/

NOUN

Chaos is a state of complete disorder.

EG *Their concerts often ended in chaos.*

chap /tʃæp/
chaps

NOUN

AN INFORMAL WORD

a man

EG *"You're a very lucky chap," he*

said.

chapter /'tʃæptər/
chapters

NOUN

one of the parts into which a book is divided

EG *Turn to Chapter 1.*

character /'kærɪktər/
characters

NOUN

1 The character of a person or place is all the qualities that make them distinct.

EG *There was another, gentler side to his character.*

2 The characters in a film, play, or book are the people in it.

EG *All the characters are very believable.*

3 a person

EG *He's an odd character.*

characteristic /kærɪktə'rɪstɪk/
characteristics

NOUN

1 a quality that is typical of a particular person or thing

EG *He inherited his physical characteristics from his father.*

ADJECTIVE

2 typical of a particular person or thing

EG *That's very characteristic of him.*

charge /tʃɑːdʒ/
charges charging charged

VERB

1 If someone charges you money, they ask you to pay it for something you have bought or received.

EG *They charge a small fee for their services.*

EG *How much did he charge you?*

2 When the police charge someone, they formally accuse

them of having committed a crime.

EG *He was arrested and charged with a variety of offences.*

3 If you **charge** a **battery**, you pass an electrical current through it to make it store electricity.

EG *Alex had forgotten to charge the battery.*

4 If you charge somewhere, you move there quickly and aggressively.

EG *She charged into the room.*

NOUN

5 the price that you have to pay for something

EG *No charge is made for repairs.*

EG *Admission is free of charge.*

6 a formal accusation that a person is guilty of a crime and has to go to court

EG *He may still face criminal charges.*

7 If you are **in charge of** someone or something, you are responsible for them.

EG *I left him in charge of the shop while I went out.*

charity /'tʃærɪtɪ/
charities

NOUN

1 an organization that raises money to help people who are ill, poor, or disabled

EG *The Red Cross is a registered charity.*

2 Charity is money or other help that is given to poor, disabled, or ill people.

EG *... to raise money for charity*

charm /tʃɑːm/
charms charming charmed

NOUN

1 Charm is the quality of being attractive and pleasant.

EG *... a man of great personal*

A
B
C
D
E
F
G
H
I
J
K
L
M
N
O
P
Q
R
S
T
U
V
W
X
Y
Z

charm

VERB
2 If you charm someone, you use your charm to please them.
EG *I was charmed by his courtesy.*

charming /'tʃɑːmɪŋ/

ADJECTIVE
very pleasant and attractive
EG *He's a very charming man.*

chart /tʃɑːt/
charts charting charted

NOUN
1 a diagram or table showing information
EG *He noted the score on his chart.*

VERB
2 If you chart something, you observe and record it carefully.
EG *We charted their movements.*

charter /'tʃɑːtər/
charters

ADJECTIVE
1 A charter flight or plane is one which is hired for use by a particular person or group.
EG *... charter flights to Spain*

NOUN
2 a formal document describing the rights or aims of an organization
EG *... the United Nations charter*

chase /tʃeɪs/
chases chasing chased

VERB
1 If you chase someone or something, you run after them or follow them in order to catch them or make them leave a place.
EG *She chased the thief for 100 yards.*
EG *Many farmers will chase you off their land.*

NOUN
2 the activity of chasing someone or something
EG *... a high-speed car chase*

chat /tʃæt/
chats chatting chatted

NOUN
1 a friendly, informal talk with someone
EG *I had a chat with John.*

VERB
2 When people chat, they talk to each other in a friendly and informal way.
EG *They were chatting about their holidays.*

chat up

VERB
AN INFORMAL USE
If you chat someone up, you talk to them in a friendly way, because you are attracted to them.
EG *He spent most of the evening chatting up one of my friends.*

cheap /tʃiːp/
cheaper cheapest

ADJECTIVE
1 Something that is cheap costs very little money.
EG *Tickets are still unbelievably cheap.*
2 Something that is cheap is of poor quality.
EG *Beware of cheap imitations.*
3 A cheap joke or remark is unfair and unkind.
EG *She accused him of making cheap jokes at her expense.*

cheat /tʃiːt/
cheats cheating cheated

VERB
1 If someone cheats in a game or exam, they break the rules in order to do better.
EG *Students may be tempted to cheat.*
2 If someone **cheats** you **out of**

something, they get it from you by behaving dishonestly.
EG ... an attempt to cheat them out of their pensions

NOUN
3 a person who cheats
EG He's a liar and a cheat.

check /tʃɛk/
checks checking checked

VERB
1 If you check something, you examine it in order to make sure that everything is all right.
EG Always check your change before leaving the shop.

NOUN
2 an inspection to make sure that everything is all right
EG ... airport security checks
3 Checks are different coloured squares which form a pattern.
EG Styles include stripes and checks.
4 In American English, the check in a restaurant is the bill.
EG Could we have the check, please?
5 the usual American spelling of **cheque**

ADJECTIVE
6 Check or **checked** means marked with a pattern of squares.
EG ... a man in a check suit

check in
VERB
When you check in at a hotel or airport, you arrive and sign your name or show your ticket.
EG Let's check in first, then go for a coffee.

check out
VERB
1 When you check out of a hotel, you pay your bill and leave.
EG They packed and checked out.
2 If you check someone or something out, you find out about

them.
EG Maybe we should go to the library and check it out.

check up
VERB
If you **check up** on someone or something, you find out information about them.
EG She kept phoning the office to check up on me.

checkbook /'tʃɛkbʊk/
see **chequebook**

checkout /'tʃɛkaʊt/
checkouts

NOUN
a counter in a supermarket where customers pay for their goods
EG There was a long queue at the checkout.

cheek /tʃiːk/
cheeks

NOUN
Your cheeks are the sides of your face below your eyes.
EG She kissed him lightly on both cheeks.

cheeky /'tʃiːkɪ/
cheekier cheekiest

ADJECTIVE
slightly rude or disrespectful, often in an amusing way
EG Martin gave her a cheeky grin.

cheer /tʃɪər/
cheers cheering cheered

VERB
1 When people cheer, they shout with approval or in order to show support for a person or team.
EG The crowd cheered as he entered the stadium.

NOUN
2 a shout of approval or support
EG A great cheer went up.
3 People sometimes say

A
B
C
D
E
F
G
H
I
J
K
L
M
N
O
P
Q
R
S
T
U
V
W
X
Y
Z

"Cheers" to each other just before they drink an alcoholic drink.
EG *He raised his glass. "Cheers!" he said.*

cheer up

VERB

When you cheer up, or when something cheers you up, you feel more cheerful.
EG *Come on, cheer up!*
EG *Her friends tried to cheer her up.*

cheerful /'tʃɪəful/

ADJECTIVE

1 A cheerful person is happy.
EG *I had never seen her so cheerful.*
2 Cheerful things are pleasant and make you feel happy.
EG *The nursery is a bright and cheerful place.*

cheese /tʃiːz/

NOUN

Cheese is a solid food made from milk.
EG *... a piece of cheese*

chef /ʃef/
chefs

NOUN

a head cook in a restaurant or hotel
EG *... a famous French chef*

chemical /'kemɪkl/
chemicals

NOUN

1 Chemicals are substances made by the use of chemistry.
EG *... the use of chemicals in agriculture*

ADJECTIVE

2 involved in chemistry or using chemicals
EG *... a chemical reaction*
EG *... chemical weapons*

chemist /'kemɪst/
chemists

NOUN

A chemist or a **chemist's** is a shop where medicines and cosmetics are sold.
EG *She went into a chemist's and bought some aspirin.*

chemistry /'kemɪstrɪ/

NOUN

Chemistry is the scientific study of substances and the ways in which they change when they are combined.
EG *He has a degree in chemistry.*

cheque /tʃek/
cheques
US **check**

NOUN

A cheque is a printed form on which you write an amount of money that you have to pay. You sign the cheque and your bank pays the money from your account.
EG *I'd like to pay by cheque.*

chequebook /'tʃekbuk/
chequebooks
US **checkbook**

NOUN

a book of cheques
EG *Someone had stolen his chequebook.*

cherry /'tʃerɪ/
cherries

NOUN

a small, round fruit with a red or black skin and a hard stone in the centre
EG *... a bowl of cherries*

chess /tʃes/

NOUN

Chess is a board game for two people in which each player has 16 pieces, including a king. The aim is to trap your opponent's

king.
EG *Do you play chess?*

chest /tʃest/
chests

NOUN

1 the front part of your body between your shoulders and your waist
EG *He was shot in the chest.*

2 a large wooden box, used for storing things
EG *... a treasure chest*

chew /tʃu:/
chews chewing chewed

VERB

When you chew something, you use your teeth to break it up in your mouth before swallowing it.
EG *Eat slowly and chew your food well.*

chicken /'tʃɪkɪn/
chickens

NOUN

a bird kept on a farm for its eggs and meat; also the meat of this bird
EG *... roast chicken*

chief /tʃi:f/
chiefs

NOUN

1 the leader of a group or organization
EG *... the police chief*

ADJECTIVE

2 most important
EG *... one of the chief sources of oil*

child /tʃaɪld/
children

NOUN

1 a young person who is not yet an adult
EG *... when I was a child*

2 Someone's child is their son or daughter.
EG *Her children are all married.*

childhood /'tʃaɪldhud/
childhoods

NOUN

Someone's childhood is the time when they are a child.
EG *She had a happy childhood.*

childish /'tʃaɪldɪʃ/

ADJECTIVE

immature and foolish
EG *... childish behaviour*

children /'tʃɪldrən/
the plural of **child**

chilly /'tʃɪlɪ/
chillier chilliest

ADJECTIVE

rather cold
EG *It was a chilly afternoon.*

chimney /'tʃɪmnɪ/
chimneys

NOUN

a pipe above a fire through which smoke can go up into the air
EG *Thick smoke poured from the chimney.*

chin /tʃɪn/
chins

NOUN

the part of your face below your mouth
EG *He stroked his chin thoughtfully.*

Chinese /tʃaɪ'ni:z/

ADJECTIVE

1 belonging or relating to China
EG *... a Chinese restaurant*

NOUN

2 someone who comes from China
EG *... a group of Chinese*
☑ 'Chinese' is both the singular and plural.

3 Chinese refers to any of the languages spoken in China.
EG *The book was in Chinese.*

A
B
C
D
E
F
G
H
I
J
K
L
M
N
O
P
Q
R
S
T
U
V
W
X
Y
Z

A
B
C
D
E
F
G
H
I
J
K
L
M
N
O
P
Q
R
S
T
U
V
W
X
Y
Z

chip /tʃɪp/
chips chipping chipped

NOUN

1 Chips are thin strips of fried potato that are eaten hot.
EG … *fish and chips*

2 In American English, chips are the same as crisps.
EG … *a packet of chips*

3 a tiny piece of silicon inside a computer which is used to form electronic circuits
EG … *computer chips*

4 a small piece of an object that has been broken off
EG *He was burning wood chips.*

5 the mark made on an object when a piece breaks off
EG *The vase had a small chip in it.*

VERB

6 If you chip an object, you break a small piece off it.
EG *The singer chipped his tooth on a microphone.*

chocolate /'tʃɒklɪt/
chocolates

NOUN

1 Chocolate is a sweet food made from cocoa beans.
EG … *a bar of chocolate*

2 a sweet made of chocolate
EG … *a box of chocolates*

choice /tʃɔɪs/
choices

NOUN

1 a range of different things that are available to choose from
EG … *a wider choice of treatments*

2 something that you choose
EG *You've made a good choice.*

3 If you have **no choice** or **little choice** but to do something, you cannot avoid doing it.
EG *I had no choice but to go with him.*

choir /'kwaɪəʳ/
choirs

NOUN

a group of singers, for example in a church
EG … *the church choir*

choke /tʃəuk/
chokes choking choked

VERB

1 If you **choke on** something, it prevents you from breathing properly.
EG *He choked on a fish bone.*

2 To choke someone means to squeeze their neck until they are dead.
EG *She choked him with his tie.*

chook /tʃuk/
chooks

NOUN

AN INFORMAL WORD

In Australian and New Zealand English, a chook is a chicken.
EG … *a frozen chook*

choose /tʃuːz/
chooses choosing chose chosen

VERB

1 If you choose something, you decide to have it.
EG *They will be able to choose their own leaders.*

2 If you choose to do something, you decide to do it.
EG *He chose to live in Kenya.*

chop /tʃɒp/
chops chopping chopped

VERB

1 If you chop something, you cut it into pieces with a knife or axe.
EG *Chop the onion into thin strips.*

NOUN

2 a small piece of lamb or pork containing a bone, usually cut

chicken

from the ribs
EG *... lamb chops*

chorus /'kɔːrəs/
choruses

NOUN
a part of a song which is repeated
after each verse
EG *Everyone joined in the chorus.*

chose /tʃəuz/
past tense of **choose**

chosen /'tʃəuzn/
past participle of **choose**

christen /'krɪsn/
**christens christening
christened**

VERB
When a baby is christened, it is
given its Christian names and
made a member of the Christian
church.
EG *She was born in March and
christened in June.*

Christian /'krɪstɪən/
Christians

NOUN
1 a person who believes in Jesus
Christ and his teachings
EG *He was a devout Christian.*

ADJECTIVE
2 relating to Jesus Christ and his
teachings
EG *... the Christian faith*

Christianity /krɪstɪˈænɪtɪ/

NOUN
Christianity is a religion based on
the teachings of Jesus Christ.
EG *... the spread of Christianity*

**Christian name Christian
names**

NOUN
Some people refer to their first
names as their Christian names.
EG *I told him to call me by my*

Christian name, but he continued to
address me as 'Mr Byrne'.

Christmas /'krɪsməs/

NOUN
Christmas is the period around the
25th of December, when
Christians celebrate the birth of
Jesus Christ.
EG *I have to work at Christmas this
year.*
EG *Merry Christmas!*

Christmas Day

NOUN
Christmas Day is the 25th of
December.
EG *We usually spend Christmas Day
at my parents'.*

Christmas Eve

NOUN
Christmas Eve is the 24th of
December.
EG *The office is open on Christmas
Eve.*

chunk /tʃʌŋk/
chunks

NOUN
a thick piece of something
EG *... chunks of ice*

church /tʃɜːtʃ/
churches

NOUN
1 a building where Christians go
for religious services
EG *... one of Britain's oldest
churches*
2 If you **go to church** or if you
are **in church**, you attend a
religious service.
EG *Did you go to church on Sunday?*
EG *I didn't see you in church this
week.*
3 In the Christian religion, a
church is one of the groups with
their own particular beliefs,

A
B
C
D
E
F
G
H
I
J
K
L
M
N
O
P
Q
R
S
T
U
V
W
X
Y
Z

customs, and ministers.
EG ... the Catholic Church

cigar /sɪˈgɑːʳ/
cigars

NOUN

a roll of dried tobacco leaves,
which people smoke
EG He was sitting alone smoking a
big cigar.

cigarette /sɪgəˈret/
cigarettes

NOUN

a thin tube of paper containing
tobacco, which people smoke
EG ... a packet of cigarettes

cinema /ˈsɪnəmə/
cinemas

NOUN

1 a place where people go to
watch films
EG How often do you go to the
cinema?

2 Cinema is the business of
making films.
EG ... one of the great works of
Hollywood cinema

circle /ˈsɜːkl/
circles circling circled

NOUN

1 a round shape in which every
point on the edge is the same
distance from the centre
EG The students sit in a circle on the
floor.

2 a group of people, usually with
the same interests
EG He has a small circle of friends.

3 an area of seats on an upper
floor of a theatre
EG Where shall we sit, stalls or
circle?

VERB

4 To circle something means to
move around it in a circle.

EG ... a lion circling its cage

circular /ˈsɜːkjʊləʳ/

ADJECTIVE

in the shape of a circle
EG ... a large circular hole

circumstances
/ˈsɜːkəmstənsɪz/

PLURAL NOUN

1 The circumstances of a situation
or event are the conditions that
affect what happens.
EG ... the circumstances
surrounding his resignation
EG He did well in the circumstances.

2 Someone's circumstances are
their position and conditions in life.
EG Her circumstances had changed.

circus /ˈsɜːkəs/
circuses

NOUN

a travelling show that takes place
in a large tent, with performers
such as clowns and trained animals
EG My real ambition was to work in
a circus.

citizen /ˈsɪtɪzn/
citizens

NOUN

The citizens of a country or city are
the people who live in it or belong
to it.
EG ... an American citizen

city /ˈsɪtɪ/
cities

NOUN

a large town where many people
live and work
EG ... the city of Cambridge
EG ... a busy city centre

civil /ˈsɪvɪl/

ADJECTIVE

relating to the citizens of a country
EG ... civil rights

civilian /sɪˈvɪlɪən/
civilians

NOUN

a person who is not in the armed forces

EG ... *the safety of civilians caught up in the fighting*

civilization /sɪvɪlaɪˈzeɪʃən/
civilizations; also spelt
civilisation

NOUN

a society which has a highly developed organization and culture

EG ... *the ancient civilizations of Central America*

civil war **civil wars**

NOUN

a war between groups of people who live in the same country

EG ... *the Spanish Civil War*

claim /kleɪm/
claims claiming claimed

VERB

1 If you claim that something is the case, you say that it is the case.

EG *He claimed he was Scottish.*

EG ... *a man claiming to be a journalist*

2 If you claim something, you ask for it because you believe you have a right to it.

EG *The money will be given to charity if no one claims it.*

3 If someone **claims responsibility for** something, they say that they are responsible for it.

EG *No one has yet claimed responsibility for the bomb.*

NOUN

4 a statement that something is the case

EG *He rejected claims that he had had affairs with six women.*

5 a demand for something that

you believe you have a right to

EG *She will make a claim for compensation.*

clamp /klæmp/
clamps clamping clamped

NOUN

1 a device that holds something firmly in place

EG ... *a dozen bottles held in place by clamps*

VERB

2 When you **clamp** one thing **to** another, you fasten them together with a clamp.

EG ... *special trays that were clamped to the arm of a chair*

clap /klæp/
claps clapping clapped

VERB

1 When you clap, or when you **clap** your **hands**, you hit your hands together to show your appreciation.

EG *The audience clapped enthusiastically.*

EG *They clapped their hands in time to the music.*

2 If you clap something somewhere, you put it there quickly and firmly.

EG *I clapped a hand over her mouth.*

clash /klæʃ/
clashes clashing clashed

VERB

1 If people **clash with** each other, they fight or argue.

EG *Youths clashed with police in the streets.*

2 Colours or ideas that clash are very different from each other and are therefore opposed.

EG *The red door clashed with the softer tone of the walls.*

EG *On this issue their views clashed.*

3 If one event **clashes with**

A B C D E F G H I J K L M N O P Q R S T U V W X Y Z

another, they happen at the same time and so you cannot go to both.
EG *His wedding clashed with the Cup Final.*

NOUN

4 a fight or argument
EG *There were clashes between fans outside the stadium.*

class /klɑːs/
classes classing classed

NOUN

1 A class of people or things is a group of them of a particular type.
EG *... the relationship between different social classes*

2 a group of pupils or students that are taught together, or a lesson that they have together
EG *If classes were smaller, children would learn more.*
EG *I have a history class at 10.*

VERB

3 If someone or something is **classed as** a particular thing, they are considered as belonging to that group of things.
EG *At 19 you're still classed as a teenager.*

classic /'klæsɪk/
classics

ADJECTIVE

1 typical and therefore a good model or example of something
EG *... a classic example of British fair play*

2 of very high quality
EG *... one of the classic films of all time*

NOUN

3 something of the highest quality
EG *The race was a classic.*

classical /'klæsɪkl/

ADJECTIVE

1 traditional in style, form, or content

EG *... classical music*

2 relating to ancient Greece or Rome
EG *... plays set in classical times*

classroom /'klɑːsrʊm/
classrooms

NOUN

a room in a school where lessons take place
EG *... a classroom full of noisy pupils*

---

clause /klɔːz/
clauses

NOUN

A **clause** is a group of words that work together to express an idea or describe a situation. A simple sentence contains one clause.
EG *Matthew ate a cake.*
EG *Anna crossed the street.*
You can add several clauses together to make a more complex sentence.
EG *Matthew ate a cake **which was covered in chocolate**.*
EG *Anna crossed the street **after looking carefully in both directions**.*

---

claw /klɔː/
claws

NOUN

An animal's claws are the hard, curved nails at the end of its feet.
EG *The cat tried to cling to the table with its claws.*

clean /kliːn/
cleaner cleanest; cleans cleaning cleaned

ADJECTIVE

1 free from dirt or unwanted marks
EG *... a clean white shirt*
EG *The room was spotlessly clean.*

2 If something such as a book or a

joke is clean, it is not rude and does not involve bad language.
EG *They show only clean, decent movies.*

3 free from fault or error
EG *... a clean driving licence*

VERB
4 If you clean something, you remove dirt from it.
EG *It took half an hour to clean the bath.*

clear /klɪəʳ/
clearer clearest; clears clearing cleared

ADJECTIVE
1 easy to understand, see, or hear
EG *I gave a clear account of the incident.*
EG *... the clearest pictures ever taken of Pluto*
EG *... in a clear voice*

2 obvious
EG *It was clear from his letter that he was still angry.*
EG *He made it clear he did not want to talk.*

3 easy to see through
EG *... a clear liquid*

4 free from obstacles or unwanted things
EG *The runway is clear, go ahead and land.*

VERB
5 If you clear unwanted things **from** a place, you remove them.
EG *Firemen were still clearing rubble from houses.*

6 If you clear a fence or other obstacle, you jump over it without touching it.
EG *He cleared the wall with only inches to spare.*

7 When fog or mist clears, it disappears.
EG *The fog is expected to clear by late morning.*

8 If someone is **cleared of** a crime, they are proved to be not guilty.
EG *He was cleared of all charges.*

clear up

VERB
1 When you clear up, or when you clear a place up, you tidy a place and put things away.
EG *Your room's a mess, go and clear it up.*

2 When a problem or mystery is cleared up, it is solved or explained.
EG *The mystery was cleared up when I discovered they were twins.*

clench /klɛntʃ/
clenches clenching clenched

VERB
1 When you clench your **fist**, you curl your fingers up tightly.
EG *... angry protesters with clenched fists*

2 When you clench your **teeth**, you squeeze them together tightly.
EG *Slowly he released his breath through clenched teeth.*

clerk /klɑːk/
clerks

NOUN
a person who keeps records or accounts in an office, bank, or law court
EG *... a bank clerk*

clever /ˈklɛvəʳ/
cleverer cleverest

ADJECTIVE
1 intelligent and quick to understand things
EG *My sister was very clever at school.*

2 very effective or skilful
EG *... a clever plan*

A B C D E F G H I J K L M N O P Q R S T U V W X Y Z

client /'klaɪənt/
clients

NOUN

someone who pays a professional person or company for a service
EG … one of the firm's most valued clients

cliff /klɪf/
cliffs

NOUN

a high area of land with a very steep side, usually next to the sea
EG The car rolled over the edge of the cliff.

climate /'klaɪmɪt/
climates

NOUN

The climate of a place is the general weather conditions that are typical of it.
EG The climate was dry in the summer.

climax /'klaɪmæks/
climaxes

NOUN

The climax of something is the most exciting moment in it, usually near the end.
EG Reaching the Olympics was the climax of her career.

climb /klaɪm/
climbs climbing climbed

VERB

1 If you climb something such as a tree, mountain, or ladder, you move towards the top of it.
EG He climbed the stairs to his bedroom.

2 If you climb somewhere, you move there, usually with difficulty.
EG We climbed over the wall.
EG The girls climbed into the back of the car.

NOUN

3 a movement upwards
EG … the long climb up the hill

cling /klɪŋ/
clings clinging clung

VERB

If you cling to something, you hold onto it tightly.
EG He was clinging to the edge of the roof.

clinic /'klɪnɪk/
clinics

NOUN

a building where people go for medical advice or treatment
EG … a maternity clinic

clip /klɪp/
clips clipping clipped

NOUN

1 a small metal or plastic object that is used for holding things together
EG She took the clip out of her hair.

2 a short piece of a film that is shown separately
EG I've seen a clip from that film.

VERB

3 If you clip one thing to another, you fasten them together with a clip.
EG Keep the list clipped to the notebook.

4 If you clip something, you cut small pieces from it in order to shape it.
EG I saw an old man out clipping his hedge.

cloakroom /'kləʊkrum/
cloakrooms

NOUN

1 a room for coats
EG Give your coat to the cloakroom attendant.

2 a room with toilets and sinks in a public building

EG *I have to find the cloakroom.*

clock /klɒk/
clocks

NOUN

a device, often mounted on a wall, that shows you what the time is
EG *... the church clock*

clockwise /ˈklɒkwaɪz/

ADVERB

in the same direction as the hands on a clock
EG *He told the children to start moving clockwise around the room.*

close /kləʊz/
closes closing closed

VERB

1 If you close something such as a door or window, or if it closes, you move it so that it is no longer open.
EG *He heard the door close behind him.*
EG *She closed her eyes and fell asleep.*

2 If a shop closes at a certain time, it does not do business after that time.
EG *Many libraries close on Saturday afternoons.*

3 If you close a meeting, conversation, or event, or if it closes, it comes to an end.
EG *He closed the meeting with a short prayer.*
EG *The competition closes next Saturday.*

close down

VERB

If a business closes down, all work stops there permanently.
EG *Many small stores have been forced to close down.*

close /kləʊs/
closer closest

ADJECTIVE

1 Something that is **close to** something else is near to it.
EG *... a restaurant close to their home*
EG *She lives quite close.*

2 People who are **close to** each other are very friendly and know each other well.
EG *He's very close to his brother.*
EG *... a close friend of mine.*

3 If a competition is close, the competitors are nearly equal and the winner wins by only a small amount.
EG *It's close but we think we'll win.*

4 A close inspection of something is very careful and thorough.
EG *Let's have a closer look.*

closed /kləʊzd/

ADJECTIVE

1 If a door or window is closed, it is not open.
EG *The door was closed, so I waited outside.*

2 If a shop or office is closed, it is not doing business.
EG *I went to the travel agent's but it was closed.*

cloth /klɒθ/
cloths

NOUN

1 Cloth is fabric made by a process such as weaving.
EG *... a piece of cloth*

2 A cloth is a piece of material that is used for wiping or protecting things.
EG *Clean it with a damp cloth.*

clothes /kləʊðz/

PLURAL NOUN

Clothes are the things that people wear, such as shirts and dresses.
EG *She went upstairs to change her clothes.*

A B C D E F G H I J K L M N O P Q R S T U V W X Y Z

A
B
C
D
E
F
G
H
I
J
K
L
M
N
O
P
Q
R
S
T
U
V
W
X
Y
Z

clothing /'kləʊðɪŋ/

NOUN

Clothing is the clothes that people wear.
EG *What is your favourite item of clothing?*

cloud /klaʊd/
clouds

NOUN

1 a mass of tiny drops of water that is seen as a white or grey patch in the sky
EG *The sun was behind the clouds.*
2 A cloud of smoke or dust is a mass of it floating in the air.
EG *The car pulled away, raising a cloud of dust.*

cloudy /'klaʊdɪ/
cloudier cloudiest

ADJECTIVE

1 full of clouds
EG *... a cloudy sky*
2 difficult to see through
EG *... a glass of cloudy liquid*

clown /klaʊn/
clowns

NOUN

a circus performer who wears funny clothes and make-up and does silly things to make people laugh
EG *... a clown wearing huge red shoes*

club /klʌb/
clubs clubbing clubbed

NOUN

1 an organization of people with a particular interest, who meet regularly; also the place where they meet
EG *... a youth club*
EG *I called in at the club for a drink.*
2 a team which competes in sports competitions

EG *He has joined Liverpool Football Club.*
3 a nightclub
EG *Sometimes we went dancing at a club.*
4 a thick, heavy stick that is used as a weapon
EG *... men armed with knives and clubs*
5 a stick that a golf player uses to hit the ball
EG *... a set of golf clubs*

VERB

6 To club someone means to hit them hard with a heavy object.
EG *Riot police clubbed a student to death.*

clue /kluː/
clues

NOUN

something that helps to solve a problem or mystery
EG *... a crossword clue*
EG *There are no clues to the girl's killer.*

clumsy /'klʌmzɪ/
clumsier clumsiest

ADJECTIVE

1 Someone who is clumsy moves or handles things in an awkward way.
EG *... a large, clumsy man*
2 Something that is clumsy is said or done without thought or skill.
EG *... his clumsy attempts to impress her*

clung /klʌŋ/
past participle and past tense of **cling**

clutch /klʌtʃ/
clutches clutching clutched

VERB

1 If you clutch something, you hold it tightly.

EG *Michelle clutched my arm.*

NOUN

2 In a car, the clutch is the foot pedal that you press when changing gear.

EG *She let out the clutch and pulled slowly away.*

cm

an abbreviation for 'centimetres'

EG *He had grown by 2.5 cm.*

coach /kəutʃ/
coaches coaching coached

NOUN

1 a large bus that takes passengers on long journeys

EG *I hate travelling by coach.*

2 a section of a train that carries passengers

EG *... the front four coaches*

3 someone who coaches a person or sports team

EG *... a football coach*

VERB

4 If someone coaches you, they help you to get better at a sport or a subject.

EG *She had been coached by a former Wimbledon champion.*

coal /kəul/

NOUN

Coal is hard black rock from under the ground that is burned as a fuel.

EG *... a lump of coal*

coast /kəust/
coasts coasting coasted

NOUN

1 the edge of the land where it meets the sea

EG *... the west coast of Scotland*

VERB

2 If a vehicle coasts somewhere, it moves there with the engine switched off.

EG *We coasted quietly down the hill.*

coat /kəut/
coats coating coated

NOUN

1 a piece of clothing with sleeves which you wear over your other clothes

EG *He put on his coat and left.*

2 An animal's coat is the fur or hair on its body.

EG *Vitamin B6 will improve the condition of your dog's coat.*

3 A coat of paint is a layer of it.

EG *The front door needs a new coat of paint.*

VERB

4 To **coat** something **with** something means to cover it with a thin layer of something.

EG *... nuts coated with chocolate*

cockroach /'kɔkrəutʃ/
cockroaches

NOUN

a large dark-coloured insect, often found in dirty rooms

EG *There are cockroaches in my room.*

cocktail /'kɔkteɪl/
cocktails

NOUN

an alcoholic drink made from several ingredients

EG *... a champagne cocktail*

coconut /'kəukənʌt/
coconuts

NOUN

a very large nut with white flesh, milky juice, and a hard hairy shell

EG *He split the coconut open with his knife.*

code /kəud/
codes

NOUN

1 a system of replacing the letters or words in a message with other

letters or words, so that nobody can understand the message unless they know the system
EG *The message was in code.*

2 a group of numbers and letters which is used to identify something
EG *... the telephone code for Melbourne*

coffee /'kɒfɪ/
coffees

NOUN
Coffee is the roasted beans of the coffee plant; also a hot drink made from this substance.
EG *... a cup of coffee*
EG *Two coffees, please.*

coffin /'kɒfɪn/
coffins

NOUN
a box in which a dead body is buried
EG *The coffin was lowered into the ground.*

coin /kɔɪn/
coins

NOUN
a small metal disc which is used as money
EG *... a handful of coins*

coincide /kəʊɪn'saɪd/
coincides coinciding coincided

VERB
1 If one event **coincides with** another, they happen at about the same time.
EG *The exhibition coincides with the 50th anniversary of his death.*

2 When two people's ideas or opinions coincide, they agree.
EG *Their views coincided.*

coincidence /kəʊ'ɪnsɪdəns/
coincidences

NOUN

A coincidence is what happens when two or more things occur at the same time by chance.
EG *... a series of amazing coincidences*
EG *I had moved to London, and by coincidence Helen had too.*

cold /kəʊld/
colder coldest; colds

ADJECTIVE
1 Something or someone that is cold has a very low temperature.
EG *... cold water*
EG *It was windy and Jake felt cold.*

2 If it is cold, the air temperature is very low.
EG *It's so cold out today.*

3 Someone who is cold does not show much affection.
EG *What a cold, unfeeling woman she was.*

NOUN
4 You can refer to cold weather as **the cold.**
EG *She was complaining about the cold.*

5 If you have a cold, you have a minor illness in which you sneeze and may have a sore throat.
EG *I had a bad cold, so I stayed at home.*

collapse /kə'læps/
collapses collapsing collapsed

VERB
1 If something such as a building or a person collapses, they fall down suddenly.
EG *These houses are liable to collapse in a heavy storm.*
EG *Jimmy collapsed on the floor.*

2 If something such as a system or a business collapses, it suddenly stops working.
EG *His business empire collapsed.*

NOUN

3 A building's or a person's collapse is what happens when they fall down suddenly.

EG ... an inquiry into the bridge's collapse

EG Three days after his collapse he was sitting up.

4 The collapse of something such as a system or business is what happens when it stops working.

EG ... the collapse of his marriage

collar /ˈkɒlər/
collars

NOUN

1 The collar of a shirt or coat is the part round the neck which is usually folded over.

EG His tie was pulled loose and his collar hung open.

2 a leather band round the neck of a dog or cat

EG She bought a new collar and chain for her dog.

colleague /ˈkɒliːg/
colleagues

NOUN

Your colleagues are the people you work with.

EG ... a business colleague

collect /kəˈlɛkt/
collects collecting collected

VERB

1 If you collect things, you gather them together for a special purpose or as a hobby.

EG They were collecting money for charity.

EG He collects antique furniture.

2 If you collect someone or something **from** somewhere, you call there and take them away.

EG We had to collect her from school.

3 When things collect in a place,

they gather there over a period of time.

EG Food collects in holes in the teeth.

collection /kəˈlɛkʃən/
collections

NOUN

1 a group of similar things that have been acquired over a period of time

EG ... a collection of paintings

2 Collection is the act of collecting something.

EG ... services such as rubbish collection

3 the organized collecting of money, for example for charity, or the sum of money collected

EG There was a collection for a present.

college /ˈkɒlɪdʒ/
colleges

NOUN

1 a place where students study after they have left school

EG ... the local technical college

2 one of the institutions into which some universities are divided

EG ... a student at Trinity College, Cambridge

collide /kəˈlaɪd/
collides colliding collided

VERB

If a moving object **collides with** something, it hits it.

EG Two trains collided head-on.

EG Racing up the stairs, he almost collided with Daisy.

colony /ˈkɒlənɪ/
colonies

NOUN

a country that is controlled by a more powerful country

EG ... one of France's former North African colonies

A
B
C
D
E
F
G
H
I
J
K
L
M
N
O
P
Q
R
S
T
U
V
W
X
Y
Z

colour /ˈkʌlər/
colours colouring coloured
US **color**

NOUN
1 the appearance that something has as a result of reflecting light
EG *"What colour is your car?" — "Red."*
2 Someone's colour is the normal colour of their skin.
EG *... discrimination on the grounds of colour*

VERB
3 If something colours your opinion, it affects the way you think about something.
EG *Anger had coloured her judgement.*

colourful /ˈkʌləful/
US **colorful**

ADJECTIVE
Something that is colourful has bright colours.
EG *... colourful flowers*

column /ˈkɒləm/
columns

NOUN
1 a tall, solid cylinder, especially one supporting a part of a building
EG *The house had two white columns.*
2 a group of people or vehicles moving in a long line
EG *... a column of tanks*
3 In a newspaper or magazine, a column is a regular section written by the same person.
EG *He writes a column for The Wall Street Journal.*

comb /kəum/
combs combing combed

NOUN
1 a flat object with long thin pointed parts which you use for tidying your hair

EG *He ran a comb through his hair.*

VERB
2 When you comb your hair, you tidy it with a comb.
EG *He combed his hair carefully.*

combat /ˈkɒmbæt/
combats combating combated

NOUN
1 Combat is fighting.
EG *... his first experience of combat*

VERB
2 If people combat something, they try to stop it happening or developing.
EG *... a way to combat crime*

combination /kɒmbɪˈneɪʃən/
combinations

NOUN
a mixture of things
EG *I did it for a combination of reasons.*

combine /kəmˈbaɪn/
combines combining combined

VERB
1 If you combine things, you join them together to make a single thing.
EG *Combine all the ingredients.*
2 If someone combines one activity with another, they do them both at the same time.
EG *It is possible to combine a career with being a mother.*

come /kʌm/
comes coming came come

VERB
1 If you come to a place, you move there or arrive there.
EG *I first came to England ten years ago.*
EG *Come here!*
2 If something comes to a place,

it reaches as far as that place.
EG *The sea water came up to his waist.*

3 You use **come to** to say that someone or something reaches a particular state.
EG *They came to power in 1997.*
EG *We had come to a decision.*

4 When a particular time or event comes, it happens.
EG *The peak of his career came early in 1990.*

5 If you **come from** a place, you were born there or it is your home.
EG *Half the students come from Japan.*

6 A time or event **to come** is a future time or event.
EG *The public will thank them in years to come.*

come about

VERB

The way something comes about is the way it happens.
EG *The discovery came about through a series of accidents.*

come across

VERB

If you come across something, you find it by chance.
EG *I came across some old photos while I was packing.*

come on

VERB

1 You say "Come on" to someone to encourage them to do something.
EG *Come on, let's dance.*

2 When a machine or an electric light comes on, it starts working.
EG *Suddenly all the lights came on.*

3 If something is coming on, it is making progress.
EG *How's your new book coming on?*

come up

VERB

1 If an event is coming up, it is about to happen.
EG *There are elections coming up.*

2 If something comes up in a conversation or meeting, it is mentioned or discussed.
EG *Your name came up last night.*

come up with

VERB

If you come up with a plan or idea, you suggest it.
EG *Whoever came up with that idea?*

comedian /kə'mi:dɪən/
comedians

NOUN

an entertainer whose job is to make people laugh
EG *He worked as a comedian in a club.*

comedy /'kɒmɪdɪ/
comedies

NOUN

1 a play, film, or television programme that is intended to make people laugh
EG *... a new TV comedy*

2 Comedy is something that amuses people in books, plays, films, or real life.
EG *... a career in comedy*

comfort /'kʌmfət/
comforts comforting comforted

NOUN

1 Comfort is the state of being physically relaxed.
EG *Now you can shop from the comfort of your own home.*

2 Comfort is a feeling of relief from worry or unhappiness.
EG *These thoughts give me great comfort.*

A B C D E F G H I J K L M N O P Q R S T U V W X Y Z

A B C D E F G H I J K L M N O P Q R S T U V W X Y Z

PLURAL NOUN

3 comforts are things which make your life easier and more pleasant

EG ... all the comforts of home

VERB

4 If you comfort someone, you make them less worried or unhappy.

EG Ned put his arm around her, trying to comfort her.

comfortable /'kʌmfətəbl/

ADJECTIVE

1 If you are comfortable, you are physically relaxed.

EG Lie down on your bed and make yourself comfortable.

2 Something that is comfortable makes you feel relaxed.

EG ... a comfortable bed

3 If you feel comfortable in a particular situation, you are not anxious or embarrassed.

EG I don't feel very comfortable with the idea.

comic /'kɒmɪk/

comics

ADJECTIVE

1 funny

EG ... a comic novel

NOUN

2 an entertainer who tells jokes

EG ... one of Britain's best-loved comics

3 a magazine that contains stories told in pictures

EG Joe loved to read Superman comics.

comma /'kɒmə/

commas

NOUN

The **comma** is the symbol , that indicates a short pause in a sentence.

EG Anna likes swimming, but Matthew prefers fishing.

EG I made this soup with carrots, onions, and potatoes.

In large numbers written as figures, a comma can be used after the figures which represent thousands.

EG He spends between £1,000 and £20,000 a year.

command /kə'mɑːnd/

commands commanding commanded

VERB

1 If you **command** someone **to do** something, you order them to do it.

EG She commanded me to lie down.

2 If you command something such as respect, you receive it because you are popular or important.

EG He commands respect from all who know him.

NOUN

3 an order to do something

EG I closed my eyes at his command.

4 Your **command** of something is your knowledge of it and your ability to use this knowledge.

EG ... a good command of English

comment /'kɒment/

comments commenting commented

VERB

1 If you **comment on** something, you make a remark about it.

EG The President refused to comment on the rumours.

NOUN

2 a remark about something

EG She received many comments about her appearance.

commentary /'kɒməntəri/

commentaries

NOUN

a description of an event which is broadcast on radio or television while the event is happening

EG *He turned on his car radio to listen to the commentary on the match.*

commentator /'kɒmənteɪtəʳ/
commentators

NOUN

someone who gives a radio or television commentary

EG *... a football commentator*

commercial /kə'mɜːʃəl/
commercials

ADJECTIVE

1 relating to the buying and selling of goods

EG *... a major centre of commercial activity*

2 Commercial organizations and products involve producing goods in order to make a profit.

EG *The project was a commercial failure.*

NOUN

3 an advert on television or radio

EG *She switched to another channel during the commercials.*

commit /kə'mɪt/
commits committing committed

VERB

1 If someone commits a crime or sin, they do something illegal or bad.

EG *They believe they know who committed the murder.*

2 If you **commit yourself** to something, you accept it fully or state that you will do it.

EG *Mary had committed herself to becoming a teacher.*

3 If someone is **committed to** a

hospital or prison, they are officially sent there.

EG *Eventually he was committed to a mental hospital.*

commitment /kə'mɪtmənt/
commitments

NOUN

1 Commitment is a strong belief in an idea or system.

EG *... a commitment to the ideas of socialism*

2 something that regularly takes up some of your time

EG *... business commitments*

committee /kə'mɪtɪ/
committees

NOUN

a group of people who make decisions on behalf of a larger group

EG *Both he and his wife are on the committee.*

☑ You can use either a singular or a plural verb after 'committee': *the committee was selected*; *the committee were selected*.

common /'kɒmən/
**commoner commonest;
commons**

ADJECTIVE

1 Something that is common exists in large numbers or happens often.

EG *McGregor is a common name there.*

EG *Earthquakes are not common in this country.*

2 If something is common to two or more people, they all have it or use it.

EG *I realized we had a common interest.*

3 If you describe someone as common, you mean they do not have good taste or good manners.

A B C D E F G H I J K L M N O P Q R S T U V W X Y Z

EG *She was often common and rude.*

NOUN

4 an area of grassy land where the public is allowed to go
EG *... Clapham Common*

5 If two things or people have something **in common**, they have similar features or interests.
EG *My brother and I have much in common.*

common sense

NOUN

Your common sense is your natural ability to behave sensibly and make good judgments.
EG *Use your common sense.*

Commonwealth
/ˈkɒmənwɛlθ/

NOUN

The Commonwealth is an association of countries that used to be ruled by Britain.
EG *... the decision by Pakistan to rejoin the Commonwealth*

communicate /kəˈmjuːnɪkeɪt/
communicates
communicating
communicated

VERB

1 When people communicate with each other, they exchange information, usually by talking or writing to each other.
EG *They communicated regularly by e-mail.*

2 If you communicate an idea or a feeling, you make someone aware of it.
EG *He was having trouble communicating his ideas.*

communication
/kəmjuːnɪˈkeɪʃən/
communications

NOUN

1 Communication is the process by which people or animals exchange information.
EG *... a highly effective system of communication*

PLURAL NOUN

2 communications are the systems by which people communicate or broadcast information, especially using electricity or radio waves
EG *All normal communications were cut.*

communism /ˈkɒmjunɪzəm/

NOUN

Communism is the political belief that all people are equal and that workers should control society.
EG *... the collapse of communism in Eastern Europe*

community /kəˈmjuːnɪtɪ/
communities

NOUN

1 all the people living in a particular area
EG *... all sections of the local community*

2 a particular group within a society
EG *... the Asian community*

commute /kəˈmjuːt/
commutes commuting
commuted

VERB

People who commute travel a long distance to work every day.
EG *Mike commutes to London every day.*

compact disc compact discs

NOUN

a small disc on which sound, especially music, is recorded
EG *The soundtrack is available on compact disc.*

companion /kəm'pænjən/
companions

NOUN

someone who you travel with or
spend time with

EG *He has been her constant
companion for the last four months.*

company /'kʌmpənɪ/
companies

NOUN

1 a business that sells goods or
provides a service

EG *... a record company*

2 Someone's company is the time
they spend with you.

EG *I enjoyed her company.*

3 If you **keep** someone
company, you spend time with
them.

EG *Why don't you stay here and
keep Emma company?*

comparative /kəm'pærətɪv/
comparatives

NOUN OR ADJECTIVE

Many adjectives have a basic form
and two other forms. The
comparative and **superlative**
forms are used when you make
comparisons.

The comparative form is usually
made by adding the ending *-er* to
the basic form of the adjective. It
shows that someone or something
has more of something than the
person or thing they are being
compared with.

EG *Matthew is **taller** than Anna.*

You can also make comparatives by
using the words *more* or *less* with
the basic form of the adjective.

EG *She is **more beautiful** than her
sister.*

See also **superlative**.

compare /kəm'pɛəʳ/
**compares comparing
compared**

VERB

1 If you **compare** one thing
with or **to** another, you consider
them together and see in what
ways they are different or similar.

EG *... studies comparing Russian
children with those in Britain*

2 If you **compare** one thing **to**
another, you say it is like the other
thing.

EG *His voice is often compared to
Pavarotti's.*

comparison /kəm'pærɪsn/
comparisons

NOUN

If you make a comparison, you
consider two things together and
see in what ways they are different
or similar.

EG *... a comparison of the British
and German economies*

compartment
/kəm'pɑːtmənt/
compartments

NOUN

1 a section of a railway carriage

EG *We shared the compartment
with a group of Japanese tourists.*

2 one of the separate parts of an
object

EG *... a special compartment inside
his wallet*

compatible /kəm'pætɪbl/

ADJECTIVE

If people or things are compatible,
they can live or work together
successfully.

EG *We weren't really compatible
with each other.*

compel /kəm'pɛl/
**compels compelling
compelled**

A
B
C
D
E
F
G
H
I
J
K
L
M
N
O
P
Q
R
S
T
U
V
W
X
Y
Z

compel

VERB

To **compel** someone **to do** something means to force them to do it.

EG ... *laws compelling cyclists to wear a helmet*

compensate /'kɒmpənseɪt/
compensates compensating compensated

VERB

1 If you **compensate** someone **for** something, you give them money to replace something lost or damaged.

EG *Farmers may be compensated for the losses they have suffered.*

2 If one thing **compensates for** another, it does something which removes or reduces the other thing's bad effects.

EG *The trip more than compensated for the hardship.*

compete /kəm'piːt/
competes competing competed

VERB

1 When people or firms **compete for** something, they try to get that thing for themselves and stop the other from getting it.

EG *Banks and building societies are competing fiercely for business.*

2 If you **compete in** a contest or game, you take part in it.

EG *He has decided not to compete in the race.*

competent /'kɒmpɪtənt/

ADJECTIVE

Someone who is competent at something is efficient and effective at it.

EG ... *a very competent engineer*

competition /kɒmpɪ'tɪʃən/
competitions

NOUN

1 When there is competition between people, they are all trying to get something that not everyone can have.

EG *There's a lot of competition for places.*

2 an event in which people take part to find who is best at something

EG ... *a crossword competition*

competitor /kəm'petɪtər/
competitors

NOUN

a person or company that is competing to become the most successful

EG *The bank isn't performing as well as its main competitors.*

complain /kəm'pleɪn/
complains complaining complained

VERB

1 If you **complain about** something, you say that you are not satisfied with it.

EG *The neighbours complained to the police about the noise.*

2 If you **complain of** pain or illness, you say that you have it.

EG *He complained of a pain in the chest.*

complaint /kəm'pleɪnt/
complaints

NOUN

If you make a complaint, you complain about something.

EG *We've had a complaint from one of our customers.*

complete /kəm'pliːt/
completes completing completed

ADJECTIVE

1 to the greatest degree possible

EG ... *a complete surprise*

2 If something is complete, none of it is missing.
EG ... *the complete works of Shakespeare*

3 When a task is complete, it is finished.
EG *The planning stage is now complete.*

VERB
4 If you complete something, you finish it.
EG *He has just completed his first novel.*

5 If you complete a form, you fill it in.
EG *Simply complete the form below.*

complex /'kɒmplɛks/
complexes

ADJECTIVE
1 Complex things have many different parts and are hard to understand.
EG ... *a very complex problem*

NOUN
2 a group of buildings that is used for a particular purpose
EG ... *a hotel and restaurant complex*

complexion /kəm'plɛkʃən/
complexions

NOUN
the quality of the skin on your face
EG ... *a healthy glowing complexion*

complicated /'kɒmplɪkeɪtɪd/

ADJECTIVE
Something that is complicated has many parts and is difficult to understand.
EG ... *a complicated voting system*

complication /kɒmplɪ'keɪʃən/
complications

NOUN
something that makes a situation more difficult to deal with

EG *They divided the bill equally between them to avoid complications.*

compliment /'kɒmplɪmənt/
compliments complimenting complimented

NOUN
1 If you **pay** someone **a compliment**, you tell them that you admire something about them.
EG *Remember to pay your partner plenty of compliments.*

VERB : /'kɒmplɪment/
☑ Note that you pronounce the verb differently from the noun.
2 If you compliment someone, you pay them a compliment.
EG *They complimented me on the way I looked.*

compose /kəm'pəʊz/
composes composing composed

VERB
1 If something is **composed of** particular things or people, they are its parts or members.
EG *The committee is composed of leaders from the local community.*

2 When someone composes a piece of music, a letter, or a speech, they write it.
EG *Vivaldi composed many fine concertos.*

composer /kəm'pəʊzə'/
composers

NOUN
someone who writes music
EG ... *Beethoven and other great composers*

comprehensive /kɒmprɪ'hɛnsɪv/
comprehensives

ADJECTIVE

A B C D E F G H I J K L M N O P Q R S T U V W X Y Z

A B C D E F G H I J K L M N O P Q R S T U V W X Y Z

1 Something that is **comprehensive** includes everything necessary or relevant.
EG *… a comprehensive guide*
NOUN
2 a school where children of all abilities are taught together
EG *… an inner-city comprehensive*

compromise /'kɒmprəmaɪz/
compromises compromising compromised
NOUN
1 an agreement in which people accept less than they originally wanted
EG *In the end they reached a compromise.*
VERB
2 When people compromise, they agree to accept less than they originally wanted.
EG *He simply refuses to compromise.*

compulsory /kəm'pʌlsərɪ/
ADJECTIVE
If something is compulsory, you have to do it.
EG *School attendance is compulsory.*

computer /kəm'pju:tər/
computers
NOUN
an electronic machine that can quickly make calculations or store and find information
EG *The data are then fed into a computer.*

conceal /kən'si:l/
conceals concealing concealed
VERB
To conceal something means to hide it.
EG *He had concealed his gun.*
EG *The hat concealed her hair.*

conceive /kən'si:v/

conceives conceiving conceived
VERB
1 If you cannot **conceive of** something, you cannot imagine it or believe it.
EG *He couldn't conceive of anyone arguing with his results.*
2 If you conceive an idea or a plan, you think of it and work out how it could be done.
EG *He conceived the idea while travelling in Russia.*
3 When a woman conceives, she becomes pregnant.
EG *My wife is unable to conceive.*

concentrate /'kɒnsəntreɪt/
concentrates concentrating concentrated
VERB
1 If you **concentrate on** something, you give it all your attention.
EG *He sat back and concentrated on his driving.*
2 When something is concentrated somewhere, it is all there rather than in several places.
EG *They are mostly concentrated in urban areas.*

concentration
/kɒnsən'treɪʃən/
NOUN
Concentration on something involves giving it all your attention.
EG *Neil kept interrupting, breaking my concentration.*

concept /'kɒnsept/
concepts
NOUN
an abstract or general idea
EG *… the concept of justice*

concern /kən'sɜːn/
concerns concerning

concerned

NOUN

1 Concern is worry about something or someone.
EG *There's no cause for concern.*

2 If something is your concern, it is your duty or responsibility.
EG *That's not my concern.*

VERB

3 If something concerns you or if you are **concerned about** it, it worries you.
EG *... the matter that most concerned me*
EG *I've been concerned about you lately.*

4 If something concerns you, it affects or involves you.
EG *These are matters which do not concern them.*

concerning /kən'sə:nɪŋ/

PREPOSITION

You use 'concerning' to say what something is about.
EG *... questions concerning his private life*

concert /'kɒnsət/
concerts

NOUN

a public performance by musicians
EG *... a rock concert*

conclude /kən'klu:d/
concludes concluding concluded

VERB

1 If you conclude that something is true, you decide that it is true using the facts you know.
EG *He concluded that she had been right.*

2 When you conclude something, you finish it.
EG *At that point I intended to conclude the interview.*

conclusion /kən'klu:ʒən/
conclusions

NOUN

1 When you **come to a conclusion**, you decide that something is true after thinking about it carefully.
EG *I've come to the conclusion that he was lying.*

2 The conclusion of something is its ending.
EG *... at the conclusion of the meeting*

concrete /'kɒŋkri:t/

NOUN

1 Concrete is a building material made by mixing cement, sand, and water.
EG *The posts had to be set in concrete.*

ADJECTIVE

2 real and physical, rather than abstract
EG *He had no concrete evidence.*

condemn /kən'dem/
condemns condemning condemned

VERB

1 If you condemn something, you say it is bad and unacceptable.
EG *Teachers condemned the new plans.*

2 If someone **is condemned to** a punishment, they are given it.
EG *She was condemned to death.*

condition /kən'dɪʃən/
conditions

NOUN

1 the state that someone or something is in
EG *The boat is in good condition.*

2 something which must happen in order for something else to be possible
EG *One of the conditions of our*

A
B
C
D
E
F
G
H
I
J
K
L
M
N
O
P
Q
R
S
T
U
V
W
X
Y
Z

release was that we had to leave the country immediately.

3 an illness or medical problem
EG ... a heart condition

PLURAL NOUN

4 The **conditions** in which people live or do things are the factors that affect their comfort, safety, or success.
EG The living conditions were awful.

condom /'kɒndəm/
condoms

NOUN

a rubber covering which a man wears during sex to prevent pregnancy or disease
EG Some men refuse to wear a condom.

conduct /kən'dʌkt/
conducts conducting conducted

VERB

1 When you conduct an activity, you do it.
EG I decided to conduct an experiment.

2 A FORMAL USE
The way you **conduct yourself** is the way that you behave.
EG ... if he conducts himself well

NOUN : /'kɒndʌkt/

☑ Note that you pronounce the noun differently from the verb.

3 The conduct of an activity is the way that it is done.
EG ... criticisms about the conduct of the trial

4 Your conduct is your behaviour.
EG ... the conduct of English football fans

conference /'kɒnfərəns/
conferences

NOUN

a meeting at which formal discussions take place

EG ... the Conservative Party conference

confess /kən'fɛs/
confesses confessing confessed

VERB

If you **confess to** something, you admit that you did it.
EG Your son has confessed to his crimes.

confession /kən'fɛʃən/
confessions

NOUN

If you make a confession, you admit that you have done something wrong.
EG I have a confession to make.

confidence /'kɒnfɪdns/

NOUN

1 If you have **confidence in** someone, you feel you can trust them.
EG I have complete confidence in you.

2 Someone who has confidence is sure of their own abilities or qualities.
EG Working in a group gives you more confidence.

confident /'kɒnfɪdənt/

ADJECTIVE

1 If you are confident about something, you are sure it will happen the way you want it to.
EG I am confident that we will succeed.

2 Someone who is confident is sure of their own abilities or qualities.
EG Gradually he became more confident and relaxed.

confidential /kɒnfɪ'dɛnʃəl/

ADJECTIVE

Confidential information is meant

to be kept secret.

EG *Any information you give us will be treated as confidential.*

confine /kən'faɪn/
confines confining confined

VERB

1 If something **is confined to** a particular place or group, it exists only there.

EG *The problem is not confined to Germany.*

2 If you **confine yourself to doing** something, it is the only thing that you do.

EG *They confined themselves to discussing the weather.*

3 If you **are confined to** a place, you cannot leave it.

EG *She was confined to bed for two days.*

PLURAL NOUN : /'kɒnfaɪnz/

☑ Note that you pronounce the noun differently from the verb.

4 The **confines** of a place are its outer edges.

EG *... outside the confines of the prison*

confirm /kən'fɜːm/
confirms confirming confirmed

VERB

1 To confirm something means to say or show that it is true.

EG *Police confirmed that they had received a call.*

EG *These new statistics confirm our fears.*

2 If you confirm an arrangement or appointment, you say that it is definite.

EG *I'd like to confirm my booking.*

conflict /'kɒnflɪkt/
conflicts conflicting conflicted

NOUN

1 Conflict is disagreement and argument.

EG *... conflict between workers and management*

2 a war or battle

EG *... a military conflict*

VERB : /kən'flɪkt/

☑ Note that you pronounce the verb differently from the noun.

3 If something such as an idea or interest **conflicts with** another, they are different and it seems impossible for them both to be true.

EG *... an opinion which conflicted with my own*

confront /kən'frʌnt/
confronts confronting confronted

VERB

1 If you **are confronted with** a problem or task, you have to deal with it.

EG *She was confronted with severe money problems.*

2 If you confront someone, you meet them face to face, especially when you are going to fight or argue with them.

EG *The candidates confronted each other during a televised debate.*

confuse /kən'fjuːz/
confuses confusing confused

VERB

1 If you **confuse** someone or something **with** someone or something else, you mix them up and think that one of them is the other.

EG *You must be confusing me with someone else.*

2 If you confuse someone, you make them uncertain about what is happening or what to do.

EG *You're just trying to confuse me.*
3 If something confuses a situation, it makes it more complicated.
EG *Her comments only confused the issue.*

confusion /kən'fjuːʒən/

NOUN

1 If there is confusion about something, it is not clear what the true situation is.
EG *There's still some confusion about the number of casualties.*
2 Confusion is disorder.
EG *In all the confusion, he managed to escape.*

congratulate /kən'grætjuleɪt/
**congratulates
congratulating
congratulated**

VERB

If you **congratulate** someone **on** something, you express pleasure at it or you praise them for it.
EG *She congratulated him on the birth of his son.*
EG *I must congratulate her on passing her exams.*

congratulations
/kəngrætjuːˈleɪʃənz/

PLURAL NOUN

You say "congratulations" to someone in order to congratulate them.
EG *Congratulations! You have a healthy baby boy.*

Congress /ˈkɒŋgrɛs/

NOUN

Congress is the elected group of politicians that is responsible for making the law in the USA.
EG *The issue will be debated in Congress.*

conjunction /kənˈdʒʌŋkʃən/
conjunctions

NOUN

A **conjunction** is a word that joins two words or two parts of a sentence together.
EG *I ordered fish **and** chips.*
EG *I will come **if** I have time.*

connect /kəˈnɛkt/
**connects connecting
connected**

VERB

1 If you **connect** one thing **to** another, you join them together.
EG *Connect the pipe to the tap.*
2 If one thing or person **is connected with** another, there is a link between them.
EG *Police say she is not connected with the inquiry.*

connection /kəˈnɛkʃən/
connections

NOUN

1 a link or relationship between things
EG *He had no connection with the police.*
2 the point where two wires or pipes are joined together
EG *… a loose connection*
3 If you get a connection at a station or airport, you continue your journey by catching another train, bus, or plane.
EG *My flight was late, so I missed my connection.*

PLURAL NOUN

4 Someone's **connections** are the people they know.
EG *He had powerful connections in the army.*

conscience /ˈkɒnʃəns/
consciences

NOUN

the part of your mind that tells you what is right and wrong
EG *I had a guilty conscience and gave the money back.*

conscious /'kɒnʃəs/
ADJECTIVE
1 If you are **conscious of** something, you are aware of it.
EG *She was not conscious of the time.*
2 A conscious action or effort is done deliberately.
EG *I made a conscious decision not to speak.*
3 Someone who is conscious is awake, rather than asleep or unconscious.
EG *Still conscious, she was taken to hospital.*

consciousness /'kɒnʃəsnɪs/
NOUN
1 Your consciousness is your mind, thoughts, beliefs, and attitudes.
EG *… drugs that can alter consciousness*
2 If you **lose consciousness**, you become unconscious.
EG *She banged her head and lost consciousness.*

consent /kən'sɛnt/
consents consenting consented
NOUN
1 Consent is permission to do something.
EG *Nothing can be done without both parents' consent.*
2 Consent is agreement about something.
EG *By common consent it was the best game of these championships.*
VERB
3 If you **consent to** something, you agree to do it or allow it to happen.

EG *He finally consented to go.*

consequence /'kɒnsɪkwəns/
consequences
NOUN
The consequences of something are its results or effects.
EG *He didn't consider the likely consequences of his action.*

consequently /'kɒnsɪkwəntlɪ/
ADVERB
as a result
EG *He broke his back and was consequently confined to a wheelchair.*

conservative /kən'sɜːvətɪv/
conservatives
NOUN
1 In Britain, the Conservatives or the Conservative Party are the main right-of-centre political party.
EG *In 1951 the Conservative Party was returned to power.*
ADJECTIVE
2 In Britain, Conservative views and policies are those of the Conservative Party.
EG *… official Conservative policy*
3 Someone who is conservative is not willing to accept changes or new ideas.
EG *You tend to get more conservative as you get older.*
4 A conservative estimate or guess is a cautious or moderate one.
EG *Conservative estimates put her wealth at £5 million.*

consider /kən'sɪdər/
considers considering considered
VERB
1 If you consider something to be the case, you think or judge that it is the case.
EG *The manager does not consider*

him a good team member.

2 If you consider something, you think about it carefully.

EG *If an offer is made, we will consider it.*

considerable /kən'sɪdərəbl/

ADJECTIVE

A considerable amount of something is a lot of it.

EG *... a considerable sum of money*

consideration
/kənsɪdə'reɪʃən/
considerations

NOUN

1 Consideration is careful thought about something.

EG *... a decision demanding careful consideration*

2 Someone who shows consideration pays attention to the needs and feelings of other people.

EG *He showed no consideration for his daughters.*

3 A consideration is something that should be thought about when you are planning or deciding something.

EG *Money was also a consideration.*

considering /kən'sɪdərɪŋ/

PREPOSITION

You use 'considering' to show that you are taking a particular fact into account when giving an opinion.

EG *He's quite cheerful, considering what he's been through.*

consist /kən'sɪst/
consists consisting consisted

VERB

Something that **consists of** particular things is formed from them.

EG *His diet consisted of bread, cheese and beer.*

consistent /kən'sɪstənt/

ADJECTIVE

1 If you are consistent, you keep doing something the same way.

EG *... one of our most consistent players*

2 If one fact or idea is **consistent with** another, they do not contradict each other.

EG *This result is consistent with earlier findings.*

conspiracy /kən'spɪrəsɪ/
conspiracies

NOUN

If there is a conspiracy, a group of people plan something wrong or illegal.

EG *He believes Kennedy's murder was the result of a conspiracy.*

constable /'kʌnstəbl/
constables

NOUN

a police officer of the lowest rank

EG *Thanks for your help, Constable.*

constant /'kɒnstənt/

ADJECTIVE

1 Something that is constant happens all the time or is always there.

EG *... a city under constant attack*

2 If an amount or level is constant, it stays the same.

EG *... a constant temperature*

constituency /kən'stɪtjuənsɪ/
constituencies

NOUN

a town or area represented by an MP

EG *There are 14,000 voters in the constituency.*

construct /kən'strʌkt/
constructs constructing constructed

VERB

If you construct something, you

build or make it.
EG *The French constructed a series of fortresses along the coast.*

consult /kən'sʌlt/
consults consulting consulted

VERB
1 If you consult someone, you ask for their opinion or advice.
EG *Consult your doctor about how much exercise you should do.*
2 If you consult a book or map, you look at it for information.
EG *Consult the chart on page 44 for the correct cooking times.*

consume /kən'sjuːm/
consumes consuming consumed

VERB
1 If you consume something, you eat or drink it.
EG *Martha consumed nearly a pound of cheese a day.*
2 If something consumes fuel or energy, it uses it up.
EG *It consumes a tiny amount of electricity.*

consumer /kən'sjuːməʳ/
consumers

NOUN
someone who buys things or uses services
EG *... two new magazines for teenage consumers*

contact /'kɒntækt/
contacts contacting contacted

NOUN
1 If you are **have contact with** someone, or if you are **in contact with** them, you regularly talk to them or write to them.
EG *He has very little contact with his family.*

EG *I'm no longer in contact with her.*
2 When there is contact between things, they are touching each other.
EG *There was no physical contact between them.*
3 A contact is someone you know in a place or organization who helps you or gives you information.
EG *He has contacts in government.*

VERB
4 If you contact someone, you telephone them or write to them.
EG *I can be contacted at the following address.*

contain /kən'teɪn/
contains containing contained

VERB
1 If a substance contains something, that thing is a part of it.
EG *Alcohol contains sugar.*
2 The things a box or room contains are the things inside it.
EG *The bag contained a Christmas card.*
3 A FORMAL USE
To contain something means to stop it increasing or spreading.
EG *... efforts to contain the disease*

container /kən'teɪnəʳ/
containers

NOUN
something such as a box or a bottle that you keep things in
EG *... a plastic container for food*

content /'kɒntɛnt/
contents

PLURAL NOUN
1 The contents of something are the things inside it.
EG *She emptied the contents of the bag onto the table.*
2 The contents of a piece of writing or a film are what is

expressed in it.

EG *The letter's contents were never disclosed.*

ADJECTIVE : /kən'tɛnt/

☑ Note that you pronounce the adjective differently from the noun.

3 If you are content, you are happy and satisfied with your life.

EG *He says his daughter is quite content.*

4 If you are **content to do** something, you are willing to do it rather than wanting something more or better.

EG *He would be content to receive a letter from her.*

contest /'kɒntɛst/
contests

NOUN

a competition or game

EG *... a writing contest*

context /'kɒntɛkst/
contexts

NOUN

The context of something is the matters related to it which help to explain it.

EG *... the historical context in which Shakespeare wrote*

continent /'kɒntɪnənt/
continents

NOUN

1 a very large area of land, such as Africa or Asia

EG *She loved the African continent.*

2 In Britain, the rest of Europe excluding Britain is sometimes called **the Continent**.

EG *On the Continent this is regarded as quite normal.*

continue /kən'tɪnjuː/
**continues continuing
continued**

VERB

1 If you **continue doing** something or **continue to do** it, you do not stop doing it.

EG *She is determined to continue working.*

EG *He continued to smoke, despite the dangers.*

2 If something continues, it does not stop.

EG *The war looks likely to continue.*

3 You say that someone or something continues when they start again after stopping.

EG *She continued after a pause.*

continuous /kən'tɪnjuəs/

ADJECTIVE

Something that is continuous happens or exists without stopping.

EG *... a continuous stream of phone calls*

contract /'kɒntrækt/
**contracts contracting
contracted**

NOUN

1 a legal agreement about the sale of something or work done for money

EG *He was given a two-year contract.*

VERB : /kən'trækt/

☑ Note that you pronounce the verb differently from the noun.

2 When something contracts, it gets smaller or shorter.

EG *When you are anxious, your muscles contract.*

contradict /kɒntrə'dɪkt/
**contradicts contradicting
contradicted**

VERB

If you contradict someone, you say that what they have just said is wrong.

EG *He didn't dare to contradict her.*

contrast /'kɒntrɑːst/
contrasts contrasting contrasted

NOUN

1 a great difference between things

EG ... *the contrast between town and country*

VERB : /kən'trɑːst/

☑ Note that you pronounce the verb differently from the noun.

2 If you **contrast** one thing **with** another, you describe or emphasize the differences between them.

EG *She contrasted the situation then with the present crisis.*

contribute /kən'trɪbjuːt/
contributes contributing contributed

VERB

1 If you **contribute to** something, you do something to make it successful.

EG *The elderly have much to contribute to the community.*

2 If you **contribute** money **to** something, you help to pay for it.

EG *The US is contributing $4 million in loans to the fund.*

contribution /kɒntrɪ'bjuːʃən/
contributions

NOUN

1 If you make a contribution to something, you do something to make it successful.

EG *He was awarded a prize for his contribution to world peace.*

2 a sum of money that you give in order to help pay for something

EG ... *companies that make charitable contributions*

control /kən'trəʊl/
controls controlling controlled

NOUN

1 Control of a country or organization is the power to make important decisions about how it is run.

EG *He was forced to give up control of the company.*

2 Your control of something is your ability to make it work the way you want it to.

EG *He lost control of the car.*

3 If something is **out of control**, nobody has any power over it.

EG *The fire was out of control.*

PLURAL NOUN

4 The **controls** on a machine are the switches or other devices that are used to operate it.

EG *She explained the controls of the washing machine.*

VERB

5 Someone who controls a country or organization has the power to make decisions about how it is run.

EG *He now controls the entire business.*

6 Something that controls a machine or system makes it work the way you want it to.

EG ... *the computer system that controls the lighting*

7 If you **control yourself**, you make yourself behave calmly when you are angry or upset.

EG *I couldn't control myself, I just screamed at him.*

controversial /kɒntrə'vɜːʃl/

ADJECTIVE

Something that is controversial causes a lot of discussion and argument, because many people disapprove of it.

EG *The changes are bound to be controversial.*

A B C D E F G H I J K L M N O P Q R S T U V W X Y Z

convenient /kən'viːnɪənt/
ADJECTIVE
If something is convenient, it is easy to use or it makes something easy to do.
EG *I find credit cards the most convenient way to pay.*
EG *It was more convenient to eat in the kitchen.*

convention /kən'venʃən/
conventions
NOUN
1 an accepted way of behaving or doing something
EG *It's just a social convention that men don't wear skirts.*
2 a large meeting of an organization or political group
EG *... the Democratic Convention*

conventional /kən'venʃənl/
ADJECTIVE
1 Someone who is conventional thinks or behaves in an ordinary and normal way.
EG *He was a conventional man who was easily shocked.*
2 A conventional method or product is one that is usually used.
EG *Conventional tests produced the same result.*

conversation /kɒnvə'seɪʃən/
conversations
NOUN
When people have a conversation, they talk to each other.
EG *I had a conversation with Roger about fishing.*

convert /kən'vɜːt/
converts converting
converted
VERB
1 To **convert** one thing **into** another means to change it so that it becomes the other thing.

EG *The body converts these substances into vitamins.*
2 If someone converts you, they persuade you to change your religious or political beliefs.
EG *If you try to convert him, he'll just walk away.*
NOUN : /'kɒnvɜːt/
☑ Note that you pronounce the noun differently from the verb.
3 someone who has changed their religious or political beliefs
EG *She was a convert to Roman Catholicism.*

convict /kən'vɪkt/
convicts convicting
convicted
VERB
1 If someone **is convicted of** a crime, they are found guilty of it in a law court.
EG *He was convicted of murder.*
NOUN : /'kɒnvɪkt/
☑ Note that you pronounce the noun differently from the verb.
2 someone who is serving a prison sentence
EG *... a football team for ex-convicts*

conviction /kən'vɪkʃən/
convictions
NOUN
1 a strong belief or opinion
EG *We had an absolute conviction that we were right.*
2 If someone has a conviction, they have been found guilty of a crime.
EG *He will appeal against his conviction.*

convince /kən'vɪns/
convinces convincing
convinced
VERB
If you **convince** someone **of** something or if you convince them

that it is true, you persuade them that it is true.
EG *I soon convinced him of my innocence.*
EG *She convinced me that I was wrong.*

cook /kuk/
cooks cooking cooked

VERB
1 If you cook food, you prepare it for eating by heating it.
EG *Let me cook you a nice hot meal.*

NOUN
2 someone who prepares and cooks food
EG *He's a very good cook.*

cooker /'kukər/
cookers

NOUN
a large metal device for cooking food, consisting of a grill, an oven, and some heated rings
EG *... an electric cooker*

cookery /'kukəri/

NOUN
Cookery is the activity of preparing and cooking food.
EG *... a cookery class*

cookie /'kuki/
cookies

NOUN
In American English, a cookie is a small, sweet, flat cake.
EG *... a jar of cookies*
☑ The usual British word is *biscuit*.

cool /ku:l/
cooler coolest; cools cooling cooled

ADJECTIVE
1 Something cool has a low temperature but is not cold.
EG *... a cool breeze*
EG *... a cool drink of milk*
2 If you are cool in a difficult

situation, you stay calm.
EG *He managed to keep cool throughout the whole affair.*

VERB
3 When something cools, it becomes less warm.
EG *Allow the liquid to cool.*

co-operate /kəu'ɒpəreɪt/
co-operates co-operating co-operated

VERB
1 When people co-operate, they work or act together.
EG *The French and British co-operated on the project.*
2 If you co-operate, you do what someone asks you to do.
EG *He has agreed to co-operate with the police.*

cop /kɒp/
cops

NOUN
AN INFORMAL WORD
a policeman or policewoman
EG *... a New York cop*

cope /kəup/
copes coping coped

VERB
If you **cope with** a problem or task, you deal with it successfully.
EG *She has had to cope with losing all her money.*
EG *I can't cope.*

copper /'kɒpər/

NOUN OR ADJECTIVE
Copper is a soft reddish-brown metal.
EG *... copper wire*

copy /'kɒpi/
copies copying copied

NOUN
1 If you make a copy of something, you produce something that looks like that

A B C D E F G H I J K L M N O P Q R S T U V W X Y Z

thing.

EG *... a copy of my letter*

2 A copy of a book, newspaper, or record is one of many identical ones produced at the same time.

EG *... a copy of today's newspaper*

VERB

3 If you copy what someone does, you do the same thing.

EG *Children often copy the behaviour of those they admire.*

4 If you copy something, you make a copy of it.

EG *He copied the information into a notebook.*

core /kɔːʳ/
cores

NOUN

1 the hard central part of a fruit such as an apple

EG *Peel the apple and remove the core.*

2 the central or most important part of something

EG *... the earth's core*

EG *... the core of the problem*

cork /kɔːk/
corks

NOUN

a piece of wood or plastic that is pushed into the end of a bottle to close it

EG *The cork broke as he tried to remove it.*

corkscrew /'kɔːkskruː/
corkscrews

NOUN

a device for pulling corks out of bottles

EG *... a penknife with a corkscrew attached*

corner /'kɔːnəʳ/
corners cornering cornered

NOUN

1 a place where two sides or edges of something meet

EG *... in the corner of the living room*

EG *... a street corner*

VERB

2 If you corner a person or animal, you force them into a place they cannot escape from.

EG *The gang was cornered by police.*

correct /kə'rɛkt/
corrects correcting corrected

ADJECTIVE

1 If something is correct, there are no mistakes in it.

EG *That's the correct answer.*

2 The correct thing or method in a particular situation is the most suitable one.

EG *... the correct course of action*

VERB

3 If you correct something which is wrong, you make it right.

EG *He asked her to correct his English.*

correspond /kɔrɪs'pɒnd/
corresponds corresponding corresponded

VERB

1 If one thing **corresponds to** another, they are very similar or connected.

EG *This map corresponds to the other closely.*

2 When people correspond, they write to each other.

EG *We corresponded regularly.*

corridor /'kɒrɪdɔːʳ/
corridors

NOUN

a passage in a building or train

EG *Turn left at the end of the corridor.*

A
B
C
D
E
F
G
H
I
J
K
L
M
N
O
P
Q
R
S
T
U
V
W
X
Y
Z

corrupt /kəˈrʌpt/
**corrupts corrupting
corrupted**

ADJECTIVE

1 Corrupt people act dishonestly
or illegally in return for money or
power.
EG ... *corrupt MPs*

VERB

2 To corrupt someone means to
make them dishonest or immoral.
EG *Power has totally corrupted him.*

corruption /kəˈrʌpʃən/

NOUN

Corruption is dishonesty and
illegal behaviour by people in
positions of power.
EG *The President faces 54 charges
of corruption and tax evasion.*

cosmetic /kɒzˈmɛtɪk/
cosmetics

PLURAL NOUN

1 cosmetics are substances such
as lipstick or face powder
EG *Many millions of pounds are
spent on cosmetics.*

ADJECTIVE

2 Cosmetic changes improve the
appearance of something without
changing its basic character.
EG *Critics say the changes are
purely cosmetic.*

cost /kɒst/
costs costing cost

NOUN

1 The cost of something is the
amount of money that is needed
to buy it, do it, or make it.
EG *The cost of the equipment can
be spread over two years.*

2 The cost of achieving something
is the loss or injury that is involved
in achieving it.
EG ... *the total cost in human misery*

VERB

3 You use 'cost' to talk about the
amount of money you have to pay
for things.
EG *How much does it cost?*
EG *It cost me £10.*

4 If a mistake costs you
something, you lose that thing
because of the mistake.
EG *The error cost him his job.*

costume /ˈkɒstjuːm/
costumes

NOUN

1 a set of clothes worn by an actor
during a performance
EG *The actors make their own
costumes.*

2 Costume is the clothing worn in
a particular place or during a
particular period.
EG ... *men in eighteenth-century
costume*

cosy /ˈkəʊzɪ/
cosier cosiest
US **cozy**

ADJECTIVE

1 A cosy place is warm and
comfortable.
EG ... *her cosy new flat*

2 Cosy activities are pleasant and
friendly.
EG ... *a cosy chat*

cot /kɒt/
cots

NOUN

a small bed for a baby, with bars
or panels round it to stop the baby
falling out
EG *She laid Anna in her cot.*

cottage /ˈkɒtɪdʒ/
cottages

NOUN

a small house, usually in the
country
EG *They used to have a cottage in*

the north of Scotland.

cotton /'kɒtn/

NOUN

1 Cotton is a type of cloth that is used to make clothes.

EG ... a cotton shirt

2 Cotton is thread that is used for sewing.

EG ... a needle and cotton

cotton wool

NOUN

Cotton wool is soft white cotton, often used for applying creams to your skin.

EG Clean the wound with a little cotton wool.

couch /kautʃ/
couches

NOUN

a long, soft piece of furniture for sitting or lying on

EG She was sitting beside her grandmother on the couch.

cough /kɒf/
coughs coughing coughed

VERB

1 When you cough, you force air out of your throat with a sudden harsh noise.

EG Graham began to cough violently.

NOUN

2 an illness that makes you cough a lot

EG I've got a terrible cough.

3 the noise you make when you cough

EG She heard a polite cough behind her.

could /kud/

☑ 'Could' is a modal verb and the past tense of 'can'. There are no forms ending in -s, -ing, or -ed.

VERB

1 You use 'could' to say that you were able or allowed to do something.

EG He could see that something was wrong.

EG She could leave if she wanted to.

2 You use 'could' to say that something might happen or might be true.

EG It could rain.

3 You use 'could' when you are asking for something politely.

EG Could you tell me how to get to the station?

council /'kaunsl/
councils

NOUN

1 a group of people who have been elected to look after the affairs of a town, district, or county

EG ... a member of Cheshire County Council

ADJECTIVE

2 In Britain, council houses or flats are owned by the local council and people pay rent to live in them.

EG There is a shortage of council housing.

count /kaunt/
counts counting counted

VERB

1 When you count, you say all the numbers in order up to a particular number.

EG He counted to twenty.

2 If you count all the things in a group, you add them up to see how many there are.

EG I counted the money to see if it was correct.

3 If something counts in a situation, it is important or valuable.

EG It's as if my opinions just don't count.

4 If something **counts as** a particular thing, it is regarded as being that thing.
EG *I'm not sure whether this counts as business expenses.*

NOUN
5 a number reached by counting
EG *At the last count I had over 500 CDs.*

6 If you **keep count of** something, you keep a record of how often it happens.
EG *Who's keeping count of the score?*

7 If you **lose count of** something, you cannot remember how often it has happened.
EG *She'd lost count of all the interviews she'd attended.*

count on
VERB
If you can count on someone or something, you can rely on them.
EG *You can count on me.*

counter /'kauntər/
counters
NOUN
a long, flat surface over which goods are sold in a shop
EG *... the shop assistant behind the counter*

countless /'kauntlɪs/
ADJECTIVE
very many
EG *There had been countless demonstrations.*

country /'kʌntrɪ/
countries
NOUN
1 one of the political areas that the world is divided into
EG *... maps of European countries*
2 the country is land away from towns and cities
EG *... a house in the country*

countryside /'kʌntrɪsaɪd/
NOUN
The countryside is land away from towns and cities.
EG *I've always loved the English countryside.*

county /'kauntɪ/
counties
NOUN
a region with its own local government
EG *... in the county of Yorkshire*

couple /'kʌpl/
couples coupling coupled
NOUN
1 A couple is two people who are married or having a sexual or romantic relationship.
EG *... an elderly couple*
2 A **couple of** things or people means two of them.
EG *... a couple of weeks ago*
VERB
3 If one thing **is coupled with** another, the two things are combined.
EG *... high quality coupled with low prices*

coupon /'ku:pɒn/
coupons
NOUN
1 a piece of printed paper issued by a company or shop, which allows you to pay less than usual for something
EG *Bring the coupon below to any of our stores and pay just £9.99.*
2 a form, for example in a newspaper, which you fill in to ask for information or to enter a competition
EG *Simply fill in the coupon below.*

courage /'kʌrɪdʒ/
NOUN

A
B
C
D
E
F
G
H
I
J
K
L
M
N
O
P
Q
R
S
T
U
V
W
X
Y
Z

A
B
C

Courage is the quality shown by people who do things knowing they are dangerous or difficult.

EG *The team showed a lot of courage.*

D

course /kɔːs/
courses

E
F

NOUN

1 a series of lessons or lectures

EG *... the other students on my French course*

G
H

2 a piece of land where races take place or golf is played

EG *... a golf course*

I
J

3 the route a ship or aircraft takes

EG *The captain changed course to avoid the storm.*

K

4 one of the parts of a meal

EG *The first course was soup.*

L
M

5 A course or a **course of action** is one of the things that you can do in a situation.

EG *The best course would be to say nothing.*

N
O

6 If something happens **in the course of** a period of time, it happens during that period.

EG *Ten people died in the course of the day.*

P
Q
R

7 You say **of course** to show that something is totally expected or that you are sure about something.

EG *Of course she wouldn't do that.*

EG *"Do you mind?" — "Of course not."*

S
T

court /kɔːt/
courts

U
V

NOUN

1 a place where legal matters are decided

EG *He is due to appear in court next week.*

EG *The court awarded him almost a million pounds.*

W
X
Y
Z

2 a place where a game such as

tennis or badminton is played

EG *... a tennis court*

3 the place where a king or queen lives

EG *... the court of Louis XIV*

cousin /ˈkʌzn/
cousins

NOUN

Your cousin is the child of your uncle or aunt.

EG *He's my cousin.*

cover /ˈkʌvəʳ/
covers covering covered

VERB

1 If you cover something, you put something else over it to protect it or hide it.

EG *She covered her face with her hands.*

2 If something covers something else, it forms a layer over it.

EG *Snow covered the hills.*

3 If you cover a particular distance, you travel that distance.

EG *They covered 20 kilometres a day.*

4 An insurance policy that covers something guarantees that money will be paid if that thing is lost, stolen, or damaged.

EG *... travel insurance covering you against theft*

5 If you cover a subject, you discuss it in a lecture, course, or book.

EG *We've covered a wide range of subjects today.*

NOUN

6 something that is put over an object to protect it or keep it warm

EG *She put the cover on her typewriter.*

7 The cover of a book or magazine is its outside.

EG *The price is on the back cover.*

8 Insurance cover is a guarantee that money will be paid if something is lost, stolen, or damaged.
EG *The policy provides unlimited cover for hospital charges.*

9 Cover is trees, rocks, or other places where you can shelter or hide.
EG *There was a sudden storm, so we ran for cover.*

cover up
VERB
If you cover up something that you do not want people to know about, you hide it from them.
EG *He suspects there's a conspiracy to cover up the crime.*

cow /kau/
cows
NOUN
a large animal that is kept on farms for its milk
EG *… a herd of cows*

coward /ˈkauəd/
cowards
NOUN
someone who is easily frightened and avoids dangerous or difficult situations
EG *She accused him of being a coward.*

cowboy /ˈkaubɔɪ/
cowboys
NOUN
a man who is employed to look after cattle in America
EG *… a cowboy film*

cozy /ˈkəuzɪ/
see **cosy**

crab /kræb/
crabs
NOUN
a sea creature with four pairs of legs, two claws, and a flat, round body covered by a shell
EG *… crab soup*

crack /kræk/
cracks cracking cracked
VERB
1 If something cracks or if something cracks it, it becomes damaged, with lines appearing on its surface.
EG *The plate cracked as he took it from the oven.*
EG *A stone had cracked the window.*

2 If you crack a problem or code, you solve it.
EG *After years of research he finally cracked the code.*
NOUN
3 one of the lines that appears on something when it cracks
EG *The plate had a crack in it.*

4 a narrow gap
EG *She saw him through a crack in the curtains.*

craft /krɑ:ft/
crafts
NOUN
1 an activity that involves making things such as pots or cloth with your hands
EG *… traditional arts and crafts*

2 a boat, plane, or space vehicle
EG *Dozens of small craft set out from the shore.*
☑ When 'craft' refers to a vehicle, the plural is *craft*.

cram /kræm/
crams cramming crammed
VERB
If you **cram** people or things **into** a place, you put so many in it that it is completely full.
EG *He crammed the bank notes into his pocket.*

A
B
C
D
E
F
G
H
I
J
K
L
M
N
O
P
Q
R
S
T
U
V
W
X
Y
Z

A
B
C
D
E
F
G
H
I
J
K
L
M
N
O
P
Q
R
S
T
U
V
W
X
Y
Z

crash /kræʃ/
crashes crashing crashed

NOUN
1 an accident in which a moving vehicle hits something and is damaged
EG ... *a car crash*

2 a sudden loud noise
EG *The tray fell to the floor with a terrific crash.*

VERB
3 If a vehicle crashes, it hits something and is badly damaged.
EG *His car crashed into the rear of a van.*

crawl /krɔːl/
crawls crawling crawled

VERB
1 When you crawl, you move around on your hands and knees.
EG *I crawled towards the door.*

2 When an insect or vehicle crawls somewhere, it moves there very slowly.
EG *I watched the moth crawl up the lampshade.*

crazy /ˈkreɪzɪ/
crazier craziest

ADJECTIVE
AN INFORMAL WORD
1 very strange or foolish
EG *The guy is crazy.*
EG ... *a crazy idea*

2 If you are **crazy about** something or someone, you like them very much.
EG *She's crazy about dancing.*

cream /kriːm/
creams

NOUN
1 Cream is a thick, yellowish-white liquid taken from the top of milk.
EG ... *strawberries and cream*

2 a substance that you can rub into your skin to make it soft or protect it
EG ... *skin cream*

ADJECTIVE
3 yellowish-white
EG ... *cream silk stockings*

crease /kriːs/
creases creasing creased

NOUN
1 an irregular line that appears on cloth or paper when it is crushed or folded
EG *She smoothed down the creases in her dress.*

2 a straight line on something that has been pressed or folded neatly
EG *She made a crease in the paper.*

VERB
3 If cloth or paper creases or if you crease it, lines appear on it.
EG *His clothes were creased, as if he had slept in them.*

create /kriːˈeɪt/
creates creating created

VERB
To create something means to cause it to happen or exist.
EG *They hope to create more jobs in the area.*

creative /kriːˈeɪtɪv/

ADJECTIVE
Creative people are good at inventing and developing new ideas.
EG ... *one of our most creative film directors*

creature /ˈkriːtʃər/
creatures

NOUN
any living thing that is not a plant
EG ... *a hedge in which many small creatures live*

credit /ˈkrɛdɪt/
credits

NOUN

1 Credit is a system where you pay for goods after you have received them.
EG ... to buy goods on credit

2 If you **get the credit for** something, people praise you for it.
EG Andy should get some of the credit for the team's win.

PLURAL NOUN
3 The list of people who helped make a film, record, or television programme is called **the credits**.
EG His name didn't appear in the credits.

credit card credit cards

NOUN
a plastic card that allows you to buy goods on credit
EG I usually pay by credit card.

creep /kri:p/
creeps creeping crept

VERB
If you creep somewhere, you move there quietly and slowly.
EG I crept back into the kitchen.

crew /kru:/
crews

NOUN
1 The crew of a ship, aeroplane, or space vehicle are the people who operate it.
EG One member of the crew was shot.

2 people with special technical skills who work together
EG ... a camera crew

cricket /'krɪkɪt/

NOUN
Cricket is an outdoor game played by two teams who take turns at scoring by hitting a ball with a bat.
EG During the summers we played cricket.

crime /kraɪm/

crimes

NOUN
an action for which you can be punished by law
EG A crime had been committed.
EG Crime is on the increase.

criminal /'krɪmɪnl/
criminals

NOUN
1 someone who has committed a crime
EG Most of his friends are criminals.

ADJECTIVE
2 involving or related to crime
EG ... a criminal offence

crisis /'kraɪsɪs/
crises

NOUN
a serious or dangerous situation
EG ... the country's economic crisis

crisp /krɪsp/
crisper crispest; crisps

ADJECTIVE
1 Something that is crisp is pleasantly fresh and firm.
EG ... crisp lettuce leaves

NOUN
2 Crisps are thin, hard slices of fried potato that are eaten cold as a snack.
EG ... a packet of cheese and onion crisps

critic /'krɪtɪk/
critics

NOUN
1 someone who writes reviews of books, films, plays, or musical performances
EG ... a film critic

2 A critic of a person or system is someone who criticizes them publicly.
EG ... the government's critics

critical /'krɪtɪkl/

A
B
C
D
E
F
G
H
I
J
K
L
M
N
O
P
Q
R
S
T
U
V
W
X
Y
Z

A
B
C
D
E
F
G
H
I
J
K
L
M
N
O
P
Q
R
S
T
U
V
W
X
Y
Z

ADJECTIVE

1 A critical time or situation is a very important one.

EG *This was a critical moment.*

2 If you are **critical of** something or someone, you criticize them.

EG *… several intellectuals who have been critical of the regime*

criticise /'krɪtɪsaɪz/
criticises criticising criticised

another spelling of **criticize**

criticism /'krɪtɪsɪzəm/
criticisms

NOUN

1 Criticism is the action of expressing disapproval of someone or something.

EG *The Government came in for severe criticism.*

2 A criticism is a statement that expresses disapproval.

EG *I don't mean this as a criticism.*

criticize /'krɪtɪsaɪz/
criticizes criticizing criticized; also spelt **criticise**

VERB

If you criticize someone or something, you say what you think is wrong with them.

EG *He criticized the police for their handling of the matter.*

crop /krɒp/
crops

NOUN

Crops are plants such as wheat and potatoes that are grown for food.

EG *The farmers here still harvest their crops by hand.*

cross /krɒs/
crosses crossing crossed

VERB

1 If you cross something such as a room or a road, you go to the other side of it.

EG *She was killed while crossing the road.*

2 Lines or roads that cross meet and go across each other.

EG *… at the point where the two roads cross*

3 If you cross your arms or legs, you put one on top of the other.

EG *She sat back and crossed her legs.*

NOUN

4 a vertical line with a shorter horizontal line across it or any object shaped like this, especially one which is a Christian symbol

EG *She wears a cross on a silver chain.*

5 a written mark shaped like an X

EG *I put a cross on the map where my house was.*

ADJECTIVE

6 Someone who is cross is rather angry.

EG *She's very cross with you.*

cross out

VERB

If you cross out words on a page, you draw a line through them.

EG *He crossed out the first sentence and wrote it again.*

crossing /'krɒsɪŋ/
crossings

NOUN

1 a place where you can cross a road safely

EG *Always cross at the crossing.*

2 a boat journey to the other side of a sea

EG *It was a very rough crossing.*

crossword /'krɒswɜːd/
crosswords

NOUN

A crossword or **crossword**

puzzle is a word game in which you work out answers to clues and write them in the white squares of a pattern of black and white squares.
EG *He always did the crossword in the Times.*

crouch /kraʊtʃ/
crouches crouching crouched

VERB
If you are crouching, you are leaning forward with your legs bent.
EG *We were crouching in the bushes.*

crowd /kraʊd/
crowds crowding crowded

NOUN
1 a large group of people gathered together
EG *A huge crowd had gathered.*

VERB
2 When people **crowd around** someone or something, they gather closely together around them.
EG *The children crowded around him.*

crowded /'kraʊdɪd/

ADJECTIVE
A crowded place is full of people.
EG *... a crowded pub*

crown /kraʊn/
crowns

NOUN
a circular object, made of gold or jewels, which a king or queen wears on their head
EG *... a picture of the Queen wearing her crown*

crucial /'kruːʃl/

ADJECTIVE
Something that is crucial is very important.

EG *He has a crucial role to play.*

cruel /'kruːəl/
crueller cruellest

ADJECTIVE
Cruel people deliberately cause pain or distress.
EG *Children can be so cruel.*

cruelty /'kruːəltɪ/

NOUN
Cruelty is behaviour that deliberately causes pain or distress.
EG *... cruelty to animals*

cruise /kruːz/
cruises cruising cruised

NOUN
1 a holiday in which you travel on a ship and visit places
EG *They were planning to go on a world cruise.*

VERB
2 When a vehicle cruises, it moves at a constant moderate speed.
EG *... a police car cruised past*

crumb /krʌm/
crumbs

NOUN
Crumbs are very small pieces of bread or cake.
EG *I brushed the crumbs from my trousers.*

crumble /'krʌmbl/
crumbles crumbling crumbled

VERB
When something crumbles, or when you crumble it, it breaks into small pieces.
EG *The old paper crumbled beneath his fingers.*
EG *Crumble the cheese into a bowl.*

crush /krʌʃ/
crushes crushing crushed

VERB
1 To crush something means to

A B C D E F G H I J K L M N O P Q R S T U V W X Y Z

squeeze it hard so that its shape is destroyed.

EG *He crushed the empty can.*

2 To crush someone means to defeat them completely.

EG *... an attempt to crush the rebels*

crutch /krʌtʃ/
crutches

NOUN

a stick which someone with an injured foot or leg uses to support them while walking

EG *I was on crutches for a while.*

cry /kraɪ/
cries crying cried

VERB

1 When you cry, tears come from your eyes, usually because you are unhappy or hurt.

EG *I hung up the phone and started to cry.*

2 If you cry something, you shout it or say it loudly.

EG *"See you soon!" they cried.*

NOUN

3 a shout or other loud sound made with your voice

EG *No-one heard his cries for help.*

cube /kjuːb/
cubes

NOUN

a solid shape with six square surfaces which are all the same size

EG *... ice cubes*

cucumber /ˈkjuːkʌmbəʳ/
cucumbers

NOUN

a long, thin, green vegetable which is eaten raw

EG *... a cheese and cucumber sandwich*

cuddle /ˈkʌdl/
cuddles cuddling cuddled

VERB

1 If you cuddle someone, you hold them closely in your arms as a way of showing your affection.

EG *They used to kiss and cuddle in front of everyone.*

NOUN

2 If you **give** someone **a cuddle**, you cuddle them.

EG *I wanted to give him a cuddle.*

cult /kʌlt/
cults

NOUN

1 a small religious group, especially one which is considered strange

EG *She belongs to a cult which worships trees.*

ADJECTIVE

2 very popular or fashionable among a particular group of people

EG *Since her death she has become a cult figure.*

culture /ˈkʌltʃəʳ/
cultures

NOUN

1 Culture refers to the arts and to people's appreciation of them.

EG *Popular culture today is dominated by TV.*

2 A culture is a particular society, considered in relation to its ideas, customs, and art.

EG *... people from different cultures*

cunning /ˈkʌnɪŋ/

ADJECTIVE

A cunning person or plan achieves things in a clever way, often by deceiving people.

EG *Be careful, he's quite cunning.*

cup /kʌp/
cups

NOUN

1 a small, round container with a

handle, which you drink from
EG *... a cup of tea*

2 a large metal container with two handles, given as a prize in some sports and competitions
EG *They paraded the cup around the stadium.*

cupboard /'kʌbəd/
cupboards

NOUN

1 a piece of furniture with doors and shelves
EG *... kitchen cupboards*

2 a very small room for storing things in
EG *... the cupboard at the end of the hall*

curb /kə:b/
see **kerb**

cure /kjuər/
cures curing cured

VERB

1 If a doctor or a medical treatment cures someone or cures their illness, they make the person well again.
EG *Almost overnight I was cured.*

NOUN

2 A **cure for** an illness or a problem is something that brings it to an end.
EG *There is still no cure for the common cold.*

curiosity /kjuərɪˈɒsɪti/

NOUN

Curiosity is the desire to know about things.
EG *To satisfy my curiosity, I arranged to meet her.*

curious /'kjuərɪəs/

ADJECTIVE

1 Someone who is **curious about** something wants to know more about it.

EG *She was curious about all aspects of my past.*

2 Something that is curious is unusual or difficult to understand.
EG *A curious thing happened.*

curl /kə:l/
curls curling curled

NOUN

1 Curls are lengths of hair shaped in tight curves and circles.
EG *... the little girl with blonde curls*

VERB

2 If something curls somewhere, it moves there in a curve or circle.
EG *Smoke was curling up the chimney.*

currency /'kʌrnsɪ/
currencies

NOUN

The money used in a country is referred to as its currency.
EG *... when you exchange foreign currency at the airport*
EG *... a single European currency*

current /'kʌrnt/
currents

NOUN

1 a continuous, flowing movement of water or air
EG *She was swept out to sea by the strong current.*

2 A current or an **electric current** is a flow of electricity through a wire or circuit.
EG *A powerful electric current is passed through the liquid.*

ADJECTIVE

3 Something that is current is happening, being done, or being used now.
EG *The current situation is very different.*

current affairs

PLURAL NOUN

A B C D E F G H I J K L M N O P Q R S T U V W X Y Z

Current affairs are political events which are discussed in the media.
EG ... a current affairs programme

curry /'kʌrɪ/
curries

NOUN
Curry is an Indian dish made with hot spices.
EG I went for a curry last night.

curse /kəːs/
curses cursing cursed

VERB
1 If you curse, you swear because you are angry.
EG I put the phone down, cursing loudly.

NOUN
2 A curse is what you say when you curse.
EG Groans and curses filled the air.

3 a magic spell that is supposed to cause unpleasant things to happen to someone
EG Maybe there's a curse on my family.

curtain /'kəːtn/
curtains

NOUN
Curtains are hanging pieces of material which can be pulled across a window to keep out the light or to prevent people from looking in.
EG Her bedroom curtains were drawn.

curve /kəːv/
curves curving curved

NOUN
1 a smooth, gradually bending line
EG ... the curve of his lips

VERB
2 When something curves, it moves in a curve or has the shape of a curve.

EG The lane curved away to the right.

cushion /'kuʃən/
cushions

NOUN
a soft object which you put on a seat to make it more comfortable
EG He put a cushion behind his back.

custom /'kʌstəm/
customs

NOUN
1 a traditional activity
EG ... an ancient Chinese custom

2 something that is usually done at a particular time or in particular circumstances
EG It was my custom to interview every applicant personally.

3 customs is the place at a border, airport, or harbour where you have to declare any goods that you are bringing into a country
EG We went through customs without any problems.

customer /'kʌstəmər/
customers

NOUN
A shop's or firm's customers are the people who buy its goods or services.
EG The shop was full of customers.

cut /kʌt/
cuts cutting cut

VERB
1 If you cut something, you use a knife or other sharp tool to mark it or to remove parts of it.
EG Cut the tomatoes in half.
EG You've had your hair cut.

2 If you **cut** a part of your body, you injure yourself on a sharp object and

bleed.
EG *I cut myself shaving.*
EG *Robert cut his knee on a rusty nail.*
3 If you cut the amount of something, you reduce it.
EG *Our principal aim is to cut costs.*

NOUN
4 a mark made with a knife or other sharp tool
EG *He made a number of cuts in the wood.*
5 an injury caused by a sharp object
EG *He escaped with cuts and bruises.*
6 a reduction in something
EG *... another cut in interest rates*

cut down
VERB
1 If you cut down a tree, you cut through its trunk so that it falls to the ground.
EG *Most of the trees have now been cut down.*
2 If you **cut down on** something, you use or do less of it.
EG *He wants to cut down on coffee.*

cut off
VERB
1 If you cut something off, you remove it with a knife or a similar tool.
EG *He threatened to cut off my hair.*
2 To cut someone or something off means to separate them from things they are normally connected with.
EG *Without a car we felt very cut off.*
3 If a supply of something is cut off, you no longer get it.
EG *The water had been cut off.*

cut out
VERB
1 If you cut something out, you remove it with scissors or a similar tool.
EG *I cut the picture out and pinned it to my wall.*
2 If you cut out something, you stop doing it.
EG *It's best to cut out all alcohol during pregnancy.*

cute /kju:t/
ADJECTIVE
pretty or attractive
EG *... a cute little dog*

cycle /'saɪkl/
cycles cycling cycled
VERB
1 When you cycle, you ride a bicycle.
EG *I usually cycle to work.*
NOUN
2 a bicycle
EG *... a cycle race*
3 a series of events which is continually repeated
EG *... the cycle of births and deaths*

cyclist /'saɪklɪst/
cyclists
NOUN
someone who rides a bicycle
EG *... a cyclist in a yellow jacket*

cynical /'sɪnɪkl/
ADJECTIVE
Someone who is cynical believes that people always behave selfishly or dishonestly.
EG *It has made me very cynical about politicians.*

A
B
C
D
E
F
G
H
I
J
K
L
M
N
O
P
Q
R
S
T
U
V
W
X
Y
Z

Dd

dad /dæd/
or **daddy** /'dædɪ/
dads or **daddies**

NOUN

AN INFORMAL WORD

Your dad or your daddy is your father.

EG *He's living with his mum and dad.*

daft /dɑːft/
dafter daftest

ADJECTIVE

stupid and not sensible

EG *That's a daft question.*

daily /'deɪlɪ/

ADJECTIVE

1 occurring every day

EG *... my daily visit to the gym*

2 relating to a single day or to one day at a time

EG *... the average daily wage*

dam /dæm/
dams

NOUN

a barrier built across a river to hold back water

EG *... the Aswan Dam*

damage /'dæmɪdʒ/
damages damaging damaged

VERB

1 To damage something means to harm or spoil it.

EG *A fire had severely damaged the school.*

NOUN

2 Damage is injury or harm that is caused to something.

EG *The bomb caused extensive damage to the restaurant.*

damned /dæmd/

ADJECTIVE

AN INFORMAL WORD

Damned is a swear word that is used to express anger or for emphasis.

EG *It's a damned nuisance.*

damp /dæmp/
damper dampest

ADJECTIVE

slightly wet

EG *... a damp towel*

dance /dɑːns/
dances dancing danced

VERB

1 When you dance, you move around in time to music.

EG *Would you like to dance?*

NOUN

2 a series of rhythmic movements which you do in time to music

EG *... a very energetic dance*

3 a social event where people dance with each other

EG *... the school dance*

danger /'deɪndʒəʳ/
dangers

NOUN

1 Danger is the possibility that someone may be harmed or killed.

EG *Your life is in danger.*

2 A danger is something or someone that can hurt or harm you.

EG *... the dangers of smoking*

dangerous /'deɪndʒrəs/

ADJECTIVE

Something that is dangerous is likely to hurt or harm you.

EG *It's dangerous to drive when you're tired.*

dare /dɛəʳ/

dares daring dared

VERB

1 If you **dare to do** something, you have the courage to do it.
EG *Nobody dared to complain.*
☑ You can leave out the word 'to' after 'dare': *nobody dared complain*. The form *dares* is never used in a question or in a negative statement. You use *dare* instead: *dare she tell?; he dare not enter.*

2 If you **dare** someone **to do** something, you challenge them to prove they are not frightened of doing it.
EG *I dare you to ask him his name.*

dark /dɑːk/
darker darkest

ADJECTIVE

1 When it is dark, there is not enough light to see properly.
EG *It was too dark to see what was happening.*

2 Something that is dark is black or a shade close to black.
EG *... a dark suit*

NOUN

3 the dark is the lack of light in a place
EG *I've always been afraid of the dark.*

darling /'dɑːlɪŋ/
darlings

NOUN

You call someone darling if you love them or like them very much.
EG *Thank you, darling.*

dart /dɑːt/
darts darting darted

NOUN

1 a small pointed object which is designed to be thrown or shot
EG *... a poison dart*

2 darts is a game in which the players throw darts at a round board divided into numbered sections
EG *... a game of darts*
☑ Although it looks like a plural, 'darts' is a singular noun: *darts is his favourite game.*

VERB

3 If you dart somewhere, you move there quickly and suddenly.
EG *She darted across the empty street.*

dash /dæʃ/
dashes dashing dashed

VERB

1 If you dash somewhere, you rush there.
EG *She suddenly dashed down to the cellar.*

NOUN

2 a sudden movement or rush
EG *... the 100-mile dash to the hospital*

The **dash** is the symbol — that marks a sudden change in the flow of a sentence.
EG *I'm not sure — what was the question again?*

---

dashboard /'dæʃbɔːd/
dashboards

NOUN

the instrument panel in a car
EG *... a flashing light on the dashboard*

data /'deɪtə/

NOUN

Data is information, usually in the form of facts or statistics.
EG *The study was based on data from 2,100 women.*
☑ 'Data' is really a plural word, but it is usually used as a singular: *data is fed into the computer.*

A B C D E F G H I J K L M N O P Q R S T U V W X Y Z

date /deɪt/
dates dating dated

NOUN

1 a particular day or year
EG *What's the date today?*
EG *His date of birth is June 28, 1954.*

2 If you **have a date with** someone, especially someone of the opposite sex, or if you **go on a date** with them, you have an appointment to meet them.
EG *I've got a date with Lucy.*
EG *It's ages since I've been on a date.*

3 Something that is **out of date** is old-fashioned and no longer useful.
EG *Computers go out of date so quickly.*

VERB

4 If you are dating someone, you have a romantic relationship with them.
EG *He's been dating her for several weeks.*

5 If you date something, you find out when it began or was made.
EG *Scientists are still trying to date the stone.*

6 If something **dates from** a particular time, that is when it happened or was made.
EG *The treasure dates from the 6th century B.C.*

daughter /ˈdɔːtəʳ/
daughters

NOUN

Your daughter is your female child.
EG *I have two daughters and a son.*

daughter-in-law
/ˈdɔːtərɪnlɔː/
daughters-in-law

NOUN

Your daughter-in-law is the wife of your son.
EG *... his daughter-in-law, Carol*

dawn /dɔːn/
dawns

NOUN

1 the time in the morning when light first appears in the sky
EG *Nancy woke at dawn.*

2 the beginning of something
EG *... the dawn of a new age*

day /deɪ/
days

NOUN

1 one of the seven 24-hour periods of time in a week, measured from one midnight to the next
EG *Nobody has seen them for several days.*

2 Day is the part of the day when it is light.
EG *The snack bar is open during the day.*

3 You can refer to a period of time as a particular day or particular days.
EG *... in my grandfather's day*
EG *... these days*

daylight /ˈdeɪlaɪt/

NOUN

Daylight is the part of the day when it is light.
EG *There wasn't much daylight left.*

dead /dɛd/

ADJECTIVE

1 no longer living
EG *Both her parents are dead.*

2 no longer used or no longer functioning
EG *... a dead language*
EG *The phone went dead.*

ADVERB

3 precisely or exactly
EG *Suddenly another boat*

appeared, dead ahead.

deadline /'dɛdlaɪn/
deadlines

NOUN

a time or date before which
something must be done
EG *We missed the deadline because
of all the delays.*

deadly /'dɛdlɪ/
deadlier deadliest

ADJECTIVE

likely or able to cause death
EG *… a deadly disease*
EG *… deadly weapons*

deaf /dɛf/
deafer deafest

ADJECTIVE

Deaf people are unable to hear
anything or unable to hear well.
EG *She's been deaf since birth.*

deal /diːl/
deals dealing dealt

NOUN

1 an agreement or arrangement,
especially in business
EG *… the best business deal I ever
did*

2 **a good deal** or **a great deal
of** something is a lot of it
EG *They spent a great deal of
money on the house.*

VERB

3 If you **deal with** something,
you do what is necessary to
achieve the result you want.
EG *He must learn to deal with stress.*

4 If someone **deals in** a particular
type of goods, they buy and sell
those goods.
EG *She deals in antiques.*

5 When you deal cards, you give
them out to the players in a game
of cards.
EG *He dealt them each six cards.*

dear /dɪəʳ/
dears; dearer dearest

NOUN

1 You can call someone 'dear' as a
sign of affection.
EG *What's the matter, dear?*

ADJECTIVE

2 much loved
EG *He's a very dear friend.*

3 Something that is dear costs a
lot of money.
EG *They're far too dear.*

☑ 'Dear' is used before a person's
name, or before *Sir* or *Madam*, to
begin a letter: *Dear Mr Collins;
Dear Madam.*

death /dɛθ/
deaths

NOUN

Death is the end of the life of a
person or animal.
EG *… the tenth anniversary of his
death*
EG *… the danger of death from
starvation*

debate /dɪ'beɪt/
debates debating debated

NOUN

1 Debate is argument or
discussion.
EG *There has been a lot of debate
about this.*

2 a formal discussion in which
opposing views are expressed
EG *… a debate on public spending*

VERB

3 When people debate something,
they discuss it in a formal manner.
EG *The meeting will debate the
issue today.*

debt /dɛt/
debts

NOUN

1 A debt is a sum of money that
you owe someone.

EG *He is still paying off his debts.*

2 Debt is the state of owing money.

EG *He got into debt as a student.*

decade /ˈdɛkeɪd/
decades

NOUN

a period of ten years

EG *... the last decade of the 19th century*

decaffeinated /diˈkæfɪneɪtɪd/

ADJECTIVE

Decaffeinated coffee or tea has had most of the caffeine removed.

EG *... a cup of decaffeinated coffee*

decay /dɪˈkeɪ/
decays decaying decayed

VERB

1 When things decay, they rot or go bad.

EG *The bodies had already started to decay.*

NOUN

2 Decay is the process of decaying.

EG *... dental decay*

deceive /dɪˈsiːv/
deceives deceiving deceived

VERB

If you deceive someone, you make them believe something that is not true.

EG *I was really hurt that he had deceived me.*

December /dɪˈsɛmbər/

NOUN

December is the twelfth month of the year.

EG *They are due to arrive in early December.*

decent /ˈdiːsənt/

ADJECTIVE

1 acceptable in standard or quality

EG *He gets a decent pension.*

2 honest and respectable

EG *... a decent man*

decide /dɪˈsaɪd/
decides deciding decided

VERB

1 If you **decide to do** something, you choose to do it.

EG *Why did you decide to get married?*

2 If you decide that something is the case, you form that opinion about it.

EG *He decided that she must be right.*

3 If something decides a situation, it makes a particular result certain.

EG *The cup final was decided on penalties.*

decimal /ˈdɛsɪməl/
decimals

ADJECTIVE

1 A decimal system involves counting in units of ten.

EG *... the decimal system of metric weights and measures*

NOUN

2 a fraction written in the form of a dot followed by numbers representing tenths, hundredths, and so on

EG *... mathematical concepts such as decimals and fractions*

decision /dɪˈsɪʒən/
decisions

NOUN

a choice or judgment that is made about something

EG *I think you made the right decision.*

deck /dɛk/
decks

NOUN

1 A deck on a bus or ship is a

downstairs or upstairs area.
EG ... *the top deck of the bus*
EG ... *a luxury liner with five passenger decks*

2 A **tape deck** or **record deck** is a piece of equipment on which you play tapes or records.
EG ... *the tape deck in my car*

declare /dɪ'klɛəʳ/
declares declaring declared

VERB

1 If you declare something, you say it firmly and forcefully.
EG *She declared that she would fight on.*

2 To declare something means to announce it officially or formally.
EG *He was declared insane.*

3 If you declare goods or earnings, you say what you have bought or earned, in order to pay tax on it.
EG *The customs officer asked if he had anything to declare.*

decline /dɪ'klaɪn/
declines declining declined

VERB

1 If something declines, it becomes smaller or weaker.
EG *The number of staff has declined in recent years.*

2 If you decline something, you politely refuse to accept it or do it.
EG *I declined his offer of a drink.*

NOUN

3 a gradual weakening or decrease
EG ... *a decline in the birth rate*

decorate /'dɛkəreɪt/
decorates decorating decorated

VERB

1 If you decorate something, you make it more attractive by adding things to it.
EG *He decorated his office with pictures.*

2 If you decorate a room or building, you put paint or paper on the walls and ceiling.
EG *He paid someone to decorate the bedroom.*

decoration /dɛkə'reɪʃən/
decorations

NOUN

Decorations are features that you add to something to make it more attractive.
EG *We put up the Christmas decorations.*

decrease /diː'kriːs/
decreases decreasing decreased

VERB

1 If something decreases or if you decrease it, it becomes less or smaller.
EG *The number of people getting married has decreased.*
EG *Try to decrease the amount of coffee you drink.*

NOUN : /'diːkriːs/
☑ Note the change in stress.

2 A **decrease in** something is a reduction in its amount or size.
EG ... *a decrease in the number of people out of work*

dedicate /'dɛdɪkeɪt/
dedicates dedicating dedicated

VERB

1 If you **dedicate yourself to** something, you give your time and energy to it.
EG *She has dedicated her life to caring for others.*

2 If you **dedicate** a book or piece of music **to** someone, you say that it is written for them, as a sign of respect or affection.
EG *He dedicated all his books to his wife.*

A
B
C
D
E
F
G
H
I
J
K
L
M
N
O
P
Q
R
S
T
U
V
W
X
Y
Z

deduct /dɪ'dʌkt/
**deducts deducting
deducted**

VERB

If you deduct an amount from a total, you take it away from the total.

EG *Marks will be deducted for poor spelling.*

deep /diːp/
deeper deepest

ADJECTIVE

1 If something is deep, it extends a long way down from the surface.

EG *... a deep hole*

2 You use 'deep' to talk about how much something measures from the surface to the bottom.

EG *The water was only three feet deep.*

3 great or intense

EG *... his deep love of his country*

4 A deep sound is a low one.

EG *... a deep voice*

deer /dɪəʳ/

☑ The plural is *deer*.

NOUN

A deer is a large wild animal. Male deer usually have large, branching horns.

EG *... a herd of deer*

defeat /dɪ'fiːt/
defeats defeating defeated

VERB

1 If you defeat someone, you win a victory over them.

EG *The team hasn't been defeated all year.*

NOUN

2 Defeat is the state of being beaten or of failing.

EG *He refused to admit defeat.*

3 A defeat is an occasion on which someone is beaten or fails to achieve something.

EG *It was a crushing defeat for the government.*

defence /dɪ'fɛns/
defences
US **defense**

NOUN

1 Defence is action that is taken to protect someone or something from attack.

EG *They carried sticks for defence.*

EG *... the Ministry of Defence*

2 A defence is the arguments that are used to support something that has been criticized.

EG *He drew up a defence of his economic policy.*

defend /dɪ'fɛnd/
**defends defending
defended**

VERB

1 If you defend someone or something, you protect them from harm or danger.

EG *He tried to defend himself but was badly beaten.*

2 If you defend a person or their ideas, you argue in support of them.

EG *The decision was unpopular and hard to defend.*

defense /dɪ'fɛns/
see **defence**

defensive /dɪ'fɛnsɪv/

ADJECTIVE

1 intended or designed for protection

EG *... defensive weapons*

2 Someone who is defensive feels unsure and threatened.

EG *Don't get defensive, I was only joking.*

deficiency /dɪ'fɪʃənsɪ/
deficiencies

NOUN

a lack of something
EG ... a vitamin deficiency

define /dɪˈfaɪn/
defines defining defined

VERB
If you define something, you say
what it is or what it means.
EG Culture can be defined in many
ways.

definite /ˈdɛfɪnɪt/

ADJECTIVE
1 clear and unlikely to be changed
EG It's too soon to give a definite
answer.
2 true rather than being
someone's guess or opinion
EG We haven't heard anything
definite yet.

definitely /ˈdɛfɪnɪtlɪ/

ADVERB
You use 'definitely' to emphasize
that something is certain and will
not change.
EG I'm definitely going to contact
her.

definition /dɛfɪˈnɪʃən/
definitions

NOUN
a statement that explains the
meaning of a word or idea
EG What's your definition of a good
holiday?

degree /dɪˈgriː/
degrees

NOUN
1 an amount of a feeling or quality
EG This will provide a high degree of
protection.
2 a unit of measurement for
temperatures and angles; often
written as ° after a number
EG It is 20°C.
EG ... a ninety-degree angle
3 a university qualification that

you gain after completing a course
of study
EG She has a degree in English.

delay /dɪˈleɪ/
delays delaying delayed

VERB
1 If you **delay doing** something,
you do not do it until a later time.
EG They wanted to delay getting
married until they were older.
2 If something delays you, it
makes you late or slows you down.
EG The flight was delayed for an
hour.
NOUN
3 If there is a delay, something
does not happen until later than
planned or expected.
EG The fog caused serious delays.

deliberate /dɪˈlɪbərət/

ADJECTIVE
If something that you do is
deliberate, you intended to do it.
EG It was a deliberate insult.

delicious /dɪˈlɪʃəs/

ADJECTIVE
Delicious food or drink has an
extremely pleasant taste.
EG ... a wide selection of delicious
meals

delight /dɪˈlaɪt/
**delights delighting
delighted**

NOUN
1 Delight is great pleasure or joy.
EG Andrew roared with delight.
VERB
2 If something delights you, or if
you **are delighted** by it, it gives
you a lot of pleasure.
EG ... music that has delighted
audiences all over the world
EG I'm delighted to see you again.

A
B
C
D
E
F
G
H
I
J
K
L
M
N
O
P
Q
R
S
T
U
V
W
X
Y
Z

deliver /dɪ'lɪvəʳ/
delivers delivering delivered

VERB

1 If you deliver something somewhere, you take it there.
EG *The postman at last delivered the letter.*

2 If you deliver a lecture or speech, you give it.
EG *He delivered an emotional speech.*

3 If someone delivers a baby, they help with the birth of the baby.
EG *... the woman who'd delivered all three of her children*

delivery /dɪ'lɪvərɪ/
deliveries

NOUN

1 Delivery is the act of bringing letters or goods to someone's house or office.
EG *Please allow 28 days for delivery.*

2 A delivery of letters or goods is an occasion when they are delivered.
EG *I got a delivery of fresh eggs this morning.*

demand /dɪ'mɑːnd/
demands demanding demanded

VERB

1 If you demand something, you ask for it forcefully.
EG *I demanded an explanation from him.*

2 If a situation demands a particular quality, it needs it.
EG *What this demands is hard work.*
EG *... the high standards demanded of doctors*

NOUN

3 a forceful request for something
EG *... my demand for a clean towel*

4 If there is **demand** for something, a lot of people want to buy it or have it.
EG *Demand for coal is down.*

PLURAL NOUN

5 The **demands** of a job or activity are the efforts that are needed in order to do it.
EG *... the demands of a new job*

democracy /dɪ'mɔkrəsɪ/
democracies

NOUN

1 Democracy is a system of government in which the people choose their leaders by voting for them in elections.
EG *... the spread of democracy in Eastern Europe*

2 a country in which the people choose their government by voting for it
EG *... a modern democracy such as ours*

democratic /demə'krætɪk/

ADJECTIVE

1 governed by representatives who are elected by the people
EG *... a democratic society*

2 A democratic system is one in which everyone is equally involved.
EG *We work in a very democratic way.*

demonstrate /'demənstreɪt/
demonstrates demonstrating demonstrated

VERB

1 To demonstrate something means to show that it is true.
EG *This demonstrates exactly what I mean.*

2 If you demonstrate something to somebody, you show them how to do it or how it works.
EG *She demonstrated how to apply the make-up.*

3 If people demonstrate, they march or gather together to show

that they oppose or support something.
EG ... *the students who had demonstrated against the government*

demonstration
/demən'streɪʃən/
demonstrations

NOUN
1 a march or gathering in which people show their support for something or their opposition to it
EG ... *when police broke up the demonstration*
2 a talk or explanation that shows how to do something
EG ... *the first public demonstration of television*
3 a clear proof of something
EG ... *a demonstration of the power of reason*

dense
/dɛns/
denser densest

ADJECTIVE
1 thickly crowded or packed together
EG ... *the dense crowd*
2 difficult to see through
EG ... *dense black smoke*

dent
/dɛnt/
dents denting dented

VERB
1 To dent something means to damage it by hitting it and making a hollow in its surface.
EG ... *a dented tin can*

NOUN
2 a hollow in the surface of something, caused by hitting it
EG *There was a dent in the bonnet of the car.*

dentist
/'dɛntɪst/
dentists

NOUN

a person who is qualified to treat people's teeth; you also refer to the place where a dentist works as **the dentist's**
EG *Visit your dentist twice a year for a check-up.*

deny
/dɪ'naɪ/
denies denying denied

VERB
1 If you deny something, you say that it is not true.
EG *She denied all the accusations.*
2 If you deny someone something, you refuse to give it to them.
EG *They were denied permission to attend.*

deodorant
/diː'əʊdərənt/
deodorants

NOUN
a substance that you put on your body to hide or reduce the smell of sweat
EG ... *a can of deodorant*

depart
/dɪ'pɑːt/
departs departing departed

VERB
To **depart from** a place means to leave it and start a journey to another place.
EG ... *the train now departing from Platform 5*

department
/dɪ'pɑːtmənt/
departments

NOUN
one of the sections into which an organization is divided
EG ... *the cosmetics department at Selfridges*

department store
department stores

NOUN
a large shop which sells many different kinds of goods
EG ... *a New York department store*

A B C D E F G H I J K L M N O P Q R S T U V W X Y Z

departure /dɪˈpɑːtʃər/

NOUN

Departure is the act of leaving a place or a job.

EG ... *the President's departure for Helsinki*

EG ... *his departure from the post*

depend /dɪˈpɛnd/
depends depending depended

1 If one thing **depends on** another, it is influenced by it.

EG *The cooking time depends on the size of the potato.*

VERB

2 If you **depend on** someone or something, you trust them and rely on them.

EG *You can depend on me.*

deposit /dɪˈpɒzɪt/
deposits

NOUN

a sum of money that you give in part payment for goods or services

EG ... *a £50 deposit is required when ordering*

depressed /dɪˈprɛst/

ADJECTIVE

1 If you are depressed, you are sad and feel you cannot enjoy anything.

EG *She's very depressed about the whole situation.*

2 A depressed place has a lot of unemployment and poverty.

EG ... *depressed industrial areas*

depression /dɪˈprɛʃən/
depressions

NOUN

1 a state of mind in which someone feels unhappy and has no energy or enthusiasm

EG *He's been suffering from depression.*

2 a time when there is a lot of unemployment and poverty

EG ... *the Great Depression of the 1930s*

deprive /dɪˈpraɪv/
deprives depriving deprived

VERB

If you **deprive** someone **of** something, you take it away from them or prevent them from having it.

EG *She was deprived of her passport at Immigration.*

depth /dɛpθ/
depths

NOUN

1 The depth of something is the measurement or distance between its top and bottom.

EG *The water was 12 to 18 inches in depth.*

2 The depth of something such as an emotion is its intensity.

EG ... *the depth of her hostility*

deputy /ˈdɛpjʊtɪ/
deputies

NOUN

Someone's deputy is a person who acts on their behalf when they are away.

EG ... *the Deputy Chairman*

derive /dɪˈraɪv/
derives deriving derived

VERB

1 A FORMAL USE

If you **derive** something **from** someone or something, you get it from them.

EG *He derives so much pleasure from music.*

2 If something **is derived from** something else, it comes from that thing.

EG *The name is derived from a Greek word.*

descend /dɪ'sɛnd/
descends descending descended

VERB
If you descend, you move downwards.
EG *She suddenly descended to the cellar.*
EG *... as we descend the stairs*

describe /dɪs'kraɪb/
describes describing described

VERB
If you describe someone or something, you say what they are like.
EG *We asked her to describe his face.*

description /dɪs'krɪpʃən/
descriptions

NOUN
A description of someone or something is an account which explains what they are like.
EG *The police have issued a description of the man.*

desert /'dɛzət/
deserts deserting deserted

NOUN
1 an area of land, usually in a hot region, which has almost no water, rain, trees, or plants
EG *... the Sahara Desert*

VERB : /dɪ'zɜːt/
☑ Note that you pronounce the verb differently from the noun.
2 If someone deserts you, they leave you and no longer help or support you.
EG *His clients had deserted him.*

deserve /dɪ'zɜːv/
deserves deserving deserved

VERB
If you deserve something, you earn it or have a right to it because of your qualities or actions.
EG *He deserves a rest.*
EG *They deserved to win.*

design /dɪ'zaɪn/
designs designing designed

VERB
1 If you design something, you plan what it should be like.
EG *Who designed the costumes?*

NOUN
2 a drawing from which something can be built or made
EG *... his design for a new office block*
3 a pattern of lines, colours, or shapes
EG *... curtains and wallpaper with the same design*

desirable /dɪ'zaɪərəbl/

ADJECTIVE
Something that is desirable is worth having or doing.
EG *... a desirable job*

desire /dɪ'zaɪəʳ/
desires desiring desired

VERB
1 A FORMAL USE
If you desire something, you want it.
EG *He gave me everything I desired.*

NOUN
2 a strong feeling of wanting something
EG *She had no desire to stay up all night.*

desk /dɛsk/
desks

NOUN
a table which you sit at in order to write or work
EG *... a writing desk*
EG *... the information desk*

desperate /'dɛspərɪt/

ADJECTIVE
If you are desperate, you are in such a bad situation that you will do anything to change it.
EG ... a desperate attempt to save their marriage

despite /dɪsˈpaɪt/
PREPOSITION
You use 'despite' to introduce a fact which makes the other part of the sentence surprising.
EG He fell asleep despite all the coffee he'd drunk.

dessert /dɪˈzɜːt/
desserts
NOUN
a sweet food that you eat at the end of a meal
EG For dessert there was ice cream.

destination /ˌdɛstɪˈneɪʃən/
destinations
NOUN
Your destination is the place you are going to.
EG I reached my destination two hours late.

destined /ˈdɛstɪnd/
ADJECTIVE
If something is **destined to** happen, or if someone is **destined for** something, that thing will definitely happen.
EG Their problems seem destined to continue.
EG I was destined for fame and fortune.

destroy /dɪsˈtrɔɪ/
destroys destroying destroyed
VERB
To destroy something means to damage it so much that it is completely ruined.
EG The building was completely destroyed.
EG He destroyed my confidence.

destruction /dɪsˈtrʌkʃən/
NOUN
Destruction is the act of destroying something or the state of being destroyed.
EG ... the destruction of the environment
EG ... causing enormous destruction

detail /ˈdiːteɪl/
details
NOUN
1 A detail of something is one of its individual facts or features.
EG I remember every detail of the party.
PLURAL NOUN
2 details about something are information about it
EG See the bottom of this page for details of how to apply.

detailed /ˈdiːteɪld/
ADJECTIVE
containing a lot of details
EG ... a detailed account of the incident

detain /dɪˈteɪn/
detains detaining detained
VERB
1 To detain someone means to force them to stay.
EG She was being detained for questioning.
2 If you detain someone, you delay them.
EG I mustn't detain you.

detect /dɪˈtɛkt/
detects detecting detected
VERB
If you detect something, you notice or find it.
EG Cancer can be detected by X-rays.

detective /dɪˈtɛktɪv/
detectives

NOUN

a person, for example a police officer, whose job is to investigate crimes

EG *Detectives are appealing for witnesses to come forward.*

deter /dɪˈtəːr/
deters deterring deterred

VERB

To **deter** someone **from doing** something means to make them not want to do it.

EG *They hope it will deter criminals from carrying guns.*

determination
/dɪtəːmɪˈneɪʃən/

NOUN

Determination is the quality that you show when you have decided to do something and you will not let anything stop you.

EG *... his determination to win the match*

determine /dɪˈtəːmɪn/
determines determining determined

VERB

1 If something determines what will happen, it controls it.

EG *... the genes responsible for determining your sex*

2 To determine something means to discover the facts about it.

EG *They are still trying to determine exactly what happened.*

determined /dɪˈtəːmɪnd/

ADJECTIVE

If you are **determined to do** something, you will not let anything stop you from doing it.

EG *She was determined to succeed.*

EG *... a most determined man*

detour /ˈdiːtuər/
detours

NOUN

If you **make a detour** on a journey, you go by a longer or less direct route.

EG *He made a detour so he could pass by his old school.*

develop /dɪˈvɛləp/
develops developing developed

VERB

1 When a person or thing develops, they grow or become more advanced.

EG *As children develop, their needs change.*

2 If you develop something, you help it to grow or succeed.

EG *We must develop closer ties with Germany.*

3 When a photographic film **is developed**, photographs are produced from it.

EG *... after the film was developed*

development /dɪˈvɛləpmənt/
developments

NOUN

1 Development is gradual growth or progress.

EG *... the development of young children*

2 A development is a new stage in a series of events.

EG *... the latest developments in technology*

device /dɪˈvaɪs/
devices

NOUN

a machine or tool that is used for a particular purpose

EG *... a device to warn you when the batteries need changing*

A
B
C
D
E
F
G
H
I
J
K
L
M
N
O
P
Q
R
S
T
U
V
W
X
Y
Z

A
B
C
D
E
F
G
H
I
J
K
L
M
N
O
P
Q
R
S
T
U
V
W
X
Y
Z

devil /ˈdɛvl/
devils

NOUN

1 In Christianity and some other religions, **the Devil** is the most powerful evil spirit.
EG ... the battle between God and the Devil

2 A devil is an evil spirit.
EG ... devils with horns and tails

devise /dɪˈvaɪz/
devises devising devised

VERB

If you devise something, you invent it or design it.
EG We devised a way of helping him.

devote /dɪˈvəʊt/
devotes devoting devoted

VERB

If you devote your time or energy to something, or if you **devote yourself to** it, you spend all your time or energy on it.
EG He abandoned politics and devoted himself to business.

devoted /dɪˈvəʊtɪd/

ADJECTIVE

very loving and loyal
EG ... his devoted wife
EG They are devoted to one another.

diagnose /daɪəɡˈnəʊz/
diagnoses diagnosing diagnosed

VERB

To diagnose an illness or problem means to identify what is wrong.
EG Her illness was diagnosed as cancer.

diagram /ˈdaɪəɡræm/
diagrams

NOUN

a drawing that shows or explains something
EG He drew a quick diagram of the route.

dial /ˈdaɪəl/
dials dialling dialled

NOUN

1 The dial on a clock or meter is the part where the time or a measurement is shown.
EG The dial on the clock showed 5 minutes to 7.

VERB

2 If you dial a number on a telephone, you press the buttons to select the number you want.
EG He lifted the phone and dialled her number.

dialogue /ˈdaɪəlɒɡ/
dialogues
US **dialog**

NOUN

1 In a novel, play, or film, dialogue is conversation.
EG He writes great dialogue.

2 Dialogue is discussion between people or groups.
EG ... a direct dialogue between the two nations

diamond /ˈdaɪəmənd/
diamonds

NOUN

a hard, bright, precious stone
EG ... a pair of diamond earrings

diaper /ˈdaɪəpər/
diapers

NOUN

In American English, a diaper is a piece of thick cloth or paper which you put round a baby's bottom.
EG He refused to change her diaper.
☑ The usual British word is nappy.

diary /ˈdaɪərɪ/
diaries

NOUN

a book for writing things in, with a separate space for each day of the year

EG *He took out his diary to check if he would be busy.*

dice /daɪs/
☑ The plural is *dice*.

NOUN
a small cube on which each side is marked with dots representing the numbers one to six
EG *He rolled the dice.*

dictate /dɪk'teɪt/
dictates dictating dictated

VERB
1 If you dictate something, you say it aloud for someone else to write down.
EG *He dictated a letter to his secretary.*
2 If one thing is dictated by another, it is caused or influenced by it.
EG *What we wear is largely dictated by convention.*

dictator /dɪk'teɪtər/
dictators

NOUN
a ruler who has complete power in a country
EG *... the dictator of a small African state*

dictionary /'dɪkʃənrɪ/
dictionaries

NOUN
a book in which words are listed alphabetically and explained or translated into another language
EG *She told him to look the word up in a dictionary.*

did /dɪd/
past tense of **do**

die /daɪ/
dies dying died

VERB
1 When people, animals, or plants die, they stop living.

EG *My mother died of cancer.*
EG *Most of the trees are dying.*
2 When things die or **die out**, they stop existing.
EG *That custom has died out now.*
3 When something dies, **dies away,** or **dies down,** it becomes less intense and disappears.
EG *The footsteps died away.*

diet /'daɪət/
diets

NOUN
1 Your diet is the usual food that you eat.
EG *... a vegetarian diet*
2 If you are **on a diet,** you only eat certain foods because you are trying to lose weight.
EG *No cake for me, I'm on a diet.*

differ /'dɪfər/
differs differing differed

VERB
1 If two or more things differ, they are unlike each other.
EG *The story differed from the one he told his wife.*
2 If people differ, they disagree about something.
EG *This is where we differ.*

difference /'dɪfrəns/
differences

NOUN
1 The difference between things is the way in which they are unlike each other.
EG *There are many differences between the two societies.*
2 The difference between two amounts is the amount by which one is less than another.
EG *Compare the two figures and write down the difference.*
3 If something **makes a difference**, it changes a situation.

A
B
C
D
E
F
G
H
I
J
K
L
M
N
O
P
Q
R
S
T
U
V
W
X
Y
Z

A B C D E F G H I J K L M N O P Q R S T U V W X Y Z

EG *She punished him but it made no difference.*

different /'dɪfrənt/

ADJECTIVE

1 If one thing is **different from** another, it is not like the other thing.

EG *London is different from most European capitals.*

EG *We have totally different views.*

☑ In American English, speakers also say that one thing is *different than* another.

2 Things that are different are distinct and separate, although of the same kind.

EG *... different brands of toothpaste*

difficult /'dɪfɪkəlt/

ADJECTIVE

1 Something that is difficult is not easy to do, understand, or solve.

EG *I found it difficult to get out of bed.*

EG *Some of the ideas are very difficult.*

2 Someone who is difficult behaves in an unreasonable way.

EG *... a difficult child*

difficulty /'dɪfɪkəltɪ/
difficulties

NOUN

1 A difficulty is a problem.

EG *The main difficulty is lack of time.*

2 Difficulty is the fact or quality of being difficult.

EG *Students complained about the difficulty of the questions.*

dig /dɪg/
digs digging dug

VERB

1 If you dig, or if you dig a hole, you make a hole in the ground.

EG *Rescue workers are still digging through the rubble.*

EG *He dug a hole in the lawn.*

2 If you **dig** one thing **into** another, or if one thing **digs into** another, the first thing presses hard against the second.

EG *The straps were digging into his shoulders.*

digger /'dɪgər/
diggers

NOUN

AN INFORMAL WORD

In Australian and New Zealand English, a digger or **Digger** is a soldier.

EG *Four World War I Diggers will lead the parade.*

digital /'dɪdʒɪtl/

ADJECTIVE

Digital systems record or send information in the form of thousands of very small signals.

EG *... digital television*

dignity /'dɪgnɪtɪ/

NOUN

Dignity is behaviour which is serious, calm, and controlled.

EG *She conducted herself with dignity.*

dilute /daɪˈluːt/
dilutes diluting diluted

VERB

If you dilute a liquid, you add water or another liquid to it to make it weaker.

EG *Dilute the juice with water.*

dim /dɪm/
dimmer dimmest; dims
dimming dimmed

ADJECTIVE

1 not bright or not easy to see

EG *The lights were dim.*

EG *... the dim outline of a small boat*

VERB

2 If you dim a light, or if it dims, it becomes less bright.
EG *Someone dimmed the lights.*

dimension /daɪˈmɛnʃən/
dimensions

NOUN

1 a particular aspect of something
EG *Works of art have a spiritual dimension.*

2 The dimensions of something are its measurements or its size.
EG *... the dimensions of the room*
EG *... a problem of major dimensions*

diminish /dɪˈmɪnɪʃ/
diminishes diminishing diminished

VERB

If something diminishes, it becomes smaller or less important.
EG *The threat of war has diminished.*

dine /daɪn/
dines dining dined

VERB

A FORMAL WORD

If you dine, you have dinner.
EG *We dined together in the hotel.*

dinkum /ˈdɪŋkəm/

ADJECTIVE

AN INFORMAL WORD

In Australian and New Zealand English, dinkum or **fair dinkum** means genuine.
EG *... a fair dinkum offer*

dinner /ˈdɪnəʳ/
dinners

NOUN

1 Dinner is the main meal of the day, eaten either in the evening or at lunchtime.
EG *She invited us to her house for dinner.*

2 a formal social occasion in the evening, at which a meal is served
EG *The Club holds an annual dinner.*

dip /dɪp/
dips dipping dipped

VERB

1 If you **dip** something **into** a liquid, you put it in and then quickly take it out again.
EG *She dipped her fingers into the water.*

2 If something dips, it makes a downward movement.
EG *The sun dipped below the horizon.*

diploma /dɪˈpləumə/
diplomas

NOUN

a qualification awarded by a college or university
EG *... a diploma in social work*

diplomat /ˈdɪpləmæt/
diplomats

NOUN

an official who negotiates with another country on behalf of his or her own country
EG *... a senior German diplomat*

direct /daɪˈrɛkt/
directs directing directed

ADJECTIVE

1 Direct means going somewhere in a straight line or by the shortest route.
EG *... a direct train service from Calais to Strasbourg*

2 If someone's behaviour is direct, they are honest and say what they mean.
EG *He avoided giving a direct answer.*

3 A direct relationship between two things or people is one which involves only those two things or people.

A
B
C
D
E
F
G
H
I
J
K
L
M
N
O
P
Q
R
S
T
U
V
W
X
Y
Z

EG *He seemed to be in direct contact with the criminals.*

VERB

4 If you **direct** one thing **at** another thing, you aim or point it at that thing.

EG *They directed their anger at the politicians.*

5 If you **direct** someone somewhere, you tell them how to get there.

EG *Could you direct me to the station?*

6 Someone who directs a film or play organizes the way it is made and performed.

EG *The film was directed by Howard Hawks.*

direction /dɪˈrɛkʃən/
directions

NOUN

1 the general line that someone or something is moving or pointing in

EG *The town was ten miles away in the opposite direction.*

PLURAL NOUN

2 directions are instructions that tell you how to do something or how to get somewhere

EG *He gave Dan directions to the computer room.*

director /dɪˈrɛktər/
directors

NOUN

1 The directors of a company are its senior managers.

EG *... the board of directors*

2 The director of a film or play is the person who decides how it is made and performed.

EG *... the film director Franco Zeffirelli*

directory /dɪˈrɛktərɪ/
directories

NOUN

a book which gives lists of information such as people's names, addresses, and telephone numbers

EG *... the telephone directory*

dirt /dɜːt/

NOUN

1 Dirt is any substance such as dust, mud, or stains.

EG *I started to wash off the dirt.*

2 You can refer to the earth on the ground as the dirt.

EG *He drew a circle in the dirt with a stick.*

dirty /ˈdɜːtɪ/
dirtier dirtiest

ADJECTIVE

1 marked or covered with dirt

EG *The kids have got their clothes dirty.*

2 unfair or dishonest

EG *... a dirty fight*

3 Dirty jokes or books refer to sex in a way that many people find shocking.

EG *He told a dirty joke about the Queen.*

dis- /dɪs/

PREFIX

Dis- is added to the beginning of some words to form a word that means the opposite.

EG *... disadvantage*

EG *... disprove*

disability /dɪsəˈbɪlɪtɪ/
disabilities

NOUN

an illness or injury that restricts someone's way of life

EG *... people with disabilities*

disabled /dɪsˈeɪbld/

ADJECTIVE

Disabled people have an illness or injury that restricts their way of life.

A
B
C
D
E
F
G
H
I
J
K
L
M
N
O
P
Q
R
S
T
U
V
W
X
Y
Z

EG ... the problems faced by disabled people in the workplace

disagree /dɪsəˈgriː/
disagrees disagreeing disagreed

VERB

1 If you **disagree with** someone, you have a different opinion to them about something.
EG My wife disagrees with me about this.
EG They still communicate even though they disagree.

2 If you **disagree with** an action or proposal, you believe it is wrong.
EG He strongly disagreed with her policies.

disappear /dɪsəˈpɪər/
disappears disappearing disappeared

VERB

1 If someone or something disappears, they go where they cannot be seen or found.
EG ... a Japanese woman who disappeared 13 years ago

2 If something disappears, it stops existing or happening.
EG The pain suddenly disappeared.

disappoint /dɪsəˈpɔɪnt/
disappoints disappointing disappointed

VERB

If someone or something disappoints you, they are not as good as you had hoped or do not do what you had hoped.
EG I'm sorry if this reply disappoints you.

disapprove /dɪsəˈpruːv/
disapproves disapproving disapproved

VERB

If you disapprove of something or

someone, you believe they are wrong or bad.
EG Everyone disapproved of their marrying so young.

disaster /dɪˈzɑːstər/
disasters

NOUN

1 a very bad accident such as an earthquake or a plane crash
EG It was the second air disaster in the region.

2 a complete failure
EG The party was a disaster.

disc /dɪsk/
discs

NOUN

a flat round object
EG ... a compact disc
EG ... a floppy disc

discard /dɪsˈkɑːd/
discards discarding discarded

VERB

If you discard something, you get rid of it because you do not want it.
EG Read the instructions before discarding the box.

discipline /ˈdɪsɪplɪn/
disciplines disciplining disciplined

NOUN

1 Discipline is the practice of making people obey rules and punishing them when they break them.
EG ... problems of discipline in the classroom

2 Discipline is the ability to behave and work in a controlled way.
EG The job requires discipline and dedication.

VERB

To discipline someone means to

A B C D E F G H I J K L M N O P Q R S T U V W X Y Z

punish them.
EG *The company is not going to discipline anybody.*

disc jockey disc jockeys
NOUN
a person who introduces and plays pop records on the radio or at a night club
EG *… a Radio One disc jockey*

disclose /dɪs'kləuz/
discloses disclosing disclosed
VERB
If you disclose new or secret information, you tell it to someone.
EG *He will not disclose the names of his patients.*

disco /'dɪskəu/
discos
NOUN
a place where people dance to pop music
EG *Afterwards we went to a disco.*

discount /'dɪskaunt/
discounts
NOUN
a reduction in the price of something
EG *All full-time staff get a 20% discount on goods.*

discourage /dɪs'kʌrɪdʒ/
discourages discouraging discouraged
VERB
1 If something or someone discourages you, they cause you to lose your enthusiasm for something.
EG *Don't let such problems discourage you.*
2 If you discourage someone from doing something, or if you discourage it, you try to persuade them not to do it.

EG *… a campaign to discourage children from smoking*

discover /dɪs'kʌvər/
discovers discovering discovered
VERB
If you discover something, you find or learn about it for the first time.
EG *A few days later her body was discovered.*
EG *She discovered that they'd escaped.*

discovery /dɪs'kʌvərɪ/
discoveries
NOUN
The discovery of something is the act of finding it or learning about it for the first time.
EG *… the discovery of millions of pounds in cash*
EG *I felt I'd made an incredible discovery.*

discriminate /dɪs'krɪmɪneɪt/
discriminates discriminating discriminated
VERB
1 To discriminate between things means to recognize the differences between them.
EG *He's incapable of discriminating between a good idea and a bad one*
2 To discriminate against a person or group means to treat them unfairly, usually because of their race, colour, or sex.
EG *The divorce laws discriminate against men.*

discuss /dɪs'kʌs/
discusses discussing discussed
VERB
When people discuss something, they talk about it in detail.
EG *I will be discussing the situation*

with colleagues tomorrow.

discussion /dɪsˈkʌʃən/
discussions

NOUN

a conversation or piece of writing in which a subject is considered in detail

EG *We had a long discussion about the proposals.*

disease /dɪˈziːz/
diseases

NOUN

an illness which affects people, animals, or plants

EG *... heart disease*

disguise /dɪsˈɡaɪz/
disguises disguising disguised

VERB

1 If you **disguise yourself,** you change your appearance so that people will not recognize you.

EG *She disguised herself as a man.*

2 If you disguise a feeling, you hide it or pretend that it is something else.

EG *I tried to disguise my disappointment.*

NOUN

3 A disguise is something you wear or a change you make to your appearance so that people will not recognize you.

EG *He was wearing a ridiculous disguise.*

disgust /dɪsˈɡʌst/
disgusts disgusting disgusted

NOUN

1 Disgust is a strong feeling of dislike or disapproval.

EG *He spoke of his disgust at the way he had been treated.*

VERB

2 If something disgusts you, you strongly dislike it or disapprove of it.

EG *I was disgusted by her behaviour.*

dish /dɪʃ/
dishes

NOUN

1 a shallow container for cooking or eating from

EG *Whose turn is it to wash the dishes?*

2 food of a particular kind or food cooked in a particular way

EG *There are plenty of vegetarian dishes to choose from.*

disk /dɪsk/
another spelling of **disc**

dislike /dɪsˈlaɪk/
dislikes disliking disliked

VERB

If you dislike something or someone, you think they are unpleasant.

EG *She disliked most of his friends.*

dismiss /dɪsˈmɪs/
dismisses dismissing dismissed

VERB

1 If you dismiss something, you decide that it is not important enough for you to think about.

EG *I considered the idea briefly, then dismissed it.*

2 If an employer dismisses an employee, they tell that person to leave their job.

EG *He was dismissed for incompetence.*

3 If someone in authority dismisses you, they tell you to leave.

EG *She dismissed the rest of the class.*

A B C D E F G H I J K L M N O P Q R S T U V W X Y Z

A
B
C
D
E
F
G
H
I
J
K
L
M
N
O
P
Q
R
S
T
U
V
W
X
Y
Z

disorder /dɪsˈɔːdər/
disorders

NOUN

1 Disorder is a state of being untidy or badly organized.
EG *The room was in complete disorder.*

2 A disorder is a physical or mental problem or illness.
EG *... a stomach disorder*

display /dɪsˈpleɪ/
displays displaying displayed

VERB

1 If you display something, you show it to people.
EG *... war veterans proudly displaying their medals*

2 If you display an emotion, you behave in a way that shows you feel it.
EG *He displayed almost no fear.*

NOUN

3 an arrangement of things designed to attract people's attention
EG *... a display of rare books*

dispose /dɪsˈpəuz/
disposes disposing disposed

VERB

If you **dispose of** something, you get rid of it.
EG *He told police how he had disposed of the murder weapon.*

dispute /dɪsˈpjuːt/
disputes disputing disputed

NOUN

1 an argument
EG *... a bitter dispute between neighbours*

VERB

2 If you dispute a fact or theory, you say that it is incorrect or untrue.
EG *Nobody disputed that she was clever.*

disqualify /dɪsˈkwɒlɪfaɪ/
disqualifies disqualifying disqualified

VERB

If someone is **disqualified from** a competition or activity, they are officially stopped from taking part in it.
EG *He was disqualified from driving for 18 months.*

dissolve /dɪˈzɒlv/
dissolves dissolving dissolved

VERB

If you **dissolve** something **in** a liquid, or if it dissolves, it mixes with the liquid and disappears.
EG *Dissolve the salt in a little boiled water.*
EG *Heat gently until the sugar dissolves.*

distance /ˈdɪstns/
distances

NOUN

1 The distance between two points is the amount of space between them.
EG *... the distance between the town and the sea*

2 Distance is the fact of being far away.
EG *We phone each other regularly, so the distance is less of a problem.*

distant /ˈdɪstnt/

ADJECTIVE

1 far away in space or time
EG *... a distant figure on the hill*
EG *... in the distant past*

2 A distant relative is one that you are not closely related to.
EG *He's a distant relative of my father.*

3 Someone who is distant is cold and unfriendly.
EG *He found her polite but distant.*

distinct /dɪsˈtɪŋkt/

ADJECTIVE

1 If one thing is **distinct from** another, there is an important difference between them.
EG ... *a word with two distinct meanings*
EG ... *a view quite distinct from those he had previously expressed*

2 If something is distinct, you can hear, smell, see, or sense it clearly.
EG *She had a distinct feeling that someone was watching her.*

distinctive /dɪsˈtɪŋktɪv/

ADJECTIVE

Something that is distinctive has a special quality which makes it easy to recognize.
EG ... *a distinctive voice*

distinguish /dɪsˈtɪŋgwɪʃ/
distinguishes distinguishing distinguished

VERB

1 If you can **distinguish** one thing **from** another, you can see or understand the difference between them.
EG *He seems unable to distinguish right from wrong.*

2 If you can distinguish something, you can see, hear or taste it.
EG *I heard shouting but couldn't distinguish the words.*

distort /dɪsˈtɔːt/
distorts distorting distorted

VERB

1 If you distort a statement or an argument, you change it so that it is untrue.
EG *She accused the journalist of distorting her views.*

2 If something is distorted, it is changed so that it seems strange or unclear.

EG *There was a problem with the phone, making his voice distorted.*

distract /dɪsˈtrækt/
distracts distracting distracted

VERB

If something distracts you, it stops you from concentrating.
EG *Playing video games sometimes distracts him from his homework.*

distress /dɪsˈtres/
distresses distressing distressed

NOUN

1 Distress is extreme sadness, suffering, or pain.
EG *Such problems can cause enormous distress.*

2 If someone or something is **in distress**, they are in danger and need help.
EG *The ship was in distress.*

VERB

3 If something distresses you, it causes you to be upset or worried.
EG *Her death had profoundly distressed me.*

distribute /dɪsˈtrɪbjuːt/
distributes distributing distributed

VERB

1 If you distribute things, you hand them out or deliver them.
EG *Soldiers are distributing food and blankets to the survivors.*

2 If you **distribute** something **among** people, you share it among them.
EG *Distribute the chores among all the family members.*

district /ˈdɪstrɪkt/
districts

NOUN

an area of a town or country

A B C D E F G H I J K L M N O P Q R S T U V W X Y Z

EG *... a working-class district of Paris*

disturb /dɪsˈtəːb/
disturbs disturbing disturbed

VERB
1 If you disturb someone, you interrupt what they are doing or interrupt their peace.
EG *She slept in a separate room so as not to disturb him.*
2 If something disturbs you, it makes you feel upset or worried.
EG *dreams so vivid that they disturbed me for days*

disturbance /dɪsˈtəːbəns/
disturbances

NOUN
1 Disturbance is the state of being disturbed.
EG *This will cause less disturbance to your everyday life.*
2 A disturbance is an incident in which people behave violently in public.
EG *The disturbances spread to more than thirty cities.*

ditch /dɪtʃ/
ditches

NOUN
a channel cut into the ground at the side of a road or field
EG *The car ended up in a ditch.*

dive /daɪv/
dives diving dived
☑ In American English, the past tense is *dove*.

VERB
1 If you dive, you jump head-first into water with your arms above your head.
EG *She was standing by the pool, about to dive in.*
2 If you dive, you go under the

surface of a sea or lake using special equipment to help you breathe.
EG *They spent the afternoon diving.*
3 When birds or animals dive, they move quickly downwards through the air or water.
EG *The shark dived down and swam under the boat.*

divert /daɪˈvəːt/
diverts diverting diverted

VERB
To divert something means to change its course or direction.
EG *Police are diverting traffic away from the Square.*

divide /dɪˈvaɪd/
divides dividing divided

VERB
1 When you divide something, or when it divides, it separates it into two or more parts.
EG *... an attempt to divide the country into two distinct regions*
2 If something divides two areas, it forms a barrier between them.
EG *... the frontier dividing Mexico from the United States*
3 If you **divide** a larger number **by** a smaller number, you calculate how many times the larger number contains the smaller number.
EG *... 35 divided by 7 is 5*

division /dɪˈvɪʒən/
divisions

NOUN
1 Division is the act of separating something into two or more parts.
EG *... the division of the country into two states*
2 one of the parts into which an organization is divided
EG *... the Research Division*

divorce /dɪˈvɔːs/
divorces divorcing divorced

NOUN

1 Divorce is the formal and legal ending of a marriage.
EG *… marriages that end in divorce*

VERB

2 When a married couple **get divorced,** or when one partner divorces the other, their marriage is legally ended.
EG *They got divorced two years ago.*
EG *She's divorcing her husband.*

DIY

NOUN

DIY is the activity of making or repairing things in your home. DIY is an abbreviation for 'do-it-yourself'.
EG *… a DIY store*

dizzy /ˈdɪzɪ/
dizzier dizziest

ADJECTIVE

If you feel dizzy, you feel that you are losing your balance and are about to fall.
EG *The champagne made me slightly dizzy.*

DJ DJs

NOUN

A DJ is a disc jockey.
EG *Who is your favourite DJ?*

do /duː/
does doing did done; dos

VERB

1 You use 'do' to form questions and negatives and to give emphasis to the main verb of a sentence.
EG *What do you think?*
EG *I don't understand.*
EG *That does look nice.*
✓ *Do not, does not,* and *did not* are often shortened to *don't, doesn't,* and *didn't.*

2 If someone does a task or activity, they perform it.
EG *He just didn't want to do any work.*

3 If you ask someone what they do, you want to know what their job is.
EG *What will you do when you leave school?*

4 If you **do well** at something, you are successful. If you **do badly,** you are unsuccessful.
EG *She did well at school.*
EG *They didn't do too badly.*

5 You use 'do' to say that something has a particular result.
EG *The bomb did a lot of damage.*

6 If you **do** something **about** a problem, you try to solve it.
EG *He didn't like it, but there wasn't much he could do about it.*

7 If something **will do,** it is satisfactory.
EG *Give them a present — anything will do.*

8 If one thing **has** something **to do with** another thing, or if it **is** something **to do with** it, the two things are connected.
EG *The argument had something to do with money.*
EG *It's nothing to do with you.*

NOUN

9 AN INFORMAL USE
a party or other social event
EG *We're having a little do on Saturday.*

do up

VERB

1 If you do something up, you fasten it.
EG *Do your coat up.*

2 To do up an old building means to repair and decorate it.
EG *They're doing up the old cinema.*

A
B
C
D
E
F
G
H
I
J
K
L
M
N
O
P
Q
R
S
T
U
V
W
X
Y
Z

A
B
C
D
E
F
G
H
I
J
K
L
M
N
O
P
Q
R
S
T
U
V
W
X
Y
Z

dock /dɒk/
docks docking docked

NOUN
1 an area in a harbour where ships are loaded, unloaded, or repaired
EG *He works at the docks.*

VERB
2 When a ship docks, it is brought into a dock.
EG *The vessel docked at Liverpool.*

doctor /'dɒktər/
doctors

NOUN
1 a person who is qualified in medicine and treats people who are ill; you also refer to the surgery or clinic where a doctor works as **the doctor's**
EG *If the symptoms persist, call your doctor.*
2 Doctor is the title given to someone who has been awarded the highest academic degree by a university.
EG *She is a doctor of philosophy.*

document /'dɒkjumənt/
documents documenting documented

NOUN
1 a piece of paper which provides an official record of something
EG *... travel documents*
VERB : /'dɒkjumɛnt/
☑ Note that you pronounce the verb differently from the noun.
2 If you document something, you make a detailed record of it.
EG *... a book documenting his prison experiences*

documentary /dɒkju'mɛntərɪ/
documentaries

NOUN
a radio or television programme, or a film, which gives information about real events

EG *... a documentary about the police*

dodge /dɒdʒ/
dodges dodging dodged

VERB
If you dodge something, you avoid it by quickly moving aside.
EG *The band ran from the stage, dodging beer cans as they went.*

does /dʌz/
the third person singular of the present tense of **do**

dog /dɒg/
dogs

NOUN
an animal that is often kept as a pet or used to guard things
EG *A dog was barking outside.*

doll /dɒl/
dolls

NOUN
a child's toy which looks like a small person or baby
EG *... a little girl playing with a doll*

dollar /'dɒlər/
dollars

NOUN
A dollar is a unit of money in the USA, Canada, and some other countries. It is worth 100 cents and is represented by the symbol '$'.
EG *She gets paid ten dollars an hour.*

dome /dəum/
domes

NOUN
a round roof
EG *... the dome of St Paul's Cathedral*

domestic /də'mɛstɪk/

ADJECTIVE
1 happening or existing within

one particular country
EG *... both domestic and international flights*

2 involving or concerned with the home and family
EG *... routine domestic tasks*

dominate /'dɒmɪneɪt/
dominates dominating dominated

VERB

1 To dominate a situation means to be the most powerful or important thing or person in it.
EG *The news was dominated by the war.*

2 If one person dominates another, they have power over them.
EG *... men who are dominated by their wives*

donate /dəˈneɪt/
donates donating donated

VERB

1 If you **donate** something **to** a charity, you give it to them.
EG *... people who donate clothes to Oxfam*

2 If you donate your blood or a part of your body, you allow doctors to use it to help someone who is ill.
EG *... people who donate their organs for use after death*

done /dʌn/
past participle of **do**

donkey /'dɒŋkɪ/
donkeys

NOUN

an animal like a horse, but smaller and with longer ears
EG *... a ride on a donkey*

donor /'dəʊnəʳ/
donors

NOUN

someone who gives some of their blood or a part of their body to help a person who is ill
EG *... a kidney donor*

doomed /duːmd/

ADJECTIVE

Someone or something that is doomed is certain to fail.
EG *... a doomed attempt to rescue her children*

door /dɔːʳ/
doors

NOUN

a swinging or sliding panel that is used for opening or closing the entrance to a building, room, cupboard, or vehicle
EG *I knocked at the door but there was no answer.*

doorway /'dɔːweɪ/
doorways

NOUN

an opening in a wall for a door
EG *He stood in the doorway, smiling.*

dose /dəʊs/
doses

NOUN

a measured amount of a medicine or drug
EG *It's quite harmless in doses.*

dot /dɒt/
dots

NOUN

a very small, round mark
EG *... a black dot in the middle of a circle*

double /'dʌbl/
doubles doubling doubled

ADJECTIVE

1 twice the usual size
EG *... a double whisky*

2 consisting of two parts
EG *... a pair of double doors*

A
B
C
D
E
F
G
H
I
J
K
L
M
N
O
P
Q
R
S
T
U
V
W
X
Y
Z

A B C D E F G H I J K L M N O P Q R S T U V W X Y Z

VERB

3 If something doubles, or if you double it, it becomes twice as large.

EG *The number of staff has doubled over the last year.*

EG *He offered to double her salary.*

4 If one person or thing **doubles as** another person or thing, they have a second job or use as well as their main one.

EG *Their home doubles as an office.*

NOUN

5 A double or a **double room** is a room that is intended to be used by two people.

EG *The hotel said there were no double rooms available.*

6 Your double is someone who looks exactly like you.

EG *He believes everyone has a double somewhere.*

7 doubles is a game of tennis or badminton which two people play against two other people

EG *... the final of the women's doubles*

☑ Although it looks like a plural noun, 'doubles' is singular: *the doubles was a close match.*

doubt /daut/
doubts doubting doubted

NOUN

1 Doubt is a feeling of uncertainty about whether something is true or possible.

EG *There is no doubt that he tries hard.*

EG *This raises serious doubts about his motives.*

VERB

2 If you doubt something, you think that it is probably not true or possible.

EG *He doubted whether he would learn anything new.*

doubtful /'dautful/

ADJECTIVE

unlikely or uncertain

EG *It is doubtful whether he will play again.*

dove /dəuv/
see **dive**

down /daun/

PREPOSITION OR ADVERB

1 Down means towards the ground, towards a lower level, or in a lower place.

EG *A man came down the stairs.*

EG *She nodded and looked down.*

PREPOSITION

2 If you go down a road or river, you go along it.

EG *He walked a few miles down the road.*

ADVERB

3 If you **put** something **down**, you place it on a surface.

EG *He put his glass down on the table.*

4 If an amount of something **goes down**, it decreases.

EG *My weight went down to seventy pounds.*

ADJECTIVE

5 If you are down, you feel depressed.

EG *He's been a bit down since the accident.*

downstairs /'daun'stɛəz/

ADVERB

1 If you go downstairs in a building, you go down the stairs towards the ground floor.

EG *He followed her downstairs.*

ADJECTIVE OR ADVERB

2 If someone or something is downstairs in a building, they are on a lower floor or on the ground floor.

EG *... a downstairs flat*

EG ... *the people who live downstairs*

downtown /'daun'taun/

ADJECTIVE OR ADVERB
in or towards the centre of a city
EG ... *downtown Chicago*
EG *He works downtown.*

downwards /'daunwədz/ or downward /'daunwəd/

ADVERB OR ADJECTIVE
If you move or look downwards, you move or look towards the ground or towards a lower level.
EG *His eyes travelled downwards.*
EG *She slipped on the downward slope.*

doze /dəuz/
dozes dozing dozed

VERB
When you doze, you sleep lightly for a short period.
EG *He sat in the chair, dozing.*

dozen /'dʌzn/
dozens

NOUN
A dozen things are twelve of them.
EG ... *two dozen eggs*

Dr /'dɒktər/
Dr is an abbreviation for Doctor.
EG ... *a letter for Dr John Hardy*

draft /drɑːft/
drafts drafting drafted

NOUN
1 an early version of a piece of writing
EG ... *the first draft of an article he was writing*
2 the usual American spelling of **draught**

VERB
3 When you draft a piece of writing, you write the first version of it.

EG *He drafted a letter to the paper.*
4 If people **are drafted** somewhere, they are moved there to do a particular job.
EG *Extra police officers had to be drafted in.*
5 If you **are drafted**, you are ordered to serve in the armed forces.
EG ... *after he was drafted into the US army*

drag /dræg/
drags dragging dragged

VERB
1 If you drag a heavy object somewhere, you pull it there slowly and with difficulty.
EG *He dragged his chair towards the table.*
2
NOUN
Men **in drag** are male entertainers who wear women's clothing.
EG *The band were all in drag.*

drain /dreɪn/
drains draining drained

VERB
1 If you drain something or if it drains, liquid flows out of it or off it.
EG *Drain the pasta well.*
EG *All the sewage drains off into the river.*
2 If something drains your strength or resources, it uses them up.
EG *The dispute drained him of energy.*

NOUN
3 a pipe that carries water or waste products away from a place, or an opening in a surface that leads to the pipe
EG ... *a blocked drain*

A
B
C
D
E
F
G
H
I
J
K
L
M
N
O
P
Q
R
S
T
U
V
W
X
Y
Z

drama /'drɑːmə/
dramas

NOUN

1 a serious play for the theatre, television, or radio
EG ... *a new TV drama*

2 Drama is plays and the theatre in general.
EG ... *an expert in Greek drama*

3 You can refer to the exciting aspects of a situation as drama.
EG ... *the drama of real life*

dramatic /drə'mætɪk/

ADJECTIVE

A dramatic change or event happens suddenly and is very noticeable.
EG ... *a dramatic improvement*

drank /dræŋk/
past tense of **drink**

drastic /'dræstɪk/

ADJECTIVE

A drastic course of action is extreme and is usually taken urgently.
EG *It's time for drastic action.*

draught /drɑːft/
draughts
US **draft**

NOUN

1 a current of cold air
EG *There was a draught coming from the door.*

2 draughts is a game for two people played on a chessboard with round pieces
EG ... *a game of draughts*
☑ Although it looks like a plural, 'draughts' is a singular noun: *draughts is his favourite game.*

ADJECTIVE

3 Draught beer is served straight from barrels rather than in bottles.
EG ... *a pint of draught lager*

draw /drɔː/
draws drawing drew drawn

VERB

1 When you draw something, you use a pen or pencil to make a picture of it.
EG *We ought to draw a map.*

2 You can use 'draw' to show that something moves somewhere or is moved there.
EG *The taxi slowly drew away.*
EG *He drew his chair closer to the fire.*

3 If you draw a comparison or a conclusion, you decide that it exists or is true.
EG *What conclusions do you draw from all this?*

4 If you draw money out of a bank account, you take it out.
EG *He drew £100 out of his savings account.*

5 If you **draw the curtains,** you pull them so that they cover or uncover the window.
EG *She drew the curtains while she got changed.*

NOUN

6 the result of a game or competition in which nobody wins
EG *The match ended in a draw.*

draw up

VERB

If you draw up a plan, document, or list, you prepare it and write it out.
EG *The lawyers drew up a contract.*

drawer /'drɔːr/
drawers

NOUN

a part of a desk or other piece of furniture that is shaped like a box and slides in and out
EG *He kept the document in a locked drawer in his desk.*

drawing /'drɔːɪŋ/
drawings

NOUN

a picture made with a pen or pencil
EG *She did a drawing of me.*

dread /drɛd/
dreads dreading dreaded

VERB

If you dread something, you feel very worried and frightened about it.
EG *He was dreading the journey.*

dreadful /'drɛdful/

ADJECTIVE

very bad or unpleasant
EG *The weather was dreadful.*

dream /driːm/
dreams dreaming dreamed
or **dreamt**

NOUN

1 a series of events that you experience in your mind while asleep
EG *I had a strange dream last night.*
2 a situation or event which you often think about because you would very much like it to happen
EG *... his dream of winning the lottery*

VERB

3 When you dream, you see events in your mind while you are asleep.
EG *He dreamt that he was back at school.*
4 When you **dream of** something happening, you often think about it because you would very much like it to happen.
EG *He dreamt of becoming a writer.*
5 If you say you **would not dream of doing** something, you are emphasizing that you would not do it.
EG *I wouldn't dream of making fun*

of you.

dress /drɛs/
dresses dressing dressed

NOUN

1 A dress is a piece of clothing worn by a woman or girl that covers her body and part or all of her legs.
EG *... a woman in a black dress*
2 Dress is any clothing.
EG *... men in evening dress*

VERB

3 When you dress or **get dressed,** you put clothes on.
EG *She told him to wait while she got dressed.*

drew /druː/
past tense of **draw**

drift /drɪft/
drifts drifting drifted

VERB

1 When something drifts, it is carried along by the wind or by water.
EG *The boat drifted out to sea.*
2 When people drift somewhere, they move there slowly or without a plan.
EG *She and her husband drifted apart.*
EG *He drifted from job to job.*

drill /drɪl/
drills drilling drilled

NOUN

1 a tool for making holes
EG *... an electric drill*
2 a routine procedure or routine training
EG *... a fire drill*

VERB

3 If you **drill into** something, or if you **drill a hole,** you make a hole using a drill.
EG *This meant drilling into the*

A
B
C
D
E
F
G
H
I
J
K
L
M
N
O
P
Q
R
S
T
U
V
W
X
Y
Z

A
B
C
D
E
F
G
H
I
J
K
L
M
N
O
P
Q
R
S
T
U
V
W
X
Y
Z

bedroom wall.
EG *I drilled five holes in the wall.*

drink /drɪŋk/
drinks drinking drank drunk

VERB

1 When you drink a liquid, you take it into your mouth and swallow it.
EG *He drank some tea.*

2 To drink means to drink alcohol.
EG *He was smoking and drinking too much.*

NOUN

3 an amount of liquid that you drink
EG *I'll get you a drink of water.*

4 an alcoholic drink
EG *Let me buy you a drink.*

drip /drɪp/
drips dripping dripped

VERB

1 When liquid drips somewhere, it falls in small drops.
EG *Rain dripped from his cap.*

2 When an object drips, drops of liquid fall from it.
EG *The kitchen tap was dripping.*

NOUN

3 a small, individual drop of liquid
EG *Drips of water rolled down the walls.*

4 a medical device for passing liquid into the blood of a patient
EG *I had to be put on a drip.*

drive /draɪv/
drives driving drove driven

VERB

1 If you drive a vehicle, you operate it and control its movements.
EG *… a man driving a small white car*
EG *She never learned to drive.*

2 If you drive someone

somewhere, you take them there in a vehicle.
EG *His daughter drove him to the station.*

3 If something or someone **drives** you **to do** something, they cause you to do it.
EG *Jealousy can drive people to kill.*

4 If you **drive** a post or nail **into** something, you push it in or hammer it in.
EG *He drove the nails into the wall with a hammer.*

5 If something drives a machine, it supplies the power that makes it work.
EG *The wheels are driven by an electric motor.*

NOUN

6 a journey in a vehicle
EG *It's a 30-mile drive to the lake.*

7 a private road that leads from a public road to a person's house
EG *They turned off the road and into the drive.*

drizzle /'drɪzl/

NOUN

Drizzle is light rain.
EG *The rain had turned to drizzle.*

drop /drɒp/
drops dropping dropped

VERB

1 If you drop something, or if it drops, it falls straight down.
EG *I dropped my glasses and broke them.*
EG *The book dropped onto the floor.*

2 If a level or amount drops, it becomes less.
EG *The temperature drops quickly at night.*

3 If your voice drops, or if you drop your voice, you speak more quietly.
EG *He dropped his voice and*

glanced at the door.
4 If you **drop** something or someone somewhere, you deposit or leave them there.
EG *He dropped her outside her house.*

NOUN
5 A **drop** of liquid is a very small quantity of it.
EG *A drop of blood slid down his leg.*
6 A **drop in** something is a decrease in it.
EG *... a huge drop in income*

drought /draʊt/
droughts
NOUN
a long period during which there is no rain
EG *... one of the worst droughts this century*

drove /drəʊv/
past tense of **drive**

drown /draʊn/
drowns drowning drowned
VERB
When someone drowns, or when they are drowned, they die because they have gone under water and cannot breathe.
EG *She fell into the water and drowned.*

drug /drʌg/
drugs drugging drugged
NOUN
1 a chemical that is given to people to treat illness or disease
EG *... a new drug in the fight against cancer*
2 Drugs are substances that some people smoke, swallow, or inject because of their stimulating effects.
EG *She was sure Leo was taking drugs.*
VERB

3 To drug a person or animal means to give them a drug in order to make them unconscious.
EG *They drugged the guard dog.*

drugstore /ˈdrʌgstɔːʳ/
drugstores
NOUN
In American English, a drugstore is a shop where medicines, cosmetics, and some other goods are sold.
EG *... a raid on a drugstore*

drum /drʌm/
drums
NOUN
1 a musical instrument consisting of a skin stretched tightly over a round frame
EG *He plays the drums in a band.*
2 an object or container shaped like a drum
EG *... an oil drum*

drunk /drʌŋk/
drunks
1 Drunk is the past participle of **drink**
ADJECTIVE
2 If someone is drunk, they have consumed too much alcohol.
EG *He got drunk and fell over.*
NOUN
3 A drunk is someone who is drunk, or who often gets drunk.
EG *A drunk tried to tell me his life story.*

dry /draɪ/
drier or **dryer driest; dries drying dried**
ADJECTIVE
1 Something that is dry contains no water or liquid.
EG *The paint was still not dry.*
EG *... a period of dry weather*
2 Dry wine does not taste sweet.

A B C D E F G H I J K L M N O P Q R S T U V W X Y Z

A
B
C
D
E
F
G
H
I
J
K
L
M
N
O
P
Q
R
S
T
U
V
W
X
Y
Z

EG ... *a glass of dry white wine*

VERB

3 When you dry something, or when it dries, liquid is removed from it.

EG *She helped me to dry the dishes.*

EG *Allow your hair to dry naturally.*

dry-clean /ˈdraɪˈkliːn/
dry-cleans dry-cleaning dry-cleaned

VERB

When clothes are dry-cleaned, they are cleaned with a liquid chemical rather than with water.

EG *He took his suit to be dry-cleaned.*

dual /ˈdjuəl/

ADJECTIVE

having two parts, functions, or aspects

EG ... *his dual role within the Party*

duck /dʌk/
ducks ducking ducked

NOUN

1 a bird that lives in water and has short legs and a large, flat beak

EG *There were ducks on the pond.*

VERB

2 If you duck, you move your head quickly downwards in order to avoid being hit or seen.

EG *He ducked below the wall as she walked past.*

due /djuː/

ADJECTIVE

1 If something is due at a particular time, it is expected to happen or arrive at that time.

EG *The train is due at 8 o'clock.*

2 **due to** means because of

EG *Headaches can be due to stress.*

dug /dʌg/

past participle and past tense of **dig**

dull /dʌl/
duller dullest

ADJECTIVE

1 not interesting

EG *He's a nice man, but rather dull.*

2 not bright, sharp, or clear

EG ... *a dull day*

dumb /dʌm/
dumber dumbest

ADJECTIVE

1 unable to speak

EG ... *a young deaf and dumb man*

2 AN INFORMAL USE
stupid

EG *I've met a lot of dumb people.*

dummy /ˈdʌmɪ/
dummies

NOUN

1 a rubber or plastic object which a baby sucks on

EG ... *a baby sucking on a dummy*

2 a model of a person, often used to display clothes

EG ... *a shop-window dummy*

dump /dʌmp/
dumps dumping dumped

VERB

1 If something is dumped somewhere, it is put there because it is no longer wanted.

EG ... *chemicals that are dumped into seas and lakes*

2 AN INFORMAL USE
If you dump something somewhere, you put it there in a quick or careless way.

EG *We dumped our bags at the hotel.*

NOUN

3 a place where rubbish is left

EG ... *a rubbish dump*

4 AN INFORMAL USE
You refer to a place as a dump when it is unattractive and

unpleasant to live in.
EG *This town is such a dump.*

during /'djuəriŋ/
PREPOSITION
If something happens during a period of time, it happens throughout that time or at a particular moment within that time.
EG *Plants need to be protected during bad weather.*
EG *It had snowed during the night.*

dust /dʌst/
dusts dusting dusted
NOUN
1 Dust is very small, dry particles of earth, sand, or dirt.
EG *The furniture was covered in dust.*
VERB
2 When you dust furniture or other objects, you remove dust from them using a dry cloth.
EG *She cleared the desk and dusted it.*

dustbin /'dʌstbin/
dustbins
NOUN
a large container for rubbish
EG *Half the rubbish was still in the dustbin.*

dusty /'dʌsti/
dustier dustiest
ADJECTIVE
covered with dust
EG *... a dusty old piano*

Dutch /dʌtʃ/
ADJECTIVE
1 belonging or relating to Holland
EG *... the Dutch prime minister*
NOUN
2 Dutch is the main language spoken in Holland.

EG *... his knowledge of Dutch*

duty /'dju:ti/
duties
NOUN
1 If something is your duty, you believe that you ought to do it because it is your responsibility.
EG *It is our duty to try and help.*
2 Duty is tax that is paid to the government on goods that you buy.
EG *... the duty on petrol*
3 If someone such as a policeman or nurse is **on duty**, they are working. If they are **off duty**, they are not working.
EG *Extra police were on duty that day.*
EG *When do you go off duty?*
PLURAL NOUN
4 Your **duties** are the tasks which you do as part of your job.
EG *They helped nurses with their basic duties.*

duty-free /'dju:ti'fri:/
ADJECTIVE
Duty-free goods are sold at airports or on planes or ships at a cheaper price than usual because they are not taxed.
EG *... duty-free cigarettes*

dye /daɪ/
dyes dyeing dyed
VERB
1 If you dye something, you change its colour by soaking it in a special liquid.
EG *She dyed her hair blonde.*
NOUN
2 a substance which is used to change the colour of something such as cloth or hair
EG *... a bottle of hair dye*

A
B
C
D
E
F
G
H
I
J
K
L
M
N
O
P
Q
R
S
T
U
V
W
X
Y
Z

Ee

each /iːtʃ/

ADJECTIVE, ADVERB, OR PRONOUN

1 Each thing or person in a group is every one of them, considered as individuals.

EG *Each time she went out, she bought a plant.*

EG *Tickets cost six pounds each.*

EG *She asked three doctors and each gave a different diagnosis.*

PRONOUN

2 If people do something to **each other**, each person does it to the other or others.

EG *They smiled at each other.*

☑ Whenever you use 'each other', you can also use one another: *they smiled at one another.*

eager /ˈiːgəʳ/

ADJECTIVE

If you are **eager to do** or have something, you very much want to do it or have it.

EG *He's eager to earn some money.*

ear /ɪəʳ/
ears

NOUN

Your ears are the parts of your body on either side of your head with which you hear sounds.

EG *He whispered something in her ear.*

early /ˈəːlɪ/
earlier earliest

ADJECTIVE AND ADVERB

1 before the arranged or expected time

EG *He was early for our meeting.*

EG *They arrived early.*

2 near the beginning of a period of time or an event

EG *... the early 1970s*

EG *... an incident that occurred earlier in the match*

earn /əːn/
earns earning earned

VERB

1 If you earn money, you get it in return for work that you do.

EG *She earns £25,000 a year.*

2 If you earn something such as praise, you receive it because you deserve it.

EG *He has earned my respect.*

earnings /ˈəːnɪŋz/

PLURAL NOUN

Your earnings are the money that you earn.

EG *Average weekly earnings rose last month.*

earring /ˈɪərɪŋ/
earrings

NOUN

Earrings are pieces of jewellery which you attach to your ears.

EG *He wore a gold earring in his left ear.*

earth /əːθ/

NOUN

1 The **Earth** is the planet on which we live.

EG *The Earth moves around the sun.*

2 The earth is the surface of the Earth.

EG *The earth shook.*

3 Earth is the substance on the surface of the earth in which plants grow.

EG *... a huge pile of earth*

earthquake /ˈəːθkweɪk/
earthquakes

NOUN

a shaking of the ground caused by

movement of the earth's surface
EG *... buildings designed to withstand earthquakes*

ease /iːz/
eases easing eased
NOUN
1 The ease of something is how easy it is.
EG *I was surprised at the ease of his victory.*
VERB
2 When something eases, or when you ease it, it becomes less intense.
EG *The rain had eased.*
EG *I gave him some brandy to ease the pain.*

easily /ˈiːzɪlɪ/
ADVERB
1 without difficulty
EG *She won the race easily.*
2 without a doubt
EG *The cost could easily be higher.*

east /iːst/
NOUN
1 The east is the direction in which you look to see the sun rise.
EG *The road runs from east to west.*
2 The east of a place is the part which is towards the east.
EG *... a village in the east of the country*
ADJECTIVE OR ADVERB
3 in or towards the east
EG *... the east side of the camp*
EG *The entrance faces east.*

Easter /ˈiːstəʳ/
NOUN
Easter is a Christian festival that is held in the spring.
EG *They usually go on holiday at Easter.*

eastern /ˈiːstən/
ADJECTIVE
in or from the east

EG *... a remote eastern corner of the country*

easy /ˈiːzɪ/
easier easiest
ADJECTIVE
1 If something is easy, you can do it without difficulty.
EG *The shower is easy to install.*
2 An easy life or time is comfortable and without any problems.
EG *She hasn't had an easy life.*
ADVERB
3 If you **take it easy**, you relax and do not do very much.
EG *Her boss told her to take it easy for a few days.*

eat /iːt/
eats eating ate eaten
VERB
1 When you eat food, you chew it and swallow it.
EG *I ate my chicken quickly.*
2 When you eat, you have a meal.
EG *We like to eat early.*

echo /ˈɛkəʊ/
echoes echoing echoed
NOUN
1 a sound caused by a noise being reflected off a surface
EG *He heard the echo of his footsteps along the corridor.*
VERB
2 If a sound echoes, it is reflected off a surface so that it can be heard again.
EG *His cry echoed back from the mountain.*

ecological /iːkəˈlɒdʒɪkəl/
ADJECTIVE
concerning the relationship between living things and their environment
EG *... ecological disasters such as*

the burning of the rainforest

economic /iːkə'nɒmɪk/

ADJECTIVE

concerning the management of the money, industry, and trade of a country

EG *... China's economic reforms*

economics /iːkə'nɒmɪks/

NOUN

Economics is the study of the way in which money, industry, and trade are organized in a country.

EG *... a degree in economics*

☑ Although it looks like a plural, 'economics' is a singular noun: *economics is his favourite subject.*

economy /ɪ'kɒnəmɪ/
economies

NOUN

1 The economy of a country is the system by which money, industry, and trade are organized.

EG *... changes in the Indian economy*

ADJECTIVE

2 Economy goods or services are cheaper than usual.

EG *He travelled economy class.*

edge /ɛdʒ/
edges

NOUN

1 The edge of something is a border or line where it ends or meets something else.

EG *... a hill on the edge of town*

2 The edge of a blade is its thin, sharp side.

EG *... the sharp edge of the sword*

edit /'ɛdɪt/
edits editing edited

VERB

1 If you edit a piece of writing, you correct it so that it is suitable for publication.

EG *... an edited version of the speech*

2 To edit a book means to collect pieces of writing by different authors and prepare them for publication.

EG *... a collection of essays edited by Ellen Knight*

3 To edit a film or television programme means to select different parts of it and arrange them in a particular order.

EG *He taught me how to edit film.*

edition /ɪ'dɪʃən/
editions

NOUN

1 An edition of a book or magazine is a particular version of it that is printed at one time.

EG *A paperback edition is now available.*

2 An edition of a television or radio programme is a single programme that is one of a series.

EG *... tonight's edition of Panorama*

editor /'ɛdɪtər/
editors

NOUN

1 a person who is in charge of a newspaper or magazine

EG *... the editor of the Times*

2 a person who checks and corrects texts before they are published

EG *He worked more closely with his editor on his second book.*

3 a person who edits a film or television programme

EG *... a documentary film editor at the BBC*

editorial /ɛdɪ'tɔːrɪəl/
editorials

ADJECTIVE

1 involved in preparing a newspaper, book, or magazine for

publication
EG ... *the editorial staff*

NOUN
2 an article in a newspaper or
magazine which gives the opinion
of the editor or publisher on a
particular subject
EG ... *a front-page editorial on the
war*

educate /ˈɛdjukeɪt/
**educates educating
educated**

VERB
1 When someone **is educated**,
they are taught at a school or
college.
EG *He was educated abroad.*

2 If you educate people, you
improve their understanding of a
particular subject.
EG ... *an attempt to educate
teenagers about the dangers of
drugs*

education /ɛdjuˈkeɪʃən/

NOUN
Education means learning and
teaching.
EG ... *an important factor in a
child's education*

effect /ɪˈfɛkt/
effects

NOUN
1 a change or reaction that is
caused by something or that is the
result of something
EG ... *the effect of divorce on
children*
EG ... *long-lasting psychological
effects*

2 the overall impression that
someone or something creates
EG *The moonlight created a
wonderful effect.*

effective /ɪˈfɛktɪv/

ADJECTIVE
Something that is effective has the
intended results.
EG ... *the most effective way of
teaching a foreign language*

efficient /ɪˈfɪʃənt/

ADJECTIVE
capable of doing something well,
without wasting time or energy
EG *She is the most efficient person I
know.*
EG *Cycling is the most efficient form
of transport.*

effort /ˈɛfət/
efforts

NOUN
1 Effort is the physical or mental
energy that is needed to do
something.
EG *He stood up slowly and with
great effort.*

2 an attempt to do something
EG *I went to keep-fit classes in an
effort to lose weight.*

e.g.
e.g. means 'for example'
EG ... *products made from cream,
e.g. cheese, butter, etc*

egg /ɛg/
eggs

NOUN
1 a rounded object produced by
female birds, reptiles, fishes, and
insects, from which a baby
creature later emerges
EG ... *a baby bird hatching from its
egg*

2 a hen's egg that is eaten as food
EG ... *bacon and eggs*

eight /eɪt/
eights
the number 8
EG *A spider has eight legs.*

eighteen /eɪˈtiːn/

A
B
C
D
E
F
G
H
I
J
K
L
M
N
O
P
Q
R
S
T
U
V
W
X
Y
Z

A
B
C
D
E
F
G
H
I
J
K
L
M
N
O
P
Q
R
S
T
U
V
W
X
Y
Z

the number 18

EG ... *eighteen holes*

eighteenth /eɪˈtiːnθ/

ADJECTIVE

The eighteenth item in a series is the one counted as number eighteen.

EG ... *the eighteenth hole*

eighth /eɪtθ/

eighths

ADJECTIVE

1 The eighth item in a series is the one counted as number eight.

EG ... *the eighth floor*

NOUN

2 one of eight equal parts

EG ... *an eighth of the money*

eightieth /ˈeɪtɪəθ/

ADJECTIVE

The eightieth item in a series is the one counted as number eighty.

EG ... *the eightieth year*

eighty /ˈeɪtɪ/

eighties

the number 80

EG ... *eighty years*

EG ... *a woman in her eighties*

either /ˈaɪðəʳ/

ADJECTIVE OR PRONOUN

1 You use 'either' to refer to each of two possible alternatives.

EG *You can spell it either way.*

EG *Either of these schemes would cost billions of pounds.*

CONJUNCTION

2 You use 'either' in front of the first of two alternatives or possible options linked by 'or'.

EG *You can either come with me or stay here.*

ADJECTIVE

3 You use 'either' to refer to both of two things.

EG ... *on either side of the road*

☑ The usual negative form of 'either' is *neither*: *neither of these books.*

elastic /ɪˈlæstɪk/

NOUN

Elastic is rubber material which stretches when you pull it and returns to its original shape when you let it go.

EG ... *a piece of elastic*

elbow /ˈɛlbəʊ/

elbows

NOUN

Your elbows are the joints where your arms bend in the middle.

EG *He hurt his elbow while playing tennis.*

elder /ˈɛldəʳ/

eldest

ADJECTIVE

The elder of two people is the one who was born first.

EG ... *his elder brother*

EG ... *the eldest child in the family*

☑ 'Elder' and 'eldest' can only be used when talking about the age of people within families. You use 'older' and 'oldest' to talk about the age of other people or things.

elderly /ˈɛldəlɪ/

ADJECTIVE

Someone who is elderly is old.

EG ... *an elderly couple*

elect /ɪˈlɛkt/

elects electing elected

VERB

When people elect someone, they choose that person to represent them, by voting for them.

EG *He's just been elected president.*

election /ɪˈlɛkʃən/

elections

NOUN

1 a process in which people

choose one or more people to hold an official position by voting for them
EG *Who did you vote for at the election?*
2 Election is the process of electing someone.
EG *... the election of the Labour government in 1964*

electric /ɪˈlɛktrɪk/

ADJECTIVE
powered or produced by electricity
EG *... an electric guitar*
EG *... an electric current*

electrical /ɪˈlɛktrɪkl/

ADJECTIVE
powered by electricity
EG *... electrical equipment*

electrician /ɪlɛkˈtrɪʃən/
electricians

NOUN
a person whose job is to install and repair electrical equipment
EG *He's a qualified electrician.*

electricity /ɪlɛkˈtrɪsɪtɪ/

NOUN
Electricity is a form of energy that is carried by wires and that provides power for heating, lighting and machines.
EG *... powered by electricity*

electronic /ɪlɛkˈtrɒnɪk/

ADJECTIVE
An electronic device contains computer chips or other small parts which control the electric current passing through it.
EG *expensive electronic equipment*

elegant /ˈɛlɪgənt/

ADJECTIVE
Someone or something that is elegant is pleasing to look at.
EG *... an elegant restaurant*

EG *She looked beautiful and elegant.*

element /ˈɛlɪmənt/
elements

NOUN
a part of something which combines with other parts to make a whole
EG *... one of the key elements of the plan*

elephant /ˈɛlɪfənt/
elephants

NOUN
a very large animal with a long trunk
EG *... a herd of African elephants*

elevator /ˈɛlɪveɪtər/
elevators

NOUN
In American English, an elevator is a device that carries people up and down inside a building.
EG *They took the elevator to the fifth floor.*
☑ The usual British word is *lift*.

eleven /ɪˈlɛvn/
the number 11
EG *... eleven players*

eleventh /ɪˈlɛvnθ/

ADJECTIVE
The eleventh item in a series is the one counted as number eleven.
EG *... the eleventh floor*

eligible /ˈɛlɪdʒəbl/

ADJECTIVE
Someone who is **eligible for** something is entitled to it.
EG *You may be eligible for a grant.*

eliminate /ɪˈlɪmɪneɪt/
eliminates eliminating eliminated

VERB
1 If you eliminate something or someone, you remove them

A
B
C
D
E
F
G
H
I
J
K
L
M
N
O
P
Q
R
S
T
U
V
W
X
Y
Z

completely.
EG *The police eliminated him from their inquiries.*
2 If a team or a person **is eliminated from** a competition, they are defeated and take no further part.
EG *He was eliminated from the 400 metres in the semi-finals.*

else /ɛls/
ADVERB
1 'Else' means other than the thing you are talking about or more than the thing you are talking about
EG *I never wanted to live anywhere else.*
EG *What else did you buy?*
2 You say **or else** to introduce a possibility or alternative.
EG *He's either a genius or else he's mad.*

elsewhere /ɛlsˈwɛəʳ/
ADVERB
in or to another place
EG *The song is popular in Europe and elsewhere.*
EG *If you're not satisfied, then go elsewhere.*

e-mail or **email** /ˈiːmeɪl/
e-mails e-mailing e-mailed
1
VERB
If you e-mail someone, or if you e-mail something to them, you send them a message from your computer.
EG *He e-mailed her the latest figures.*
2
NOUN
E-mail is a system of sending messages from one computer to another.
EG *Most of the work was done by e-mail.*

3 a message sent from one computer to another
EG *She sent him an e-mail explaining the situation.*

embarrass /ɪmˈbærəs/
embarrasses embarrassing embarrassed
VERB
If you embarrass someone, you make them feel ashamed or awkward.
EG *I won't embarrass you by asking for details.*

embassy /ˈɛmbəsɪ/
embassies
NOUN
the building in which an ambassador and his or her staff work
EG *... the Chinese embassy*

emerge /ɪˈmɜːdʒ/
emerges emerging emerged
VERB
1 If someone **emerges from** a place, they come out of it so that they can be seen.
EG *I saw the woman emerge from a shop.*
2 If something emerges, it becomes known.
EG *It later emerged that he was already married.*

emergency /ɪˈmɜːdʒənsɪ/
emergencies
NOUN
an unexpected and serious situation which must be dealt with quickly
EG *In an emergency, contact your doctor.*

emotion /ɪˈməʊʃən/
emotions
NOUN
a strong feeling, such as love or

fear
EG *Jealousy is such a destructive emotion.*

emotional /ɪ'məʊʃənl/
ADJECTIVE
1 relating to feelings and emotions
EG *... emotional problems*
2 If someone is emotional, they show their feelings openly.
EG *He became quite emotional when I said goodbye.*

emphasis /'ɛmfəsɪs/
NOUN
Emphasis is special importance that is given to something.
EG *Too much emphasis is placed on research.*

emphasize /'ɛmfəsaɪz/
emphasizes emphasizing emphasized; also spelt **emphasise**
VERB
If you emphasize something, you indicate that it is very important.
EG *He emphasized the differences between the two methods.*

empire /'ɛmpaɪər/
empires
NOUN
a group of countries that is controlled by one country
EG *... the Roman empire*

employ /ɪm'plɔɪ/
employs employing employed
VERB
1 If you employ someone, you pay them to work for you.
EG *More than 3,000 people are employed in the industry.*
2 If you employ something for a particular purpose, you make use of it.
EG *... the clever advertising*

employed by cigarette companies

employee /ɪm'plɔɪ'i:/
employees
NOUN
a person who is paid to work for a company or organization
EG *Most of the company's employees are women.*

employer /ɪm'plɔɪər/
employers
NOUN
Your employer is the person or organization that you work for.
EG *He was sent to Rome by his employer.*

employment /ɪm'plɔɪmənt/
NOUN
Employment is work that you are paid for.
EG *She was unable to find employment.*

empty /'ɛmptɪ/
emptier emptiest; empties emptying emptied
ADJECTIVE
1 Something that is empty has nothing or nobody inside it.
EG *His glass was empty.*
EG *... an empty room*
2 without purpose, value, or meaning
EG *... empty promises*
VERB
3 If you empty something, or if you empty its contents, you remove the contents.
EG *He emptied the box onto the table.*

enable /ɪ'neɪbl/
enables enabling enabled
VERB
If something or someone **enables** you **to do** something, they make it possible for you to do it.

A B C D E F G H I J K L M N O P Q R S T U V W X Y Z

EG *The new test enables doctors to detect the disease early.*

encounter /ɪnˈkaʊntəʳ/
encounters encountering encountered
VERB
1 If you encounter someone or something, you meet them or are faced with them.
EG *Did you encounter any problems?*
NOUN
2 a meeting, especially when it is difficult or unexpected
EG *… her first encounter with her mother-in-law*

encourage /ɪnˈkʌrɪdʒ/
encourages encouraging encouraged
VERB
1 If you encourage someone, you give them the confidence to do something.
EG *When things aren't going well, he always encourages me.*
2 If you **encourage** someone **to do** something, you try to persuade them to do it.
EG *We want to encourage people to visit the area.*

end /end/
ends ending ended
NOUN
1 The end of a period of time or an event is the last part of it.
EG *… at the end of August*
EG *I cried at the end of the film.*
2 The end of something is the farthest point of it.
EG *… the room at the end of the passage*
3 the purpose for which something is done
EG *… the use of taxpayers' money for political ends*
VERB

4 If something ends, or if you end it, it finishes.
EG *The war was about to end.*
EG *I decided to end our relationship.*

ending /ˈendɪŋ/
endings
NOUN
The ending is the final part of something, especially of a film, play, or book.
EG *… a film with a happy ending*

endless /ˈendlɪs/
ADJECTIVE
Something that is endless continues so long that it seems that it will never end.
EG *… endless meetings and discussions*

enemy /ˈenəmɪ/
enemies
NOUN
Your enemy is someone who intends to harm you.
EG *He had powerful friends, but powerful enemies too.*

energy /ˈenədʒɪ/
energies
NOUN
1 Energy is the physical strength that is needed to do active things.
EG *He was saving his energy for next week's race.*
2 Energy is the power which drives machinery.
EG *… nuclear energy*

engage /ɪnˈgeɪdʒ/
engages engaging engaged
VERB
If you **engage in** an activity, you do it.
EG *I have never engaged in such activities.*

engaged /ɪnˈgeɪdʒd/
ADJECTIVE

1 When two people are engaged, they have agreed to marry each other.

EG *They've been engaged for two years.*

2 If a telephone line is engaged, it is already being used by the person you are trying to phone.

EG *The number was always engaged.*

engagement /ɪnˈɡeɪdʒmənt/
engagements

NOUN

1 an appointment that you have with someone

EG *… a diary full of social engagements*

2 an agreement that two people have made to get married

EG *… an engagement party*

engine /ˈɛndʒɪn/
engines

NOUN

1 The engine of a vehicle is the part that produces the power to make it move.

EG *He got in the car and started the engine.*

2 the large vehicle that pulls a railway train

EG *… a steam engine*

English /ˈɪŋɡlɪʃ/

ADJECTIVE

1 belonging or relating to England

EG *He said he was English.*

NOUN

2 English is the main language spoken in Great Britain, Ireland, the United States, Canada, Australia, and many other countries.

EG *She doesn't speak English.*

enjoy /ɪnˈdʒɔɪ/
enjoys enjoying enjoyed

VERB

1 If you enjoy something, it gives you pleasure.

EG *I enjoy dancing.*

2 If you **enjoy yourself**, you are happy and have fun.

EG *We really enjoyed ourselves at the party.*

enjoyable /ɪnˈdʒɔɪəbl/

ADJECTIVE

Something that is enjoyable gives you pleasure.

EG *It was more enjoyable than I expected.*

enormous /ɪˈnɔːməs/

ADJECTIVE

very large in size or amount

EG *The bedroom is enormous.*

EG *There's an enormous amount to see.*

enough /ɪˈnʌf/

ADJECTIVE OR ADVERB

1 as much or as many as required

EG *He did not have enough money for a coffee.*

EG *He was not employed long enough to get a pension.*

NOUN

2 Enough is the quantity that is necessary for something.

EG *There's not enough to go round.*

ADVERB

3 to a fairly large degree

EG *The rest of the evening passed pleasantly enough.*

enquire /ɪnˈkwaɪəʳ/
enquires enquiring enquired

VERB

If you **enquire about** something or someone, you ask for information about them.

EG *He enquired about my health.*

EG *He enquired whether I was married.*

A B C D E F G H I J K L M N O P Q R S T U V W X Y Z

A
B
C
D
E
F
G
H
I
J
K
L
M
N
O
P
Q
R
S
T
U
V
W
X
Y
Z

enquiry /ɪnˈkwaɪərɪ/
enquiries

NOUN

1 a question that you ask in order to get information

EG *He made some enquiries and found she had left her job.*

2 an official investigation

EG *... a murder enquiry*

ensure /ɪnˈʃʊəʳ/
ensures ensuring ensured

VERB

If you ensure that something happens, you make certain that it happens.

EG *We make every effort to ensure the information given is correct.*

enter /ˈentəʳ/
enters entering entered

VERB

1 When you enter a place, you go into it.

EG *He knocked before entering the room.*

2 If you enter an organization or institution, you become a member of it.

EG *He entered Parliament in 1979.*

3 If you enter a competition, you take part in it.

EG *He entered the race without telling anyone.*

4 If you enter something in a diary or a list, you write it down.

EG *Enter your name below.*

entertain /entəˈteɪn/
entertains entertaining entertained

VERB

1 If you entertain people, you do something that amuses or interests them.

EG *... games and ideas to entertain children*

2 If you entertain guests, you

invite them to your home and give them food or drink.

EG *They entertained all the right people.*

entertainment
/entəˈteɪnmənt/

NOUN

Entertainment is anything that people watch for pleasure, such as shows or films.

EG *The entertainment was provided by a dance group.*

enthusiasm /ɪnˈθuːzɪæzəm/

NOUN

Enthusiasm is great eagerness to do something or to be involved in something.

EG *... her enthusiasm for the theatre*

enthusiastic /ɪnθuːzɪˈæstɪk/

ADJECTIVE

If you are **enthusiastic about** something, you show how much you like it by the way that you talk or behave.

EG *They are very enthusiastic about the idea.*

EG *... an enthusiastic response*

entire /ɪnˈtaɪəʳ/

ADJECTIVE

You use 'entire' to emphasize that you are speaking about the whole of something.

EG *He had spent his entire life in the village.*

entirely /ɪnˈtaɪəlɪ/

ADVERB

wholly and completely

EG *... an entirely new approach*

entitle /ɪnˈtaɪtl/
entitles entitling entitled

VERB

1 If you **are entitled to** something, you have the right to have it or do it.

EG *Children and pensioners are entitled to a discount.*

2 If a book, film, or other work of art is **entitled** something, that is its name.

EG *... a poem entitled 'Christmas'*

entrance /'ɛntrns/
entrances

NOUN

1 The entrance of a building or area is its doorway or gate.

EG *She was waiting at the entrance to the church.*

2 A person's entrance is their arrival in a place, or the way in which they arrive.

EG *He wanted to make a dramatic entrance.*

entry /'ɛntrɪ/
entries

NOUN

1 Entry is the act of entering a place.

EG *No entry after 11 pm.*

2 Someone's entry into an organization is the act of joining it.

EG *... the country's entry into the European Community*

3 something which you write in order to take part in a competition

EG *Send your entry to the address below.*

4 something written in a diary or list

EG *... the entry for March 23*

envelope /'ɛnvələup/
envelopes

NOUN

the paper cover in which you send a letter through the post

EG *... a self-addressed envelope*

environment /ɪn'vaɪərnmənt/
environments

NOUN

1 Your environment is your surroundings, especially the conditions in which you live or work.

EG *... a good environment to grow up in*

2 The environment is the natural world around us.

EG *... the waste which is dumped in the environment*

environmental
/ɪnvaɪərn'mɛntl/

ADJECTIVE

concerned with the protection of the natural world

EG *... environmental groups*

envy /'ɛnvɪ/
envies envying envied

VERB

1 If you envy someone, you wish that you had what they have.

EG *I envied her relationship with our mother.*

NOUN

2 Envy is the feeling of wanting to have what someone else has.

EG *Her sisters watched with envy.*

episode /'ɛpɪsəud/
episodes

NOUN

1 an event or period of time, especially one that is important or unusual

EG *After this episode, she found it impossible to trust him.*

2 one of the programmes in a series on television or radio

EG *I never miss an episode of Neighbours.*

equal /'iːkwl/
equals equalling equalled

ADJECTIVE

1 If two things are equal, or if one thing is **equal** to another, they

A B C D E F G H I J K L M N O P Q R S T U V W X Y Z

are the same in size, number, or value.

EG … *an equal number of men and women*

EG … *an amount equal to their monthly income*

2 If people are equal, they all have the same rights and are treated in the same way.

EG … *the commitment to equal opportunities*

VERB

3 To equal a score or record means to be as good as it is.

EG *He equalled the world record.*

equip /ɪ'kwɪp/
equips equipping equipped

VERB

If a person or thing **is equipped with** something, they have it or are provided with it.

EG *The boat was equipped with all the latest technology.*

EG *We had been equipped with ample supplies.*

equipment /ɪ'kwɪpmənt/

NOUN

Equipment is all the things such as tools or machines that are used for a particular purpose.

EG *The band needed new equipment.*

EG … *various pieces of equipment*

☑ 'Equipment' refers to all of the things that are used, not to an individual tool or machine.

equivalent /ɪ'kwɪvələnt/

ADJECTIVE

1 If one amount or value is **equivalent to** another, they are the same.

EG … *a sum equivalent to six months' wages*

NOUN

2 If one thing is **the equivalent**

of another, it has the same use, value or effect.

EG *One glass of wine is the equivalent of half a pint of beer.*

erect /ɪ'rɛkt/
erects erecting erected

VERB

1 To erect something means to build it.

EG *The building was erected in 1900.*

ADJECTIVE

2 straight and upright

EG *Stand erect, with your arms at your side.*

erotic /ɪ'rɒtɪk/

ADJECTIVE

involving or causing sexual desire

EG … *an erotic film*

error /'ɛrər/
errors

NOUN

a mistake or something which you have done wrong

EG *There was an error in the calculations.*

erupt /ɪ'rʌpt/
erupts erupting erupted

VERB

1 When a volcano erupts, it throws out a lot of hot rock and ash.

EG *Scientists say the volcano could erupt again soon.*

2 When a situation erupts, it begins suddenly and violently.

EG *A family row erupted.*

escalator /'ɛskəleɪtər/
escalators

NOUN

a mechanical set of stairs that moves up or down

EG *The lift wasn't working, so we used the escalator.*

escape /ɪsˈkeɪp/
escapes escaping escaped

VERB

1 If you **escape from** someone or something, you succeed in getting away from them.

EG *Two prisoners had escaped from the jail.*

2 If you **escape** something unpleasant or difficult, you succeed in avoiding it.

EG *She was lucky to escape serious injury.*

NOUN

3 an act of escaping from a particular place or situation

EG *It was a daring escape.*

4 a situation or activity which distracts you from something unpleasant

EG *Television provides an escape for many people.*

especially /ɪsˈpɛʃlɪ/

ADVERB

You use 'especially' to show that something applies more to one thing or person than to any other.

EG *Regular eye tests are important, especially for the elderly.*

essay /ˈɛseɪ/
essays

NOUN

a short piece of writing on a particular subject, especially one written as an exercise by a student

EG *They had to write an essay on pollution.*

essential /ɪˈsɛnʃl/
essentials

ADJECTIVE

1 Something that is essential is absolutely necessary.

EG *It is essential that you seek legal advice.*

EG *Play is an essential part of a child's development.*

PLURAL NOUN

2 The **essentials** are things that are absolutely necessary.

EG *The flat contained the basic essentials.*

establish /ɪsˈtæblɪʃ/
establishes establishing established

VERB

1 If someone establishes an organization or system, they create it.

EG *The school was established in 1989 by an Italian professor.*

2 If you establish a fact, or if you establish that something is true, you discover that it is definitely true.

EG *Our first task is to establish the cause of death.*

EG *Medical tests established that she was not their own child.*

establishment /ɪsˈtæblɪʃmənt/
establishments

NOUN

1 The establishment of an organization or system is the act of setting it up.

EG *… the establishment of the regional government in 1980*

2 a shop, business, or other organization or institution

EG *… a scientific research establishment*

estate /ɪsˈteɪt/
estates

NOUN

1 a large area of land in the country that is owned by one person or organization

EG *… Lord Wyville's estate in Yorkshire*

2 an area of land which has been

developed for housing or industry

EG ... *a housing estate*

EG ... *an industrial estate*

estate agent estate agents

NOUN

a person who works for a company that sells houses and land; you also refer to a company that sells houses and land as an estate agent or an **estate agent's**

EG *The estate agent showed us round the flat.*

estimate /'ɛstɪmeɪt/

estimates estimating estimated

VERB

1 If you estimate an amount or quantity, you calculate it approximately.

EG *The damage is estimated at £100 million.*

NOUN : /'ɛstɪmət/

☑ Note that you pronounce the noun differently from the verb.

2 an approximate calculation of an amount or quantity

EG *The final cost was twice the original estimate.*

etc /ɪt'sɛtrə/

'etc' is used at the end of a list to indicate that there are other items that you could also mention

EG ... *a packed programme of events: dances, shows, coach tours, etc*

eternal /ɪ'tɜːnl/

ADJECTIVE

Something that is eternal lasts forever.

EG ... *the search for eternal youth*

ethical /'ɛθɪkl/

ADJECTIVE

Ethical means influenced by a system of moral beliefs about right and wrong.

EG ... *teenagers who become vegetarian for ethical reasons*

ethics /'ɛθɪks/

PLURAL NOUN

Ethics are moral beliefs about right and wrong.

EG *The medical profession has a code of ethics.*

ethnic /'ɛθnɪk/

ADJECTIVE

relating to different racial or cultural groups

EG ... *ethnic minorities*

EU

an abbreviation for **European Union**

euro /'juərəu/

euros

NOUN

a unit of money used by most countries belonging to the European Union

EG *The price was given in both pounds and euros.*

Europe /'juərəp/

NOUN

Europe is the continent to which the United Kingdom belongs.

EG ... *the whole of Europe*

European /juərə'piːən/

Europeans

ADJECTIVE

1 belonging or relating to Europe

EG ... *most European countries*

NOUN

2 someone who comes from Europe

EG ... *a blond European*

European Union

NOUN

a group of European countries

who have joined together for economic and trade purposes
EG *... members of the European Union*

evacuate /ɪˈvækjueɪt/
evacuates evacuating evacuated

VERB

1 If someone is evacuated, they are removed from a place of danger to a place of safety.
EG *A crowd of shoppers had to be evacuated from a store after a bomb scare.*

2 If you evacuate a place, you move out of it for a period of time, usually because it is dangerous.
EG *The entire building was evacuated.*

eve /iːv/
eves

NOUN

The eve of an event is the day before it or the time just before it.
EG *... on the eve of the battle*

even /ˈiːvn/

ADJECTIVE

1 An even surface is smooth and flat.
EG *The road wasn't very even.*

2 An even measurement or rate stays at about the same level.
EG *It's important to have an even temperature.*

3 An even number is one that can be divided exactly by two, such as 2, 4 and 6.
EG *... houses with even numbers*

4 If there is an even distribution of something, all the parts of it are equal in size or amount.
EG *Divide the pastry into six even pieces.*

ADVERB

5 You use 'even' to suggest that

something is unexpected or surprising.
EG *He hasn't even got a bank account.*

6 You use 'even' to indicate that something is greater in degree than something else.
EG *He was speaking even more slowly than usual.*

7 You use **even if** or **even though** to introduce something that is surprising in relation to the rest of the sentence.
EG *Even if you're on a diet, you can still enjoy your food.*
EG *She was too kind to say anything, even though she was jealous.*

evening /ˈiːvnɪŋ/
evenings

NOUN

the part of the evening between the end of the afternoon and the time you go to bed
EG *... at 6 o'clock in the evening*

event /ɪˈvent/
events

NOUN

1 something that happens, especially when it is unusual or important
EG *... recent events in Europe*

2 an organized activity, such as a sports match
EG *... major sporting events*

eventually /ɪˈventʃuəlɪ/

ADVERB

in the end, especially after a lot of delays or problems
EG *I eventually arrived three hours late.*

ever /ˈevər/

ADVERB

1 at any time

A
B
C
D
E
F
G
H
I
J
K
L
M
N
O
P
Q
R
S
T
U
V
W
X
Y
Z

EG *Have you ever been to Australia?*
EG *I won't ever mention it again.*
EG *It's the worst film I've ever seen.*

2 You use **ever since** to emphasize that something has been true since the time mentioned, and is still true.
EG *He has loved trains ever since he was a child.*

3 AN INFORMAL USE
ever so means very
EG *Thank you ever so much.*

every /'ɛvrɪ/

ADJECTIVE
1 You use 'every' to refer to all the members of a group or all the parts of something.
EG *Every shop in the town was closed.*

2 You use 'every' to indicate that something happens at regular intervals.
EG *A burglary occurs every three minutes in London.*

3 You use 'every' before some nouns to emphasize what you are saying.
EG *He has every chance of succeeding.*

4 If something happens **every other** day or week, it happens on alternate days or weeks.
EG *Meetings are held every other week.*

everybody /'ɛvrɪbɒdɪ/

PRONOUN
1 all the people in a group
EG *Everybody at work likes him.*

2 all the people in the world
EG *Everybody needs to relax sometimes.*
☑ 'Everybody' and 'everyone' mean the same. They are both followed by a singular form of the verb.

everyone /'ɛvrɪwʌn/

PRONOUN
1 all the people in a group
EG *He told everyone about it.*

2 all the people in the world
EG *Everyone gets lonely sometimes.*
☑ 'Everyone' and 'everybody' mean the same. They are both followed by a singular form of the verb.

everything /'ɛvrɪθɪŋ/

PRONOUN
all the parts of something or the whole of something
EG *We had everything we needed.*
EG *Is everything all right?*

everywhere /'ɛvrɪwɛəʳ/

ADVERB
in or to all places
EG *There was litter everywhere.*
EG *We went everywhere together.*

evidence /'ɛvɪdns/

NOUN
1 Evidence is anything that causes you to believe that something is true or exists.
EG *There is no evidence to support this theory.*

2 Evidence is information that is used in a court of law to try to prove something.
EG *... a vital piece of evidence*

evil /'iːvl/

NOUN
1 Evil refers to all the wicked or bad things that happen in the world.
EG *... a conflict between good and evil*

ADJECTIVE
2 Someone or something that is evil is very wrong or bad and causes harm to people.
EG *She's an evil woman.*

ex- /ɛks/

PREFIX

former

EG ... her ex-husband

exact /ɪgˈzækt/

ADJECTIVE

1 correct and complete in every detail

EG ... an exact replica of the ship

2 precise

EG I don't remember her exact words.

exactly /ɪgˈzæktlɪ/

ADVERB

1 Exactly means precisely, and not just approximately.

EG ... at exactly 5 o'clock

EG They're exactly the same.

2 You say 'Exactly' when you are agreeing with someone or emphasizing that what they are saying is true.

EG "I suppose he was late as usual." — "Exactly."

exaggerate /ɪgˈzædʒəreɪt/

exaggerates exaggerating exaggerated

VERB

If you exaggerate, or if you exaggerate something, you make something seem better, worse, bigger, or more important than it really is.

EG Don't exaggerate.

EG She sometimes exaggerates the demands of her job.

exam /ɪgˈzæm/

exams

NOUN

an official test that aims to find out your knowledge or skill in a subject

EG Did you pass your exams?

examination /ɪgzæmɪˈneɪʃən/

examinations

NOUN

1 an exam

EG ... a three-hour written examination

2 If you make an examination of something, you inspect it very carefully.

EG I carried out a detailed examination of the house.

examine /ɪgˈzæmɪn/

examines examining examined

VERB

If you examine something, you inspect it carefully.

EG He examined her passport.

EG Another doctor examined her but could find nothing wrong.

example /ɪgˈzɑːmpl/

examples

NOUN

1 something which represents or is typical of a particular group of things

EG ... a good example of early Spanish music

2 If you say someone is an **example to** people, you mean that they behave in a good way which people should copy.

EG He is an example to us all.

3 You use **for example** to give an example of something you are talking about.

EG Take my own situation, for example.

exceed /ɪkˈsiːd/

exceeds exceeding exceeded

VERB

If something exceeds a particular amount, it is greater than that amount.

EG ... the first aircraft to exceed the speed of sound

excellent /ˈɛksələnt/

ADJECTIVE

very good indeed

EG *She did an excellent job.*

except /ɪkˈsɛpt/

PREPOSITION

You use 'except' or **except for** to introduce the only thing or person that a statement does not apply to.

EG *All my family were musicians except my father.*

EG *There was nobody there except for the police.*

exception /ɪkˈsɛpʃən/
exceptions

NOUN

somebody or something that is not included in a general statement

EG *Normally I don't drink, but tonight is an exception.*

exceptional /ɪkˈsɛpʃənl/

ADJECTIVE

1 extremely clever or skilful

EG *She was an exceptional teacher.*

2 unusual and likely to happen very rarely

EG *... in exceptional circumstances*

excess /ɪkˈsɛs/

ADJECTIVE

1 more than is needed or allowed

EG *... the causes of excess weight*

EG *... excess baggage*

NOUN

2 in excess of a particular amount means more than that amount

EG *... a fortune in excess of 150 million pounds*

excessive /ɪkˈsɛsɪv/

ADJECTIVE

too great in amount or degree

EG *... the use of excessive force*

exchange /ɪksˈtʃeɪndʒ/
exchanges exchanging exchanged

VERB

1 If people exchange things, they give them to each other at the same time.

EG *We exchanged addresses.*

2 If you **exchange** something **for** something else, you replace it with that thing.

EG *I exchanged the shoes for a bigger pair.*

NOUN

3 the act of giving or receiving something in return for something else

EG *... an exchange of letters*

excite /ɪkˈsaɪt/
excites exciting excited

VERB

If something excites you, it makes you feel very happy and enthusiastic.

EG *I only do work that excites me.*

excitement /ɪkˈsaɪtmənt/

NOUN

Excitement is the state of being excited.

EG *There was enormous excitement when she finally arrived.*

exclamation mark
exclamation marks

NOUN

The **exclamation mark** is the symbol ! that is used after you write something that expresses a strong emotion, such as anger, surprise, or excitement.

EG *I can't believe it!*

exclude /ɪksˈkluːd/
excludes excluding excluded

VERB

1 If you exclude something, you choose not to include or consider it.

EG *The song was rewritten to exclude any reference to sex.*

2 If you **exclude** someone **from** a place or activity, you prevent them from entering or taking part.

EG *Women were excluded from the classes.*

exclusive /ɪksˈkluːsɪv/

ADJECTIVE

1 available only to people who are rich or important

EG *… an exclusive club*

2 used or owned by only one person or group

EG *Our group will have exclusive use of the boat.*

excuse /ɪksˈkjuːs/
excuses excusing excused

NOUN

1 a reason which you give to explain why something has been done, has not been done, or will not be done

EG *He kept finding excuses not to go home.*

VERB : /ɪksˈkjuːz/

☑ Note that you pronounce the verb differently from the noun.

2 If you excuse someone's behaviour, you give reasons for why they behaved in that way.

EG *That doesn't excuse my mother's behaviour.*

3 If you **excuse** somebody **for** something wrong they have done, you forgive them for it.

EG *I simply couldn't excuse him for what he'd said.*

4 If someone **is excused from** a duty or responsibility, they are told that they do not have to do it.

EG *She asked to be excused from swimming lessons.*

5 You say **excuse me** when you want to get somebody's attention or to apologize for an interruption or for rude behaviour.

EG *Excuse me, are you Mr Evans?*

EG *Excuse me, but there is something I must point out.*

execute /ˈeksɪkjuːt/
executes executing executed

VERB

1 If someone is executed, they are killed as a punishment for a crime.

EG *The following month the King was executed.*

2 If you execute something such as a plan or an action, you carry it out or perform it.

EG *The crime was planned and executed with great care.*

executive /ɪgˈzekjutɪv/
executives

NOUN

a person who is employed by a company at a senior level

EG *… an advertising executive*

exercise /ˈeksəsaɪz/
exercises exercising exercised

NOUN

1 Exercise is any activity which you do in order to get fit or remain healthy.

EG *Lack of exercise can lead to depression.*

2 Exercises are a series of movements which you do in order to get fit or remain healthy.

EG *I do special exercises to strengthen my stomach.*

3 Exercises are activities which you do in order to practise a particular skill.

A
B
C
D
E
F
G
H
I
J
K
L
M
N
O
P
Q
R
S
T
U
V
W
X
Y
Z

EG ... *piano exercises*

VERB
4 When you exercise, you do activities which help you to get fit and remain healthy.
EG *How often do you exercise?*

exhaust /ɪgˈzɔːst/
exhausts exhausting exhausted

VERB
1 If something exhausts you, it makes you very tired.
EG *The journey had exhausted her.*
2 If you exhaust a supply of something such as money or food, you use it up completely.
EG *They soon exhausted their supply of water.*

NOUN
3 The exhaust is the pipe which carries the gas or steam out of the engine of a vehicle.
EG *Black smoke was pouring from the exhaust.*

exhibit /ɪgˈzɪbɪt/
exhibits exhibiting exhibited

VERB
1 If you exhibit your feelings or abilities, you show them.
EG *He still exhibited signs of stress.*
2 When an object of interest is exhibited, it is put in a public place for people to look at.
EG *Some of his sketches were exhibited at the gallery.*

NOUN
3 something which is displayed in a museum or art gallery
EG *Our local museum has over a thousand exhibits.*

exhibition /ɛksɪˈbɪʃən/
exhibitions

NOUN
an event at which objects of interest are displayed to the public

EG ... *an exhibition of Japanese art*

exist /ɪgˈzɪst/
exists existing existed

VERB
If something exists, it is present in the world as a real thing.
EG *She tried to pretend her problems simply didn't exist.*

existence /ɪgˈzɪstəns/

NOUN
1 The existence of something is the fact that it is present in the world as a real thing.
EG ... *a discussion about the existence of God*
2 a way of life
EG *He leads a comfortable existence.*

exit /ˈɛksɪt/
exits

NOUN
1 a doorway through which you can leave a public place
EG *He walked towards the exit.*
2 a place where traffic can leave a motorway
EG *Take the next exit.*
3 If you refer to someone's exit from a place, you mean that they have left it.
EG ... *after his hasty exit*

expand /ɪksˈpænd/
expands expanding expanded

VERB
If something expands, or if you expand it, it becomes larger.
EG ... *a rapidly expanding universe*
EG *He owned a bookshop and wanted to expand the business.*

expect /ɪksˈpɛkt/
expects expecting expected

VERB
1 If you expect something to happen, you believe that it will

---

EG *The trial is expected to end today.*

EG *I expect she'll come along later.*

2 If you are expecting someone or something, you believe that they are going to arrive or to happen.

EG *I'm expecting an important letter.*

3 If you expect something, you believe that it is your right to get it or have it.

EG *I'm expecting you to help me.*

expectation /ɛkspɛk'teɪʃən/
expectations

NOUN

Your expectations are your beliefs that a particular thing will happen.

EG *Sales have far exceeded expectations.*

EG *... in the expectation of success*

expense /ɪks'pɛns/
expenses

NOUN

1 Expense is the money that something costs.

EG *... the expense of buying a new car*

PLURAL NOUN

2 expenses are the money that someone spends in connection with their work, which is paid back to them by their employer

EG *... travelling expenses*

expensive /ɪks'pɛnsɪv/

ADJECTIVE

If something is expensive, it costs a lot of money.

EG *Wine is so expensive in this country.*

EG *... an expensive car*

experience /ɪks'pɪərɪəns/
experiences experiencing experienced

expectation – experiment

1 Experience is all the things that you have done or that have happened to you.

EG *Everyone learns best from personal experience.*

2 An experience is something that you do or something that happens to you, especially something new or unusual.

EG *The funeral was a painful experience.*

3 Experience is knowledge or skill in a particular job or activity, which you have gained from doing that job or activity.

EG *He was rejected because he lacked experience.*

VERB

4 If you experience something, it happens to you or you are affected by it.

EG *We had never experienced this kind of holiday before.*

experienced /ɪks'pɪərɪənst/

ADJECTIVE

Someone who is experienced has been doing a particular job or activity for a long time and knows a lot about it.

EG *... the most experienced player in the team*

experiment /ɪks'pɛrɪmənt/
experiments experimenting experimented

NOUN

1 a scientific test which aims to prove or discover something

EG *The astronauts will conduct a series of medical experiments.*

VERB

2 If you **experiment on** something, you do a scientific test on it to prove or discover something.

EG *... a professor who had been experimenting on rabbits*

expert /'ɛkspəːt/
experts

NOUN

a person who is very skilled at something or who knows a lot about a particular subject
EG *... an expert on Greek drama*

explain /ɪks'pleɪn/
explains explaining explained

VERB

If you explain something, you give information about it or reasons for it so that it can be understood.
EG *She tried to explain her decision to me.*
EG *That explains why she was so upset.*

explanation /ɛksplə'neɪʃən/
explanations

NOUN

a detailed description of something or an account of why it happened
EG *He could offer no explanation for his behaviour.*

explode /ɪks'pləud/
explodes exploding exploded

VERB

If something such as a bomb explodes, it bursts with great force.
EG *The bomb exploded, killing both men.*

explore /ɪks'plɔː^r/
explores exploring explored

VERB

If you explore a place, you travel around it to discover what it is like.
EG *The best way to explore the region is by boat.*

explosion /ɪks'pləuʒən/
explosions

NOUN

a sudden violent burst of energy, for example one caused by a bomb
EG *Six soldiers were injured in the explosion.*

export /ɛks'pɔːt/
exports exporting exported

VERB

1 To export goods means to sell them to another country.
EG *The nation also exports beef.*

NOUN : /'ɛkspɔːt/
☑ Note the change in stress.

2 Exports are goods which are sold to another country.
EG *Oil exports are expected to increase this year.*

expose /ɪks'pəuz/
exposes exposing exposed

VERB

1 To expose something means to uncover it and make it visible.
EG *For a moment his whole back was exposed.*

2 To **expose** a person **to** something dangerous means to put them in a situation in which it might harm them.
EG *... workers who are exposed to dangerous chemicals*

express /ɪks'prɛs/
expresses expressing expressed

VERB

1 When you express an idea or feeling, you show what you think or feel by saying or doing something.
EG *He expressed his admiration for my work.*

ADJECTIVE

2 very fast
EG *... an express train*

expression /ɪksˈprɛʃən/
expressions

NOUN
1 The expression of ideas or feelings is the act of showing them through words, actions, or art.
EG *... the expression of emotion through laughter or tears*
2 Your expression is the look on your face which shows what you are thinking or feeling.
EG *His expression suddenly changed.*
3 a word or phrase
EG *... an Irish expression meaning 'fun'*

extend /ɪksˈtɛnd/
extends extending extended

VERB
1 If something extends for a particular distance or time, it continues for that distance or time.
EG *The caves extend for 18 km.*
EG *... a career that extended from 1894 to 1920*
2 If you extend something, you make it larger or longer.
EG *We're thinking of extending the house.*
EG *They have extended the deadline by 24 hours.*

extent /ɪksˈtɛnt/

NOUN
The extent of a situation is how great, important or serious it is.
EG *The full extent of the damage is not yet known.*
EG *To a large extent, that's true.*

external /ɛksˈtɜːnl/

ADJECTIVE
existing or happening on the outside of something
EG *... the external walls of the house*

extra /ˈɛkstrə/

ADJECTIVE OR ADVERB
more than is usual, necessary, or expected
EG *Extra staff have been hired to deal with the complaints.*
EG *You may be charged extra for this service.*

extract /ɪksˈtrækt/
extracts extracting extracted

VERB
To **extract** something **from** a place means to get it out, often by force.
EG *He tried to extract his pole from the mud.*

extraordinary /ɪksˈtrɔːdnrɪ/

ADJECTIVE
very unusual or surprising
EG *What an extraordinary thing to say!*

extreme /ɪksˈtriːm/
extremes

ADJECTIVE
1 very great in degree or intensity
EG *... people living in extreme poverty*
2 at the furthest point or edge of something
EG *... the extreme northwestern corner of Spain*

NOUN
3 the highest or furthest degree of something
EG *... extremes of temperature*

extremely /ɪksˈtriːmlɪ/

ADVERB
Extremely means very.
EG *She's extremely intelligent.*
EG *You did extremely well.*

eye /aɪ/
eyes

NOUN
Your eyes are the parts of your

A B C D E F G H I J K L M N O P Q R S T U V W X Y Z

body with which you see.

EG *I opened my eyes and looked up.*

eyebrow /'aɪbrau/
eyebrows

NOUN

Your eyebrows are the lines of hair which grow above your eyes.

EG *He raised his eyebrows and turned away.*

eyesight /'aɪsaɪt/

NOUN

Your eyesight is your ability to see.

EG *He has very poor eyesight.*

A B C D E F G H I J K L M N O P Q R S T U V W X Y Z

Ff

fabric /ˈfæbrɪk/
fabrics

NOUN
Fabric is cloth.
EG ... silk and other delicate fabrics

fabulous /ˈfæbjuləs/

ADJECTIVE
EG ... a fabulous dress

face /feɪs/
faces facing faced

NOUN
1 the front part of your head from your chin to your forehead
EG His face was covered in sweat.
2 a surface or side of something
EG ... the north face of the mountain

VERB
3 If you face something or someone, you are opposite them and look in their direction.
EG They stood facing each other.
4 If you **are faced with** something difficult or unpleasant, you have to deal with it.
EG We are faced with a serious problem.

facility /fəˈsɪlɪtɪ/
facilities

NOUN
Facilities are buildings, equipment or services that are provided for a particular purpose.
EG ... excellent shopping facilities

fact /fækt/
facts

NOUN
1 a piece of information that is true or something that has actually happened
EG ... a long list of facts and figures
EG This doesn't alter the fact that he was wrong.
2 in fact and **as a matter of fact** mean 'actually' or 'really' and are used for emphasis or when making an additional comment
EG This was, in fact, what happened.

factor /ˈfæktər/
factors

NOUN
EG ... one of the main factors in our success

factory /ˈfæktərɪ/
factories

NOUN
a building or group of buildings where goods are made in large quantities
EG ... a furniture factory

fade /feɪd/
fades fading faded

VERB
When something fades, it slowly becomes less bright or less loud.
EG The light was fading.
EG The sound of the engine faded into the distance.

fail /feɪl/
fails failing failed

VERB
1 If you fail an exam, your marks are too low and you do not pass.
EG I failed my driving test twice.
2 If someone or something **fails to do** something, they do not do it.
EG The bomb failed to explode.
EG He failed to win enough votes.

A

3 If something fails, it stops working properly.
EG *His grandmother's eyesight began to fail.*

failure /ˈfeɪljəʳ/
failures
NOUN
1 Failure is a lack of success in doing something.
EG *The attempt ended in failure.*
2 Your **failure to do** something that you were expected to do is the fact that you do not do it.
EG *... a statement explaining his failure to attend.*
3 an unsuccessful person, thing, or action
EG *He felt like a failure.*

faint /feɪnt/
fainter faintest; faints fainting fainted
ADJECTIVE
1 A sound, colour, or feeling that is faint is not strong or intense.
EG *Their voices grew fainter.*
2 If you **feel faint**, you feel dizzy and unsteady.
EG *I was feeling faint, so I sat down.*
VERB
3 If you faint, you lose consciousness for a short time.
EG *She almost fainted when he told her the news.*

fair /feəʳ/
fairer fairest; fairs
ADJECTIVE
1 reasonable and just
EG *a fair trial*
EG *It doesn't seem fair to leave him behind.*
2 A fair amount, size or distance is quite large.
EG *It cost a fair amount.*
3 Fair hair or skin is light or pale.
EG *... a little girl with long fair hair*

4 When the weather is fair, it is not cloudy or raining.
EG *... a long period of fair weather*
NOUN
5 a form of outdoor entertainment in which people pay to ride on machines or try to win prizes in games
EG *The children begged to be taken to the fair.*
6 an event at which people display or sell goods
EG *... a craft fair*

fairly /ˈfeəlɪ/
ADVERB
1 to quite a large degree
EG *He's fairly bright.*
EG *We did fairly well.*
2 in a just and reasonable way
EG *... solving their problems quickly and fairly*

faith /feɪθ/
faiths
NOUN
1 Faith is a feeling of confidence or trust in something.
EG *People have lost faith in politicians.*
2 a particular religion
EG *... students of all faiths and nationalities*

faithful /ˈfeɪθfʊl/
ADJECTIVE
1 loyal to someone or something and continuing to support them
EG *... one of his most faithful supporters*
2 accurate and truthful
EG *The script is faithful to the novel.*

fall /fɔːl/
falls falling fell fallen
VERB
1 If someone or something falls, they move quickly downwards.

EG *Bombs were falling all around us.*

2 If someone or something falls or **falls down** or **falls over**, they move from an upright position, so that they are lying on the ground.
EG *I hit him so hard he fell over.*

3 If something falls, it decreases in amount, value or strength.
EG *Her weight fell to under seven stones.*

4 When rain or snow falls, it comes down from the sky.
EG *Over an inch of rain fell in just over ten minutes.*

5 If, for example, you **fall ill**, **fall asleep**, or **fall in love**, you become ill, or begin to sleep, or begin to love someone.
EG *She was twelve years old when she first fell in love.*

NOUN
6 If you have a fall, you fall over.
EG *He had a nasty fall as he left the shop.*

7 A **fall in** something is a reduction in its amount, value or strength.
EG *… a sharp fall in the value of the pound*

8 In American English, the autumn is called the fall.
EG *… in the fall of 1991*

fall out

VERB
If someone's hair or teeth fall out, they separate from their body.
EG *The cancer treatment made his hair fall out.*

false /fɔːls/

ADJECTIVE
1 not true or not correct
EG *He gave the police a false name.*

2 not real or genuine but intended to seem real
EG *… a set of false teeth*

fame /feɪm/

NOUN
Fame is the state of being very well-known.
EG *The film earned him international fame.*

familiar /fəˈmɪlɪəʳ/

ADJECTIVE
1 well-known or easy to recognize
EG *The room was full of familiar faces.*

2 If you are **familiar with** something, you know it or understand it well.
EG *He was not very familiar with the area.*

family /ˈfæmɪlɪ/
families

NOUN
a group of people who are related to each other, especially parents and their children
EG *… the Wilkins family*
EG *… mothers with large families*
☑ You can use either a singular or a plural verb after 'family': *the whole family was there*; *the whole family were there*.

famous /ˈfeɪməs/

ADJECTIVE
very well-known
EG *… a famous writer*
EG *… a city famous for its food*

fan /fæn/
fans

NOUN
1 If you are a fan of someone or something, you admire them and are very interested in them.
EG *I'm a big fan of their music.*

2 a device that keeps a room or machine cool by creating a draught of air
EG *… an electric fan*

A B C D E F G H I J K L M N O P Q R S T U V W X Y Z

A
B
C
D
E
F
G
H
I
J
K
L
M
N
O
P
Q
R
S
T
U
V
W
X
Y
Z

fancy /'fænsɪ/
fancies fancying fancied;
fancier fanciest

VERB
1 If you fancy something, you
want to have it or do it.
EG *Do you fancy a cup of tea?*

ADJECTIVE
2 special or unusual
EG *... dressed up in fancy clothes*

fantastic /fæn'tæstɪk/

ADJECTIVE
1 wonderful and very pleasing
EG *... a fantastic sunset*
2 extremely large in degree or
amount
EG *He earns a fantastic amount.*

fantasy /'fæntəsɪ/
fantasies

NOUN
1 A fantasy is an imagined story or
situation.
EG *... sexual fantasies*
2 Fantasy is the activity of
imagining things.
EG *She can't distinguish between
fantasy and reality.*

far /fɑːʳ/
farther farthest; further
furthest

ADVERB
1 If something is far from other
things, there is a great distance or
time between them.
EG *The shop's not far from here.*
EG *Christmas seemed so far away.*
2 You use 'far' in questions and
statements about distances.
EG *How far is it to London?*
EG *She followed him as far as the
river.*
3 very much or to a great extent
EG *He eats far too much.*
4 so far means until the present

moment
EG *So far, we've done well.*
5 You can say **as far as I know**
or **so far as I recall** to indicate
that you are not sure of something.
EG *As far as I know, he's still alive.*

ADJECTIVE
6 Far means very distant or the
more distant of two things.
EG *... in the far south of Africa*
EG *... the far end of the room*
☑ When you are talking about
distances, you can use 'farther'
and 'farthest' or 'further' and
'furthest': *farther into the jungle*;
further into the jungle. If you are
talking about the extent of
something, you can only use
'further' and 'furthest': *a further
delay.*

fare /fɛəʳ/
fares faring fared

NOUN
1 The fare is the money that you
pay for a journey on a bus, train,
taxi, boat or plane.
EG *He barely had enough for the
bus fare.*

VERB
2 How someone fares in a
particular situation is how
successful they are.
EG *The team have not fared well
this season.*

farm /fɑːm/
farms

NOUN
an area of land together with
buildings, used for growing crops
and raising animals
EG *Both boys liked to work on the
farm.*

farmer /'fɑːməʳ/
farmers

NOUN

a person who owns or manages a farm

EG *… a pig farmer*

farther /'fɑːðəʳ/
a comparative form of **far**

farthest /'fɑːðɪst/
a superlative form of **far**

fascinating /'fæsɪneɪtɪŋ/

ADJECTIVE
very interesting
EG *… the most fascinating place I've ever visited*

fashion /'fæʃən/
fashions

NOUN
1 A fashion is a style of dress or way of behaving that is popular at a particular time.
EG *… the latest Paris fashions*
EG *Long hair was the fashion back then.*

2 If you do something **in** a particular **fashion**, you do it that way.
EG *He greeted us in his usual friendly fashion.*

fashionable /'fæʃnəbl/

ADJECTIVE
Something that is fashionable is very popular at a particular time.
EG *… one of London's most fashionable restaurants*

fast /fɑːst/
faster fastest; fasts fasting fasted

ADJECTIVE OR ADVERB
1 moving, acting, or happening with great speed
EG *… a fast car*
EG *He works very fast.*

ADVERB
2 You use 'fast' to talk about the speed of someone or something.
EG *How fast were you driving?*

ADJECTIVE
3 If a clock is fast, it shows a time that is later than the real time.
EG *My watch was ten minutes fast.*

VERB
4 If you fast, you eat no food for a period of time, usually for religious reasons.
EG *They fasted for three days.*

NOUN
5 a period of time during which someone does not eat food
EG *The fast had affected his health.*

fasten /'fɑːsn/
fastens fastening fastened

VERB
If you fasten something, you close it or attach it firmly to something else.
EG *She got in the car and fastened her seat belt.*

fat /fæt/
fatter fattest

ADJECTIVE
1 Someone who is fat weighs too much.
EG *I can eat what I like without getting fat.*

2 A fat object is very thick or wide.
EG *… a fat wallet*

NOUN
3 Fat is the extra flesh that animals and humans have under their skin, which is used to store energy.
EG *… an operation to remove a layer of fat*

4 Fat is a substance obtained from animals and plants and used in cooking.
EG *Avoid dishes cooked in fat.*

fatal /'feɪtl/

ADJECTIVE
1 A fatal accident or illness causes someone's death.
EG *… a fatal heart attack*

2 A fatal action has harmful results.
EG *The mistake was fatal to my plans.*

fate /feɪt/
fates

NOUN

1 Fate is a power that some people believe controls everything that happens.
EG *Fate seemed to be working against him.*

2 Someone's fate is what happens to them.
EG *She was resigned to her fate.*

father /ˈfɑːðəʳ/
fathers

NOUN

1 Your father is your male parent.
EG *His father was a painter.*

2 In some Christian churches, priests are referred to as 'Father'.
EG *I'd like your advice, Father.*

father-in-law /ˈfɑːðərɪnlɔː/
fathers-in-law

NOUN

Your father-in-law is the father of your husband or wife.
EG *She had yet to meet her father-in-law.*

fault /fɔːlt/
faults faulting faulted

NOUN

1 If something bad is your fault, you are to blame for it.
EG *It was all his fault.*

2 a weakness or flaw in someone or something
EG *His biggest fault was his desire to do too much.*

VERB

3 If you cannot fault someone or something, you cannot find any reason to criticize them.
EG *You can't fault his enthusiasm.*

favour /ˈfeɪvəʳ/
favours favouring favoured
US **favor**

NOUN

1 If you regard someone or something with favour, you like or support them.
EG *... whether he can find favour with a new audience*

2 If you **do** someone **a favour**, you do something which helps them.
EG *Can you do me a favour?*

3 Something that is **in** your **favour** is a help or advantage to you.
EG *The arguments seemed to be in our favour.*

4 If you are **in favour of** something, you agree with it and think it should happen.
EG *I'm in favour of the new proposals.*

VERB

5 If you favour something or someone, you prefer that person or thing.
EG *Some people favour a different approach.*

favourite /ˈfeɪvrɪt/
favourites
US **favorite**

ADJECTIVE

1 Your favourite person or thing is the one you like best.
EG *She's my favourite writer.*

NOUN

2 Someone's favourite is the person or thing they like best.
EG *I like all sports, but soccer is my favourite.*

3 the animal or person that is expected to win a race or contest
EG *The race was won by the favourite.*

fax /fæks/
faxes faxing faxed

NOUN

1 a machine that sends and receives documents electronically along a telephone line
EG *The fax wasn't working.*

2 a copy of a document sent electronically along a telephone line
EG *I sent him a fax.*

VERB

3 If you fax a document, you send it electronically along a telephone line.
EG *Ask your secretary to fax it to me.*

fear /fɪər/
fears fearing feared

NOUN

1 Fear is the feeling of worry you have when you think that you are in danger or that something bad might happen.
EG *She was shaking with fear.*
EG *... his fears about the forthcoming operation*

VERB

2 If you fear something unpleasant, you are worried that it might happen.
EG *Artists feared that their pictures would be forgotten.*

feast /fiːst/
feasts

NOUN

a large and special meal for many people
EG *... a wedding feast*

feather /ˈfɛðər/
feathers

NOUN

A bird's feathers are the light soft things covering its body.
EG *The floor of the cage was covered in feathers.*

feature /ˈfiːtʃər/
features featuring featured

NOUN

1 A particular feature of something is an interesting or important part of it.
EG *Such practices are an essential feature of Hindu life.*

2 Your features are your eyes, nose, mouth, and other parts of your face.
EG *His features expressed alarm.*

VERB

3 When a film or exhibition features someone or something, they are an important part of it.
EG *The series features top stars from the world of sport.*

February /ˈfɛbruəri/

NOUN

February is the second month of the year.
EG *She died in February.*

fed /fɛd/

past participle and past tense of **feed**

federal /ˈfɛdərəl/

ADJECTIVE

In a federal country or system, a group of states is controlled by a central government.
EG *... a federal republic*

fed up

ADJECTIVE

AN INFORMAL EXPRESSION

If you are **fed up with** someone or something, you are unhappy or bored with them.
EG *I'm fed up with having no money.*

fee /fiː/
fees

NOUN

a charge or payment for a job,

A B C D E F G H I J K L M N O P Q R S T U V W X Y Z

feed /fiːd/
feeds feeding fed

VERB

1 If you **feed** a person or animal, you give them food.
EG *She feeds the pigeons every day.*
2 When an animal or baby **feeds**, it eats.
EG *... insects that feed on wood*
3 If you **feed** something **into** a container or machine, you put it there.
EG *The information was fed into a computer.*

feel /fiːl/
feels feeling felt

VERB

1 If you **feel** an emotion or a sensation, you experience it or become aware of it.
EG *I felt very angry.*
EG *She felt a sharp pain in her arm.*
2 If you **feel** something, you touch it.
EG *The doctor felt my head.*
3 If you talk about how something **feels**, you are describing the emotions connected with it.
EG *It felt good to be travelling again.*
4 If something **feels** warm or cold, for example, you notice that it is warm or cold when you touch it.
EG *The stone felt smooth and nice.*
5 If you **feel** that something is the case, you believe that it is the case.
EG *She feels he treated her badly.*
6 If you **feel like** something or **feel like doing** something, you want to have it or do it.
EG *I felt like having a party.*

NOUN

7 The **feel** of something is how it feels to you when you touch it.

EG *He remembered the feel of her skin.*

feeling /ˈfiːlɪŋ/
feelings

NOUN

1 an emotion
EG *It gave me a feeling of satisfaction.*
2 a physical sensation
EG *I had a strange feeling in my neck.*

PLURAL NOUN

3 Your **feelings** are your attitudes or emotions.
EG *I had mixed feelings about meeting him.*
EG *I didn't want to hurt Max's feelings.*

feet /fiːt/
the plural of **foot**

fell /fɛl/
past tense of **fall**

fellow /ˈfɛləu/
fellows

ADJECTIVE

1 You use 'fellow' to describe people who have something in common with you.
EG *... his fellow teachers*

NOUN

2 AN OLD-FASHIONED OR INFORMAL USE
a man
EG *I knew a fellow by that name.*

felt /fɛlt/
past participle and past tense of **feel**

female /ˈfiːmeɪl/
females

NOUN

1 a woman or girl
EG *More females than males are affected.*

ADJECTIVE

2 concerning or relating to females
EG *... a female singer*

feminine /ˈfɛmɪnɪn/

ADJECTIVE
relating to women or considered
to be typical of women
EG *... traditional feminine roles*

feminism /ˈfɛmɪnɪzəm/

NOUN
Feminism is the belief that women
should have the same rights and
opportunities as men.
EG *... a lifelong supporter of
feminism*

fence /fɛns/
fences

NOUN
a wooden or wire barrier between
two areas of land
EG *... a garden fence*

ferry /ˈfɛrɪ/
ferries ferrying ferried

NOUN
1 a boat that carries people and
vehicles across short stretches of
water
EG *... a passenger ferry*

VERB
2 To ferry people or goods
somewhere means to transport
them there, usually on a short,
regular journey.
EG *... a fleet of buses ferrying
people to the concert*

festival /ˈfɛstɪvəl/
festivals

NOUN
an organized series of events or
performances
EG *... the Cannes Film Festival*

fetch /fɛtʃ/
fetches fetching fetched

VERB
1 If you fetch something, you go

to where it is and bring it back.
EG *Sylvia fetched a towel from the
bathroom.*

2 If something fetches a particular
sum of money, it is sold for that
amount.
EG *The house is expected to fetch
around a million pounds.*

fever /ˈfiːvər/
fevers

NOUN
If you have a fever, your
temperature is higher than usual
because you are ill.
EG *Symptoms include fever and
weight loss.*

few /fjuː/
fewer fewest

ADJECTIVE
1 You use 'few' to refer to a small
number of things or people.
EG *The next few days should be
interesting.*
EG *... a few close friends*

2 You use 'few' to indicate that a
number of things or people is
smaller than expected or desired.
EG *She had few friends.*
☑ You use 'fewer' to talk about
things that can be counted: *fewer
than five visits*. When you are
talking about amounts that cannot
be counted, you should use 'less':
less money.

PRONOUN
3 a few of means a small number
of
EG *I'm giving a party for a few of
the teachers.*

4 few of means a smaller number
than expected or desired
EG *Few of the houses still had lights
on.*

fiction /ˈfɪkʃən/

NOUN

A
B
C
D
E
F
G
H
I
J
K
L
M
N
O
P
Q
R
S
T
U
V
W
X
Y
Z

Fiction is stories about imaginary people and events.
EG ... *a writer of fiction*

field /fi:ld/
fields

NOUN

1 an area of land where crops are grown or animals are kept
EG ... *a field of wheat*

2 an area of land where sports are played
EG ... *a football field*

3 a particular subject or area of interest
EG *She is an expert in this field.*

fierce /fɪəs/
fiercer fiercest

ADJECTIVE

very aggressive or intense
EG ... *a fierce dog*
EG ... *a fierce storm*

fifteen /fɪf'ti:n/
the number 15
EG ... *fifteen days*

fifteenth /fɪf'ti:nθ/

ADJECTIVE

The fifteenth item in a series is the one counted as number fifteen.
EG ... *the fifteenth day*

fifth /fɪfθ/
fifths

ADJECTIVE

1 The fifth item in a series is the one counted as number five.
EG ... *the fifth day*

NOUN

2 one of five equal parts
EG ... *a fifth of the population*

fiftieth /'fɪftɪnθ/

ADJECTIVE

The fiftieth item in a series is the one counted as number fifty.
EG ... *their fiftieth wedding*

anniversary

fifty /'fɪftɪ/
fifties
the number 50
EG ... *fifty metres*
EG ... *the nineteen-fifties*

fight /faɪt/
fights fighting fought

VERB

1 When people fight, they take part in a battle, a boxing match, or in some other attempt to hurt or kill someone.
EG *He fought in the Second World War.*
EG *She used to fight with her sister.*

2 If you fight something, or if you **fight against** it, you try in a determined way to stop it happening.
EG ... *the equipment needed to fight the fire*
EG *I've fought all my life against racism.*

3 If you **fight for** something, or if you **fight to do** it, you try in a determined way to achieve it.
EG *They declared they would fight for justice.*
EG *He fought to remain conscious.*

NOUN

4 a situation in which people hit or try to hurt each other
EG *He had a big fight with his dad.*

5 a determined attempt to prevent or achieve something
EG ... *the fight against drug addiction*
EG ... *the fight for independence*

figure /'fɪɡəʳ/
figures figuring figured

NOUN

1 a written number or the amount a number stands for, especially when expressed as a statistic

EG *He wrote the figure down on a piece of paper.*
EG *... new government figures*
2 the shape of a person whom you cannot see clearly
EG *... a figure in a blue dress*
3 Your figure is the shape of your body.
EG *She has a great figure.*
4 a person
EG *He was a major figure in the trial.*
VERB
5 To **figure in** something means to appear in it or be included in it.
EG *... the many people who have figured in his life*

file /faɪl/
files filing filed
NOUN
1 a cardboard or plastic container in which documents are kept
EG *... a bookshelf crammed with files*
EG *The police probably have a file on him.*
2 A computer file is a set of related data with its own name.
EG *He copied the file onto a floppy disk.*
3 a tool with rough surfaces, used for making hard materials smooth
EG *... a nail file*
VERB
4 When someone files a document, they put it in its correct place with similar documents.
EG *They are filed alphabetically under the author's name.*
5 If you file something, you smooth or shape it with a file.
EG *She carried on filing her nails.*

fill /fɪl/
fills filling filled
VERB
1 If you fill something or if it **fills up**, it becomes full.
EG *Fill a saucepan with water.*
EG *The stadium soon began to fill up.*
2 If something fills a space, it is so big that there is very little room left.
EG *The text fills 231 pages.*
3 If something fills a need or gap, it causes the need or gap to disappear.
EG *... a sense of fun that filled a gap in his life*
fill in
VERB
If you fill in a form, you write information in the spaces on it.
EG *Just fill in the form below.*

film /fɪlm/
films filming filmed
NOUN
1 a series of moving pictures which can be shown in a cinema or on television
EG *... one of my favourite films*
2 a strip of thin plastic that you use in a camera to take photographs
EG *... a roll of film*
3 a very thin layer of powder or liquid
EG *A film of dust covered every surface.*
VERB
4 If you film someone or something, you use a camera to take moving pictures of them.
EG *A camera crew was filming her for French TV.*

filthy /ˈfɪlθɪ/
ADJECTIVE
1 very dirty
EG *... a pair of filthy jeans*
2 disgusting
EG *... a filthy habit*

A
B
C
D
E
F
G
H
I
J
K
L
M
N
O
P
Q
R
S
T
U
V
W
X
Y
Z

final /'faɪnl/
finals

ADJECTIVE
1 The final thing in a series is the last one or the one that happens at the end.
EG … *on the final morning of the festival*
2 A decision that is final cannot be changed or questioned.
EG *The judges' decision is final.*
NOUN
3 the last game or contest in a series, which decides the overall winner
EG … *the Cup Final*

finally /'faɪnəli/
ADVERB
1 If something finally happens, it happens after a long delay.
EG *Finally, he answered the phone.*
2 You use 'finally' to introduce a final point or topic.
EG *Finally, I would like to thank my wife.*

finance /faɪ'næns/
finances financing financed
VERB
1 To finance a project or purchase means to provide the money to pay for it.
EG *These funds are used to finance the purchase of equipment.*
NOUN
2 Finance is the management of money.
EG … *Canada's Minister of Finance*
PLURAL NOUN
3 Your **finances** are the amount of money that you have.
EG … *advice on how to manage your finances*

financial /faɪ'nænʃəl/
ADJECTIVE
relating to or involving money

EG *They have had financial difficulties.*

find /faɪnd/
finds finding found
VERB
1 If you find someone or something, you see them or learn where they are.
EG *He eventually found the book under his bed.*
2 If you find something that you need or want, you succeed in getting it.
EG *I must find a job.*
3 If you find that something is the case, you become aware of it or realize it.
EG *She came home to find he had already left.*
4 If you find something boring or exciting, you are bored or excited by it.
EG *I found the book very interesting.*
5 Something that **is found** in a particular place lives or exists there.
EG *These substances are found in many foods.*
6 When a court **finds** a person **guilty** or **not guilty**, they decide that the person is guilty or innocent.
EG *He was found guilty and sentenced to life imprisonment.*

find out
VERB
If you find something out, you learn or discover something.
EG *He wants to find out what happened.*

fine /faɪn/
finer finest; fines fining fined
ADJECTIVE
1 very good
EG … *one of London's finest*

theatres

2 satisfactory or acceptable
EG *Come on in, the water's fine.*

3 If you say that you are fine, you mean that you are feeling well and quite happy.
EG *"How are you?" — "I'm fine."*

4 When the weather is fine, it is sunny and not raining.
EG *... a fine summer's day*

5 Something that is fine is very narrow or small.
EG *... the fine hairs on her arm*

NOUN

6 a sum of money that is paid as a punishment
EG *The fine for smoking on buses is still quite small.*

VERB

7 Someone who is fined has to pay a sum of money as a punishment.
EG *He was fined £10,000.*

finger /'fɪŋgəʳ/
fingers

NOUN

Your fingers are the long parts of your hands with which you hold things and pick them up.
EG *He wore a ring on each of his fingers.*

fingernail /'fɪŋgəneɪl/
fingernails

NOUN

Your fingernails are the hard areas on the ends of your fingers.
EG *He was cutting his fingernails.*

fingerprint /'fɪŋgəprɪnt/
fingerprints

NOUN

Your fingerprints are the unique marks made by the tip of your fingers when you touch something.
EG *The police took his fingerprints.*

finish /'fɪnɪʃ/
finishes finishing finished

VERB

1 When you finish something, you do the last part of it and complete it.
EG *She hopes to finish the book by Christmas.*

2 When something finishes, it ends.
EG *The film finished around 10 o'clock.*

NOUN

3 The finish of something is the last part of it.
EG *I missed the finish of the match.*

fire /'faɪəʳ/
fires firing fired

NOUN

1 Fire is the flames produced when something burns.
EG *... a huge ball of fire*

2 A fire is a mass of burning material.
EG *We lit a fire on the beach.*

3 A fire is a device that uses electricity or gas to heat a room.
EG *... a gas fire*

4 If something is **on fire**, it is burning.
EG *Moments later the whole house was on fire.*

5 If you **set fire to** something, you start it burning.
EG *... two boys who set fire to a car*

6 If someone **opens fire**, they start shooting.
EG *The soldiers opened fire on the crowd.*

VERB

7 If you fire a gun or bullet, you operate the gun so that the bullet is released.
EG *He fired the gun into the air.*

8 AN INFORMAL USE

If an employer fires someone, they dismiss that person from their job.
EG ... a letter telling her she was fired

fire brigade fire brigades
NOUN
The fire brigade is the organization which has the job of putting out fires.
EG He called the fire brigade.

fire engine fire engines
US fire truck
NOUN
a large vehicle that carries equipment for putting out fires
EG Three fire engines were immediately sent to the scene.

fire escape fire escapes
NOUN
an emergency exit or set of stairs for use if there is a fire
EG The fire escape was blocked by a desk.

fireman /ˈfaɪəmən/ firemen
NOUN
a person whose job is to put out fires
EG Two firemen were injured in the blaze.

fire truck
see fire engine

firework /ˈfaɪəwɜːk/ fireworks
NOUN
a small object which produces coloured sparks or smoke when lit
EG ... a firework display

firm /fɜːm/ firmer firmest; firms
ADJECTIVE
1 Something that is firm is fairly hard and does not change shape very much when it is pressed.
EG ... a firm mattress
2 A firm grasp or push is one which is strong or controlled.
EG His handshake was firm and confident.
3 Someone who is firm behaves in a fairly strict way and will not change their mind.
EG You have to be firm with children.
NOUN
4 a business that sells or produces something
EG ... a firm of engineers

first /fɜːst/
ADJECTIVE OR ADVERB
1 happening, coming, or done before all the others of the same kind
EG ... the first week of June
EG ... the first time I went abroad
EG Green came first in the 100 metres.
ADJECTIVE
2 more important than anything else
EG Her essay won first prize.
ADVERB
3 for the first time
EG They first met in 1946.
NOUN
4 You use at first to refer to what happens at the beginning of something.
EG At first, he seemed surprised.

first aid
NOUN
First aid is medical treatment given to an injured person.
EG ... a first aid kit

first-class /ˈfɜːstˈklɑːs/
ADJECTIVE
1 Something that is first-class is of the highest quality.

EG *The food was first-class.*

2 First-class accommodation is the most expensive accommodation on a plane, ship, or train.
EG *... a first-class cabin*

3 First-class postage is the quickest and most expensive kind of postage.
EG *... a first-class stamp*

fish /fɪʃ/
fishes fishing fished
☑ The plural can be either *fish* or *fishes*, but *fish* is more common.
NOUN
1 a creature with a tail and fins that lives in water
EG *How many fish did you catch?*

2 Fish is the flesh of a fish eaten as food.
EG *Dry white wine is best with fish.*
VERB
3 If you fish, you try to catch fish.
EG *His father taught him to fish.*

fist /fɪst/
fists
NOUN
a hand with the fingers curled tightly towards the centre
EG *He swore and shook his fist at me.*

fit /fɪt/
fits fitting fitted; fitter fittest
VERB
1 If something fits, it is the right shape or size for a particular person or position.
EG *The dress didn't fit, so she took it back.*
EG *... a computer that fits into your pocket*

2 If you fit something somewhere, you put it there.
EG *She fitted her key in the lock.*
NOUN

3 If someone has a fit, they lose consciousness and their body shakes violently.
EG *Without the drugs he would have many more fits.*

4 A fit of laughter, coughing, rage, or panic is a sudden uncontrolled expression of it.
EG *She shot him in a fit of jealous rage.*
ADJECTIVE
5 Someone who is fit is healthy and physically strong.
EG *Regular exercise is the best way to keep fit.*

6 good enough or suitable
EG *She's not fit to be a mother.*

five /faɪv/
fives
the number 5
EG *... five brothers*

fix /fɪks/
fixes fixing fixed
VERB
1 If you fix something somewhere, you attach it there securely.
EG *He fixed the clock to the wall.*

2 If you fix something that is broken, you repair it.
EG *I need to get my TV fixed.*

3 If you fix something, you decide what it will be or you arrange it.
EG *A date for the wedding has not yet been fixed.*

flag /flæg/
flags
NOUN
a piece of coloured cloth, used as the symbol of a country or as a signal
EG *... the American flag*

flake /fleɪk/
flakes
NOUN

A
B
C
D
E
F
G
H
I
J
K
L
M
N
O
P
Q
R
S
T
U
V
W
X
Y
Z

A B C D E F G H I J K L M N O P Q R S T U V W X Y Z

a small thin piece of something

EG *... flakes of rust*

flame /fleɪm/
flames

NOUN

a hot bright stream of gas that comes from something that is burning

EG *The flames were so hot that the road melted.*

flap /flæp/
flaps flapping flapped

VERB

1 If something flaps, or if you flap it, it moves quickly up and down or from side to side.

EG *The flag was flapping in the wind.*

EG *The bird flapped its wings furiously.*

NOUN

2 a loose piece of something such as cloth or skin that is attached at one edge

EG *He pulled back the tent flap.*

flash /flæʃ/
flashes flashing flashed

NOUN

1 a sudden short burst of light

EG *... a flash of lightning*

VERB

2 If a light flashes, or if you flash it, it shines suddenly and briefly.

EG *He noticed a flashing light on the dashboard.*

EG *A driver flashed his headlights at her.*

3 If something flashes past, it moves or happens very quickly.

EG *Something white flashed past the car.*

flat /flæt/
flats; flatter flattest

NOUN

1 a set of rooms for living in, that is part of a larger building

EG *... a block of flats*

ADJECTIVE

2 Something that is flat is level and smooth.

EG *... a flat roof*

3 A flat object is not very tall or deep.

EG *... a square flat box*

4 A flat tyre or ball has not got enough air in it.

EG *We had a flat tyre and had to stop.*

5 A flat battery has lost its electrical charge.

EG *When he tried to start the car, the battery was flat.*

flavour /ˈfleɪvəʳ/
flavours flavouring flavoured
US **flavor**

NOUN

1 The flavour of food is its taste.

EG *This cheese has a very strong flavour.*

VERB

2 If you flavour food, you add something to give it a particular taste.

EG *... strawberry-flavoured sweets*

flaw /flɔː/
flaws

NOUN

A flaw in a theory or argument is a mistake which makes it less effective.

EG *All of these studies have serious flaws.*

flee /fliː/
flees fleeing fled

VERB

If you **flee from** someone or something, or if you flee them, you escape from them by running away.

EG *Many people have fled from their homes.*

EG *... refugees fleeing persecution*

fleet /fliːt/
fleets
NOUN

a group of ships or vehicles owned by the same organization or travelling together

EG *... a fleet of ships*

flesh /flɛʃ/
NOUN

Your flesh is the soft part of your body between the bones and the skin.

EG *... the flesh on her thighs*

flew /fluː/
past tense of **fly**

flexible /ˈflɛksəbl/
ADJECTIVE

1 Something that is flexible can be bent easily without breaking.

EG *... brushes with long, flexible bristles*

2 Someone or something that is flexible is able to adapt easily to changing circumstances.

EG *Our plans are very flexible.*

flight /flaɪt/
flights
NOUN

1 a journey made by aeroplane

EG *The flight to Karachi was delayed.*

2 Flight is the action of flying or the ability to fly.

EG *... the flight of a bird across a window*

3 A **flight of stairs** or a **flight of steps** is a row of them.

EG *The office was up three flights of stairs.*

fling /flɪŋ/
flings flinging flung
VERB

If you fling something somewhere, you throw it there using a lot of force.

EG *Peter flung his shoes into the corner.*

float /fləʊt/
floats floating floated
VERB

1 If something is floating in a liquid, it is lying just below the surface of the liquid.

EG *A branch was floating down the river.*

2 If something floats in the air, it hangs in the air or moves slowly through it.

EG *... a leaf floating on the breeze*

flock /flɒk/
flocks flocking flocked
NOUN

1 a group of birds, sheep, or goats

EG *They kept a small flock of sheep.*

VERB

2 If people flock somewhere, they go there in large numbers.

EG *People will flock to see this film.*

flood /flʌd/
floods flooding flooded
NOUN

1 If there is a flood, a large amount of water covers an area that is usually dry.

EG *More than 70 people were killed in the floods.*

2 A **flood of** something is a large amount of it occurring suddenly.

EG *There was a flood of complaints.*

VERB

3 If water floods an area that is usually dry, or if the area floods, it becomes covered with water.

EG *He left the tap running and flooded the kitchen.*

4 If people or things **flood into** a place or **flood out of** a place, they arrive or leave in large numbers.
EG ... *the refugees who are flooding out of the country*

floor /flɔːʳ/
floors
NOUN
1 the part of a room that you walk on
EG *Jack's sitting on the floor, watching TV.*
2 one of the levels in a building
EG ... *the fifth floor of the hospital*
3 the ground at the bottom of a valley or ocean
EG ... *the ocean floor*

floppy disk floppy disks;
also spelt **floppy disc**
NOUN
a small magnetic disk on which computer data is stored
EG *He copied the file onto a floppy disk.*

flour /'flauəʳ/
NOUN
Flour is a white or brown powder made by grinding grain, and used in bread, cakes, and pastry.
EG *Mix the butter into the flour.*

flow /fləu/
flows flowing flowed
VERB
1 If something flows somewhere, it moves there in a steady and continuous manner.
EG *A stream flowed gently down into the valley.*
EG ... *new measures to help traffic flow more freely*
NOUN
2 A flow of something is a steady continuous movement of it.

EG *There's a good flow of information.*
EG ... *increases in blood flow*

flower /'flauəʳ/
flowers flowering flowered
NOUN
1 A flower is the brightly-coloured part of a plant, which grows at the end of a stem.
EG ... *a bunch of flowers*
VERB
2 When a plant flowers, it produces flowers.
EG *Some of them had never flowered before.*

flown /fləun/
past participle of **fly**

flu /fluː/
NOUN
Flu is an illness similar to a bad cold, but more serious. Flu is short for 'influenza'.
EG *She's got flu.*

fluent /'fluːənt/
ADJECTIVE
Someone who is **fluent in** a foreign language can speak it correctly and without hesitating.
EG *He's fluent in Japanese.*
EG *She speaks fluent German.*

fluid /'fluːɪd/
fluids
NOUN
A fluid is a liquid.
EG *Make sure that you drink plenty of fluids.*

flung /flʌŋ/
past participle and past tense of **fling**

fly /flaɪ/
flies flying flew flown
NOUN
1 an insect with two wings

A
B
C
D
E
F
G
H
I
J
K
L
M
N
O
P
Q
R
S
T
U
V
W
X
Y
Z

EG *The butcher's window was full of dead flies.*

2 The front opening on a pair of trousers is called the fly or the **flies**.

EG *The zip on his flies had broken.*

VERB

3 When a bird, insect, or aircraft flies, it moves through the air.

EG *The bird flew away.*

4 If you fly somewhere, you travel there in an aircraft.

EG *He flew to Los Angeles.*

5 When a pilot flies an aircraft, he or she controls its movement.

EG *He flew a small plane to Cuba.*

6 If someone or something flies somewhere, they move there very quickly.

EG *She flew downstairs and opened the door.*

focus /ˈfəukəs/
focuses focusing focused

☑ When you add the endings *-es, -ing, -ed* to the verb, you can use either a single 's' or a double 's' before the ending. Either way is correct, but the first way is much more common.

VERB

1 If you **focus** your eyes or a camera **on** something, you adjust your eyes or the camera so that the image is clear.

EG *She focused her eyes on the horizon.*

2 If you **focus on** a particular topic, or if you focus your attention on it, you concentrate on it and deal with it.

EG *Recently he has focused all his attention on his career.*

NOUN

3 The **focus of** something is the main thing that it is concerned

with.

EG *The focus of the conversation shifted during the meal.*

4 If an image is in **focus**, the edges of the image are clear and sharp.

EG *Make sure the picture is in focus.*

fog /fɒg/

NOUN

Fog is a thick mist caused by tiny drops of water in the air.

EG *The crash happened in thick fog.*

foil /fɔɪl/
foils foiling foiled

VERB

1 If you foil an attempt at something, you prevent it from succeeding.

EG *The robbery was foiled by an off-duty policeman.*

NOUN

2 Foil is thin, paper-like sheets of metal used to wrap food.

EG *... aluminium foil*

fold /fəuld/
folds folding folded

VERB

1 If you fold something, you bend it so that one part lies over another.

EG *He folded the letter and put it back in the envelope.*

NOUN

2 a crease or bend in paper or cloth

EG *Make three folds in the paper.*

folk /fəuk/
folks

NOUN

1 Folk or **folks** are people.

EG *These are the folk I was telling you about.*

ADJECTIVE

2 Folk music and folk art are traditional or typical of a particular

A
B
C
D
E
F
G
H
I
J
K
L
M
N
O
P
Q
R
S
T
U
V
W
X
Y
Z

people.

EG ... *Irish folk music*

follow /'fɒləʊ/
follows following followed

VERB

1 If you follow someone, you move along behind them.
EG *We followed him up the steps.*

2 If you follow a path or a sign, you go somewhere using the path or sign to direct you.
EG *I followed the signs to the motorway.*

3 If you follow instructions or advice, you do what the instructions or advice say.
EG *She followed his advice and sold the house.*

4 Something that follows a particular thing happens after it.
EG ... *in the days following her death*

5 If something follows from something else, it is true as a result of it.
EG *Just because she's pretty, it doesn't follow that she can sing.*

6 If you follow an explanation or the plot of a story, you understand it.
EG *Can you follow what he's saying?*

follower /'fɒləʊəʳ/
followers

NOUN

The followers of a person or belief are the people who support them.
EG ... *the Party's most loyal followers*

fond /fɒnd/
fonder fondest

ADJECTIVE

If you are **fond of** someone or something, you like them.
EG *I'm very fond of him.*

food /fuːd/
foods

NOUN

Food is what people and animals eat.
EG ... *supplies of food and water*
EG ... *frozen foods*

fool /fuːl/
fools fooling fooled

NOUN

1 A fool is someone who shows poor judgement and is not sensible.
EG *You're a fool if you believe him.*

VERB

2 If you fool someone, you deceive or trick them.
EG *Don't be fooled by his appearance.*

foolish /'fuːlɪʃ/

ADJECTIVE

Foolish behaviour is not sensible and shows poor judgement.
EG *It would be foolish to take such a risk.*

foot /fʊt/

NOUN

1 the part of your body at the end of your leg
EG *She shouted and stamped her feet.*

2 the part of something that is farthest from the top
EG ... *the foot of the mountain*

3 a unit of length equal to 12 inches or about 30.5 centimetres
EG ... *a prison cell 10 feet long and 6 feet wide*

☑ The plural can be either 'foot' or 'feet': *six foot tall.*

football /'fʊtbɔːl/
footballs

NOUN

1 Football is any game in which

the ball can be kicked, especially soccer.
EG ... a group of boys playing football
2 a ball used in any of these games
EG ... a leather football

footpath /ˈfʊtpɑːθ/
footpaths
NOUN
a path for people to walk on, especially in the countryside
EG ... a footpath along the river

footstep /ˈfʊtstɛp/
footsteps
NOUN
the sound made by someone's feet when they are walking
EG They heard footsteps in the corridor.

for /fɔːr/
PREPOSITION
1 If something is for someone, they are intended to have it or benefit from it.
EG ... a table for two
EG I have some advice for you.
2 You use 'for' when explaining the reason, cause, or purpose of something.
EG This is my excuse for going to Italy.
EG ... a room for rent
3 You use 'for' to express a quantity, time, or distance.
EG They sold their house for over a million pounds.
EG We talked for a couple of minutes.
EG I drove on for a few more miles.
4 You use 'for' after words like 'time,' 'space,' 'money' and 'energy' to say whether there is enough of it for a particular purpose.
EG Do you have time for another

drink?
EG There isn't room for another bed.
5 If you are for something, you support it or approve of it.
EG Are you for or against the proposal?

forbid /fəˈbɪd/
forbids forbidding forbade forbidden
VERB
If you **forbid** someone **to do** something, or if you forbid something, you order that it must not be done.
EG I forbid you to leave.
EG The rules forbid the use of force.

force /fɔːs/
forces forcing forced
VERB
1 If you **force** someone **to do** something, you make them do it.
EG I can't force you to stay.
2 If you force something, you use a lot of strength to move or open it.
EG Police forced the door of the flat and arrested him.
NOUN
3 Force is violence or great strength.
EG The rebels seized power by force.
4 The force of something is its strength or power.
EG The force of the explosion shook the building.
5 Someone or something that is a force in a situation has a lot of influence on it.
EG She became a major force in women's tennis.
6 Forces are organized groups of people, especially soldiers or police.
EG ... the decision to send American forces to the region
7 Forces of a particular kind are

A B C D E F G H I J K L M N O P Q R S T U V W X Y Z

processes or events that seem to be outside human control.
EG ... *the forces of nature*
EG ... *market forces*

forecast /ˈfɔːkɑːst/
forecasts forecasting
forecast or **forecasted**

NOUN
1 a prediction of what will happen
EG ... *the weather forecast*

VERB
2 If you forecast an event, you predict what will happen.
EG *He forecast that house prices would start to rise again.*

foreground /ˈfɔːgraund/

NOUN
In a picture, the foreground is the part that seems nearest to you.
EG ... *the tall figure in the foreground*

forehead /ˈfɒrɪd/
foreheads

NOUN
the flat area at the front of your head, above your eyebrows and below where your hair grows
EG *He kissed her on the forehead.*

foreign /ˈfɒrɪn/

ADJECTIVE
1 belonging to or involving a country that is not your own
EG ... *a foreign language*
EG ... *foreign travel*
2 If something is **foreign to** you, it is unfamiliar.
EG *Such ideas were completely foreign to him.*

foreigner /ˈfɒrɪnər/
foreigners

NOUN
someone who belongs to a country that is not your own
EG *They are discouraged from*

talking to foreigners.

forest /ˈfɒrɪst/
forests

NOUN
a large area of trees growing close together
EG ... *two boys who had got lost in the forest*

forever /fəˈrevər/

ADVERB
permanently or continually
EG *I knew the fun wouldn't last forever.*

forget /fəˈget/
forgets forgetting forgot
forgotten

VERB
1 If you forget something, you cannot remember it.
EG *I forgot his name.*
EG *She forgot where she parked the car.*
2 If you **forget to do** something, you do not remember to do it.
EG *He forgot to lock the door.*
3 If you forget something that you had intended to bring with you, you do not remember to bring it.
EG *She forgot her passport, so we had to go home.*

forgive /fəˈgɪv/
forgives forgiving forgave
forgiven

VERB
If you forgive someone who has done something wrong, you stop being angry with them.
EG *He has never forgiven her for what she said.*

forgot /fəˈgɒt/
past tense of **forget**

forgotten /fəˈgɒtn/
past participle of **forget**

fork /fɔːk/
forks

NOUN
an object consisting of three or four thin points on the end of a handle, used for eating food
EG *... knives and forks*

form /fɔːm/
forms forming formed

NOUN
1 A form of something is a type or kind of it.
EG *... a new form of weapon*
2 The form of something is its shape.
EG *... a brooch in the form of a lizard*
3 A form is a sheet of paper with questions and spaces for you to fill in the answers.
EG *You will be asked to fill in a form.*
4 In sport, a person's form refers to their ability or success over a period of time.
EG *His form this season has been brilliant.*

VERB
5 When a particular shape forms or is formed, people or things are arranged so that this shape is made.
EG *They formed a circle and sang.*
6 The things that form something are the things it consists of.
EG *... the events that form the basis of her novel*
7 When someone forms something or when it forms, it is created, organized, or started.
EG *The League was formed in 1959.*

formal /ˈfɔːməl/

ADJECTIVE
1 Formal speech or behaviour is correct and serious, rather than relaxed and friendly.

EG *... a formal letter of apology*
2 A formal action or event is an official one.
EG *... a formal dinner*

format /ˈfɔːmæt/
formats

NOUN
The format of something is the way it is arranged and presented.
EG *I met with him to explain the format of the programme.*

former /ˈfɔːmər/

ADJECTIVE
1 You use 'former' to indicate what someone or something used to be, but no longer is.
EG *... a former tennis champion*

NOUN
2 You use **the former** to refer to the first of two things that you have just mentioned.
EG *If I had to choose between happiness and money, I would choose the former.*

formula /ˈfɔːmjʊlə/
formulae or **formulas**

NOUN
1 a group of letters, numbers, or symbols which stand for a mathematical or scientific rule
EG *... a mathematical formula*
2 a plan for dealing with a particular problem
EG *... a peace formula*

forth /fɔːθ/

ADVERB
A FORMAL WORD
1 If you go forth from a place, you leave it.
EG *... when Columbus set forth on his epic voyage of discovery*
2 If you **bring** something **forth**, you make it visible.
EG *He brought forth a slim volume*

of poetry.

fortieth /ˈfɔːtɪɪθ/

ADJECTIVE

The fortieth item in a series is the one counted as number forty.

EG *... her fortieth birthday*

fortnight /ˈfɔːtnaɪt/
fortnights

NOUN

a period of two weeks

EG *I hope to be back in a fortnight.*

fortunate /ˈfɔːtʃənɪt/

ADJECTIVE

Someone or something that is fortunate is lucky.

EG *He was fortunate to survive.*

EG *It was fortunate that the water was so shallow.*

fortunately /ˈfɔːtʃənɪtlɪ/

ADVERB

You use 'fortunately' to indicate that a situation is good or lucky.

EG *Fortunately, no one was hurt.*

fortune /ˈfɔːtʃən/
fortunes

NOUN

1 Fortune or **good fortune** is good luck.

EG *He'd had a bit of good fortune at the racetrack.*

2 You can say that a large amount of money is **a fortune**.

EG *The holiday cost them a fortune.*

PLURAL NOUN

3 The **fortunes** of someone or something are the extent to which they are successful or unsuccessful.

EG *The film follows the fortunes of two women.*

forty /ˈfɔːtɪ/
forties

the number 40

EG *... forty days*

EG *... men in their forties*

forward /ˈfɔːwəd/
forwards forwarding forwarded

ADVERB

1 Forward or **forwards** means in the front or towards the front.

EG *We moved forward to get a better view.*

EG *She fell forwards.*

2 Forward or **forwards** means developing or progressing.

EG *They just couldn't see any way forward.*

3 Forward or **forwards** means in or towards a future time.

EG *It's time to look forward, not back.*

VERB

4 If you **forward** a letter **to** someone, you send it to them at their new address after it has been sent to their old address.

EG *We promised to forward all his mail to him.*

foster /ˈfɒstər/
fosters fostering fostered

VERB

1 If someone fosters a child, they look after the child for a period in their home, but do not become its legal parent.

EG *She has fostered more than a hundred children.*

2 If you foster a feeling, activity, or idea, you help it to develop.

EG *We have a responsibility to foster good relations with them.*

ADJECTIVE

3 Foster parents are people who foster a child.

EG *Jack was placed with foster parents.*

fought /fɔːt/

past participle and past tense of **fight**

foul /faʊl/
fouler foulest; fouls fouling fouled

ADJECTIVE

1 Something that is foul is very unpleasant, especially because it is dirty or obscene.
EG ... a foul smell
EG ... foul language

VERB

2 To foul something means to make it dirty.
EG Dogs must not be allowed to foul the pavement.

3 In sport, if a player fouls another player, they touch them in a way that breaks the rules.
EG He was sent off for fouling the goalkeeper.

NOUN

4 In sport, a foul is an action that breaks the rules.
EG ... a foul on the goalkeeper

found /faʊnd/
founds founding founded

1 Found is the past tense and past participle of **find**

VERB

2 If someone founds an organization or company, they create it.
EG The Party was founded in 1893.

foundation /faʊnˈdeɪʃən/
foundations

NOUN

1 The foundation of a belief or way of life is the ideas or attitudes on which it is based.
EG The issue threatens the very foundation of our community.

PLURAL NOUN

2 The **foundations** of a building are the layer of concrete or bricks below the ground on which it is built.

EG We wanted to lay the foundations before the winter.

fountain /ˈfaʊntɪn/
fountains

NOUN

a structure consisting of a jet of water forced into the air by a pump
EG Children were playing in the fountains.

four /fɔːr/
fours

1 the number 4
EG ... four children

PLURAL NOUN

2 If you are **on all fours**, you are on your hands and knees.
EG She crawled to the window on all fours.

fourteen /fɔːˈtiːn/
the number 14
EG ... fourteen men

fourteenth /fɔːˈtiːnθ/

ADJECTIVE

The fourteenth item in a series is the one counted as number fourteen.
EG ... the fourteenth man

fourth /ˈfɔːθ/
fourths

ADJECTIVE

1 The fourth item in a series is the one counted as number four.
EG ... the fourth floor

NOUN

2 In American English, a fourth is one of four equal parts of something.
EG ... three-fourths of those interviewed
☑ The British word is *quarter*.

fox /fɒks/
foxes

NOUN

a wild animal which looks like a

A
B
C
D
E
F
G
H
I
J
K
L
M
N
O
P
Q
R
S
T
U
V
W
X
Y
Z

dog and has reddish-brown fur and a thick tail
EG ... *a fox that had wandered into the city*

fraction /ˈfrækʃən/
fractions

NOUN

1 In mathematics, a fraction is a part of a whole number.
EG ... *a lesson on decimals and fractions*

2 a tiny proportion or amount of something
EG *She hesitated for a fraction of a second.*

fracture /ˈfræktʃəʳ/
fractures fracturing fractured

NOUN

1 a crack or break in something, especially a bone
EG ... *a hip fracture*

VERB

2 If something fractures, or if you fracture it, it breaks.
EG ... *a fractured skull*

fragile /ˈfrædʒaɪl/

ADJECTIVE

easily broken or damaged
EG ... *fragile glass*
EG ... *a fragile relationship*

fragment /ˈfrægmənt/
fragments fragmenting fragmented

NOUN

1 a small piece or part of something
EG ... *fragments of glass*

VERB : /frægˈment/

☑ Note that you pronounce the verb differently from the noun.

2 If something fragments, it breaks into small pieces.
EG *The Party was in danger of*

fragmenting.

frame /freɪm/
frames framing framed

NOUN

1 the structure surrounding a door, window, or picture
EG ... *a wooden picture frame*

2 an arrangement of connected bars over which something is built
EG ... *a house with a timber frame*

VERB

3 If you frame a picture, you put it into a frame.
EG ... *a framed photograph of his wife*

framework /ˈfreɪmwɜːk/
frameworks

NOUN

1 a structure that forms a support or frame for something
EG ... *wooden shelves on a steel framework*

2 a set of rules or ideas which you use to decide what to do
EG ... *within the framework of the regulations*

frank /fræŋk/
franker frankest

ADJECTIVE

If you are frank, you say things in an open and honest way.
EG ... *a frank discussion*

fraud /frɔːd/
frauds

NOUN

1 Fraud is the crime of getting money by deceiving someone.
EG *He was jailed for two years for fraud.*

2 A fraud is someone or something that deceives people in a dishonest way.
EG *Many so-called psychics are frauds.*

freak /friːk/
freaks

NOUN

1 someone whose appearance or behaviour is very unusual
EG *Successful black women are sometimes looked upon as freaks.*

ADJECTIVE

2 A freak event is very unusual.
EG *... a freak accident*

free /friː/
freer freest; frees freeing freed

ADJECTIVE

1 If something is free, you can have it without paying for it.
EG *... a free brochure*
EG *Admission is free.*

2 Something that is free is not controlled or limited.
EG *... free elections*
EG *Women should be free to dress as they please.*

3 Someone who is free is no longer a prisoner.
EG *He walked from the court a free man.*

4 To be **free of** something unpleasant means not to be affected by it.
EG *She wanted her aunt's life to be free of worry.*

5 If someone is free, they are not busy.
EG *Are you free for dinner?*

6 If a seat or table is free, it is not being used.
EG *Is this seat free?*

VERB

7 If you free someone or something that is trapped, you release them.
EG *Firemen tried to free the injured man.*

8 When a prisoner is freed, he or she is released.
EG *Two of the hostages have now been freed.*

9 If you **free** someone **of** something unpleasant, you remove it from them.
EG *This will free us of most of our debts.*

freedom /friːdəm/

NOUN

1 If you have the freedom to do something, you are allowed to do it.
EG *They were given complete freedom to go wherever they liked.*
EG *... freedom of speech*

2 When prisoners gain their freedom, they are released or they escape.
EG *He looked forward to the day he would gain his freedom.*

3 When there is **freedom from** something unpleasant, people are not affected by it.
EG *... freedom from hunger*

freeway /friːweɪ/
freeways

NOUN

In American and Australian English, a freeway is a road designed for fast travel over long distances.
EG *... an accident on the freeway*
☑ The British word is *motorway*.

freeze /friːz/
freezes freezing froze frozen

VERB

1 When a liquid freezes, or when something freezes it, it becomes solid because it is very cold.
EG *As the temperature fell, the water began to freeze.*

2 If you freeze food, you put it in a freezer to preserve it.

A B C D E F G H I J K L M N O P Q R S T U V W X Y Z

EG *You can freeze the soup at this stage.*

3 If you freeze, you suddenly stop moving because there is danger.
EG *A light came on and she froze.*

freezer /ˈfriːzəʳ/
freezers

NOUN

a large refrigerator in which you can store food for a long time
EG *... à freezer full of ice cream*

freezing /ˈfriːzɪŋ/

ADJECTIVE

extremely cold
EG *It's freezing in here.*
EG *I'm freezing.*

French /frentʃ/

ADJECTIVE

1 belonging or relating to France
EG *... a French film*

NOUN

2 French is the main language spoken in France.
EG *It sounded better in French.*

frequency /ˈfriːkwənsɪ/
frequencies

NOUN

1 The frequency of an event is how often it happens.
EG *The frequency of her visits increased.*

2 The frequency of a sound or radio wave is the rate at which it vibrates.
EG *You can't hear sounds of such a high frequency.*

frequent /ˈfriːkwənt/

ADJECTIVE

If something is frequent, it happens often.
EG *She gives frequent performances of her work.*

fresh /freʃ/

fresher freshest

ADJECTIVE

1 A fresh thing replaces a previous one or is added to it.
EG *The footprints had been filled in by fresh snow.*

2 Fresh food has been obtained or prepared recently, and is not frozen or from a tin.
EG *... locally caught fresh fish*

3 Fresh water is not salty, for example the water in a river or lake.
EG *Fresh water was in short supply.*

4 If you are **fresh from** something, you have experienced it recently.
EG *... a teacher fresh from college*

Friday /ˈfraɪdɪ/
Fridays

NOUN

Friday is the day between Thursday and Saturday.
EG *He was born on Friday the thirteenth of May.*

fridge /frɪdʒ/
fridges

NOUN

an electrically cooled container in which you store food to keep it fresh
EG *The milk is in the fridge.*

fried /fraɪd/

past participle and past tense of **fry**

friend /frend/
friends

NOUN

A friend is someone you know well and like, but who is not related to you.
EG *She's my best friend.*
EG *We've been friends for many years.*

A B C D E F G H I J K L M N O P Q R S T U V W X Y Z

friendly /'frɛndlɪ/
friendlier friendliest

ADJECTIVE

1 If you are **friendly** to someone, you behave in a kind and pleasant way to them.
EG *He was very friendly to us.*
EG *... a friendly young man*

2 If you are **friendly with** someone, you like them and enjoy spending time with them.
EG *I'm friendly with her mother.*

friendship /'frɛndʃɪp/
friendships

NOUN

1 A friendship is a relationship between friends.
EG *... the end of a good friendship*

2 Friendship is the state of being friends with someone.
EG *... after seven years of friendship*

frighten /'fraɪtn/
frightens frightening frightened

VERB

If something or someone frightens you, they make you feel afraid.
EG *She knew he was trying to frighten her.*

frightened /'fraɪtnd/

ADJECTIVE

If you are **frightened of** someone or something, you are afraid of them.
EG *She was frightened of flying.*

fringe /frɪndʒ/
fringes

NOUN

1 the hair that hangs over your forehead
EG *... a long fringe that almost covered her eyes*

2 a decoration on clothes and other objects, consisting of a row of hanging threads
EG *... a jacket with leather fringes*

PLURAL NOUN

3 The **fringes** of a place are the parts farthest from its centre.
EG *... an area on the fringes of the city*

frog /frɒg/
frogs

NOUN

a small creature with big eyes and long back legs, which it uses for jumping
EG *The pond was home to several frogs.*

from /frɒm/

PREPOSITION

1 You use 'from' to say what the source, origin, or starting point of something is.
EG *... a present from his wife*
EG *... people from a city 100 miles away*
EG *She ran from the room.*

2 If you take something from an amount, you reduce the amount by that much.
EG *The money will be deducted from your salary.*

3 You use 'from' when stating the range of something.
EG *From 1977 to 1983 he lived abroad.*

front /frʌnt/
fronts

NOUN

1 The front of something is the part that faces forward.
EG *Stand at the front of the line.*
EG *... a jacket with six buttons down the front*

2 Something that is **in front** is ahead of others in a moving group.
EG *Don't drive too close to the car in front.*

A B C D E F G H I J K L M N O P Q R S T U V W X Y Z

3 If you are **in front** in a competition, you are winning.
EG *We were now three points in front.*

4 If something is **in front of** another thing, it is facing it or near the front of it.
EG *She sat down in front of the mirror.*

ADJECTIVE
5 The front part of something is the part that is nearest to the front.
EG *... the front seat of the car*

frontier /'frʌntɪər/
frontiers

NOUN
a border between two countries
EG *They were questioned at the frontier.*

frown /fraʊn/
frowns frowning frowned

VERB
1 If you frown, you move your eyebrows closer together, because you are annoyed, worried, or puzzled.
EG *He frowned at her anxiously.*

NOUN
2 an expression on the face of someone who is frowning
EG *A frown appeared on his face.*

froze /frəʊz/
past tense of **freeze**

frozen /'frəʊzn/
past participle of **freeze**

fruit /fruːt/

NOUN
Fruit is the part of a plant that contains the seeds. Apples, oranges, and bananas are all fruit.
EG *Try to eat at least one piece of fruit a day.*

frustrate /frʌs'treɪt/
frustrates frustrating

frustrated

VERB
1 If something frustrates you, it causes you problems and makes you upset.
EG *Everyone gets frustrated with their work.*

2 To frustrate something such as a plan means to prevent it.
EG *They deliberately frustrated my attempts to find work.*

fry /fraɪ/
fries frying fried

VERB
When you fry food, you cook it in a pan containing hot fat.
EG *... fried fish*

ft. /fʊt, fiːt/
an abbreviation for 'foot' or 'feet'
EG *... flying at 1,000 ft.*

fuel /'fjuːəl/
fuels fuelling fuelled

NOUN
1 Fuel is a substance such as coal or petrol that is burned to provide heat or power.
EG *... the fuel necessary to heat their homes*

VERB
2 A machine or vehicle that is **fuelled by** a substance works by burning that substance.
EG *... power stations fuelled by oil*

fulfil /fʊl'fɪl/
fulfils fulfilling fulfilled
US **fulfill**

VERB
1 If you fulfil a promise, hope, or duty, you carry it out or achieve it.
EG *Sadly, she never fulfilled her dream of becoming an actress.*

2 If something fulfils you, it gives you satisfaction.
EG *... a fulfilling job*

full /ful/
fuller fullest

ADJECTIVE

1 Something that is full contains as much as it is possible to hold.
EG *The car park was full.*

2 If a place is **full of** people or things, it contains a lot of them.
EG *... a box full of toys*

3 to the greatest possible extent
EG *The radio was playing at full volume.*

4 complete or whole
EG *Full details will be sent to you.*

ADVERB

5 completely or wholly
EG *Turn the taps full on.*

---

full stop full stops

NOUN

The **full stop** is the symbol . that marks the end of a sentence.
EG *The train is leaving.*
It is also used after some initials.
EG *... D.H. Lawrence*

---

full-time /'ful'taɪm/

ADJECTIVE OR ADVERB

If you work full-time, you work for the whole of each normal working week.
EG *... a full-time job*
EG *She works full-time.*

fun /fʌn/
NOUN

1 Fun is pleasant, enjoyable and amusing activity.
EG *We had so much fun.*

2 If someone or something is fun, you enjoy being with them or you enjoy doing it.
EG *She's great fun.*
EG *Computers can be a lot of fun.*

3 If you **make fun of** someone or something, you tease them or make jokes about them.
EG *They all made fun of my plan.*

function /'fʌŋkʃən/
functions functioning functioned

NOUN

1 The function of something is the thing it was designed to do.
EG *The proper function of criticism is to bring about change for the better.*

VERB

2 When something functions, it operates or works.
EG *Sometimes the lift didn't function at all.*

fund /fʌnd/
funds funding funded

NOUN

1 an amount of money that is collected for a particular purpose
EG *... a pension fund*

PLURAL NOUN

2 **funds** are amounts of money that are available to be spent
EG *The concert will raise funds for cancer research.*

VERB

3 To fund something means to provide money for it.
EG *... research funded by the government*

fundamental /fʌndə'mentl/
ADJECTIVE

basic and central
EG *Fundamental changes are required.*

funeral /'fju:nərəl/
funerals

NOUN

a ceremony at which someone who has died is buried or cremated
EG *His funeral is next Thursday.*

funny /ˈfʌnɪ/
funnier funniest

ADJECTIVE

1 Funny things are amusing and make you smile or laugh.
EG ... *a funny story*
2 strange or puzzling
EG *You get a lot of funny people in the library.*

fur /fɜːʳ/

NOUN

Fur is the thick hair that grows on the bodies of many animals.
EG ... *the bear's thick fur*
EG *women in fur coats*

furious /ˈfjʊərɪəs/

ADJECTIVE

1 extremely angry
EG *He's furious at the way he's been treated.*
2 involving great energy or effort
EG ... *months of furious debate*

furnish /ˈfɜːnɪʃ/
furnishes furnishing furnished

VERB

If you furnish a room, you put furniture into it.
EG ... *a furnished flat*

furniture /ˈfɜːnɪtʃəʳ/

NOUN

Furniture is moveable objects such as tables, chairs and wardrobes.

EG *There was no furniture left in the flat.*
EG *Each piece of furniture has been carefully chosen.*

☑ 'Furniture' refers to a number of objects, not to an individual table or chair.

further /ˈfɜːðəʳ/
1 a comparative form of **far**

ADJECTIVE

2 additional or more
EG *For further information, write to ...*

furthest /ˈfɜːðɪst/
a superlative form of **far**

fuss /fʌs/

NOUN

Fuss is unnecessarily anxious or excited behaviour.
EG *I don't know what all the fuss is about.*

future /ˈfjuːtʃəʳ/

NOUN

1 The future is the period of time after the present.
EG *He is already making plans for the future.*
2 **in future** means from now on
EG *Be more careful in future.*

ADJECTIVE

3 relating to or occurring at a time after the present
EG ... *the UK's future role in Europe*

gain /geɪn/
gains gaining gained

VERB

1 If you gain something, you get it gradually.

EG *I spent years trying to gain the right qualifications.*

2 If you **gain from** a situation, you get an advantage from it.

EG *We all hope to gain from the company's success.*

NOUN

3 an increase

EG *... a gain of 15%*

gale /geɪl/
gales

NOUN

an extremely strong wind

EG *Gales are forecast for the weekend.*

gallery /'gælərɪ/
galleries

NOUN

a building or room where works of art are shown

EG *... an art gallery*

gallon /'gæln/
gallons

NOUN

a unit of measurement for liquids equal to eight pints, or about 4.56 litres in Britain and 3.79 litres in America

EG *... a gallon of petrol*

gallop /'gæləp/
gallops galloping galloped

VERB

When a horse gallops, it runs very fast, so that all four feet are briefly off the ground at the same time.

EG *The horse galloped away.*

gamble /'gæmbl/
gambles gambling gambled

VERB

1 When people gamble, they bet money on the result of a contest or race.

EG *John gambled heavily on the horses.*

2 If you **gamble** something, you risk losing it in the hope of gaining an advantage.

EG *The company gambled everything on the new factory.*

NOUN

3 A gamble is a risky action that you take in the hope of gaining an advantage.

EG *The gamble finally paid off.*

game /geɪm/
games

NOUN

1 an activity with a set of rules which is played by individuals or teams against each other

EG *... the wonderful game of football*

2 In sport, a game is a match.

EG *They have lost their last three games.*

gang /gæŋ/
gangs ganging ganged

NOUN

a group of people who join together for some purpose, for example to commit a crime

EG *... a gang of masked robbers*

gang up

VERB

AN INFORMAL USE

If people **gang up on** you, they join together against you.

EG *The other children were ganging*

A B C D E F G H I J K L M N O P Q R S T U V W X Y Z

up on her.

gap /gæp/

gaps

NOUN

1 a space between two things or a hole in something solid
EG *He watched through a gap in the fence.*

2 A gap between things, people, or ideas is a great difference between them.
EG *... the growing gap between rich and poor*

garage /'gærɑːʒ/

garages

NOUN

1 a building in which you can keep a car
EG *He put the car in the garage.*

2 a place where cars are repaired or where petrol is sold
EG *... a local garage*

garbage /'gɑːbɪdʒ/

NOUN

In American English, garbage is rubbish, especially waste from a kitchen.
EG *Which day is the garbage collected?*

garden /'gɑːdn/

gardens

NOUN

an area of land next to a house, with plants, trees and grass
EG *... the back garden*

garment /'gɑːmənt/

garments

NOUN

a piece of clothing
EG *... a basket full of assorted garments*

gas /gæs/

gases; gasses gassing gassed

☑ The plural of the noun 'gas' is *gases*. The verb forms of 'gas' are spelt with a double 's'.

NOUN

1 any substance that is not liquid or solid, such as the substances that form the Earth's atmosphere or the fuel used for heating and cooking
EG *... a light, colourless gas*
EG *... a gas cooker*

2 In American English, gas is petrol.
EG *... a tank of gas*

VERB

3 If someone gasses people or animals, they kill them with poison gas.
EG *Thousands of people were gassed.*

gasoline /'gæsəliːn/

NOUN

In American English, gasoline is petrol.
EG *... the price of gasoline*

gasp /gɑːsp/

gasps gasping gasped

VERB

1 If you gasp, you take a short, quick breath through your mouth, for example because you are surprised or in pain.
EG *She gasped when he told her the news.*

NOUN

2 a short, quick breath through the mouth
EG *... a gasp of surprise*

gate /geɪt/

gates

NOUN

a barrier which is used at the entrance to a garden or field
EG *He opened the gate and approached the house.*

gather /ˈgæðəʳ/
gathers gathering gathered

VERB

1 When people **gather**, they come together in a group.
EG *We gathered around the fireplace.*

2 If you **gather** a number of things, you bring them together in one place.
EG *They gathered nuts and berries for food.*

3 If something **gathers** speed or strength, it gradually becomes faster or stronger.
EG *The raft gathered speed as it approached the waterfall.*

4 You use **I gather** to introduce information that you have found out about someone or something.
EG *I gather he lives abroad.*

gathering /ˈgæðərɪŋ/
gatherings

NOUN

a meeting of people for a particular purpose
EG *... a social gathering*

gave /geɪv/
past tense of **give**

gay /geɪ/
gays

ADJECTIVE

1 Someone who is **gay** is homosexual.
EG *... gay men*

NOUN

2 a homosexual person, especially a homosexual man
EG *... gays and lesbians*

☑ The most common meaning of 'gay' now is 'homosexual'. In some older books it may have its old-fashioned meaning of 'lively and full of fun'.

gaze /geɪz/
gazes gazing gazed

VERB

1 If you **gaze at** someone or something, you look steadily at it for a long time.
EG *He was gazing at himself in the mirror.*

NOUN

2 Someone's **gaze** refers to the way they are looking at something.
EG *... without shifting his gaze from the TV*

gear /gɪəʳ/
gears

NOUN

1 a piece of machinery, especially in a car or on a bicycle, which controls the rate at which energy is converted into movement
EG *The car was in fourth gear.*

2 The **gear** for an activity is the clothes or equipment that you need for it.
EG *We took off our riding gear.*

gender /ˈdʒɛndəʳ/
genders

NOUN

Gender is the sex of a person or animal.
EG *... discrimination on the grounds of gender*

gene /dʒiːn/
genes

NOUN

the part of a cell in a living thing which controls its characteristics and which is passed on to the next generation
EG *Is there a gene for intelligence?*

general /ˈdʒɛnərəl/
generals

ADJECTIVE

1 relating to the whole of

A B C D E F G H I J K L M N O P Q R S T U V W X Y Z

something or to most things in a group

EG *There has been a general improvement in health.*

2 true, suitable, or relevant in most situations

EG *... a topic of general interest*

3 including or involving a range of different things

EG *... a general hospital*

NOUN

4 an army officer of very high rank

EG *... the General's visit to Sarajevo*

5 in general is used to indicate that a statement is true in most cases or that it applies to most people or things

EG *In general, people supported us.*

general election general elections

NOUN

an election for a new government, which all the people of a country may vote in

EG *... when a general election is held*

generate /'dʒɛnəreɪt/
generates generating generated

VERB

To generate something means to create or produce it.

EG *... using wind power to generate electricity*

EG *The factory will generate new jobs.*

generation /dʒɛnəˈreɪʃən/
generations

NOUN

1 all the people of a similar age

EG *... the younger generation*

2 the period of time that it takes for children to grow up and have children of their own

EG *Within a few generations this*

knowledge will be lost.

generous /'dʒɛnərəs/

ADJECTIVE

1 A generous person gives more of something, especially money, than is usual or expected.

EG *It was very generous of him to lend us the money.*

2 Something that is generous is larger than usual or expected.

EG *... a generous portion of spaghetti*

genetic /dʒɪˈnɛtɪk/

ADJECTIVE

involving or relating to genes

EG *... genetic engineering*

genius /'dʒiːnɪəs/
geniuses

NOUN

1 A genius is a highly intelligent, creative, or talented person.

EG *... a mathematical genius*

2 Genius is very great ability or skill in something.

EG *... a writer of genius*

gentle /'dʒɛntl/
gentler gentlest

ADJECTIVE

mild and calm; not violent or rough

EG *... a gentle man*

EG *... a gentle breeze*

gentleman /'dʒɛntlmən/
gentlemen

NOUN

1 a man who is polite and well-educated

EG *He is such a gentleman.*

2 You can refer politely to any man as a gentleman.

EG *This way please, gentlemen.*

gents /dʒɛnts/

NOUN

AN INFORMAL WORD

the gents is a public toilet for men

EG *I hurried to the gents.*

☑ Although it looks like a plural, 'gents' is a singular noun: *the gents is upstairs.*

genuine /ˈdʒɛnjuɪn/

ADJECTIVE

real and exactly what it appears to be

EG *It's made of genuine silver.*

geography /dʒɪˈɒgrəfɪ/

NOUN

Geography is the study of the physical features of the earth.

EG *… a geography teacher*

germ /dʒəːm/
germs

NOUN

a very small organism that causes disease

EG *Chlorine is widely used to kill germs.*

German /ˈdʒəːmən/
Germans

ADJECTIVE

1 belonging or relating to Germany

EG *the German football team*

NOUN

2 someone who comes from Germany

EG *… a joke about two Germans*

3 German is the main language spoken in Germany, Austria and parts of Switzerland.

EG *She knew a few words of German.*

gesture /ˈdʒɛstjəʳ/
gestures

NOUN

1 a movement of your hands or head that communicates a message or feeling

EG *She made an angry gesture with her fist.*

2 an action that expresses your attitude or intentions

EG *The march is intended as a gesture of support.*

get /gɛt/
gets getting got

☑ In American English, the past participle is *gotten.*

VERB

1 'Get' often means the same as 'become'.

EG *It was beginning to get dark.*

2 If you get something, you obtain or receive it.

EG *… how to get enough food*

EG *I got your message.*

3 If you get something or someone, you fetch them.

EG *I'll get you a cup of coffee.*

4 If you get something done, you arrange for it to be done.

EG *I'm going to get my car repaired.*

EG *I'll get him to phone you.*

5 If someone or something gets into a particular state or situation, they start being in that state or situation.

EG *… you might get into trouble*

EG *I managed to get it clean.*

6 If you get a train, bus, or plane, you travel on it.

EG *You can get a bus there.*

7 If you get somewhere, you move or arrive there.

EG *It was late when she got home.*

8 If you get a joke or get the point of something, you understand it.

EG *I didn't get the point of that story.*

get away

VERB

If you get away, you escape.

A B C D E F G H I J K L M N O P Q R S T U V W X Y Z

EG *I tried to grab him, but he got away.*

get on

VERB

1 If you **get on with** someone, you have a friendly relationship with them.

EG *I get on very well with his wife.*

2 If you **get on with** a task, you start doing it or continue doing it.

EG *Jane got on with her work while he talked.*

3 If you are getting on well or badly, you are making good or bad progress.

EG *How are you getting on?*

get over

VERB

If you get over a bad experience or an illness, you recover from it.

EG *She still hasn't got over his death.*

get through

VERB

1 If you get through a task, you complete it.

EG *I'll never get through this book.*

2 If you **get through to** someone, you make them understand what you are saying.

EG *She simply couldn't get through to him.*

3 If you get through on the telephone, you succeed in talking to someone.

EG *I've been phoning all day but I can't get through.*

get up

VERB

1 If you get up from a chair, you stand up.

EG *He got up and answered the door.*

2 When you get up, you get out of bed.

EG *I got up early this morning.*

ghost /gəust/
ghosts

NOUN

the spirit of a dead person

EG *She claims she saw her father's ghost.*

giant /'dʒaɪənt/
giants

NOUN

1 a huge person in a myth or legend

EG *... a tale of monsters and giants*

ADJECTIVE

2 much larger than other similar things

EG *... a giant Christmas tree*

gift /gɪft/
gifts

NOUN

1 something that you give someone as a present

EG *... suggestions for Christmas gifts*

2 a natural skill or ability

EG *He has a gift for comedy.*

gigantic /dʒaɪˈgæntɪk/

ADJECTIVE

extremely large

EG *... a gigantic TV screen*

giggle /'gɪgl/
giggles giggling giggled

VERB

If someone giggles, they laugh in a child-like, helpless way.

EG *Both girls began to giggle.*

gin /dʒɪn/

NOUN

Gin is a strong, colourless alcoholic drink made from grain and berries.

EG *... a glass of gin and tonic*

girl /gəːl/
girls

NOUN

a female child or young woman
EG ... an 11-year-old girl
EG I have two children, a girl and a boy.

girlfriend /'gɜːlfrend/
girlfriends

NOUN

Someone's girlfriend is the woman or girl with whom they are having a romantic or sexual relationship.
EG Has he got a girlfriend?

give /gɪv/
gives giving gave given

1 If you give someone something or **give** it **to** them, you hand it to them.
EG I gave her the money.
EG Give it to me.
2 If you give someone something or **give** it **to** them, you provide it for them.
EG He gave my husband a job.
EG She often gives money to charity.
3 You use 'give' to express physical actions...
EG He gave my hand a squeeze.
4 If you give a speech or performance, you speak or perform in public.
EG Rosa gave a lovely performance.
5 If you give a party, you organize it.
EG I gave a dinner party for a few friends.

give in

VERB

If you give in, you admit that you are defeated.
EG Her parents finally gave in and let her borrow the car.

give up

VERB

1 If you give something up, you stop doing it.

EG He's trying to give up smoking.
2 If you give up, you admit that you cannot do something.
EG I give up, what's the answer?

glad /glæd/
gladder gladdest

ADJECTIVE

happy and pleased
EG I'm glad I changed my mind.
EG We were glad to see him go.

glance /glɑːns/
glances glancing glanced

VERB

1 If you **glance at** someone or something, you look at them quickly.
EG He glanced at his watch.

NOUN

2 a quick look
EG The boys exchanged glances.

glass /glɑːs/
glasses

NOUN

1 Glass is the hard, clear substance that windows and bottles are made from.
EG ... a pane of glass
2 A glass is a container made from glass which you can drink from; also the amount contained in a glass.
EG ... a row of glasses
EG ... a glass of water

PLURAL NOUN

3 **glasses** are two lenses in a frame, which some people wear over their eyes in order to see better
EG He took off his glasses.
EG ... a new pair of glasses

glimpse /glɪmps/
glimpses glimpsing glimpsed

NOUN

A
B
C
D
E
F
G
H
I
J
K
L
M
N
O
P
Q
R
S
T
U
V
W
X
Y
Z

1 a brief sight of something
EG *They caught a glimpse of their hero.*

VERB
2 If you glimpse something, you see it briefly.
EG *... a village they had glimpsed through the trees*

global /ˈgləʊbl/
ADJECTIVE
concerning the whole world
EG *... global warming*

globe /gləʊb/
NOUN
You can refer to the world as the globe.
EG *... performers from around the globe*

gloomy /ˈgluːmɪ/
ADJECTIVE
1 Something that is gloomy is dark and depressing.
EG *... a gloomy winter day*
2 Someone who is gloomy is unhappy and has no hope.
EG *They are gloomy about their chances of success.*

glove /glʌv/
gloves
NOUN
Gloves are articles of clothing which you wear over your hands for warmth or protection.
EG *... a pair of gloves*

glow /gləʊ/
glows glowing glowed
VERB
1 If something glows, it shines with a dull, steady light.
EG *A light glowed behind the curtains.*
NOUN
2 a dull, steady light
EG *... the glow of the fire*

glue /gluː/
glues gluing or **glueing glued**
NOUN
1 a substance used for sticking things together
EG *... a tube of glue*
VERB
2 If you glue one object to another, you stick them together using glue.
EG *Glue the two halves together.*

go /gəʊ/
goes going went gone
VERB
1 If you go somewhere, you move or travel there.
EG *She went to Rome.*
EG *I'm going home.*
2 You can use 'go' to mean become.
EG *She felt she was going mad.*
3 If you are **going to do** something, you intend to do it.
EG *I'm going to buy a new car.*
4 If you **go to** school, work, or church, you attend it regularly.
EG *His son went to a top university.*
5 If a road goes somewhere, it ends there or passes through there.
EG *Does this road go to the station?*
6 If you go swimming or go for a walk, for example, you spend time swimming or walking.
EG *Shall we go for a walk?*
7 You can use 'go' to describe the state that someone or something is in.
EG *Our arrival went unnoticed.*
8 If something goes well, it is successful. If it goes badly, it is unsuccessful.
EG *The party went really well.*
9 If a machine is going, it is working.
EG *My car still isn't going.*

10 You can use 'go' when repeating a song, story, or saying.
EG *... or so the story goes*

11 If your money or time **goes on** something, you spend your money or time on it.
EG *Most of my money goes on bills.*

12 If one thing **goes with** another, they look or taste nice together.
EG *Red wine doesn't go with fish.*

13 If there is a certain amount of time **to go**, that amount of time is left before something else happens.
EG *I've got one more year of my course to go.*

NOUN

14 If it is your go in a game, it is your turn to do something.
EG *Whose go is it?*

15 If you **have a go at** something, you attempt to do it.
EG *I'd always wanted to have a go at skating.*

go off

VERB

1 If a bomb or gun goes off, it explodes or fires.
EG *The gun went off by accident.*

2 If you go off someone or something, you stop liking them.
EG *I'm beginning to go off the idea.*

go on

VERB

1 If someone or something **goes on doing** something, they continue to do it.
EG *Unemployment is likely to go on rising.*

2 Something that is going on is happening.
EG *I looked away while this was going on.*

go out

VERB

If a light or flame goes out, it stops shining or burning.
EG *Suddenly all the lights went out.*

goal /gəul/
goals

NOUN

1 In games like football and hockey, the goal is the space into which the players try to get the ball in order to score.
EG *The ball missed the goal by inches.*

2 In games like football and hockey, if a player scores a goal, they get the ball into the goal.
EG *They beat us by four goals to three.*

3 Your goal is something that you hope to achieve.
EG *Our goal is to raise as much money as possible.*

goalkeeper /'gəulki:pəʳ/
goalkeepers

NOUN

the player, in games like football and hockey, whose job is to stop the ball from going into the goal
EG *... the England goalkeeper*

goat /gəut/
goats

NOUN

an animal similar to a sheep, with a beard and horns
EG *... goat's cheese*

god /gɒd/
gods

NOUN

1 The name **God** is given to the being who is believed by Christians, Jews, and Muslims to have created and to rule the world.
EG *Do you believe in God?*

2 any of the beings that are

A
B
C
D
E
F
G
H
I
J
K
L
M
N
O
P
Q
R
S
T
U
V
W
X
Y
Z

believed in many religions to have power over an aspect of the world
EG ... the Greek god of wine, Dionysus

goes /gəuz/
the third person singular of the present tense of **go**

gold /gəuld/
NOUN
1 Gold is a valuable, yellow-coloured metal, used for making jewellery.
EG ... the price of gold
ADJECTIVE
2 made of gold
EG ... gold coins

golden /'gəuldən/
ADJECTIVE
bright yellow
EG ... an endless golden beach

golf /gɒlf/
NOUN
Golf is a game in which players use special clubs to hit a ball into holes that are spread out over a large area of land.
EG ... a golf course

gone /gɒn/
past participle of **go**

good /gud/
better best; goods
ADJECTIVE
1 pleasant or enjoyable
EG We had a really good time.
2 of a high quality
EG The food was very good indeed.
3 sensible or valid
EG ... a good reason for staying home
4 kind and showing consideration
EG He was very good to her.
EG That's very good of you.
5 well-behaved

EG Have the children been good?
6 You can say **good morning**, **good afternoon**, or **good evening** when you are greeting someone in the morning, afternoon, or evening.
EG Good morning, how are you today?
7 as good as means almost
EG His career is as good as over.
NOUN
8 Good refers to things that are considered to be morally right.
EG ... the forces of good and evil
9 Good refers to anything which is desirable or which benefits someone.
EG The break has done me good.
EG I'm telling you this for your own good!
10 for good means forever
EG The theatre closed down for good.
PLURAL NOUN
11 goods are objects that are sold in shops
EG ... a wide range of electrical goods

goodbye /gud'baɪ/
NOUN
You say goodbye when you are leaving someone or ending a telephone conversation.
EG He left without saying goodbye.
EG Goodbye, Jane.

goodnight /gud'naɪt/
NOUN
You say goodnight late in the evening before you leave someone or go to sleep.
EG She went upstairs to say goodnight to the children.
EG Goodnight, darling.

gorgeous /'gɔːdʒəs/
ADJECTIVE

extremely pleasant or attractive
EG *... a gorgeous man*
EG *It's a gorgeous day.*

gossip /'gɒsɪp/
gossips gossiping gossiped

NOUN
1 Gossip is informal conversation, often about other people.
EG *They enjoy spreading gossip about their colleagues.*

VERB
2 If you gossip, you talk informally with someone, especially about other people.
EG *I mustn't stand here gossiping with you.*

got /gɒt/
1 Got is the past tense and past participle of **get**
2 You can use **have got** instead of the more formal 'have' when talking about possessing things.
EG *I've got a coat just like that.*
3 You can use **have got to** instead of the more formal 'have to' when talking about something that must be done.
EG *I've got to go to the dentist's.*

gotten /'gɒtn/
In American English, gotten is the past participle of **get**

govern /'gʌvən/
governs governing governed

VERB
1 If someone governs a country, they officially control it.
EG *... the party that governs the country*
2 Something that governs a situation influences or controls it.
EG *Much of our behaviour is governed by habit.*

government /'gʌvnmənt/

governments

NOUN
1 The government is the group of people who govern a country.
EG *... new measures by the government*
☑ You can use either a singular or a plural verb after 'the government': *the government is unpopular; the government are unpopular.*
2 Government is the control and organization of a country.
EG *... our system of government*

gown /gaun/
gowns

NOUN
1 a long, formal dress
EG *... a wedding gown*
2 a long black cloak worn by people such as judges and lawyers
EG *... lawyers in their gowns*

GP GPs

NOUN
A GP is a doctor who treats all types of illness and who works in the community rather than in a hospital. GP is an abbreviation for 'general practitioner'.
EG *She phoned her GP for advice.*

grab /græb/
grabs grabbing grabbed

VERB
1 If you grab something, you take it or pick it up roughly.
EG *I grabbed him by the neck.*
2 If you grab an opportunity, you take advantage of it eagerly.
EG *She grabbed the chance to go to New York.*

grade /greɪd/
grades grading graded

VERB
1 If someone grades things, they

A B C D E F G H I J K L M N O P Q R S T U V W X Y Z

judge them according to their quality.

EG *The college does not grade students' work.*

NOUN

2 The grade of something is its quality.

EG *... different grades of paper*

3 Your grade in an exam is the mark that you get.

EG *I got a grade B.*

4 In schools in the United States, a grade is a group of classes for children of a similar age.

EG *She's in the sixth grade.*

gradual /'grædjuəl/

ADJECTIVE

A gradual change or process happens slowly over a long period of time.

EG *Losing weight is a gradual process.*

gradually /'grædjuəli/

ADVERB

happening slowly over a long period of time

EG *Gradually her condition improved.*

graduate /'grædjuit/
graduates graduating graduated

NOUN

1 a person who has completed a first degree at a university

EG *... a history graduate*

VERB : /'grædjueɪt/

☑ Note that you pronounce the verb differently from the noun.

2 A student who has graduated has completed a first degree at a university.

EG *She graduated from Manchester University last year.*

☑ In America, someone who has completed a course at a high

school is called a *high school graduate*. You can also say that someone has *graduated from high school*.

grain /greɪn/
grains

NOUN

1 Grain is a cereal plant, such as wheat, that has been harvested for food.

EG *... a bag of grain*

2 A grain of wheat, rice, or other cereal plant is a seed from it.

EG *... grains of rice*

3 A grain of sand or salt is a tiny piece of it.

EG *Each grain of sand is different.*

gram /græm/
grams; also spelt **gramme**

NOUN

a unit of weight equal to one thousandth of a kilogram

EG *It only weighs a few grams.*

grammar /'græmər/

NOUN

Grammar is the rules of a language that state how words can be combined to form sentences.

EG *... the basic rules of English grammar*

grammar school grammar schools

NOUN

1 in Britain, a secondary school for pupils of high academic ability

EG *Both her children went to grammar school.*

2 in Australia, a private school, usually one controlled by a church

EG *... a $6000-a-year grammar school*

3 in the USA and Canada, a state school for younger children

EG *... a 6-year-old at grammar*

school

gramme /græm/
grammes
another spelling of **gram**

grand /grænd/
grander grandest

ADJECTIVE
1 splendid or impressive
EG ... *a grand house*
2 very important or ambitious
EG ... *a grand scheme to take over the world*

NOUN
3 AN INFORMAL USE
a thousand pounds or a thousand dollars
EG ... *a car costing twenty grand*

grandad /grændæd/
grandads

NOUN
AN INFORMAL WORD
Your grandad is your grandfather.
EG *My grandad is 85.*

grandchild /ˈɡræntʃaɪld/
grandchildren

NOUN
Someone's grandchildren are the children of their son or daughter.
EG *She has three grandchildren.*

granddaughter /ˈɡrændɔːtər/
granddaughters

NOUN
Someone's granddaughter is the daughter of their son or daughter.
EG ... *a photo of my granddaughter*

grandfather /ˈɡrændfɑːðər/
grandfathers

NOUN
Your grandfather is your father's father or your mother's father.
EG *His grandfather was a professor.*

grandma /ˈɡrænmɑː/
grandmas

NOUN
AN INFORMAL WORD
Your grandma is your grandmother.
EG *Thanks, Grandma.*

grandmother /ˈɡrænmʌðər/
grandmothers

NOUN
Your grandmother is your father's mother or your mother's mother.
EG *Both my grandmothers are Scottish.*

grandparent /ˈɡrændpeərənt/
grandparents

NOUN
Your grandparents are the parents of your father or mother.
EG *She was raised by her grandparents.*

grandson /ˈɡrænsʌn/
grandsons

NOUN
Someone's grandson is the son of their son or daughter.
EG ... *her grandson's birthday*

granny /ˈɡrænɪ/
grannies

NOUN
AN INFORMAL WORD
Your granny is your grandmother.
EG *She lives with her granny.*

grant /ɡrɑːnt/
grants granting granted

NOUN
1 an amount of money that an official body gives to someone for a particular purpose
EG *He was given a grant to carry out repairs.*

VERB
2 If someone in authority grants you something, they give it to you.
EG *Permission was granted a few weeks ago.*

3 If you **take** something **for granted**, you believe it without thinking about it.
EG *He took it for granted that he would be offered the job.*

4 If you **take** someone **for granted**, you benefit from them without showing that you are grateful.
EG *I'm tired of being taken for granted.*

grape /greɪp/
grapes

NOUN
a small green or purple fruit, eaten raw or used to make wine
EG *... a bunch of grapes*

grapefruit /'greɪpfruːt/
☑ The plural can be either *grapefruit* or *grapefruits*.

NOUN
a large, round, yellow fruit
EG *... a grapefruit knife*

graphic /'græfɪk/
graphics

ADJECTIVE
1 A graphic description of something unpleasant is very detailed and realistic.
EG *The film contains graphic scenes of violence.*

PLURAL NOUN
2 graphics are drawings and pictures composed of simple lines and strong colours
EG *... computer-generated graphics*

grasp /grɑːsp/
grasps grasping grasped

VERB
1 If you grasp something, you hold it firmly.
EG *He grasped both my hands.*

2 If you grasp an idea, you understand it.

EG *The concepts were difficult to grasp.*

NOUN
3 a firm hold
EG *The gun slipped from her grasp.*

4 Your **grasp of** something is your understanding of it.
EG *He has a good grasp of the basics.*

grass /grɑːs/
NOUN
Grass is the common green plant that grows on lawns and in parks.
EG *... the grass around the tent*

grate /greɪt/
grates grating grated

VERB
If you grate food, you slice it into small pieces by rubbing it against a tool called a grater.
EG *... grated cheese*

grateful /'greɪtful/
ADJECTIVE
If you are **grateful for** something that someone has given you or done for you, you are pleased and want to thank them.
EG *I'm grateful to you for your help.*
EG *I can't tell you how grateful I am.*

grave /greɪv/
graves; graver gravest

NOUN
1 a place where a dead person is buried
EG *He visits her grave every Sunday.*

ADJECTIVE
2 A FORMAL USE
very serious
EG *... a grave crisis*

gravel /'grævl/
NOUN
Gravel is small stones used for making roads and paths.
EG *... a gravel path*

graveyard /'greɪvjɑːd/
graveyards

NOUN

an area of land where dead people
are buried

EG ... *a funeral in a graveyard*

gravy /'greɪvɪ/

NOUN

Gravy is a brown sauce made from
meat juices.

EG ... *roast beef and gravy*

gray /greɪ/
see **grey**

grease /griːs/
greases greasing greased

NOUN

1 Grease is a substance used for
oiling machines.

EG *Most of the grease ended up on
his hands.*

2 Grease is an oily substance
produced by your skin.

EG *His hair is thick with grease.*

3 Grease is melted animal fat, used
in cooking.

EG ... *bacon grease*

VERB

4 If you grease something, you
put grease on it.

EG *Lightly grease a baking tray.*

great /greɪt/
greater greatest

ADJECTIVE

1 very large in size, amount, or
degree

EG ... *a great black cloud of smoke*

EG *She had great difficulty in
staying awake.*

2 very important

EG ... *a great artist*

3 very good

EG *That's a great idea.*

great- /greɪt/

PREFIX

'Great-' is used before words like
grandmother and grandfather to
refer to a relative who is a further
generation away from you. For
example, your great-grandmother
is the mother of one of your
grandparents.

EG *She has five grandchildren and
twelve great-grandchildren.*

Great Britain

NOUN

Great Britain is the island
consisting of England, Scotland,
and Wales.

EG ... *in Great Britain and Northern
Ireland*

greedy /'griːdɪ/
greedier greediest

ADJECTIVE

Someone who is greedy wants
more of something such as food or
money than is necessary or fair.

EG ... *greedy bosses who give
themselves big pay rises*

Greek /griːk/
Greeks

ADJECTIVE

1 belonging or relating to Greece

EG ... *Greek food*

NOUN

2 someone who comes from
Greece

EG ... *the ancient Greeks*

3 Greek is the main language
spoken in Greece.

EG ... *a book in Greek*

green /griːn/
greener greenest; greens

ADJECTIVE OR NOUN

1 Green is the colour of grass or
leaves.

EG ... *a shiny green apple*

EG ... *decorated in bright green*

NOUN

2 a smooth flat area of grass
EG ... *the village green*

ADJECTIVE

3 'Green' is used to describe political movements which are concerned with environmental issues.
EG ... *the Green Party*

greenhouse /ˈgriːnhaus/
greenhouses

NOUN

a glass building in which people grow plants that need to be kept warm
EG ... *the greenhouse where he grew his tomatoes*

greet /griːt/
greets greeting greeted

VERB

1 If you greet someone, you say something friendly like 'hello' to them when you meet them.
EG *He hurried to greet his guests.*

2 If something **is greeted** in a particular way, people react to it in that way.
EG *The announcement was greeted with surprise.*

grew /gruː/
past tense of **grow**

grey /greɪ/
greyer greyest; greys
US **gray**

ADJECTIVE OR NOUN

Grey is the colour of ashes, or of clouds when it is raining.
EG *His hair is going grey.*
EG ... *a dark shade of grey*

greyhound /ˈgreɪhaund/
greyhounds

NOUN

a thin dog with long legs that can run very fast
EG ... *a greyhound race*

grief /griːf/

NOUN

1 Grief is extreme sadness.
EG ... *her grief at her husband's suicide*

2 If someone or something **comes to grief**, they fail or are injured.
EG *Many marriages come to grief over lack of money.*
EG *She came to grief at the final hurdle.*

grill /grɪl/
grills grilling grilled

NOUN

1 a part of a cooker where food is cooked by heat from above
EG *Place the fish under a hot grill.*

VERB

2 If you grill food, you cook it under a grill.
EG ... *grilled chicken*

grin /grɪn/
grins grinning grinned

VERB

1 If you grin, you smile broadly.
EG *Nancy grinned at him.*

NOUN

2 a broad smile
EG *He had a big grin on his face.*

grind /graɪnd/
grinds grinding ground

VERB

1 If you grind something such as pepper or coffee, you crush it into a fine powder.
EG ... *freshly ground coffee*

2 If you grind something into a surface, you press it hard into the surface.
EG *He ground his cigar stub into the ashtray.*

3 If something **grinds to a halt**, it slows down and stops.
EG *Progress ground to a halt.*

grip /grɪp/
grips gripping gripped

VERB

1 If you grip something, you hold it firmly.

EG *She gripped the rope.*

2 If something grips you, you give all your attention to it.

EG *The whole community has been gripped by fear.*

NOUN

3 a firm hold

EG *She released her grip on the bag.*

groan /grəʊn/
groans groaning groaned

VERB

1 If you groan, you make a long, low sound of pain, unhappiness, or disapproval.

EG *He began to groan with pain.*

NOUN

2 the sound you make when you groan

EG *... a groan of disappointment*

gross /grəʊs/
grosser grossest

ADJECTIVE

1 very bad

EG *He was dismissed for gross misconduct.*

2 very ugly, rude, or disgusting

EG *Don't be so gross!*

3 A gross amount is the total amount before anything has been deducted.

EG *... a gross income of £30,000 a year*

ground /graʊnd/
grounds grounding grounded

1 Ground is the past tense and past participle of **grind**

NOUN

2 the ground is the surface of the earth or the floor of a room

EG *They sat on the ground.*

3 Ground is land, especially land that is used for a particular purpose.

EG *... a patch of waste ground*

EG *... the city's football ground*

4 'Ground' is used in expressions such as **gain ground** and **new ground** to refer to the progress that someone or something makes.

EG *The Conservatives are gaining ground, according to recent polls.*

EG *These novels are breaking new ground.*

PLURAL NOUN

5 the grounds of a large building are the garden or area of land which surrounds it

EG *... the grounds of the university*

6 A FORMAL USE

The **grounds for** something are the reasons for it.

EG *You have no grounds for complaint.*

VERB

7 If an aircraft **is grounded**, it is not allowed to fly.

EG *The minister ordered all the planes to be grounded.*

ground floor **ground floors**

NOUN

The ground floor of a building is the floor that is level or almost level with the ground outside.

EG *I live on the ground floor.*

group /gru:p/
groups grouping grouped

NOUN

1 A group of things or people is a number of them that are linked in some way.

EG *... a small group of friends*

EG *... members of an environmental group*

2 a number of musicians who

perform pop music together

EG *He's a drummer in a group.*

VERB

3 When things or people are grouped together, they are linked in some way.

EG *... the problems caused by grouping all drugs together*

☑ You can use either a singular or a plural verb after the noun 'group': *the group is quite large*; *the group are quite large*.

grow /grəu/

grows growing grew grown

VERB

1 When someone or something grows, they get bigger or increase.

EG *Children grow at different rates.*

EG *Their influence continues to grow.*

2 If a tree or plant grows somewhere, it is alive there.

EG *Trees and bushes grew all along the path.*

3 When people grow plants, they plant them and look after them.

EG *Similar plants were grown by the ancient Greeks.*

4 If a man grows a beard or moustache, he lets it develop by not shaving.

EG *I'm thinking of growing a beard.*

5 You use 'grow' to say that someone or something gradually changes into a different state.

EG *He's growing old.*

grow on

VERB

AN INFORMAL USE

If something grows on you, you gradually come to like it.

EG *The place was beginning to grow on me.*

grow up

VERB

When a child grows up, they become an adult.

EG *She grew up in Tokyo.*

growth /grəuθ/

NOUN

1 The growth of something is its increase in size or importance.

EG *... the growth of the fishing industry*

2 The growth of a person, animal or plant is its development and increase in size.

EG *... the idea that smoking stunts your growth*

guarantee /gærən'ti:/

guarantees guaranteeing guaranteed

NOUN

1 A guarantee is a written promise by a company that if a product develops a fault, it will be replaced or repaired free of charge.

EG *... a five-year guarantee*

2 If something is a guarantee of something else, it makes it certain that it will happen.

EG *There is no guarantee that this will work.*

VERB

3 If something or someone guarantees something, they make certain that it will happen.

EG *Money doesn't guarantee success.*

EG *I can't guarantee that he'll come.*

4 If a product is guaranteed, it has a guarantee.

EG *All products are guaranteed for three years.*

guard /gɑːd/

guards guarding guarded

VERB

1 If you guard a person or object, you watch them carefully, either to protect them or to stop them from

escaping.
EG *She was guarded night and day.*

NOUN
2 a person whose job is to guard a person, object, or place
EG *... a prison guard*

guess /gɛs/
guesses guessing guessed

VERB
1 If you guess something, you form an opinion about it without knowing all the facts.
EG *She guessed that he was in his late forties.*
EG *Someone might have guessed our secret.*

NOUN
2 an attempt to give an answer or opinion about something without knowing all the facts
EG *If you don't know the answer, have a guess.*

guest /gɛst/
guests

NOUN
1 someone who has been invited to stay at your home or attend an event
EG *She was a guest at the wedding.*
2 The guests in a hotel are the people staying there.
EG *I seemed to be the only guest.*

guidance /'gaɪdəns/

NOUN
Guidance is help and advice.
EG *The other staff looked to him for guidance.*

guide /gaɪd/
guides guiding guided

NOUN
1 someone who shows you round places, or leads the way through difficult country
EG *... a tour guide*

2 a book which gives information about a particular place or subject
EG *... The Rough Guide to Paris*

VERB
3 If you guide someone in a particular direction, you lead them in that direction.
EG *He took her arm and guided her through the door.*
4 If something guides you, it influences your actions or decisions.
EG *He let himself be guided by his instincts.*

guideline /'gaɪdlaɪn/
guidelines

NOUN
a piece of official advice about how something should be done
EG *... new government guidelines on the teaching of religion*

guilt /gɪlt/

NOUN
1 Guilt is an unhappy feeling of having done something wrong.
EG *Her emotions ranged from anger to guilt.*
2 Someone's guilt is the fact that they have done something wrong.
EG *I'm not convinced of his guilt.*

guilty /'gɪltɪ/
guiltier guiltiest

ADJECTIVE
1 If someone is **guilty of** doing something illegal or wrong, they did it.
EG *Both men were found guilty of murder.*
EG *She was advised to plead guilty.*
2 If you feel guilty, you are unhappy because you think you have done something wrong.
EG *There's no reason to feel guilty.*

A B C D E F G H I J K L M N O P Q R S T U V W X Y Z

guitar /gɪˈtɑːʳ/
guitars
NOUN
a musical instrument with six strings and a long neck
EG ... *an electric guitar*

gulf /gʌlf/
gulfs
NOUN
1 a very large bay
EG ... *the Gulf of Mexico*
2 a wide difference between two things or people
EG ... *the growing gulf between rich and poor*

gum /gʌm/
gums
NOUN
1 Gum is a flavoured substance that people chew but do not swallow.
EG ... *a stick of chewing gum*
2 Your gums are the firm flesh in which your teeth are set.
EG *The toothbrush had made his gums bleed.*

gun /gʌn/
guns
NOUN
a weapon which fires bullets or shells
EG *He aimed the gun and fired.*

gust /gʌst/
gusts
NOUN
a sudden rush of wind
EG *A gust of wind blew his hat off.*

guy /gaɪ/
guys
NOUN
AN INFORMAL WORD
a man
EG *He's an interesting guy.*

gym /dʒɪm/
gyms
NOUN
a room with special equipment for doing physical exercise
EG ... *the school gym*

Hh

abit /'hæbɪt/
habits

NOUN

A habit is something that you do often or regularly.

EG *He had a habit of smiling at everyone he saw.*

ad /hæd/

past participle and past tense of **have**

2 Had is often shortened to 'd: *he'd seen her before.*

air /heəʳ/
hairs

NOUN

1 Hair is the fine, thread-like material that grows on your head and body.

EG *He has black hair.*

EG *... the hairs on the back of his neck.*

2 You only talk about 'hairs' when you are referring to individual pieces of hair. When you are talking about all the hairs on your head, you say 'hair'.

3 An animal's hair is the rough, thread-like material that covers its body.

EG *I am allergic to cat hair.*

EG *There were dog hairs on the carpet.*

aircut /'heəkʌt/
aircuts

NOUN

1 If you have a haircut, someone cuts your hair for you.

EG *I need a haircut.*

2 A haircut is the style in which your hair has been cut.

EG *Who's the guy with the funny haircut?*

hairdresser /'heədresəʳ/
hairdressers

NOUN

a person who is trained to cut and style people's hair; you also refer to the shop where a hairdresser works as a hairdresser or a **hairdresser's**

EG *She works in a hairdresser's.*

hairy /'heərɪ/
hairier hairiest

ADJECTIVE

covered in hair

EG *... long hairy legs*

half /hɑːf/
halves

NOUN, ADJECTIVE, OR ADVERB

1 Half refers to one of two equal parts that make up a whole.

EG *... the second half of the match*

EG *They chatted for another half hour.*

EG *The bottle was only half full.*

ADVERB

2 You can use 'half' to say that something is only partly true.

EG *I half expected him to hit me.*

PREPOSITION

3 **half past** refers to a time that is thirty minutes after a particular hour

EG *... half past twelve*

halfway /'hɑːfweɪ/

ADVERB

at the middle of the distance between two points in space or time

EG *He stopped halfway down the ladder.*

EG *... halfway through the term*

hall /hɔːl/
halls

NOUN

1 the room just inside the front entrance of a house which leads into other rooms
EG *The lights were on in the hall.*

2 a large room or building used for public events
EG *... a concert hall*

halt /hɔːlt/
halts halting halted

VERB

1 When a person or vehicle halts, or when something halts them, they stop moving along.
EG *They halted at a short distance from the house.*

2 When an activity or process halts, or when something halts it, it stops completely.
EG *... an attempt to halt the country's economic decline*

NOUN

3 When something **comes to a halt**, it stops moving or developing.
EG *The elevator came to a halt.*

ham /hæm/

NOUN

Ham is meat from the back leg of a pig, usually eaten cold.
EG *... a ham sandwich*

hamburger /'hæmbɜːgər/
hamburgers

NOUN

a flat disc of chopped meat, fried and served in a bread roll
EG *A hamburger and large fries, please.*

hammer /'hæmər/
hammers hammering hammered

NOUN

1 a tool consisting of a heavy piece of metal at the end of a handle, used for hitting nails into things
EG *He dropped the hammer on his foot.*

VERB

2 If you hammer something, you hit it repeatedly with a hammer.
EG *Hammer a wooden peg into the hole.*

hamper /'hæmpər/
hampers hampering hampered

VERB

1 If something hampers you, it makes it difficult for you to do what you are trying to do.
EG *I was hampered by a lack of information.*

NOUN

2 a large basket with a lid, used for carrying food
EG *... a picnic hamper*

hand /hænd/
hands handing handed

NOUN

1 Your hands are the parts of your body at the ends of your arms, below the wrist.
EG *He put his hands in his pockets.*

2 If someone **has a hand in** something, they are involved in doing it or creating it.
EG *She had a hand in its design.*

3 If you **give** someone **a hand**, you help them to do something.
EG *Come and give me a hand in the garden.*

4 You use **on the one hand** and **on the other hand** to introduce the two parts of an argument or discussion that has two different points of view.
EG *On the one hand the house seems a bit expensive. On the other hand, it's just what we're looking f*

5 If you do something **by hand**, you do it using your hands rather than a machine.
EG *Each item was sewn by hand.*

6 The hands of a clock or watch are the thin pieces of metal or plastic that indicate what time it is.
EG *… the hour hand*

VERB
7 If you hand someone something or **hand** it **to** them, you give it to them.
EG *I asked him to hand it to me.*

handbag /ˈhændbæg/ **handbags**

NOUN
a small bag used mainly by women to carry money and personal items
EG *Her keys were stolen from her handbag.*

handful /ˈhændful/ **handfuls**

NOUN
1 A handful of something is the amount of it that you can hold in your hand.
EG *He picked up a handful of seeds.*

2 A handful of people or things is a small number of them.
EG *Only a handful of people knew.*

handicapped /ˈhændɪkæpt/

ADJECTIVE
A handicapped person has a physical or mental disability.
EG *Alex was mentally handicapped.*

handkerchief /ˈhæŋkətʃɪf/ **handkerchiefs**

NOUN
a small square of fabric used for blowing your nose
EG *… a folded white handkerchief*

handle /ˈhændl/ **handles handling handled**

NOUN
1 the part of a tool, bag, or cup that you hold in order to pick it up or use it
EG *… the broom handle*

2 a knob or bar that is attached to a door and used to open and close it
EG *I turned the handle and stepped inside.*

VERB
3 If you handle an object, you hold it or touch it with your hands.
EG *Wear rubber gloves when handling such substances.*

4 If you handle something, you deal with it successfully.
EG *I have learned how to handle pressure.*

handsome /ˈhænsəm/

ADJECTIVE
A handsome man has an attractive face.
EG *He's tall, dark and handsome.*

handwriting /ˈhændraɪtɪŋ/

NOUN
Someone's handwriting is their style of writing with a pen or pencil.
EG *The address was in Anna's handwriting.*

handy /ˈhændɪ/ **handier handiest**

ADJECTIVE
1 useful
EG *… handy hints on looking after indoor plants*

2 convenient and nearby
EG *Keep a pencil and paper handy.*

hang /hæŋ/ **hangs hanging hung**

VERB
1 If you hang something in a high place, or if it hangs there, it is

attached there so that it does not touch the ground.

EG ... a young woman hanging clothes on a washing line

EG His jacket hung from a hook on the door.

2 If someone **is hanged**, they are killed by suspending them by a rope around the neck.

EG He was hanged after being found guilty of spying.

☑ When 'hang' means to kill someone, the past tense and past participle are hanged.

hang about or hang around

VERB

AN INFORMAL USE

If you hang about or hang around somewhere, you stay or wait there.

EG ... a strange character who used to hang around outside the office

hang on

VERB

1 If you **hang on to** something, you hold it tightly or keep it.

EG She hung on to his legs to stop him from falling.

EG ... the President's attempts to hang on to power

2 AN INFORMAL USE

If someone asks you to hang on, they want you to wait.

EG Hang on, I'll be with you in a minute.

hang up

VERB

1 If you hang something up somewhere, or if it hangs up there, it is attached there so that it does not touch the ground.

EG The prisoners climbed onto the roof and hung up a banner.

EG ... the coats hanging up in the hall

2 If you hang up when you are speaking on the telephone, you put down the telephone and end the call.

EG Don't hang up on me!

happen /'hæpən/
happens happening happened

VERB

1 When something happens, it occurs or takes place.

EG Tell me what happened.

EG ... the best thing that has ever happened to me

2 If you **happen to do** something, you do it by chance.

EG I happened to notice his name in the paper.

happiness /'hæpɪnɪs/

NOUN

a feeling of great pleasure or joy

EG Money can't buy happiness.

happy /'hæpɪ/
happier happiest

ADJECTIVE

1 full of pleasure or joy

EG ... a confident, happy child

EG ... a happy childhood

2 If you are **happy with** something, you are satisfied with

EG I wasn't very happy with what I'd written.

3 If you are **happy to do** something, you are willing to do

EG I would be happy to help.

harbour /'hɑːbəʳ/
harbours
us **harbor**

NOUN

a protected area of deep water where boats can be moored

EG ... as the boat approached the harbour

hard /hɑːd/
harder hardest

ADJECTIVE OR ADVERB

1 Something that is hard requires a lot of effort.
EG *... hard work*
EG *They tried hard to attract tourists.*

2 Hard means with a lot of force.
EG *... a hard punch*
EG *I kicked a dustbin very hard.*
ADJECTIVE

3 Something that is hard is firm and does not bend or break easily.
EG *... the hard wooden floor*

4 Something that is hard is difficult.
EG *... a hard problem*
EG *It's hard to know what he means.*

5 Someone who is hard shows no pity or is not kind.
EG *Don't be hard on him.*

6 Hard drugs are very strong illegal drugs.
EG *... heroin and other hard drugs*

hardly /'hɑːdlɪ/
ADVERB

1 almost not or not quite
EG *I could hardly believe it.*
EG *There was hardly anyone there.*

2 certainly not
EG *It's hardly a secret.*

harm /hɑːm/
harms harming harmed
VERB

1 If you harm someone or something, you injure or damage them.
EG *The gang seemed anxious not to harm anyone.*
NOUN

2 Harm is injury or damage.
EG *To cut taxes now would do more harm than good.*

harmful /'hɑːmful/
ADJECTIVE

Harmful things have a bad effect on someone or something.
EG *... the harmful effects of smoking*

harmless /'hɑːmlɪs/
ADJECTIVE

Something that is harmless has no bad effects.
EG *... a harmless substitute for tobacco*

harsh /hɑːʃ/
harsher harshest
ADJECTIVE

1 Harsh living conditions or climates are severe and unpleasant.
EG *... harsh weather conditions*

2 Harsh actions or remarks are unkind and show no sympathy.
EG *... harsh criticism*

harvest /'hɑːvɪst/
harvests
NOUN

1 the harvest is the act of gathering a crop, or the time when this is done
EG *... at the start of the harvest*

2 A harvest is a crop that has been gathered.
EG *A big harvest is expected this year.*

has /hæz/
third person singular of the present tense of **have**
☑ *Has* is often shortened to *'s*: *he's got a gun.*

hasty /'heɪstɪ/
hastier hastiest
ADJECTIVE

Something that is hasty is done quickly and without preparation.
EG *... a hasty decision*

hat /hæt/
hats
NOUN

a covering for the head

EG ... *a large straw hat*

hatch /hætʃ/
hatches hatching hatched

VERB
1 When an egg hatches, or when a bird or reptile hatches, the egg breaks open and the young bird or reptile emerges.
EG *The young disappeared soon after they had hatched.*

2 If you hatch a plot, you plan it.
EG *He accused them of hatching a plot to kill him.*

NOUN
3 a small covered opening in a floor, wall, or ceiling
EG *He passed the plates through the serving hatch.*

hate /heɪt/
hates hating hated

VERB
1 If you hate someone or something, you dislike them very much.
EG *I hate the way he dresses.*

NOUN
2 Hate is a very strong feeling of dislike.
EG *... feelings of love or hate*

hatred /'heɪtrɪd/
NOUN
Hatred is a very strong feeling of dislike.
EG *... his hatred of his parents*

haunt /hɔːnt/
haunts haunting haunted

VERB
1 If a ghost haunts a place, it is seen or heard there regularly.
EG *His ghost is said to haunt the attic.*

2 If a memory or fear haunts you, it continually worries you.
EG *The decision to leave her children now haunts her.*

have /hæv/
has having had

☑ *Have, has* and *had* are often shortened to *'ve, 's* and *'d: I've nothing to say; she's been sick; he'd seen her before.*

AUXILIARY VERB
1 You use 'have' to form the past tense or to express completed actions.
EG *They have never met.*
EG *I have lost my watch.*

2 If you **have to do** something, you must do it.
EG *He had to go to Germany.*

VERB
3 If you have something, you own or possess it.
EG *We have two tickets for the concert.*
EG *Do you have any brothers or sisters?*
EG *She has blue eyes.*

4 If you have something, you experience it.
EG *I have an idea!*
EG *He had a marvellous time.*

5 If you have something in a particular position or state, it is in that position or state.
EG *Mary had her eyes closed.*
EG *They had the curtains open.*

6 If you have something done, someone does it for you or it happens to you.
EG *You've had your hair cut.*
EG *We had all our money stolen.*

7 When a woman has a baby, she gives birth to it.
EG *She had the baby last week.*

hazard /'hæzəd/
hazards

NOUN
A hazard is something which coul

be dangerous to you.
EG *... health hazards*

he /hiː/

PRONOUN
You use 'he' to refer to a man,
boy, or male animal.
EG *He lives in California.*

head /hed/
heads heading headed

NOUN
1 Your head is the part of your
body which has your eyes, brain,
and mouth in it.
EG *He shook his head sadly.*

2 Your head is your mind.
EG *I can't get that song out of my
head.*

3 The head of something is the
top or front of it, or the most
important end of it.
EG *... at the head of the list*
EG *... the head of the queue*
EG *... flower heads*

4 The head of a group or
organization is the person in
charge.
EG *... heads of government from
over 100 countries*

5 When you toss a coin, the side
called **heads** is the one with the
picture of a head on it.
EG *Heads or tails?*

VERB
6 If something heads a list or
group, it is at the top of it.
EG *Paris heads the list of Europe's
most expensive cities.*

7 If someone heads a group or
organization, they are in charge of
it.
EG *Bryce heads the sales team.*

8 If a piece of writing **is headed**
a particular title, it has that title.
EG *One chapter is headed "Beating
the System".*

9 If something **is heading for** a
particular place or outcome, it is
moving towards that place or
outcome.
EG *... a truck heading for the border*
EG *She's heading for a nervous
breakdown.*

10 If you head a ball, you hit it
with your head.
EG *He headed the ball across the
goal.*

headache /'hedeɪk/
headaches

NOUN
a pain in your head
EG *I've got a headache.*

headlight /'hedlaɪt/
headlights

NOUN
A vehicle's headlights are the large
bright lights at the front.
EG *He flashed his headlights at me.*

headline /'hedlaɪn/
headlines

NOUN
1 A headline is the title of a
newspaper story, printed in large
letters at the top of it.
EG *The headline said simply, "New
Planet Discovered".*

PLURAL NOUN
2 the headlines are the main
points of the radio or television
news
EG *Here are the headlines.*

headquarters /'hedkwɔːtəz/

PLURAL NOUN
The headquarters of an
organization are its main offices.
EG *... the army's headquarters in
Buenos Aires*
☑ You can use either a singular or
a plural verb after 'headquarters':
the headquarters is in New York;
the headquarters are in New York.

heal /hiːl/
heals healing healed

VERB

If something heals or if you heal it, it becomes healthy or normal again.

EG *His leg needs support while the bone is healing.*

EG *... an attempt to heal the wounds in the party*

health /hɛlθ/

NOUN

1 Your health is the condition of your body.

EG *Smoking is bad for your health.*

2 Health is a state in which you are fit and well.

EG *They nursed me back to health.*

healthy /'hɛlθɪ/
healthier healthiest

ADJECTIVE

1 Someone who is healthy is not ill.

EG *She was a very healthy child.*

2 Something that is healthy is good for you.

EG *... a healthy diet*

heap /hiːp/
heaps heaping heaped

NOUN

1 A heap of things is an untidy pile of them.

EG *... a heap of clothes*

VERB

2 If you heap things somewhere, you put them in a pile.

EG *She heaped more carrots onto Michael's plate.*

hear /hɪəʳ/
hears hearing heard

VERB

1 When you hear sounds, you are aware of them because they reach your ears.

EG *I could hear someone laughing upstairs.*

2 When you **hear from** someone, they write to you or phone you.

EG *I haven't heard from him in years.*

3 If you hear some news or information, someone tells you about it.

EG *Where did you hear of this school?*

EG *I heard that he was forced to resign.*

hearing /'hɪərɪŋ/

NOUN

Hearing is the sense which makes it possible for you to be aware of sounds.

EG *My hearing is poor.*

heart /hɑːt/
hearts

NOUN

1 Your heart is the organ in your chest that pumps the blood around your body.

EG *... the beating of his heart*

2 Your heart is thought of as the centre of your emotions, especially of love.

EG *She's got a good heart.*

EG *His heart filled with pride.*

EG *... matters of the heart*

3 The **heart of** something is its most central or important part.

EG *... in the heart of the city*

EG *... the heart of the problem*

4 Heart is courage, determination, or enthusiasm.

EG *They were losing heart.*

heart attack **heart attacks**

NOUN

If someone has a heart attack, their heart suddenly beats irregularly or stops completely.

EG *He died of a heart attack.*

heat /hiːt/
heats heating heated

NOUN

1 Heat is warmth or the quality of being hot.

EG *... the fierce heat of the sun*

2 The heat of something is its temperature.

EG *Adjust the heat of the oven.*

3 a contest or race in a competition which decides who will compete in the final

EG *She was eliminated in the heats.*

VERB

4 When you heat something, or when you **heat** it **up**, you raise its temperature.

EG *She heated up a pie for me.*

heaven /ˈhɛvn/

NOUN

In some religions, heaven is the place where God lives and where good people go when they die.

EG *She told them their mother was now in heaven.*

heavy /ˈhɛvɪ/
heavier heaviest

ADJECTIVE

1 Someone or something that is heavy weighs a lot.

EG *... a heavy suitcase*

2 You use 'heavy' to talk about how much someone or something weighs.

EG *How heavy are you?*

3 great in degree or amount

EG *... heavy casualties*

4 solid in appearance

EG *... heavy shoes*

5 involving a lot of force

EG *... a heavy blow*

hedge /hɛdʒ/
hedges

NOUN

a row of bushes along the edge of a garden, field, or road

EG *... a man cutting his hedge*

heel /hiːl/
heels

NOUN

1 Your heel is the back part of your foot, below your ankle.

EG *He had a plaster on his heel.*

2 The heel of a shoe is the raised part on the bottom at the back.

EG *... shoes with high heels*

height /haɪt/
heights

NOUN

1 The height of a person or object is their measurement from bottom to top.

EG *... a man of average height*

2 Height is the quality of being tall.

EG *His height causes him a lot of problems.*

3 The height of something is the distance that it is above the ground.

EG *The plane began to lose height.*

4 A height is a high position or place.

EG *He's afraid of heights.*

5 The height of something is the time when it is most successful or intense.

EG *... at the height of the tourist season*

heir /ɛəʳ/
heirs

NOUN

Someone's heir is the person who is entitled to inherit their property or title.

EG *... the heir to the throne*

held /hɛld/

past participle and past tense of **hold**

helicopter /ˈhɛlɪkɒptəʳ/
helicopters

NOUN

an aircraft with spinning blades instead of wings, which allow it to take off vertically

EG ... *a sea rescue involving two helicopters*

hell /hɛl/

NOUN

1 In some religions, hell is the place where the Devil lives and where wicked people are punished after they die.

EG ... *the fiery pit of hell*

2 AN INFORMAL USE

If you say that something is hell, you mean it is very unpleasant.

EG *Bullies can make your life hell.*

hello /həˈləʊ/

INTERJECTION

You say 'hello' as a greeting or when you answer the phone.

EG *Hello, Ray, how are you?*

helmet /ˈhɛlmɪt/
helmets

NOUN

a hard hat which you wear to protect your head

EG ... *a cycling helmet*

help /hɛlp/
helps helping helped

VERB

1 If someone or something helps you, they make something easier or better for you.

EG *She helped me wash the dishes.*

EG *The drugs have helped to ease the pain.*

2 If you **help yourself to** something, you serve yourself or take it for yourself.

EG *Help yourself to a beer.*

3 If you **can't help** something,

you cannot control it or stop it happening.

EG *I can't help feeling sorry for him.*

NOUN

4 Help is the assistance that someone or something gives you when you are in difficulty or danger.

EG *Thanks for your help.*

EG *The book wasn't much help.*

EG *He was screaming for help.*

helpful /ˈhɛlpfʊl/

ADJECTIVE

1 If someone is helpful, they help you in some way.

EG *The staff were very helpful.*

2 Something that is helpful makes a situation easier or better.

EG *You may find it helpful to take notes.*

helpless /ˈhɛlplɪs/

ADJECTIVE

If you are helpless, you are unable to protect yourself or to do anything useful.

EG ... *a helpless child*

hen /hɛn/
hens

NOUN

a female chicken

EG ... *a barn full of hens*

her /həːʳ/

PRONOUN OR ADJECTIVE

You use 'her' to refer to a woman, girl, or female animal that has already been mentioned.

EG *They gave her the job.*

EG *I went with Erica and her boyfriend.*

herb /həːb/
herbs

NOUN

a plant whose leaves are used as a medicine or to flavour food

EG *... herbs and spices*

herd /hɜːd/
herds herding herded

NOUN
1 a large group of animals
EG *... a herd of cattle*

VERB
2 If you herd animals or people somewhere, you make them move there as a group.
EG *We were herded onto the bus.*

here /hɪəʳ/

ADVERB
1 You use 'here' to mean the place where you are.
EG *She was here a minute ago.*
EG *Here's the taxi.*
EG *Come here!*

2 You use 'here' to mean in the place mentioned or indicated.
EG *... if you'll just sign here*

3 You use 'here' to refer to a time or situation that is happening now.
EG *Here's your chance to win a luxury holiday.*

4 here and there means in several different places
EG *He could only understand a few words here and there.*

heritage /'hɛrɪtɪdʒ/

NOUN
A country's heritage is all the traditions and possessions that have continued over many years.
EG *The building is an important part of our heritage.*

hero /'hɪərəʊ/
heroes

NOUN
1 the main male character in a book, film, or play
EG *... the author's decision to make his hero a photographer*

2 a person who has done something brave or good
EG *... a war hero*

heroin /'hɛrəʊɪn/

NOUN
Heroin is a powerful drug that is used to prevent pain and taken illegally by some people for pleasure.
EG *... a heroin addict*

heroine /'hɛrəʊɪn/
heroines

NOUN
1 the main female character in a book, film, or play
EG *The heroine works in TV.*

2 a woman who has done something brave or good
EG *... one of the heroines of the struggle*

hers /hɜːz/

PRONOUN
You use 'hers' to refer to something that belongs or relates to a woman, girl, or female animal.
EG *He'd never seen eyes as green as hers.*
EG *I'm a great friend of hers.*

herself /hɜːˈsɛlf/

PRONOUN
1 You use 'herself' to refer to a woman, girl, or female animal that has already been mentioned.
EG *She pulled herself out of the water.*

2 You use 'herself' to emphasize 'she'.
EG *She herself is Irish.*
EG *Louise herself had had a similar experience.*

hesitate /'hɛzɪteɪt/
hesitates hesitating hesitated

VERB
If you hesitate, you pause or show

uncertainty.

EG *She hesitated before replying.*

EG *Don't hesitate to ask for help.*

heterosexual

/ˌhɛtərəʊˈsɛksjuəl/

ADJECTIVE

Someone who is heterosexual is sexually attracted to people of the opposite sex.

EG *... heterosexual couples*

hi /haɪ/

INTERJECTION

AN INFORMAL WORD

You say 'hi' when you are greeting someone.

EG *Hi, Ingrid.*

hiccups /ˈhɪkʌps/ also spelt hiccoughs

PLURAL NOUN

Hiccups are short, uncontrolled sounds in your throat, often caused by eating or drinking something too quickly.

EG *She had hiccups throughout the film.*

hide /haɪd/
hides hiding hid hidden

VERB

1 If you hide something, you put it where it cannot be seen, or you prevent it from being discovered.

EG *She hid the book under a cushion.*

EG *He was unable to hide his disappointment.*

2 If you hide, you go somewhere where you cannot easily be seen or found.

EG *She hid behind a tree.*

high /haɪ/
higher highest; highs

ADJECTIVE OR ADVERB

1 tall or a long way above the ground

EG *... the high walls of the prison*

EG *He jumped high into the air.*

2 great in degree, quantity, or intensity

EG *high winds*

EG *Interest rates are likely to go even higher.*

ADJECTIVE

3 You use 'high' to talk about how much something measures from the bottom to the top.

EG *... a statue nine inches high*

EG *How high is the building?*

☑ You do not use 'high' to talk about the height of people. You use 'tall': *he was six feet tall*.

4 Something that is high is towards the top of a scale of importance or quality.

EG *This is one of our highest priorities.*

EG *... service of a very high standard*

5 AN INFORMAL USE

Someone who is **high on** a drug is affected by having taken it.

EG *He was too high on drugs to remember much.*

NOUN

6 a high point or level

EG *Morale reached a new high.*

highlight /ˈhaɪlaɪt/
highlights highlighting highlighted

VERB

1 If you highlight a point or problem, you draw attention to it.

EG *The report highlights a number of problem areas.*

PLURAL NOUN

2 The **highlights** of an event are the most exciting or interesting parts of it.

EG *The highlights of the match were shown on TV.*

highly /ˈhaɪlɪ/

ADVERB
extremely
EG *It is highly unlikely I'll be able to attend.*
EG *... highly skilled craftsmen*

high street high streets

NOUN
the main street in a town, where most of the shops are
EG *Health food shops are opening in every high street.*

highway /'haɪweɪ/ highways

NOUN
In American English, a highway is a main road, especially one that connects towns or cities.
EG *... a six-lane highway*

hilarious /hɪ'leərɪəs/

ADJECTIVE
very funny
EG *... a hilarious film.*

hill /hɪl/ hills

NOUN
a rounded area of land that is higher than the land surrounding it
EG *... a monument on the top of a hill*

him /hɪm/

PRONOUN
You use 'him' to refer to a man, boy, or male animal that has already been mentioned.
EG *He wants you to ring him back.*

himself /hɪm'self/

PRONOUN
1 You use 'himself' to refer to a man, boy, or male animal that has already been mentioned.
EG *He poured himself a whisky.*
2 You use 'himself' to emphasize 'he'.
EG *He himself can't swim.*

EG *The judge told me so himself.*

Hindu /'hɪnduː/ Hindus

NOUN
1 a person who believes in the Indian religion of Hinduism
EG *... an area mainly populated by Hindus*
ADJECTIVE
2 belonging or relating to Hinduism
EG *... a Hindu temple*

hint /hɪnt/ hints hinting hinted

NOUN
1 an indirect suggestion
EG *He gave no hint of what his plans might be.*
2 a helpful piece of advice
EG *The book offers handy hints on looking after indoor plants.*
VERB
3 If you hint that something is the case, you suggest it indirectly.
EG *The President hinted that he might make some changes.*

hip /hɪp/ hips

NOUN
Your hips are the two areas at the sides of your body between your waist and the tops of your legs.
EG *She put her hands on her hips.*

hire /'haɪər/ hires hiring hired

VERB
1 If you hire something, you pay money to use it for a period of time.
EG *Shall we hire a car for the weekend?*
2 If you hire someone, you pay them to do a job for you.
EG *He hired a top lawyer to defend*

A B C D E F G H I J K L M N O P Q R S T U V W X Y Z

him.

NOUN

3 Something that is **for hire** is available for people to hire.

EG *'Cycles for hire'*

his /hɪz/

ADJECTIVE OR PRONOUN

You use 'his' to refer to something that belongs or relates to a man, boy, or male animal.

EG *He spent most of his time abroad.*

EG *She's a good friend of his.*

historical /hɪˈstɒrɪkl/

ADJECTIVE

1 occurring in the past, or relating to the study of the past

EG *... historical events*

EG *... manuscripts of historical interest*

2 describing or representing the past

EG *... a historical novel*

history /ˈhɪstəri/
histories

NOUN

1 History is the study of the past.

EG *He's studying history at university.*

2 The history of a person, place, or subject is the set of facts that are known about them.

EG *... the boy's medical history*

hit /hɪt/
hits hitting hit

VERB

1 If you hit someone or something, you strike them with a lot of force, using your hand or an object held in your hand.

EG *He hit me on the head.*

EG *She hit the ball hard across the net.*

2 When a moving object hits

another object, it strikes it with a lot of force.

EG *The car had apparently hit a wall.*

3 If something hits a person, place, or thing, it affects them badly.

EG *... the earthquake which hit Peru*

NOUN

4 a record, play, or film that is very popular and successful

EG *The song became a massive hit.*

hitchhike /ˈhɪtʃhaɪk/
hitchhikes hitchhiking
hitchhiked

VERB

If you hitchhike, you travel by getting lifts from passing vehicles.

EG *He hitchhiked around Europe.*

HIV

NOUN

1 HIV is a virus that reduces people's resistance to illness and can cause AIDS.

EG *... people with HIV*

2 If someone is **HIV positive**, they are infected with HIV. If they are **HIV negative**, they are not infected with HIV.

EG *He admitted he was HIV positive.*

hobby /ˈhɒbi/
hobbies

NOUN

something that you do for pleasure in your spare time

EG *Do you have any hobbies?*

hockey /ˈhɒki/

NOUN

Hockey is a game in which two teams use long sticks with curved ends to try to hit a small ball into the other team's goal.

EG *... a hockey stick*

hold /həuld/

holds holding held

VERB

1 When you hold something, you carry or support it, using your hands or arms.
EG *Hold the baby while I load the car.*

2 If you hold something in a particular position, you keep it in that position.
EG *He held the door open for her.*

3 If something holds a particular amount, it can contain that amount.
EG *The case holds up to forty cassettes.*

4 'Hold' often means the same as 'have'.
EG *Some of the views he held were very strange.*
EG *The police plan to hold an investigation.*
EG *You can't hold a proper conversation with him.*

5 If you hold someone **responsible** for something, you consider that they are responsible for it.
EG *I will hold you personally responsible if we fail.*

6 If someone asks you to hold when you are speaking on the telephone, they want you to wait for a short time.
EG *The line is engaged — will you hold?*

7 If you are held in a place, you are kept there as a prisoner.
EG *I was held overnight in a cell.*

NOUN

8 Your **hold on** something is the fact that you are holding it.
EG *He released his hold on the camera.*

9 If someone or something has a **hold over** you, they have power or influence over you.
EG *The party has a considerable hold over him.*

10 If you **grab hold of** something or **catch hold of** it, you close your hand tightly around it.
EG *He grabbed hold of the rope.*

11 If you **get hold of** someone or something, you manage to get them or find them.
EG *It's hard to get hold of guns in this country.*

hold on

VERB

1 If you **hold on to** something, you keep your hand firmly round it.
EG *He was trying to hold on to a rock when he fell.*

2 If you **hold on to** something, you keep it and prevent other people from getting it.
EG *… a politician who knew how to hold on to power*

3 If someone asks you to hold on, they want you to wait for a short time.
EG *Hold on a minute, I'll be right back.*

hole /həul/
holes

NOUN

an opening or hollow space in something
EG *… socks with holes in them*
EG *He dug a deep hole in the garden.*

holiday /'hɒlɪdeɪ/
holidays

NOUN

1 a period of time spent away from home for pleasure
EG *We're going to Scotland for our holidays.*
EG *I went on holiday to Greece.*

A B C D E F G H I J K L M N O P Q R S T U V W X Y Z

2 a day when people do not go to work or school because of a national festival

EG *New Year's Day is a public holiday.*

☑ If you talk about 'your holidays', you mean a time spent away from home. If you talk about 'the holidays', you mean a time when people do not go to work or school.

hollow /'hɔləʊ/

ADJECTIVE

1 Something that is hollow has a hole or space inside it.

EG *... a hollow tree*

2 A statement or situation that is hollow has no real value or worth.

EG *... a hollow threat*

holy /'həʊlɪ/
holier holiest

ADJECTIVE

1 Something that is holy relates to God or to a particular religion.

EG *This is a holy place.*

2 Someone who is holy is religious and leads a pure and good life.

EG *... a holy man*

home /'həʊm/
homes

NOUN

1 Your home is the house or flat where you live.

EG *They stayed at home and watched TV.*

EG *She wanted to go home.*

2 Your home is the place or country where you live or feel that you belong.

EG *She has made Switzerland her home.*

3 a building in which elderly or ill people live and receive care

EG *... a home for handicapped children*

homeless /'həʊmlɪs/

ADJECTIVE

Someone who is homeless has nowhere to live.

EG *... the growing number of homeless families*

homesick /'həʊmsɪk/

ADJECTIVE

If you are homesick, you are unhappy because you are away from home and miss your family and friends.

EG *She's feeling a little homesick.*

homework /'həʊmwɜːk/

NOUN

Homework is school work given to pupils to do at home.

EG *Have you done your homework?*

homosexual /hɔməʊ'seksjʊəl/

ADJECTIVE

Someone who is homosexual is sexually attracted to people of the same sex.

EG *... a homosexual relationship*

honest /'ɔnɪst/

ADJECTIVE

Someone who is honest always tells the truth and does not try to deceive people.

EG *... an honest man*

EG *I'll be honest with you.*

honesty /'ɔnɪstɪ/

NOUN

Honesty is the quality of being honest.

EG *I can answer you with complete honesty.*

honey /'hʌnɪ/

NOUN

Honey is a sweet substance made by bees and eaten as food.

EG *... a jar of honey*

honeymoon /'hʌnɪmuːn/

honeymoons

NOUN

a holiday taken by a couple who have just got married

EG *They went to Bermuda for their honeymoon.*

honour /ˈɒnəʳ/
honours honouring honoured
US **honor**

NOUN

1 Your honour is your good reputation and the respect that other people have for you.

EG *He felt that his honour was at stake.*

2 An honour is an award given to someone for something they have done.

EG *She was showered with honours, among them an Oscar.*

3 If you describe doing something as an honour, you mean that you feel privileged to do it.

EG *It's an honour to work with her.*

VERB

4 If you honour someone, you give them special praise or attention, or an award.

EG *He was honoured by the Pope.*

5 If you say that you are **honoured to do** something, you mean that you feel privileged to do it.

EG *I feel honoured to have been chosen.*

hood /hud/
hoods

NOUN

1 a loose covering for the head, usually part of a coat or jacket

EG *... pulling her hood up against the rain*

2 In American English, the hood of a car is the cover over the engine at the front.

EG *The mechanic had the hood up to work on the engine.*

☑ The usual British word is *bonnet.*

hook /huk/
hooks hooking hooked

NOUN

1 a curved piece of metal or plastic that is used for catching things or for holding things up

EG *... a fish hook*

EG *... curtain hooks*

VERB

2 If you **hook** one thing **to** or **onto** another, you attach it there using a hook.

EG *He hooked the caravan to the car.*

hooray /huːˈreɪ/
another spelling of **hurray**

hop /hɒp/
hops hopping hopped

VERB

1 If you hop, you jump on one foot.

EG *... a game in which everyone had to hop*

2 When animals or birds hop, they jump with two feet together.

EG *... frogs hopping across the road*

3 AN INFORMAL USE

If you hop somewhere, you move there quickly and easily.

EG *We were late, so we hopped into a taxi.*

hope /həup/
hopes hoping hoped

VERB

1 If you hope that something will happen, you want or expect it to happen.

EG *I hope he agrees.*

EG *"Is he coming to the party?" — "I hope so."*

2 If you **hope to do** something, you think that it is possible or likely that you will do it.
EG *She hopes to arrive next Monday.*
NOUN
3 Hope is the wish or expectation that things will go well in the future.
EG *... the hopes and dreams of our ancestors*
EG *There is little hope of success.*

hopeful /'həupful/
ADJECTIVE
If you are hopeful, you are fairly confident that something you want to happen will happen.
EG *Surgeons are hopeful that her sight can be saved.*

hopeless /'həuplɪs/
ADJECTIVE
1 without hope
EG *They feel hopeless about their prospects.*
2 certain to be unsuccessful
EG *... a hopeless situation*

horizon /hə'raɪzn/
horizons
NOUN
The horizon is the distant line where the sky seems to touch the land or sea.
EG *The sun had already sunk below the horizon.*

horizontal /hɒrɪ'zɒntl/
ADJECTIVE
flat and parallel with the ground
EG *... a pattern of vertical and horizontal lines*

horn /hɔːn/
horns
NOUN
1 On a vehicle, a horn is a warning device which makes a loud noise.
EG *He beeped his horn at her.*

2 On a cow or goat, the horns are the hard, pointed things that grow from its head.
EG *... the horns of a bull*

horrible /'hɒrɪbl/
ADJECTIVE
very unpleasant
EG *... a horrible little boy*

horror /'hɒrər/
horrors
NOUN
Horror is a strong feeling of alarm caused by something very unpleasant.
EG *He gazed in horror at the knife.*
EG *... the horrors of war*

horse /hɔːs/
horses
NOUN
a large animal which people can ride
EG *... a man on a horse*

hospital /'hɒspɪtl/
hospitals
NOUN
a place where sick people are looked after by doctors and nurses
EG *... a children's hospital*
EG *... when my mother went into hospital*

host /həust/
hosts hosting hosted
NOUN
1 The host at a party is the person who invited the guests and who provides the food or drink.
EG *He was always the perfect host.*
2 A **host of** things is a large number of them.
EG *... for a whole host of reasons*
VERB
3 If a person or place hosts an event, they organize it or act as host at it.

EG *... when Barcelona hosted the Olympic Games*

hostage /'hɒstɪdʒ/
hostages

NOUN
a person who is illegally held prisoner and threatened with harm unless certain demands are met
EG *... before the two hostages were released*

hostel /'hɒstl/
hostels

NOUN
a large house where people can stay cheaply for a short time
EG *... a youth hostel*

hostile /'hɒstaɪl/

ADJECTIVE
If someone is hostile to you, they behave aggressively towards you.
EG *... a hostile audience*

hot /hɒt/
hotter hottest

ADJECTIVE
1 Someone or something that is hot has a high temperature.
EG *Aren't you hot in that coat?*
EG *... hot water*
EG *It's so hot today.*

2 You can say that food is hot when it has a burning taste caused by spices.
EG *... a hot curry*

hot dog **hot dogs**

NOUN
a long bread roll with a sausage in it
EG *... a hot dog with ketchup and mustard*

hotel /həʊ'tɛl/
hotels

NOUN
a building where people stay, paying for their room and meals
EG *... a five-star hotel*

hour /'aʊər/
hours

NOUN
1 a period of 60 minutes
EG *The journey took three hours.*
EG *... half an hour later*

PLURAL NOUN
2 The **hours** during which something happens are the period of time during which it happens.
EG *Phone us during office hours.*

house /haʊs/
houses housing housed

NOUN
1 a building where people live, or the people who live there
EG *... her parents' house in Kent*
EG *His cries woke the whole house.*

2 a particular type of building or company
EG *... the opera house*
EG *... a publishing house*

VERB : /haʊz/
☑ Note that you pronounce the verb differently from the noun.

3 If a building houses something, that thing is kept in the building.
EG *The gallery houses the university's art collection.*

House of Commons

NOUN
The House of Commons is the more powerful of the two parts of the British Parliament. Its members are elected by the public.
EG *The House of Commons has rejected the proposal.*

House of Lords

A
B
C
D
E
F
G
H
I
J
K
L
M
N
O
P
Q
R
S
T
U
V
W
X
Y
Z

NOUN
The House of Lords is the less powerful of the two parts of the British Parliament. Its members are not elected.
EG ... a member of the House of Lords

housewife /'hauswaɪf/
housewives

NOUN
a married woman who does not have a paid job, but instead looks after her home and children
EG ... a housewife and mother of three

housing /'hauzɪŋ/

NOUN
Housing is the buildings that people live in.
EG ... the serious shortage of housing

hover /'hɒvəʳ/
hovers hovering hovered

VERB
When a bird, insect, or aircraft hovers, it stays in the same position in the air.
EG A helicopter hovered overhead.

how /hau/

ADVERB
1 You use 'how' to ask about the way that something happens.
EG How did you find out?
EG We still don't know how he died.

2 You use 'how' to ask about amounts and quantities.
EG How much does it cost?
EG I wonder how old he is.

3 You use 'how' when you asking about someone's health or about the success of something.
EG How are you?
EG How was your holiday?

4 You use 'how' to emphasize the degree to which something is true.
EG I didn't realize how heavy you were.

5 You use expressions such as **how about...** or **how would you like...** when you are making a suggestion or an offer.
EG How about a drink?
EG How would you like to earn some money?

however /hau'ɛvəʳ/

ADVERB
1 You use 'however' when you are adding a comment which contrasts with what has just been said.
EG Much of the house needs repairing. However, the roof is new.

2 You use 'however' to say that something makes no difference to a situation.
EG However hard she tried, nothing seemed to work.

hug /hʌg/
hugs hugging hugged

VERB
1 If you hug someone, you put your arms round them and hold them close to you.
EG Lynn and I hugged each other.

NOUN
2 the act of hugging someone
EG There were lots of hugs and kisses.

huge /hju:dʒ/
huger hugest

ADJECTIVE
extremely large in amount, size, or degree
EG ... a huge success
EG ... a huge crowd

hum /hʌm/

hums humming hummed

VERB

1 If something hums, it makes a continuous low noise.
EG *The generator hummed faintly.*

2 If you hum, you sing with your lips closed.
EG *She was humming to herself.*

NOUN

3 a continuous low noise
EG *... the hum of the fridge*

human /'hju:mən/ humans

ADJECTIVE

1 relating to or concerning people
EG *... the human race*
EG *The crash was the result of human error.*

NOUN

2 a person
EG *Pollution affects animals as well as humans.*

human being human beings

NOUN

a person
EG *... the first human being in space*

humanity /hju:'mænɪtɪ/

NOUN

Humanity is people in general.
EG *I have faith in humanity.*

humour /'hju:mə^r/ humours humouring humoured
us **humor**

NOUN

1 Humour is the quality of being funny.
EG *He failed to see the humour of the situation.*

2 Humour is the ability to find certain things amusing.
EG *Helen's got a peculiar sense of humour.*

VERB

3 If you humour someone, you try to please them, so that they will not become upset.
EG *He nodded, partly to humour her.*

hundred /'hʌndrəd/ hundreds

the number 100
EG *... one hundred miles*
EG *... hundreds of people*

hundredth /'hʌndrədθ/ hundredths

ADJECTIVE

1 The hundredth item in a series is the one counted as number one hundred.
EG *... the hundredth year*

NOUN

2 one of a hundred equal parts
EG *... a hundredth of a second*

hung /hʌŋ/

past participle and past tense of **hang**

hunger /'hʌŋgə^r/

NOUN

Hunger is the need or desire to eat.
EG *His hunger prevented him from concentrating.*
EG *Thousands could die of hunger.*

hungry /'hʌŋgrɪ/ hungrier hungriest

ADJECTIVE

When you are hungry, you want food.
EG *Are you hungry?*

hunt /hʌnt/ hunts hunting hunted

VERB

1 When people hunt, they chase and kill wild animals for food or

A
B
C
D
E
F
G
H
I
J
K
L
M
N
O
P
Q
R
S
T
U
V
W
X
Y
Z

sport.

EG As a child I learned to hunt and fish.

2 If you **hunt for** something, you search for it.

EG ... the weeks he'd spent hunting for a flat

NOUN

3 the act of searching for something

EG ... the hunt for the missing child

hurl /hɜːl/
hurls hurling hurled

VERB

If you hurl something, you throw it with great force.

EG Groups of angry youths hurled stones at police.

hurray /hu'reɪ/
or **hurrah** or **hooray**

INTERJECTION

People sometimes say "hurray" when they are very happy or excited.

EG It's Friday! Hurray!

hurricane /'hʌrɪkən/
hurricanes

NOUN

a very violent storm with strong winds

EG ... the hurricane that destroyed the town

hurry /'hʌrɪ/
hurries hurrying hurried

VERB

1 If you hurry somewhere, you go there quickly.

EG She hurried through the empty streets.

2 If you **hurry to do** something, you try to do it quickly or soon.

EG She hurried to apologise for her remarks.

3 If you hurry someone or something, or if you **hurry** them **up**, you try to make something happen more quickly.

EG ... an attempt to hurry up the process

NOUN

4 If you are **in a hurry**, you want to do something quickly.

EG He was in a hurry to leave.

5 If you do something **in a hurry**, you do it quickly.

EG She left town in a hurry.

hurry up

VERB

If you tell someone to hurry up, you want them to do something more quickly.

EG Hurry up, we'll be late.

hurt /hɜːt/
hurts hurting hurt

VERB

1 If you hurt someone, you cause them physical pain.

EG Sorry, did I hurt you?

2 If a part of your body hurts, you feel pain there.

EG My leg really hurts.

3 If you hurt a part of your body or **hurt yourself**, you injure yourself.

EG He fell and hurt his back.

EG Have you hurt yourself?

4 If you hurt someone, you upset them by being unkind towards them.

EG I didn't want to hurt his feelings.

ADJECTIVE

5 If you are hurt, you are injured.

EG His comrades asked him if he was hurt.

6 If you feel hurt, you are upset because of someone's unkindness towards you.
EG *He felt hurt by all the lies.*

husband /'hʌzbənd/
husbands

NOUN

A woman's husband is the man she is married to.
EG *She married her first husband in 1982.*

hut /hʌt/
huts

NOUN

a small, simple building, with only one or two rooms
EG *... a wooden hut in the forest*

hyphen /'haɪfn/
hyphens

NOUN

The **hyphen** is the symbol - that joins two different parts together in some words.
EG *Anna was re-elected president.*
EG *She is left-handed.*

A
B
C
D
E
F
G
H
I
J
K
L
M
N
O
P
Q
R
S
T
U
V
W
X
Y
Z

Ii

I /aɪ/

PRONOUN

You use 'I' to refer to yourself.

EG *I like your hat.*

EG *Jim and I are getting married.*

ice /aɪs/

NOUN

Ice is water that has frozen solid.

EG *There was ice on the roads.*

ice cream ice creams

NOUN

Ice cream is a very cold sweet food made from frozen cream.

EG *I'll get you some ice cream.*

EG *She bought the children ice creams.*

ice-skate /ˈaɪsskeɪt/
**ice-skates ice-skating
ice-skated**

NOUN

1 Ice-skates are boots with a metal blade on the bottom, which you wear when skating on ice.

EG *... a pair of ice-skates*

VERB

2 If you ice-skate, you move about on ice wearing ice-skates.

EG *We went ice-skating.*

ID

NOUN

ID is a document such as a driving licence or passport, which states who you are. ID is short for 'identification'.

EG *Could I see some ID, please?*

idea /aɪˈdɪə/
ideas

NOUN

1 a plan or possible course of action

EG *I've got a brilliant idea.*

2 an opinion or belief

EG *He has some strange ideas about women.*

3 If you have an idea of something, you have a general but not a detailed knowledge of it.

EG *Could you give me an idea of the cost?*

EG *I have no idea where he is.*

ideal /aɪˈdɪəl/

ADJECTIVE

The ideal person or thing for a particular purpose is the best possible one.

EG *He's the ideal person for the job.*

identical /aɪˈdentɪkl/

ADJECTIVE

exactly the same

EG *... identical twins*

EG *Her dress was identical to mine.*

identification
/aɪdentɪfɪˈkeɪʃən/

NOUN

1 Identification is a document such as a driving licence or passport, which states who you are.

EG *Unfortunately I had no identification on me.*

2 The identification of someone or something is the act of identifying them.

EG *... the early identification of a disease*

identify /aɪˈdentɪfaɪ/
**identifies identifying
identified**

VERB

1 If you identify someone or something, you are able to recognize them or name them.

EG *... the task of identifying the*

body

2 If you **identify with** someone, you understand their feelings and ideas.

EG *She identifies closely with the characters she plays.*

identity /aɪˈdɛntɪtɪ/
identities

NOUN

Your identity is who you are.

EG *The police soon established his true identity.*

idiot /ˈɪdɪət/
idiots

NOUN

someone who is stupid or foolish

EG *I was an idiot to have believed her.*

i.e.

i.e. means 'that is' and is used before giving more information

EG *... strategic points, i.e. airports or military bases*

if /ɪf/

CONJUNCTION

1 You use 'if' to introduce the circumstances in which an event or situation might happen or might have happened.

EG *I'll stay if I can.*

EG *She gets angry if I interrupt her.*

EG *Is there a bus? If not, I'll walk.*

2 whether

EG *I asked her if she wanted to come shopping.*

ignore /ɪgˈnɔːʳ/
ignores ignoring ignored

VERB

If you ignore someone or something, you deliberately take no notice of them.

EG *I ignored his unkind remarks.*

ill /ɪl/

ADJECTIVE

1 unhealthy or sick

EG *I was feeling ill.*

2 harmful or unpleasant

EG *Did you suffer any ill effects?*

illegal /ɪˈliːgl/

ADJECTIVE

forbidden by the law

EG *... an illegal organization*

EG *Birth control was illegal there until 1978.*

illness /ˈɪlnɪs/
illnesses

NOUN

1 Illness is the state or experience of being ill.

EG *... the treatment of mental illness*

2 An illness is a particular disease.

EG *... common illnesses such as coughs and colds*

illustrate /ˈɪləstreɪt/
illustrates illustrating illustrated

VERB

1 If something illustrates a fact, it shows that the fact is true.

EG *This incident illustrates the weakness of the system.*

2 If you illustrate a point when you are speaking, you make its meaning clearer, often by giving examples.

EG *Let me give another example to illustrate my point.*

3 If a book is illustrated, it has pictures in it.

EG *... an illustrated Bible*

image /ˈɪmɪdʒ/
images

NOUN

1 a mental picture

EG *The name conjures up images of sun and sand.*

2 a picture or photograph

EG *... her image on the TV screen*

3 the appearance which a person or organization presents to the public
EG *The tobacco industry has been trying to improve its image.*

imaginary /ɪˈmædʒɪnərɪ/
ADJECTIVE
Something that is imaginary exists only in someone's mind.
EG *... the creation of an imaginary world*

imagination /ɪmædʒɪˈneɪʃən/
imaginations
NOUN
Your imagination is your ability to form pictures and ideas in your mind, especially new or exciting ideas.
EG *She has a vivid imagination.*
EG *The approach shows a lack of imagination.*

imagine /ɪˈmædʒɪn/
imagines imagining imagined
VERB
1 If you imagine something, you form a picture or idea of it in your mind.
EG *Can you imagine how I felt?*
2 If you imagine something, you think you have experienced it but actually you have not.
EG *I must have imagined the whole thing.*
3 If you imagine that something is true, you think it is true.
EG *I imagine he's dead now.*

imitate /ˈɪmɪteɪt/
imitates imitating imitated
VERB
If you imitate someone or something, you copy them.
EG *He walked behind her, imitating everything she did.*

immediate /ɪˈmiːdɪət/
ADJECTIVE
1 Something that is immediate happens or is done without delay.
EG *The announcement had an immediate effect.*
2 very close in time, space, or relationship
EG *... in the immediate neighbourhood*
EG *... his immediate superior*

immediately /ɪˈmiːdɪətlɪ/
ADVERB
1 If something happens immediately, it happens without any delay.
EG *She answered his letter immediately.*
EG *The reasons for this may not be immediately obvious.*
2 very close in time or space
EG *... immediately behind the house*

immense /ɪˈmens/
ADJECTIVE
very large in size or amount
EG *... an immense cloud of smoke*
EG *I felt immense relief.*

immigrant /ˈɪmɪɡrənt/
immigrants
NOUN
someone who has come to live in a country from another country
EG *... illegal immigrants*

immigration /ɪmɪˈɡreɪʃən/
NOUN
1 Immigration is the fact or process of people coming into a country in order to live and work there.
EG *... stricter controls on immigration*
2 Immigration is the place at a port, airport, or border where officials check people's passports.

279

immoral – important

A B C D E F G H I J K L M N O P Q R S T U V W X Y Z

EG *She was interviewed for an hour at immigration.*

immoral /ɪˈmɒrl/

ADJECTIVE

If you describe someone or their behaviour as immoral, you mean that their behaviour is morally wrong.

EG *... people who think that abortion is immoral*

immune /ɪˈmjuːn/

ADJECTIVE

If you are **immune to** a disease, you cannot be affected by it.

EG *This test will show whether you're immune to the disease.*

impact /ˈɪmpækt/
impacts

NOUN

1 If something has or makes an **impact on** a situation or person, it has a strong effect on them.

EG *Her speech had a powerful impact on everyone.*

EG *He wanted to make an immediate impact on the audience.*

2 The impact of one object on another is the force with which it hits it.

EG *The track should absorb the impact of the runner's foot.*

impatient /ɪmˈpeɪʃənt/

ADJECTIVE

1 If you are impatient, you are annoyed because you do not want to wait for something.

EG *Some countries are growing impatient with the slow pace of reform.*

2 If you are **impatient to do** something, you are eager to do it and do not want to wait.

EG *He was impatient to get home.*

implication /ɪmplɪˈkeɪʃən/

implications

NOUN

The implications of something are the things that are likely to happen as a result of it.

EG *... the political implications of his decision*

imply /ɪmˈplaɪ/
implies implying implied

VERB

If you imply that something is the case, you suggest it in an indirect way.

EG *Are you implying that it was my fault?*

import /ɪmˈpɔːt/
imports importing imported

VERB

1 When a country or company imports a product, they buy it from another country for use in their own country.

EG *... the cost of importing goods from Europe*

NOUN : /ˈɪmpɔːt/

☑ Note the change in stress.

2 Imports are products bought from another country for use in your own country.

EG *... imports and exports*

importance /ɪmˈpɔːtns/

NOUN

The importance of something is its quality of being important.

EG *... the importance of safety in car design*

important /ɪmˈpɔːtnt/

ADJECTIVE

1 Something that is important is very valuable, necessary, or significant.

EG *Her sons are the most important thing in her life.*

EG *Money simply isn't important to*

him.

2 An important person has a lot of influence or power.

EG *... the most important man on the island*

impose /ɪmˈpəuz/
imposes imposing imposed

VERB

1 If you **impose** something **on** people, you force them to accept it.

EG *Parents should beware of imposing their own tastes on their children.*

2 If someone **imposes on** you, they expect you to do something for them which you do not want to do.

EG *We didn't want to impose on them by staying longer.*

impossible /ɪmˈpɒsɪbl/

ADJECTIVE

Something that is impossible cannot happen or be done.

EG *That's impossible!*

EG *The law is impossible to enforce.*

impress /ɪmˈpres/
impresses impressing impressed

VERB

1 If someone or something impresses you, they cause you to admire them.

EG *... a group of students who were trying to impress their girlfriends*

2 If you **impress** something **on** someone, you make them understand the importance of it.

EG *I had always impressed the need for safety on him.*

impression /ɪmˈpreʃən/
impressions

NOUN

An impression of someone or

something is the way they look or seem to you.

EG *What were your first impressions of college?*

EG *He gave the impression of not caring.*

impressive /ɪmˈpresɪv/

ADJECTIVE

If something is impressive, you admire it.

EG *The film's special effects are particularly impressive.*

imprison /ɪmˈprɪzn/
imprisons imprisoning imprisoned

VERB

If someone **is imprisoned**, they are locked up or kept somewhere.

EG *He was imprisoned for 18 months for drug offences.*

improve /ɪmˈpruːv/
improves improving improved

VERB

If something improves or if you improve it, it gets better.

EG *The weather is beginning to improve.*

EG *He wants to improve his French.*

improvement
/ɪmˈpruːvmənt/
improvements

NOUN

If there is an **improvement** in something, it becomes better.

EG *... the dramatic improvement in his finances*

EG *There's still room for improvement.*

impulse /ˈɪmpʌls/
impulses

NOUN

a strong urge to do something

EG *She felt a sudden impulse to*

confide in someone.

in /ɪn/

PREPOSITION

1 You use 'in' to indicate the place where something is or the place where it is contained.
EG … a school in England
EG He put the plate in the cupboard.

2 You use 'in' to indicate the thing that something is part of.
EG … the best scene in the film
EG There are twelve students in my class.

3 You use 'in' to indicate the time when something happens.
EG I arrived in the afternoon.
EG She was born in 1960.

4 You use 'in' to indicate how long something takes or how long it will be before something happens.
EG She wrote the book in two years.
EG I'll be back in a minute.

5 You use 'in' to indicate the way that something is or the way that it is done.
EG The house was in ruins.
EG Dave looked up in surprise.

ADVERB

6 If you are in, you are present at your home or place of work.
EG My brother wasn't in when I called.

7 If someone or something comes in, they enter a place.
EG They shook hands and went in.

in- /ɪn/

PREFIX

In- is added to the beginning of some words to form a word with the opposite meaning.
EG … inappropriate
EG … indirect

in. /ɪntʃ, 'ɪntʃɪz/
ins.

an abbreviation for 'inch' or

'inches'
EG … 5 ft. 10 in.

incentive /ɪn'sentɪv/
incentives

NOUN

If something is an **incentive to do** something, it encourages you to do it.
EG There was little incentive to continue.

inch /ɪntʃ/
inches

NOUN

a unit of length equal to about 2.54 centimetres
EG His face was a few inches from hers.

incident /'ɪnsɪdnt/
incidents

NOUN

an event, often one that involves something unpleasant
EG … a dramatic shooting incident

inclined /ɪn'klaɪnd/

ADJECTIVE

If you are **inclined to do** something, you often do that thing or you want to do that thing.
EG … or, if you are so inclined, you can go sailing
EG No one felt inclined to argue with him.

include /ɪn'kluːd/
includes including included

VERB

If one thing includes another, the second thing is part of the first thing.
EG A good British breakfast always includes sausages.
EG Meals are included in the price.

including /ɪn'kluːdɪŋ/

PREPOSITION

You use 'including' to give

examples of things that are part of the group of things that you are talking about.

EG *Six people, including two police officers, were injured.*

income /'ɪnkʌm/
incomes

NOUN
the money that a person earns
EG *... families on low incomes*

income tax

NOUN
Income tax is a part of your income that you have to pay regularly to the government.
EG *... the basic rate of income tax*

increase /ɪn'kriːs/
increases increasing increased

VERB
1 If something increases, or if you increase it, it becomes larger in number, level, or amount.
EG *The population continues to increase.*
EG *The government has increased the amount of money available.*

NOUN : /'ɪnkriːs/
☑ Note the change in stress.
2 An **increase in** something is a rise in the number, level, or amount of it.
EG *... a sharp increase in road accidents*

incredible /ɪn'krɛdɪbl/

ADJECTIVE
1 wonderful
EG *I had an incredible holiday.*
2 difficult to believe
EG *It's incredible that he survived.*

indeed /ɪn'diːd/

ADVERB
You use 'indeed' to emphasize what you are saying.

EG *The wine was very good indeed.*
EG *Yes indeed, I quite agree.*

independent /ɪndɪ'pɛndnt/

ADJECTIVE
1 Something that is independent is separate from other people or things, so that it is not affected by them.
EG *Results are assessed by an independent panel.*
EG *... the newly independent countries of Eastern Europe*
2 Someone who is independent does not need other people's help.
EG *... a fiercely independent woman*

index /'ɪndɛks/
indexes

NOUN
an alphabetical list at the back of a book, referring to items in the book
EG *He looked for his name in the index.*

Indian /'ɪndɪən/
Indians

ADJECTIVE
1 belonging or relating to India
EG *... an Indian film*

NOUN
2 someone who comes from India
EG *... a successful young Indian*
3 someone descended from the people who lived in North, South, or Central America before Europeans arrived
EG *... the culture of the South American Indians*

indicate /'ɪndɪkeɪt/
indicates indicating indicated

VERB
1 If something indicates something, it shows that it is true.
EG *... a gesture which clearly indicated his relief*

2 If you indicate something, you point to it.
EG *He took my coat and indicated the chair beside him.*

3 If you indicate an opinion or intention, you mention it.
EG *He has indicated that he may leave.*

4 If the driver of a vehicle indicates, they operate flashing lights to show which way they are going to turn.
EG *... a driver who had failed to indicate*

individual /ɪndɪˈvɪdjuəl/
individuals

ADJECTIVE

1 relating to one particular person or thing
EG *Each family needs individual attention.*

NOUN

2 a person
EG *... wealthy individuals*

indoor /ˈɪndɔːr/

ADJECTIVE

situated or happening inside a building
EG *... an indoor market*

indoors /ɪnˈdɔːz/

ADVERB

inside a building
EG *Perhaps we should go indoors.*

indulge /ɪnˈdʌldʒ/
indulges indulging indulged

VERB

If you **indulge in** something, you allow yourself to do something that you enjoy.
EG *Only rarely will she indulge in a glass of wine.*

industrial /ɪnˈdʌstrɪəl/

ADJECTIVE

relating to industry

EG *... industrial equipment*

industry /ˈɪndəstrɪ/
industries

NOUN

1 Industry is the work and processes involved in making things in factories.
EG *... the use of robots in industry*

2 A particular industry is all the people and processes involved in manufacturing a particular thing.
EG *... the film industry*

inevitable /ɪnˈevɪtəbl/

ADJECTIVE

certain to happen
EG *If the case succeeds, it's inevitable that other trials will follow.*

infant /ˈɪnfənt/
infants

NOUN

a baby or very young child
EG *... young mums with infants in prams*

infect /ɪnˈfekt/
infects infecting infected

VERB

If someone or something infects someone, they cause them to have a disease.
EG *... people infected with HIV*

infection /ɪnˈfekʃən/
infections

NOUN

1 Infection is the state of being infected.
EG *... a very small risk of infection*

2 a disease caused by germs
EG *... a chest infection*

inferior /ɪnˈfɪərɪər/

ADJECTIVE

Something that is **inferior to** another thing is not as good as it.
EG *Comprehensive schools were*

A
B

regarded as inferior to grammar schools.
EG *The tapes were of inferior quality.*

infinite /'ɪnfɪnɪt/

C
D
E

ADJECTIVE
without any limit or end
EG ... *an infinite number of possibilities*

F
G
H
I
J
K
L

infinitive /ɪn'fɪnɪtɪv/
infinitives

NOUN
The **infinitive** is the form of a verb that has no endings added to indicate the tense or the person. The infinitive is often used after the word to in certain verb phrases.
EG *It was not easy **to find** a new job.*
EG *I want **to go** home.*

M
N
O
P

inflation /ɪn'fleɪʃən/

NOUN
Inflation is an increase in the price of goods and services in a country.
EG ... *an increase in the rate of inflation*

Q
R
S
T
U

inflict /ɪn'flɪkt/
inflicts inflicting inflicted

VERB
If someone or something **inflicts** something unpleasant **on** you, they make you suffer it.
EG ... *sports that inflict cruelty on animals*

V
W
X
Y
Z

influence /'ɪnfluəns/
influences influencing influenced

NOUN
1 Influence is the power to make other people do what you want.
EG *She has no influence on him at all.*
2 An influence is the effect that

someone or something has.
EG ... *driving under the influence of alcohol*

VERB
3 If you influence someone or something, you have an effect on them.
EG *I didn't want him to influence my choice.*

inform /ɪn'fɔːm/
informs informing informed

VERB
If you inform someone of something, you tell them about it.
EG *My daughter informed me that she was pregnant.*

informal /ɪn'fɔːml/

ADJECTIVE
relaxed and casual
EG ... *an informal meeting*

information /ɪnfə'meɪʃən/

NOUN
Information about something is knowledge about it.
EG *For further information, contact the number below.*
EG ... *a fascinating piece of information*
☑ Information refers to all of the things that are known about something, not to an individual fact.

ingredient /ɪn'griːdɪənt/
ingredients

NOUN
Ingredients are the things that something is made from, especially in cookery.
EG *Mix the ingredients in a bowl.*

inhabit /ɪn'hæbɪt/
inhabits inhabiting inhabited

VERB
If you inhabit a place, you live there.

EG ... *the people who inhabit these islands*

inhabitant /ɪnˈhæbɪtnt/
inhabitants

NOUN

The inhabitants of a place are the people who live there.
EG ... *the inhabitants of Glasgow*

inherit /ɪnˈherɪt/
inherits inheriting inherited

VERB

1 If you inherit money or property, you receive it from someone who has died.
EG ... *paintings that he inherited from his father*

2 If you inherit a characteristic from a parent or ancestor, you are born with it.
EG *Her children have inherited her love of sport.*

initial /ɪˈnɪʃl/
initials

ADJECTIVE

1 You use 'initial' to describe something that happens at the beginning of a process.
EG *My initial reaction was shock.*

NOUN

2 Your initials are the capital letters which begin each word of your name.
EG *Please give your surname and initials.*

inject /ɪnˈdʒekt/
injects injecting injected

VERB

1 If a doctor or nurse **injects** you **with** a substance, they use a needle to put the substance into your body.
EG *His son was injected with strong drugs.*

2 If you **inject** something new

into a situation, you add it.
EG *She tried to inject some fun into their relationship.*

injection /ɪnˈdʒekʃən/
injections

NOUN

If you have an injection, a doctor or nurse puts a substance into your body using a needle.
EG *They gave me an injection to help me sleep.*

injure /ˈɪndʒəʳ/
injures injuring injured

VERB

If you injure someone, you damage part of their body.
EG *Several policemen were injured in the riots.*

injury /ˈɪndʒərɪ/
injuries

NOUN

An injury is damage done to someone's body.
EG *Fortunately, her injuries were not serious.*
EG *He escaped without injury.*

ink /ɪŋk/

NOUN

Ink is the coloured liquid used for writing or printing.
EG *The letter was written in green ink.*

inland /ɪnˈlænd/

ADVERB

towards or near the middle of a country, away from the coast
EG *Most of them live further inland.*

ADJECTIVE : /ˈɪnlənd/
☑ Note the change in stress.
towards or near the middle of a country, away from the coast
EG ... *an inland sea*

inn /ɪn/
inns

A
B
C
D
E
F
G
H
I
J
K
L
M
N
O
P
Q
R
S
T
U
V
W
X
Y
Z

A
B
C
D
E
F
G
H
I
J
K
L
M
N
O
P
Q
R
S
T
U
V
W
X
Y
Z

NOUN
a small hotel or pub
EG *... the Waterside Inn*

inner /'ɪnəʳ/
ADJECTIVE
The inner parts of something are
the parts that are inside and close
to the centre.
EG *... the inner city*

innocent /'ɪnəsnt/
ADJECTIVE
1 not guilty of a crime
EG *She was sure he was innocent of
the crime.*
2 not involved in a conflict
EG *They are killing innocent women
and children.*
3 without experience of evil or
unpleasant things
EG *She seemed so young and
innocent.*

inquire /ɪn'kwaɪəʳ/
inquires inquiring inquired;
also spelt **enquire**
VERB
If you **inquire about** someone
or something, you ask for
information about them.
EG *He inquired about my health.*
EG *He inquired whether I was
married.*

inquiry /ɪn'kwaɪərɪ/
inquiries; also spelt **enquiry**
NOUN
1 a question that you ask in order
to get information
EG *He made some inquiries and
discovered she had moved.*
2 an official investigation
EG *... an independent inquiry into
the incident*

insect /'ɪnsɛkt/
insects
NOUN

a small creature with six legs, and
usually wings
EG *... ants, wasps and other insects*

insert /ɪn'sɜːt/
inserts inserting inserted
VERB
If you **insert** an object **into**
something, you put it inside.
EG *He inserted the key into the lock.*

inside /ɪn'saɪd/
insides
ADVERB, PREPOSITION, OR ADJECTIVE
1 Someone or something that is
inside a place, container, or object
is in it or surrounded by it.
EG *I sat inside and waited.*
EG *... inside the house*
EG *... an inside pocket*
NOUN
2 The inside of something is the
part that its sides surround or
contain.
EG *I painted the inside of the house.*
3 inside out means with the
inside part facing outwards
EG *Her umbrella blew inside out.*

insist /ɪn'sɪst/
insists insisting insisted
VERB
If you **insist on** something, you
demand it forcefully.
EG *She insisted on joining us.*

inspect /ɪn'spɛkt/
**inspects inspecting
inspected**
VERB
If you **inspect** something, you
examine or check it carefully.
EG *He raised his hand so she could
inspect the wound.*

inspire /ɪn'spaɪəʳ/
inspires inspiring inspired
VERB
If someone or something inspires

you, they give you new ideas and enthusiasm.
EG ... *a musician who inspired a whole generation*

install /ɪnˈstɔːl/
installs installing installed

VERB
If you **install** a piece of equipment in a place, you put it there so that it is ready to use.
EG *They had installed a new computer.*

instance /ˈɪnstəns/
instances

NOUN
1 a particular example or occurrence of something
EG ... *another instance of corruption*

2 You use **for instance** to give an example of something you are talking about.
EG *In some countries, for instance Spain, the problem is more serious.*

instant /ˈɪnstənt/
instants

NOUN
1 a moment or short period of time
EG *The pain disappeared in an instant.*
EG *For an instant, he was tempted to run.*

ADJECTIVE
2 immediate and without delay
EG *The record was an instant success.*

instead /ɪnˈstɛd/

ADVERB
If you do one thing **instead of** another, you do the first thing and not the second thing.
EG *They took the stairs instead of the lift.*
EG *Try exercising instead of sitting in front of the TV all night.*

instinct /ˈɪnstɪŋkt/
instincts

NOUN
a natural tendency to do something
EG *My first instinct was to run away.*

institute /ˈɪnstɪtjuːt/
institutes

NOUN
an organization for teaching or research
EG ... *a research institute*

institution /ɪnstɪˈtjuːʃən/
institutions

NOUN
1 a large, important organization, for example a university or bank
EG ... *the largest financial institution in Hong Kong*

2 a place such as a mental hospital, children's home, or prison, where people are looked after
EG ... *a mental institution*

instruct /ɪnˈstrʌkt/
instructs instructing instructed

VERB
1 If you **instruct** someone **to do** something, you tell them to do it.
EG *I've been instructed to take you to London.*

2 If someone **instructs** you **in** a subject or skill, they teach you about it.
EG *He instructed them in basic survival techniques.*

instructions /ɪnˈstrʌkʃənz/

PLURAL NOUN
1 Instructions are information on how to do something.
EG *Simply follow the instructions below.*

2 Instructions are what someone

A B C D E F G H I J K L M N O P Q R S T U V W X Y Z

tells you to do.

EG *He claimed he was just following instructions.*

instrument /'instrəmənt/
instruments

NOUN

1 a tool or device

EG *... a special instrument for cutting through metal*

2 A musical instrument is an object such as a piano or guitar, which you play in order to make music.

EG *Which instruments do you play?*

insult /ɪn'sʌlt/
insults insulting insulted

VERB

1 If you insult someone, you offend them by being rude to them.

EG *I didn't mean to insult you.*

NOUN : /'ɪnsʌlt/

☑ Note the change in stress.

2 a rude remark which offends someone

EG *They hurled insults at each other.*

insurance /ɪn'ʃuərəns/

NOUN

Insurance is an arrangement in which you pay money to a company so that if there is an accident or damage, the company will pay you a sum of money.

EG *Always remember to take out travel insurance.*

insure /ɪn'ʃuər/
insures insuring insured

VERB

If you insure something, you pay money to a company so that if there is an accident or damage, the company will pay you a sum of money.

EG *Unfortunately, the necklace was not insured.*

intact /ɪn'tækt/

ADJECTIVE

complete and undamaged

EG *Few of the buildings have remained intact.*

intellectual /ɪntə'lɛktjuəl/
intellectuals

ADJECTIVE

1 involving thought, ideas, and understanding

EG *... the intellectual development of children*

NOUN

2 someone who enjoys thinking about complicated ideas

EG *... writers, artists and other intellectuals*

intelligence /ɪn'tɛlɪdʒəns/

NOUN

Your intelligence is your ability to understand and learn things.

EG *... a woman of exceptional intelligence*

intelligent /ɪn'tɛlɪdʒnt/

ADJECTIVE

An intelligent person is able to think and learn things quickly and well.

EG *... the most intelligent man I have ever met*

intend /ɪn'tɛnd/
intends intending intended

VERB

1 If you intend to do something, you have decided or planned to do it.

EG *She intended to move back to France.*

2 If something is intended for a particular purpose, it is planned to have that purpose.

EG *Today's announcement was intended as a warning.*

intense /ɪnˈtɛns/

ADJECTIVE

very great in strength or amount

EG *… intense heat*

intensive /ɪnˈtɛnsɪv/

ADJECTIVE

involving a lot of effort over a short time

EG *… an intensive training course*

intention /ɪnˈtɛnʃən/
intentions

NOUN

An intention is an idea or plan of what you are going to do.

EG *… his intention to return to Berlin*

EG *I have no intention of resigning.*

intercourse /ˈɪntəkɔːs/

NOUN

Intercourse or **sexual intercourse** is the act of having sex.

EG *She denied they had ever had intercourse.*

interest /ˈɪntrɪst/
**interests interesting
interested**

NOUN

1 If you have an **interest** in something, you want to know more about it.

EG *He showed no interest in the idea.*

2 Your interests are the things that you enjoy doing.

EG *His interests include cooking and photography.*

3 Interest is an extra payment that you receive if you have invested money, or an extra payment that you make if you have borrowed money.

EG *Does your bank account pay interest?*

PLURAL NOUN

4 If something is **in the interests of** a person or group, it will benefit them.

EG *Did he act in the best interests of the company?*

VERB

5 If something interests you, you want to know more about it.

EG *This is the area that most interests me.*

interested /ˈɪntrɪstɪd/

ADJECTIVE

If you are **interested in** something, you want to know more about it.

EG *I'm not very interested in sport.*

interesting /ˈɪntrɪstɪŋ/

ADJECTIVE

If you find something interesting, it attracts you or holds your attention.

EG *… a very interesting book*

EG *It will be interesting to see how he reacts.*

interfere /ɪntəˈfɪəʳ/
**interferes interfering
interfered**

VERB

1 If you **interfere in** a situation, you try to influence it, although it does not concern you.

EG *She has no right to interfere in my affairs.*

EG *I wish everyone would stop interfering.*

2 Something that **interferes with** a situation has a damaging effect on it.

EG *He didn't intend to let a lack of money interfere with his plans.*

interior /ɪnˈtɪərɪəʳ/
interiors

NOUN

the inside part of something

A
B
C
D
E
F
G
H
I
J
K
L
M
N
O
P
Q
R
S
T
U
V
W
X
Y
Z

EG ... *the interior of the building*

interjection /ɪntəˈdʒɛkʃən/
interjections

NOUN

An **interjection** is a word that expresses a strong emotion, such as anger, surprise, or excitement. For example, 'Congratulations!' and 'Hurray!' are interjections.

internal /ɪnˈtɜːnl/

ADJECTIVE

happening inside a person, place, or object
EG ... *internal bleeding*
EG ... *internal mail*

international /ɪntəˈnæʃənl/

ADJECTIVE

involving different countries
EG ... *an international agreement*

Internet /ˈɪntənɛt/

NOUN

the Internet is a worldwide network of computer links which allows computer users to communicate with each other
EG *He spends most of his spare time on the Internet.*

interpret /ɪnˈtɜːprɪt/
interprets interpreting interpreted

VERB

1 If you interpret what someone says or does, you decide what it means.
EG *His refusal can be interpreted in a number of ways.*

2 If you interpret what someone is saying, you immediately translate it into another language.
EG *She spoke little English, so her husband had to interpret for us.*

interpretation

/ɪntəːprɪˈteɪʃən/
interpretations

NOUN

An interpretation of something is an opinion of what it means.
EG *The government put a different interpretation on the figures.*

interrupt /ɪntəˈrʌpt/
interrupts interrupting interrupted

VERB

1 If you interrupt someone, you start talking while they are talking
EG *He interrupted me every time I tried to speak.*

2 If someone or something interrupts a process or activity, they stop it continuing for a time.
EG *She was forced to interrupt her holiday to deal with the problem.*

interval /ˈɪntəvl/
intervals

NOUN

1 a period of time between two events or dates
EG *The ferry service has started again after an interval of 12 years.*

2 a short break during a play or concert
EG *Wine was served during the interval.*

intervene /ɪntəˈviːn/
intervenes intervening intervened

VERB

If you **intervene in** a situation, you become involved in it and try to change it.
EG *The situation calmed down when police intervened.*
EG *He refused to intervene in the dispute.*

interview /ˈɪntəvjuː/
interviews interviewing interviewed

NOUN

a meeting at which an employer asks you questions in order to find out if you are suitable for a job
EG *I had an interview for a job.*

2 a conversation in which a journalist asks a famous person questions
EG *... an interview with the film's director*

VERB

3 When an employer interviews you, they ask you questions in order to find out if you are suitable for a job.
EG *He was interviewed for a management job.*

4 When a journalist interviews a famous person, they ask them questions.
EG *She was interviewed live on TV.*

intimate /'ɪntɪmət/

ADJECTIVE

1 If two people are intimate, there is a close relationship between them.
EG *They are intimate friends.*

2 An intimate matter is very private and personal.
EG *He wrote about the intimate details of his family life.*

into /'ɪntu/

PREPOSITION

1 If you go into a place or object, you go inside it.
EG *She got into the car.*
EG *He smuggled the gun into the country.*

2 If you bump or crash into something, you hit it accidentally.
EG *The car hit the kerb and smashed into the wall.*

3 If you get into a particular state, you start being in that state.
EG *He's always getting into trouble.*

4 If one thing changes into another thing, it becomes that thing.
EG *He tried to turn it into a joke.*

5 If something is divided into a number of pieces, it is divided so that it becomes several smaller pieces.
EG *Cut the cake into slices.*

6 An investigation into an event or subject is concerned with that event or subject.
EG *... research into AIDS*

7 AN INFORMAL USE
If you are into something, you like it very much.
EG *She's really into healthy food.*

introduce /ɪntrə'djuːs/
introduces introducing introduced

VERB

1 If you introduce something into a place or system, you cause it to exist there for the first time.
EG *The Government has introduced a number of further measures.*

2 If you introduce one person to another, you tell them each other's name so that they can get to know each other.
EG *Let me introduce my wife.*

introduction /ɪntrə'dʌkʃən/
introductions

NOUN

1 The introduction of something into a place or system is the act of causing it to exist there for the first time.
EG *... the introduction of student loans*

2 a piece of writing at the beginning of a book, which tells you what the book is about
EG *... with an introduction by Stephen Hawking*

A
B
C
D
E
F
G
H
I
J
K
L
M
N
O
P
Q
R
S
T
U
V
W
X
Y
Z

A B C D E F G H I J K L M N O P Q R S T U V W X Y Z

invade /ɪnˈveɪd/
invades invading invaded

VERB

If a foreign army invades a country, it enters it by force.
EG ... when the Romans invaded Britain

invalid /ˈɪnvəlɪd/
invalids

NOUN

someone who is so ill that they need to be looked after
EG I hate being treated as an invalid.

invalid /ɪnˈvælɪd/

ADJECTIVE

not valid
EG The election was stopped and declared invalid.

invariably /ɪnˈveərɪəblɪ/

ADVERB

If something invariably happens, it always happens.
EG They invariably get it wrong.

invasion /ɪnˈveɪʒən/
invasions

NOUN

If there is an invasion of a country, a foreign army enters it by force.
EG ... after the Roman invasion of Britain

invent /ɪnˈvent/
invents inventing invented

VERB

1 If you invent something, you are the first person to think of it or make it.
EG Writing had not been invented at that time.

2 If you invent a story or excuse, you claim that it is true when it is not.
EG Every time it happened, he invented a different excuse.

invention /ɪnˈvenʃən/
inventions

NOUN

1 An invention is a machine or system that has been invented by someone.
EG The spinning wheel is a Chinese invention.

2 Invention is the act of inventing something.
EG ... before the invention of the telephone

inverted commas

PLURAL NOUN

See **quotation marks**.

invest /ɪnˈvest/
invests investing invested

VERB

1 If you invest money, you try to increase its value, for example by buying property or shares.
EG He wants advice on how to invest the money.

2 If you invest in something useful, you buy it because it will help you do something better.
EG The company has invested in a huge new computer system.

3 If you invest money, time, or energy in something, you spend money, time, or energy trying to make it successful.
EG He's invested so much time in the idea.

investigate /ɪnˈvestɪɡeɪt/
investigates investigating investigated

VERB

If someone investigates something, they try to find out all the facts about it.
EG Police are still investigating how the accident happened.

nvestigation /ɪnvestɪ'geɪʃən/
investigations

NOUN

an attempt to find out all the facts about something

EG *He ordered an investigation into the affair.*

EG *He is under investigation for corruption.*

nvestment /ɪn'vestmənt/
investments

NOUN

1 Investment is the activity of investing money.

EG *… an attempt to encourage investment*

2 An investment is a sum of money that you invest, or the thing that you invest in it.

EG *… a better return on your investments*

EG *… people's desire to buy a house as an investment*

nvisible /ɪn'vɪzɪbl/

ADJECTIVE

If something is invisible, you cannot see it because it is hidden, very small, or imaginary.

EG *The star is invisible to the naked eye.*

nvitation /ɪnvɪ'teɪʃən/
invitations

NOUN

a written or spoken request to come to an event such as a party or meeting

EG *… a wedding invitation*

nvite /ɪn'vaɪt/
invites inviting invited

VERB

1 If you **invite** someone **to** an event, you ask them to come to it.

EG *I wasn't invited to the party.*

2 If you **invite** someone **to do**

something, you ask them to do it.

EG *Andrew has been invited to speak at the conference.*

involve /ɪn'vɒlv/
involves involving involved

VERB

1 If a situation involves something, that thing is a necessary part of it.

EG *His work involves a lot of travelling.*

2 If a situation involves someone, they are taking part in it.

EG *… a riot involving a group of students*

involved /ɪn'vɒlvd/

ADJECTIVE

1 If you are **involved in** something, you are taking part in it or connected with it.

EG *More women should be involved in politics.*

2 The things involved in a job or system are the necessary parts of it.

EG *There's quite a lot of work involved.*

Irish /'aɪrɪʃ/

ADJECTIVE

1 belonging or relating to the Republic of Ireland, or to the whole of Ireland

EG *… an Irish actor*

NOUN

2 a language spoken in some parts of Ireland

EG *… students of Irish*

iron /'aɪən/
irons ironing ironed

NOUN

1 Iron is a hard dark metal which is used to make steel.

EG *… a huge iron gate*

2 An iron is a device which you heat up and rub over clothes in order to remove creases.

A B C D E F G H I J K L M N O P Q R S T U V W X Y Z

EG *... an electric iron*

VERB
3 If you iron clothes, you use a hot iron to remove creases from them.
EG *... a freshly ironed shirt*

ironic /aɪˈrɒnɪk/

ADJECTIVE
1 If you make an ironic remark, you say something that you do not mean, as a joke.
EG *They called him Mr Popularity, but they were being ironic.*
2 An ironic situation is strange or amusing because it is the opposite of what you expect.
EG *It seems ironic that the people he writes about never actually read his books.*

irregular /ɪˈrɛgjʊləʳ/

ADJECTIVE
Something that is irregular is not smooth or straight, or does not form a regular pattern.
EG *The paint was drying in irregular patches.*
EG *He works irregular hours.*

irrelevant /ɪˈrɛləvənt/

ADJECTIVE
not directly connected with a subject
EG *He either ignored the questions or gave irrelevant answers.*

irresistible /ɪrɪˈzɪstɪbl/

ADJECTIVE
1 uncontrollable
EG *... an irresistible urge to yawn*
2 extremely attractive
EG *Women found him irresistible.*

irritate /ˈɪrɪteɪt/

irritates irritating irritated

VERB
If something irritates you, it annoys you.
EG *Her laugh really irritates me.*

is /ɪz/
the third person, present tense of
be
☑ *Is* is often shortened to *'s*: *she's going home; her mother's a writer.*

Islam /ˈɪzlɑːm/

NOUN
Islam is the Muslim religion, which teaches that there is only one God, Allah, and Mohammed is his prophet.
EG *... a convert to Islam*

island /ˈaɪlənd/

islands

NOUN
a piece of land surrounded on all sides by water
EG *... the island of Crete*

isle /aɪl/

isles

NOUN
A FORMAL WORD
an island
EG *... the Isle of Man*

isolated /ˈaɪsəleɪtɪd/

ADJECTIVE
1 An isolated place is a long way from large towns and is difficult to reach.
EG *... an isolated farmhouse*
2 If you feel isolated, you feel lonely and without help.
EG *She feels very isolated at home.*

issue /ˈɪʃuː/

issues issuing issued

NOUN
1 an important subject that people are talking about
EG *... a major political issue*
2 a particular edition of a newspaper or magazine
EG *... the latest issue of Scientific American*

VERB

3 If someone issues a statement or warning, they say it formally and publicly.
EG *He has issued a statement denying the allegations.*

4 If you are issued with something, it is officially given to you.
EG *Staff will be issued with new uniforms.*

it /ɪt/
PRONOUN

1 You use 'it' to refer to something that has already been mentioned, or to a situation that you have just described.
EG *The course was so wet that it was considered dangerous.*
EG *It was a difficult decision.*

2 You use 'it' to talk about your feelings or point of view.
EG *It was nice meeting you again.*
EG *It's a pity you weren't there.*

3 You use 'it' when you are reporting a situation or event.
EG *It's well-known that he's gay.*
EG *It's supposed to be harmless.*

4 You use 'it' to make statements about the weather, time, or date.
EG *It was raining.*
EG *It's half past eight.*
EG *It's the 28th of June.*

5 You use 'it' to ask someone who they are, or to tell them who you are.
EG *Who is it?*
EG *It's me.*

Italian /ɪˈtæljən/
Italians
ADJECTIVE

1 belonging or relating to Italy
EG *... Italian clothes*
NOUN

2 someone who comes from Italy
EG *... two young Italians*

3 Italian is the main language spoken in Italy.
EG *... a poem in Italian*

itch /ɪtʃ/
itches itching itched
VERB

When a part of your body itches, you have an unpleasant feeling that makes you want to scratch it.
EG *My nose is really itching.*

item /ˈaɪtəm/
items
NOUN

one of a collection or list of things
EG *... various items of clothing*
EG *... the next item on the agenda*

its /ɪts/
ADJECTIVE OR PRONOUN

'Its' refers to something that belongs or relates to a thing, child, or animal.
EG *Her youngest child is fighting for its life.*
EG *We have our traditions, France has its.*

☑ Do not confuse *its* and *it's*. *Its* means 'belonging to it': *the cat has hurt its paw*. *It's* is short for 'it is' or 'it has': *it's green; it's been snowing again.*

itself /ɪtˈsɛlf/
PRONOUN

1 'Itself' refers to the same thing, child, or animal that has already been mentioned.
EG *Paris prides itself on its luxurious hotels.*

2 'Itself' is used to emphasize the thing you are referring to.
EG *Life itself is a learning process.*

A
B
C
D
E
F
G
H
I
J
K
L
M
N
O
P
Q
R
S
T
U
V
W
X
Y
Z

Jj

jacket /'dʒækɪt/
jackets

NOUN

1 a short coat

EG … a leather jacket

2 an outer covering for something

EG … a book jacket

jail /dʒeɪl/
jails jailing jailed

NOUN

1 a building where people convicted of a crime are locked up

EG He served six months in jail for theft.

VERB

2 If someone **is jailed**, they are locked up in a jail.

EG He was jailed for 20 years.

jam /dʒæm/
jams jamming jammed

NOUN

1 a food made by boiling fruit and sugar together until it sets

EG … strawberry jam

2 a situation where there are so many vehicles on the road that they cannot move

EG … a traffic jam

VERB

3 If you jam something somewhere, you push it there roughly.

EG He jammed his hat onto his head.

4 If something jams, or if you jam it, it becomes stuck or unable to work properly.

EG The second time he fired, his gun jammed.

January /'dʒænjuərɪ/

NOUN

January is the first month of the year.

EG They met on January 2nd.

Japanese /dʒæpə'niːz/

ADJECTIVE

1 belonging or relating to Japan

EG … Japanese food

NOUN

2 someone who comes from Japan

EG … a group of Japanese

☑ 'Japanese' is both singular and plural.

3 Japanese is the main language spoken in Japan.

EG He is studying Japanese.

jar /dʒɑːʳ/
jars

NOUN

a glass container with a lid, used for storing food

EG … a jar of coffee

jaw /dʒɔː/
jaws

NOUN

1 Your jaw is the part of your face below your mouth.

EG His jaw dropped in surprise.

2 A person's or animal's jaws are their mouth and teeth.

EG The dog held a snake in its jaws.

jazz /dʒæz/

NOUN

Jazz is a style of popular music with a strong rhythm, invented by black American musicians in the early twentieth century.

EG The pub has live jazz on Sundays.

jealous /'dʒɛləs/

ADJECTIVE

1 A jealous person feels angry or bitter because they think that

another person is trying to take a lover or friend away from them.
EG ... an insanely jealous woman

2 If you are **jealous of** another person's possessions or qualities, you feel angry or bitter because you do not have them.
EG She was jealous of his wealth.

jeans /dʒiːnz/

PLURAL NOUN

Jeans are casual trousers, usually made from strong, blue material.
EG ... a pair of blue jeans

jerk /dʒɜːk/
jerks jerking jerked

VERB
1 If you jerk something, you give it a sudden, sharp pull.
EG I jerked the fishing rod back and lost the fish.
2 If something jerks, it moves suddenly and sharply.
EG The car jerked to a halt.

jet /dʒɛt/
jets

NOUN
1 an aeroplane which is able to fly very fast
EG ... her private jet
2 A jet of liquid or gas is a strong, fast, thin stream of it.
EG ... a jet of water

Jew /dʒuː/
Jews

NOUN
a person who practises the religion of Judaism
EG ... the history of the Jews

jewel /'dʒuːəl/
jewels

NOUN
a precious stone that is used to decorate valuable things such as rings or necklaces

EG ... a gold box containing precious jewels

jewellery /'dʒuːəlrɪ/
US **jewelry**

NOUN
Jewellery is things such as rings and necklaces that people wear to look more attractive.
EG ... a lot of jewellery
EG ... an expensive piece of jewellery
☑ 'Jewellery' refers to a number of objects, not to an individual ring or necklace.

Jewish /'dʒuːɪʃ/

ADJECTIVE
belonging or relating to the religion of Judaism or to Jews
EG ... a Jewish festival

job /dʒɒb/
jobs

NOUN
1 the work that someone does to earn money
EG She's got a new job.
2 a duty or responsibility
EG He was given the job of tending the fire.
3 If someone **does** or **makes a good job of** something, they do it well.
EG He didn't do a very good job of explaining himself.
EG He hasn't made a good job of mending that fence.

jockey /'dʒɒkɪ/
jockeys

NOUN
someone who rides a horse in a race
EG ... last year's champion jockey

jog /dʒɒg/
jogs jogging jogged

VERB

A
B
C
D
E
F
G
H
I
J
K
L
M
N
O
P
Q
R
S
T
U
V
W
X
Y
Z

1 If you jog, you run slowly, usually as a form of exercise.
EG *He jogs twice a week.*

NOUN

2 a slow run
EG *He went for an early morning jog.*

join /dʒɔɪn/
joins joining joined

VERB

1 If you join someone, you go to where they are.
EG *Why don't you join us inside for a drink?*

2 When two things join, or when one thing joins another, they come together.
EG *The two streams join and form a river.*
EG *This road joins the motorway at junction 16.*

3 If you join a club or organization, you become a member of it.
EG *He joined the Army five years ago.*

join in

VERB

If you join in an activity, you take part in it.
EG *Thousands of people are expected to join in the celebrations.*

joint /dʒɔɪnt/
joints

ADJECTIVE

1 shared by or belonging to two or more people
EG *… a joint bank account*

NOUN

2 a part of your body such as your elbow or knee where two bones meet and are able to move together
EG *Her joints ache if she exercises.*

joke /dʒəuk/
jokes joking joked

NOUN

1 something that you say in order to make people laugh
EG *He made a joke about poisoning his wife.*

VERB

2 If you joke, you say something amusing or tell a funny story.
EG *She often jokes about her appearance.*

3 If you **are joking**, you say something that is not true, as a joke.
EG *Don't get upset, I was only joking.*

journal /dʒɜ:nl/
journals

NOUN

a magazine that deals with a specialized subject
EG *… scientific journals*

journalist /dʒɜ:nəlɪst/
journalists

NOUN

a person whose job is to collect news and to write or talk about it
EG *She worked as a journalist on The Times.*

journey /dʒɜ:nɪ/
journeys journeying journeyed

NOUN

1 the act of travelling from one place to another
EG *… during the journey to the airport*

VERB

2 A FORMAL USE
If you journey somewhere, you travel there.
EG *He intended to journey up the Amazon.*

joy /dʒɔɪ/

A B C D E F G H I J K L M N O P Q R S T U V W X Y Z

joys

NOUN

1 Joy is a feeling of great happiness.

EG *She cried with joy.*

2 A joy is something that gives you pleasure.

EG *That's one of the joys of being a chef.*

judge /dʒʌdʒ/
judges judging judged

NOUN

1 the person in a law court who decides how the law should be applied and how criminals should be punished

EG *The judge adjourned the case until next Tuesday.*

2 the person who chooses the winner of a competition

EG *... a panel of judges*

VERB

3 If you judge someone or something, you form an opinion about them based on the information that you have.

EG *It's hard to judge her age.*

judgment /'dʒʌdʒmənt/
judgments; also spelt **judgement**

NOUN

1 an opinion that you have after thinking carefully about something

EG *In your judgment, what has changed over the past few years?*

2 Judgment is the ability to make sensible guesses and decisions.

EG *No one has questioned my judgment before.*

jug /dʒʌg/
jugs

NOUN

a container used for holding or pouring liquids

EG *... a jug of water*

juice /dʒuːs/

NOUN

Juice is the liquid that can be obtained from fruit or other food.

EG *... a glass of orange juice*

July /dʒuːˈlaɪ/

NOUN

July is the seventh month of the year.

EG *... the weather in July*

jump /dʒʌmp/
jumps jumping jumped

VERB

1 When you jump, you push your feet against the ground and move quickly upwards into the air.

EG *She was jumping up and down to keep warm.*

EG *She jumped out of the window to avoid him.*

2 If you jump something, you leap off the ground and move over or across it.

EG *Both horses jumped the final fence beautifully.*

3 If something **makes** you **jump**, it surprises you and causes you to make a sudden movement.

EG *A sudden noise made her jump.*

NOUN

4 a leap into the air, sometimes over an object

EG *... the longest ever jump by a man*

jumper /'dʒʌmpər/
jumpers

NOUN

a knitted piece of clothing for the top half of the body

EG *... a woolly jumper*

June /dʒuːn/

NOUN

June is the sixth month of the year.

EG *His birthday is in June.*

A B C D E F G H I J K L M N O P Q R S T U V W X Y Z

jungle /'dʒʌŋgl/
jungles

NOUN

a dense forest in a very hot country

EG … lost in the jungle

junior /'dʒuːniər/

ADJECTIVE

1 A junior official or employee holds a lower position in an organization.

EG … a junior minister

2 If you are someone's junior, you are younger than they are.

EG … a woman 12 years his junior

junk /dʒʌŋk/

NOUN

Junk is old or second-hand things.

EG The garage was full of junk.

jury /'dʒuəri/
juries

NOUN

a group of people in a law court who have been randomly selected to listen to the facts about a crime and to decide whether the accused person is guilty or not

EG The jury found him guilty of murder.

☑ You can use either a singular or a plural verb after 'jury': the jury was undecided; the jury were undecided .

just /dʒʌst/

ADVERB

1 If something has just happened, it happened a very short time ago.

EG I've just bought a new car.

2 If you are just doing something, you will finish doing it very soon.

EG I'm just getting changed.

3 If you just do something, you do it by a very small amount.

EG We just got there in time.

4 simply or only

EG It was just an excuse not to cut the grass.

5 exactly

EG It's just what she wanted.

ADJECTIVE

6 right or acceptable according to particular moral principles

EG She arrived at a just decision.

justice /'dʒʌstɪs/

NOUN

Justice is fairness in the way that people are treated.

EG The families of his victims are demanding justice.

justification /dʒʌstɪfɪ'keɪʃən/
justifications

NOUN

A justification for something is an acceptable reason or explanation for it.

EG The only justification for a zoo is educational.

justify /'dʒʌstɪfaɪ/
justifies justifying justified

VERB

If you justify an action or idea, you prove or explain why it is reasonable or necessary.

EG How can you justify what you've done?

kangaroo /ˌkæŋɡəˈruː/
kangaroos

NOUN

a large Australian animal with
strong back legs which it uses for
jumping

EG … *a shop selling kangaroo meat*

keen /kiːn/
keener keenest

ADJECTIVE

1 Someone who is keen is
enthusiastic about something.
EG *She's a keen amateur
photographer.*

2 If you are **keen on doing**
something or **keen to do** it, you
very much want to do it.
EG *You're not keen on going, are
you?*
EG *He seems keen to learn.*

keep /kiːp/
keeps keeping kept

VERB

1 To keep someone or something
in a particular condition or place
means to make them stay in that
condition or place.
EG *The noise kept him awake.*
EG *They want to keep her in
hospital for another week.*

2 If you keep something, you
continue to have it.
EG *The city of Leningrad was
deciding whether to keep its name.*

3 If you keep something
somewhere, you store it there.
EG *She kept her money under the
mattress.*

4 If you **keep doing** something
or **keep on doing** it, you do it
repeatedly or continuously.
EG *I kept phoning the hospital.*

EG … *but he kept on trying*

5 If someone or something **keeps**
you **from doing** something,
they prevent you from doing it.
EG *What can we do to keep it from
happening again?*

6 If you keep a promise or
appointment, you do what you
said you would do.
EG *I always keep my promises.*

7 If you **keep** something **from**
someone, you do not tell them
about it.
EG *He kept the truth from his wife.*

8 If you keep a record of a series of
events, you write down what
happened.
EG *She began to keep a diary.*

9 If something keeps you, it delays
you.
EG *What kept you?*

kerb /kɜːb/
kerbs
US **curb**

NOUN

the raised edge of a pavement,
which separates it from the road
EG *She stepped off the kerb without
looking.*

kettle /ˈketl/
kettles

NOUN

a covered container in which you
boil water
EG *I'll put the kettle on and make us
some tea.*

key /kiː/
keys

NOUN

1 a specially shaped piece of metal
that fits in a lock and is turned in
order to open it

EG *... a set of car keys*
EG *... the keys to his flat*

2 The keys on a typewriter or piano are the buttons that you press in order to operate or play it.
EG *Her fingers seemed to dance over the piano keys.*

3 In music, a key is a scale of notes.
EG *... in the key of A minor*

ADJECTIVE
4 The key person or thing in a group is the most important one.
EG *... a key figure in the government*

keyboard /ˈkiːbɔːd/
keyboards

NOUN
a set of keys on a piano, typewriter, or computer
EG *... a computer keyboard*

kick /kɪk/
kicks kicking kicked

VERB
1 If you kick someone or something, you hit them with your foot.
EG *She kicked him in the leg.*

NOUN
2 If you give something a kick, you hit it with your foot.
EG *He received several kicks to the head.*

3 AN INFORMAL USE
If you **get a kick out of** something, you enjoy it very much.
EG *I got a kick out of seeing my name in print.*

kick off

VERB
When a football team kicks off, they begin playing.
EG *They kicked off late because of crowd trouble.*

kid /kɪd/
kids kidding kidded

NOUN
1 AN INFORMAL WORD
a child
EG *They've got three kids.*
EG *... when I was a kid*

VERB
2 If you **are kidding,** you say something that is not true, as a joke.
EG *I'm not kidding, I really did win the lottery.*

kidnap /ˈkɪdnæp/
kidnaps kidnapping kidnapped

VERB
If someone is kidnapped, they are taken away by force and something is demanded in exchange for their return.
EG *... a plot to kidnap the President*

kidney /ˈkɪdnɪ/
kidneys

NOUN
Your kidneys are the two organs in your body that remove waste matter from your blood.
EG *... kidney disease*

kill /kɪl/
kills killing killed

VERB
1 If someone kills a person, animal, or plant, they cause them to die.
EG *Six people were killed in the crash.*
EG *She killed him with a hammer.*

2 AN INFORMAL USE
If something **is killing** you, it is causing you a lot of pain.
EG *My back's killing me.*

kilo /ˈkiːləu/
kilos

NOUN
a kilogram
EG *It weighs around 5 kilos.*

kilogram /ˈkɪləʊgræm/
kilograms; also spelt
kilogramme

NOUN
a unit of weight equal to 1000
grams or about 2.2 pounds
EG ... *a kilogram of butter*

kilometre /ˈkɪləmiːtəʳ/
kilometres
US **kilometer**

NOUN
a unit of distance equal to 1000
metres or about 0.62 miles
EG ... *about 20 kilometres from the
border*

kind /kaɪnd/
kinds; kinder kindest

NOUN
1 A particular kind of thing is one
of the types or sorts of that thing.
EG *I'm not the kind of man to get
married.*
EG *All kinds of people were there.*
ADJECTIVE
2 caring and helpful
EG *She was very kind to me.*
EG *It was kind of you to come.*

king /kɪŋ/
kings

NOUN
a man who is a member of the
royal family of his country, and
who is the leader of that country
EG ... *the king of Spain*

kingdom /ˈkɪŋdəm/
kingdoms

NOUN
a country that is governed by a
king or queen
EG ... *the United Kingdom*

kiss /kɪs/
kisses kissing kissed

VERB
1 When you kiss someone, you
touch them with your lips in order
to show your affection.
EG *She kissed him on the cheek.*
EG *They stopped under a tree and
kissed.*

NOUN
2 When you give someone a kiss,
you kiss them.
EG *She stood waiting for a kiss.*

kit /kɪt/
kits

NOUN
a collection of objects or clothes
that you use for a sport or other
activity
EG ... *a football kit*
EG ... *a tool kit*

kitchen /ˈkɪtʃɪn/
kitchens

NOUN
a room used for cooking and
preparing food
EG *Come and help me in the
kitchen.*

kitten /ˈkɪtn/
kittens

NOUN
a very young cat
EG *Their cat had just had kittens.*

km /ˈkɪləmiːtəʳ, ˈkɪləmiːtəz/
☑ The plural can be either *km* or
kms.
an abbreviation for kilometre or
kilometres
EG ... *25kms from London*

knee /niː/
knees

NOUN
Your knees are the parts of your
body where your legs bend.
EG *The snow came up to his knees.*

kneel /niːl/
kneels kneeling kneeled or
knelt

A
B
C
D
E
F
G
H
I
J
K
L
M
N
O
P
Q
R
S
T
U
V
W
X
Y
Z

VERB

When you kneel or **kneel down,** you bend your legs and lower your body until your knees are touching the ground.

EG *She knelt down beside him.*

knew /njuː/

past tense of **know**

knickers /'nɪkəz/

PLURAL NOUN

Knickers are underwear worn by women and girls, with holes for the legs and elastic around the waist.

EG *... six pairs of knickers*

knife /naɪf/

knives; knifes knifing knifed

NOUN

1 a sharp metal tool used for cutting things or as a weapon

EG *... a knife and fork*

2 If someone knifes a person, they stab them with a knife.

EG *She was knifed in the back.*

knight /naɪt/

knights knighting knighted

VERB

If someone **is knighted,** they are given the title 'Sir' before their name.

EG *He was knighted by the Queen.*

knit /nɪt/

knits knitting knitted

VERB

If you knit a piece of clothing, you make it from wool, using knitting needles or a machine.

EG *She knitted him a scarf.*

knives /naɪvz/

the plural of **knife**

knob /nɒb/

knobs

NOUN

a round handle or switch

EG *... a door knob*

EG *... by turning the knob on the radio*

knock /nɒk/

knocks knocking knocked

VERB

1 If you **knock on** a door or window, you hit it with your hand.

EG *She went to his flat and knocked on the door.*

2 If you knock something, you touch it or hit it roughly so that it moves or falls over.

EG *He accidentally knocked the picture off the shelf.*

EG *She rushed out of the room, knocking over the lamp.*

NOUN

3 a firm blow on something solid

EG *There was a knock at the door.*

knock out

VERB

If you knock someone out, you cause them to become unconscious.

EG *He hit me so hard that he nearly knocked me out.*

knot /nɒt/

knots

NOUN

1 a fastening made by passing one end of a piece of string or fabric through a loop and pulling it tight

EG *One lace had broken and been tied in a knot.*

2 a unit of speed for ships and aircraft, equal to about 1.85 kilometres per hour

EG *... speeds of up to 30 knots*

know /nəʊ/

knows knowing knew known

VERB

1 If you know something, you have it in your mind and you do not need to learn it.
EG *Do you know his name?*
EG *Sara doesn't know much about art.*

2 If you know a person, place, or thing, you are familiar with them.
EG *I've known him for five years.*
EG *He knew London well.*

3 If you **know how to do** something, you have the necessary skills to do it.

EG *He doesn't know how to swim.*

4 If you **know of** something, you have heard about it.
EG *I know of the place, but I've never been there.*

knowledge /ˈnɒlɪdʒ/

NOUN

Knowledge is all the information that someone knows about a subject.
EG *… the latest advances in scientific knowledge*
EG *My knowledge of French is poor.*

label /'leɪbl/
labels labelling labelled

NOUN
1 a piece of paper or plastic attached to something and giving information about it
EG … the label on the bottle

VERB
2 If you label something, you put a label on it.
EG Some of the boxes weren't even labelled.

labour /'leɪbər/
US labor

NOUN
1 Labour is hard work.
EG … the result of two years' labour
2 Labour refers to the people who work in a country or industry.
EG … a shortage of skilled labour
3 In Britain, Labour or the Labour Party is the main left-of-centre political party.
EG They always votes Labour.
4 Labour is the last stage of pregnancy when a woman gives birth to a baby.
EG She went into labour late last night.

lace /leɪs/
laces lacing laced

NOUN
1 Lace is a very fine decorated cloth, made with a lot of holes in it.
EG … a tablecloth edged with lace
2 Laces are the thin pieces of material that are used to fasten shoes.
EG He knelt and tied his laces.

VERB
3 When you lace your shoes or **lace** them **up**, you tie a bow in the laces.
EG Her fingers were too cold to lace her shoes up.

lack /læk/
lacks lacking lacked

NOUN
1 If there is a **lack of** something, there is not enough of it or there is none of it.
EG Despite his lack of experience, he got the job.

VERB
2 If someone or something lacks something, or if they are **lacking in** something, they do not have enough or any of that thing.
EG What the film lacks is a good ending.
EG Francis was lacking in stamina.

lad /læd/
lads

NOUN
AN INFORMAL WORD
a boy or young man
EG He's a big lad for his age.

ladder /'lædər/
ladders

NOUN
a wooden or metal frame used for climbing something, consisting of two long poles with short bars in between
EG … a man climbing a ladder

lady /'leɪdɪ/
ladies

NOUN
1 You can refer to a woman as a lady, especially when you are being polite or showing respect.
EG Your table is ready, ladies.
2 Lady is a title used in front of the names of some women from the

upper classes, such as a lord's wife.
EG *... Lord and Lady Keeble*

3 People sometimes refer to a public toilet for women as **the ladies**.
EG *At the station, she rushed into the ladies.*

lager /ˈlɑːgəʳ/
lagers

NOUN
Lager is a kind of light beer.
EG *... a pint of lager*

laid /leɪd/
past participle and past tense of **lay**

lain /leɪn/
past participle of **lie**

lake /leɪk/
lakes

NOUN
an area of fresh water surrounded by land
EG *We went fishing in the lake.*

lamb /læm/
lambs

NOUN
1 A lamb is a young sheep.
EG *... a newborn lamb*

2 Lamb is the meat from a lamb.
EG *... a leg of lamb*

lamp /læmp/
lamps

NOUN
a device that produces light
EG *... a table lamp*

land /lænd/
lands landing landed

NOUN
1 Land is an area of ground.
EG *... good agricultural land*

2 Land is the part of the earth that is not covered by water.
EG *... a search over land and sea*

3 A land is a country.
EG *... in a foreign land*

VERB
4 When someone or something lands somewhere, they reach the ground after moving through the air.
EG *The ball landed in the middle of the road.*

5 When a aircraft lands, it arrives back on the ground after a journey.
EG *He woke up just before we landed.*

landing /ˈlændɪŋ/
landings

NOUN
1 a flat area at the top of a set of stairs in a building
EG *I ran out onto the landing.*

2 the act of bringing an aircraft down to the ground
EG *It was a very smooth landing.*

landscape /ˈlændskeɪp/
landscapes

NOUN
The landscape is everything you can see when you look across an area of land.
EG *... Arizona's desert landscape*

lane /leɪn/
lanes

NOUN
1 a narrow road, especially in the country
EG *... a quiet country lane*

2 one of the parallel strips into which a road is divided
EG *... the inside lane on the motorway*

language /ˈlæŋgwɪdʒ/
languages

NOUN
1 A language is a system of words used by the people of a particular

A
B
C
D
E
F
G
H
I
J
K
L
M
N
O
P
Q
R
S
T
U
V
W
X
Y
Z

A B C D E F G H I J K L M N O P Q R S T U V W X Y Z

country or area to communicate with each other.
EG ... *a foreign language*
2 The language in which something is written or performed is the style in which it is expressed.
EG *Some of the language in the film shocked me.*

lap /læp/
laps lapping lapped

NOUN
1 Your lap is the flat area formed by your thighs when you are sitting down.
EG *She sat with her hands in her lap.*
2 In a race, a lap is the distance that someone has travelled when they have gone round the course once.
EG *They had completed six laps of the track.*

VERB
3 If you lap someone in a race, you pass them when they are still on the previous lap.
EG *He is in danger of being lapped.*
4 When water laps against something, it gently moves against it in little waves.
EG *The water lapped against the shore.*
5 When an animal laps a drink or **laps** it **up**, it drinks the liquid by using its tongue.
EG ... *a cat lapping up milk from a dish*

large /lɑːdʒ/
larger largest

ADJECTIVE
Someone or something that is large is bigger than usual or average.
EG ... *a large room*
EG ... *a large amount of cash*

EG ... *large numbers of people*

largely /'lɑːdʒlɪ/
ADVERB
You use 'largely' to say that a statement is mostly but not completely true.
EG *The public are largely unaware of this.*

laser /'leɪzər/
lasers

NOUN
a narrow ray of concentrated light produced by a special machine; also the machine that produces this light
EG ... *developments in laser technology*

last /lɑːst/
lasts lasting lasted

ADJECTIVE
1 The last thing or event is the most recent one.
EG ... *last year*
EG *A lot had changed since my last visit.*
2 The last person or thing is the one that comes after all the others of the same kind.
EG ... *the last guest to arrive*
EG ... *the last three pages of the book*
3 The last one of a group of things is the only one that remains after all the others have gone.
EG ... *the last piece of pizza*

ADVERB
4 If you last did something on a particular occasion, you have not done it since then.
EG *They last met in Rome.*
5 If something happens last, it happens after everything else.
EG *He added the milk last.*

VERB
6 If something lasts, it continues

to exist or happen.
EG *This weather won't last.*
EG *Her speech lasted fifty minutes.*
7 If something lasts for a particular time, it remains in good condition for that time.
EG *... a battery that lasts twice as long as most other batteries*

NOUN
8 at last means after a long time
EG *The coffee arrived at last.*

late /leɪt/
later latest

ADVERB OR ADJECTIVE
1 Late means near the end of a period of time.
EG *... late in the evening*
EG *... the late 1960s*
EG *It's getting late, we'd better go.*
2 Late means after the time that was arranged or expected, or after the usual time.
EG *Steve arrived late.*
EG *We had a late lunch.*

ADJECTIVE
3 A FORMAL USE
Late means dead.
EG *... my late grandmother*

lately /'leɪtlɪ/
ADVERB
Lately means recently.
EG *His health hasn't been too good lately.*

later /'leɪtər/
1 the comparative of **late**

ADVERB OR ADJECTIVE
2 You use 'later' or **later on** to refer to a time that is after the present one.
EG *Later on I'll be talking to Patty Davis.*
EG *... at a later date*

latest /'leɪtɪst/
1 the superlative of **late**

ADJECTIVE
2 most modern or most recent
EG *... the latest developments in technology*
EG *... her latest book*

Latin /'lætɪn/
NOUN
Latin is the language that was spoken in ancient Rome.
EG *... books in Greek and Latin*

latter /'lætər/
ADJECTIVE
1 You use 'latter' to refer to the second of two things that are mentioned.
EG *I prefer the latter option.*
2 You use 'latter' to refer to the second or later part of something...
EG *... during the latter part of his career*

NOUN
3 You use **the latter** to refer to the second of two things that are mentioned.
EG *... sandwiches and cakes (the latter bought from Mrs Paul's bakery)*

laugh /lɑːf/
laughs laughing laughed
VERB
1 When you laugh, you make a noise which shows that you are amused or happy.
EG *The British don't laugh at the same jokes as the French.*
2 If you **laugh at** someone or something, you mock them or make joke about them.
EG *They all used to laugh at me because I was fat.*
NOUN
3 the noise you make when you laugh
EG *She has a very sexy laugh.*

A
B
C
D
E
F
G
H
I
J
K
L
M
N
O
P
Q
R
S
T
U
V
W
X
Y
Z

laughter /'lɑːftər/

NOUN

Laughter is people laughing.

EG ... the sound of laughter

launch /lɔːntʃ/
launches launching launched

VERB

1 To launch a ship means to put it into water for the first time.

EG ... when the ship was launched in 1926

2 To launch a rocket means to send it into space.

EG They plan to launch two more satellites this year.

3 When a company launches a new product, it makes it available to the public.

EG ... all the promotion involved in launching new products

laundry /'lɔːndri/
laundries

NOUN

1 A laundry is a business that washes and irons clothes and sheets.

EG He takes his sheets to a laundry.

2 Laundry is dirty clothes and sheets that are being washed, are about to be washed, or have just been washed.

EG ... the room where I hang the laundry

lavatory /'lævətəri/
lavatories

NOUN

a toilet

EG ... a public lavatory

law /lɔː/
laws

NOUN

1 the law is the system of rules developed by the government of a country, which tells people what

they are allowed to do

EG It's against the law to make obscene phone calls.

EG ... not a good reason for breaking the law

2 Law is the profession of people such as lawyers and judges, or the study of this subject.

EG ... a career in law

EG ... a law degree

3 one of the rules established by a government, which tells people what they are allowed to do

EG ... a new law to protect privacy

4 a scientific rule which explains how things work in the physical world

EG ... the law of gravity

lawn /lɔːn/
lawns

NOUN

an area of grass that is kept cut short

EG They were sitting on the lawn.

lawyer /'lɔːjər/
lawyers

NOUN

a person who is qualified to advise people about the law and represent them in court

EG ... the lawyer for the defence

lay /leɪ/
lays laying laid

1 Lay is the past tense of some senses of **lie**.

VERB

2 When you lay something somewhere, you place it there.

EG Lay a sheet of newspaper on the floor.

EG ... workmen digging up the road to lay pipes

3 If you **lay the table**, you put things such as knives and forks on the table ready for a meal.

EG *The table was laid for lunch.*
4 When a bird lays an egg, an egg comes out of its body.
EG *My canary has laid an egg.*

layer /'leɪəʳ/
layers

NOUN
a layer of something is a flat piece of it that covers a surface or that is between two other things
EG *A fresh layer of snow covered the street.*
EG *... the ozone layer*

lazy /'leɪzɪ/
lazier laziest

ADJECTIVE
Someone who is lazy does not want to work or make an effort.
EG *I was too lazy to learn how to read music.*

lb /paund z/
☑ The plural can be either *lb* or *lbs*.
an abbreviation for pound or pounds, when 'pound' refers to weight
EG *... 3lb of sugar*

lead /liːd/
leads leading led

VERB
1 If you lead someone somewhere, you take them there.
EG *A nurse led me to a large room.*
2 If a road or door leads somewhere, you can get to that place by following the road or going through the door.
EG *... a door leading to the garden*
3 If you lead in a race or competition, you are winning.
EG *Henman currently leads by two sets to one.*
4 If one thing **leads to** another, it causes the second thing to happen.

EG *... the incident that led to the war*
5 If you lead a busy life or a dull life, your life is busy or dull.
EG *She leads such an interesting life.*
6 Someone who leads a group of people is in charge of them.
EG *He led the country between 1949 and 1984.*

NOUN
7 If you **take** the **lead** in a race or competition, you start winning. If you are **in the lead**, you are winning.
EG *England took the lead with a goal from Owen.*
EG *Suddenly we were in the lead.*
8 a length of leather or chain attached to a dog's collar, used for controlling the dog
EG *... a woman with a dog on a lead*
9 If the police have a lead, they have a clue which might help them to solve a crime.
EG *Police say they have no leads so far.*

lead /lɛd/
NOUN
Lead is a soft, grey, heavy metal.
EG *... lead poisoning*

leader /'liːdəʳ/
leaders

NOUN
1 the person who is in charge of an organization or group of people
EG *... the Conservative leader*
2 the person who is winning in a race or competition
EG *... the leader after the first lap*

leaf /liːf/
leaves

NOUN
one of the parts of a tree or plant that is flat, thin, and usually green

A B C D E F G H I J K L M N O P Q R S T U V W X Y Z

EG *The leaves were already beginning to fall from the trees.*

leaflet /'li:flɪt/
leaflets

NOUN

a piece of paper containing information about a particular subject

EG *Campaigners were handing out leaflets.*

league /li:g/
leagues

NOUN

a group of people, clubs, or countries that have joined together for a particular purpose or because they share a common interest

EG *... the Football League*

leak /li:k/
leaks leaking leaked

VERB

1 If a container or other object leaks, it has a hole which lets gas or liquid escape.

EG *The roof leaks.*

2 If a liquid or gas leaks, it escapes from a container.

EG *The gas had apparently leaked from the cylinder.*

3 If someone in an organization leaks information, they give the information to someone who is not supposed to have it.

EG *The letter was leaked to the press.*

NOUN

4 If a container or other object has a leak, it has a hole which lets gas or liquid escape.

EG *The explosion was blamed on a gas leak.*

lean /li:n/
leans leaning leant or **leaned; leaner leanest**

VERB

1 When you lean in a particular direction, you bend your body in that direction.

EG *She leant out of the window and waved.*

2 When you **lean on** something, you rest your body against it for support.

EG *A man was leaning on the railing.*

3 If you lean something somewhere, you place it there so that its weight is supported.

EG *He leant his bike against the wall.*

ADJECTIVE

4 If meat is lean, it does not have very much fat.

EG *... beautiful meat, lean and tender*

leap /li:p/
leaps leaping leapt or **leaped**

VERB

1 If you leap somewhere, you jump a long distance or jump high in the air.

EG *He leapt from a window and escaped.*

NOUN

2 a jump over a long distance or high in the air

EG *... a leap of over 3 metres*

learn /lə:n/
learns learning learnt or **learned**

VERB

1 When you learn something, you gain knowledge or a skill through study or training.

EG *She wants to learn Chinese.*

EG *He's learning to play the piano.*

2 If you **learn of** something, you find out about it.

EG *She had first learnt of the fire*

that morning.

lease /liːs/
leases leasing leased

NOUN

1 a legal agreement which allows someone to use a house or flat in return for rent

EG *The lease still has five years left to run.*

VERB

2 If you lease something such as a house or a car, or if someone **leases** it **to** you, they allow you to use it in return for regular payments.

EG *He leased an apartment.*

EG *She hopes to lease the building to students.*

least /liːst/

ADJECTIVE, ADVERB, OR PRONOUN

1 You use **the least** to refer to the smallest amount or extent of something.

EG *… the cheese with the least fat*

EG *… the least experienced player in the team*

EG *The least you can do is give me some advice.*

ADVERB

2 You use **at least** to show that you are referring to the minimum amount of something, and that the true amount may be greater.

EG *At least 200 people were injured.*

3 You use **at least** when you are mentioning an advantage that still exists in a bad situation.

EG *At least he's still alive.*

leather /ˈlɛðər/

NOUN

Leather is animal skin, which is used to make shoes, clothes, and other things.

EG *… a leather jacket*

leave /liːv/

leaves leaving left

VERB

1 When you leave a place or person, you go away from them.

EG *They left the hotel early.*

EG *My flight leaves in less than an hour.*

EG *Bill left me for another woman.*

2 If you leave something somewhere, you put it there before you go away.

EG *I left my bags in the car while I did some shopping.*

EG *I left a message for you at work.*

3 If you leave something somewhere, you forget to take it with you.

EG *I must have left my keys at home.*

4 If you leave a job or organization, you stop being a part of it.

EG *He left school with no qualifications.*

5 If something leaves an amount of something, that amount remains available after the rest has been used.

EG *That won't leave us any money for food.*

6 If something leaves a mark or impression, it causes it.

EG *The operation will leave a scar.*

EG *She left a lasting impression on him.*

7 If you **leave** money or property **to** someone, you arrange for it to be given to them after you have died.

EG *He left everything to his wife.*

8 If you **leave** someone **alone**, you do not bother them.

EG *He kept phoning me — he wouldn't leave me alone.*

NOUN

9 a period of holiday or absence

A
B
C
D
E
F
G
H
I
J
K
L
M
N
O
P
Q
R
S
T
U
V
W
X
Y
Z

A B C D E F G H I J K L M N O P Q R S T U V W X Y Z

from a job

EG *Why don't you take a few days' leave?*

leaves /liːvz/

the plural of **leaf**

lecture /ˈlɛktʃəʳ/
lectures

NOUN

a formal talk that is intended to teach people about a subject, especially at a university

EG *He's giving a lecture on modern art.*

led /lɛd/

past tense and past participle of **lead**

left /lɛft/

1 Left is the past tense and past participle of **leave**

NOUN

2 The left is one of two opposite sides, positions, or directions. If you are facing north and you turn to the left, you will be facing west.

EG *To my left was a small cottage.*

EG *In Britain cars drive on the left.*

3 People and political groups that hold socialist views are referred to as **the left**.

EG *The change has been opposed by the left.*

ADJECTIVE OR ADVERB

4 Left means on or towards the left of something.

EG *... a cut over his left eye*

EG *Turn left into Govan Road.*

ADJECTIVE

5 If a certain amount of something is left or **left over**, it remains when the rest has gone.

EG *They have two games left to play.*

EG *Was there any money left over?*

left-handed /lɛftˈhændɪd/

ADJECTIVE OR ADVERB

Someone who is left-handed does things such as writing with their left hand.

EG *I noticed she was left-handed.*

EG *He threw the ball left-handed.*

left-wing /ˈlɛftˈwɪŋ/

ADJECTIVE

A left-wing person or group has political ideas that are based on socialism.

EG *... because they considered him too left-wing*

leg /lɛg/
legs

NOUN

1 Your legs are the two long parts of your body that you stand on and walk with.

EG *... a pain in his left leg*

2 The legs of a pair of trousers are the parts that cover your legs.

EG *The grass had stained his trouser legs.*

3 The legs of a table or chair are the parts which rest on the floor and support it.

EG *His ankles were tied to the legs of the chair.*

4 A leg of a journey or a sports match is one part of it.

EG *The first leg of the journey was by boat.*

legal /ˈliːgl/

ADJECTIVE

1 relating to the law

EG *... the Dutch legal system*

2 allowed by the law

EG *What I did was perfectly legal.*

legend /ˈlɛdʒənd/
legends

NOUN

1 a very old and popular story

EG *... according to an old Irish*

legend
2 someone who is very famous
EG *... Hollywood legend Audrey Hepburn*

legitimate /lɪˈdʒɪtɪmət/
ADJECTIVE
Something that is legitimate is reasonable or acceptable according to existing laws or standards.
EG *... the legitimate government*
EG *That's a perfectly legitimate fear.*

leisure /ˈlɛʒəʳ/
NOUN
Leisure is the time when you do not have to work and can do things that you enjoy.
EG *... a relaxing way to fill my leisure time*

lemon /ˈlɛmən/
lemons
NOUN
a yellow fruit with a sour taste
EG *... a slice of lemon*

lemonade /lɛməˈneɪd/
NOUN
a clear, sweet drink, traditionally made from lemons, water, and sugar
EG *... a glass of lemonade*

lend /lɛnd/
lends lending lent
VERB
1 If you lend someone something or **lend** it **to** them, you let them have it for a period of time.
EG *Will you lend me your jacket?*
EG *I lent my bicycle to Harold.*
2 If a person or bank lends you money, they give you money and you agree to pay it back later.
EG *He lent me ten pounds for a taxi.*

length /lɛŋθ/
lengths
NOUN
1 The length of something is the distance from one end to the other.
EG *... the length of the fish*
EG *It grows to a length of five metres.*
2 The length of an event or activity is the amount of time that it continues.
EG *... his film, over two hours in length*
3 The length of something is the fact that it is long rather than short.
EG *I was surprised at the length of his fingernails.*
EG *... the length of time it took him to make up his mind*
PLURAL NOUN
4 If you **go to great lengths** to achieve something, you do extreme things in order to achieve it.
EG *People have gone to great lengths to raise the money.*

lens /lɛnz/
lenses
NOUN
a thin, curved piece of glass or plastic which makes things appear larger or clearer
EG *... a camera lens*
EG *... the sunglasses with the green lenses*

lent /lɛnt/
past participle and past tense of **lend**

lesbian /ˈlɛzbɪən/
lesbians
NOUN
a homosexual woman
EG *... a youth group for lesbians and gays*

less /lɛs/
ADJECTIVE, ADVERB, OR PRONOUN

1 Less means a smaller amount of something, or to a smaller extent.
EG *A shower uses less water than a bath.*
EG *She was less frightened of him now.*
EG *They left less than three weeks ago.*

☑ You use 'less' to talk about things that cannot be counted: *less time*. When you are talking about things that can be counted, you should use 'fewer': *fewer students*.

PREPOSITION
2 You use 'less' to show that one number or amount is to be subtracted from another.
EG *He earns £50,000 a year, less tax.*

lesson /'lɛsn/
lessons

NOUN
1 a fixed period of time during which people are taught something
EG *Joanna was taking piano lessons.*
2 an experience that makes you understand something important
EG *There's one major lesson to be learned from all this.*

let /lɛt/
lets letting let

VERB
1 If you **let** someone **do** something, you allow them to do it.
EG *He let me carry on talking.*
EG *Her parents won't let her eat sweets.*
2 If you let someone into a place or out of a place, you allow them to enter or leave.
EG *I'd better let the dog out.*
3 If someone lets a house or flat that they own, they rent it out.

EG *I've decided to let my flat.*
4 You can say **let's** when you are making a suggestion.
EG *Let's go home.*
5 If you **let go of** someone or something, you stop holding them.
EG *She let go of Mona's hand.*
6 If you **let** someone **know** something, you make sure that they know about it.
EG *If you're interested, let me know.*

lethal /'li:θl/

ADJECTIVE
Something that is lethal can kill you.
EG *... a lethal weapon*

letter /'lɛtər/
letters

NOUN
1 a message written on paper and sent to someone, usually through the post
EG *I wrote her a long letter.*
2 Letters are written symbols which go together to make words.
EG *... the letter E*

lettuce /'lɛtɪs/
lettuces

NOUN
a vegetable with large green leaves that you eat in salads
EG *... a lettuce leaf*

level /'lɛvl/
levels

NOUN
1 a point on a scale which measures the amount, importance, or difficulty of something
EG *... the lowest level of inflation for years*
2 The level of something is its height.
EG *He held the gun at waist level.*

A
B
C
D
E
F
G
H
I
J
K
L
M
N
O
P
Q
R
S
T
U
V
W
X
Y
Z

ADJECTIVE

3 A surface that is **level** is completely flat.
EG ... *an area of level ground*

4 If one thing is **level with** another, it is at the same height.
EG *She knelt down so that her face was level with the boy's.*

ADVERB

5 If you **draw level with** someone, you get closer to them until you are beside them.
EG *He drew level with the car in front and shouted through the window.*

liable /'laɪəbl/

ADJECTIVE

1 If you say that something is **liable to** happen, you mean that it will probably happen.
EG ... *equipment that is liable to break*

2 If you are **liable for** something, you are legally responsible for it.
EG ... *since you are not liable for the debt*

liar /'laɪər/
liars

NOUN

a person who tells lies
EG *She accused him of being a liar.*

liberal /'lɪbərl/
liberals

NOUN

1 someone who tolerates a wide range of behaviour or opinions
EG ... *a nation of liberals*

ADJECTIVE

2 If someone has liberal views, they tolerate a wide range of behaviour or opinions.
EG ... *liberal views on drugs*

Liberal Democrat Liberal Democrats

NOUN

The Liberal Democrats or the Liberal Democrat Party is the third largest political party in Britain and the main centre party.
EG ... *the role of the Liberal Democrats*

liberty /'lɪbətɪ/

NOUN

Liberty is the freedom to do what you want to do and go where you want to go.
EG ... *prisoners who complain about loss of liberty*

library /'laɪbrərɪ/
libraries

NOUN

a building in which books are kept, especially a public building from which people can borrow books
EG ... *the local library*

licence /'laɪsns/
licences
US **license**

NOUN

an official document which gives you permission to do, use, or own something
EG ... *a driving licence*

license /'laɪsns/
licenses licensing licensed

VERB

If someone licenses an activity, they give official permission for it to be done.
EG *The ferry was licensed to carry a hundred people.*

lick /lɪk/
licks licking licked

VERB

If you lick something, you move your tongue over it.
EG *The dog licked the man's hand excitedly.*

A B C D E F G H I J K L M N O P Q R S T U V W X Y Z

lid /lɪd/
lids

NOUN

the top of a container, which you open in order to reach what is inside

EG ... *a saucepan lid*

lie /laɪ/
lies lying lay lain

☑ The past tense of this verb 'lie' is *lay*. Do not confuse it with the verb 'lay' meaning 'put'.

VERB

1 If someone or something lies somewhere, they rest there in a flat position.

EG *There was a child lying on the ground.*

EG *Broken glass lay scattered on the carpet.*

2 If you say where someone or something lies, you are saying where they are or what their position is.

EG *The farm lies between two valleys.*

EG *Tait is currently lying in second place.*

lie /laɪ/
lies lying lied

VERB

1 If you lie, you say something that you know is not true.

EG *He lied about his age.*

NOUN

2 something you say which you know is not true

EG *All the boys told lies about their adventures.*

life /laɪf/
lives

NOUN

1 Life is the state of being alive.

EG ... *a baby's first few minutes of life*

2 Your life is your existence from the time you are born until the time you die.

EG *He spent the last five years of his life abroad.*

3 If you refer to the life in a place, you are talking about the amount of activity there.

EG *The town was full of life.*

lifestyle /'laɪfstaɪl/
lifestyles

Your lifestyle is the way that you live.

EG *The baby's arrival meant a change of lifestyle.*

lifetime /'laɪftaɪm/
lifetimes

NOUN

Your lifetime is the period of time during which you are alive.

EG *I've seen a lot of changes in my lifetime.*

lift /lɪft/
lifts lifting lifted

VERB

1 If you lift something, you move it to a higher position.

EG *He lifted the glass to his mouth.*

2 When fog or mist lifts, it clears away.

EG *Around midday the fog lifted.*

3 If people in authority lift a rule or law, they end it.

EG *The ban was finally lifted in 1998.*

NOUN

4 a device that carries people or goods from one floor to another in a building

EG *We took the lift to the top floor.*

5 If you **give** someone **a lift**, you drive them from one place to another.

EG *Jenny gave me a lift to the shops.*

light /laɪt/
lights lighting lighted or **lit;
lighter lightest**

NOUN
1 Light is the brightness from the
sun, moon, fire, or lamps, that lets
you see things.
EG *It was difficult to see in the dim
light.*
2 a lamp or other device that gives
out brightness
EG *Remember to turn the lights out.*
3 If you give someone **a light**,
you give them a match or lighter
to light their cigarette.
EG *Do you have a light?*

ADJECTIVE
4 If it is light, there is enough light
from the sun to see things.
EG *It was still light when we arrived.*
5 A light colour is pale.
EG *... a light blue shirt*
6 A light object does not weigh
much.
EG *Modern tennis rackets are very
light.*

VERB
7 A place that is lit by something
has light shining in it.
EG *The room was lit by a single
bulb.*
EG *The moon lit the road ahead.*
8 If you light a fire or cigarette,
you make it start burning.
EG *She drew the curtains and lit the
fire.*

lighter /ˈlaɪtər/
lighters

NOUN
a device for lighting cigarettes
EG *... a disposable lighter*

lighting /ˈlaɪtɪŋ/

NOUN
The lighting in a place is the way
that it is lit.

EG *... the absence of street lighting*

lightning /ˈlaɪtnɪŋ/

NOUN
Lightning is the bright flashes of
light in the sky that you sometimes
see during a storm.
EG *... a flash of lightning*
EG *... thunder and lightning*

like /laɪk/
likes liking liked

VERB
1 If you like someone or
something, you think they are
interesting, enjoyable, or attractive.
EG *I don't know why she doesn't
like football.*
EG *That's one of the things I like
about you.*
2 If you say that you would like
something or **would like to do**
something, you mean that you
want it.
EG *I'd like a cup of tea.*
EG *Would you like to come back for
coffee?*

PREPOSITION
3 If one thing is like another, it is
similar to it.
EG *It's a bit like his last film.*
4 If you ask what someone or
something is like, you are asking
about their qualities.
EG *What's your new boss like?*
5 You use 'like' to give an example
of the thing that you have just
mentioned.
EG *... big cities like New York*
6 If you **feel like doing**
something, you want to do it.
EG *I feel like celebrating.*

likely /ˈlaɪklɪ/
likelier likeliest

ADJECTIVE
Something that is likely will
probably happen or is probably

A B C D E F G H I J K L M N O P Q R S T U V W X Y Z

true.

EG *Is he likely to agree?*

EG *It's more likely that she forgot.*

likewise /'laɪkwaɪz/

ADVERB

You use 'likewise' when you are saying that two things are similar or the same.

EG *It's very popular in Spain, likewise in Italy.*

EG *She sat down and he did likewise.*

limb /lɪm/

limbs

NOUN

Your limbs are your arms and legs.

EG *He was very tall with long limbs.*

limit /'lɪmɪt/

limits limiting limited

NOUN

1 A limit is the largest or smallest amount of something that is possible or allowed.

EG *He was being tested to his limits.*

EG *... the speed limit*

VERB

2 If you limit something, you prevent it from developing or becoming bigger.

EG *He did all he could to limit the damage.*

limited /'lɪmɪtɪd/

ADJECTIVE

Something that is limited is not very great in amount or extent.

EG *We have a limited amount of time.*

limp /lɪmp/

limps limping limped;
limper limpest

VERB

1 If you limp, you walk in an uneven way because you have hurt your leg or foot.

EG *... as he limped off the pitch at half-time*

NOUN

2 an uneven way of walking

EG *Since the accident she has walked with a limp.*

ADJECTIVE

3 Something that is limp is soft or weak.

EG *... a limp handshake*

line /laɪn/

lines lining lined

NOUN

1 a long, thin mark

EG *Draw a line down the centre of the page.*

2 a number of people or things that are arranged in a row

EG *... a line of women queueing for bread*

3 a route along which someone or something moves

EG *... a railway line*

4 a long piece of string or wire

EG *She put her washing on the line.*

5 In a piece of writing or a song, a line is a number of words together.

EG *How does the next line go?*

VERB

6 If people or things line a place, they are present along its edges.

EG *Crowds lined the streets.*

line up

VERB

When people line up, they form a queue.

EG *The children lined up behind their teacher.*

link /lɪŋk/

links linking linked

NOUN

1 a relationship or connection between two things

EG *... the link between alcohol and violence*

2 a physical connection between two things or places
EG ... *a high-speed rail link between the two cities*

VERB
3 If something links places or things, it joins them together.
EG ... *a canal linking the rivers*
4 If you link one person or thing to another, you claim there is a connection between them.
EG *The police are not linking him to the murder.*

lion /'laɪən/
lions

NOUN
a large member of the cat family that is found in Africa. Male lions have long hair on their head and neck.
EG ... *a lion cub*

lip /lɪp/
lips

NOUN
Your lips are the two outer edges of your mouth.
EG ... *with a cigarette between his lips*

lipstick /'lɪpstɪk/
lipsticks

NOUN
Lipstick is a coloured substance which women wear on their lips.
EG *She was wearing red lipstick.*
EG ... *a range of glossy lipsticks*

liquid /'lɪkwɪd/
liquids

NOUN
a substance such as water, which is not solid and can be poured
EG ... *a glass containing some unknown liquid*

list /lɪst/
lists listing listed

NOUN
1 a set of words or items written one below the other
EG ... *the hotel's wine list*
EG ... *a shopping list*

VERB
2 If you list a number of things, you write them or say them one after another.
EG *She listed all the reasons why I ought to leave.*

listen /'lɪsn/
listens listening listened

VERB
If you **listen to** someone who is talking or **listen to** a sound, you give your attention to them.
EG *Sonia was not listening to him.*
EG *He spent his time listening to the radio.*
EG *Are you listening?*

lit /lɪt/
past participle and past tense of **light**

liter /'li:tər/
see **litre**

literally /'lɪtrəlɪ/
ADVERB
You use 'literally' to emphasize what you are saying, especially when you are exaggerating.
EG *There were literally hundreds of people there.*
EG *I literally crawled to the car.*

literary /'lɪtərərɪ/
ADJECTIVE
connected with literature
EG ... *a literary critic*

literature /'lɪtrɪtʃər/
NOUN
Novels, plays, and poetry are referred to as literature.
EG ... *a Professor of English Literature*

A
B
C
D
E
F
G
H
I
J
K
L
M
N
O
P
Q
R
S
T
U
V
W
X
Y
Z

A
B
C
D
E
F
G
H
I
J
K
L
M
N
O
P
Q
R
S
T
U
V
W
X
Y
Z

litre /'liːtər/
litres
us **liter**

NOUN

a unit of liquid volume equal to about 1.76 British pints or 2.11 American pints

EG … *15 litres of water*

litter /'lɪtər/
litters littering littered

NOUN

1 Litter is rubbish in the street and other public places.

EG *People have always dropped litter.*

VERB

2 If things litter a place, they are scattered all over it.

EG *Glass littered the pavement.*

little /'lɪtl/

ADJECTIVE

1 small in size

EG … *a little house*

2 short in time or distance

EG … *a little way down the road*

3 a little bit means to a small extent

EG *He's a little bit young for such a job.*

ADVERB OR PRONOUN

4 a little of something is a small amount of it

EG *He seemed a little anxious.*

EG *Pour a little of the sauce over the chicken.*

5 Little means not much.

EG *I had very little money left.*

EG *Little is known about his childhood.*

☑ If you have *a little food*, you have some food, but if you have *little food*, you do not have as much as you would like.

live /lɪv/
lives living lived

VERB

1 To live means to be alive.

EG *She lived at the end of the sixteenth century.*

2 If you live in a place, that is where your home is.

EG *He still lives with his parents.*

3 The way someone lives is the kind of life they have.

EG *We live quite simply.*

live /laɪv/

ADJECTIVE OR ADVERB

1 Live television or radio is broadcast while the event is taking place.

EG … *a live football match*

EG *The concert will be shown live.*

ADJECTIVE

2 Live animals or plants are alive, rather than dead or artificial.

EG … *a basket of live crabs*

lively /'laɪvlɪ/

ADJECTIVE

full of life and enthusiasm

EG … *lively conversation*

liver /'lɪvər/
livers

NOUN

Your liver is a large organ in your body which cleans your blood.

EG … *liver disease*

lives /laɪvz/
the plural of **life**

living /'lɪvɪŋ/

ADJECTIVE

1 If someone is living, they are alive.

EG … *her only living relative*

NOUN

2 The work that you do **for a living** is the work that you do in order to earn an income.

EG *What does he do for a living?*

living room living rooms

NOUN

the room in a house where people relax

EG *We were in the living room watching TV.*

load /ləud/

loads loading loaded

VERB

1 If you load a vehicle or container, you put things into it.

EG *... after they'd finished loading the truck*

2 If you load a gun, you put a bullet into it.

EG *He carried a loaded gun.*

NOUN

3 A load is something large or heavy which is being carried.

EG *... a tractor with a big load of hay*

4 AN INFORMAL USE

A **load of** something, or **loads of** something, means a lot of it.

EG *He's got loads of money.*

loaf /ləuf/

loaves

NOUN

a large piece of bread in a shape that can be cut into slices

EG *... a loaf of crusty bread*

loan /ləun/

loans loaning loaned

NOUN

1 a sum of money that you borrow

EG *... a bank loan*

VERB

2 If you **loan** someone something or **loan** it **to** them, you lend it to them.

EG *He never loaned his car to anyone.*

loaves /ləuvz/

the plural of **loaf**

lobster /'lɒbstər/

lobsters

NOUN

a sea creature with a hard shell, two front claws, and eight legs

EG *For dinner we had lobster.*

local /'ləukl/

locals

ADJECTIVE

1 existing in or belonging to the area where you live

EG *... the local newspaper*

NOUN

2 The locals are the people who live in a particular area.

EG *That's where the locals go to drink.*

locate /ləu'keɪt/

locates locating located

VERB

1 If you locate someone or something, you find them.

EG *The police were unable to locate him.*

2 If something **is located** in a place, it is in that place.

EG *The restaurant is located near the cathedral.*

location /ləu'keɪʃən/

locations

NOUN

A location is a place, especially the place where something is situated.

EG *She couldn't remember the exact location of the church.*

lock /lɒk/

locks locking locked

VERB

1 If you lock something, you fasten it with a key.

EG *She forgot to lock the door.*

2 If you lock a person or thing somewhere, you put them there and fasten the lock.

A
EG *They locked him in a cell.*
EG *I was locked out of the house.*
NOUN
3 a device which prevents something from being opened except with a key
EG *He heard a key in the lock.*

locker /'lɒkəʳ/
lockers
NOUN
a small cupboard for someone's personal belongings, for example in a changing room
EG *... a left-luggage locker*

log /lɒg/
logs
NOUN
a thick piece of wood which has been cut from a tree
EG *He dumped the logs beside the fire.*

logic /'lɒdʒɪk/
NOUN
Logic is a way of reasoning involving a series of statements, each of which must be true if the statement before it is true.
EG *I don't follow the logic of your argument.*

logical /'lɒdʒɪkl/
ADJECTIVE
A logical conclusion or result is the only reasonable one.
EG *There is only one logical conclusion.*

lone /ləʊn/
ADJECTIVE
A lone person or thing is the only one in a particular place.
EG *He was shot by a lone gunman.*

lonely /'ləʊnlɪ/
lonelier loneliest
ADJECTIVE
1 If you are lonely, you are

unhappy because you feel alone.
EG *... lonely people who just want to talk*
2 A lonely place is one which very few people visit.
EG *... lonely country roads*

long /lɒŋ/
longer longest; longs longing longed
ADJECTIVE
1 great in length or distance
EG *... a long dress*
EG *... a long road*
EG *His new book is very long.*
ADJECTIVE OR ADVERB
2 continuing for a great amount of time
EG *There had been no rain for a long time.*
EG *It won't take long.*
3 You use 'long' to talk about amounts of time.
EG *The journey is 5 hours long.*
EG *How long can you stay?*
4 You use 'long' to talk about the distance that something measures from one end to the other.
EG *... an insect three inches long*
EG *How long is the tunnel?*
ADVERB
5 If you say that you **won't be long**, you mean that you will arrive or return soon.
EG *I'm just going out — I won't be long.*
6 If something **no longer** happens, it used to happen but does not happen now.
EG *Food shortages are no longer a problem.*
7 If one thing is true **as long as** another thing is true, it is true only if the other thing is true.
EG *As long as there's no more rain, the match will go ahead.*

VERB

8 If you **long for** something, or if you **long to do** it, you want it to happen very much.

EG *He longed for the winter to be over.*

EG *I'm longing to meet her.*

loo /luː/
loos

NOUN

AN INFORMAL WORD

a toilet

EG *I need to go to the loo.*

look /luk/
looks looking looked

VERB

1 If you **look** in a particular direction, you turn your eyes in order to see what is there.

EG *He looked at his watch.*

EG *She turned to look out of the window.*

2 If you **look for** someone or something, you try to find them.

EG *I'm looking for my keys.*

3 If you **look at** a subject or situation, you study it or judge it.

EG *Let's look at the implications of this.*

4 If you describe the way that someone or something **looks**, you are describing their appearance.

EG *The house looks lovely.*

EG *He looked as if he was going to cry.*

NOUN

5 If you **have** or **take a look** at something, you look at it.

EG *Lucy took a last look in the mirror.*

6 The **look** on your face is the expression on it.

EG *... with a look of disgust*

PLURAL NOUN

7 If you talk about someone's **looks**, you are talking about how attractive they are.

EG *She was beginning to lose her looks.*

look after
VERB

If you **look after** someone or something, you take care of them.

EG *His sister looks after the children at weekends.*

look forward to
VERB

If you are **looking forward to** something, you want it to happen because you think you will enjoy it.

EG *I'm really looking forward to going on holiday.*

look out
VERB

You say "look out" to warn someone of danger.

EG *Look out! There's a car coming.*

loop /luːp/
loops looping looped

NOUN

1 a curved or circular shape in something long such as a piece of string

EG *... loops of wire*

VERB

2 If you **loop** rope or string around an object, you place it in a loop around the object.

EG *He looped the rope over the wood.*

loose /luːs/
looser loosest

ADJECTIVE

1 Something that is loose is not firmly held or fixed in place.

EG *... a loose tooth*

ADVERB

2 If people or animals **break loose** or are **set loose**, they are freed after they have been held or

A B C D E F G H I J K L M N O P Q R S T U V W X Y Z

imprisoned.
EG *She broke loose from his embrace.*

lord /lɔːd/
lords

NOUN
a man who has a high rank in the upper classes
EG *She married a lord.*

lorry /'lɒrɪ/
lorries

NOUN
a large vehicle for transporting goods by road
EG *... a seven-ton lorry*

lose /luːz/
loses losing lost

VERB
1 If you lose something, you cannot find it, or you no longer have it because it has been taken from you.
EG *I lost my keys.*
EG *He lost his place in the team.*
2 If you lose a fight or an argument, you are beaten.
EG *They haven't lost a single match.*
3 If you lose something, you begin to have less of it.
EG *... the best way to lose weight*
EG *The company was losing money.*
4 If you lose a relative or friend, they die.
EG *She lost her brother in the war.*

loss /lɒs/
losses

NOUN
The loss of something is the fact of no longer having it or of having less of it.
EG *... the loss of her sight*
EG *Big job losses are expected.*

lost /lɒst/
1 Lost is the past tense and past

participle of **lose**

ADJECTIVE
2 If you are lost, you do not know where you are.
EG *I suddenly realized I was lost.*
3 If something is lost, you cannot find it.
EG *... the hunt for the lost umbrella*

lot /lɒt/
lots

NOUN
1 a lot of something, or lots of something, is a large amount of it
EG *A lot of my friends are Irish.*
EG *He drank lots of milk.*
2 a lot means very much or very often
EG *He doesn't earn a lot.*
EG *They go out quite a lot.*
3 a group of people or things
EG *We were sent two lots of documents.*
4 the lot means the whole of an amount
EG *He bet his wages and lost the lot.*

lotion /'ləʊʃən/
lotions

NOUN
a liquid that you put on your skin to protect it or make it softer
EG *... suntan lotion*

lottery /'lɒtərɪ/
lotteries

NOUN
a type of gambling in which people buy numbered tickets from which a winner is selected at random
EG *... the National Lottery*

loud /laʊd/
louder loudest

ADJECTIVE OR ADVERB
A loud noise produces a lot of sound.

EG ... *a loud explosion*
EG *He turned the television up very loud.*

lounge /laundʒ/
lounges lounging lounged
NOUN
1 a room in a house, hotel, or airport where people can sit and relax
EG ... *the airport departure lounge*
VERB
2 If you lounge somewhere, you spend your time there in a relaxed and lazy way.
EG *They spent the afternoons lounging around the swimming pool.*

love /lʌv/
loves loving loved
VERB
1 If you love someone, you have strong feelings of affection for them.
EG *Oh, Amy, I love you.*
2 If you love something, you like it very much.
EG *We both love fishing.*
3 If you **would love to do** something, you want very much to do it.
EG *I would love to live there.*
NOUN
4 Love is a strong feeling of affection for someone or something.
EG ... *our love for each other*
EG ... *his love of football*
5 If you are **in love with** someone, you feel strongly attracted to them romantically or sexually.
EG *We were madly in love with each other.*
6 When two people **make love**, they have sex.
EG ... *the first time they made love*

lovely /'lʌvlɪ/
lovelier loveliest
ADJECTIVE
very beautiful or pleasant
EG *You look lovely.*
EG ... *a lovely day*

lover /'lʌvər/
lovers
NOUN
1 A person's lover is someone that they have a sexual relationship with but are not married to.
EG *They became lovers a week later.*
2 Someone who is a lover of something is very fond of it.
EG ... *art lovers*

low /ləʊ/
lower lowest; lows
ADJECTIVE OR ADVERB
1 Something that is low is close to the ground or measures a short distance from the ground to the top.
EG *The sun was low in the sky.*
EG ... *a low table*
EG ... *an aircraft flying very low*
ADJECTIVE
2 small in value or amount
EG ... *people on low incomes*
EG *The lowest number of accidents for 5 years.*
3 poor in quality
EG ... *work of a very low standard*
NOUN
4 A low is a level or amount that is less than before.
EG *The dollar fell to a new low.*

lower /'ləʊər/
lowers lowering lowered
1 Lower is the comparative of **low**
ADJECTIVE
2 The lower one of a pair of things is the bottom one.
EG ... *the lower deck of the bus*
VERB

3 If you lower something, you move it downwards.
EG *They lowered the coffin into the grave.*

4 To lower an amount, value, or quality means to make it less.
EG *... the decision to lower interest rates*

loyal /ˈlɔɪəl/
ADJECTIVE
If you are loyal, you are firm in your friendship or support for someone or something.
EG *... a loyal friend*
EG *They had remained loyal to the president.*

luck /lʌk/
NOUN
1 Luck or **good luck** is anything good that happens to you which is not a result of your own efforts.
EG *We had no luck with the weather.*
EG *The success owed more to good luck than good planning.*

2 bad luck is anything bad that happens to you which is not a result of your own efforts
EG *He's had a lot of bad luck recently.*

3 You say **good luck** to someone when you are wishing them success.
EG *Good luck in your exams!*

lucky /ˈlʌkɪ/
luckier luckiest
ADJECTIVE
1 If someone is lucky, they are in a desirable situation.
EG *I'm lucky in having an excellent teacher.*

2 Someone who is lucky has a lot of good luck.
EG *He had always been lucky at cards.*

3 Something that is lucky has good effects or consequences.
EG *It's lucky that no one was injured.*

luggage /ˈlʌgɪdʒ/
NOUN
Your luggage is the bags and suitcases that you take with you when you travel.
EG *Leave your luggage in the hotel.*
EG *How many pieces of luggage did you have?*
☑ 'Luggage' refers to all of your suitcases and bags, not to an individual suitcase or bag.

lump /lʌmp/
lumps
NOUN
1 a solid piece of something
EG *... a lump of wood*

2 a small, hard piece of flesh on someone's body
EG *She had a lump removed from her breast.*

lunch /lʌntʃ/
lunches
NOUN
a meal eaten in the middle of the day
EG *... a light lunch*
EG *We all went out for lunch.*

lunchtime /ˈlʌntʃtaɪm/
lunchtimes
NOUN
Lunchtime is the period of the day when people eat lunch.
EG *Could we meet at lunchtime?*

lung /lʌŋ/
lungs
NOUN
Your lungs are the two organs inside your chest with which you breathe.
EG *... lung cancer*

A B C D E F G H I J K L M N O P Q R S T U V W X Y Z

luxury /'lʌkʃərɪ/
luxuries

NOUN

1 Luxury is great comfort, especially among expensive and beautiful surroundings.

EG *... a life of luxury*

2 A luxury is something that you enjoy very much but do not often have, usually because it is expensive.

EG *Foreign holidays are a luxury we can no longer afford.*

lying /'laɪɪŋ/
present participle of **lie**

lyrics /'lɪrɪks/

PLURAL NOUN

The lyrics of a song are its words.

EG *... with lyrics by Tim Rice*

A
B
C
D
E
F
G
H
I
J
K
L
M
N
O
P
Q
R
S
T
U
V
W
X
Y
Z

Mm

machine /mə'ʃi:n/
machines

NOUN

a piece of equipment which uses electricity or power from an engine to make it work

EG *... a machine to pump water out of mines*

machinery /mə'ʃi:nərɪ/

NOUN

Machinery is machines in general.

EG *They import most of their machinery.*

EG *... a piece of machinery*

mad /mæd/
madder maddest

ADJECTIVE

1 Someone who is mad has a mental illness which causes them to behave in strange ways.

EG *She was afraid of going mad.*

2 If you describe someone as mad, you mean that they are very foolish.

EG *He said we were mad to share a flat.*

3 AN INFORMAL USE

Someone who is mad is angry.

EG *She was mad at me for waking her up.*

4 AN INFORMAL USE

If you are **mad about** someone or something, you like them very much.

EG *Alan was mad about golf.*

madam /'mædəm/

'Madam' is a formal way of addressing a woman.

EG *This way, madam.*

made /meɪd/

past participle and past tense of **make**

magazine /mægə'zi:n/
magazines

NOUN

a weekly or monthly publication with articles and photographs

EG *... a women's magazine*

magic /'mædʒɪk/

NOUN

1 In myths and stories, magic is a special power that can make impossible things happen.

EG *They believe in magic.*

2 Magic is the art of performing tricks to entertain people.

EG *... a book on magic*

magnet /'mægnɪt/
magnets

NOUN

a piece of iron which attracts iron or steel towards it

EG *... a fridge magnet*

magnificent /mæg'nɪfɪsnt/

ADJECTIVE

extremely beautiful or impressive

EG *The scenery is magnificent.*

EG *... a magnificent achievement*

maid /meɪd/
maids

NOUN

a woman who is employed to cook or clean in another person's house

EG *A maid brought me breakfast.*

maiden name maiden names

NOUN

the surname that a woman had before she married

EG *Please give your married name and maiden name.*

mail /meɪl/
mails mailing mailed

NOUN

1 Mail is the letters and parcels delivered to you by the post office.

EG *Was there any mail today?*

2 Mail is the system used for collecting and delivering letters and parcels.

EG *You will be contacted by mail.*

VERB

3 If you mail a letter, you send it by post.

EG *I mailed a letter to you yesterday.*

mail order

NOUN

Mail order is a system of buying goods by post.

EG *... a mail order catalogue*

main /meɪn/
mains

ADJECTIVE

1 most important

EG *... the main entrance*

EG *My main concern is to protect the children.*

PLURAL NOUN

2 the mains are the large pipes or wires that carry gas, water, or electricity to a building

EG *... a radio that plugs into the mains*

mainly /'meɪnlɪ/

ADVERB

You use 'mainly' to show that a statement is true in most cases.

EG *The staff were mainly Russian.*

maintain /meɪn'teɪn/
maintains maintaining
maintained

VERB

1 If you maintain something, you make it continue or keep it at a particular rate or level.

EG *I've tried to maintain contact with the children.*

EG *... the need to maintain high standards*

2 If you maintain a machine or a building, you keep it in good condition.

EG *The house costs a fortune to maintain.*

3 If you maintain that something is true, you believe it is true and say so.

EG *He maintained his innocence throughout the trial.*

majesty /'mædʒɪstɪ/

NOUN

You say **His Majesty** when you are talking about a king, and **Her Majesty** when you are talking about a queen.

EG *His Majesty requests your presence.*

major /'meɪdʒəʳ/
majors

ADJECTIVE

1 more important or more serious than other things

EG *Drug abuse is a major problem here.*

NOUN

2 an army officer of the rank immediately above captain

EG *... Major Alan Bulman*

majority /mə'dʒɒrɪtɪ/
majorities

NOUN

1 The majority of people or things in a group is more than half of them.

EG *The majority of people in our survey agreed.*

2 In an election or vote, a majority is the difference between the number of votes gained by the winner and the number gained by the person or party that comes second.

A B C D E F G H I J K L M N O P Q R S T U V W X Y Z

EG *The decision was passed by a wide majority.*

make /meɪk/
makes making made

VERB

1 If you make something, you produce or prepare it.

EG *Sheila makes all her own clothes.*

EG *I always make the dinner on Fridays.*

2 If someone or something **makes** you **do** something, they cause you to do it.

EG *The smoke made him cough.*

EG *She made him tidy his room.*

3 If you make something, you do it or offer it.

EG *He was about to make a speech.*

EG *Can I make a suggestion?*

4 If you **make it** somewhere, you succeed in arriving there.

EG *So did you make it to America?*

NOUN

5 The make of a product is the name of the company that made it.

EG *What make of car do you drive?*

make of

VERB

If you ask someone what they make of something, you are asking them what they think of it.

EG *What did you make of his speech?*

make up

VERB

1 If a number of people or things make up something, they are the members or parts of it.

EG *Women make up 13 per cent of the police force.*

2 If you make something up, you invent it.

EG *I'm not making it up, it really happened.*

3 If two people make up or **make it up** after a quarrel, they become friends again.

EG *She came back and they made it up.*

4 To **make up for** something that is lost or damaged means to replace it or compensate for it.

EG *... an extra payment to make up for the stress you've been caused*

5 If you **make up** your **mind**, you come to a decision.

EG *I can't make up my mind which book to buy.*

make-up /'meɪkʌp/

NOUN

Make-up is coloured creams and powders which women put on their faces to make themselves look more attractive.

EG *... women who wear too much make-up*

male /meɪl/
males

NOUN

1 a man or boy

EG *... the average American male*

ADJECTIVE

2 concerning or affecting men rather than women

EG *... a deep male voice*

man /mæn/
men; mans manning manned

NOUN

1 an adult male human being

EG *... a young man*

2 Human beings in general are sometimes referred to as man or men.

EG *... the most dangerous substance known to man*

EG *All men are equal.*

VERB

3 If you man something, you are in charge of it or you operate it.

EG *The station is seldom manned in the evening.*

manage /'mænɪdʒ/
manages managing managed

VERB

1 If you **manage to do** something, you succeed in doing it.
EG *We managed to find somewhere to sit.*

2 If you manage an organization or business, you are responsible for controlling it.
EG *Within two years he was managing the company.*

management /'mænɪdʒmənt/

NOUN

1 Management is the control and organizing of something.
EG *The zoo needed better management.*

2 The management is the people who control an organization.
EG *The management is doing its best.*

☑ You can use either a singular or a plural verb after 'the management': *the management is unpopular; the management are unpopular.*

manager /'mænɪdʒər/
managers

NOUN

a person responsible for running a business or organization
EG *... a bank manager*

mankind /mæn'kaɪnd/

NOUN

You use 'mankind' to refer to all human beings.
EG *... a threat to mankind*

manner /'mænər/
manners

NOUN

1 The manner in which you do something is the way you do it.
EG *... to conduct themselves in a professional manner*

PLURAL NOUN

2 If you have good **manners**, you behave very politely.
EG *She dressed well and had beautiful manners.*

mansion /'mænʃən/
mansions

NOUN

a very large house
EG *... a country mansion*

manual /'mænjuəl/
manuals

ADJECTIVE

1 Manual work involves physical strength rather than mental skill.
EG *... skilled manual workers*

2 Manual equipment is operated by hand rather than by electricity or by a motor.
EG *... a manual typewriter*

NOUN

3 a book which tells you how to use a machine
EG *... the instruction manual*

manufacture /mænju'fæktʃər/
manufactures manufacturing manufactured

VERB

1 To manufacture goods means to make them in a factory.
EG *... goods manufactured abroad*

NOUN

2 The manufacture of goods is the making of them in a factory.
EG *... the manufacture of nuclear weapons*

many /'mɛnɪ/

ADJECTIVE OR PRONOUN

1 If there are many people or

A
B
C
D
E
F
G
H
I
J
K
L
M
N
O
P
Q
R
S
T
U
V
W
X
Y
Z

things, there are a large number of them.
EG *Many people would agree.*
EG *Many of these countries have huge debts.*
EG *Many are too weak to walk.*
2 You use 'many' to talk about how great a number or quantity is.
EG *How many tickets do you require?*
EG *No one knows how many were killed.*

☑ You only use 'many' to talk about things that can be counted. You should use 'much' if you want to talk about a large amount of something: *too much money.*

map /mæp/
maps
NOUN
a detailed drawing of an area as it would appear if you saw it from above
EG *... a map of the city centre*

marathon /'mærəθən/
marathons
NOUN
a race in which people run 26 miles
EG *... the London Marathon*

marble /'mɑːbl/
NOUN
Marble is a very hard, cold stone which is often polished to show the coloured patterns in it.
EG *... a marble fireplace*

march /mɑːtʃ/
marches marching marched
NOUN
1 an organized protest in which a large group of people walk somewhere together
EG *She'd been on a few marches before.*
VERB
2 When soldiers march, they walk

with quick regular steps as a group.
EG *... soldiers marching down the street*

March /mɑːtʃ/
NOUN
March is the third month of the year.
EG *... the prospect of snow in March*

margarine /mɑːdʒə'riːn/
NOUN
Margarine is a substance similar to butter, made from vegetable oil and animal fat.
EG *... a tub of margarine*

margin /'mɑːdʒɪn/
margins
NOUN
1 If you win a contest by a large or small margin, you win it by a large or small amount.
EG *... a winning margin of fifty points*
2 the blank space at each side of a written or printed page
EG *... a tick in the margin*

marine /mə'riːn/
marines
NOUN
1 a soldier who is trained for duties at sea as well as on land
EG *... a US marine*
ADJECTIVE
2 relating to or involving the sea
EG *... marine life*

mark /mɑːk/
marks marking marked
NOUN
1 a small stain or damaged area on a surface
EG *I can't get this mark off the wall.*
2 a written or printed symbol
EG *He made a few marks in the margin.*
3 a score given to a student for

homework or for an exam

EG *She did well to get such a good mark.*

4 Behaviour which is a **mark of** something is a sign of that thing.

EG *They removed their hats as a mark of respect.*

VERB

5 If something marks a surface, it stains or damages it in some way.

EG *... a sofa badly marked by cigarette burns*

6 If you mark something, you write a symbol on it or identify it in some other way.

EG *... a report marked Top Secret*

7 When a teacher marks a student's work, they decide how good it is and give it a mark.

EG *He was marking essays in his study.*

8 If an event marks a point or stage in something, it shows that that point or stage has been reached.

EG *The announcement marks the end of an extraordinary few days.*

marked /mɑːkt/

ADJECTIVE

very obvious

EG *... a marked improvement*

market /'mɑːkɪt/

markets marketing marketed

NOUN

1 a place where goods are bought and sold, usually outdoors

EG *... an antiques market*

2 The market for a product is the number of people who want to buy it.

EG *... the housing market*

VERB

3 To market a product means to sell it in an organized way.

EG *... a pen first marketed by a Japanese firm*

marmalade /'mɑːməleɪd/

NOUN

Marmalade is a type of jam made from oranges or lemons.

EG *... toast and marmalade*

marriage /'mærɪdʒ/

marriages

NOUN

1 the relationship between a husband and wife

EG *... a happy marriage*

2 Marriage is the act of marrying someone.

EG *I opposed her marriage to Ben.*

marry /'mærɪ/

marries marrying married

VERB

1 When a man and woman **get married** or marry, they become each other's husband and wife during a special ceremony.

EG *Laura just got married to Jake.*

EG *He wants to marry her.*

2 When someone such as a priest or vicar marries a couple, he or she is in charge of their marriage ceremony.

EG *The local vicar has agreed to marry us.*

marvellous /'mɑːvləs/

US **marvelous**

ADJECTIVE

wonderful or excellent

EG *... a marvellous actor*

masculine /'mæskjulɪn/

ADJECTIVE

typical of men, rather than women

EG *... the masculine world of motor racing*

mask /mɑːsk/

masks masking masked

A
B
C
D
E
F
G
H
I
J
K
L
M
N
O
P
Q
R
S
T
U
V
W
X
Y
Z

NOUN
1 something you wear over your face for protection or as a disguise
EG ... *actors wearing masks*

VERB
2 If you mask something, you cover it so that it is protected or cannot be seen.
EG *Her eyes were masked by sunglasses.*

mass /mæs/
masses

NOUN
1 A **mass** of something is a large amount of it.
EG *She had a mass of red hair.*
2 Mass is a Christian religious service in which people eat bread and drink wine in order to remember the last meal of Jesus Christ
EG *She went to Mass each day.*

PLURAL NOUN
3 the masses are the ordinary people in society
EG ... *opera for the masses*

ADJECTIVE
4 involving or affecting a large number of people
EG ... *weapons of mass destruction*

massage /'mæsɑːʒ/
massages massaging massaged

VERB
1 If you massage someone or a part of their body, you rub their body in order to help them relax or to relieve pain.
EG *He continued massaging my shoulders.*

NOUN
2 a treatment which involves rubbing the body
EG *She asked me if I wanted a massage.*

massive /'mæsɪv/
ADJECTIVE
extremely large
EG ... *a massive iceberg*

master /'mɑːstəʳ/
masters mastering mastered

NOUN
1 a man who has authority over others, such as the employer of servants or the owner of slaves or animals
EG ... *a dog walking next to its master*

VERB
2 If you master something, you succeed in learning how to do it or understand it.
EG *I never mastered French.*

masterpiece /'mɑːstəpiːs/
masterpieces

NOUN
an extremely good painting, novel, film, or other work of art
EG ... *one of the true masterpieces of English literature*

mat /mæt/
mats

NOUN
1 a small piece of material that you put on a table to protect it from a hot plate or cup
EG ... *a set of table mats*
2 a small piece of carpet or other thick material that you put on the floor
EG *There was a letter on the mat.*

match /mætʃ/
matches matching matched

NOUN
1 an organized game of football, cricket, or some other sport
EG ... *a football match*
2 a small, wooden stick that produces a flame when you strike

A
B
C
D
E
F
G
H
I
J
K
L
M
N
O
P
Q
R
S
T
U
V
W
X
Y
Z

it against a rough surface
EG ... *a box of matches*

VERB
3 If one thing matches another, or if they match, the two things look similar or look good together.
EG *The lampshades matched the curtains.*

mate /meɪt/
mates mating mated

NOUN
1 AN INFORMAL USE
Your mates are your friends.
EG *He's in the pub with his mates.*
2 An animal's mate is its sexual partner.
EG *The males guard their mates closely.*

VERB
3 When animals mate, they have sex in order to produce young.
EG ... *when a female is ready to mate*

material /mə'tɪərɪəl/
materials

NOUN
1 Material is cloth.
EG ... *the thick material of her skirt*
2 Material is a solid substance.
EG ... *the recycling of all materials*

PLURAL NOUN
3 The equipment for a particular activity can be referred to as **materials**.
EG ... *building materials*

mathematics /mæθə'mætɪks/

NOUN
Mathematics is the study of numbers, quantities, and shapes.
EG ... *a professor of mathematics*
☑ Although it looks like a plural, 'mathematics' is a singular noun: *mathematics is his favourite subject.*

maths /mæθs/

NOUN
Maths is mathematics.
EG *He taught science and maths.*
☑ Like 'mathematics', 'maths' is a singular noun: *maths is his favourite subject.*

matter /'mætər/
matters mattering mattered

NOUN
1 A matter is a task or situation that you have to deal with.
EG *This is a matter for the police.*
EG *Getting angry won't help matters.*
2 Matter is any substance.
EG ... *how matter behaves at extreme temperatures*
3 If you ask **What's the matter?**, you are asking what is wrong.
EG *You're very quiet. What's the matter?*

VERB
4 If something matters, it is important.
EG ... *what really matters*
EG *It doesn't matter to me how old she is.*

mattress /'mætrɪs/
mattresses

NOUN
a thick, rectangular pad that is put on a bed to make it comfortable to sleep on
EG ... *a feather mattress*

mature /mə'tjʊər/
matures maturing matured

VERB
1 When a child or young animal matures, it becomes an adult.
EG *Children mature earlier these days.*

ADJECTIVE
2 fully grown or developed
EG *We're both mature adults.*

A
B
C
D
E
F
G
H
I
J
K
L
M
N
O
P
Q
R
S
T
U
V
W
X
Y
Z

maximum /'mæksɪməm/

ADJECTIVE

1 The maximum amount is the most that is possible or allowed.

EG ... *the car's maximum speed*

NOUN

2 The maximum is the most that is possible or allowed.

EG ... *a maximum of two years in prison*

may /meɪ/

might

☑ 'May' is a modal verb. There are no forms ending in -s, -ing, or -ed.

VERB

1 If something may happen, it is possible that it will happen.

EG *We may have some rain today.*

EG *It might have been an accident.*

2 If someone may do something, they are allowed to do it.

EG *May I come in?*

☑ This sense is usually only used in polite questions.

3 You can use 'may' when saying that, although something is true, something else is also true.

EG *I may be 50 but I'm still a good swimmer.*

May /meɪ/

NOUN

May is the fifth month of the year.

EG ... *after their holiday in May*

maybe /'meɪbi:/

ADVERB

You use 'maybe' to express uncertainty, for example when you do not know that something is definitely true.

EG *I met him once, maybe twice.*

EG *Maybe I should lie about my age.*

EG *"Will Gerald be there?" — "Maybe not."*

mayonnaise /meɪə'neɪz/

NOUN

Mayonnaise is a sauce made from eggs, oil, and vinegar, and usually eaten with salad.

EG ... *a jar of mayonnaise*

mayor /meər/

mayors

NOUN

a person who has been elected to represent the people of a town or city

EG ... *the Mayor of New York*

me /mi:/

PRONOUN

You use 'me' to refer to yourself.

EG ... *decisions that would affect me for the rest of my life*

EG *He gave me the book.*

EG *Hi, it's me.*

meal /mi:l/

meals

NOUN

an occasion when people eat, or the food that they eat at that time

EG *She talked to him throughout the meal.*

EG ... *a delicious meal*

mean /mi:n/

means meaning meant; meaner meanest

VERB

1 If you ask what something means, you want someone to explain it to you or you want to know what it refers to.

EG *What does that word actually mean?*

EG *I don't know what you mean by that.*

EG *I thought you meant the tall woman over there.*

2 If you mean what you say, you believe it and you are serious about it.

EG *He says he loves me but does he really mean it?*

3 If something **means** a lot to you, it is important to you.
EG *Winning means so much to her.*

4 If one thing **means** another thing, it shows that the second thing is true or makes it happen.
EG *Major roadworks will mean long delays.*

5 If you **mean to do** something, you intend to do it.
EG *I didn't mean to hurt you.*

ADJECTIVE
6 Someone who is **mean** is unwilling to spend much money.
EG *Don't be mean with the tip.*

7 If you are **mean to** someone, you are unkind to them.
EG *He apologized for being so mean to her.*

NOUN
8 A **means** of doing something is a method or thing which makes it possible to do it.
EG *They didn't provide me with any means of transport.*
EG *Victims were identified by several means.*

9 If you do something **by means of** a particular method or thing, you use that method or thing to do it.
EG *The tests were marked by means of a computer.*

meaning /ˈmiːnɪŋ/
meanings

NOUN
The **meaning** of a word or action is the thing that it refers to or expresses.
EG *... two words with similar meanings*
EG *What was the meaning of that smile?*

meant /mɛnt/
1 the past tense and past participle of **mean**

ADJECTIVE
2 If something is **meant to** happen, that is what was intended.
EG *I'm meant to be at work now.*

3 If something is **meant to** have a particular quality, people believe or say that it has that quality.
EG *It's meant to be a really good film.*

meantime /ˈmiːntaɪm/

NOUN
in the meantime means in the period of time between two events or while something else is happening
EG *I'll call the nurse; in the meantime, you must rest.*

meanwhile /ˈmiːnwaɪl/

ADVERB
in the period of time between two events or while something else is happening
EG *He crawled to the window, meanwhile removing his gun.*

measure /ˈmɛʒəʳ/
measures measuring measured

VERB
1 If you **measure** something, you find out how big or good it is by using particular procedures or instruments.
EG *We measured how tall he was.*
EG *He measures his success by the number of letters he receives.*

2 If something **measures** a particular distance, that is how long or wide it is.
EG *... fragments of glass measuring a few millimetres across*

NOUN
3 an action that is intended to

achieve a particular result
EG ... *new measures to combat crime*

4 A **measure of** something is a certain amount of it.
EG *We've had a measure of success.*

measurement /'mɛʒəmənt/
measurements

NOUN
the result that you obtain when you measure something
EG *We took lots of measurements.*

meat /miːt/
NOUN
Meat is the flesh of animals that people cook and eat.
EG *Meat and fish are quite expensive there.*

mechanic /mɪˈkænɪk/
mechanics
NOUN
someone whose job is to repair and maintain machines and engines
EG ... *a car mechanic*

mechanical /mɪˈkænɪkl/
ADJECTIVE
relating to machines and engines
EG *The train had stopped due to a mechanical problem.*

medal /'mɛdl/
medals
NOUN
a small, metal disc that is given as an award or a prize
EG ... *after winning three Olympic gold medals*

media /'miːdɪə/
PLURAL NOUN
You can refer to the television, radio, and newspapers as **the media**.
EG ... *the media's fascination with the Royal Family*

☑ Although 'media' is a plural noun, it is often used as a singular: *the media is obsessed with violence.*

mediaeval /mɛdrˈiːvl/
another spelling of **medieval**

medical /'mɛdɪkl/
medicals
ADJECTIVE
1 relating to the prevention and treatment of illness and injuries
EG ... *medical treatment*
NOUN
2 a thorough examination of your body by a doctor
EG *He failed his army medical.*

medicine /'mɛdsɪn/
medicines
NOUN
1 Medicine is the treatment of illness and injuries by doctors and nurses.
EG ... *a career in medicine*
2 a substance that you drink to help cure an illness
EG ... *a bottle of cough medicine*

medieval /mɛdrˈiːvl/
or **mediaeval**
ADJECTIVE
relating to the period between about 1100 AD and 1500 AD, especially in Europe
EG ... *a medieval castle*

meditate /'mɛdɪteɪt/
meditates meditating meditated
VERB
1 If you **meditate on** something, you think about it very deeply.
EG *He meditated on the problem.*
2 If you meditate, you remain in a calm, silent state for a period of time, often as part of a religious training.

EG *She meditates for ten minutes every day.*

medium /'miːdɪəm/
mediums or **media**

ADJECTIVE

1 If something is of medium size or degree, it is neither large nor small.
EG *He was of medium height.*

NOUN

2 a means that you use to communicate something
EG *... through the medium of television*

meet /miːt/
meets meeting met

VERB

1 If you meet someone, you happen to be in the same place as them.
EG *We met by chance.*
EG *He's the kindest person I've ever met.*

2 If you meet a visitor, you go to be with them when they arrive.
EG *Her parents met her off the boat.*

3 When people meet, they gather together for a purpose.
EG *I'll meet you at the beach tomorrow.*

4 If something meets a need or requirement, it fulfils it.
EG *... services intended to meet the needs of the elderly*

meeting /'miːtɪŋ/
meetings

NOUN

1 an event at which people discuss things or make decisions
EG *... a business meeting*

2 an occasion when you meet someone
EG *He remembers his first meeting with Alice.*

melody /'mɛlədɪ/
melodies

NOUN

a tune
EG *He knew the melody but couldn't remember the words.*

melon /'mɛlən/
melons

NOUN

a large, juicy fruit with a green or yellow skin and many seeds inside
EG *... a slice of melon*

melt /mɛlt/
melts melting melted

VERB

When something melts or when you melt it, it changes from a solid to a liquid because it has been heated.
EG *The snow had melted.*
EG *Melt the butter in a saucepan.*

member /'mɛmbəʳ/
members

NOUN

A member of a group is one of the people or things belonging to it.
EG *... older members of the family*

Member of Parliament
Members of Parliament

NOUN

a person who has been elected to represent people in a country's parliament
EG *... the Member of Parliament for Chingford*

membership /'mɛmbəʃɪp/

NOUN

1 Membership of an organization is the state of being a member of it.
EG *... the rules governing membership of the party*

2 The membership of an organization is the people who belong to it or the number of

A
B
C
D
E
F
G
H
I
J
K
L
M
N
O
P
Q
R
S
T
U
V
W
X
Y
Z

A B C D E F G H I J K L M N O P Q R S T U V W X Y Z

people who belong to it.
EG *Membership fell to half a million.*

memorable /'mɛmərəbl/

ADJECTIVE
If something is memorable, it is
likely to be remembered because it
is special or unusual.
EG *... a memorable victory*

memory /'mɛmərɪ/
memories

NOUN
1 Your memory is your ability to
remember things.
EG *The details are still fresh in my
memory.*
EG *I have an excellent memory.*
EG *He claimed to have lost his
memory.*
2 A memory is something that you
remember about the past.
EG *He had happy memories of his
schooldays.*
3 A computer's memory is its
capacity to store information.
EG *... 64 megabytes of memory*

men /mɛn/
the plural of **man**

mend /mɛnd/
mends mending mended

VERB
If you mend something that is
broken, you repair it.
EG *They took a long time mending
the roof.*

mental /'mɛntl/

ADJECTIVE
relating to the mind and the
process of thinking
EG *... the mental development of
children*
EG *... a mental hospital*

mention /'mɛnʃən/
**mentions mentioning
mentioned**

VERB
1 If you mention something, you
say something about it, usually
briefly.
EG *I thought I mentioned it to you.*

NOUN
2 a brief comment about someone
or something
EG *He made no mention of his
criminal past.*

menu /'mɛnjuː/
menus

NOUN
a list of the food and drink that
you can buy in a restaurant
EG *Could we see the menu?*

mere /mɪər/

ADJECTIVE
You use 'mere' to emphasize how
unimportant or small something is.
EG *Tickets are a mere £7.50.*

merely /'mɪəlɪ/

ADVERB
You use 'merely' to emphasize that
something is only what you say
and not better or more important.
EG *Michael is now merely a good
friend.*

mess /mɛs/
messes messing messed

NOUN
1 If a something is a mess or **in a
mess**, it is dirty or untidy.
EG *I'm sorry the room's such a mess.*
EG *Her hair was in a terrible mess.*
2 If a situation is a mess or **in a
mess**, it is full of problems.
EG *I've made a real mess of my life.*
EG *The economy is now in a mess.*

mess about or **mess around**

VERB
If you mess about or mess around,
you spend time doing silly or
casual things.

A B C D E F G H I J K L M N O P Q R S T U V W X Y Z

EG *Stop messing about and get a job.*

mess up

VERB

If you mess something up, you spoil it or do it wrong.

EG *He'd already messed up one career.*

message /'mɛsɪdʒ/
messages

NOUN

a piece of information or a request that you send someone or leave for them

EG *I got a message you were trying to reach me.*

met /mɛt/

past participle and past tense of **meet**

metal /'mɛtl/
metals

NOUN

Metal is a hard substance such as iron, steel, copper, or lead.

EG *... a lamp made of wood and metal*

EG *... a metal bar*

meter /'mi:tər/
meters

NOUN

a device that measures and records something

EG *... a parking meter*

see **metre**

method /'mɛθəd/
methods

NOUN

a particular way of doing something

EG *... the traditional method of making wine*

metre /'mi:tər/
metres

US **meter**

a unit of length equal to 100 centimetres

EG *The scarves are 2.3 metres long.*

metric /'mɛtrɪk/

ADJECTIVE

relating to the system of measurement that uses metres, grams, and litres

EG *... the metric system*

mice /maɪs/

the plural of **mouse**

microphone /'maɪkrəfəun/
microphones

NOUN

a device that is used to record sounds or make them louder

EG *... as he stepped up to the microphone to sing*

microwave /'maɪkrəuweɪv/
**microwaves microwaving
microwaved**

NOUN

1 an oven which cooks food very quickly by means of radiation

EG *Just pop it in the microwave for 2 minutes.*

VERB

2 If you microwave food, you cook it in a microwave.

EG *... not suitable for microwaving*

midday /mɪd'deɪ/

NOUN

Midday is twelve o'clock in the middle of the day.

EG *At midday we all went home.*

middle /'mɪdl/
middles

NOUN

1 The middle of something is the part furthest from the edges, ends, or surface.

EG *Howard stood in the middle of the room.*

A
B
C
D
E
F
G
H
I
J
K
L
M
N
O
P
Q
R
S
T
U
V
W
X
Y
Z

2 The middle of an event is the part that comes after the first part and before the last part.
EG *I woke up in the middle of the night.*

ADJECTIVE
3 The middle thing in a series is the one with an equal number of things on each side.
EG *The middle drawer contained stockings.*

middle-aged /mɪdl'eɪdʒd/

ADJECTIVE
Middle-aged people are between the ages of about 40 and 60.
EG *His parents are middle-aged.*

middle class middle classes

NOUN
The middle class or the middle classes are the people in a society who are not working class or upper class, for example managers and lawyers.
EG *... the rise of the middle class*

midnight /'mɪdnaɪt/

NOUN
Midnight is twelve o'clock at night.
EG *The gates are locked at midnight.*

might /maɪt/

☑ 'Might' is a modal verb. There are no forms ending in -s, -ing, or -ed.
1 Might is the past tense of **may**

VERB
2 You use 'might' to say that something will possibly happen or is possibly true.
EG *I might not be back until tomorrow.*
EG *You might be right.*

3 You use 'might' as a polite way of making suggestions or requests.
EG *I thought we might go for a drive.*
EG *Might I trouble you for some*

sugar?

mild /maɪld/
milder mildest

ADJECTIVE
Something that is mild is not very strong or severe.
EG *The weather was mild for December.*
EG *I felt only mild surprise.*

mile /maɪl/
miles

NOUN
a unit of distance equal to 1760 yards or about 1.6 kilometres
EG *The nearest doctor is five miles away.*

military /'mɪlɪtərɪ/

ADJECTIVE
related to or involving the armed forces of a country
EG *... a military base*

milk /mɪlk/
milks milking milked

NOUN
1 Milk is the white liquid produced by cows and goats, which people drink and make into butter and cheese.
EG *... a pint of milk*

2 Milk is the white liquid that a baby drinks from its mother's breasts.
EG *... a mother's milk*

VERB
3 When someone milks a cow or goat, they remove milk from its body.
EG *... helping her father to milk the cows*

mill /mɪl/
mills

NOUN
1 a building where grain is crushed to make flour

EG *... on the site an old mill*

2 a factory for making materials such as steel, wool, or cotton
EG *... a cotton mill*

millennium /mɪˈlɛnɪəm/
millennia or **millenniums**

NOUN
a period of 1000 years
EG *... celebrations to mark the millennium*

millimetre /ˈmɪlɪmiːtər/
millimetres
US **millimeter**

NOUN
a unit of length equal to one tenth of a centimetre
EG *... tiny insects a few millimetres long*

million /ˈmɪljən/
millions
the number 1,000,000
EG *... a million dollars*
EG *... millions of pounds*

millionaire /mɪljəˈnɛər/
millionaires

NOUN
someone who has money or property worth at least a million pounds or dollars
EG *By the time he died, he was a millionaire.*

millionth /ˈmɪljənθ/
millionths

ADJECTIVE
1 The millionth item in a series is the one counted as number one million.
EG *... the millionth customer to visit the shop*

NOUN
2 one of a million equal parts
EG *... a millionth of a second*

min. /ˈmɪnɪts/
an abbreviation for 'minute' or

'minutes'
EG *... 2 hrs 10 min*

mind /maɪnd/
minds minding minded

NOUN
1 Your mind is your ability to think, together with all the thoughts you have and your memory.
EG *You must be strong in mind and body.*
EG *He couldn't get her reply out of his mind.*

2 If you **change** your **mind**, you change a decision that you have made or an opinion that you have.
EG *I was going to vote for him, but I changed my mind.*

VERB
3 If you **do not mind** something, you are not annoyed or bothered by it.
EG *I hope you don't mind me phoning you at home.*

4 If you **do not mind** what happens or what something is like, you do not have a strong preference about it.
EG *I don't mind where we go.*

5 If you say that you **wouldn't mind** something, you mean that you would quite like it.
EG *I wouldn't mind a coffee.*

6 If you tell someone to mind something, you are warning them to be careful.
EG *Mind that plate, it's hot.*

mine /maɪn/
mines

PRONOUN
1 You use 'mine' to refer to something that belongs or relates to yourself.
EG *Her hand was inches from mine.*
EG *He's a good friend of mine.*

A
B
C
D
E
F
G
H
I
J
K
L
M
N
O
P
Q
R
S
T
U
V
W
X
Y
Z

NOUN
2 a place where deep holes or tunnels are dug under the ground in order to extract minerals
EG … *a coal mine*
3 a bomb hidden in the ground or underwater, which explodes when something touches it
EG … *an unexploded mine*

mineral /'mɪnərəl/
minerals
NOUN
a substance such as tin, salt, or coal that is formed naturally in rocks and in the earth
EG … *rich mineral deposits*

miniature /'mɪnətʃər/
ADJECTIVE
a tiny copy of something much larger
EG … *a miniature version of the Eiffel Tower*

minimum /'mɪnɪməm/
ADJECTIVE
1 A minimum amount is the smallest amount that is possible or allowed.
EG … *the minimum height for a policeman*
NOUN
2 A minimum is the smallest amount that is possible or allowed.
EG *This will take a minimum of one hour.*

minister /'mɪnɪstər/
ministers
NOUN
1 a person who is in charge of a particular government department
EG … *the Minister of Defence*
2 a religious leader or official, especially in a Protestant church
EG … *a Baptist minister*

ministry /'mɪnɪstrɪ/

ministries
NOUN
a government department
EG … *the Ministry of Justice*

minor /'maɪnər/
ADJECTIVE
less important or serious than other things
EG … *a minor injury*

minority /maɪ'nɒrɪtɪ/
minorities
NOUN
1 The minority of people or things in a group is a number of them forming less than half of the group.
EG *Only a small minority of people want this.*
2 A minority is a group of people of a particular race or religion living in a place where most people are of a different race or religion.
EG … *the region's ethnic minorities*

minus /'maɪnəs/
PREPOSITION
1 You use 'minus' to show that one number is being subtracted from another.
EG *Ten minus six equals four.*
ADJECTIVE
2 'Minus' before a number means that the number is less than zero.
EG … *temperatures of minus 65 degrees*

minute /'mɪnɪt/
minutes
NOUN
1 a unit of time equal to sixty seconds
EG *The pizza takes about 20 minutes to cook.*
2 a short period of time
EG *See you in a minute.*

minute /maɪ'njuːt/

ADJECTIVE
extremely small
EG *Only a minute amount is needed.*

miracle /ˈmɪrəkl/
miracles

NOUN
a surprising and fortunate event, especially one that is believed to have been caused by God
EG *It was a miracle no one was killed.*
EG *... the miracles performed by Jesus*

mirror /ˈmɪrəʳ/
mirrors

NOUN
an object made of glass in which you can see your reflection
EG *She stared at herself in the mirror.*

miscarriage /ˈmɪskærɪdʒ/
miscarriages

NOUN
If a woman has a miscarriage, she gives birth to a baby before it is properly formed and it dies.
EG *She has had several miscarriages.*

miserable /ˈmɪzərəbl/

ADJECTIVE
1 If you are miserable, you are very unhappy.
EG *... a job which made me really miserable*
2 If a place or a situation is miserable, it makes you feel depressed.
EG *... a miserable little flat*

misery /ˈmɪzəri/

NOUN
Misery is great unhappiness.
EG *All that money brought him nothing but misery.*

misleading /mɪsˈliːdɪŋ/

ADJECTIVE

If something is misleading, it gives you a wrong idea or impression.
EG *It would be misleading to say that we were friends.*

miss /mɪs/
misses missing missed

VERB
1 If you miss something that you are aiming at, you fail to hit it.
EG *His shot missed the target.*
2 If you miss something, you do not notice it.
EG *You can't miss it. It's on the second floor.*
3 If you miss someone or something, you feel sad because they are no longer with you.
EG *The boys miss their father.*
4 If you miss a bus, plane, or train, you arrive too late to catch it.
EG *He missed the last bus home.*
5 If you miss an event or activity, you fail to attend it.
EG *I had to miss my French lesson.*
6 'Miss' is used before the name of a girl or unmarried woman.
EG *Did you know Miss West?*
7 an occasion when you miss something that you were aiming at
EG *What a terrible miss by Shearer!*

missile /ˈmɪsaɪl/
missiles

NOUN
1 a weapon that moves long distances through the air and explodes when it reaches its target
EG *... nuclear missiles*
2 any object that is thrown as a weapon
EG *Rioters hurled missiles at the police.*

missing /ˈmɪsɪŋ/

ADJECTIVE

If someone or something is missing, you cannot find them.
EG *He's been missing for four years.*

mission /'mɪʃən/
missions

NOUN

an important task that someone has to do
EG *He flew back to Rome, his mission accomplished.*

mist /mɪst/
mists

NOUN

Mist consists of many tiny drops of water in the air, which make it hard to see clearly.
EG *… a sea mist*

mistake /mɪs'teɪk/
mistakes mistaking mistook mistaken

NOUN

1 If you **make a mistake**, or if you do something wrong **by mistake**, you do something wrong without intending to.
EG *… a spelling mistake*
EG *I think you've made a mistake in your calculations.*
EG *He switched the alarm off by mistake.*

VERB

2 If you **mistake** someone or something **for** another person or thing, you wrongly think that they are the other person or thing.
EG *I mistook him for the owner of the house.*

mistaken /mɪs'teɪkən/

ADJECTIVE

If you are **mistaken about** someone or something, you are wrong about them.
EG *I can see I was mistaken about you.*

mistook /mɪs'tuk/
past tense of **mistake**

mistress /'mɪstrɪs/
mistresses

NOUN

A married man's mistress is a woman he is having a sexual relationship with, but who is not his wife.
EG *She was his mistress for three years.*

mix /mɪks/
mixes mixing mixed

VERB

If two things mix, or if you **mix** one thing **with** another, they combine to form a single thing.
EG *Oil and water don't mix.*
EG *Mix the flour with the water.*

mix up

VERB

If you mix up two things or people, you think that one of them is the other one.
EG *People often mix us up.*

mixture /'mɪkstʃər/
mixtures

NOUN

1 two or more things mixed together
EG *… with a mixture of fear and excitement*

2 a substance consisting of other substances which have been mixed together
EG *Spoon the mixture into glasses.*

mm /'mɪlɪmi:tər, 'mɪlɪmi:təz/
an abbreviation for 'millimetres'
EG *… 45 mm of rain*

moan /məun/
moans moaning moaned

VERB

1 If you moan, you make a low, miserable sound because you are

in pain or unhappy.
EG *He lay on his bed moaning.*

2 If you **moan about**
something, you complain about it.
EG *She's always moaning about
how busy she is.*

NOUN

3 a low cry of pain or unhappiness
EG *She let out a faint moan.*

mob /mɒb/
mobs

NOUN

a large, disorganized crowd of
people
EG *A violent mob attacked the bus.*

mobile /ˈməʊbaɪl/

ADJECTIVE

able to move or be moved easily
EG *He's much more mobile since
getting his new wheelchair.*
EG *... a mobile phone*

mock /mɒk/
mocks mocking mocked

VERB

1 If you mock someone, you tease
them or try to make them look
foolish.
EG *I'm serious, don't mock me.*

ADJECTIVE

2 not genuine
EG *His voice was raised in mock
horror.*

modal /ˈməʊdl/
modals

ADJECTIVE OR NOUN

A **modal verb** or a **modal** is a type
of auxiliary verb. It is used with
another verb to show that an action
is, for instance, possible, necessary,
or intended. 'Can', 'could', 'may',
'might', 'must', 'ought', 'shall',
'should', 'will', and 'would' are
modal verbs.

EG *I **couldn't** do it without your
help.*
EG *You **should** listen to your
mother.*

mode /məʊd/
modes

NOUN

A mode of something is one of the
different forms it can take.
EG *... road, rail and other modes of
transport*

model /ˈmɒdl/
models modelling modelled

NOUN OR ADJECTIVE

1 a smaller copy of something that
shows what it looks like or how it
works
EG *... tiny models of famous ships*
EG *... a model railway*

NOUN

2 a system that people might
want to copy
EG *... the Chinese model of
economic reform*

3 a type or version of a machine
EG *Which model of washing
machine did you choose?*

4 a person who poses for a painter
or photographer
EG *... an artist's model*

5 a person who wears the clothes
that are being displayed at a
fashion show
EG *... a fashion model*

ADJECTIVE

6 A model wife or a model student
is an excellent example of a wife or
student.
EG *As a girl she had been a model
pupil.*

VERB

7 If one thing **is modelled on**
another thing, the first thing is
made so that it is like the second

A
B
C
D
E
F
G
H
I
J
K
L
M
N
O
P
Q
R
S
T
U
V
W
X
Y
Z

thing.

EG *Most of the characters are modelled on the author's friends.*

moderate /ˈmɒdərət/

moderates moderating moderated

ADJECTIVE

1 Moderate political opinions or policies are not extreme.

EG *... a man of very moderate views*

2 A moderate amount of something is neither large nor small.

EG *... moderate exercise*

VERB : /ˈmɒdəreɪt/

☑ Note that you pronounce the verb differently from the noun.

3 If you moderate something or if it moderates, it becomes less extreme or violent.

EG *They hope he will moderate his views.*

EG *The crisis has moderated somewhat.*

modern /ˈmɒdən/

ADJECTIVE

1 relating to the present time

EG *... modern society*

2 new and involving the latest ideas or equipment

EG *... modern technology*

modernize /ˈmɒdənaɪz/

modernizes modernizing modernized; also spelt **modernise**

VERB

To modernize something means to replace old methods or equipment with new ones.

EG *... a plan to modernize the factory*

modest /ˈmɒdɪst/

ADJECTIVE

1 quite small in size or amount

EG *... a modest flat*

EG *... a modest improvement*

2 Someone who is modest does not boast about their abilities or possessions.

EG *He is modest about his achievements.*

modify /ˈmɒdɪfaɪ/

modifies modifying modified

VERB

If you modify something, you change it slightly in order to improve it.

EG *They intend to modify the existing rules.*

moisture /ˈmɔɪstʃər/

NOUN

Moisture is tiny drops of water in the air or on a surface.

EG *The plant retains the moisture.*

mom /mɒm/

moms

NOUN

AN INFORMAL WORD

In American English, your mom is your mother.

EG *We waited for Mom and Dad to get home.*

☑ The British spelling is **mum**.

moment /ˈməumənt/

moments

NOUN

1 a very short period of time

EG *He paused for a moment.*

2 The moment at which something happens is the point in time at which it happens.

EG *At that moment, the doorbell rang.*

3 If something is happening **at the moment**, it is happening now.

EG *He's abroad at the moment.*

monarchy /'mɒnəkɪ/
monarchies

NOUN

a system in which a king or queen rules over a country
EG … the future of the monarchy

Monday /'mʌndɪ/
Mondays

NOUN

Monday is the day between Sunday and Tuesday.
EG On Monday morning he phoned in sick.

money /'mʌnɪ/

NOUN

Money is the coins or notes that you use to buy things.
EG I need to earn some money.
EG How much money do you have on you?

monitor /'mɒnɪtər/
monitors monitoring monitored

VERB

1 If you monitor something, you regularly check its condition and progress.
EG Her health will be monitored daily.

NOUN

2 a machine that is used to check or record things
EG … a heart monitor

monk /mʌŋk/
monks

NOUN

a member of a male religious community
EG … a Buddhist monk

monkey /'mʌŋkɪ/
monkeys

NOUN

an animal that has a long tail and climbs trees

EG … a monkey on a branch

monster /'mɒnstər/
monsters

NOUN

a large, imaginary creature that looks very frightening
EG … like a monster from a science-fiction film

month /mʌnθ/
months

NOUN

1 one of the twelve periods that a year is divided into
EG We leave next month.
EG … in the month of May
2 any period of four weeks
EG She spent a few months with us.

monthly /'mʌnθlɪ/

ADJECTIVE OR ADVERB

happening or appearing once a month
EG … a monthly magazine
EG I get paid monthly.

mood /muːd/
moods

NOUN

Your mood is the way you are feeling at a particular time.
EG She was in a really good mood.
EG He was in no mood to celebrate.

moon /muːn/
moons

NOUN

an object like a small planet that travels round a planet, especially the bright object in the sky that moves round the earth
EG … the first man on the moon
EG … the moons of Jupiter

moor /muər/
moors mooring moored

NOUN

1 a high area of open land
EG … the Yorkshire moors

A B C D E F G H I J K L **M** N O P Q R S T U V W X Y Z

VERB

2 If you moor a boat, you attach it to the land with a rope.
EG *She moored the barge on the right bank of the river.*

moral /'mɔrl/
morals

ADJECTIVE

1 relating to beliefs about what is right and wrong
EG *... moral values*

2 If you give someone **moral support**, you encourage them in what they are doing.
EG *They need moral as well as financial support.*

PLURAL NOUN

3 morals are attitudes and beliefs concerning right and wrong behaviour
EG *They have no morals.*

morale /mɔ'rɑːl/

NOUN

Morale is the amount of confidence and hope that people have.
EG *The morale of the troops was high.*

more /mɔːr/

ADJECTIVE OR PRONOUN

1 More means a greater number or extent than something else.
EG *He's got more money than me.*
EG *... a survey of more than 1,500 schools*

2 You use 'more' to refer to an additional thing or amount of something.
EG *He found a few more clues.*
EG *Would you like some more?*

ADVERB

3 More means to a greater degree or extent.
EG *I was more amused than concerned.*

EG *We can talk more later.*

4 You use 'more' to show that something is repeated.
EG *Repeat the exercise once more.*

5 You use 'more' to form comparatives.
EG *You look more beautiful than ever.*
EG *He did it more carefully the second time.*

✔ You do not use 'more' to form the comparative form of short adjectives. The comparative of 'fast' is *faster*, not *more fast*.

6 If something is **more or less** true, it is almost but not completely true.
EG *The conference is more or less over.*

morning /'mɔːnɪŋ/
mornings

NOUN

1 the early part of the day until lunchtime
EG *The next morning I got up early.*

2 the part of the day between midnight and noon
EG *He was born at three in the morning.*

mortal /'mɔːtl/
mortals

ADJECTIVE

1 unable to live forever
EG *Remember that you are mortal.*

NOUN

2 an ordinary person
EG *Musicians, like the rest of us, are mere mortals.*

mortgage /'mɔːgɪdʒ/
mortgages mortgaging mortgaged

NOUN

1 a loan which you get from a bank or building society in order to buy a house

EG *He had problems getting a mortgage.*

VERB

2 If you **mortgage** your house, you use it as a guarantee to a company in order to borrow money from them.

EG *They had to mortgage their home to pay the bills.*

Moslem /ˈmɒzləm/
another spelling of **Muslim**

mosque /mɒsk/
mosques

NOUN

a building where Muslims go to attend religious services

EG *... the city's newest mosque*

mosquito /mɒsˈkiːtəʊ/
mosquitoes or **mosquitos**

NOUN

Mosquitoes are small flying insects which bite people in order to suck their blood.

EG *... a mosquito bite*

most /məʊst/

ADJECTIVE OR PRONOUN

1 You use 'most' to refer to the majority of a group of things or people or the largest part of something.

EG *Most people don't share your views.*

EG *Most of the book is true.*

2 the most means a larger amount than anyone or anything else

EG *She has the most talent.*

EG *... the most he had ever earned*

PRONOUN

3 You say **at most** or **at the most** when stating the maximum number that is possible or likely.

EG *She is sixteen at most.*

4 If you **make the most of**

something, you get the maximum use or advantage from it.

EG *They made the most of their chances.*

ADVERB

5 You use 'most' to show that something happens more often or is more true than anything else.

EG *What she feared most was becoming like her mother.*

6 You use 'most' to form superlatives.

EG *... the most beautiful women in the world*

☑ You do not use 'most' to form the superlative form of short adjectives. The superlative of 'fast' is *fastest*, not *most fast*.

mostly /ˈməʊstlɪ/

ADVERB

You use 'mostly' to show that a statement is generally true.

EG *Her friends are mostly men.*

motel /məʊˈtɛl/
motels

NOUN

a hotel for people who are travelling by car

EG *... a motel next to the freeway*

moth /mɒθ/
moths

NOUN

an insect like a butterfly which usually flies at night

EG *... like a moth to a flame*

mother /ˈmʌðəʳ/
mothers

NOUN

Your mother is the woman who gave birth to you or who brought you up.

EG *... my mother and father*

EG *She's a housewife and mother of two.*

A
B
C
D
E
F
G
H
I
J
K
L
M
N
O
P
Q
R
S
T
U
V
W
X
Y
Z

mother-in-law /'mʌðərɪnlɔː/
mothers-in-law

NOUN

Your mother-in-law is the mother of your husband or wife.

EG ... *dinner with my mother-in-law*

motion /'məʊʃən/
motions

NOUN

1 Motion is movement.

EG ... *the motion of the ship*

EG *Apply with a brush, using circular motions.*

2 a proposal which people discuss and vote on at a meeting

EG *The motion was defeated.*

motivate /'məʊtɪveɪt/
motivates motivating motivated

VERB

1 If you are motivated by something, it makes you behave in a particular way.

EG *He is motivated by duty rather than ambition.*

2 If you motivate someone, you make them feel determined to do something.

EG ... *a manager who knows how to motivate his players*

motive /'məʊtɪv/
motives

NOUN

a reason or purpose for doing something

EG *There was no motive for the attack.*

motor /'məʊtər/
motors

NOUN

a part of a vehicle or machine that uses electricity or fuel to produce movement so that the vehicle or machine can work

EG *She got in and started the motor.*

motorbike /'məʊtəbaɪk/
motorbikes

NOUN

a vehicle with two wheels and an engine

EG ... *a man on a motorbike*

motorist /'məʊtərɪst/
motorists

NOUN

a person who drives a car

EG ... *a tax aimed at motorists*

motorway /'məʊtəweɪ/
motorways

NOUN

a wide road built for fast travel over long distances

EG ... *the M1 motorway*

mount /maʊnt/
mounts mounting mounted

VERB

1 To mount a campaign or event means to organize it and carry it out.

EG ... *a new campaign mounted by the police*

2 If something is mounting, it is increasing.

EG *Economic problems are mounting.*

3 A FORMAL USE

If you mount something, you go to the top of it.

EG *He mounted the steps.*

4 If you mount a horse or bicycle, you climb on to it.

EG *They mounted their bikes and rode off.*

NOUN

5 'Mount' is used as part of the name of a mountain.

EG ... *Mount Everest*

mountain /'maʊntɪn/
mountains

NOUN

a very high piece of land with steep sides

EG *… Britain's highest mountain*

mouse /maʊs/
mice

NOUN

1 a small furry animal with a long tail

EG *… a house infested with rats and mice*

2 a computer device that you move by hand in order to perform operations without using the keyboard

EG *… the left-hand button on the mouse*

moustache /məsˈtɑːʃ/
moustaches
US **mustache**

NOUN

A man's moustache is the hair that grows on his upper lip.

EG *He was short and had a moustache.*

mouth /maʊθ/
mouths mouthing mouthed

NOUN

1 Your mouth is your lips, or the space behind them where your tongue and teeth are.

EG *She clamped her hand over his mouth.*

EG *His mouth was full of peas.*

VERB : /maʊð/

✓ Note that you pronounce the verb differently from the noun.

2 If you mouth something, you form words with your lips without making any sound.

EG *He mouthed "Thank you" to the jurors.*

move /muːv/
moves moving moved

VERB

1 When you move something, or when it moves, its position changes.

EG *A traffic warden asked him to move his car.*

EG *The train began to move.*

2 If you move or **move house**, you go to live in a different place.

EG *She had often considered moving to London.*

EG *… the problems of moving house*

3 If something moves you, it causes you to feel a deep emotion.

EG *Her story moved us to tears.*

NOUN

4 a movement

EG *We were watching his every move.*

5 an act of moving house

EG *The move to London was not without its problems.*

6 an action that you take in order to achieve something

EG *Being honest may not be a good move.*

movement /ˈmuːvmənt/
movements

NOUN

1 Movement involves changing position or going from one place to another.

EG *He heard a movement behind him.*

EG *… the movement of refugees across borders*

2 a group of people who share the same beliefs or aims

EG *… the peace movement*

movie /ˈmuːvɪ/
movies

NOUN

In American English, a movie is a cinema film.

EG *… a horror movie*

moving /'muːvɪŋ/

ADJECTIVE

Something that is moving makes you feel deep sadness or emotion.

EG ... a very moving experience

MP MPs

NOUN

a person who has been elected to parliament to represent people from a particular area. MP is an abbreviation for 'Member of Parliament'.

EG ... the MP for West Lancashire

mph

an abbreviation for 'miles per hour'

EG ... at a speed of 60 mph

Mr /'mɪstəʳ/

'Mr' is used before a man's name when you are speaking or referring to him.

EG Mr Grant told me to come.

Mrs /'mɪsɪz/

'Mrs' is used before the name of a married woman when you are speaking or referring to her.

EG Hello, Mrs Miles.

Ms /mɪz/

'Ms' is used before a woman's name when you are speaking or referring to her. Both married and unmarried women can be addressed as 'Ms'.

EG ... Ms Sara Brown

much /mʌtʃ/

ADVERB

1 You use 'much' to indicate the great size, extent, or intensity of something.

EG He's much taller than you.

EG She hasn't changed much.

EG Thank you very much.

2 If something does not happen much, it does not happen often.

EG He doesn't go out much.

ADJECTIVE OR PRONOUN

3 You use 'much' to talk about the size or amount of something.

EG How much money do you need?

EG She knows how much this upsets me.

☑ You only use 'much' to talk about something that cannot be counted. You should use 'many' if you want to talk about a large number of things: too many books.

mud /mʌd/

NOUN

Mud is wet earth.

EG Their lorry got stuck in the mud.

muddy /'mʌdɪ/
muddier muddiest

ADJECTIVE

covered in mud

EG ... a muddy field

mug /mʌg/
mugs mugging mugged

NOUN

1 a large, deep cup

EG ... a mug of sweet tea

VERB

2 If someone mugs you, they attack you in order to steal your money.

EG He has been mugged several times.

multi- /'mʌltɪ/

PREFIX

'Multi-' is used to form words that refer to something that has many parts or aspects.

EG ... a multi-storey car park

EG ... a multi-millionaire

multiply /'mʌltɪplaɪ/
multiplies multiplying multiplied

VERB

1 When something multiplies, it increases greatly in number or

amount.
EG *As the trip wore on, the dangers multiplied.*

2 When you **multiply** one number **by** another, you calculate the total you would get if you added the first number to itself a particular number of times.
EG *6 multiplied by 3 is 18.*

mum /mʌm/
mums

NOUN
AN INFORMAL WORD
Your mum is your mother.
EG *He misses his mum.*

mumble /'mʌmbl/
mumbles mumbling mumbled

VERB
If you mumble something, you say it very quietly and not very clearly.
EG *He mumbled a few words of thanks.*

mummy /'mʌmi/
mummies

NOUN
1 USED ESPECIALLY BY CHILDREN
Your mummy is your mother.
EG *Mummy, I'm tired!*

2 a dead body which was preserved long ago by being rubbed with special oils and wrapped in cloth
EG *... an Egyptian mummy*

murder /'mɜːdər/
murders murdering murdered

NOUN
1 Murder is the deliberate killing of a person.
EG *He was found guilty of murder.*
EG *... the second murder this week*

VERB
2 If someone murders a person,

they kill them deliberately.
EG *... a man who murdered his wife*

murmur /'mɜːmər/
murmurs murmuring murmured

VERB
If you murmur something, you say it very quietly.
EG *He turned and murmured something to the professor.*

muscle /'mʌsl/
muscles

NOUN
Your muscles are the internal parts of your body which you expand or contract when you make a movement.
EG *... your stomach muscles*

museum /mjuːˈziəm/
museums

NOUN
a public building where interesting or valuable objects are kept and displayed
EG *... the Natural History Museum*

mushroom /'mʌʃrum/
mushrooms

NOUN
a plant with a short stem and a round top and no leaves, flowers, or roots. You can eat some types of mushroom.
EG *... a mushroom omelette*

music /'mjuːzɪk/

NOUN
1 Music is the pattern of sounds performed by people singing or playing instruments.
EG *... pop music*

2 Music is the written symbols that represent musical sounds.
EG *I taught myself to read music.*

musical /'mjuːzɪkl/
musicals

A
B
C
D
E
F
G
H
I
J
K
L
M
N
O
P
Q
R
S
T
U
V
W
X
Y
Z

ADJECTIVE

1 concerned with playing or studying music

EG ... *a musical instrument*

NOUN

2 a play or film that uses singing and dancing in the story

EG ... *a Broadway musical*

musician /mjuːˈzɪʃən/
musicians

NOUN

a person who plays a musical instrument as their job or hobby

EG *He was a brilliant musician.*

Muslim /ˈmʌzlɪm/
Muslims; also spelt **Moslem**

NOUN

1 a person who believes in Islam and lives according to its rules

EG ... *a devout Muslim*

ADJECTIVE

2 relating to Islam

EG ... *Britain's Muslim population*

must /mʌst/

☑ 'Must' is a modal verb. It has only one form. There are no forms ending in -*s*, -*ing*, or -*ed*.

VERB

1 If something must happen, it is very important or necessary that it happens.

EG *You mustn't let them upset you.*

EG *You must be over 18 to get in.*

2 If you tell someone they must do something, you are suggesting that they do it.

EG *You must try this pudding — it's delicious.*

3 You use 'must' to show that you are fairly sure about something.

EG *He must be twenty years older than her.*

NOUN

4 a must is something that is

absolutely necessary

EG *The museum is a must for all visitors.*

mustache /məsˈtɑːʃ/
see **moustache**

mustard /ˈmʌstəd/

NOUN

Mustard is a yellow or brown paste made from seeds which tastes spicy.

EG ... *a pot of mustard*

mutter /ˈmʌtər/
mutters muttering muttered

VERB

If you mutter something, you say it very quietly.

EG *Rory muttered something under his breath.*

mutual /ˈmjuːtʃuəl/

ADJECTIVE

You use 'mutual' to describe something that is experienced or shared by both of two people.

EG *They had a mutual interest in rugby.*

my /maɪ/

ADJECTIVE

You use 'my' to refer to something that belongs or relates to yourself.

EG *I invited him back to my flat.*

myself /maɪˈself/

PRONOUN

1 You use 'myself' to refer to yourself.

EG *I asked myself what I would have done.*

EG *I looked at myself in the mirror.*

2 You use 'myself' to emphasize 'I'.

EG *I don't understand it myself.*

3 If you say something such as 'I did it myself', you mean that you did it without any help.

EG *I installed the computer myself.*

A B C D E F G H I J K L M N O P Q R S T U V W X Y Z

mysterious /mɪsˈtɪərɪəs/
ADJECTIVE
strange or not understood
EG *He died in mysterious circumstances.*

mystery /ˈmɪstərɪ/
mysteries
NOUN
something that is not understood or known about
EG *Her identity remains a mystery.*

myth /mɪθ/
myths
NOUN
1 a story which was made up long ago to explain natural events or to justify religious beliefs
EG *… a Greek myth*
2 an untrue belief or explanation
EG *It's a myth that men are better drivers than women.*

A
B
C
D
E
F
G
H
I
J
K
L
M
N
O
P
Q
R
S
T
U
V
W
X
Y
Z

Nn

nail /neɪl/

nails nailing nailed

NOUN

1 a small, pointed piece of metal which you hammer into objects to hold them together

EG *Someone was hammering a nail into the wall.*

2 Your nails are the thin hard areas covering the ends of your fingers and toes.

EG *I sat there biting my nails.*

VERB

3 If you nail something somewhere, you fix it there using a nail.

EG *The windows were all nailed shut.*

naked /'neɪkɪd/

ADJECTIVE

not wearing any clothes

EG *... her naked body*

name /neɪm/

names naming named

NOUN

1 a word that you use to identify a person, place, or thing

EG *His name is Michael.*

EG *They changed the name of the street.*

VERB

2 When you name someone or something, you give them a name.

EG *Her father had named her Lucy.*

3 If you name someone, you identify them by stating their name.

EG *One of the victims has been named as John Barr.*

napkin /'næpkɪn/

napkins

NOUN

a small piece of cloth or paper which you use to wipe your hands and mouth after eating

EG *... a paper napkin*

nappy /'næpɪ/

nappies

NOUN

a piece of thick cloth or paper which you put round a baby's bottom

EG *... a disposable nappy*

narrow /'nærəʊ/

narrower narrowest; narrows narrowing narrowed

ADJECTIVE

1 Something that is narrow measures a small distance from one side to the other.

EG *... the town's narrow streets*

VERB

2 If something narrows, it becomes less wide.

EG *The track narrowed ahead.*

nasty /'nɑːstɪ/

nastier nastiest

ADJECTIVE

very unpleasant

EG *... a nasty shock*

EG *She was so nasty to me.*

nation /'neɪʃən/

nations

NOUN

a country

EG *... the Arab nations*

national /'næʃənl/

ADJECTIVE

1 relating to the whole of a country

EG *... a national newspaper*

2 typical of a particular country

EG *... women in Polish national*

dress

nationality /ˌnæʃəˈnælɪtɪ/
nationalities

NOUN
Nationality is the fact of being a
citizen of a particular country.
EG *Asked his nationality, he said
British.*

native /ˈneɪtɪv/
natives

ADJECTIVE
1 Your native country is the
country where you were born.
EG *... his first visit to his native
country since 1948*
2 Your native language is the
language that you first learned to
speak.
EG *French is not my native
language.*

NOUN
3 A **native of** a place is someone
who was born there.
EG *... a native of Barbados*

natural /ˈnætʃrəl/

ADJECTIVE
1 normal and to be expected
EG *It is only natural for youngsters
to crave excitement.*
2 existing or happening in nature
EG *... a natural disaster like an
earthquake*
3 A natural ability is one that you
were born with.
EG *... his natural talent as an
engineer*

nature /ˈneɪtʃər/
natures

NOUN
1 Nature is animals, plants, and all
the other things in the world that
are not made by people.
EG *The night sky is one of the most
beautiful sights in nature.*

2 The nature of a person or thing
is their basic quality or character.
EG *She liked his warm, generous
nature.*
EG *... the ambitious nature of the
programme*

naughty /ˈnɔːtɪ/
naughtier naughtiest

ADJECTIVE
1 A child who is naughty behaves
badly.
EG *She shouted at him whenever he
was naughty.*
2 slightly rude or indecent
EG *... a naughty magazine*

navy /ˈneɪvɪ/
navies

NOUN
the part of a country's armed
forces that fights at sea
EG *He had formerly been in the
Navy.*

near /nɪər/
**nearer nearest; nears
nearing neared**

PREPOSITION, ADJECTIVE, OR ADVERB
1 If something is near a place or
near to it, it is a short distance
from it.
EG *... a cottage near the river*
EG *My office is quite near.*
EG *He crouched as near to the door
as he could.*
2 If something is near a particular
state or **near to** it, it has almost
reached it.
EG *This view is fairly near the truth.*
EG *... standing there in near
darkness*
EG *Her mother was near to tears.*

PREPOSITION OR ADVERB
3 If something happens near a
particular time or **near to** it, it
happens just before or just after
that time.

A B C D E F G H I J K L M N O P Q R S T U V W X Y Z

EG *... near the beginning of the play*
EG *The announcement, so near to Christmas, came as a shock.*

VERB

4 When you are nearing a particular place or time, you are approaching it and will soon reach it.
EG *The dog began to bark as he neared the door.*
EG *He must be nearing fifty.*

nearby /nɪə'baɪ/

ADJECTIVE OR ADVERB

a short distance away
EG *... a nearby restaurant*
EG *... someone who lived nearby*

nearly /'nɪəlɪ/

ADVERB

not completely but almost
EG *It's nearly 8 o'clock.*
EG *I've nearly finished.*

neat /niːt/

neater neatest

ADJECTIVE

1 tidy and smart
EG *She put her clothes in a neat pile.*
EG *He's always so neat.*

2 A neat alcoholic drink does not have anything added to it.
EG *... a small glass of neat vodka*

necessary /'nɛsɪsrɪ/

ADJECTIVE

Something that is necessary is needed or must be done.
EG *We will do whatever is necessary.*
EG *It might be necessary to leave fast.*

necessity /nɪ'sɛsɪtɪ/

necessities

NOUN

1 Necessity is the need to do something.
EG *He'd learned the necessity of hiding his feelings.*

2 A necessity is something that you need in order to live.
EG *Water is a basic necessity of life.*

neck /nɛk/

necks

NOUN

Your neck is the part of your body which joins your head to the rest of your body.
EG *She wore a chain round her neck.*

necklace /'nɛklɪs/

necklaces

NOUN

a piece of jewellery which a woman wears round her neck
EG *... a necklace of white beads*

need /niːd/

needs needing needed

VERB

1 If you need something or **need to do** it, you cannot achieve what you want without it.
EG *I need some help.*
EG *I need to make a phone call.*

2 If an object or place needs something doing to it, that action must or should be done.
EG *The building needs a few repairs.*

3 If you say that someone **needn't do** something or that they **don't need to do** it, you are suggesting that they should not do it.
EG *Look, you needn't shout.*
EG *You don't need to wait for me.*

NOUN

4 a strong feeling that you must have or do something
EG *I felt the need to write about it.*

5 If there is a **need for** something, that thing would improve the situation.
EG *There is a need for more schools like this.*

PLURAL NOUN

6 Your **needs** are the things that you need to have.
EG *He had more than enough money for his needs.*

needle /'ni:dl/
needles

NOUN
1 a small, thin piece of metal with a hole at one end and a sharp point at the other, used for sewing
EG *... a needle and thread*
2 Knitting needles are long thin pieces of steel or plastic, used for knitting.
EG *... a pair of knitting needles*
3 a sharp instrument that is used to inject someone
EG *She left the needle sticking in his arm.*
4 the thin piece of metal or plastic on a dial which moves to show a measurement
EG *... the needle of a compass*

negative /'nɛgətɪv/

ADJECTIVE
1 A negative answer means 'no'.
EG *The question brought a negative response.*
2 Something that is negative is unpleasant or harmful.
EG *The news is not all negative.*
3 Someone who is negative sees only the bad aspects of a situation.
EG *Why are you so negative about everything?*
4 If a medical or scientific test is negative, it shows that something has not happened or is not present.
EG *The pregnancy test was negative.*

neglect /nɪ'glɛkt/
neglects neglecting neglected

VERB
1 If you neglect someone or something, you do not look after

them properly.
EG *He neglected his duties.*

NOUN
2 Neglect is failure to look after someone or something properly.
EG *Most of her plants died from neglect.*

negotiate /nɪ'gəʊʃɪeɪt/
negotiates negotiating negotiated

VERB
When people negotiate, they talk about a situation in order to reach an agreement about it.
EG *... the Prime Minister's refusal to negotiate with terrorists*

negotiation /nɪgəʊʃɪ'eɪʃən/
negotiations

NOUN
Negotiations are discussions between people with different interests.
EG *... before the negotiations broke down*
EG *... four years of negotiation*

neighbour /'neɪbər/
neighbours
US **neighbor**

NOUN
Your neighbour is someone who lives next door to you or near you.
EG *... visits from friends and neighbours*

neighbourhood /'neɪbəhud/
neighbourhoods
US **neighborhood**

NOUN
a district where people live
EG *... a safe neighbourhood*

neither /'naɪðər/

CONJUNCTION, ADJECTIVE, OR PRONOUN
1 You use 'neither' to make a negative statement that refers to

A B C D E F G H I J K L M N O P Q R S T U V W X Y Z

each of two things or people.

EG *I never learned to swim and neither did she.*

EG *Neither option appeals to me.*

EG *Neither of us felt like going out.*

CONJUNCTION

2 You use **neither** together with **nor** to link two things which are not true or do not happen.

EG *He spoke neither English nor German.*

EG *The play is neither as funny nor as clever as he thinks.*

nephew /ˈnɛvjuː/
nephews

NOUN

Your nephew is the son of your sister or brother.

EG *He'd bought his nephew a present.*

nerve /nɜːv/
nerves

NOUN

1 Nerves are long, thin structures that send messages between your brain and other parts of your body.

EG *... a trapped nerve*

2 Nerve is courage.

EG *She didn't have the nerve to approach him.*

PLURAL NOUN

3 If you talk about someone's **nerves**, you mean their ability to remain calm in a difficult situation.

EG *It needs confidence and strong nerves.*

4 You can refer to someone's feelings of anxiety as **nerves**.

EG *I don't suffer from nerves.*

5 If someone or something **gets on** your **nerves**, they irritate you.

EG *This place really gets on my nerves.*

nervous /ˈnɜːvəs/
ADJECTIVE

worried or frightened

EG *I was nervous about meeting him.*

nest /nɛst/
nests

NOUN

a place that birds, insects, and other animals make to lay eggs in or rear their young in

EG *... a bird's nest*

net /nɛt/
nets

NOUN

1 a piece of material made of threads that cross each other with small spaces in between

EG *... a fishing net*

2 the **Net** is the same as the Internet

EG *He heard about it on the Net.*

ADJECTIVE

3 A net result or amount is final, after everything has been considered or included.

EG *... a net profit of 171 million pounds*

network /ˈnɛtwɜːk/
networks

NOUN

1 a large number of lines or roads which cross each other at many points

EG *... a network of paths*

2 a large number of people or things that work together as a system

EG *... their widespread network of offices*

neutral /ˈnjuːtrəl/
ADJECTIVE

1 People who are neutral do not support either side in a disagreement or war.

EG *They have remained neutral*

throughout the conflict.

NOUN

2 Neutral is the position between the gears of a vehicle in which the gears are not connected to the engine.

EG *Graham put the van in neutral and jumped out.*

never /ˈnɛvəʳ/

ADVERB

at no time in the past, present, or future

EG *I've never met him.*

EG *Such decisions are never easy.*

EG *You'll never see her again.*

nevertheless /nɛvəðəˈlɛs/

ADVERB

You use 'nevertheless' when saying something that contrasts with what has just been said.

EG *All that is true, but it's incredible nevertheless.*

new /njuː/
newer newest

ADJECTIVE

1 recently made or created

EG *... a new hotel*

EG *These ideas aren't new.*

2 recently discovered

EG *... a new virus*

3 not used or owned before

EG *... sales of new cars*

4 different or unfamiliar

EG *I have to find somewhere new to live.*

EG *... a name which was new to me*

news /njuːz/

NOUN

1 News is information about things that have happened recently.

EG *Chris had some good news about his sister.*

2 News is information that is

published in newspapers and broadcast on radio and television.

EG *... some of the top stories in the news*

☑ Although it looks like a plural, 'news' is a singular noun: *news is just coming in.*

newspaper /ˈnjuːzpeɪpəʳ/
newspapers

NOUN

a publication, on large sheets of folded paper, that is produced regularly and contains news and articles

EG *The man behind them was reading a newspaper.*

New Year

NOUN

New Year is the time when people celebrate the start of a year.

EG *Happy New Year!*

EG *The restaurant was closed over New Year.*

next /nɛkst/

ADJECTIVE OR ADVERB

1 The next thing, person, or event is the one that comes immediately after the present one.

EG *What time is the next train?*

EG *He did not know what would happen next.*

ADJECTIVE

2 You use 'next' to refer to a particular time which follows immediately after the present one.

EG *She's due to arrive next Friday.*

EG *Let's go there next week.*

3 The next place or person is the one nearest to you.

EG *Stop at the next corner.*

ADVERB

4 If one thing is **next to** another, it is at the side of it.

EG *She sat down next to him.*

A B C D E F G H I J K L M N O P Q R S T U V W X Y Z

nice /naɪs/
nicer nicest
 ADJECTIVE
pleasant or attractive
EG ... *a nice meal*
EG *He was very nice to me.*

nickname /'nɪkneɪm/
nicknames
 NOUN
an informal name for someone or something
EG *Red got his nickname because of his red hair.*

niece /niːs/
nieces
 NOUN
Your niece is the daughter of your sister or brother.
EG ... *her five-year-old niece*

night /naɪt/
nights
 NOUN
1 Night is the time between sunset and sunrise when it is dark.
EG *He didn't leave the house all night.*
2 The night is the time between the end of the afternoon and the time that you go to bed.
EG *So where were you on Friday night?*

nightclub /'naɪtklʌb/
nightclubs
 NOUN
a place where people go late in the evening to drink and dance
EG ... *one of the liveliest nightclubs in New York*

nightmare /'naɪtmɛəʳ/
nightmares
 NOUN
1 a very frightening dream
EG *She had a nightmare about a vicious dog.*
2 a very unpleasant or frightening situation
EG *The whole journey was a nightmare.*

nil /nɪl/
 NOUN
Nil means zero or nothing. It is used especially in sports scores.
EG *We lost by two goals to nil.*

nine /naɪn/
nines
the number 9
EG ... *nine puppies*

nineteen /naɪn'tiːn/
the number 19
EG ... *nineteen years*

nineteenth /naɪn'tiːnθ/
 ADJECTIVE
The nineteenth item in a series is the one counted as number nineteen.
EG ... *the nineteenth floor*

ninetieth /'naɪntɪɪθ/
 ADJECTIVE
The ninetieth item in a series is the one counted as number ninety.
EG ... *the ninetieth year*

ninety /'naɪntɪ/
nineties
the number 90
EG ... *ninety kilometres*
EG ... *the nineteen-nineties*

ninth /naɪnθ/
ninths
 ADJECTIVE
1 The ninth item in a series is the one counted as number nine.
EG ... *the ninth day*
 NOUN
2 one of nine equal parts
EG ... *a ninth of the people*

nipple /'nɪpl/
nipples
 NOUN

Your nipples are the two small pieces of hard flesh on your chest.
EG *The breastfeeding had made her nipples sore.*

no /nəʊ/

INTERJECTION

1 You use 'no' to give a negative answer to a question or to refuse something.
EG *"Is she back yet?" — "No."*
EG *"Would you like a drink?" — "No, thanks."*

2 You use 'no' to agree with a question that already contains a negative.
EG *"Don't you like it?" — "No, I don't."*

ADJECTIVE

3 none at all or not at all
EG *No letters survive from this period.*
EG *She gave no reason.*

4 'No' is used in notices and instructions to say that something is forbidden.
EG *… a 'No Smoking' sign*
EG *No talking after lights out.*

ADVERB

5 'No' is used with the comparative form of an adjective or adverb to mean 'not'.
EG *… no later than 24th July*

noble /'nəʊbl/
nobler noblest

ADJECTIVE

honest, brave, and not selfish
EG *It seems to me that you did a noble thing.*

nobody /'nəʊbədɪ/

PRONOUN

Nobody means the same as no-one.
EG *Nobody realizes how bad things are.*

nod /nɒd/
nods nodding nodded

VERB

1 When you nod, you move your head up and down, usually to show agreement.
EG *She nodded in agreement.*

NOUN

2 a movement of your head up and down
EG *Todd agreed with a nod of his head.*

noise /nɔɪz/
noises

NOUN

a sound, especially one that is loud or unpleasant
EG *He heard a noise under his window.*
EG *There were complaints about the level of noise.*

noisy /'nɔɪzɪ/
noisier noisiest

ADJECTIVE

making a lot of noise or full of noise
EG *… a noisy crowd*
EG *It was so noisy there.*

non- /nɒn/

PREFIX

'Non' is added to the beginning of some words to form the negative of those words.
EG *… a non-smoker*
EG *… non-alcoholic beer*

none /nʌn/

PRONOUN

not a single thing or person, or not even a small amount of something
EG *None of us knew how to treat her.*
EG *They asked me for fresh ideas, but I had none.*

nonetheless /'nʌnðə'lɛs/

ADVERB

A
B
C
D
E
F
G
H
I
J
K
L
M
N
O
P
Q
R
S
T
U
V
W
X
Y
Z

A FORMAL WORD
You use 'nonetheless' when saying something that contrasts with what has just been said.
EG *We felt we had proved a point to him, nonetheless.*

nonsense /'nɒnsəns/

NOUN
Nonsense is foolish or meaningless words or behaviour.
EG *... all that poetic nonsense about love*
EG *"I'm putting on weight." — "Nonsense!"*

noon /nuːn/

NOUN
Noon is midday.
EG *An inspection will be held at noon today.*

no-one /'nəuwʌn/
or **no one**

PRONOUN
not a single person
EG *... a job that no-one wants*

nor /nɔːr/

CONJUNCTION
You use 'nor' after 'neither' or after a negative statement to add something else that the negative statement applies to.
EG *They had neither the time nor the money for the sport.*
EG *If you're not going, then nor will I.*

normal /'nɔːməl/

ADJECTIVE
usual and ordinary
EG *I try to lead a normal life.*
EG *Is it normal to worry about such things?*

normally /'nɔːməlɪ/

ADVERB
1 You use 'normally' to refer to what usually happens or what you usually do.
EG *Normally it rains in July.*
EG *I don't normally like dancing.*
2 in a way that is normal
EG *The baby is developing normally.*

north /nɔːθ/

NOUN
1 The north is the direction on your left when you are looking towards where the sun rises.
EG *... a group of islands further to the north*
2 The north of a place is the part which is towards the north.
EG *... a school in the north of England*

ADJECTIVE OR ADVERB
3 in or towards the north
EG *... the north coast of Crete*
EG *We were travelling north.*

North America

NOUN
North America is the continent that consists of the United States of America and Canada.
EG *... a tour of North America*

north-east /nɔːθ'iːst/

NOUN, ADVERB, OR ADJECTIVE
North-east is halfway between north and east.
EG *... a town in the north-east*
EG *They sailed north-east.*
EG *... the north-east corner of Skye*

northern /'nɔːðən/

ADJECTIVE
in or from the north
EG *... northern cities*

north-west /nɔːθ'wɛst/

NOUN, ADVERB, OR ADJECTIVE
North-west is halfway between north and west.
EG *... a housing development in the north-west of Mexico City*
EG *We were heading north-west.*

A
B
C
D
E
F
G
H
I
J
K
L
M
N
O
P
Q
R
S
T
U
V
W
X
Y
Z

EG ... the north-west corner of
France

nose /nəuz/
noses

NOUN

the part of your face which sticks
out above your mouth and which
you use for smelling and breathing
EG Keeler scratched his nose.

nostril /'nɔstrɪl/
nostrils

NOUN

Your nostrils are the two openings
in your nose which you breathe
through.
EG ... the hair in his nostrils

not /nɔt/
☑ Not is often shortened to n't
and added to the end of words
such as 'is', 'have' and 'do': I don't
know; he isn't joking.

ADVERB

1 You use 'not' to make a sentence
negative.
EG He was not there.
EG Why didn't you do it months
ago?
2 You use 'not' to represent the
negative of a word or phrase that
has just been used.
EG "Have you found Paula?" —
"I'm afraid not."
EG I don't care whether he comes or
not.
3 You use 'not' to make
suggestions.
EG Why don't you join us?
4 You use 'not' to say that there
are exceptions to something that
is generally true, or that
something is not the whole truth.
EG Not every applicant was young.
EG She's not only pretty, she's
smart too.
5 You use 'not' when you are

contrasting two things.
EG Training is an investment, not a
cost.

note /nəut/
notes noting noted

NOUN

1 a short letter
EG I'll leave a note for Karen.

2 something that you write down
that helps you to remember
something
EG You should take notes during the
meeting.

3 a musical sound of a particular
pitch, or a written symbol that
represents it
EG She taught them a few simple
notes on the piano.

4 a piece of paper money
EG ... a five pound note

5 an atmosphere, feeling, or
quality
EG The film ends on a positive note.

6 If you **take note of** something,
you pay attention to it because
you think it is important.
EG You should take note of the
weather conditions.

VERB

7 If you note a fact, you become
aware of it.
EG Please note that there are a
limited number of tickets.

8 If you note something or **note
down** it, you write it down.
EG He noted down the address.

nothing /'nʌθɪŋ/

PRONOUN

not a single thing
EG He said nothing to reporters.
EG There is nothing wrong with the
car.
EG He was dressed in jeans and
nothing else.

notice /'nəutɪs/
notices noticing noticed

VERB

1 If you notice something, you become aware of it.

EG *She noticed a bird sitting on the fence.*

EG *I noticed he was acting strangely.*

NOUN

2 a written announcement

EG *... a 'No Vacancies' notice in the window*

3 Notice is advance warning about something.

EG *I was given four days' notice to prepare for the wedding.*

4 If someone **brings** something **to** your **notice**, they make you aware of it.

EG *I'm glad he brought it to my notice.*

5 If you **take** no **notice of** someone or something, you do not pay attention to them.

EG *No one took any notice of what I said.*

noticeable /'nəutɪsəbl/

ADJECTIVE

very obvious and easy to see

EG *... a noticeable improvement*

notion /'nəuʃən/
notions

NOUN

an idea or belief

EG *... old-fashioned notions about love*

notorious /nəu'tɔːrɪəs/

ADJECTIVE

well-known for something bad

EG *The area has become notorious for violence against tourists.*

nought /nɔːt/
noughts

the number 0

EG *... a score of nought*

EG *... a string of noughts*

noun /naun/
nouns

NOUN

A **noun** is a word that refers to a person, a thing, or an idea. For example, 'president', 'table', and 'beauty' are nouns.

Proper nouns are words which give the name of a particular person, place, or object. They begin with capital letters. For example, 'John Smith', 'New York', and 'The Bank of England' are proper nouns.

novel /'nɒvl/
novels

NOUN

1 a book that tells a long story about imaginary people and events

EG *... a novel about rural life*

ADJECTIVE

2 new and interesting

EG *... a very novel experience*

novelist /'nɒvəlɪst/
novelists

NOUN

a person who writes novels

EG *... England's most popular romantic novelist*

November /nəu'vɛmbər/

NOUN

November is the eleventh month of the year.

EG *... a party in November*

novice /'nɒvɪs/
novices

NOUN

someone who is not yet experienced at something

EG *Most of us are novices on the computer.*

now /nau/

ADVERB

1 You use 'now' to refer to the present time.
EG *I must go now.*
EG *She should know that by now.*
EG *... in three days from now*

2 You can say 'Now' to introduce new information into an account.
EG *Now, this is the interesting part.*

3 If something happens **now and then**, it happens sometimes but not regularly.
EG *Now and then they heard the roar of a truck.*

4 **just now** means a very short time ago
EG *You looked pretty upset just now.*

CONJUNCTION

5 You use 'now' or **now that** to show that two events are connected or may be connected.
EG *Things have got better now that he's older.*

nowhere /'nəuwɛəʳ/

ADVERB

not anywhere
EG *There was nowhere to hide.*
EG *This kind of forest exists nowhere else in the world.*

nuclear /'nju:klɪəʳ/

ADJECTIVE

relating to the energy produced when atoms are split
EG *... a nuclear power station*
EG *... nuclear war*

nude /nju:d/

ADJECTIVE

not wearing any clothes
EG *... a nude model*

nuisance /'nju:sns/
nuisances

NOUN

someone or something that is annoying or causing problems
EG *I'm sorry to have been such a nuisance.*
EG *It's a nuisance that you live so far away.*

numb /nʌm/

ADJECTIVE

If a part of your body is numb, you cannot feel anything there.
EG *My feet felt numb from the cold.*

number /'nʌmbəʳ/
numbers numbering numbered

NOUN

1 a word or symbol that is used for counting or calculating something
EG *Fred said that thirteen was his lucky number.*
EG *... number 3, Argyll Street*

2 Someone's number is the series of numbers that you dial when you telephone them.
EG *Have you got their number?*

3 A **number of** things or people means several of them.
EG *Sam told a number of lies.*
EG *... a large number of accidents*

VERB

4 If you number something, you give it a number in a series and write the number on it.
EG *I haven't numbered the pages.*

numerous /'nju:mərəs/

ADJECTIVE

existing or happening in large numbers
EG *... numerous aunts and cousins*

nun /nʌn/
nuns

NOUN

a member of a female religious community
EG *... a school run by nuns*

A
B
C
D
E
F
G
H
I
J
K
L
M
N
O
P
Q
R
S
T
U
V
W
X
Y
Z

nurse /nɜːs/
nurses nursing nursed

NOUN

1 a person whose job is to look after people who are ill
EG *He gave the nurse some instructions about my diet.*

VERB

2 If you nurse someone, you look after them when they are ill.
EG *They nursed me back to health.*

nursery /ˈnɜːsərɪ/
nurseries

NOUN

a place where young children are looked after while their parents are working
EG *The company ran its own nursery.*

nut /nʌt/
nuts

NOUN

1 a fruit with a hard shell and a centre that can be eaten
EG *Suzanne mixed fruit, nuts, and cereal for breakfast.*

2 a piece of metal with a hole in the middle which a bolt screws into
EG *It was held down by nuts along the bottom.*

nylon /ˈnaɪlɒn/

NOUN

Nylon is a type of strong artificial material.
EG *... nylon stockings*

obey /ə'beɪ/
obeys obeying obeyed

VERB

If you obey a person or an order,
you do what you are told to do.
EG *You will be expected to obey the
rules.*

object /'ɒbdʒɪkt/
objects objecting objected

NOUN

1 anything solid that you can
touch or see, and that is not alive
EG *... the large black object he was
carrying*

2 an aim or purpose
EG *The object of the exercise is to
raise money.*

When people talk about the **object**
of a verb or of a sentence, they
mean the person or thing that is
affected by the action, rather than
the person or thing that does it.
EG *The cat chased **a mouse**.*

VERB : /əb'dʒɛkt/
☑ Note that you pronounce the
verb differently from the noun.

3 If you **object to** something,
you dislike it or disapprove of it.
EG *I strongly object to that
statement.*

objection /əb'dʒɛkʃən/
objections

NOUN

If you have an objection to
something, you dislike it or
disapprove of it.
EG *I have no objection to banks
making money.*
EG *No-one raised any objections to
the change.*

objective /əb'dʒɛktɪv/
objectives

NOUN

1 Your objective is something that
you are trying to achieve.
EG *His main objective was to win.*

ADJECTIVE

2 based on facts and not
influenced by personal feelings
EG *A journalist should be completely
objective.*

obligation /ɒblɪ'geɪʃən/
obligations

NOUN

something that you must do
because it is your duty
EG *You're under no obligation to
buy anything.*

obscene /əb'siːn/

ADJECTIVE

Something that is obscene is likely
to offend people because it refers
to sex.
EG *... obscene language*

observation /ɒbzə'veɪʃən/
observations

NOUN

1 Observation is the act of
watching something carefully.
EG *... careful observation of the
movement of the planets*

2 something that you have seen or
noticed
EG *This report is based on my own
observations.*

3 a remark
EG *I wish to make a few general
observations about your work.*

observe /əb'zɜːv/
**observes observing
observed**

A
B
C
D
E
F
G
H
I
J
K
L
M
N
O
P
Q
R
S
T
U
V
W
X
Y
Z

VERB
1 If you observe someone or something, you watch them carefully.
EG *Professor Stern studies and observes the behaviour of babies.*
2 If you observe something, you notice it.
EG *It was difficult to observe any change in his expression.*
3 A FORMAL USE
If you observe a law or custom, you obey it or follow it.
EG *Motorists were forced to observe speed restrictions.*

obsessed /əb'sɛst/
ADJECTIVE
If you are **obsessed with** something or someone, you think about them all the time.
EG *He was obsessed with football.*

obstacle /'ɒbstəkl/
obstacles
NOUN
something which is in your way or which makes it difficult to do something
EG *... obstacles in the road*
EG *... the greatest obstacle to success*

obstruct /əb'strʌkt/
obstructs obstructing obstructed
VERB
If something obstructs a road or path, it blocks it.
EG *Lorries have completely obstructed the entrance.*

obtain /əb'teɪn/
obtains obtaining obtained
VERB
A FORMAL WORD
If you obtain something, you get it.
EG *Evans was trying to obtain a false passport.*

obvious /'ɒbvɪəs/
ADJECTIVE
easy to see or understand
EG *It was obvious that he wasn't going to answer.*
EG *... an obvious weakness*

occasion /ə'keɪʒən/
occasions
NOUN
1 a time when something happens
EG *I met her on only one occasion.*
2 an important event
EG *The first night was quite an occasion.*

occasionally /ə'keɪʒənəlɪ/
ADVERB
sometimes but not often
EG *I visit him occasionally.*

occupation /ˌɒkjʊ'peɪʃən/
occupations
NOUN
1 a job or profession
EG *... moving from one occupation to another*
2 a pastime
EG *Parachuting is a dangerous occupation.*
3 The occupation of a country is its invasion and control by a foreign army.
EG *... the French occupation of North Africa*

occupy /'ɒkjʊpaɪ/
occupies occupying occupied
VERB
1 The people who occupy a building are the people who live or work there.
EG *... houses occupied by the elderly*
2 If a seat or place **is occupied**, someone is using it so that it is not available.
EG *... three beds, two of which were*

occupied

3 When people occupy a place, they move into it and take control of it.
EG *Students occupied the building.*

occur /əˈkəːʳ/
occurs occurring occurred
VERB
1 If something occurs, it happens or exists.
EG *The attack occurred at a swimming pool.*
EG *The phrase often occurs in the Bible.*
2 If a thought or idea **occurs to** you, you suddenly think of it.
EG *That possibility hadn't occurred to them.*

ocean /ˈəuʃən/
oceans
NOUN
The ocean is the sea.
EG *He stood gazing out at the ocean.*
EG *... the Pacific Ocean*

o'clock /əˈklɒk/
ADVERB
You use 'o'clock' after numbers from one to twelve to say what time it is.
EG *... four o'clock in the afternoon*

October /ɒkˈtəubəʳ/
NOUN
October is the tenth month of the year.
EG *... a short holiday in October*

odd /ɒd/
odder oddest; odds
ADJECTIVE
1 Something odd is strange or unusual.
EG *... an odd coincidence*
2 You use 'odd' when you are not mentioning the exact type or

frequency of something.
EG *She helped me with odd jobs around the house.*
EG *He likes the odd drink.*
3 Odd things are things that do not belong to the same set or pair.
EG *... odd socks*
4 Odd numbers are numbers that cannot be divided exactly by two.
EG *... the houses with odd numbers*
PLURAL NOUN
5 You can refer to the probability of something happening as **the odds** that it will happen.
EG *What are the odds on him winning?*

of /ɒv, əv/
PREPOSITION
1 consisting of or containing
EG *... a collection of short stories*
EG *... a cup of tea*
2 belonging to or connected with
EG *... the cover of the book*
EG *... the mayor of Los Angeles*
✓ When 'of' means 'belonging to', it can be replaced by 's: *the cover of the book* means the same as *the book's cover*.
3 forming part of a larger group or thing
EG *... a blade of grass*
EG *... a piece of bread*
4 You use 'of' to talk about amounts, ages, and dates.
EG *... a rise of 15 per cent*
EG *... a woman of 26*
EG *... the fourth of July*
5 You use 'of' when naming something or describing a characteristic of something.
EG *... the city of Canberra*
EG *... a woman of great influence*

off /ɒf/
PREPOSITION OR ADVERB
1 You use 'off' to indicate the

A
B
C
D
E
F
G
H
I
J
K
L
M
N
O
P
Q
R
S
T
U
V
W
X
Y
Z

A
B
C
D
E
F
G
H
I
J
K
L
M
N
O
P
Q
R
S
T
U
V
W
X
Y
Z

removal of something.
EG *He took his feet off the desk.*
EG *She picked up the spoon and wiped the dirt off.*

2 You use 'off' to indicate movement away from or out of a place.
EG *They had just stepped off the plane.*
EG *She got up and marched off.*

3 You use 'off' to indicate that something is separated or distant from a place.
EG *... an island off the coast of Australia*
EG *The whole area has been fenced off.*

4 Time off is time when you do not go to work.
EG *He couldn't get time off work.*
EG *It was Frank's night off.*

ADJECTIVE
5 not switched on
EG *Her bedroom light was off.*

6 cancelled or postponed
EG *The concert was off.*

7 Food that is off has gone sour or bad.
EG *This milk is off.*

offence /ə'fens/
offences
US **offense**

NOUN
a crime
EG *Rape is a serious offence.*

offend /ə'fend/
offends offending offended

VERB
If you offend someone, you upset them.
EG *I didn't mean to offend her.*

offense /ə'fens/
see **offence**

offer /'ɔfər/

offers offering offered

VERB
1 If you offer something to someone, you ask them if they would like it.
EG *She offered him a cup of tea.*
EG *Greg offered to teach him to ski.*

NOUN
2 something that someone says they will give you or do for you
EG *He refused the offer of a drink.*

office /'ɔfɪs/
offices

NOUN
1 a room where people work at desks
EG *I arrived at the office early.*

2 a department of an organization, especially a government department
EG *Contact your local tax office.*

officer /'ɔfɪsər/
officers

NOUN
a person with a position of authority in the armed forces, the police, or a government organization
EG *... army officers*

official /ə'fɪʃl/
officials

ADJECTIVE
1 approved by the government or by someone in authority
EG *... the official figures*

2 done or used by someone in authority as part of their job
EG *... an official visit*

NOUN
3 a person who holds a position of authority in an organization
EG *... a senior official at the American embassy*

often /'ɔfn/

ADVERB

1 If something happens often, it happens many times or much of the time.

EG *She often spent Sunday with them.*

EG *That doesn't happen very often.*

2 You use 'often' to talk about the frequency of something.

EG *How often do you brush your teeth?*

EG *John came as often as he could.*

oh /əu/

INTERJECTION

You use 'oh' to introduce a comment on something that has just been said, or to express a feeling such as surprise, pain, or joy.

EG *"You don't understand." — "Oh, I think I do."*

EG *"Oh my God," he moaned.*

oil /ɔɪl/
oils oiling oiled

NOUN

1 Oil is a smooth, thick liquid that is found underground and used as a fuel.

EG *The Middle East has vast resources of oil.*

2 Oil is a smooth, thick liquid made from plants or fish and used in cooking.

EG *... olive oil*

VERB

3 If you oil something, you put oil in it or on it.

EG *The machine needs to be oiled regularly.*

OK also spelt okay
AN INFORMAL WORD

ADJECTIVE OR ADVERB

1 If something is OK, it is acceptable.

EG *Is it OK if I come alone?*

EG *Tell me if this sounds OK.*

ADJECTIVE

2 If someone is OK, they are safe and well.

EG *She immediately asked if I was okay.*

INTERJECTION

3 You can say 'OK' to show that you agree with something.

EG *"Shall I call you on Friday?" — "OK."*

4 You can use 'OK?' to ask whether someone understands and accepts what you have said.

EG *We'll meet tomorrow. OK?*

old /əuld/
older oldest

ADJECTIVE

1 Someone or something that is old has lived or existed for a long time.

EG *... an old lady*

EG *... old clothes*

2 You use 'old' to talk about the age of someone or something.

EG *This photo is five years old.*

EG *How old are you now?*

3 You use 'old' to talk about something that is no longer used or something that has been replaced by something else.

EG *... when Jane returned to her old flat*

old-fashioned /ˈəuldˈfæʃnd/

ADJECTIVE

Something which is old-fashioned is no longer used, done, or believed by most people.

EG *... a pair of old-fashioned shoes*

EG *She has some very old-fashioned ideas.*

on /ɒn/

PREPOSITION

1 Someone or something that is on an object or surface is

A
B
C
D
E
F
G
H
I
J
K
L
M
N
O
P
Q
R
S
T
U
V
W
X
Y
Z

supported by it or attached to it.
EG *The woman was sitting on the sofa.*
EG *... the pictures on the wall*

2 If you are on a bus, plane, or train, you are inside it.
EG *She liked to read on the bus.*

3 If something happens on a particular day, that is when it happens.
EG *It's his birthday on Monday.*

4 If something is done on an instrument or machine, it is done using that instrument or machine.
EG *I could do all my work on the computer.*

5 A book or talk on a particular subject is about that subject.
EG *... a new book on alternative medicine*

6 You use 'on' when mentioning an event that was followed by another one.
EG *On hearing this, she screamed.*

ADVERB
7 If you have a piece of clothing on, you are wearing it.
EG *Bob already had his coat on.*

8 You use 'on' to say that someone is continuing to do something.
EG *They walked on in silence.*

ADJECTIVE
9 If a machine or electric light is on, it is working.
EG *The light was on upstairs.*

10 If an event is on, it is taking place.
EG *Tomorrow's race is definitely on.*
EG *What's on at the cinema?*

once /wʌns/

ADVERB
1 If something happens once, it happens one time only.
EG *Mary only went to Manchester*

once.
EG *They meet once a month.*

2 If something was once true, it was true in the past, but is no longer true.
EG *The island was once covered by trees.*

CONJUNCTION
3 If something happens once another thing has happened, it happens immediately afterwards.
EG *I'll go back to the hotel once the game is over.*

NOUN
4 If you do something **at once**, you do it immediately.
EG *We must go home at once.*

5 If several things happen **at once**, they all happen at the same time.
EG *Everybody was talking at once.*

one /wʌn/
ones

1 the number 1
EG *They had three sons and one daughter.*
EG *... one thousand years ago*

ADJECTIVE
2 'One' can be used instead of 'a', for example to give emphasis or to talk about a time in the past or future.
EG *There is one thing I still don't understand.*
EG *... one day last week*

3 If you refer to **the one** person or thing of a particular kind, you mean the only person or thing of that kind.
EG *He was the one man who could save the country.*

PRONOUN
4 You use 'one' to refer to the same thing or person that you have mentioned earlier.
EG *They are selling their house to*

move to a smaller one.
EG We are the only ones who know.

5 A FORMAL USE
You can use 'one' to refer to people in general.
EG One never knows what might happen.

6 one another means the same as 'each other'
EG They smiled at one another.

oneself /wʌn'sɛlf/

PRONOUN
A FORMAL WORD

1 You use 'oneself' to refer to yourself or to people in general.
EG … a way of making oneself feel sophisticated

2 To do something oneself means to do it without any help.
EG There are some things one must do oneself.

3 You use 'oneself' to emphasize that something happens to you rather than to people in general.
EG It is better to die oneself than to kill.

onion /'ʌnjən/
onions

NOUN
a small, round vegetable with a very strong smell and taste
EG … fried onions

only /'əʊnlɪ/

ADVERB

1 You use 'only' to indicate that what you are saying refers to one particular person or thing.
EG Only Tony was able to continue.
EG He only reads poetry.

2 You use 'only' to introduce a condition which must happen before something else can happen.
EG You will only be paid if you win.

3 You use 'only' to emphasize that something is unimportant or small.

EG I was only joking.
EG It only costs £5.

4 You use 'only' to introduce something which happens immediately after something else.
EG She tried phoning them, only to find the number engaged.

5 If something has **only just** happened, it happened a very short time ago.
EG I've only just arrived.

6 If you **only just** succeed in doing something, you succeed by a very small degree.
EG They only just managed to survive.

ADJECTIVE

7 If you talk about the only person or thing in a situation, you mean that there are no others.
EG She was the only woman in the team.

8 If you are an only child, you have no brothers or sisters.
EG She was the only child of a wealthy family.

CONJUNCTION

9 but or except
EG He was like you, only taller.
EG I would go, only I'm busy.

onto /'ɒntu/
or **on to**

PREPOSITION

1 If you put something onto an object, you put it on it.
EG I lowered myself onto the bed.

2 If you get onto a bus, train, or plane, you get on it.
EG … as I got onto the train

open /'əʊpn/
opens opening opened

VERB

1 When you open something, or when it opens, it is moved so that it is no longer closed.

EG *She opened the door.*

EG *... the moment her eyes opened*

2 When a shop or office opens, it is unlocked and the people in it start working.

EG *The bank opens at nine o'clock.*

ADJECTIVE

3 Something that is open is not closed or fastened.

EG *Her eyes were open.*

EG *... an open window*

4 When a shop or office is open, it is unlocked and the people in it are working.

EG *The restaurant is now open on Sundays.*

5 Someone who is open is honest and does not deceive people.

EG *He was quite open about his debts.*

opening /ˈəʊpnɪŋ/
openings

ADJECTIVE

1 The opening event in a series is the first one.

EG *... the opening game of the season*

NOUN

2 The opening of a book or film is the first part of it.

EG *That would make a great opening for a novel.*

3 a hole or gap

EG *... a narrow opening in the fence*

opera /ˈɒpərə/
operas

NOUN

a play in which the words are sung rather than spoken

EG *... an opera about Joan of Arc*

operate /ˈɒpəreɪt/
**operates operating
operated**

VERB

1 The way that something

operates is the way it works.

EG *We are shocked at the way some businesses operate.*

EG *Calculators operate on the same principle.*

2 When you operate a machine, you make it work.

EG *The manual shows you how to operate the computer.*

3 When surgeons operate, they cut open a person's body to remove or repair a damaged part.

EG *... after they decided to operate on him*

operation /ɒpəˈreɪʃən/
operations

NOUN

1 a complex, planned event

EG *... the rescue operation*

2 a form of medical treatment in which a surgeon cuts open a person's body to remove or repair a damaged part

EG *Peacock had just had an operation on his back.*

opinion /əˈpɪnjən/
opinions

NOUN

a belief or view

EG *In my opinion, he's wrong.*

EG *She has strong opinions about television.*

opponent /əˈpəʊnənt/
opponents

NOUN

someone who is against you in an argument or contest

EG *... an outspoken opponent of the president*

EG *Norris twice knocked down his opponent.*

opportunity /ɒpəˈtjuːnɪtɪ/
opportunities

NOUN

a chance to do something that you want to do
EG *I had an opportunity to go to New York.*

opposed /ə'pəuzd/

ADJECTIVE
If you are **opposed to** something, you disagree with it.
EG *He was totally opposed to the idea.*

opposite /'ɔpəzɪt/
opposites

PREPOSITION OR ADVERB
1 If one thing is opposite another, it is facing it.
EG *... the shop opposite the station*
EG *... the house opposite*

ADJECTIVE
2 The opposite part of something is the part farthest away from you.
EG *... the opposite side of town*
3 If things are opposite, they are completely different.
EG *... a word with the opposite meaning*

NOUN
4 If two things are **the opposite of** one another, they are completely different.
EG *He was the complete opposite of Raymond.*
EG *They're complete opposites.*

opposition /ɔpə'zɪʃən/

NOUN
1 If there is **opposition to** something, people disagree with it and try to prevent it.
EG *There was strong opposition to this proposal.*
2 the **Opposition** refers to the political parties that do not form part of a country's government
EG *... the Leader of the Opposition*

opt /ɔpt/

opts opting opted

VERB
If you **opt for** something or **opt to do** something, you choose it or choose to do it.
EG *Many children of farmers opt for a different career.*
EG *I opted to spend my second year in Edinburgh.*

optimistic /ɔptɪ'mɪstɪk/

ADJECTIVE
hopeful about the future
EG *She is optimistic that an agreement can be reached.*

option /'ɔpʃən/
options

NOUN
a choice between two or more things
EG *What other options are there?*

or /ɔːr/

CONJUNCTION
1 You use 'or' to link two alternatives.
EG *Tea or coffee?*
EG *I don't know if she'll come or not.*
☑ You do not use 'or' after *neither*. You use 'nor' instead: *he speaks neither English nor German.*
2 You can use 'or' to mean 'if not'.
EG *She had to have the operation, or she would die.*

orange /'ɔrɪndʒ/
oranges

ADJECTIVE OR NOUN
1 Orange is a colour between red and yellow.
EG *... an orange jacket*
EG *It was painted a vivid orange.*

NOUN
2 a round, sweet fruit with a thick orange skin
EG *... orange juice*

A B C D E F G H I J K L M N O P Q R S T U V W X Y Z

A
B
C
D
E
F
G
H
I
J
K
L
M
N
O
P
Q
R
S
T
U
V
W
X
Y
Z

orchestra /ˈɔːkɪstrə/
orchestras

NOUN

a large group of musicians who play musical instruments together
EG … the London Symphony Orchestra

☑ You can use either a singular or a plural verb after 'orchestra': *the orchestra was preparing; the orchestra were preparing*.

order /ˈɔːdəʳ/
orders ordering ordered

NOUN

1 a command given by someone in authority
EG *The lieutenant gave the order to arrest them.*

2 Order is a situation in which everything is in the correct place or everything is peaceful and calm.
EG *She longed for some order in her life.*
EG *The police arrived to restore order.*

3 An order is something that you ask to be brought or sent to you, and that you are going to pay for.
EG *A waiter came to take their order.*

4 If things are arranged or done **in** a particular **order**, they are arranged or done in that sequence.
EG *The names were listed in alphabetical order.*

5 If you do something **in order to** achieve a particular thing, you do it because you want to achieve that thing.
EG *Naseem came to Britain in order to study.*

VERB

6 If you **order** someone **to do** something, you tell them firmly to do it.
EG *He ordered his men to stop firing.*
EG *Croft ordered an investigation.*

7 When you order something that you are going to pay for, you ask for it to be brought or sent to you.
EG *Jim ordered another plate of cakes.*

ordinary /ˈɔːdnrɪ/

ADJECTIVE

not special or different in any way
EG … *ordinary people*
EG … *an ordinary day*

organ /ˈɔːgən/
organs

NOUN

1 Your organs are parts of your body that have a particular purpose, for example your heart or lungs.
EG … *internal organs*

2 a large musical keyboard instrument
EG … *the church organ*

organise /ˈɔːgənaɪz/
another spelling of **organize**

organization /ɔːgənaɪˈzeɪʃən/
organizations; also spelt
organisation

NOUN

1 an official group of people
EG … *a powerful political organization*

2 The organization of something is the act of planning and arranging it.
EG *There's a complete lack of organization.*

organize /ˈɔːgənaɪz/
organizes organizing organized; also spelt **organise**

VERB

If you organize an event, you plan and arrange it.
EG *We decided to organize a concert for Easter.*

origin /ˈɒrɪdʒɪn/

A
B
C
D
E
F
G
H
I
J
K
L
M
N
O
P
Q
R
S
T
U
V
W
X
Y
Z

origins

NOUN

You can refer to the beginning or cause of something as its origin or **origins**.

EG *The origins of the custom are not known.*

original /əˈrɪdʒɪnl/

originals

ADJECTIVE

1 Original refers to something that existed at the beginning of a process, rather than later.

EG *... the original owner of the cottage*

2 full of imagination or new ideas

EG *... a highly original thinker*

3 a work of art or a document that is not a copy or a later version

EG *The pictures on the walls were all originals.*

EG *I photocopied the form and sent the original back.*

ornament /ˈɔːnəmənt/

ornaments

NOUN

a small, attractive object that you display in your home or garden

EG *... a shelf with a few photos and ornaments on it*

other /ˈʌðəʳ/

others

ADJECTIVE OR PRONOUN

1 You use 'other' to refer to an additional thing or person of the same type.

EG *They were just like any other young couple.*

EG *Four crewmen were killed, one other was injured.*

2 You use 'other' to refer to a different thing or person from the one mentioned.

EG *You have no other choice.*

EG *Some of these methods will work, others will not.*

3 You use 'other' to refer to the second of two things or people.

EG *... at the other end of the room*

EG *... with a cigarette in one hand and a drink in the other*

4 You use 'other' to refer to the rest of the things or people in a group.

EG *All the other children had left.*

EG *... the astronomy of Copernicus, Galileo and others*

ADJECTIVE

5 the other day or **the other week** means a day or week in the recent past

EG *I saw David the other day.*

otherwise /ˈʌðəwaɪz/

ADVERB

1 'Otherwise' means 'if not'.

EG *You had to learn to swim pretty quickly, otherwise you sank.*

2 'Otherwise' means apart from the thing mentioned.

EG *She had written to her daughter, but otherwise did nothing.*

3 'Otherwise' means in a different way.

EG *Two years ago he had thought otherwise.*

ought /ɔːt/

☑ 'Ought' is a modal verb. It has only one form. There are no forms ending in -s, -ing, or -ed.

VERB

1 If you say that someone **ought to do** something, you mean that it is the right or sensible thing to do.

EG *He ought to see a doctor.*

EG *I ought to have told you.*

2 If you say that something **ought to** be the case, you mean that you expect it to be the case.

A B C D E F G H I J K L M N O P Q R S T U V W X Y Z

EG *It ought to be quite easy.*
EG *He ought to have arrived by now.*

ounce /auns/
ounces
NOUN
a unit of weight equal to one sixteenth of a pound or about 28.35 grams
EG *... three ounces of cheese*

our /'auər/
ADJECTIVE
You use 'our' to refer to something that belongs or relates to yourself and one or more other people.
EG *We recently sold our house.*
EG *There are a lot of cats in our neighbourhood.*

ours /auəz/
PRONOUN
You use 'ours' to refer to something that belongs or relates to yourself and one or more other people.
EG *... a town like ours*
EG *... a friend of ours from Korea*

ourselves /auə'sɛlvz/
PRONOUN
1 You use 'ourselves' to refer to yourself and one or more other people.
EG *We find ourselves without any real choice.*
EG *We almost made ourselves ill.*
2 You use 'ourselves' to emphasize 'we'.
EG *We ourselves were not in danger.*
3 If you say something such as 'we did it ourselves', you mean that you did it without any help.
EG *We built the house ourselves.*

out /aut/
ADVERB
1 towards the outside of a place
EG *Two dogs rushed out of the house.*
EG *He stood looking out of the window.*
EG *... a sign saying "Keep Out"*
2 outdoors
EG *They are playing out in the sunshine.*
3 If you do something **out of** a particular feeling, that feeling causes you to do it.
EG *She went along out of curiosity.*
4 If something is made **out of** a particular material, it was constructed using that material.
EG *... old instruments made out of wood*
5 If you are **out of** something, you no longer have any of it.
EG *We're out of milk again.*
6 If something is true of, for example, one **out of** two people, it is true of half of those people.
EG *Two out of three people voted against it.*
ADVERB OR ADJECTIVE
7 not at home
EG *I went out to buy a newspaper.*
EG *She was out when I rang.*
8 no longer shining or burning
EG *All the lights went out.*
EG *The fire had been out for hours.*
9 available to buy
EG *Her book comes out in July.*
EG *Their new video is out soon.*
ADJECTIVE
10 In a game or sport, if you are out, you are no longer taking part.
EG *If you land on a red square, you're out.*

outcome /'autkʌm/
outcomes
NOUN
The outcome of something is the result of it.
EG *... the outcome of the election*

outdoor /aut'dɔːʳ/
ADJECTIVE
happening or used outside
EG ... outdoor activities such as sailing

outdoors /aut'dɔːz/
ADVERB
outside rather than in a building
EG It was too cold to sit outdoors.

outer /'autəʳ/
ADJECTIVE
The outer parts of something are the parts furthest from the centre.
EG ... the outer door of the office

outfit /'autfɪt/
outfits
NOUN
a set of clothes
EG Richard and Danny wore cowboy outfits.

outing /'autɪŋ/
outings
NOUN
a trip that you make for pleasure
EG ... a family outing to London

outline /'autlaɪn/
outlines outlining outlined
VERB
1 If you outline a plan or idea, you explain it in a general way.
EG The mayor outlined his plan.
NOUN
2 a general explanation or description of something
EG ... an outline of the report
3 The outline of something is its shape.
EG ... the unmistakable outline of the cathedral

outlook /'autluk/
NOUN
1 Your outlook is your general attitude towards life.

EG My whole outlook on life had changed.
2 The outlook of a situation is the way it is likely to develop.
EG The economic outlook is bright.

outrageous /aut'reɪdʒəs/
ADJECTIVE
unacceptable or very shocking
EG ... his outrageous drunken behaviour

outside /aut'saɪd/
NOUN
1 The outside of something is the part which surrounds or contains the rest of it.
EG We wandered around the outside of the house.
ADVERB OR PREPOSITION
2 not inside
EG He stood outside and shouted.
EG Wait outside the door.
ADJECTIVE
3 On a road, the outside lane is the one for overtaking or for travelling at high speed.
EG ... the outside lane of the motorway
EG ... an outside toilet

outskirts /'autskəːts/
PLURAL NOUN
The outskirts of a city or town are the parts around the edge of it.
EG ... a flat on the outskirts of Paris

outstanding /aut'stændɪŋ/
ADJECTIVE
1 extremely good
EG ... an outstanding athlete
2 Money that is outstanding is still owed to someone.
EG I fully intend to repay the outstanding debt.

outward /'autwəd/
ADJECTIVE
1 Outward means away from a

A B C D E F G H I J K L M N O P Q R S T U V W X Y Z

A
B
C
D
E
F
G
H
I
J
K
L
M
N
O
P
Q
R
S
T
U
V
W
X
Y
Z

place.

EG *… the outward journey*

2 The outward features of something are the ones that it appears to have, rather than the ones it actually has.

EG *He never showed any outward signs of stress.*

outwards /ˈautwədz/

ADVERB

towards the outside

EG *The door opens outwards.*

oven /ˈʌvn/

ovens

NOUN

the part of a cooker that you use for baking or roasting food

EG *The turkey was roasting in the oven.*

over /ˈəuvəʳ/

PREPOSITION

1 If one thing is over another thing, it is directly above the second thing or covering it.

EG *… the picture over the fireplace*

EG *He put his hands over his eyes.*

2 If you climb or jump over something, you climb or jump across the top of it.

EG *The boys climbed over the fence and escaped.*

3 Something that is over a particular amount is more than that amount.

EG *It cost over a million dollars.*

4 If something happens over a period of time, it happens during that period.

EG *Things have improved over the last few weeks.*

5 If people disagree over something, they disagree because of it.

EG *… an argument over money*

ADVERB OR PREPOSITION

6 If you lean over or bend over, you bend your body in a particular direction.

EG *He leant over to open the door of the car.*

EG *She bent over the table, frowning.*

ADVERB

7 You use 'over' to indicate a particular position.

EG *… the man over by the window*

EG *Come over here.*

8 If something rolls over or turns over, it moves so that its other side is facing upwards.

EG *He turned the envelope over to look at the address.*

9 If something falls over or is knocked over, it falls or is knocked towards the ground.

EG *A chair was knocked over in the rush.*

ADJECTIVE

10 Something that is over is finished.

EG *The waiting was finally over.*

overall /əuvərˈɔːl/

ADJECTIVE

1 You use 'overall' to show that you are talking about a situation in general or about the whole of something.

EG *The overall quality of the work was very good.*

ADVERB

2 You use 'overall' to show that you are talking about a situation in general or about the whole of something.

EG *Overall, things are not too bad.*

overcome /əuvəˈkʌm/

overcomes overcoming overcame overcome

VERB

If you overcome a problem or a

feeling, you successfully deal with it or control it.
EG *She finally overcame her fear of flying.*

overhead /əuvəˈhɛd/

ADVERB
Overhead means above a particular place.
EG *... seagulls flying overhead*

ADJECTIVE : /ˈəuvəhɛd/
☑ Note that you pronounce the adjective differently from the adverb.
Overhead means above a particular place.
EG *... an overhead locker*

overlap /əuvəˈlæp/
overlaps overlapping overlapped

VERB
If two things overlap, a part of the first thing covers a part of the second thing.
EG *The edges must not overlap.*

overlook /əuvəˈluk/
overlooks overlooking overlooked

VERB
1 If a building overlooks a place, you can see that place from it.
EG *The room overlooked a small courtyard.*
2 If you overlook something, you ignore it or do not notice it.
EG *We are willing to overlook this foolish behaviour.*
EG *Gallagher had overlooked an important point.*

overnight /ˈəuvənait/

ADJECTIVE
1 during the night
EG *... overnight accommodation*
2 If something happens overnight, it happens quickly and unexpectedly.
EG *... an overnight success*

ADVERB : /əuvəˈnait/
☑ Note that you pronounce the adverb differently from the adjective.
3 during the night
EG *Further rain was forecast overnight.*
4 If something happens overnight, it happens quickly and unexpectedly.
EG *The problem won't disappear overnight.*

overseas /əuvəˈsiːz/

ADVERB
1 happening or existing abroad
EG *... if you're working overseas*

ADJECTIVE
2 happening or existing abroad
EG *... an overseas tour*
3 from abroad
EG *... overseas students*

overtake /əuvəˈteik/
overtakes overtaking overtook overtaken

VERB
If you overtake a person or vehicle, you pass them because you are moving faster than them.
EG *We overtook two taxis.*

overwhelmed /əuvəˈwɛlmd/

ADJECTIVE
If you are **overwhelmed by** something, it affects you very strongly.
EG *The priest appeared overwhelmed by the news.*

owe /əu/
owes owing owed

VERB
1 If you owe someone money or if you **owe** money **to** them, they have lent it to you and you have

A B C D E F G H I J K L M N O P Q R S T U V W X Y Z

A
B
C
D
E
F
G
H
I
J
K
L
M
N
O
P
Q
R
S
T
U
V
W
X
Y
Z

not yet paid it back.
EG *You still owe me five pounds.*
EG *The company owes money to more than sixty banks.*
2 If you **owe** a quality or skill **to** someone, you only have it because of them.
EG *He owes his success to his mother.*

PREPOSITION

3 You use **owing to** when you are giving the reason for something.
EG *I was late owing to a traffic jam.*

own /əun/
owns owning owned

ADJECTIVE OR PRONOUN

1 If something is your **own**, it belongs to you or is associated with you.
EG *She stayed in her own house.*
EG *Lunch isn't provided, you have to bring your own.*

PRONOUN

2 If you are **on** your **own**, you are alone.
EG *Do you mind being here on your own?*

3 If you do something **on** your **own**, you do it without any help from other people.
EG *I can do it on my own.*

VERB

4 If you **own** something, it belongs to you.
EG *Her father owns a pub.*

owner /'əunəʳ/
owners

NOUN

The owner of something is the person it belongs to.
EG *... the owner of the store*

oz /auns, 'aunsız/
an abbreviation for 'ounce' or 'ounces'
EG *... 4 oz of cheese*

p /piː/
an abbreviation for pence
EG *They cost 50p each.*

pace /peɪs/
paces pacing paced

NOUN
1 The pace of something is the speed at which it moves or happens.
EG *Many people were unhappy with the pace of change.*
EG *He quickened his pace.*

2 the distance you move when you take one step
EG *I took a pace backwards.*

VERB
3 If you pace a small area, you keep walking around it because you are anxious or impatient.
EG *He found John pacing up and down the flat.*

pack /pæk/
packs packing packed

VERB
1 If you pack, you put your belongings into a bag before leaving a place.
EG *We barely had time to pack.*
EG *Did you remember to pack the camera?*

2 If people pack a place or **pack into** a place, it becomes crowded with them.
EG *Thousands of people packed into the stadium.*

NOUN
3 a bag that you carry on your back
EG *I hid the money in my pack.*

4 a packet or collection of something
EG *... a pack of cards*

EG *... an information pack*

package /'pækɪdʒ/
packages

NOUN
a small parcel
EG *... a package addressed to his wife*

packed /pækt/
ADJECTIVE
very full
EG *The church was packed with people.*

packet /'pækɪt/
packets

NOUN
a small box or bag in which something is sold
EG *... a packet of crisps*

pad /pæd/
pads

NOUN
1 a thick, soft piece of material
EG *... shoulder pads*

2 a number of pieces of paper fixed together at one end
EG *Keep a pad and pen handy.*

padded /'pædɪd/
ADJECTIVE
Something that is padded has soft material inside it or over it to protect it or change its shape.
EG *... a padded bra*

page /peɪdʒ/
pages

NOUN
1 one side of one of the pieces of paper in a book or magazine
EG *Turn to page 4.*

2 a single sheet of paper
EG *He turned the pages of his*

A

B

notebook.

paid /peɪd/
past participle and past tense of
pay

C

D

pain /peɪn/
pains

NOUN
1 Pain is a feeling of discomfort in
your body caused by an illness or
injury.
EG … *a pill to ease the pain*
EG *I felt a sharp pain in my lower
back.*
2 Pain is unhappiness.
EG … *the pain of losing a loved one*
3 If you are **in pain**, you are
hurting.
EG *She's been in a lot of pain since
the operation.*

E

F

G

H

I

J

K

painful /ˈpeɪnful/

L

ADJECTIVE
causing physical or emotional pain
EG … *a painful injury*
EG … *the painful process of
growing up*

M

N

O

paint /peɪnt/
paints painting painted

P

NOUN
1 Paint is a coloured liquid that is
used to decorate buildings and
make pictures.
EG *The paint was still wet on the
walls.*

Q

R

S

VERB
2 If you paint something or paint a
picture of it, you make a picture of
it using paint.
EG *He painted several portraits of
her.*
3 If you paint something such as a
wall, you cover it with paint.
EG *They painted the walls white.*

T

U

V

W

X

painting /ˈpeɪntɪŋ/
paintings

Y

Z

NOUN
a picture which someone has
painted
EG … *a large oil painting of Queen
Victoria*

pair /peər/
pairs

NOUN
1 A pair of things is two things of
the same type that are meant to
be used together.
EG *A good pair of shoes is essential.*
2 You use 'pair' when referring to
certain objects which have two
main parts of the same size and
shape.
EG … *a pair of scissors*
EG *A pair of trousers was missing.*

pajamas /pəˈdʒɑːməz/
see **pyjamas**

palace /ˈpæləs/
palaces

NOUN
a large, grand house, especially
the home of a king or queen
EG … *crowds outside Buckingham
Palace*

pale /peɪl/
paler palest

ADJECTIVE
1 not strong or bright in colour
EG … *pale blue*
2 If someone looks pale, their face
is a lighter colour than usual.
EG *She looked pale and tired.*

pan /pæn/
pans

NOUN
a round metal container with a
long handle, used for cooking
things
EG … *a frying pan*

panel /ˈpænl/
panels

NOUN
1 a small group of people who are chosen to do something
EG … *a panel of judges*
2 a flat piece of wood or other material that is part of a larger object
EG … *door panels*

panic /'pænɪk/
panics panicking panicked

NOUN
1 Panic is a sudden strong feeling of fear or anxiety.
EG *The earthquake caused panic among the villagers.*

VERB
2 If you panic, you become so afraid or anxious that you cannot act sensibly.
EG *The crowd panicked when the lights went out.*

pantomime /'pæntəmaɪm/
pantomimes

NOUN
a funny musical play for children, usually performed at Christmas
EG *She took the children to a pantomime.*

pants /pænts/
PLURAL NOUN
1 Pants are an item of underwear with holes for your legs and elastic around the top.
EG … *an old pair of pants*
2 In American English, pants are trousers.
EG … *a man in brown pants*

paper /'peɪpər/
papers

NOUN
1 Paper is a material that you write on or wrap things with.
EG … *a piece of paper*
EG … *a paper bag*

2 a newspaper
EG … *the Sunday paper*

PLURAL NOUN
3 papers are official documents, for example a passport or identity card
EG *The officer asked him for his papers.*

paperback /'peɪpəbæk/
paperbacks

NOUN
a book with a thin cardboard cover
EG … *a cheap paperback*

parade /pə'reɪd/
parades parading paraded

NOUN
1 a line of people or vehicles moving together through a public place in order to celebrate something
EG … *a military parade*

VERB
2 When people parade, they walk together in a formal group, usually in front of other people.
EG *Soldiers paraded down the main street.*

paragraph /'pærəgrɑːf/
paragraphs

NOUN
a section of a piece of writing which begins on a new line
EG … *the final paragraph*

parallel /'pærəlɛl/
parallels

NOUN
1 If something has a parallel, or if there are parallels between two or more things, they are similar to each other.
EG *There are curious parallels between the two books.*

ADJECTIVE
2 If two lines or objects are

A B C D E F G H I J K L M N O P° Q R S T U V W X Y Z

A
B
C
D
E
F
G
H
I
J
K
L
M
N
O
P
Q
R
S
T
U
V
W
X
Y
Z

parallel, they are the same distance apart along the whole of their length.
EG *... 72 ships drawn up in two parallel lines*

paralyse /'pærəlaɪz/
paralyses paralysing paralysed
US **paralyze**
VERB
If someone **is paralysed** by an accident or illness, they have no feeling in part or all of their body and are unable to move.
EG *He had been paralysed in a road accident.*

parcel /'pɑːsl/
parcels
NOUN
something wrapped up in paper
EG *... parcels of food and clothes*

pardon /'pɑːdn/
pardons pardoning pardoned
NOUN
1 You say **Pardon?** or **I beg your pardon?** when you want someone to repeat something they have said.
EG *"Shall I open it?" — "Pardon?" — "Shall I open it?"*
2 You say **I beg your pardon** as a way of apologizing for accidentally doing something wrong.
EG *I beg your pardon, that was thoughtless of me.*
VERB
3 If someone who has been found guilty of a crime **is pardoned**, they are allowed to go free.
EG *Hundreds of political prisoners were pardoned and released.*

parent /'peərənt/
parents

NOUN
Your parents are your father and mother.
EG *This is where a lot of parents go wrong.*

park /pɑːk/
parks parking parked
NOUN
1 a public area with grass and trees
EG *... a walk in Regent's Park*
VERB
2 When you park a vehicle, you drive it into a position where it can be left.
EG *He found a place to park the car.*
EG *Could you park over there?*

parliament /'pɑːləmənt/
parliaments
NOUN
the group of people who make or change the laws of a country
EG *... the Scottish parliament*

part /pɑːt/
parts parting parted
NOUN
1 one of the pieces or aspects of something
EG *... in some parts of the world*
EG *... spare parts for military equipment*
2 one of the roles in a play or film
EG *Brutus is the most difficult part in the play.*
3 If you have a **part** in something, you are involved in it.
EG *He was jailed for ten years for his part in the plot.*
4 If you **take part in** an activity, you do it together with other people.
EG *He did not take part in the meeting.*
VERB
5 If things that are next to each other part, or if you part them,

A
B
C
D
E
F
G
H
I
J
K
L
M
N
O
P
Q
R
S
T
U
V
W
X
Y
Z

they move away from each other.
EG *Her lips parted and she smiled.*
EG *Leo parted the curtains.*

partial /'pɑːʃl/

ADJECTIVE
not complete or whole
EG *... a partial explanation*

participate /pɑːˈtɪsɪpeɪt/
participates participating participated

VERB
If you **participate in** an activity, you do it together with other people.
EG *Both sides agreed to participate in talks.*

---

participle /'pɑːtɪsɪpl/
participles

NOUN
A **participle** is a word formed from a verb that can be used as an adjective or in certain verb phrases. Most verbs have a **present participle** ending in *-ing* and a **past participle** ending in *-ed*.
EG *They abandoned the **sinking** ship.*
EG *He had been **warned** about this.*

---

particle /'pɑːtɪkl/
particles

NOUN
a very small piece of something
EG *... food particles in your teeth*

particular /pəˈtɪkjulər/

ADJECTIVE
1 You use 'particular' to emphasize that you are talking about one thing rather than other similar ones.
EG *One particular memory still haunts me.*
2 greater or more intense than usual
EG *Pay particular attention to the following advice.*

NOUN
3 You use **in particular** to show that what you are saying applies especially to one thing or person.
EG *The older man in particular interested him.*

particularly /pəˈtɪkjulələri/

ADVERB
1 You use 'particularly' to show that what you are saying applies especially to one thing or situation.
EG *This is hard for young children, particularly when they are ill.*
2 greater or more intense than usual
EG *It's not particularly difficult to do.*

partly /'pɑːtli/

ADVERB
to some extent but not completely
EG *It's partly my fault.*

partner /'pɑːtnər/
partners

NOUN
1 Someone's partner is the person they are married to or living with.
EG *Discuss the problem with your partner.*
2 Your partner is the person you are doing something with, for example in a dance or a game.
EG *... to dance with a partner*

part-time /'pɑːtˈtaɪm/

ADJECTIVE OR ADVERB
If you work part-time, you work for only a part of each normal working day or week.
EG *... a part-time job*
EG *She works part-time.*

party /'pɑːti/
parties

NOUN

A
B
C
D
E
F
G
H
I
J
K
L
M
N
O
P
Q
R
S
T
U
V
W
X
Y
Z

1 a social event, often in order to celebrate something

EG *We threw a huge birthday party.*

2 an organization whose members share the same political beliefs and campaign for election to government

EG *... the Labour Party*

3 a group who are doing something together

EG *... a coach party*

pass /pɑːs/
passes passing passed

VERB

1 To pass someone or something means to move past them.

EG *We passed the street where I used to live.*

2 To pass in a particular direction means to move in that direction.

EG *They passed through the gate.*

3 If you pass someone something or **pass** it **to** them, you hand it to them or give it to them.

EG *Pass the salt, please.*

EG *Officers passed the information to their superiors.*

4 If you pass a period of time in a particular way, you spend it that way.

EG *The children passed the time playing in the street.*

5 When a period of time passes, it happens and ends.

EG *Several minutes passed before anyone spoke.*

6 If you pass a test or an exam, you are considered to be of an acceptable standard.

EG *Kevin has just passed his driving test.*

7 When a new law or proposal is passed, it is formally approved.

EG *... many of the laws passed by Parliament*

NOUN

8 the transfer of the ball in a ball game to another player in the same team

EG *Cole's pass was intercepted by Merson.*

9 an official document that allows you to go somewhere

EG *Don't let anyone in unless they have a pass.*

pass out

VERB

If someone passes out, they faint or collapse.

EG *He was so drunk that he passed out.*

passage /'pæsɪdʒ/
passages

NOUN

1 a long, narrow corridor or space that connects two places

EG *... along a narrow passage towards a door*

2 a section of a book or piece of music

EG *He read a passage from Milton.*

passenger /'pæsɪndʒəʳ/
passengers

NOUN

a person travelling in a vehicle, aircraft, or ship

EG *... a flight with more than a hundred passengers on board*

passion /'pæʃən/

NOUN

Passion is a very strong feeling, especially of sexual attraction.

EG *I felt such extraordinary passion for her.*

passionate /'pæʃənɪt/

ADJECTIVE

A passionate person has very strong feelings about something.

EG *I'm a passionate believer in*

public art.

passive /'pæsɪv/

ADJECTIVE
Someone who is passive does not take action but instead lets things happen to them.
EG *The drug tends to make patients more passive.*

NOUN
When a sentence is in the **passive**, the subject of the verb is affected by the action, rather than doing it. The passive always uses a form of the verb *be* with the past participle of the verb.
EG *The house **is being repaired**.*
EG *He **was bitten** by a dog.*

---

passport /'pɑːspɔːt/
passports

NOUN
an official document which you need to show when you enter or leave a country
EG *... a British passport*

past /pɑːst/

NOUN
1 the past is the period of time before the present
EG *In the past this was never a problem.*
2 Your past is all the things that have happened to you.
EG *... stories about his past*

ADJECTIVE
3 Past things are things that happened or existed before the present.
EG *... details of his past activities*
4 You use 'past' to talk about a period of time that has just finished.
EG *... the events of the past few days*

PREPOSITION OR ADVERB
5 You use 'past' to note the time when it is thirty minutes or less after a particular hour.
EG *It's ten past eleven.*
EG *I have my lunch at half past.*
6 If you go past something, you move towards it and continue until you are on the other side.
EG *She ran past the car without seeing us.*
EG *An ambulance drove past.*

PREPOSITION
7 Something that is past a place is situated on the other side of it.
EG *The farm was just past the next village.*

paste /peɪst/
pastes pasting pasted

NOUN
1 Paste is a soft, thick mixture of a substance, which can be easily spread.
EG *... tomato paste*
EG *... wallpaper paste*

VERB
2 If you paste something somewhere, you stick it there with glue.
EG *The children were pasting gold stars on a chart.*

pastime /'pɑːstaɪm/
pastimes

NOUN
something that you enjoy doing in your spare time
EG *His favourite pastime is golf.*

pastry /'peɪstrɪ/
pastries

NOUN
1 Pastry is a mixture of flour, fat, and water that is used for making pies.
EG *... courgettes wrapped in pastry*

2 a small cake
EG *... a tray of Danish pastries*

pat /pæt/
pats patting patted
VERB
1 If you pat something, you tap it lightly with your hand held flat.
EG *"Don't worry," she said, patting me on the knee.*
NOUN
2 the action of patting something
EG *... a pat on the back*

patch /pætʃ/
patches patching patched
NOUN
1 a piece of material that is used to cover a hole in something
EG *... jackets with patches on the elbows*
2 an area of a surface that is different in appearance from the rest
EG *... the bald patch on the top of his head*
VERB
3 If you patch something that has a hole in it, you mend it by fixing something over the hole.
EG *... their patched clothes*

path /pɑːθ/
paths
NOUN
1 a strip of ground for people to walk on
EG *... the garden path*
2 Your path is the area ahead of you as you move along.
EG *A group of reporters blocked his path.*

patient /'peɪʃnt/
patients
ADJECTIVE
1 If you are patient, you stay calm in a difficult or irritating situation.
EG *I've got to be patient and wait.*
NOUN
2 a person receiving treatment from a doctor
EG *... cancer patients*

patrol /pə'trəʊl/
patrols patrolling patrolled
VERB
1 When soldiers, police, or guards patrol an area, they walk or drive around it to make sure there is no trouble.
EG *Guards patrolled the grounds.*
NOUN
2 a group of people patrolling an area
EG *... an army patrol*

pattern /'pætən/
patterns
NOUN
1 a design of shapes repeated at regular intervals
EG *... a pattern of red and gold stripes*
2 a particular way in which something is usually or repeatedly done
EG *All three attacks followed the same pattern.*

pause /pɔːz/
pauses pausing paused
VERB
1 If you pause, you stop speaking or doing something for a short time.
EG *She paused for a moment at the door.*
NOUN
2 a short period when something stops before continuing
EG *After a pause, he continued.*

pavement /'peɪvmənt/
pavements
NOUN

a path with a hard surface at the side of a road
EG *He was hurrying along the pavement.*

paw /pɔː/
paws

NOUN

The paws of an animal such as a cat, dog, or bear are its feet.
EG *The kitten was black with white paws.*

pay /peɪ/
pays paying paid

VERB

1 When you **pay** an amount of money **for** something, you give it to someone because you are buying something or you owe it to them.
EG *She paid £300,000 for the house.*
EG *When are you going to pay me that hundred pounds?*

2 When you pay a bill or debt, you give the money that you owe.
EG *He paid his bill and left.*
EG *You can pay by credit card.*

3 When you **are paid** or **get paid**, you receive your wages or salary from your employer.
EG *I get paid monthly.*

4 If it **pays to do** something, it is to your advantage to do it.
EG *They say it pays to advertise.*

5 If you **pay for** something that you have done, you suffer as a result.
EG *She committed a terrible crime and will have to pay for it.*

6 If you **pay attention to** someone or something, you give them your attention.
EG *Nobody paid attention to him.*

7 If you **pay** someone **a visit**, you visit them.

EG *Why don't you pay us a visit some time?*

NOUN

8 Your pay is your wages or salary.
EG *... complaints about their pay and conditions*

payment /ˈpeɪmənt/
payments

NOUN

1 Payment is the act of paying money.
EG *Players now expect payment for interviews.*

2 a sum of money paid
EG *... mortgage payments*

pea /piː/
peas

NOUN

Peas are small round green seeds that are eaten as a vegetable.
EG *... a tin of peas*

peace /piːs/

NOUN

1 Peace is a state of undisturbed calm and quiet.
EG *One more question and I'll leave you in peace.*

2 Peace is a state of not being involved in a war.
EG *... a commitment to world peace*

peaceful /ˈpiːsful/

ADJECTIVE

quiet and calm
EG *It's so peaceful without the children here.*

peach /piːtʃ/
peaches

NOUN

a soft, round fruit with yellow flesh and a yellow and red skin
EG *... peaches and cream*

peak /piːk/
peaks peaking peaked

NOUN

1 The peak of an activity or process is the point at which it is strongest or most successful.
EG … the peak of the morning rush hour

2 the pointed top of a mountain
EG … snow-covered peaks

VERB

3 When something peaks, it reaches its highest value or its greatest level of success.
EG His career peaked during the 1970s.

peanut /'piːnʌt/
peanuts

NOUN

Peanuts are small nuts that grow under the ground.
EG … a packet of roasted peanuts

pear /peəʳ/
pears

NOUN

a fruit which is narrow at the top and wider at the bottom
EG … a juicy pear

peasant /'pɛznt/
peasants

NOUN

a person who works on the land, especially in a poor country
EG … the work of Chinese peasants

peculiar /pɪˈkjuːlɪəʳ/

ADJECTIVE

strange and often unpleasant
EG Rachel thought it tasted peculiar.
EG He has some peculiar ideas.

pedal /'pɛdl/
pedals pedalling pedalled

NOUN

1 The pedals on a bicycle are the two parts that you push with your feet in order to make the bicycle move.

EG He rested his feet on the pedals.

VERB

2 When you pedal a bicycle, you push the pedals around with your feet to make it move.
EG She pedalled furiously up the hill..

pedestrian /pɪˈdɛstrɪən/
pedestrians

NOUN

someone who is walking
EG … streets crowded with pedestrians

peel /piːl/
peels peeling peeled

NOUN

1 The peel of a fruit is its skin.
EG … grated lemon peel

VERB

2 When you peel fruit or vegetables, you remove the skin.
EG She began peeling the potatoes.

3 If a layer of something is peeling, it is coming away from a surface.
EG Paint was peeling off the walls.

peg /pɛg/
pegs

NOUN

1 a small device which you use to fasten clothes to a washing line
EG … a clothes peg

2 a hook on a wall where you can hang things
EG His jacket hung from a peg in the hall.

pen /pɛn/
pens

NOUN

a long, thin instrument used for writing with ink
EG … a ballpoint pen

penalty /'pɛnltɪ/
penalties

NOUN

1 a punishment for breaking a rule

or law
EG ... *the death penalty*

2 In soccer, a penalty is a free kick at goal that is given to the attacking team if the defending team have committed a foul near their goal.
EG *They were awarded a penalty in the last minute.*

pence /pɛns/
a plural form of **penny**

pencil /'pɛnsl/
pencils

NOUN
a long, thin stick of wood with a black substance in the centre, used for drawing or writing
EG ... *a pencil with a rubber at the end*

penetrate /'pɛnɪtreɪt/
penetrates penetrating penetrated

VERB
If someone or something penetrates an object or area, they succeed in getting into it.
EG *They had orders to shoot anyone who penetrated the area.*

penny /'pɛnɪ/
pence or **pennies**

NOUN
1 In Britain a penny is a coin that is worth one hundredth of a pound.
EG *Beer will go up by a penny a pint.*
☑ 'Pennies' usually refers to a number of individual coins: *he took two pennies out of his pocket*. You use 'pence' when you are talking about a sum of money: *it only cost fifty pence.*

2 In American English, a penny is a coin that is worth one cent.
EG ... *a handful of pennies*

pension /'pɛnʃən/
pensions

NOUN
a regular sum of money paid to a retired or disabled person
EG *He receives a company pension.*

pensioner /'pɛnʃənəʳ/
pensioners

NOUN
a retired person who receives a pension from the state
EG ... *people on low incomes such as pensioners*

people /'piːpl/
peoples

PLURAL NOUN
1 People are men, women, and children.
EG *Thousands of people have lost their homes.*

NOUN
2 A people is all the men, women, and children of a particular country or race.
EG *It's a triumph for the American people.*

pepper /'pɛpəʳ/
peppers

NOUN
1 Pepper is a hot-tasting spice that is used to flavour food.
EG ... *salt and pepper*

2 a hollow green, red, or yellow vegetable, with sweet-flavoured flesh
EG ... *green peppers*

per /pəːʳ/

PREPOSITION
'Per' means 'each' when expressing rates and ratios.
EG ... *70 miles per hour*

per cent /pəˈsɛnt/ also spelt **percent**

ADVERB

A B C D E F G H I J K L M N O P Q R S T U V W X Y Z

You use 'per cent' to talk about amounts as a proportion of a hundred. An amount that is 10 per cent (10%) of a larger amount is equal to 10 hundredths of the larger amount.
EG *Over 80 per cent of Americans believe Presley is alive.*

percentage /pə'sɛntɪdʒ/
percentages

NOUN
a fraction of an amount expressed as a number of hundredths
EG *... the high percentage of failed marriages*

perfect /'pɜːfɪkt/
perfects perfecting perfected

ADJECTIVE
1 Something that is perfect is as good as it can possibly be.
EG *His English was perfect.*
EG *Now is the perfect time to buy a home.*

VERB : /pə'fɛkt/
☑ Note that you pronounce the verb differently from the noun.
2 If you perfect something, you make it as good as it can possibly be.
EG *... using the techniques he had perfected*

perfectly /'pɜːfɪktlɪ/

ADVERB
1 You can use 'perfectly' to emphasize what you are saying.
EG *They are perfectly safe to eat.*
2 If something is done perfectly, it could not possibly be done better.
EG *The system worked perfectly.*

perform /pə'fɔːm/
performs performing performed

VERB

1 If you perform a task or action, you do it.
EG *... people who have performed outstanding acts of bravery*
2 The way that something performs is how well it works.
EG *... a measure of how different schools are performing*
3 To perform a play or piece of music means to do it in front of an audience.
EG *This play was first performed in 411 BC.*

performance /pə'fɔːməns/
performances

NOUN
1 an entertainment provided for an audience
EG *... a performance of Bizet's Carmen*
2 Someone's or something's performance is how successful they are.
EG *... the poor performance of the economy*

perfume /'pɜːfjuːm/
perfumes

NOUN
a pleasant-smelling liquid which women put on their bodies
EG *... a bottle of perfume*

perhaps /pə'hæps/

ADVERB
You use 'perhaps' when you are not sure whether something is true or possible.
EG *It will cost hundreds, perhaps thousands, to repair.*
EG *Perhaps, in time, she'll understand.*

period /'pɪərɪəd/
periods

NOUN
1 a particular length of time

EG ... a period of a few months
EG I like Italian opera of that period.
2 When a woman has a period, she bleeds inside her body, usually once a month.
EG ... because she had missed her period
3 In American English, a period is a full stop.
EG ... putting a comma instead of a period

permanent /'pə:mənənt/
ADJECTIVE
lasting forever or present all the time
EG ... permanent damage to the brain
EG The ban is intended to be permanent.

permission /pə'mɪʃən/
NOUN
If you have permission to do something, you are allowed to do it.
EG He asked permission to leave the room.
EG They cannot leave the country without permission.

permit /pə'mɪt/
permits permitting permitted
VERB
1 If someone or something **permits** you **to do** something, they allow it or make it possible.
EG Employees are permitted to use the golf course.
EG We fly tomorrow, weather permitting.
NOUN : /'pə:mɪt/
☑ Note that you pronounce the noun differently from the verb.
2 an official document which says that you are allowed to do something

EG ... a work permit

person /'pə:sn/
☑ The usual plural of 'person' is people. Persons is only used in very formal English.
NOUN
1 a man, woman, or child
EG There was far too much for one person.
2 If you do something **in person**, you do it yourself rather than letting someone else do it for you.
EG You must collect the mail in person.

The **person** of the verb refers to whether the action is done by the speaker (the **first person**), by the person spoken to (the **second person**), or by someone else (the **third person**).

The first person form of a verb is the form used after I or we.
EG I **live** in Sweden.
EG We **live** in Sweden.

The second person form of a verb is the form used after you.
EG You **live** in Sweden.

The third person form of a verb is the form used after he, she, it, or they.
EG He **lives** in Sweden.
EG They **live** in Sweden.

personal /'pə:snl/
ADJECTIVE
1 belonging or relating to a particular person
EG That's my personal opinion.
2 Personal matters relate to your private life.
EG He had resigned for personal reasons.

A
B
C
D
E
F
G
H
I
J
K
L
M
N
O
P
Q
R
S
T
U
V
W
X
Y
Z

personality /ˌpɜːsəˈnælɪtɪ/
personalities

NOUN

1 Your personality is your character and nature.
EG *She's got a very lively personality.*

2 a famous person
EG *... television personalities*

personally /ˈpɜːsnəlɪ/

ADVERB

1 You use 'personally' to emphasize that you are giving your own opinion.
EG *Personally, I think it's a waste of time.*

2 If you do something personally, you do it yourself rather than letting someone else do it for you.
EG *I'll deal with it personally.*

3 If you know someone personally, you know them rather than just knowing about them.
EG *I've never met him personally.*

personnel /ˌpɜːsəˈnɛl/

PLURAL NOUN

The personnel of an organization are the people who work for it.
EG *... military personnel*

perspective /pəˈspɛktɪv/
perspectives

NOUN

A particular perspective is one way of thinking about something.
EG *The death of his father gave him a new perspective on life.*

persuade /pəˈsweɪd/
persuades persuading persuaded

VERB

If someone **persuades** you **to do** something, or if they persuade you that something is true, they cause you to do it or believe it by giving you good reasons for it.

EG *My husband persuaded me to come.*
EG *I managed to persuade Steve that I would support him.*

pet /pɛt/
pets

NOUN

a tame animal that you keep at home
EG *... dogs and other pets*

petrol /ˈpɛtrəl/

NOUN

Petrol is a liquid that is used as a fuel for motor vehicles.
EG *... a litre of petrol*

petty /ˈpɛtɪ/
pettier pettiest

ADJECTIVE

Petty things are small and unimportant.
EG *... endless rules and petty regulations*

phase /feɪz/
phases

NOUN

a particular stage in the development of something
EG *... the first phase of the process*

phenomenon /fəˈnɒmɪnən/
phenomena

NOUN

something that happens or exists, especially something remarkable
EG *... natural phenomena such as lightning*

philosophy /fɪˈlɒsəfɪ/
philosophies

NOUN

1 Philosophy is the study of ideas about basic things such as the nature of existence or how we should live.
EG *... traditional Chinese philosophy*

2 a set of beliefs
EG *The parties have quite different*

philosophies.

phone /fəun/
phones phoning phoned

NOUN

1 a piece of electrical equipment for talking directly to someone who is in a different place by dialling their number

EG *Jamie answered the phone.*

EG *We discussed it over the phone.*

VERB

2 If you phone someone or **phone** them **up,** you speak to them using a telephone.

EG *I'll phone him up and ask him.*

photo /'fəutəu/
photos

NOUN

a photograph

EG *We must take a photo of it!*

photograph /'fəutəgræf/
photographs photographing photographed

NOUN

1 a picture that is made using a camera

EG *Her photograph was on the front page of the paper.*

VERB

2 When you photograph someone or something, you take a picture of them using a camera.

EG *They were photographed kissing.*

phrase /freiz/
phrases

NOUN

a short group of words

EG *It was a phrase I'd never heard before.*

physical /'fizikl/

ADJECTIVE

1 concerning the body rather than the mind

EG *... a physical examination*

2 Physical things are real things that can be touched or seen.

EG *... physical objects*

physics /'fiziks/

NOUN

Physics is the scientific study of forces such as heat, light, sound, and electricity.

EG *... the laws of physics*

☑ Although it looks like a plural, 'physics' is a singular noun: *physics is his favourite subject.*

piano /pɪ'ænəu/
pianos

NOUN

a large musical instrument with a row of black and white keys, which you strike with your fingers

EG *... before I learned to play the piano*

pick /pɪk/
picks picking picked

VERB

1 If you pick someone or something, you choose them.

EG *I could not have picked a better companion.*

2 If you pick flowers or fruit, you break them off the plant and collect them.

EG *He helps his mother pick strawberries.*

3 If you pick something from a place, you take it from that place using your fingers.

EG *She picked the book off the shelf.*

NOUN

4 You can refer to the best things or people in a group as **the pick of** that group.

EG *The company gets the pick of Japan's best graduates.*

pick up

VERB

1 If you pick something up, you

lift it from a surface using your fingers.
EG *He picked up the phone immediately.*
2 If you pick someone or something **up**, you collect them from where they are waiting.
EG *We'll pick you up from the airport.*

picnic /'pɪknɪk/
picnics
NOUN
a meal eaten out of doors
EG *We're going on a picnic tomorrow.*

picture /'pɪktʃər/
pictures picturing pictured
NOUN
1 a drawing, painting, photograph, or television image of someone or something
EG *There was a picture of him in the paper.*
2 If you have a picture of something in your mind, you have an idea or impression of it.
EG *We have a picture of how we'd like things to be.*
PLURAL NOUN
3 If you go to **the pictures**, you go to see a film at the cinema.
EG *We're going to the pictures tonight.*
VERB
4 If someone **is pictured** in a newspaper or magazine, a photograph of them is printed in it.
EG *The team are pictured on many of today's front pages.*
5 If you picture something, you imagine it clearly.
EG *That is how I always picture him.*

pie /paɪ/
pies
NOUN
a dish of meat, vegetables, or fruit covered with pastry
EG *... a slice of apple pie*

piece /piːs/
pieces piecing pieced
NOUN
1 a portion or part of something
EG *... a piece of paper*
EG *Cut the ham into pieces.*
2 an individual thing of a particular kind
EG *... a good piece of advice*
EG *... a sturdy piece of furniture*
3 something that has been written or created, such as an article, a work of art, or some music
EG *There was a piece about him in the paper.*
EG *... a beautiful piece of music*
4 a coin
EG *... a 50 pence piece*
piece together
VERB
If you piece something together, you gradually put a number of things together to make something complete.
EG *Doctors pieced together the broken bones.*
EG *Francis was able to piece together what had happened.*

pier /pɪər/
piers
NOUN
a large platform which sticks out into the sea and which people can walk along
EG *... a walk along Brighton Pier*

pierce /pɪəs/
pierces piercing pierced
VERB
If a sharp object pierces something, it goes through it, making a hole.
EG *I'm having my ears pierced.*

EG *One bullet pierced his chest.*

pig /pɪg/
pigs

NOUN

a farm animal, with pink or black skin and a curly tail, that is kept for its meat

EG *... the grunting of the pigs*

pile /paɪl/
piles piling piled

NOUN

1 a quantity of things lying on top of one another

EG *... a pile of leaves*

VERB

2 If you pile things somewhere, you put them on top of one another.

EG *He was piling clothes into the suitcase.*

pill /pɪl/
pills

NOUN

1 a small, round tablet of medicine that you swallow

EG *... a sleeping pill*

2 the pill is a type of drug that women can take regularly to avoid becoming pregnant

EG *She had been on the pill for three years.*

pillow /'pɪləʊ/
pillows

NOUN

a cushion which you rest your head on when you are in bed

EG *He left a flower on the pillow for when she woke.*

pilot /'paɪlət/
pilots

NOUN

a person who is trained to fly an aircraft

EG *... an airline pilot*

pin /pɪn/
pins pinning pinned

NOUN

1 a thin, pointed piece of metal that is used to fasten things together

EG *... needles and pins*

VERB

2 If you pin something somewhere, you fasten it there with a pin.

EG *They pinned a notice to the door.*

pinch /pɪntʃ/
pinches pinching pinched

VERB

1 If you pinch something, you squeeze it between your thumb and first finger.

EG *She pinched his cheek.*

2 AN INFORMAL USE

If someone pinches something, they steal it.

EG *... the person who had pinched his wallet*

NOUN

3 A **pinch of** something is the amount that you can hold between your thumb and first finger.

EG *... a pinch of salt*

pineapple /'paɪnæpl/
pineapples

NOUN

a large fruit with sweet, yellow flesh and thick, rough, brown skin

EG *... slices of pineapple*

pink /pɪŋk/
pinker pinkest; pinks

ADJECTIVE OR NOUN

Pink is a colour between red and white.

EG *... pink lipstick*
EG *... different shades of pink*

A
B
C
D
E
F
G
H
I
J
K
L
M
N
O
P
Q
R
S
T
U
V
W
X
Y
Z

A
B
C
D
E
F
G
H
I
J
K
L
M
N
O
P
Q
R
S
T
U
V
W
X
Y
Z

pint /paɪnt/
pints

NOUN

1 a unit of measurement for liquids equal to one eighth of a gallon, or about 0.568 litres in Britain and 0.473 litres in America
EG … *a pint of milk*

2 a pint of beer
EG *Fancy a pint?*

pipe /paɪp/
pipes piping piped

NOUN

1 a long, hollow tube through which liquid or gas can flow
EG … *water pipes*

2 an object that is used for smoking tobacco, consisting of a small hollow bowl attached to a thin tube
EG … *a man smoking a pipe*

VERB

3 If liquid or gas is piped somewhere, it is transferred there through a pipe.
EG *Hot water is piped to all the rooms.*

pirate /ˈpaɪərət/
pirates

NOUN

Pirates were people who attacked and robbed ships at sea.
EG … *a famous nineteenth-century pirate*

pistol /ˈpɪstl/
pistols

NOUN

a small gun
EG … *with a pistol tucked in his belt*

pit /pɪt/
pits

NOUN

1 a large hole in the ground
EG *The bodies were thrown into a pit.*

2 a coal mine
EG … *back when all the pits were working*

pitch /pɪtʃ/
pitches pitching pitched

NOUN

1 an area of ground marked out for playing a game such as football or cricket
EG … *a football pitch*

2 The pitch of a sound is how high or low it is.
EG *He raised his voice to an even higher pitch.*

VERB

3 If you pitch something somewhere, you throw it there with a lot of force.
EG *Simon pitched the bottle into the lake.*

pity /ˈpɪtɪ/
pities pitying pitied

VERB

1 If you pity someone, you feel very sorry for them.
EG *I don't know whether to hate him or pity him.*

NOUN

2 If you feel pity for someone, you feel very sorry for them.
EG *She felt such pity for the child.*

3 If you say that something is **a pity**, you mean that you are disappointed about it and you wish it had happened differently.
EG *It's a pity you can't come.*

pizza /ˈpiːtsə/
pizzas

NOUN

a flat piece of pastry covered with cheese, tomato, and other food and baked in an oven
EG … *a mushroom pizza*

place /pleɪs/

places placing placed

NOUN

1 any point, building, or area
EG *… a good place to camp*
EG *The cellar was a very dark place.*

2 the house or flat where you live
EG *Let's all go back to my place.*

3 the position where something belongs
EG *He returned the album to its place on the shelf.*

4 a seat or position that is available for someone to occupy
EG *I found a place to park.*

5 a particular position in a race, competition, or series
EG *Last year she finished in third place.*

6 If you have a place in a team or on a course, you are allowed to join the team or course.
EG *I eventually got a place at York University.*

7 When something **takes place**, it happens.
EG *The elections will take place in November.*

VERB

8 If you place something somewhere, you put it there.
EG *She placed her hand gently on my shoulder.*

plain /pleɪn/
plainer plainest; plains

ADJECTIVE

1 very simple in style with no pattern or decoration
EG *… a plain white skirt*

2 obvious or easy to understand
EG *He made his feelings quite plain.*

3 A woman or girl who is plain is not attractive.
EG *… a shy, rather plain girl*

NOUN

4 a large, flat area of land with very few trees
EG *… the buffalo that once roamed the plains*

plan /plæn/
plans planning planned

NOUN

1 a method of achieving something that has been worked out beforehand
EG *I told them of my plan.*

PLURAL NOUN

2 If you have **plans,** you are intending to do a particular thing.
EG *What are your plans for tonight?*

VERB

3 If you plan something, you decide in detail what you are going to do.
EG *Everything must be planned in advance.*

4 If you **plan to do** something, you intend to do it.
EG *They plan to marry in the summer.*

plane /pleɪn/
planes

NOUN

1 a vehicle with wings and engines which can fly
EG *He had plenty of time to catch his plane.*

2 You can refer to a particular level of something as a particular plane.
EG *… to lift the conversation onto a higher plane*

planet /'plænɪt/
planets

NOUN

a large round object in space which moves around the sun or a star
EG *… the nine planets of the solar system*

A
B
C
D
E
F
G
H
I
J
K
L
M
N
O
P
Q
R
S
T
U
V
W
X
Y
Z

plant /plɑːnt/
plants planting planted
NOUN
1 a living thing that grows in the earth and has a stem, leaves, and roots
EG *Water each plant as often as required.*
2 a factory or power station
EG *... a car assembly plant*
VERB
3 If you plant a seed or plant, you put it into the ground.
EG *He plans to plant fruit trees and vegetables.*
4 If you plant something somewhere, you put it there secretly.
EG *... the man who planted the bomb*

plastic /'plæstɪk/
NOUN
Plastic is a light but strong material made by a chemical process.
EG *... sheets of plastic*
EG *... a plastic bag*

plate /pleɪt/
plates
NOUN
1 a flat dish that is used to hold food, or the amount of food on a plate
EG *She pushed her plate away.*
EG *... a plate of sandwiches*
2 a flat piece of metal, for example on part of a machine
EG *... heavy steel plates*

platform /'plætfɔːm/
platforms
NOUN
1 a raised structure on which someone or something can stand
EG *The speaker mounted the platform.*
2 the raised area in a railway

station where passengers get on and off trains
EG *... the train now arriving at platform 4*

play /pleɪ/
plays playing played
VERB
1 When children play, they take part in games or use toys.
EG *Polly was playing with her dolls.*
2 When you play a sport or game, you take part in it.
EG *He plays football every Sunday.*
3 When one person or team plays another, they compete against them.
EG *... when Scotland played Estonia*
4 If an actor plays a character in a play or film, they perform that role.
EG *His ambition is to play Dracula.*
5 If someone or something plays a part or a role in something, they have an effect on it.
EG *... the role that diet plays in our health*
6 If you play a musical instrument, you produce music from it.
EG *Nina had been playing the piano.*
7 If you play music, you put on a record, tape, or CD.
EG *... a radio station that plays only jazz*
NOUN
8 Play is the activity of playing a game or sport.
EG *Children's play prepares them for adulthood.*
EG *Play was abandoned due to rain.*
9 a drama performed in the theatre or on television
EG *... my favourite Shakespeare play*

player /'pleɪər/
players
NOUN
1 a person who takes part in a

sport or game
EG ... *some of Liverpool's top players*

2 a musician
EG ... *a trumpet player*

playground /ˈpleɪɡraʊnd/
playgrounds

NOUN
a special area for children to play in
EG ... *the school playground*

plea /pliː/
pleas

NOUN
an emotional request
EG ... *a plea for help*

plead /pliːd/
pleads pleading pleaded

VERB
1 If you **plead with** someone,
you ask them in an intense
emotional way to do something.
EG *She was pleading with me to
stay.*

2 When a person **pleads guilty**
or **not guilty,** they state in court
that they are guilty or not guilty of
a crime.
EG *Morris had pleaded guilty to
robbery.*

pleasant /ˈplɛznt/
ADJECTIVE
nice, enjoyable, or attractive
EG ... *a pleasant evening with
friends*
EG ... *a pleasant little town*

please /pliːz/
pleases pleasing pleased
1 You say 'please' when you are
asking someone politely to do
something.
EG *Can you help me, please?*
EG *Please come in.*

2 You say 'please' when you are
accepting something politely.
EG *"Tea?" — "Yes, please".*

VERB
3 If something pleases you, it
makes you feel happy and satisfied.
EG *You're an impossible man to
please.*

pleased /pliːzd/
ADJECTIVE
If you are pleased, you are happy
about something.
EG *I was very pleased with the
results.*
EG *They were pleased to be going
home.*

pleasure /ˈplɛʒər/
pleasures

NOUN
1 Pleasure is a feeling of
happiness, satisfaction, or
enjoyment.
EG *Seeing her win gave him great
pleasure.*

2 an activity that you enjoy
EG *Watching TV is our only pleasure.*

plenty /ˈplɛntɪ/
NOUN
If there is **plenty of** something,
there is a lot of it.
EG *We've got plenty of time.*

plot /plɒt/
plots plotting plotted

NOUN
1 a secret plan made by a group of
people
EG ... *a plot to kidnap the president*

2 The plot of a film, novel, or play
is the story.
EG *It's got a very good plot.*

VERB
3 If people **plot to do**
something, they plan it secretly.
EG *They were plotting to overthrow
the government.*

plough /plaʊ/
ploughs ploughing

A B C D E F G H I J K L M N O P Q R S T U V W X Y Z

ploughed
US **plow**

NOUN

1 a large tool that is pulled across a field to turn the soil over before planting seeds
EG *… the blades of the plough*

VERB

2 When a farmer ploughs land, they use a plough to turn over the soil.
EG *… a ploughed field*

plug /plʌg/
plugs plugging plugged

NOUN

1 a plastic object with metal pins that connects a piece of electrical equipment to an electric socket
EG *… a three-pin plug*

2 a thick, circular piece of rubber or plastic that you use to block the hole in a sink or bath
EG *She put the plug in the sink and filled it with water.*

plug in

VERB

If you plug in a piece of electrical equipment, you push its plug into an electric socket.
EG *I filled the kettle and plugged it in.*

plum /plʌm/
plums

NOUN

a small fruit with a smooth red or yellow skin and a stone in the middle
EG *… a bag of plums*

plumber /ˈplʌmə^r/
plumbers

NOUN

a person who connects and repairs water pipes
EG *He's a plumber.*

plunge /plʌndʒ/
plunges plunging plunged

VERB

1 If you plunge somewhere, especially into water, you fall or rush there.
EG *… when a bus plunged into a river*

2 If you **plunge** an object **into** something, you push it in quickly.
EG *She plunged the knife into his chest.*

3 If something plunges, it falls suddenly.
EG *His confidence plunged.*

plural /ˈpluərl/
plurals

NOUN

The **plural** of a noun is the form that is used to refer to more than one example of a person or thing. Plural nouns generally end in **-s**, for example, 'cars', 'tables', 'countries', and 'calves'.

Some nouns have the same form for both the singular and the plural, for example 'fish' and 'sheep'. A few nouns have special plural forms, for example the plural of 'man' is 'men' and the plural of 'child' is 'children'.

In this dictionary, plurals are shown in bold after the pronunciation.

plus /plʌs/

PREPOSITION

1 You use 'plus' to show that one number is being added to another.
EG *Two plus two equals four.*

2 You can use 'plus' when you mention an additional item.
EG *He wrote a history of Scotland plus a history of British literature.*

ADJECTIVE

3 'Plus' before a number means

that the number is greater than zero.

EG *... temperatures of plus 120 degrees*

4 slightly more than the number mentioned

EG *... a career of 25 years plus*

p.m.

p.m. is used after a number between one and twelve to refer to times between noon and midnight

EG *It is 10 p.m.*

pocket /'pɒkɪt/
pockets

NOUN

a kind of small bag that forms part of a piece of clothing and is used for carrying things

EG *The man stood with his hands in his pockets.*

poem /'pəʊɪm/
poems

NOUN

a piece of writing, usually in short lines, in which the words are chosen for their beauty and sound

EG *... a poem by John Keats*

poet /'pəʊɪt/
poets

NOUN

a person who writes poems

EG *He was a painter and poet.*

poetry /'pəʊɪtrɪ/

NOUN

Poetry is poems, considered as a form of literature.

EG *Durrell wrote a great deal of poetry.*

point /pɔɪnt/
points pointing pointed

NOUN

1 an opinion or fact expressed by someone

EG *That's a very good point.*

2 the point of something is its purpose

EG *What's the point in even trying?*

EG *I can't really see the point of the meeting.*

3 the point of something is the most important part of it

EG *You've completely missed the point.*

4 an aspect or quality of someone or something

EG *Science has never been my strong point.*

5 a position or time

EG *... at various points along the road*

EG *At some point during the party, a fight started.*

6 a single mark in a competition

EG *New Zealand have beaten Scotland by 21 points to 18.*

7 the thin, sharp end of something such as a needle or knife

EG *Only the point of the blade was visible.*

8 Your **point of view** is your opinion about something or your attitude towards it.

EG *Try to see things from my point of view.*

9 In spoken English, you use 'point' to refer to the dot in a decimal number that separates the whole number from the fraction.

EG *... nine point four*

☑ The word 'point' is not used in written English. It is always represented by a dot: 9.4.

VERB

10 If you **point at** someone or something or **point to** them, you hold out your finger to show where they are.

EG *He pointed at the one he wanted.*

EG *She pointed to a picture on the*

wall.

11 If you **point** something **at** someone, you aim the end of it towards them.

EG *A man pointed a gun at them.*

point out

VERB

If you point something out to someone, you draw their attention to it by pointing to it or explaining it.

EG *She pointed her boss out to us.*

EG *I pointed out that he was wrong.*

pointed /'pɔɪntɪd/

ADJECTIVE

A pointed object has a thin, sharp end.

EG *... pointed shoes*

pointless /'pɔɪntlɪs/

ADJECTIVE

Something that is pointless has no purpose.

EG *Without an audience the performance is pointless.*

poison /'pɔɪzn/

poisons poisoning poisoned

NOUN

1 Poison is a substance that harms or kills you if you swallow it or absorb it.

EG *Mercury is a known poison.*

VERB

2 To poison someone means to harm them by giving them poison.

EG *... the rumours that she had poisoned him*

poke /pəuk/

pokes poking poked

VERB

1 If you poke someone or something, you push them with your finger or a sharp object.

EG *He was poking me in the chest with a pen.*

2 If something **pokes out of** another thing, you can see part of it from underneath or behind that thing.

EG *... the handkerchief poking out of his pocket*

pole /pəul/

poles

NOUN

1 a long rounded piece of wood or metal

EG *... a telegraph pole*

2 The Earth's poles are its two opposite ends.

EG *... the North Pole*

police /pə'liːs/

PLURAL NOUN

1 The police are the official organization that is responsible for making sure that people obey the law.

EG *The police are looking for him.*

2 Police are men and women who are members of the police.

EG *Over a hundred police surrounded the area.*

☑ You refer to an individual member of the police as a *policeman* or a *policewoman*. A *police officer* can be either a man or a woman.

policy /'pɒlɪsɪ/

policies

NOUN

a set of plans and ideas, especially in politics or business

EG *What is their policy on drugs?*

polish /'pɒlɪʃ/

polishes polishing polished

NOUN

1 Polish is a substance that you put on an object to clean it and make it shine.

EG *... furniture polish*

VERB
2 If you polish something, you put polish on it or rub it with a cloth to make it shine.
EG *He never polishes his shoes.*

polite /pə'laɪt/
ADJECTIVE
Someone who is polite has good manners and is not rude to other people.
EG *Everyone was trying to be so polite.*

political /pə'lɪtɪkl/
ADJECTIVE
relating to politics
EG *... the main political parties*

politician /pɒlɪ'tɪʃən/
politicians
NOUN
a person whose job is in politics, especially a Member of Parliament
EG *... a Labour politician*

politics /'pɒlɪtɪks/
NOUN
Politics is the activity and planning concerned with achieving power and control in a country or organization.
EG *... one of the key jobs in British politics*
☑ 'Politics' is usually used as a singular noun: *politics is a strange business.*

poll /pəʊl/
polls
NOUN
a survey in which people are asked their opinions about something
EG *... an opinion poll*

pollute /pə'luːt/
pollutes polluting polluted
VERB
To pollute water, air, or land means to make it dirty and

dangerous to use or live in.
EG *... a polluted river*

pollution /pə'luːʃən/
NOUN
1 Pollution is poisonous substances that pollute water, air, or land.
EG *... all the pollution on the beach*
2 Pollution is the process of polluting water, air, or land.
EG *... the level of pollution in the river*

pond /pɒnd/
ponds
NOUN
a small, usually man-made area of water
EG *... a garden pond*

pony /'pəʊnɪ/
ponies
NOUN
a small horse
EG *... a ride on a pony*

pool /puːl/
pools pooling pooled
NOUN
1 a swimming pool
EG *... a heated indoor pool*
2 a small area of still water
EG *... a rock pool*
3 A pool of liquid or light is a small area of it.
EG *... a pool of blood*
4 Pool is a game in which players knock coloured balls into pockets around a table using long sticks called cues.
EG *... a game of pool*
5 A pool of people, money, or things is a group or collection that is used or shared by several people.
EG *... a car pool*
PLURAL NOUN
6 the pools are a competition in

which people try to guess the results of football matches
EG *He won over a million on the pools.*

VERB

7 If people pool their resources, they share them or put them together for a particular purpose.
EG *We pooled our savings to start up the business.*

poor /puəʳ/
poorer poorest

ADJECTIVE

1 Poor people have very little money and few possessions.
EG *... children from poor families*

2 Poor places are inhabited by people who are poor.
EG *... a very poor neighbourhood*

3 You use 'poor' to show sympathy.
EG *Poor Gordon!*

4 of a low quality or standard
EG *... a poor performance*

pop /pɒp/
pops popping popped

NOUN

1 Pop is modern music, usually played with electronic equipment.
EG *... a pop star*

2 a short, sharp sound
EG *The ballon burst with a loud pop.*

VERB

3 If something pops, it makes a sudden sharp sound.
EG *... as the cork popped from the bottle*

4 AN INFORMAL USE

If you pop something somewhere, you put it there quickly.
EG *I'd just popped the pie in the oven.*

5 AN INFORMAL USE

If you pop somewhere, you go there quickly.

EG *She popped out to buy him an ice cream.*

popcorn /'pɒpkɔːn/

NOUN

Popcorn is a snack consisting of grains that are heated until they grow bigger and burst.
EG *... a bag of popcorn*

Pope /pəup/
Popes

NOUN

The Pope is the head of the Roman Catholic Church.
EG *... a visit by the Pope*

popular /'pɒpjuləʳ/

ADJECTIVE

1 liked or approved of by a lot of people
EG *... the most popular politician in France*
EG *Chocolate sauce is always popular with children.*

2 involving or intended for ordinary people
EG *... the popular press*

population /pɒpju'leɪʃən/
populations

NOUN

The population of a place is the people who live there, or the number of people who live there.
EG *The country is unable to feed its population.*
EG *... a massive increase in population*

porch /pɔːtʃ/
porches

NOUN

a covered area at the entrance to a building
EG *... the front porch*

pork /pɔːk/

NOUN

Pork is meat from a pig which has

not been salted or smoked.
EG *... pork sausages*

pornography /pɔːˈnɒɡrəfɪ/
NOUN
Pornography refers to books, magazines, and films that are designed to cause sexual excitement.
EG *... a campaign against pornography*

port /pɔːt/
ports
NOUN
1 a town or area which has a harbour or docks
EG *... the Mediterranean port of Marseilles*
ADJECTIVE
2 The port side of a ship is the left side when you are facing the front.
EG *... on the port side*

portable /ˈpɔːtəbl/
ADJECTIVE
designed to be easily carried
EG *... a portable television*

porter /ˈpɔːtər/
porters
NOUN
1 a person whose job is to be in charge of the entrance of a building such as a hotel
EG *... a hotel porter*
2 a person whose job is to carry things, for example people's luggage at a railway station
EG *... a railway porter*

portion /ˈpɔːʃən/
portions
NOUN
1 A portion of something is a part of it.
EG *I spent a large portion of my life there.*
2 an amount of food that is

sufficient for one person
EG *The portions were very generous.*

portrait /ˈpɔːtreɪt/
portraits
NOUN
a picture or photograph of someone
EG *... a portrait of the Queen*

portray /pɔːˈtreɪ/
portrays portraying portrayed
VERB
When an actor, artist, or writer portrays someone or something, they represent or describe them.
EG *... the way women are portrayed in adverts*

pose /pəʊz/
poses posing posed
VERB
1 If something poses a problem or danger, it causes it.
EG *This could pose a threat to their health.*
2 If you pose a question, you ask it.
EG *... the moral questions posed by the debate*
3 If you **pose as** someone else, you pretend to be that person in order to deceive people.
EG *... a friend posing as my lawyer*
4 If you **pose for** a photograph or painting, you stay in a particular position so that someone can photograph or paint you.
EG *The ministers agreed to pose for photographs.*
NOUN
5 a way of standing, sitting, or lying
EG *The girls were photographed in a variety of poses.*

position /pəˈzɪʃən/
positions positioning

A
B
C
D
E
F
G
H
I
J
K
L
M
N
O
P
Q
R
S
T
U
V
W
X
Y
Z

positioned

NOUN

1 The position of someone or something is the place where they are.
EG *The ship's position was reported to the coastguard.*

2 When someone or something is in a particular position, they are sitting or lying in that way.
EG *I raised myself to a sitting position.*

3 The position that you are in is the situation that you are in.
EG *This puts the president in a difficult position.*

VERB

4 If you position something somewhere, you put it there.
EG *He positioned a cushion behind Joanna's back.*

positive /ˈpɒzɪtɪv/

ADJECTIVE

1 If you are positive about something, you are completely sure about it.
EG *I was positive he'd be there.*

2 If you are positive, you are confident and hopeful.
EG *I felt very positive about everything.*

3 A positive response is one that is approving or encouraging.
EG *I anticipate a positive response.*

4 If a medical or scientific test is positive, it shows that something has happened or is present.
EG *The pregnancy test was positive.*

possess /pəˈzes/
possesses possessing possessed

VERB

If you possess something, you own it or have it.
EG *… visitors who do not possess a ticket*
EG *… the practical skills that some people possess*

possession /pəˈzeʃən/
possessions

NOUN

1 If something is in your **possession,** you have it.
EG *The documents are now in our possession.*

2 Your possessions are the things that you own or that you have with you.
EG *… people who had lost all their possessions*

possibility /pɒsɪˈbɪlɪtɪ/
possibilities

NOUN

1 something that might be true or might happen
EG *We must accept the possibility that we are wrong.*

2 one of several things that can be done
EG *There are many possibilities available to you.*

possible /ˈpɒsɪbl/

ADJECTIVE

1 If something is possible, it might happen or be true.
EG *It's quite possible that I'm wrong*

2 If it is **possible to do** something, it can be done.
EG *If it's possible to find him, we will.*

3 If you do something as soon as **possible** or as quickly as **possible,** you do it as soon or as quickly as you can.
EG *I'll be there as soon as possible.*

possibly /ˈpɒsɪblɪ/

ADVERB

1 You use 'possibly' to show that you are not sure whether

A B C D E F G H I J K L M N O P Q R S T U V W X Y Z

something is true or will happen.
EG *Television is possibly to blame for this.*
2 You use 'possibly' to emphasize that you are surprised or puzzled.
EG *What could it mean?*

post /pəust/
posts posting posted
NOUN
1 the post is the system by which letters and parcels are collected and delivered
EG *The cheque is in the post.*
2 Post is letters and parcels that are delivered to you.
EG *Was there any post this morning?*
3 a job or official position in an organization
EG *She is well qualified for the post.*
4 an upright pole fixed into the ground
EG *The dog was tied to a post.*
VERB
5 If you post a letter, you send it to someone through the post.
EG *I'm posting you a cheque tonight.*
6 If you **are posted** somewhere, you are sent by your employers to work there.
EG *He was posted overseas.*

post- /pəust/
PREFIX
after a particular time or event
EG *... his post-war career*

postage /'pəustɪdʒ/
NOUN
Postage is the money that you pay to send letters and parcels by post.
EG *... plus 50p for postage and packing*

postcard /'pəustkɑːd/
postcards

NOUN
a card, often with a picture on one side, which you write on and send without an envelope
EG *She sent him a postcard from Japan.*

postcode /'pəustkəud/
postcodes
NOUN
a short sequence of letters and numbers at the end of an address
EG *Remember to add the postcode.*

poster /'pəustər/
posters
NOUN
a large notice or picture that you stick on a wall
EG *The walls are covered with posters of pop stars.*

postman /'pəustmən/
postmen
NOUN
a man whose job is to collect and deliver letters and parcels that are sent by post
EG *Has the postman been yet?*

post office post offices
NOUN
a building where you can buy stamps and post letters and parcels
EG *You can pay the bill at a post office.*

postpone /pəus'pəun/
postpones postponing postponed
VERB
If you postpone an event, you arrange for it to take place at a later time than was originally planned.
EG *The visit has now been postponed until next month.*

pot /pɒt/
pots

A B C D
NOUN
1 a deep round container for cooking food
EG ... pots and pans
2 a teapot or coffee pot
EG There's tea in the pot.

potato /pə'teɪtəu/
potatoes
NOUN
a white vegetable that has a brown or red skin and grows underground
EG ... mashed potatoes

potential /pə'tɛnʃl/
ADJECTIVE
1 You use 'potential' to say that someone or something is capable of becoming a particular kind of person or thing.
EG He's a potential world champion.
NOUN
2 If someone or something has potential, they are capable of being successful or useful.
EG The boy has great potential.

pound /paund/
pounds pounding pounded
NOUN
1 the main unit of money in Britain and in some other countries
EG Beer cost three pounds a bottle.
2 a unit of weight equal to 16 ounces or about 0.454 kilograms
EG ... a pound of cheese
VERB
3 If you pound something or **pound on** it, you hit it repeatedly with your fist.
EG Someone was pounding on the door.

pour /pɔːr/
pours pouring poured
VERB
1 If you pour a liquid out of a container, you make it flow out by tipping the container.
EG She poured the tea down the sink.
EG Let me pour you a drink.
2 If something pours somewhere, it flows there quickly and in large quantities.
EG Sweat poured down his face.
3 When it is raining heavily, you can say that it **is pouring**.
EG It's been pouring all day.

poverty /'pɒvətɪ/
NOUN
Poverty is the state of being very poor.
EG ... people living in poverty

powder /'paudər/
powders
NOUN
Powder consists of many tiny particles of a solid substance.
EG ... a fine white powder

power /'pauər/
powers powering powered
NOUN
1 Someone who has power has a lot of control over people and events.
EG ... a position of great power and influence
2 Your power to do something is your ability or right to do it.
EG I will do everything in my power to help.
EG ... the legal powers of customs officers
3 The power of something is its physical strength.
EG ... the power of the engine
4 Power is energy obtained, for example, by burning fuel or using the wind or waves.
EG ... nuclear power
VERB

A B C D E F G H I J K L M N O P Q R S T U V W X Y Z

5 Something that powers a machine provides the energy for it to work.

EG *The planes are powered by Rolls Royce engines.*

powerful /'pauəful/

ADJECTIVE

1 able to control or influence people and events

EG *... the most powerful country in the world*

2 very strong

EG *... powerful muscles*

EG *... a powerful computer*

practical /'præktɪkl/

ADJECTIVE

1 involving real situations rather than ideas or theories

EG *... practical suggestions for healthy eating*

2 Someone who is practical is able to deal effectively and sensibly with problems.

EG *You were always so practical, Maria.*

3 sensible and likely to be effective

EG *... the most practical way of preventing crime*

practically /'præktɪklɪ/

ADVERB

almost

EG *I've known him practically all my life.*

practice /'præktɪs/

practices

NOUN

1 You can refer to something that people do regularly as a practice.

EG *... the practice of kissing hands*

2 Practice is regular training in a skill or activity.

EG *I need more practice.*

3 In American English, 'practice' also the usual spelling of the verb 'practise': *she practices every day.*

practise /'præktɪs/

practises practising practised

US practice

VERB

1 If you practise, you do something regularly in order to do it better.

EG *She practises every day on the piano.*

2 When people practise a religion, custom, or craft, they take part in the activities associated with it.

EG *... a custom still practised in some areas*

praise /preɪz/

praises praising praised

VERB

1 If you praise someone or something, you express your strong approval of them.

EG *He praised the fans for their continued support.*

NOUN

2 Praise is what you say or write when you praise someone.

EG *She is full of praise for what he did.*

pray /preɪ/

prays praying prayed

VERB

When someone prays, they speak to God to give thanks or to ask for help.

EG *... all those praying for peace*

prayer /preər/

prayers

NOUN

1 Prayer is the activity of praying.

EG *The night was spent in prayer.*

2 the words that someone says when they pray

EG *I said a little prayer for her.*

pre- /priː/

PREFIX

before a particular time or event
EG *... the pre-Christmas rush*

precaution /prɪˈkɔːʃən/
precautions

NOUN

an action that is intended to prevent something from happening
EG *It's still worth taking precautions against accidents.*

precious /ˈprɛʃəs/

ADJECTIVE

Something that is precious is valuable or important and should be looked after or used carefully.
EG *... precious jewels*
EG *Her family's support is particularly precious to her.*

precise /prɪˈsaɪs/

ADJECTIVE

You use 'precise' to emphasize that you are talking about an exact thing, rather than something vague.
EG *We will never know the precise details of his death.*

precisely /prɪˈsaɪslɪ/

ADVERB

exactly
EG *... at 4 p.m. precisely*
EG *That's precisely what I mean.*

predict /prɪˈdɪkt/
predicts predicting predicted

VERB

If you predict an event, you say that it will happen.
EG *He predicted that my hair would grow back.*

prediction /prɪˈdɪkʃən/

predictions

NOUN

If you make a prediction, you say what you think will happen.
EG *What's your prediction for the match?*

prefer /prɪˈfɜːr/
prefers preferring preferred

VERB

If you **prefer** one thing **to** another, you like it better than the other thing.
EG *I preferred books to people.*
EG *I would prefer to go alone.*

preference /ˈprɛfrəns/
preferences

NOUN

If you have a preference for something, you prefer that thing to other things.
EG *Please state your preference below.*

pregnant /ˈprɛgnənt/

ADJECTIVE

A woman who is pregnant has a baby developing in her body.
EG *I hear Phyllis is pregnant again.*

prejudice /ˈprɛdʒudɪs/

NOUN

Prejudice is an unreasonable dislike of someone or something, or an unreasonable preference for one group over another.
EG *... racial prejudice*

preliminary /prɪˈlɪmɪnərɪ/

ADJECTIVE

Preliminary activities take place before something starts and in preparation for it.
EG *... the preliminary rounds of the competition*

premises /ˈprɛmɪsɪz/

PLURAL NOUN

The premises of a business are the

buildings and land that it occupies.
EG *The firm moved to new premises.*

preparation /prɛpəˈreɪʃən/
preparations

NOUN

1 Preparation is the process of getting something ready.
EG *Months of preparation lay ahead.*

PLURAL NOUN

2 preparations are the arrangements that are made for a future event
EG *… the preparations for the wedding*

prepare /prɪˈpɛəʳ/
prepares preparing prepared

VERB

1 If you prepare something, you make it ready for a particular purpose.
EG *Each report takes 1,000 hours to prepare.*
EG *… a simple meal to prepare*

2 If you **prepare for** something, you get ready for it.
EG *She told them to prepare for government.*

prepared /prɪˈpɛəd/

ADJECTIVE

1 If you are **prepared to do** something, you are willing to do it.
EG *He's not prepared to compromise.*

2 If you are **prepared for** something, you are ready for it.
EG *Be prepared for a surprise.*

preposition /prɛpəˈzɪʃən/
prepositions

NOUN

A **preposition** is a word that is used before a noun or pronoun to link it to other words. Prepositions may describe where something is, where it is going, or when it is happening.
EG *The cat sheltered **under** a bench.*
EG *The train came **into** the station.*
EG *They will arrive **on** Friday.*

prescribe /prɪˈskraɪb/
prescribes prescribing prescribed

VERB

When doctors prescribe treatment, they state what treatment a patient should have.
EG *She was prescribed antibiotics for the infection.*

prescription /prɪˈskrɪpʃən/
prescriptions

NOUN

a form on which a doctor writes the details of a medicine needed by a patient
EG *You will have to take your prescription to a chemist.*

presence /ˈprɛzns/

NOUN

1 Someone's presence in a place is the fact that they are there.
EG *His presence only made things worse.*

2 If you are **in** someone's **presence,** you are in the same place as they are.
EG *I always feel nervous in her presence.*

present /ˈprɛznt/
presents presenting presented

ADJECTIVE

1 If someone is present somewhere, they are there.
EG *He had been present at the birth of his son.*

2 A present situation is one that

A B C D E F G H I J K L M N O P Q R S T U V W X Y Z

A
B
C
D
E
F
G
H
I
J
K
L
M
N
O
P
Q
R
S
T
U
V
W
X
Y
Z

exists now rather than in the past or future.

EG ... *the present economic difficulties*

NOUN

3 the present is the period of time that is taking place now

EG ... *continuing right up to the present*

4 something that you give to someone for them to keep

EG ... *a Christmas present*

VERB : /prɪˈzɛnt/

☑ Note that you pronounce the verb differently from the adjective and the noun.

5 If you **present** someone **with** something or if you **present** it **to** them, you formally give it to them.

EG ... *before he was presented with the prize*

EG *She presented an award to the girl.*

6 Something that presents a difficulty or an opportunity causes it or provides it.

EG *This presents a problem for many consumers.*

7 If you present someone or something in a particular way, you describe them in that way.

EG *Her lawyer presented her in the most favourable light.*

preserve /prɪˈzɜːv/
preserves preserving preserved

VERB

If you preserve something, you make sure that it stays as it is and does not change or end.

EG *We will do everything to preserve peace.*

president /ˈprezɪdənt/
presidents

NOUN

1 The president of a country that has no king or queen is the leader of the country.

EG ... *the President of the United States*

2 The president of an organization is the person who has the highest position in it.

EG ... *the new president of the company*

press /prɛs/
presses pressing pressed

VERB

1 If you press something, you push it or hold it firmly against something else.

EG *He pressed the button and a door opened.*

EG *Lisa pressed his hand.*

2 If you press clothes, you iron them.

EG *Vera pressed his shirt.*

3 If you **press for** something, you try hard to persuade someone to agree to it.

EG *She was pressing for improvements to the education system.*

NOUN

4 Newspapers and the journalists who work for them are called **the press**.

EG *The British press is full of articles on the subject.*

☑ You can use either a singular or a plural verb after 'the press': *the press was unfair to her*; *the press were unfair to her.*

pressure /ˈprɛʃər/
pressures

NOUN

1 Pressure is the force that is produced by pushing on something.

EG *It bends when you put any*

pressure on it.

2 If there is pressure on you to do something, someone is trying to make you do it.
EG *He may have put pressure on her to agree.*
EG *... the pressures of modern life*

presumably /prɪˈzjuːməblɪ/

ADVERB
If you say that something is presumably true, you mean that you assume it is true.
EG *Presumably the front door was locked?*

pretend /prɪˈtend/
pretends pretending pretended

VERB
1 If you pretend that something is the case, you try to make people believe that it is, although it is not.
EG *The boy pretended to be asleep.*
2 If you pretend that you are doing something, you imagine that you are doing it.
EG *She can sunbathe and pretend she's in Spain.*

pretty /ˈprɪtɪ/
prettier prettiest

ADJECTIVE
1 attractive and pleasant
EG *... a pretty girl*
EG *... a pretty little town*
ADVERB
2 AN INFORMAL USE
quite or rather
EG *He spoke pretty good English.*

prevent /prɪˈvent/
prevents preventing prevented

VERB
If you prevent something or **prevent** it **from** happening, you stop it from happening.

EG *These methods prevent pregnancy.*
EG *Further treatment will prevent cancer from developing.*

previous /ˈpriːvɪəs/

ADJECTIVE
A previous time or thing is one that occurred before the present one.
EG *... the previous year*
EG *... a previous marriage*

previously /ˈpriːvɪəslɪ/

ADVERB
at a time before the present
EG *Previously she had very little time to work.*
EG *... ten years previously*

price /praɪs/
prices pricing priced

NOUN
1 The price of something is the amount of money that you have to pay in order to buy it.
EG *... the price of bread*
VERB
If something **is priced at** a particular amount, that is what it costs.
EG *The book is priced at £8.99.*

prick /prɪk/
pricks pricking pricked

VERB
If you prick something, you stick a sharp object into it.
EG *Prick the sausages with a fork.*

pride /praɪd/
prides priding prided

NOUN
1 Pride is a feeling of satisfaction that you have when you or people close to you have done something well.
EG *His mother looked at him with pride.*

2 Pride is a sense of dignity and self-respect.
EG *His own pride forbids him to ask for help.*

VERB
3 If you **pride yourself on** a quality or skill, you are proud of it.
EG *She prides herself on her punctuality.*

priest /priːst/
priests

NOUN
a religious leader or official, especially in some Christian churches
EG *... a Catholic priest*

primary /ˈpraɪmərɪ/

ADJECTIVE
extremely important or most important
EG *... the primary aim of his research*

primary school primary schools

NOUN
a school for children between the ages of 5 and 11
EG *She is in her third year at primary school.*

prime /praɪm/

ADJECTIVE
1 main or most important
EG *... the prime suspect*
2 of the best quality
EG *... in prime condition*

NOUN
3 If you are in your **prime**, you are at the stage in your life when you are most active or most successful.
EG *She was in her intellectual prime.*

prime minister prime ministers

NOUN

The prime minister is the leader of the government.
EG *... the former Prime Minister of Pakistan*

primitive /ˈprɪmɪtɪv/

ADJECTIVE
1 connected with a society in which people live very simply
EG *... primitive tribes*
2 very simple, basic, or old-fashioned
EG *... primitive technology*

prince /prɪns/
princes

NOUN
a male member of a royal family, especially the son of a king or queen
EG *the Prince of Wales*

princess /prɪnˈses/
princesses

NOUN
a female member of a royal family, especially the daughter of a king or queen, or the wife of a prince
EG *... Princess Anne*

principal /ˈprɪnsɪpl/

ADJECTIVE
main or most important
EG *... the principal source of food*

principle /ˈprɪnsɪpl/
principles

NOUN
1 a belief that you have about the way you should behave
EG *I try to live according to my principles.*
2 a general rule or scientific law
EG *The doctrine was based on three fundamental principles.*

print /prɪnt/
prints printing printed

VERB

1 If someone prints a newspaper or book, they reproduce it in large quantities using a mechanical process.
EG *About 10,000 copies of the pamphlet were printed.*

2 If a newspaper or magazine prints a piece of writing, it publishes it.
EG *They did not print his letter.*

3 If numbers or letters are printed on something, they appear on it.
EG *... the number printed on the receipt*

NOUN

4 The letters and numbers on the pages of a printed document are referred to as print.
EG *... columns of tiny print*

printer /'prɪntər/
printers

NOUN

a piece of computer equipment that makes paper copies of information stored in the computer
EG *... a laser printer*

prior /'praɪər/

ADJECTIVE

1 planned or done at an earlier time
EG *I have a prior engagement.*
EG *No prior knowledge is required.*

2 Something that happens **prior to** a particular time or event happens before it.
EG *... his movements prior to the shooting*

priority /praɪˈɒrɪtɪ/
priorities

NOUN

something that needs to be dealt with before everything else
EG *Her first priority is to get fit again.*

prison /'prɪzn/
prisons

NOUN

a building where criminals are kept
EG *... after he was released from prison*

prisoner /'prɪznər/
prisoners

NOUN

someone who is kept in a prison as a punishment or because they have been captured by an enemy
EG *... the large number of prisoners sharing cells*
EG *He was taken prisoner in North Africa in 1942.*

private /'praɪvɪt/
privates

ADJECTIVE

1 for the use of one person or group rather than for the general public
EG *... his father's private plane*

2 taking place between a small number of people and kept secret from others
EG *... a private conversation*

3 owned or run by individuals or companies rather than by the state
EG *... a private company*

NOUN

4 a soldier of the lowest rank
EG *... Private Ryan*

5 If you do something **in private**, you do it without other people being present.
EG *Could I talk to you in private?*

privilege /'prɪvɪlɪdʒ/
privileges

NOUN

a special right or advantage that is given to a person or group
EG *... special privileges for government officials*

A B C D E F G H I J K L M N O P Q R S T U V W X Y Z

prize /praɪz/
prizes prizing prized

NOUN
1 a reward that is given to the winner of a competition or game
EG *He won first prize.*

VERB
2 Something that **is prized** is wanted and admired because of its value or quality.
EG *These shells were highly prized by the Indians.*

pro /prəʊ/
pros

NOUN
1 AN INFORMAL USE
a professional, especially in sport
EG *... some of Europe's top pros*

PLURAL NOUN
2 The **pros and cons** of a situation are its advantages and disadvantages.
EG *... the pros and cons of getting married*

pro- /prəʊ/
PREFIX
supporting or in favour of
EG *... pro-democracy protests*

probable /ˈprɒbəbl/
ADJECTIVE
Something that is probable is likely to be true or likely to happen.
EG *... the most probable outcome*
EG *It is probable that she'll win.*

probably /ˈprɒbəblɪ/
ADVERB
Something that is probably true is likely but not certain to be true.
EG *You probably won't agree with this.*

problem /ˈprɒbləm/
problems

NOUN
1 an unsatisfactory situation that causes difficulties
EG *The main problem was my age.*
2 a puzzle or question that you solve using logical thought or mathematics
EG *... a chess problem*

procedure /prəˈsiːdʒər/
procedures

NOUN
a way of doing something, especially the correct or usual way
EG *The entire procedure takes about 15 minutes.*

proceed /prəˈsiːd/
proceeds proceeding proceeded

VERB
1 If you **proceed to do** something, you do it after doing something else.
EG *He then proceeded to tell us everything.*
2 A FORMAL USE
To proceed means to continue doing something.
EG *... before we proceed any further*
PLURAL NOUN : /ˈprəʊsiːdz/
☑ Note that you pronounce the noun differently from the verb.
3 The **proceeds** of an event are the money that is obtained from it.
EG *The proceeds from the concert will go towards famine relief.*

process /ˈprəʊsɛsɪz/
processes processing processed

NOUN
1 a series of actions or events which have a particular result
EG *... the ageing process*
2 If you are **in the process of** doing something, you have started doing it but have not yet finished.
EG *They are in the process of formulating new rules.*

VERB

3 When something such as food or information is processed, it is treated or dealt with in a particular way.

EG ... *processed foods*

EG *Your application will take a few weeks to process.*

produce /prəˈdjuːs/
produces producing produced

VERB

1 To produce something means to make it or cause it to happen.

EG *It produces a third of the nation's oil.*

EG *The drug is known to produce side effects.*

2 If you produce something from somewhere, you show it so that it can be seen.

EG *To hire a car you must produce a passport.*

3 The person who produces a play, film, or record is the person who organizes it and decides how it should be made.

EG *George Lucas produced this film.*

NOUN : /ˈprɒdjuːs/

☑ Note that you pronounce the noun differently from the verb.

4 Produce is food that is grown to be sold.

EG ... *farm produce*

product /ˈprɒdʌkt/
products

NOUN

1 something that is made to be sold

EG ... *consumer products*

2 the result of something

EG *We are all the products of our upbringing.*

production /prəˈdʌkʃən/

NOUN

Production is the process of manufacturing or growing something in large quantities.

EG ... *modern methods of production*

profession /prəˈfɛʃən/
professions

NOUN

1 a type of job that requires advanced education or training

EG ... *a demanding profession*

2 You use 'profession' to refer to all the people who have the same profession.

EG ... *the medical profession*

professional /prəˈfɛʃənl/
professionals

ADJECTIVE

1 Professional means relating to the work of someone who is qualified in a particular profession.

EG *I think you need professional advice.*

2 Professional describes activities which are done to earn money rather than as a hobby.

EG ... *a professional footballer*

3 A professional piece of work is of a very high standard.

EG ... *a very professional performance*

NOUN

4 a person who has been trained in a profession

EG *You should seek the help of a professional.*

5 someone who plays a sport to earn money rather than as a hobby

EG *He has been a professional for several years.*

professor /prəˈfɛsər/
professors

NOUN

the most senior teacher in a department of a British university,

A B C D E F G H I J K L M N O P Q R S T U V W X Y Z

or a teacher at an American college or university
EG ... Professor Cameron

profile /'prəufaɪl/
profiles

NOUN
Your profile is the outline of your face seen from the side.
EG ... his handsome profile

profit /'prɒfɪt/
profits profiting profited

NOUN
1 an amount of money that you gain when you are paid more for something than it cost you
EG They made a large profit on the deal.

VERB
2 If you **profit from** something, you gain or benefit from it.
EG I don't like to profit from other people's misfortunes.

profound /prə'faund/

ADJECTIVE
1 very great or intense
EG ... discoveries which had a profound effect on medicine
2 showing great intellectual depth or understanding
EG ... a profound question

program /'prəugræm/
programs programming programmed

NOUN
1 a set of instructions that a computer follows in order to perform a particular task
EG ... errors in computer programs

VERB
2 When someone programs a computer, they write a program and put it into the computer.
EG The computer is programmed to compare the two sets of data.

☑ In American English, 'program' is also the usual spelling of 'programme'.

programme /'prəugræm/
programmes
US **program**

NOUN
1 a planned series of events
EG ... a programme of official engagements
2 something that is broadcast on television or radio
EG ... local news programmes
3 a set of pages giving information about a play, concert, or show
EG ... a theatre programme

progress /'prəugres/
progresses progressing progressed

NOUN
1 Progress is the process of gradually improving or getting near to achieving something.
EG ... signs of progress
EG Gerry is now making real progress.
2 The progress of something is the way it develops.
EG ... news on the progress of the war
3 Something that is **in progress** has started and is still continuing.
EG A cricket match was in progress.

VERB : /prə'gres/
☑ Note that you pronounce the verb differently from the noun.
4 If you progress, you become more advanced or skilful at something.
EG He's not progressing as quickly as we'd like.
5 If events progress, they continue to happen gradually.
EG ... as the trip progressed

prohibit /prə'hɪbɪt/

A B C D E F G H I J K L M N O P Q R S T U V W X Y Z

prohibits prohibiting prohibited

VERB

If someone prohibits something or **prohibits** you **from doing** something, they forbid it or make it illegal.

EG ... *a law that prohibited the sale of alcohol*

EG *They are prohibited from owning guns.*

project /'prɒdʒɛkt/
projects projecting projected

NOUN

1 a carefully planned task that requires a lot of time or effort

EG ... *an international science project*

VERB : /prə'dʒɛkt/

☑ Note that you pronounce the verb differently from the noun.

2 Something that is projected is planned or expected.

EG ... *the projected rate of economic growth*

3 If you project an image onto a screen, you make it appear there.

EG ... *pictures projected onto a wall*

prolong /prə'lɒŋ/
prolongs prolonging prolonged

VERB

If you prolong something, you make it last longer.

EG *Foreign military aid was prolonging the war.*

prominent /'prɒmɪnənt/

ADJECTIVE

1 important or well-known

EG ... *one of Edinburgh's most prominent citizens*

2 very noticeable

EG ... *his prominent nose*

promise /'prɒmɪs/
promises promising promised

VERB

1 If you **promise to do** something, you say that you will definitely do it.

EG *He promised to wait.*

EG *Promise me that you'll come.*

2 Something that promises to have a particular quality shows signs that it will have that quality.

EG *The talk promises to be very entertaining.*

NOUN

3 a statement made by someone that they will definitely do something

EG *He made a promise to me.*

4 Someone or something that shows promise seems likely to be successful.

EG ... *a performance full of promise*

promising /'prɒmɪsɪŋ/

ADJECTIVE

Someone or something that is promising seems likely to be successful.

EG ... *one of the most promising poets of his generation*

promote /prə'məʊt/
promotes promoting promoted

VERB

1 If someone promotes something, they try to make it happen or become more popular.

EG ... *an attempt to promote economic growth*

EG ... *a tour to promote his latest album*

2 If someone **is promoted,** they are given a more important job at work.

EG *I was promoted to editor.*

A
B
C
D
E
F
G
H
I
J
K
L
M
N
O
P
Q
R
S
T
U
V
W
X
Y
Z

prompt /prɒmpt/
**prompts prompting
prompted**

VERB
1 If something **prompts** you **to
do** something, it makes you
decide to do it.
EG *Curiosity prompted him to push
at the door.*

ADJECTIVE
2 A prompt action is done without
any delay.
EG *... a prompt reply*

pronoun /'prəunaun/
pronouns

NOUN
A **pronoun** is a word that is used in
place of a noun. Pronouns may be
used instead of naming a person,
thing, or idea.
EG ***She*** *caught a fish.*
EG *He opened the letter and read* ***it***.
EG *I didn't say* ***that***.

pronounce /prə'nauns/
**pronounces pronouncing
pronounced**

VERB
When you pronounce a word, you
say it.
EG *Have I pronounced your name
correctly?*

proof /pru:f/

NOUN
If you have proof of something,
you have evidence which shows
that it is true or exists.
EG *There is no proof that he
actually said that.*

prop /prɒp/
props propping propped

VERB
If you prop an object somewhere,
you support it or rest it against
something.
EG *He propped his bike against the
wall.*

proper /'prɒpər/

ADJECTIVE
1 real or satisfactory
EG *He was no nearer having a
proper job.*
2 correct or suitable
EG *Put things in their proper place.*

property /'prɒpətɪ/
properties

NOUN
1 A person's property is the things
that belong to them.
EG *... stolen property*
2 a characteristic or quality
EG *Mint has powerful healing
properties.*

proportion /prə'pɔːʃən/
proportions

NOUN
1 The proportion of things or
people in a group is the number of
them compared to the total
number in the group.
EG *The proportion of women in the
profession had risen to 17%.*
EG *... a tiny proportion of the
population*

PLURAL NOUN
2 You can refer to the size of
something as its **proportions**.
EG *... a red umbrella of vast
proportions*

proposal /prə'pəuzl/
proposals

NOUN
a suggestion or plan
EG *... a business proposal*

propose /prə'pəuz/
**proposes proposing
proposed**

VERB

1 If you **propose** a plan or idea, you suggest it.
EG ... *the changes proposed by Britain*

2 If you **propose to do** something, you intend to do it.
EG *And how do you propose to do that?*

3 If you **propose to** someone, you ask them to marry you.
EG ... *after he had proposed to her*

prosecute /'prɒsɪkjuːt/
prosecutes prosecuting prosecuted

VERB

If someone is prosecuted, they are charged with a crime and put on trial.
EG *He was prosecuted for drunken driving.*

prospect /'prɒspɛkt/
prospects

NOUN

1 If there is a prospect of something, there is a possibility that it will happen.
EG *There was little prospect of winning.*

PLURAL NOUN

2 Someone's **prospects** are their chances of being successful.
EG ... *to improve your career prospects*

protect /prə'tɛkt/
protects protecting protected

VERB

To protect someone or something means to prevent them from being harmed.
EG *What can women do to protect themselves from heart disease?*

protection /prə'tɛkʃən/

NOUN

If something provides protection, it prevents people or things from being harmed.
EG *Such a diet offers protection against a number of diseases.*

protest /prə'tɛst/
protests protesting protested

VERB

1 If you protest, you say or show that you disapprove of something.
EG ... *students protesting against the arrests*
EG *He opened the letter before she could protest.*

NOUN : /'prəʊtɛst/
☑ Note that you pronounce the noun differently from the verb.

2 a demonstration or statement showing that you disapprove of something
EG ... *the protests against the government's proposals*

Protestant /'prɒtɪstənt/
Protestants

NOUN

a member of a Christian church which is not the Catholic church
EG ... *both Protestants and Catholics*

proud /praud/
prouder proudest

ADJECTIVE

1 If you feel proud, you feel satisfaction at something good that you are connected with.
EG ... *the proud parents*
EG *I am proud to be Welsh.*
EG *I felt proud of his efforts.*

2 Someone who is proud has a lot of dignity and self-respect.
EG *He was too proud to ask his family for help.*

A B C D E F G H I J K L M N O P Q R S T U V W X Y Z

A B C D E F G H I J K L M N O P Q R S T U V W X Y Z

prove /pruːv/
proves proving proved or
proven

VERB

1 If you prove that something is
true, you show by means of
argument or evidence that it is
definitely true.
EG *A letter from Kathleen proved
that he lived there.*

2 If something **proves to be**
true, it becomes clear that it is true.
EG *The reports proved to be
exaggerated.*

provide /prəˈvaɪd/
**provides providing
provided**

VERB

If you **provide** someone **with**
something, you give it to them or
make it available to them.
EG *They would not provide us with
any details.*
EG *Meals were not provided.*

provided /prəˈvaɪdɪd/
or **providing** /prəˈvaɪdɪŋ/

CONJUNCTION

If something will happen provided
that something else happens, or
providing it happens, the first
thing will happen only if the
second thing also happens.
EG *Providing he's fit, he'll play.*

provoke /prəˈvəʊk/
**provokes provoking
provoked**

VERB

1 If you provoke someone, you
deliberately try to make them
angry.
EG *They are ready to shoot if
provoked.*

2 If something provokes an
unpleasant reaction, it causes it.
EG *The programme provoked a*
storm of criticism.

psychiatrist /saɪˈkaɪətrɪst/
psychiatrists

NOUN

a doctor who treats people
suffering from mental illness
EG *He was sent to see a psychiatrist.*

psychological /saɪkəˈlɒdʒɪkl/

ADJECTIVE

concerned with a person's mind
and thoughts
EG *... psychological problems*

psychology /saɪˈkɒlədʒɪ/

NOUN

Psychology is the scientific study of
the mind and of the reasons for
people's behaviour.
EG *... a professor of psychology*

pub /pʌb/
pubs

NOUN

a building where people can buy
and drink alcoholic drinks
EG *He goes to the pub most nights.*

public /ˈpʌblɪk/

NOUN

1 You can refer to people in
general as **the public**.
EG *The gardens are open to the
public.*

☑ You can use either a singular or
a plural verb after 'the public': *the
public is waiting*; *the public are
waiting*.

2 If you do something **in public**,
you do it when other people are
present.
EG *... the last time she appeared in
public*

ADJECTIVE

3 relating to people in general
EG *... public opinion*

4 provided for everyone to use
EG *... public transport*

publication /pʌblɪˈkeɪʃən/

publications

NOUN

1 The publication of a book is the act of printing it and making it available.

EG *The final volume is due for publication in October.*

2 a book or magazine

EG *... a medical publication*

publicity /pʌb'lɪsɪtɪ/

NOUN

Publicity is information or advertising about an item or event.

EG *There was some advance publicity for the book.*

publish /'pʌblɪʃ/
publishes publishing published

VERB

1 When a company publishes a book, newspaper, or magazine, they print copies of it and distribute it.

EG *... before the book was published*

2 When a newspaper or magazine publishes an article or photograph, they print it.

EG *... the decision not to publish the photos*

pudding /'pudɪŋ/
puddings

NOUN

1 a cooked sweet food, usually served hot

EG *... rice pudding*

2 You can refer to the sweet course of a meal as the pudding.

EG *What's for pudding?*

puddle /'pʌdl/
puddles

NOUN

a small shallow pool of rain or other liquid

EG *He stepped over a puddle.*

pull /pul/
pulls pulling pulled

VERB

1 When you pull something, you hold it and move it towards you.

EG *I helped pull him out of the water.*

EG *Pull as hard as you can.*

2 When something is pulled by a vehicle or animal, it is attached to it and moves along behind it.

EG *... a plough pulled by four oxen*

pull away

VERB

When a vehicle pulls away, it starts moving forward.

EG *We waved as the train pulled away.*

pull up

VERB

When a vehicle pulls up, it stops.

EG *The taxi pulled up and the driver jumped out.*

pulse /pʌls/
pulses

NOUN

Your pulse is the regular beating of blood through your body, which you can feel at your wrists and elsewhere.

EG *His pulse was racing.*

pump /pʌmp/
pumps pumping pumped

NOUN

1 a machine that is used to force a liquid or gas to move in a particular direction

EG *... a petrol pump*

VERB

2 To pump a liquid or gas somewhere means to force it to flow in that direction, using a pump.

EG *... a factory that pumped its waste into the river*

A B C D E F G H I J K L M N O P Q R S T U V W X Y Z

A B C D E F G H I J K L M N O P Q R S T U V W X Y Z

punch /pʌntʃ/
punches punching punched

VERB

1 If you punch someone, you hit them hard with your fist.

EG *He was punching and kicking me.*

NOUN

2 a hard blow with the fist

EG *... a punch on the nose*

3 Punch is a drink usually made from wine or spirits mixed with fruit.

EG *... a bowl of punch*

punctuation /pʌ[n]ktjuˈeɪʃən/

NOUN

Punctuation marks are symbols that are added to writing to help the reader to understand the meaning.

'	apostrophe
(), [], {}	brackets
,	comma
—	dash
!	exclamation mark
.	full stop
-	hyphen
?	question mark
" " (or ' ')	quotation marks

You can find out more about the meaning of these symbols by looking at the individual entries.

puncture /ˈpʌŋktʃər/
punctures

NOUN

a small hole in a car or bicycle tyre, made by a sharp object

EG *Somebody helped me mend the puncture.*

punish /ˈpʌnɪʃ/
punishes punishing punished

VERB

If you punish someone, you make them suffer because they have done something wrong.

EG *People who take drugs should be helped, not punished.*

punishment /ˈpʌnɪʃmənt/
punishments

NOUN

Punishment is the act of punishing someone, or a particular way of punishing someone.

EG *He is guilty and deserves punishment.*

EG *The usual punishment is a fine.*

pupil /ˈpjuːpl/
pupils

NOUN

The pupils at a school are the children who attend it.

EG *... schools with over 1,000 pupils*

puppet /ˈpʌpɪt/
puppets

NOUN

a doll that can be moved by pulling strings or by putting your hand inside its body

EG *... a glove puppet*

puppy /ˈpʌpɪ/
puppies

NOUN

a young dog

EG *He gave one of the puppies away.*

purchase /ˈpɜːtʃɪs/
purchases purchasing purchased

A FORMAL WORD

VERB

1 When you purchase something, you buy it.

EG *... before purchasing your ticket*

NOUN

2 the act of buying something

... *the date of purchase*
3 something that you have bought
EG ... *after examining her purchases*

pure /pjʊəʳ/
purer purest

ADJECTIVE
1 not mixed with anything else
EG ... *a pure wool sweater*
2 clean and free from harmful
substances
EG ... *demands for purer water*

purely /'pjʊəlɪ/

ADVERB
completely and wholly
EG *I met her purely by chance.*

purple /'pɜːpl/
purples

ADJECTIVE OR NOUN
Purple is a colour between red and
blue.
EG ... *a purple umbrella*
EG *Purple was his favourite colour.*

purpose /'pɜːpəs/
purposes

NOUN
1 The purpose of something is the
reason for it.
EG *What is the purpose of your visit?*
2 Your purpose is the thing that
you want to achieve.
EG *Her only purpose in life was to
get rich.*
3 If you do something **on
purpose**, you do it deliberately.
EG *Was it an accident or did he do
it on purpose?*

purse /pɜːs/
purses

NOUN
1 a very small bag for carrying
money
EG *How much money have you got
in your purse?*
2 In American English, a purse is a

handbag.
EG *She reached in her purse for her
cigarettes.*

pursue /pə'sjuː/
pursues pursuing pursued

VERB
A FORMAL WORD
1 If you pursue an activity, you try
to achieve it.
EG *I decided to pursue a career in
photography.*
2 If you pursue someone, you
follow them in order to catch
them.
EG *He pursued the man who had
robbed him.*

push /pʊʃ/
pushes pushing pushed

VERB
1 If you push something or
someone, you use force to make
them move away from you.
EG *He pushed the door open.*
EG *Just turn the handle and push.*
2 If you push somewhere or **push
your way** somewhere, you use
force to move past things that are
blocking your path.
EG *He pushed his way to the front
of the queue.*
3 If you **push** someone **into**
doing something, you encourage
or force them to do it.
EG *His mother pushed him into
applying for the job.*
NOUN
4 the act of pushing something
EG ... *at the push of a button*

put /pʊt/
puts putting put

VERB
1 When you put something
somewhere, you move it into that
place or position.
EG *I'd forgotten where I'd put my*

A B C D E F G H I J K L M N O P Q R S T U V W X Y Z

A
B
C
D
E
F
G
H
I
J
K
L
M
N
O
P
Q
R
S
T
U
V
W
X
Y
Z

keys.

EG *She put down her bags on the floor.*

2 To put someone or something in a particular state or situation means to cause them to be in that state or situation.

EG *I'd put the children to bed.*

EG *This puts me in an awkward position.*

3 If you put an idea or remark in a particular way, you express it that way.

EG *He admitted to an error of judgment, as he put it.*

4 If you **put** your trust or confidence **in** someone or something, you trust them or have confidence in them.

EG *Are we right to put our confidence in computers?*

5 If you **put** time, work, or energy **into** an activity, you use it in doing that activity.

EG *He put so much work into the show.*

6 If you put information somewhere, you write or type it there.

EG *What did he put for his address?*

put off

VERB

1 If you put something off, you delay doing it.

EG *... women who put off having a baby*

2 To put someone off something means to cause them to dislike it.

EG *It was his personal habits that put me off.*

put on

VERB

1 When you put on clothing or make-up, you place it on your

body.

EG *I haven't even put any lipstick on.*

2 If you put on a record, tape, or CD, you place it on a machine and listen to it.

EG *Shall I put some music on?*

3 When people put on a show, exhibition, or service, they arrange for it to take place.

EG *British Airways is putting on an extra flight to London.*

put out

VERB

If you put out a fire, cigarette, or light, you make it stop burning or shining.

EG *He lit a cigarette and immediately put it out.*

put up

VERB

1 If people put something up, they construct or erect it.

EG *They put up their tents.*

EG *They're putting new street signs up.*

2 To put up the price of something means to cause the price to increase.

EG *They know he plans to put taxes up.*

3 If you put up resistance to something, you resist it.

EG *She put up a tremendous fight.*

4 If you **put up with** something, you tolerate it even though you find it unpleasant.

EG *Why did you put up with it for so long?*

puzzle /ˈpʌzl/

puzzles puzzling puzzled

VERB

1 If something puzzles you, you do not understand it.
EG ... *a question which has puzzled me for years*

NOUN
2 a game or question that requires a lot of thought to complete or solve

EG ... *a crossword puzzle*

pyjamas /pə'dʒɑːməz/
US **pajamas**

PLURAL NOUN
Pyjamas are loose trousers and a loose jacket that you wear in bed.
EG ... *a new pair of pyjamas*

Qq

qualification /ˌkwɒlɪfɪˈkeɪʃən/
qualifications

NOUN
1 Your qualifications are the examinations that you have passed.
EG ... *people with good academic qualifications*
2 The qualifications for an activity are the qualities or skills that you need in order to do it.
EG *Heath has all the qualifications to become a good manager.*

qualify /ˈkwɒlɪfaɪ/
qualifies qualifying qualified

VERB
1 When someone qualifies, they pass the examinations that they need in order to do a particular job.
EG *She qualified as an accountant.*
2 If you **qualify for** something, you have the right to do it or have it.
EG *You qualify for a discount.*
EG *She failed to qualify for the finals.*

quality /ˈkwɒlɪtɪ/
qualities

NOUN
1 The quality of something is how good it is.
EG *The quality of the food is very poor.*
2 a characteristic
EG ... *people with leadership qualities*

quantity /ˈkwɒntɪtɪ/
quantities

NOUN
an amount that you can measure or count
EG ... *a small quantity of water*

EG ... *large quantities of cash*

quarrel /ˈkwɒrəl/
quarrels quarrelling quarrelled

NOUN
1 an angry argument
EG *The letter led to a serious quarrel between them.*

VERB
2 If people quarrel, they have an angry argument.
EG *They were always quarrelling about trivial things.*
EG *My brother quarrelled with my father.*

quarter /ˈkwɔːtəʳ/
quarters

NOUN
1 one of four equal parts
EG ... *a quarter of a mile*
EG *Cut the peppers into quarters.*
2 When you are telling the time, 'quarter' refers to the fifteen minutes before or after the hour.
EG ... *a quarter to six*
EG ... *a quarter past ten*
3 an American or Canadian coin worth 25 cents
EG *He gave the boy a quarter.*

queen /kwiːn/
queens

NOUN
a female, royal ruler, or a woman married to a king
EG ... *Queen Victoria*
EG *The king and queen had fled.*

query /ˈkwɪərɪ/
queries querying queried

NOUN
1 a question
EG *I am not able to answer your*

query.

VERB

2 If you query something, you ask about it because you think it might not be correct.

EG *No-one queried my decision.*

question /'kwestʃən/
questions questioning questioned

NOUN

1 a sentence which asks for information

EG *Norman refused to answer any questions.*

2 a problem that needs to be discussed

EG *... the difficult question of unemployment*

3 If there is **no question** about something, there is no doubt about it.

EG *There can be no question about his ability.*

VERB

4 If you question someone, you ask them questions.

EG *I questioned her about Jane.*

5 If you question something, you express doubts about it.

EG *No-one questioned the doctor's decision.*

question mark question marks

NOUN

The **question mark** is the symbol **?** that shows that the sentence that has just finished is a question.

EG *When is the train leaving?*

queue /kju:/
queues queuing or **queueing queued**

NOUN

1 a line of people or vehicles that are waiting for something

EG *He got a tray and joined the queue.*

VERB

2 When people queue or **queue up**, they stand in a line waiting for something.

EG *He spent an hour queuing for petrol.*

quick /kwɪk/
quicker quickest

ADJECTIVE

1 moving or doing things with great speed

EG *You'll have to be quick.*

EG *He's a quick learner.*

2 lasting only a short time

EG *... a quick chat*

3 happening with very little delay

EG *... a quick end to the war*

quickly /'kwɪklɪ/

ADVERB

1 with great speed

EG *Stop me if I'm speaking too quickly.*

2 taking only a short time

EG *You can get fit quite quickly.*

3 with very little delay

EG *We need to get it back as quickly as possible.*

quid /kwɪd/

☑ The plural is *quid.*

NOUN

AN INFORMAL WORD

a pound in money

EG *It cost him 500 quid.*

quiet /'kwaɪət/
quieter quietest

ADJECTIVE

1 Someone or something that is quiet makes very little noise.

EG *The children were very quiet.*

EG *... new quieter aircraft*

2 If you are quiet, you are not

speaking.

EG *I told them to be quiet.*

3 A quiet place, time, or situation is calm and peaceful.

EG *... a quiet evening at home*

NOUN

4 Quiet is silence.

EG *Ralph asked for quiet.*

quietly /ˈkwaɪətlɪ/

ADVERB

1 making very little noise

EG *They were playing quietly upstairs.*

2 without speaking

EG *Amy stood quietly by the door.*

3 without excitement or fuss

EG *He lives quietly in the country.*

quit /kwɪt/

quits quitting quit

VERB

If you quit something, you leave it or stop doing it.

EG *Leigh quit his job as a salesman.*

EG *She's trying to quit smoking.*

quite /kwaɪt/

ADVERB

1 fairly but not very

EG *She's quite old.*

EG *It's quite a long way away.*

2 completely

EG *Our position is quite clear.*

EG *I quite agree with you.*

quiz /kwɪz/

quizzes

NOUN

a game in which someone tests your knowledge by asking you questions

EG *... a quiz about gardening*

---

quotation marks

PLURAL NOUN

Quotation marks or **inverted commas** are the symbols " " or ' ' that show where a speaker's words begin and end.

EG *"I would like some more," said Matthew.*

These symbols can also be used to indicate the title of something such as a book, a film, or a piece of music.

EG *The class had been reading 'The Little Prince'.*

---

quote /kwəut/

quotes quoting quoted

VERB

1 If you quote something that someone has written or said, you repeat their words.

EG *He sounded like he was quoting from a textbook.*

NOUN

2 A quote from something written or said is a sentence or phrase from it.

EG *The article began with a quote from Churchill.*

A B C D E F G H I J K L M N O P Q R S T U V W X Y Z

rabbit /'ræbɪt/
rabbits

NOUN
a small animal with long ears
EG ... *a pet rabbit*

race /reɪs/
races racing raced

NOUN
1 a competition to see who is fastest, for example in running or driving
EG ... *a cross-country race*
2 one of the major groups that human beings can be divided into according to their physical features
EG ... *discrimination on the grounds of race or religion*

VERB
3 If you race, you take part in a race.
EG *She has raced against some of the best in the world.*
4 If you race somewhere, you go there as quickly as possible.
EG *He raced after the others.*

racial /'reɪʃl/

ADJECTIVE
relating to the different races that people belong to
EG ... *racial discrimination*

racism /'reɪsɪzəm/

NOUN
Racism is the treatment of some people as inferior because of their race.
EG ... *the fight against racism*

rack /ræk/
racks

NOUN
a piece of equipment for holding things or hanging things on
EG ... *a luggage rack*
EG ... *a clothes rack*

radar /'reɪdɑːr/

NOUN
Radar is a way of discovering the position or speed of objects such as ships or aircraft by using radio signals.
EG ... *a radar screen*

radiation /reɪdɪ'eɪʃən/

NOUN
Radiation is the stream of particles given out by a radioactive substance.
EG ... *the long-term effects of radiation*

radiator /'reɪdɪeɪtər/
radiators

NOUN
1 a hollow metal device for heating a room, usually connected to a central heating system
EG ... *a towel drying on a radiator*
2 the part of a car that is filled with water to cool the engine
EG ... *a leak in the radiator*

radical /'rædɪkl/

ADJECTIVE
very important or basic
EG ... *a radical change in the law*

radio /'reɪdɪəu/
radios

NOUN
1 Radio is the broadcasting of programmes for the public to listen to.
EG ... *the problems faced by local radio*
2 a piece of equipment for listening to radio programmes
EG ... *a transistor radio*

A B C D E F G H I J K L M N O P Q R S T U V W X Y Z

3 Radio is a system of sending sound over a distance by means of electrical signals.

EG *They are in daily radio contact with the rebel leader.*

4 a piece of equipment for sending and receiving radio messages

EG *... a policeman who raised the alarm on his radio*

radioactive /ˌreɪdɪəʊ'æktɪv/

ADJECTIVE

Radioactive substances produce energy in the form of powerful and harmful rays.

EG *... radioactive waste*

raft /rɑːft/
rafts

NOUN

a floating platform made from long pieces of wood tied together

EG *... a bamboo raft*

rag /ræg/
rags

NOUN

1 a piece of old cloth used to clean or wipe things

EG *... an oily rag*

PLURAL NOUN

2 rags are old torn clothes

EG *... small children, some dressed in rags*

rage /reɪdʒ/
rages raging raged

NOUN

1 Rage is strong, uncontrollable anger.

EG *... a fit of rage*

VERB

2 If something such as a storm or battle rages, it continues with great force or violence.

EG *The fire raged for more than four hours.*

raid /reɪd/
raids raiding raided

VERB

1 When people raid a place, they enter it by force in order to attack it or look for something.

EG *... after police raided the firm's offices*

NOUN

2 the act of raiding a place

EG *... an armed raid on a bank*

rail /reɪl/
rails

NOUN

1 a fixed horizontal bar used as a support or for hanging things on

EG *... a hand rail*

EG *... a curtain rail*

2 Rails are the steel bars which trains run along.

EG *... after the train left the rails*

3 Rail is the railway.

EG *I plan to go by rail.*

railroad /'reɪlrəʊd/
railroads

NOUN

In American English, a railroad is a railway.

EG *... a small railroad station*

railway /'reɪlweɪ/
railways

NOUN

a route along which trains travel

EG *The road ran beside a railway.*

rain /reɪn/
rains raining rained

NOUN

1 Rain is water falling from the clouds in small drops.

EG *... after standing in the rain for an hour*

VERB

2 When rain falls, you can say that **it is raining**.

EG *It's been raining all day.*
EG *It didn't rain all week.*

rainbow /ˈreɪmbəʊ/
rainbows

NOUN

an arch of different colours that sometimes appears in the sky after it has been raining
EG *... all the colours of the rainbow*

raise /reɪz/
raises raising raised

VERB

1 If you raise something, you make it higher.
EG *He raised his hand.*

2 If you raise the level or standard of something, you increase it or improve it.
EG *... courses to raise the standard of coaching*

3 If you **raise** your **voice**, you speak more loudly.
EG *Anne raised her voice in order to be heard.*

4 To raise money for a cause means to get people to donate money towards it.
EG *... an event to raise money for local charities*

5 If you raise a child, you look after it until it is grown up.
EG *... the house where she was raised*

6 If you raise a subject, you mention it.
EG *He never raised the matter with me.*

NOUN

7 In American English, a raise is an increase in your wages or salary.
EG *Within two months Kelly got a raise.*
☑ The usual British word is *rise*.

ramp /ræmp/
ramps

NOUN

a sloping surface between two places that are at different levels
EG *I pushed her wheelchair up the ramp.*

ran /ræn/
past tense of **run**

ranch /rɑːntʃ/
ranches

NOUN

a large farm where cattle or horses are reared, especially in the USA
EG *... a cattle ranch*

random /ˈrændəm/

ADJECTIVE OR NOUN

Something that is done in a random way, or **at random**, is done without a definite plan.
EG *... a random sample of 930 women*
EG *He chose his victims at random.*

rang /ræŋ/
past tense of **ring**

range /reɪndʒ/
ranges ranging ranged

NOUN

1 a number of different things of the same kind
EG *A wide range of colours are available.*

2 a set of values on a scale
EG *The average age range is between 35 and 55.*

3 The range of something is the maximum distance over which it can reach things or detect things.
EG *... a missile with a range of 2,000 kilometres*

VERB

4 When things **range from** one point **to** another, they vary within these points on a scale.
EG *Prices range from £5 to £10.*

A B C D E F G H I J K L M N O P Q R S T U V W X Y Z

rank /ræŋk/
ranks ranking ranked

NOUN

1 Someone's **rank** is their position or grade in an organization.
EG *He eventually rose to the rank of captain.*

2 a row of people or things
EG *... a taxi rank*

PLURAL NOUN

3 the **ranks** of a group are its members
EG *We welcomed five new members to our ranks.*

VERB

4 If someone or something **is ranked** at a particular position, they are at that position on a scale.
EG *... a player who is now ranked among the world's top ten*

rap /ræp/
raps rapping rapped

NOUN

1 a quick knock or blow on something
EG *There was a sharp rap on the door.*

2 **Rap** or **rap music** is a type of music in which the words are spoken in a rapid, rhythmic way.
EG *... a rap group*

VERB

3 If you **rap** something or **rap on** it, you hit it with a series of quick blows.
EG *She turned and rapped on Simon's door.*

rape /reɪp/
rapes raping raped

VERB

1 If someone is **raped**, they are forced to have sex.
EG *... the man who had raped her*

2 **Rape** is the crime of forcing

someone to have sex.
EG *... victims of rape*

rapid /'ræpɪd/

ADJECTIVE

If something is **rapid**, it happens or moves very quickly.
EG *... rapid economic growth*
EG *His breathing became more rapid.*

rare /rɛəʳ/
rarer rarest

ADJECTIVE

1 Something that is **rare** is not common or does not happen often.
EG *... a rare flower*
EG *Such occasions are rare.*

2 Meat that is **rare** is cooked very lightly.
EG *I prefer my steak rare.*

rash /ræʃ/
rashes

ADJECTIVE

1 If you are **rash**, you do something without thinking carefully about it.
EG *Don't do anything rash.*

NOUN

2 an area of red spots that appear on your skin when you are ill or have an allergic reaction
EG *I noticed a rash on my leg.*

raspberry /'rɑːzbərɪ/
raspberries

NOUN

a small soft red fruit that grows on a bush
EG *... a bowl of raspberries*

rat /ræt/
rats

NOUN

an animal which has a long tail and looks like a large mouse
EG *... a laboratory experiment with rats*

rate /reɪt/
rates rating rated

NOUN

1 The rate at which something happens is the speed or frequency with which it happens.
EG ... the rate at which hair grows

2 A rate is the amount of money that is charged for goods or services.
EG ... special rates for students

VERB

3 If you rate someone or something as good or bad, you consider them to be good or bad.
EG He was rated as one of England's top young players.

rather /'rɑːðəʳ/

ADVERB

1 to a fairly large extent
EG We got along rather well.
EG ... rather unusual circumstances

2 If you **would rather do** something, you would prefer to do it.
EG Kids would rather play than study.

3 If you do one thing **rather than** another, you choose to do the first thing instead of the second.
EG I try to use the bike rather than the car.

ratio /'reɪʃɪəʊ/
ratios

NOUN

a relationship which shows how many times one thing is greater than another
EG The adult to child ratio is 1 to 6.

rational /'ræʃənl/

ADJECTIVE

based on reason rather than emotion
EG ... a rational decision

rattle /'rætl/
rattles rattling rattled

VERB

1 When something rattles or when you rattle it, it makes short, regular knocking sounds, for example because it is shaking.
EG Every time a train passes, the dishes rattle.
EG He rattled the bars of the cage.

NOUN

2 a baby's toy which makes a noise when it is shaken
EG ... a brightly coloured rattle

rave /reɪv/
raves raving raved

VERB

1 If someone raves, they talk in an excited and uncontrolled way.
EG He started raving about being treated badly.

2 AN INFORMAL USE
If you **rave about** something, you talk about it very enthusiastically.
EG Rachel raved about the new dishes she had tried.

ADJECTIVE

3 A **rave review** is a very enthusiastic one.
EG Stoppard's new play has received rave reviews.

NOUN

4 a large dance event with electronic music
EG ... an all-night rave

raw /rɔː/

ADJECTIVE

1 Raw food is uncooked.
EG ... raw vegetables

2 A raw substance is in its natural state before being processed.
EG ... raw materials

ray /reɪ/
rays

A B C D E F G H I J K L M N O P Q R S T U V W X Y Z

NOUN
a line of light that shines from an object such as the sun
EG ... the sun's rays

razor /ˈreɪzər/
razors

NOUN
a tool that people use for shaving
EG ... a disposable razor

re- /riː/

PREFIX
Re- is used to form words that refer to the act of repeating something. For example, to reread something means to read it again.
EG He never re-married.

reach /riːtʃ/
reaches reaching reached

VERB
1 When you reach a place, you arrive there.
EG He did not stop until he reached the door.
2 When you reach somewhere, you move your arm towards it.
EG Judy reached into her handbag.
3 If you **can reach** something, you are able to touch it by stretching out your arm or leg.
EG I can't reach that shelf.
4 If you reach someone, you contact them, usually by telephone.
EG I've been trying to reach you all morning.
5 If something reaches a place or point, it extends as far as that place or point.
EG ... a cloak that reaches to the ground
EG Unemployment has reached record levels.
6 When people reach an agreement or decision, they succeed in achieving it.

EG ... in an attempt to reach a compromise

NOUN
7 If a place or thing is **within reach**, it is possible to get to it because of its position.
EG It is located within easy reach of the motorway.
8 If something is **out of reach**, you cannot get to it because of its position.
EG Store out of reach of children.

react /riːˈækt/
reacts reacting reacted

VERB
When you **react to** something, you behave in a particular way because of it.
EG He reacted badly to the news.
EG How did she react?

reaction /riːˈækʃən/
reactions

NOUN
Your reaction to something is what you feel, say, or do because of it.
EG He was surprised that his question caused such a strong reaction.

read /riːd/
reads reading read
☑ The past tense and past participle of 'read' are spelt the same as the present tense, but they rhyme with bed.

VERB
1 When you read something that is written, you look at it and understand or say aloud the words that are there.
EG Have you read this book?
EG I read about it in the paper.
2 You can use 'read' when saying what is written somewhere.
EG The sign read, "Private: Not In Service".

ready /ˈrɛdɪ/

ADJECTIVE

1 Someone or something that is ready has reached the required stage for something or is properly prepared for something.

EG *Your glasses will be ready in a fortnight.*

EG *It took her a long time to get ready for church.*

2 If you are **ready to do** something or **ready for** something, you are willing to do it.

EG *She was always ready to give interviews.*

EG *She says she's not ready for marriage.*

real /rɪəl/

ADJECTIVE

1 Something that is real actually exists and is not imagined or invented.

EG *It wasn't a dream, it was real.*

2 Something that is real is genuine and not artificial.

EG *… real leather*

3 You can use 'real' to refer to the true or original nature of something.

EG *This was the real reason for her call.*

realise /ˈrɪəlaɪz/

realises realising realised

another spelling of **realize**

realistic /rɪəˈlɪstɪk/

ADJECTIVE

1 If you are realistic about a situation, you recognize and accept its true nature.

EG *Let's be realistic, we can't afford a bigger house.*

2 A realistic painting, story, or film represents things in a way that is like real life.

EG *His novels are more realistic than*

his plays.

reality /riːˈælɪtɪ/

NOUN

Reality is the real nature of things, rather than the way someone imagines them.

EG *… the line between fiction and reality*

realize /ˈrɪəlaɪz/

realizes realizing realized; also spelt **realise**

VERB

1 If you realize something, you become aware of it.

EG *People don't realize how serious the problem is.*

EG *… once she realized her mistake*

2 A FORMAL USE

If your hopes or fears **are realized**, what you hoped for or feared actually happens.

EG *Our worst fears were realized.*

really /ˈrɪəlɪ/

ADVERB

1 You use 'really' to emphasize a statement or to reduce the force of a negative statement.

EG *… a really good film*

EG *I really hope she comes.*

EG *I'm not really surprised.*

2 You use 'really' when you are talking about the true facts about something.

EG *What was really going on?*

3 You can say **Really?** to express surprise.

EG *"It only cost ten pounds." — "Really?"*

rear /rɪəʳ/

rears rearing reared

NOUN

1 The rear of something is the part at the back.

EG *… the rear of the building*

A
B
C
D
E
F
G
H
I
J
K
L
M
N
O
P
Q
R
S
T
U
V
W
X
Y
Z

VERB

2 If you rear children or young animals, you bring them up until they are able to look after themselves.

EG *I was reared in east Texas.*

3 When a horse rears, it raises the front part of its body, so that its front legs are in the air.

EG *The horse reared and threw off its rider.*

reason /ˈriːzn/
reasons reasoning reasoned

NOUN

1 The reason for something is the fact or situation which explains why it happens.

EG *Who would have a reason to kill her?*

EG *... the reason why Italian tomatoes have so much flavour*

2 If you **have reason to** believe or feel something, there are good reasons why you believe it or feel it.

EG *He had every reason to be upset.*

3 Reason is the ability to think and make judgments.

EG *... his lack of faith in reason*

VERB

4 If you reason that something is true, you decide it is true after considering all the facts.

EG *I reasoned that if he could do it, so could I.*

reasonable /ˈriːznəbl/

ADJECTIVE

1 fair and sensible

EG *I'm a reasonable man.*

EG *It seems reasonable to expect sales to increase.*

2 A reasonable amount is a fairly large amount.

EG *There were a reasonable number of people there.*

3 A reasonable price is fair and not

too high.

EG *The prices are reasonable.*

4 Something that is reasonable is fairly good, but not very good.

EG *"What's the food like there?" — "Reasonable"*

reassure /riːəˈʃuər/
reassures reassuring reassured

VERB

If you reassure someone, you say or do things to make them stop worrying.

EG *I tried to reassure her that everything would be OK.*

rebel /ˈrɛbl/
rebels rebelling rebelled

NOUN

1 Rebels are people who are fighting against their own country's army in order to change the political system.

EG *... fighting between rebels and government forces*

2 A rebel is someone who rejects society's values and behaves differently from other people.

EG *She had been a rebel at school.*

VERB : /rɪˈbɛl/

☑ Note that you pronounce the verb differently from the noun.

3 When someone rebels, they reject society's values and behave differently from other people.

EG *I was very young and rebelling against everything.*

recall /rɪˈkɔːl/
recalls recalling recalled

VERB

1 When you recall something, you remember it.

EG *She could not recall ever seeing him drunk.*

2 If you are recalled to a place, you are ordered to return there.

EG *Spain has recalled its ambassador.*

receipt /rɪˈsiːt/
receipts

NOUN

a piece of paper confirming that money or goods have been received

EG *I wrote her a receipt for the money.*

receive /rɪˈsiːv/
receives receiving received

VERB

1 When you receive something, you get it after someone has given or sent it to you.

EG *I received your letter of June 7.*

2 If you receive something such as injuries or the blame for something, you are injured or blamed.

EG *... the injuries she received in a car crash*

EG *He received most of the blame.*

3 If something **is received** in a particular way, people react to it in that way.

EG *The decision was received with disappointment.*

recent /ˈriːsnt/

ADJECTIVE

Something recent happened a short time ago.

EG *... her recent trip to Argentina*

recently /ˈriːsntlɪ/

ADVERB

a short time ago

EG *He recently celebrated his eightieth birthday.*

reception /rɪˈsɛpʃən/
receptions

NOUN

1 In a hotel or office, reception is the place near the entrance where appointments and enquiries are dealt with.

EG *... the young lady at reception*

2 a formal party

EG *... the wedding reception*

3 The reception that someone or something gets is the way that people react to them.

EG *... the enthusiastic reception of his book*

receptionist /rɪˈsɛpʃənɪst/
receptionists

NOUN

The receptionist in a hotel or office deals with people when they arrive, answers the telephone, and arranges appointments.

EG *... a hotel receptionist*

recipe /ˈrɛsɪpɪ/
recipes

NOUN

a list of ingredients and instructions for cooking something

EG *... a recipe for Yorkshire pudding*

reckon /ˈrɛkən/
reckons reckoning reckoned

VERB

1 AN INFORMAL USE

If you reckon that something is true, you think it is true.

EG *I reckon we'll be there by midnight.*

2 If something **is reckoned** to be a particular figure, it is calculated to be that amount.

EG *About 40% of the country is reckoned to be illiterate.*

reckon with

VERB

If you had not reckoned with something, you had not expected it and therefore were unprepared when it happened.

EG *He had not reckoned with the strength of Sally's feelings.*

A
B
C
D
E
F
G
H
I
J
K
L
M
N
O
P
Q
R
S
T
U
V
W
X
Y
Z

recognize /'rɛkəgnaɪz/
recognizes recognizing recognized; also spelt **recognise**

VERB

1 If you recognize someone or something, you realize that you know who or what they are.
EG *The receptionist recognized me at once.*

2 If you recognize something, you accept that it exists or that it is true.
EG *They have been slow to recognize the problem.*

recommend /rɛkə'mɛnd/
recommends recommending recommended

VERB

If someone **recommends** something or someone **to** you, they suggest that you would find them good or useful.
EG *He recommended the restaurant to all his friends.*
EG *Can you recommend a good doctor?*

record /'rɛkɔːd/
records recording recorded

NOUN

1 a written account of something
EG *your medical records*

2 a round, flat piece of plastic on which music has been recorded; also the music recorded on this
EG *... one of my favourite records*

3 an achievement which is the best of its type
EG *... the world record*

4 Your record is what is known about your achievements or past activities.
EG *He had a criminal record.*

VERB : /rɪ'kɔːd/

☑ Note that you pronounce the verb differently from the noun.

5 If you record information, you write it down so that it can be referred to later.
EG *He recorded everything in his diary.*

6 When music or speech is recorded, it is put on tape, record, or CD.
EG *The album was recorded in Ireland.*

ADJECTIVE : /'rɛkɔːd/

7 higher, lower, better, or worse than ever before
EG *Profits were at a record level.*

recover /rɪ'kʌvər/
recovers recovering recovered

VERB

1 If you **recover from** an illness or unhappy experience, you get well again or stop being upset by it.
EG *She is now recovering in hospital.*
EG *... a tragedy from which he never recovered*

2 If you recover a lost object or your ability to do something, you get it back.
EG *Most of the goods were never recovered.*
EG *She never recovered consciousness.*

recovery /rɪ'kʌvərɪ/
recoveries

NOUN

If a sick or injured person makes a recovery, they become well again.
EG *He made a remarkable recovery from a leg injury.*

recreation /rɛkrɪ'eɪʃən/

NOUN

Recreation is the things that you do for pleasure in your spare time.
EG *Sundays are for relaxation and*

recreation.

rectangular /rɛk'tæŋgjulər/

ADJECTIVE

Something that is rectangular has four sides whose corners are all ninety-degree angles.

EG ... a rectangular table

recur /rɪ'kəːr/

recurs recurring recurred

VERB

If something recurs, it happens again.

EG ... a recurring nightmare

recycle /riː'saɪkl/

recycles recycling recycled

VERB

If you recycle used products, you process them so that they can be used again.

EG ... recycled glass

red /rɛd/

redder reddest; reds

ADJECTIVE OR NOUN

1 Red is the colour of blood or of a ripe tomato.

EG ... a red dress

EG ... a bright splash of red

ADJECTIVE

2 Red hair is between orange and brown in colour.

EG ... her long red hair

reduce /rɪ'djuːs/

reduces reducing reduced

VERB

To reduce something means to make it smaller in size or amount.

EG It reduces the risk of heart disease.

reduction /rɪ'dʌkʃən/

reductions

NOUN

When there is a reduction in something, it is made smaller.

EG ... dramatic reductions in staff

redundant /rɪ'dʌndnt/

ADJECTIVE

1 When people are **made redundant**, they lose their jobs because there is no more work for them or no money to pay them.

EG My husband was made redundant last year.

2 When something becomes redundant, it is no longer needed.

EG ... skills that technology has made redundant

refer /rɪ'fəːr/

refers referring referred

VERB

1 If you **refer to** someone or something, you mention them or describe them in a particular way.

EG He never once referred to his recent troubles.

EG Marcia had referred to him as her dear friend.

2 If you **refer to** a book or other source of information, you look at it in order to find something out.

EG He had to keep referring to the manual.

3 If a person or problem **is referred to** another person, that person is asked to deal with them.

EG I was referred to an ear specialist.

referee /rɛfə'riː/

referees

NOUN

the official who controls a football or boxing match

EG He was sent off for arguing with the referee.

reference /'rɛfrəns/

references

NOUN

1 A reference to someone or something is a mention of them.

EG He made no reference to any agreement.

A
B
C
D
E
F
G
H
I
J
K
L
M
N
O
P
Q
R
S
T
U
V
W
X
Y
Z

2 Reference is the act of referring to someone or something for information or advice.
EG *Keep this leaflet for future reference.*

3 If someone gives you a reference when you apply for a job, they write a letter about your abilities.
EG *I've given you a marvellous reference.*

reflect /rɪˈflɛkt/
reflects reflecting reflected

VERB
1 If something reflects an attitude or situation, it shows what it is like.
EG *Dad's choice of school reflected his hopes for us.*

2 When something is reflected in a mirror or in water, you can see its image there.
EG *... the image reflected in the glass*

3 If a surface reflects light or heat, the light or heat comes back from the surface instead of passing through it.
EG *... a layer of aluminium to reflect heat*

reflection /rɪˈflɛkʃən/
reflections

NOUN
1 an image in a mirror or in water
EG *He gazed at his reflection in the mirror.*

2 If something is a reflection of something else, it shows what that thing is like.
EG *The drawings are a reflection of his own self-hate.*

reform /rɪˈfɔːm/
reforms reforming reformed

NOUN
1 Reforms are major changes to laws or institutions.
EG *... a series of economic reforms*

VERB
2 When laws or institutions are reformed, major changes are made to them.
EG *... his proposals for reforming the legal system*

refrigerator /rɪˈfrɪdʒəreɪtər/
refrigerators

NOUN
an electrically cooled container in which you store food to keep it fresh
EG *... a gas commonly used in refrigerators*

refugee /rɛfjuˈdʒiː/
refugees

NOUN
Refugees are people who have been forced to leave their country and live elsewhere.
EG *... thousands of refugees*

refund /ˈriːfʌnd/
refunds refunding refunded

NOUN
1 a sum of money which is returned to you, for example because you have returned goods to a shop
EG *You should ask for a refund.*

VERB : /rɪˈfʌnd/
☑ Note that you pronounce the verb differently from the noun.

2 If someone refunds your money, they return it to you.
EG *We guarantee to refund your money if you're not entirely satisfied.*

refusal /rɪˈfjuːzəl/
refusals

NOUN
A refusal is the fact of firmly saying or showing that you will not do, allow, or accept something.
EG *... because of his refusal to accept the deal*

refuse /rɪˈfjuːz/
refuses refusing refused

VERB

1 If you **refuse to do** something, you say or decide firmly that you will not do it.
EG *He refused to comment after the trial.*
EG *I refuse to let him bully me.*

2 If you refuse something, you do not allow it or do not accept it.
EG *The United States has refused him a visa.*
EG *He offered me another drink, which I refused.*

regard /rɪˈgɑːd/
regards regarding regarded

VERB

1 If you regard someone or something in a particular way, you think of them in that way.
EG *We all regard him as a friend.*

PREPOSITION

2 You can use **regarding** or **as regards** to indicate what you are referring to.
EG *... information regarding his current address*
EG *As regards the war, he believed in victory at any price.*

PLURAL NOUN

3 regards is used in various expressions to express friendly feelings
EG *Give my regards to your husband.*
EG *With best regards, David.*

region /ˈriːdʒən/
regions

NOUN

1 a large area of land
EG *... a remote region of the country*

2 in the region of means approximately
EG *The scheme will cost in the region of six million pounds.*

register /ˈredʒɪstər/
registers registering registered

NOUN

1 an official list or record
EG *... the electoral register*

VERB

2 When something is registered, it is recorded on an official list.
EG *The car was registered in my name.*

3 When something registers on a scale, it shows a particular value.
EG *The earthquake registered 5.3 on the Richter scale.*

regret /rɪˈgret/
regrets regretting regretted

VERB

1 If you regret something, you wish that it had not happened.
EG *I did nothing, and I've regretted it ever since.*

2 You can say that you regret something as a way of apologizing.
EG *We regret any inconvenience to passengers.*

NOUN

3 Regret is a feeling of sadness or disappointment.
EG *He feels deep regret about his friend's death.*

regular /ˈregjulər/
regulars

ADJECTIVE

1 Regular events happen at equal or frequent intervals.
EG *Take regular exercise.*
EG *The trains to London are fairly regular.*

2 If you are a regular visitor somewhere, you go there often.
EG *... regular churchgoers*

3 usual or normal

EG *It looks just like a regular cigarette.*
4 Something that is regular has a well-balanced appearance.
EG *... a regular geometrical shape*

NOUN
5 People who go to a place often are known as its regulars.
EG *... the regulars at his local pub*

regulate /ˈregjuleɪt/
regulates regulating regulated

VERB
To regulate something means to control the way it operates.
EG *Sweating helps to regulate the body's temperature.*

regulation /regjuˈleɪʃən/
regulations

NOUN
1 Regulations are official rules.
EG *... the new safety regulations*
2 Regulation is the control of something.
EG *... the regulation of the betting industry*

rehearsal /rɪˈhɜːsəl/
rehearsals

NOUN
a practice of a performance in preparation for the actual event
EG *The band was due to begin rehearsals for a concert tour.*

rehearse /rɪˈhɜːs/
rehearses rehearsing rehearsed

VERB
When people rehearse a performance of something, they practise it.
EG *The cast were only given three weeks to rehearse.*

reign /reɪn/
reigns reigning reigned

VERB
1 When a king or queen reigns, he or she is the leader of the country.
EG *... Henry II, who reigned from 1154 to 1189*
2 If something such as silence or calm reigns in a place, the place is silent or calm.
EG *A relative calm reigned over the city.*

NOUN
3 The reign of a king or queen is the period when they reign.
EG *... during the reign of Queen Victoria*

reject /rɪˈdʒekt/
rejects rejecting rejected

VERB
1 If you reject a proposal or request, you do not accept it or agree to it.
EG *The president was correct to reject the offer.*
2 If you are rejected by someone, they tell you that they do not want you.
EG *... students who are rejected by top universities*

relate /rɪˈleɪt/
relates relating related

VERB
1 If something relates to something else, it is connected or concerned with it.
EG *The statistics relate only to western Germany.*
2 If you relate to someone, you understand their thoughts and feelings.
EG *Children need to learn to relate to other children.*

related /rɪˈleɪtɪd/

ADJECTIVE
1 If two things are related, they are connected in some way.

EG *Crime and poverty are closely related.*

2 People who are related belong to the same family.

EG *We have the same name but we're not related.*

relation /rɪˈleɪʃən/
relations

NOUN

1 If there is a relation between two things, they are connected in some way.

EG *This theory bears no relation to reality.*

2 Your relations are the members of your family.

EG *... visits to friends and relations*

PLURAL NOUN

3 relations between people are their feelings and behaviour towards each other

EG *Relations between the couple had not improved.*

relationship /rɪˈleɪʃənʃɪp/
relationships

NOUN

1 The relationship between two people or groups is the way they feel and behave towards each other.

EG *... close family relationships*

2 a close friendship, especially one involving romantic or sexual feelings

EG *... when the relationship ended*

3 The relationship between two things is the way in which they are connected.

EG *... the relationship between diet and cancer*

relative /ˈrelətɪv/
relatives

ADJECTIVE

1 You use 'relative' when comparing the size or quality of two or more things.

EG *... the relative strengths of the British and German forces*

NOUN

2 Your relatives are the members of your family.

EG *Get a relative to look after the children.*

relatively /ˈrelətɪvlɪ/

ADVERB

fairly or quite

EG *It's relatively easy.*

relax /rɪˈlæks/
relaxes relaxing relaxed

VERB

1 If you relax or if something relaxes you, you become calm and less worried or tense.

EG *I ought to relax and stop worrying.*

EG *Massage is used to relax muscles.*

2 If you relax a rule, you make it less strict.

EG *The rules governing student conduct were relaxed.*

release /rɪˈliːs/
releases releasing released

VERB

1 If a prisoner or animal is released, they are set free.

EG *He was released from prison last year.*

2 If you release someone or something, you stop holding them or remove something that is holding them.

EG *He stopped and faced her, releasing her wrist.*

EG *Wade released the handbrake.*

3 When a new record, film, or document is released, it becomes available for people to buy, see, or read.

EG *He is releasing an album of love songs.*

A
B
C
D
E
F
G
H
I
J
K
L
M
N
O
P
Q
R
S
T
U
V
W
X
Y
Z

EG *Figures released yesterday show sales are up.*

NOUN

4 The release of someone is the act of setting them free.

EG *... three days after her release from hospital*

5 The release of a record, film, or document is the act of making it available.

EG *... following the release of his latest record*

relevant /'rɛləvənt/

ADJECTIVE

If something is **relevant to** a situation or person, it is important in that situation or to that person.

EG *Is socialism still relevant to people's lives?*

EG *We have passed all relevant information on to the police.*

reliable /rɪ'laɪəbl/

ADJECTIVE

1 Reliable people and things can be trusted to do what you want or to work well.

EG *Japanese cars are so reliable.*

2 Reliable information is likely to be correct, because it comes from a source that you can trust.

EG *There is no reliable information about the number of deaths.*

relief /rɪ'liːf/

NOUN

1 If you feel relief, you feel glad because something unpleasant is over or has been avoided.

EG *I breathed a sigh of relief when he left.*

2 If something provides relief from pain or distress, it stops or reduces the pain or distress.

EG *This brought considerable relief from the pain.*

relieve /rɪ'liːv/
relieves relieving relieved

VERB

If something relieves pain or an unpleasant feeling, it makes it less painful or unpleasant.

EG *Drugs can relieve much of the pain.*

relieved /rɪ'liːvd/

ADJECTIVE

If you are relieved, you feel glad because something unpleasant is over or has been avoided.

EG *We're all relieved to be back home.*

religion /rɪ'lɪdʒən/
religions

NOUN

1 Religion is belief in a god or gods.

EG *... the importance of religion*

2 a particular set of religious beliefs

EG *... the Christian religion*

religious /rɪ'lɪdʒəs/

ADJECTIVE

1 connected with religion

EG *... different religious beliefs*

2 Someone who is religious has a strong belief in a god or gods.

EG *... a very religious man*

reluctant /rɪ'lʌktənt/

ADJECTIVE

If you are **reluctant to do** something, you do not want to do it.

EG *Mr Spero was reluctant to ask for help.*

rely /rɪ'laɪ/
relies relying relied

VERB

1 If you **rely on** someone or something, you need them in order to do something.

EG *She has to rely on money from*

her parents.

2 If you can **rely on** someone **to do** something, you can trust them to do it.

EG *I know I can rely on you to sort it out.*

remain /rɪˈmeɪn/
remains remaining remained

VERB

1 If you remain in a particular place or state, you do not move from that place or do not change from that state.

EG *She remained at home, waiting for his call.*

EG *The three men remained silent.*

2 Something that remains continues to exist.

EG *Other dangers still remain.*

PLURAL NOUN

3 The **remains** of something are the parts that are left after most of it has been destroyed.

EG *... the remains of an ancient mosque*

remainder /rɪˈmeɪndəʳ/

NOUN

The remainder of something is the part that is left after the rest has gone.

EG *He gulped down the remainder of his coffee.*

remark /rɪˈmɑːk/
remarks remarking remarked

VERB

1 If you **remark on** something, you say something about it.

EG *Everyone had remarked on her new hairstyle.*

NOUN

2 If you make a remark about something, you say something about it.

EG *His remarks were repeated in all*

the papers.

remarkable /rɪˈmɑːkəbl/

ADJECTIVE

impressive or unusual

EG *... a remarkable achievement*

remedy /ˈrɛmədɪ/
remedies

NOUN

something that cures an illness or corrects a problem

EG *... a remedy for hay fever*

EG *... a remedy for unemployment*

remember /rɪˈmɛmbəʳ/
remembers remembering remembered

VERB

1 If you remember someone or something from the past, you still have an idea of them and are able to think about them.

EG *I remember her very well.*

EG *I don't remember talking to you at all.*

2 If you remember something, you suddenly become aware of it again.

EG *Then I remembered his letter, which cheered me up.*

3 If you **remember to do** something, you do it when you intend to.

EG *Did you remember to bring the camera?*

remind /rɪˈmaɪnd/
reminds reminding reminded

VERB

1 If someone reminds you of a fact or **reminds** you **to do** something, they say something which makes you think about it or remember to do it.

EG *He reminded me that he was still my boss.*

EG *Remind me to buy a bottle of wine, will you?*

A B C D E F G H I J K L M N O P Q R S T U V W X Y Z

2 If someone or something **reminds** you **of** another person or thing, they are similar to the other person or thing and make you think of them.
EG *She reminds me of my grandmother.*

remote /rɪˈməʊt/
remoter remotest
ADJECTIVE
1 far away from where most people live
EG *... villages in remote areas*
2 If there is only a remote possibility that something will happen, it is unlikely to happen.
EG *The chances of his surviving are pretty remote.*

removal /rɪˈmuːvəl/
NOUN
1 The removal of something is the act of taking it away.
EG *... the surgical removal of a tumour*
2 Removal is the process of transporting furniture from one building to another.
EG *... a removal van*

remove /rɪˈmuːv/
removes removing removed
VERB
If you remove something from a place, you take it off or away.
EG *He removed his jacket.*
EG *Three bullets were removed from his wounds.*

render /ˈrɛndəʳ/
renders rendering rendered
VERB
You can use 'render' to say that something is changed into a different state.
EG *The bomb was quickly rendered harmless.*

renew /rɪˈnjuː/
renews renewing renewed
VERB
1 If you renew an activity or relationship, you begin it again.
EG *After the war the two men renewed their friendship.*
2 If you renew a licence or contract, you extend the period of time for which it is valid.
EG *His contract is not being renewed.*

rent /rɛnt/
rents renting rented
VERB
1 If you rent something, you pay the owner a regular sum of money in exchange for being able to use it.
EG *... a rented flat*
2 If you **rent** something **to** someone, or if you **rent** it **out**, you let them use it in exchange for a regular payment.
EG *She rented out rooms to students.*
NOUN
3 Rent is the amount of money that you pay regularly for the use of land or accommodation.
EG *How much rent do you pay?*

repair /rɪˈpeəʳ/
repairs repairing repaired
NOUN
1 A repair is something that you do to mend something that is damaged.
EG *Many women know how to carry out repairs on their cars.*
VERB
2 If you repair something that is damaged, you mend it.
EG *... while the roof was being repaired*

repeat /rɪˈpiːt/

A
B
C
D
E
F
G
H
I
J
K
L
M
N
O
P
Q
R
S
T
U
V
W
X
Y
Z

repeats repeating repeated

VERB

1 If you repeat something, you say, write, or do it again.
EG *He kept repeating that he was unable to remember.*
EG *The next day I repeated the procedure.*

NOUN

2 something which is done again or happens again
EG *... a repeat of last year's final*
EG *... the number of repeats on TV*

replace /rɪˈpleɪs/
replaces replacing replaced

VERB

1 When one person or thing replaces another, the first person or thing takes the place of the second.
EG *... the lawyer who replaced Bob as chairman*

2 If you replace something that is damaged or lost, you get a new one.
EG *... a new sweater to replace the one he had lost*

3 If you replace something, you put it back where it was before.
EG *He replaced the book on the shelf.*

replacement /rɪˈpleɪsmənt/
replacements

NOUN

1 The replacement for someone or something is the person or thing that takes their place.
EG *Taylor has nominated Adams as his replacement.*

2 The replacement of someone or something is the act of replacing them by another person or thing.
EG *... the replacement of damaged or lost books*

reply /rɪˈplaɪ/

replies replying replied

VERB

1 If you reply or **reply to** something, you say or write something as an answer to it.
EG *He replied that this was impossible.*
EG *I've not replied to Lee's letter yet.*

NOUN

2 A reply is what you say or write when you answer someone.
EG *I called her name but there was no reply.*
EG *David has had twelve replies to his advert.*

report /rɪˈpɔːt/
reports reporting reported

VERB

1 If you report that something has happened, you tell someone about it.
EG *He reported the theft to the police.*
EG *I have nothing else to report.*

2 If you **report** someone **to** an authority, you make an official complaint about them.
EG *His ex-wife reported him to the police.*

3 If you **report to** a person or place, you go there and say you are ready for work.
EG *He was told to report to the manager when he arrived.*

NOUN

4 an account of an event or situation
EG *... a news report*
EG *... his school report*

reporter /rɪˈpɔːtər/
reporters

NOUN

someone who writes news articles or broadcasts news reports
EG *... a sports reporter*

A
B
C
D
E
F
G
H
I
J
K
L
M
N
O
P
Q
R
S
T
U
V
W
X
Y
Z

represent /rɛprɪˈzɛnt/
represents representing
represented

VERB
1 If someone represents you, they act on your behalf.
EG ... *lawyers representing relatives of the victims*
2 If a sign or symbol represents something, it is accepted as meaning that thing.
EG ... *where 'c' represents the speed of light*
3 If something represents a change or achievement, it is a change or achievement.
EG *This represents a major advance.*

representative
/rɛprɪˈzɛntətɪv/
representatives

NOUN
1 a person who acts on behalf of another person or group of people
EG ... *trade union representatives*
ADJECTIVE
2 If someone or something is **representative of** a group, they are typical of that group.
EG *The photos chosen are not representative of his work.*

reproduce /riːprəˈdjuːs/
reproduces reproducing
reproduced

VERB
if you reproduce something, you copy it.
EG *I won't try to reproduce his accent.*

reproduction /riːprəˈdʌkʃən/
reproductions

NOUN
a copy of something such as an antique or a painting
EG ... *a reproduction of a popular painting*

reptile /ˈrɛptaɪl/
reptiles

NOUN
an animal such as a snake, which has cold blood and lays eggs
EG ... *the reptile house at the zoo*

republic /rɪˈpʌblɪk/
republics

NOUN
a country which has a president rather than a king or queen
EG *In 1918 Austria became a republic.*

republican /rɪˈpʌblɪkən/

ADJECTIVE
If someone is republican, they favour a style of government which has a president.
EG *Some families have been republican for generations.*

reputation /rɛpjuˈteɪʃən/
reputations

NOUN
The reputation of something or someone is the opinion that people have of them.
EG *The college had a good reputation.*

request /rɪˈkwɛst/
requests requesting
requested

VERB
1 If you request something, you ask for it politely or formally.
EG *She had requested that the door be left open.*
NOUN
2 If you make a request for something, you request it.
EG *He ignored my request.*

require /rɪˈkwaɪər/
requires requiring required

VERB
1 If you require something, you

need it.

EG *If you require further information, please contact the head office.*

EG *What qualifications are required?*

2 If a law or rule **requires** you **to do** something, you have to do it.

EG *The rules require employers to provide safety training.*

requirement /rɪˈkwaɪəmənt/
requirements

NOUN

something that you must have or must do

EG *Maths is no longer a requirement for many courses.*

rescue /ˈrɛskjuː/
rescues rescuing rescued

VERB

1 If you rescue someone, you save them from a dangerous or unpleasant situation.

EG *... rescuing 20 people from the sinking ship*

EG *He had rescued her from a horrible life.*

NOUN

2 Rescue is an attempt to save someone from a dangerous or unpleasant situation.

EG *... to improve the chances of rescue*

EG *... a major air-sea rescue*

research /rɪˈsɜːtʃ/
researches researching researched

NOUN

1 Research is work that tries to discover facts about something.

EG *... cancer research*

VERB

2 If you research something, you try to discover facts about it.

EG *She spent two years researching her documentary.*

resemblance /rɪˈzɛmbləns/

NOUN

If there is a resemblance between two things or people, they are similar to each other.

EG *There was a remarkable resemblance between him and Pete.*

resemble /rɪˈzɛmbl/
resembles resembling resembled

VERB

If one thing or person resembles another, they are similar to each other.

EG *The situation resembles that of Europe in 1940.*

resent /rɪˈzɛnt/
resents resenting resented

VERB

If you resent something, you feel bitter and angry about it.

EG *I resent being dependent on her.*

reservation /rɛzəˈveɪʃən/
reservations

NOUN

1 If you have reservations about something, you are not sure that it is good or right.

EG *This is the one reservation I have about the book.*

2 If you make a reservation, you arrange for something such as a hotel room or a table in a restaurant to be kept for you.

EG *I'd like to make a reservation for next Monday.*

reserve /rɪˈzɜːv/
reserves reserving reserved

VERB

1 If you reserve something, you arrange for it to be kept specially for you.

EG *They reserved two seats on the flight.*

EG *A double room had been*

reserved for him.

NOUN

2 a supply of something for future use

EG *... the world's oil reserves*

resident /'rezɪdənt/
residents

NOUN

1 The residents of a house or area are the people who live there.

EG *... complaints by local residents*

ADJECTIVE

2 If someone is resident in a town or country, they live there.

EG *He had been resident in Brussels since 1967.*

resign /rɪ'zaɪn/
resigns resigning resigned

VERB

1 If you resign from a job, you formally announce that you are leaving it.

EG *... after he resigned as chairman*

2 If you **resign yourself to** an unpleasant situation, you accept it.

EG *He seemed to resign himself to being unemployed.*

resignation /rezɪg'neɪʃən/
resignations

NOUN

1 Someone's resignation is a formal statement of their intention to leave a job.

EG *He has accepted my resignation.*

2 Resignation is the attitude of someone who accepts an unpleasant situation or fact.

EG *She spoke with quiet resignation.*

resist /rɪ'zɪst/
resists resisting resisted

VERB

1 If you resist something, you refuse to accept it and try to prevent it.

EG *He resisted demands for a public enquiry.*

2 If you **resist doing** something, you stop yourself from doing it, although you want to do it.

EG *She cannot resist giving him advice.*

resistance /rɪ'zɪstəns/
resistances

NOUN

1 Resistance to something such as change is a refusal to accept it.

EG *... his stubborn resistance to anything new*

2 Resistance to an attack is when people fight back.

EG *The demonstrators offered no resistance.*

resolution /rezə'lu:ʃən/
resolutions

NOUN

1 a formal decision taken at a meeting

EG *The French government supported the resolution.*

2 Resolution is determination.

EG *She acted with great resolution.*

3 If you make a resolution, you decide to try very hard to do something.

EG *She made a resolution to get fit.*

EG *a New Year's resolution*

4 A FORMAL USE

The resolution of a problem is the solving of it.

EG *... a peaceful resolution to the crisis*

resolve /rɪ'zɒlv/
resolves resolving resolved

VERB

1 If you resolve a problem, you find a solution to it.

EG *We must find a way of resolving these problems.*

2 If you **resolve to do**

something, you make a firm decision to do it.
EG *He resolved to wait until she called him.*

resort /rɪ'zɔːt/
resorts resorting resorted

VERB
1 If you **resort to** a course of action, you do it because you have no other choice.
EG *... people who resort to violence*

NOUN
2 a place where people spend their holidays
EG *... a ski resort*

3 If you do something **as a last resort**, you do it because you can find no other way of solving a problem.
EG *As a last resort, they can sleep here.*

resource /rɪ'zɔːs/
resources

NOUN
The resources of a country, organization, or person are the materials, money, or skills they have.
EG *... Britain's energy resources*

respect /rɪs'pekt/
respects respecting respected

VERB
1 If you respect someone, you have a high opinion of their character or ideas.
EG *He needs the advice of people he respects.*

2 If you respect someone's rights or wishes, you avoid doing things that they would dislike or regard as wrong.
EG *I respected her wishes and remained silent.*

NOUN

3 If you have **respect for** someone, you have a high opinion of their character or ideas.
EG *I have great respect for him as an artist.*

4 If you show respect for someone, you avoid doing things that they would dislike or regard as wrong.
EG *... a complete lack of respect*

5 You can say **in this respect** and **in many respects** to show that what you are saying applies to a particular thing or number of things.
EG *In this respect we are different.*
EG *In many respects, nothing has changed.*

respectable /rɪs'pektəbl/

ADJECTIVE
1 approved of by society and regarded as morally correct
EG *... a respectable member of the community*

2 adequate or reasonable
EG *... a respectable rate of economic growth*

respectively /rɪs'pektɪvlɪ/

ADVERB
in the same order as the items just mentioned
EG *Their sons, Ben and Joe, were three and six respectively.*

respond /rɪs'pɒnd/
responds responding responded

VERB
When you **respond to** something, you react to it by doing or saying something.
EG *He is likely to respond positively to the request.*
EG *I wonder how she'll respond.*

response /rɪs'pɒns/
responses

A B C D E F G H I J K L M N O P Q R S T U V W X Y Z

NOUN
Your response to something is your reaction or reply to it.
EG *There has been no response to his remarks yet.*

responsibility /rɪspɒnsɪˈbɪlɪtɪ/
responsibilities

NOUN
1 If you have responsibility for something or someone, it is your duty to deal with it or to help them.
EG *The garden was his responsibility.*
EG *As a doctor, she has a responsibility to her patients.*
2 If you accept responsibility for something that has happened, you agree that you were to blame for it.
EG *We must all accept responsibility for our own mistakes.*

responsible /rɪsˈpɒnsɪbl/

ADJECTIVE
1 If you are **responsible for** something that has happened, it is your fault.
EG *Who's responsible for this mess?*
2 If you are **responsible for** something, it is your duty to deal with it.
EG *The children were responsible for cleaning their own rooms.*
3 A responsible person behaves properly, without needing to be supervised.
EG *... the need for responsible parents*

rest /rɛst/
rests resting rested

NOUN
1 the rest of something is all the remaining parts of it
EG *He was unable to travel with the rest of the team.*

EG *She regretted it for the rest of her life.*
☑ If you are talking about something that cannot be counted, the verb following 'rest' is singular: *the rest of the food was delicious*. If you are talking about several people or things, the verb is plural: *the rest of the boys were delighted*.
2 If you have a rest, you do not do anything active for a while.
EG *Try to get some rest.*
EG *I need a rest.*

VERB
3 If you rest, you do not do anything active for a while.
EG *Go back to bed and rest.*
4 If you rest something somewhere, or if it rests there, its weight is supported there.
EG *She rested her head on his shoulder.*

restaurant /ˈrɛstərɒŋ/
restaurants

NOUN
a place where you can buy and eat a meal
EG *... an Italian restaurant*

restore /rɪˈstɔːʳ/
restores restoring restored

VERB
To restore something means to cause it to exist again or to return to its previous state.
EG *The army was brought in to restore order.*
EG *He was anxious to restore his reputation.*

restrict /rɪsˈtrɪkt/
restricts restricting restricted

VERB
1 If you restrict something, you put a limit on it to stop it

becoming too large.
EG ... an attempt to restrict the number of cars entering the city

2 To restrict someone's movements or actions means to prevent them from moving or acting freely.
EG ... another law that restricts what we can do

restriction /rɪsˈtrɪkʃən/
restrictions

NOUN
a rule or situation that limits what you can do
EG ... financial restrictions

result /rɪˈzʌlt/
results resulting resulted

NOUN
1 The result of an action or situation is the situation that is caused by it.
EG As a result of the incident he lost his job.
EG The test had disastrous results.
2 The result of a contest, calculation, or exam is the final score, figures, or marks at the end of it.
EG ... the football results
EG ... the laboratory that calculated the results

VERB
3 If something **results in** a particular event, it causes that event to happen.
EG Half of all road accidents result in head injuries.
4 If something **results from** a particular event, it is caused by that event.
EG The fire had resulted from carelessness.

resume /rɪˈzjuːm/
resumes resuming resumed

VERB

If you resume an activity, or if it resumes, it begins again.
EG The search resumed early today.

retain /rɪˈteɪn/
retains retaining retained

VERB
A FORMAL WORD
To retain something means to keep it.
EG The plant retains moisture well.

retire /rɪˈtaɪər/
retires retiring retired

VERB
When older people retire, they leave their job and stop working.
EG Gladys retired at the age of 68.

retirement /rɪˈtaɪəmənt/

NOUN
Retirement is the time when someone retires, or the period after they have retired.
EG He is on the verge of retirement.
EG ... the house she had bought for her retirement

retreat /rɪˈtriːt/
retreats retreating retreated

VERB
If you retreat, you move away from someone or something.
EG He retreated to the kitchen to consider their quarrel.
EG ... after the French forces retreated

return /rɪˈtɜːn/
returns returning returned

VERB
1 If you return to a place or to a particular condition, you go back to that place or condition.
EG ... three days after returning to Britain
EG Life had not yet returned to normal.

2 If you return something to someone, you give it back to them.
EG *He returned her passport.*
EG *Why couldn't she return his affection?*

NOUN

3 Your return is your arrival back at a place or former condition.
EG *... since his return from Berlin*
EG *He called for an end to strikes and a return to work.*

4 The return of something is the act of giving or putting it back.
EG *... Japan's demand for the return of the islands*

5 A return or a **return ticket** is a ticket for a journey to a place and back again.
EG *... a return ticket to Manchester*

6 If you do something **in return** for what someone has done for you, you do it because of what they did.
EG *There's little I can do for him in return.*

reveal /rɪ'viːl/
reveals revealing revealed
VERB

1 If you reveal something, you tell people about it.
EG *They were not ready to reveal any details of the arrest.*

2 If you reveal something that has been hidden, you uncover it.
EG *She drew the curtains back to reveal a huge garden.*

revenge /rɪ'vɛndʒ/
NOUN
Revenge involves hurting someone who has hurt you.
EG *... to take revenge on the man who had deceived her*

reverse /rɪ'vɜːs/
reverses reversing reversed
VERB

1 When someone reverses a process or decision, they change it to its opposite.
EG *They won't reverse the decision to increase prices.*

2 If you reverse the order of things, you arrange them in the opposite order.
EG *The aim of the game is to reverse the order of the coins.*

3 When you reverse or reverse a car, you drive it backwards.
EG *She reversed into the garage.*

NOUN

4 the reverse is the opposite of what has just been said or done
EG *It's not difficult, quite the reverse.*

ADJECTIVE

5 Reverse means opposite to what has just been described.
EG *Instead of bringing peace, the meeting may have the reverse effect.*

review /rɪ'vjuː/
reviews reviewing reviewed
NOUN

1 an article or a talk on television or radio, giving an opinion of a new book, play, or film
EG *... a book review*

2 When there is a review of a situation or system, it is examined to decide whether changes are needed.
EG *The policy is due for review this year.*

VERB

3 When someone reviews a book, play, or film, they write an account expressing their opinion of it.
EG *Both films will be reviewed next week.*

4 If you review a situation or system, you examine it in order to decide whether changes are needed.

EG *The government will review the situation in June.*

revise /rɪˈvaɪz/
revises revising revised

VERB

If you revise something, you alter or correct it.
EG *I found myself revising my opinion of him.*

revive /rɪˈvaɪv/
revives reviving revived

VERB

1 When something is revived, it becomes active or successful again.
EG *... an attempt to revive the economy*

2 If you revive someone who has fainted, or if they revive, they become conscious again.
EG *She could not be revived.*

revolution /rɛvəˈluːʃən/
revolutions

NOUN

1 an attempt by a large group of people to change their country's political system, using force
EG *... the October revolution*

2 an important change in an area of human activity
EG *... the industrial revolution*

revolutionary /rɛvəˈluːʃənrɪ/
revolutionaries

ADJECTIVE

1 involving great changes
EG *... a revolutionary new system*

NOUN

2 a person who takes part in a revolution
EG *The revolutionaries laid down their arms.*

reward /rɪˈwɔːd/
rewards rewarding rewarded

NOUN

1 something you receive because you have done something good
EG *... a £50,000 reward for information leading to his arrest*
EG *... the emotional rewards of parenthood*

VERB

2 If you reward someone, you give them a reward.
EG *He held the door open for her and was rewarded with a smile.*

rhyme /raɪm/
rhymes rhyming rhymed

VERB

1 If one word **rhymes with** another or if two words rhyme, they have a very similar sound.
EG *Sally rhymes with valley.*

NOUN

2 a word that rhymes with another
EG *He couldn't find a rhyme for 'orange'.*

rhythm /ˈrɪðm/
rhythms

NOUN

a regular series of sounds, movements, or actions
EG *Her body swayed to the rhythm of the music.*

rib /rɪb/
ribs

NOUN

Your ribs are the curved bones that go from your spine to your chest.
EG *... a broken rib*

ribbon /ˈrɪbən/
ribbons

NOUN

a long, narrow piece of cloth used as a fastening or decoration
EG *She had tied back her hair with a ribbon.*

rice /raɪs/

NOUN

A
B

Rice consists of white or brown grains taken from a cereal plant.
EG ... *a bowl of fried rice*

rich /rɪtʃ/
richer richest; riches

C
D

ADJECTIVE
1 Someone who is **rich** has a lot of money or possessions.
EG *Their one aim in life is to get rich.*

E
F

2 Something that is **rich in** something contains a large amount of it.
EG *Bananas are rich in vitamin A.*

G
H

3 Rich food contains a large amount of fat, oil, or sugar.
EG ... *the dangers of eating too much rich food*

I
J

PLURAL NOUN
4 riches are valuable possessions or large amounts of money
EG *Some people want fame or riches.*

K
L

rid /rɪd/
rids ridding rid

M
N

VERB
1 A FORMAL USE
If you **rid** a place or person **of** something unpleasant, you succeed in removing it.
EG *Why couldn't he rid himself of these thoughts?*

O
P

ADJECTIVE
2 When you **get rid of** something you do not want, you remove or destroy it.
EG *I'll never get rid of these stains.*

Q
R

ridden /'rɪdn/
past participle of **ride**

S

ride /raɪd/
rides riding rode ridden

T
U

VERB
1 When you ride a horse or a bicycle, you sit on it and control it as it moves along.

V
W
X
Y
Z

EG *He mounted his horse and rode away.*

2 When you **ride** in a car, you travel in it.
EG ... *a comfortable car to ride in*

NOUN
3 a journey on a horse or bicycle, or in a vehicle
EG ... *the long ride to work*

ridiculous /rɪ'dɪkjuləs/

ADJECTIVE
very foolish
EG *It's ridiculous to suggest that we're having an affair.*

rifle /'raɪfl/
rifles

NOUN
a gun with a long barrel
EG ... *an automatic rifle*

rig /rɪg/
rigs rigging rigged

VERB
1 If someone rigs a contest, they dishonestly arrange for a particular person to succeed.
EG *She accused her opponents of rigging the vote.*

NOUN
2 a large structure used for extracting oil or gas from the ground or the sea bed
EG ... *an oil rig*

right /raɪt/
rights

NOUN
1 You use 'right' to refer to principles of morally correct behaviour.
EG *At least he knew right from wrong.*

2 If you have a **right to do** something, you are morally or legally entitled to do it. Your **rights** are the things you are entitled to do.

EG *People have the right to read whatever they want.*

EG *You must stand up for your rights.*

3 The right is one of two opposite directions, sides, or positions. If you are facing north and you turn to the right, you will be facing east.

EG *On her right was a large house.*

EG *They turned their heads slowly from left to right.*

4 the right refers to people who support the political ideas of capitalism rather than socialism

EG *... his colleagues on the right of the party*

ADJECTIVE OR ADVERB

5 correct and in agreement with the facts

EG *That clock never tells the right time.*

EG *You're absolutely right.*

EG *He guessed right about some things.*

6 on or towards the right of something

EG *His right arm was broken.*

EG *Turn right at the corner.*

7 You use 'right' to refer to actions that are considered to be morally or legally correct.

EG *I don't think it's right to leave children alone.*

EG *Treat him right and he'll be your friend forever.*

ADJECTIVE

8 The right decision, action, or person is the best or most suitable one.

EG *They decided the time was right for their escape.*

EG *She's the right person for the job.*

ADVERB

9 You can use 'right' to emphasize the exact position or time of

something.

EG *I'm right here.*

EG *I had to decide right then.*

10 You can use 'right' to indicate that you have dealt with one thing and are going on to another.

EG *Right, who's next?*

right-wing /raɪtˈwɪŋ/

ADJECTIVE

A right-wing person or group has conservative or capitalist views.

EG *... a right-wing government*

ring /rɪŋ/

rings ringing rang rung

VERB

1 If you ring someone, you phone them.

EG *She rang him at home.*

2 When a telephone or bell rings, it makes a clear, loud sound.

EG *The phone was ringing all morning.*

EG *He heard the school bell ring.*

NOUN

3 the sound made by a telephone or bell

EG *She picked the phone up after a couple of rings.*

4 a small circle of metal that you wear on your finger

EG *... a wedding ring*

5 an object or group of things in the shape of a circle

EG *... onion rings*

rinse /rɪns/

rinses rinsing rinsed

VERB

When you rinse something, you wash it in clean water.

EG *Rinse the rice before cooking.*

riot /ˈraɪət/

riots rioting rioted

NOUN

1 When there is a riot, a crowd of

people behave violently in a public place.
EG *Two other prisoners were injured in the riots.*

VERB
2 When people riot, they behave violently in a public place.
EG *They rioted in protest against the government.*

rip /rɪp/
rips ripping ripped

VERB
1 When you rip something, you tear it.
EG *I tried not to rip the paper as I unwrapped it.*

2 If you rip something **away** or **off**, you remove it quickly and with great force.
EG *One of the hinges was ripped away from the frame.*
EG *Her earring had been ripped off.*

NOUN
3 a long split in a piece of cloth or paper
EG *There were several rips in her dress.*

ripe /raɪp/
riper ripest

ADJECTIVE
Ripe fruit or grain is fully developed and ready to be eaten.
EG *... a ripe, juicy plum*

rise /raɪz/
rises rising rose risen

VERB
1 If something rises, it moves upwards.
EG *Wilson watched the smoke rise from his cigarette.*
EG *... before the sun rose*

2 A FORMAL USE
When you rise, you stand up.
EG *Luther rose slowly from the chair.*

3 A FORMAL USE

When you rise, you get out of bed.
EG *I rose early.*

4 If land rises, it slopes upwards.
EG *... the hills that rose behind him*

5 If a sound rises, it becomes higher.
EG *His voice rose almost to a scream.*

6 If an amount rises, it increases.
EG *Profits rose to over £2 million.*

NOUN
7 an increase
EG *He's due for a pay rise.*

8 Someone's rise is the process by which they become more powerful or successful.
EG *... his rise to fame*

9 If something **gives rise to** an event or situation, it causes it to happen.
EG *His lack of experience gave rise to two problems.*

risk /rɪsk/
risks risking risked

NOUN
1 If there is a risk of something unpleasant, there is a possibility that it will happen.
EG *There's a small risk that his party might lose.*
EG *... a drug that reduces the risk of infection*

2 Someone or something that is a risk is likely to cause harm or have undesirable results.
EG *Policemen face many risks these days.*
EG *You're taking a risk by telling her.*

VERB
3 If you risk something unpleasant, you do something knowing that the unpleasant thing might happen as a result.
EG *If he doesn't play, he risks losing his place in the team.*

risky /ˈrɪskɪ/

ADJECTIVE

If something is risky, it is
dangerous or could fail.
EG *It's risky to try to predict the
outcome.*

rival /ˈraɪvl/
rivals

NOUN

Someone's rival is the person they
are competing with.
EG *He is well ahead of his nearest
rival.*

river /ˈrɪvəʳ/
rivers

NOUN

a large amount of water flowing in
a long line across land
EG *... on the banks of the river*

road /rəʊd/
roads

NOUN

a long piece of hard ground built
between two places so that people
can travel along it easily
EG *There was very little traffic on
the roads.*
EG *They will travel by road to
Jordan.*

roar /rɔːʳ/
roars roaring roared

VERB

1 If something roars, it makes a
very loud noise.
EG *The crowd roared every time he
got the ball.*

NOUN

2 a very loud noise
EG *... the roar of traffic*

roast /rəʊst/
roasts roasting roasted

VERB

1 If you roast meat or other food,
you cook it using dry heat in an
oven or over a fire.
EG *They roasted a chicken over the
fire.*

ADJECTIVE

2 Roast meat has been roasted.
EG *... roast beef*

rob /rɒb/
robs robbing robbed

VERB

If someone robs a person or place,
they steal money or property from
them.
EG *He attempted to rob a bank.*

robbery /ˈrɒbərɪ/
robberies

NOUN

Robbery is the crime of stealing
money or property.
EG *The gang committed dozens of
armed robberies.*

robot /ˈrəʊbɒt/
robots

NOUN

a machine which moves and
performs tasks automatically
EG *... the use of robots in industry*

rock /rɒk/
rocks rocking rocked

NOUN

1 Rock is the hard substance
which the Earth is made of.
EG *hills of bare rock*

2 a piece of rock, either large or
small
EG *He climbed up onto the rocks.*
EG *She picked up a rock and threw
it into the lake.*

3 Rock or **rock music** is music
with a strong beat, usually
involving electric guitars and
drums.
EG *... the singer in a rock band*

VERB

4 When something rocks or when

A
B
C
D
E
F
G
H
I
J
K
L
M
N
O
P
Q
R
S
T
U
V
W
X
Y
Z

you rock it, it moves regularly backwards and forwards or from side to side.

EG *The boat rocked from side to side.*

EG *She rocked the baby in her arms.*

rocket /'rɒkɪt/
rockets

NOUN

a space vehicle, usually shaped like a long pointed tube

EG *... a space rocket*

rod /rɒd/
rods

NOUN

a long, thin bar made of wood or metal

EG *... a fishing rod*

rode /rəud/

past tense of **ride**

role /rəul/
roles

NOUN

1 The role of someone or something is their position or function in a situation.

EG *He played a major role in getting the two sides to meet.*

2 An actor's role is the character that he or she plays.

EG *He gave her a leading role in his film.*

roll /rəul/
rolls rolling rolled

VERB

1 If something rolls or if you roll it, it moves along a surface, turning over many times.

EG *The ball rolled into the net.*

EG *We rolled the stone down the hill.*

2 If you roll something or if you **roll** it **up**, you wrap it around itself so that it has a rounded shape.

EG *... a rolled-up newspaper*

NOUN

3 A roll of paper or cloth is a long piece of it that has been rolled into a tube.

EG *... a roll of film*

4 a very small, circular loaf of bread

EG *... a roll and butter*

Roman Catholic Roman Catholics

ADJECTIVE

1 relating or belonging to the branch of the Christian church that accepts the Pope as its leader

EG *... a Roman Catholic priest*

NOUN

2 someone who belongs to the Roman Catholic church

EG *Like her, Maria was a Roman Catholic.*

romance /rə'mæns/
romances

NOUN

a relationship between two people who are in love with each other

EG *... a holiday romance*

romantic /rə'mæntɪk/

ADJECTIVE

1 connected with sexual love

EG *... a romantic comedy*

EG *... a romantic dinner for two*

2 Romantic ideas are ideas that are not realistic.

EG *He has a romantic view of rural society.*

roo /ruː/
roos

NOUN

AN INFORMAL WORD

In Australian English, a roo is a kangaroo.

EG *... a baby roo*

roof /ruːf/
roofs

NOUN
The roof of a building or car is the covering on top of it.
EG ... *a white cottage with a red roof*

room /ruːm/
rooms

NOUN
1 one of the separate sections in a building
EG *He excused himself and left the room.*
EG ... *a hotel room*
2 If there is **room for** something, there is enough space for it.
EG *There wasn't enough room for his bags.*
EG *There's still plenty of room.*

root /ruːt/
roots

NOUN
1 The roots of a plant are the parts that grow underground.
EG ... *the twisted roots of an apple tree*
2 The root of a hair or tooth is the part beneath the skin.
EG *They pulled her hair out by the roots.*
3 The root of a problem is the thing that caused it.
EG *We got to the root of the problem.*

PLURAL NOUN
4 You can refer to the place or culture that you come from as your **roots**.
EG *I am proud of my Brazilian roots.*

rope /rəʊp/
ropes

NOUN
a length of thick string, made by twisting together several thinner pieces of string
EG *He tied the rope around his waist.*

rose /rəʊz/
roses

1 Rose is the past tense of **rise**
NOUN
2 a flower with a pleasant smell that grows on a bush
EG ... *a bunch of roses*

rot /rɒt/
rots rotting rotted

VERB
1 When food, wood, or other substances rot, or when something rots them, they decay and fall apart.
EG ... *the smell of rotting fish*
EG *Sugar rots your teeth.*

NOUN
2 Rot is the condition that affects things when they decay.
EG *The timber frame was not protected against rot.*

rotten /'rɒtn/

ADJECTIVE
1 Something that is rotten has decayed.
EG ... *rotten eggs*
2 AN INFORMAL USE
bad or unpleasant
EG *I think it's a rotten idea.*
EG *That's a rotten thing to say!*

rough /rʌf/
rougher roughest

ADJECTIVE
1 not smooth
EG *His hands were hard and rough.*
2 using too much force
EG *Don't be so rough or you'll break it.*
3 dangerous or violent
EG ... *a rough part of town*
4 difficult or unpleasant
EG *Teachers have had a rough time.*
5 A rough guess or estimate is one

A
B
C
D
E
F
G
H
I
J
K
L
M
N
O
P
Q
R
S
T
U
V
W
X
Y
Z

that is approximately correct.
EG *At a rough guess, it is five times more profitable.*

roughly /'rʌflɪ/

ADVERB
approximately
EG *... a woman of roughly his own age*

round /raund/
rounder roundest; rounds rounding rounded

ADJECTIVE
1 Something round is shaped like a ball or a circle.
EG *a large round loaf*

PREPOSITION OR ADVERB
☑ When 'round' is used as a preposition or an adverb, you can also use 'around': *round the table*; *around the table*. 'Around' is much more common in American English.
2 If something is round something else, it surrounds it.
EG *They were sitting round the kitchen table.*
EG *... a house with a fence all round*
3 If something goes round something else, it moves in a circle with that thing at its centre.
EG *He wants to sail round the world.*
EG *The car had crashed but the wheels continued to go round.*
4 You can refer to an area near a place as the area round it.
EG *There's nothing to do round here.*
EG *The owner showed them round.*

PREPOSITION
5 If you go round a corner or obstacle, you go to the other side of it.
EG *Suddenly a car came round the corner.*

ADVERB

6 If you turn or look round, you turn so that you are facing in a different direction.
EG *I called his name and he turned round.*
7 If you move things round, you move them so that they are in different places.
EG *He's always moving the furniture round.*
8 If you go round to someone's house, you visit them.
EG *I'll be round at 7.30.*

NOUN
9 one of a series of events, especially in a sports competition
EG *... the third round of the Cup*
EG *... a further round of talks*

VERB
10 If you round a corner or bend, you move in the direction of the corner or bend.
EG *The house disappeared as we rounded the corner.*

round up

VERB
If you round up people or animals, you gather them together.
EG *The police rounded up a number of suspects.*

route /ruːt/
routes

NOUN
a way from one place to another
EG *... the most direct route to the town centre*

routine /ruːˈtiːn/
routines

ADJECTIVE
1 Routine activities are done regularly as a normal part of a procedure.
EG *... a series of routine medical tests*

NOUN

2 the usual way or order in which you do things
EG ... *their daily routine*

row /rəʊ/
rows rowing rowed

NOUN
1 A row of people or things is several of them arranged in a line.
EG ... *a row of pretty little cottages*
EG ... *a seat in the front row*

VERB
2 When you row a boat, you make it move through the water using two long poles called oars.
EG *He rowed quickly to the shore.*

row /raʊ/
rows rowing rowed

NOUN
1 a serious argument
EG *We had a terrible row about money.*
2 If someone or something makes a row, they make a lot of noise.
EG *Our little van made an awful row.*

VERB
3 If people row, they have a noisy argument.
EG *They row all the time.*
EG *He had rowed with his girlfriend.*

royal /ˈrɔɪəl/

ADJECTIVE
belonging to or involving a queen, a king, or a member of their family
EG ... *the royal family*

royalty /ˈrɔɪəltɪ/
royalties

NOUN
1 The members of a royal family are sometimes referred to as royalty.
EG ... *a ceremony attended by royalty*

PLURAL NOUN

2 royalties are payments made to authors and musicians from the sales of their books or records
EG *He earned very little from the royalties.*

rub /rʌb/
rubs rubbing rubbed

VERB
1 If you rub something, you move your hand or a cloth backwards and forwards over it.
EG *He rubbed his eyes.*
2 If you rub a substance onto a surface, you spread it over the surface with your hand.
EG *He rubbed oil into my back.*

rubber /ˈrʌbər/
rubbers

NOUN
1 Rubber is a strong, elastic substance used for making tyres, boots, and other products.
EG ... *the smell of burning rubber*
2 a small piece of rubber that you use to remove mistakes made when writing or drawing
EG ... *a pencil with a rubber at the end*

rubbish /ˈrʌbɪʃ/

NOUN
1 Rubbish is unwanted things or waste material.
EG ... *a dustbin piled high with rubbish*

2 AN INFORMAL USE
You can refer to something foolish or something of very poor quality as rubbish.
EG *"Rubbish!" he said. "You're imagining it."*
EG *He described her book as absolute rubbish.*

rude /ruːd/
ruder rudest

A
B
C
D
E
F
G
H
I
J
K
L
M
N
O
P
Q
R
S
T
U
V
W
X
Y
Z

ADJECTIVE

1 Someone who is rude is not polite.

EG *He's rude to her friends.*

2 Something that is rude is likely to embarrass or offend people because it refers to sex or to activities such as going to the toilet.

EG *... a rude joke*

rug /rʌg/
rugs

NOUN

a small, thick carpet

EG *... a Persian rug*

rugby /'rʌgbɪ/

NOUN

Rugby is a game played by two teams, who try to carry a ball past a line at their opponents' end of the pitch.

EG *... a game of rugby*

ruin /'ru:ɪn/
ruins ruining ruined

VERB

1 If you ruin something, you destroy or spoil it completely.

EG *He has ruined his chances of ever being elected.*

EG *Dinner was ruined.*

NOUN

2 A ruin or the **ruins** of something refers to the parts that are left after it has been severely damaged.

EG *It was splendid once, but it is a ruin now.*

EG *... the ruins of an ancient monastery*

rule /ru:l/
rules ruling ruled

NOUN

1 Rules are instructions which tell you what you are allowed to do.

EG *... the rules of basketball*

EG *This was against the rules.*

2 as a rule means usually or generally

EG *As a rule, she eats dinner with us.*

VERB

3 The person or group that rules a country controls its affairs.

EG *For four centuries foreigners have ruled Angola.*

rule out

VERB

If you rule out an idea or course of action, you reject it.

EG *Murder cannot be ruled out.*

ruler /'ru:ləʳ/
rulers

NOUN

1 a person who rules a country

EG *... the rulers of the country*

2 a long, flat object with straight edges, used for measuring things or drawing straight lines

EG *... a 12-inch ruler*

rumour /'ru:məʳ/
rumours
US **rumor**

NOUN

a piece of information that people are talking about, which may or may not be true

EG *There are rumours that he is about to resign.*

run /rʌn/
runs running ran

VERB

1 When you run, you move quickly so that both feet briefly leave the ground.

EG *Antonia ran to meet them.*

2 If a road or river runs in a particular direction, that is its course.

EG *The road runs all the way to the coast.*

3 If you run your hand or an object over something, you move it over it.
EG *She ran her finger down the list.*
4 If someone runs in an election, they stand as a candidate.
EG *He announced he would run for President.*
5 If you run an organization, you are in charge of it.
EG *Is this any way to run a country?*
6 If you run an experiment, a computer program, or other process, you start it and let it continue.
EG *He ran a series of computer checks.*
7 When a machine is running, or when you are running it, it is operating.
EG *He left the car running while he went inside.*
8 If a bus or train runs somewhere, it travels there at set times.
EG *The trains run until midnight.*
9 If you run water, you turn on a tap to make it flow.
EG *We heard him running the kitchen tap.*
10 If a liquid runs somewhere, it flows there.
EG *Tears were running down her cheeks.*
11 If the dye in something runs, the colour comes out when it is washed.
EG *... colours that are guaranteed not to run*
12 If an event or contract runs for a particular time, it continues for that time.
EG *The play ran for three years in the West End.*

NOUN
13 If you go for a run, you run for pleasure or exercise.

EG *... a cross-country run*

run away

VERB
If you **run away from** a place, you leave it suddenly or secretly.
EG *I ran away from home when I was 16.*
EG *We decided to run away together.*

run out

VERB
If something runs out or if you **run out of** it, you have no more of it left.
EG *We've run out of coffee.*

run over

VERB
If a vehicle runs someone over, it knocks them down.
EG *He ran over a six-year-old child as he was driving home.*

rung /rʌŋ/
past participle of **ring**

runner-up /rʌnər'ʌp/
runners-up

NOUN
a person or team that comes second in a race or competition
EG *The runners-up will receive a case of wine.*

rural /'ruərl/

ADJECTIVE
relating to or involving the countryside
EG *... rural areas*

rush /rʌʃ/
rushes rushing rushed

VERB
1 If you rush somewhere, you go there quickly.
EG *I've got to rush.*
EG *She was rushed to hospital in an ambulance.*
2 If you rush something, you do it

in a hurry.

EG *Chew your food well and do not rush meals.*

3 If you **are rushed into** something, you do it without thinking about it for long enough.

EG *She won't be rushed into marriage.*

NOUN

4 a situation in which you need to go somewhere or do something very quickly

EG *The men left in a rush.*

EG *It was a real rush to get here on time.*

5 If there is a **rush for** something, many people are trying to get it or do it.

EG *... the rush for tickets*

Russian /'rʌʃən/
Russians

ADJECTIVE

1 belonging or relating to Russia

EG *... a Russian accent*

NOUN

2 someone who comes from Russia

EG *... a tall Russian*

3 Russian is the main language spoken in Russia.

EG *She speaks fluent Russian.*

rust /rʌst/

NOUN

Rust is a brown substance that forms on iron or steel when it comes into contact with water.

EG *... an abandoned car, covered in rust*

ruthless /'ruːθlɪs/

ADJECTIVE

very harsh or cruel

EG *... a ruthless criminal*

sack /sæk/
sacks sacking sacked

NOUN
1 a large bag made of rough material
EG *... a sack of potatoes*

2 AN INFORMAL USE
If you **get the sack**, your employer tells you that you can no longer work for them.
EG *One girl got the sack for telling lies.*

VERB
3 AN INFORMAL USE
If you are sacked, you are told by your employer that you no can longer work for them.
EG *I was sacked from my job as a postman.*

sacrifice /'sækrɪfaɪs/
sacrifices sacrificing sacrificed

VERB
1 If you sacrifice something valuable or important, you give it up in order to obtain something else.
EG *She sacrificed her marriage for her career.*

2 If someone sacrifices an animal, they kill it in a special religious ceremony.
EG *The priest sacrificed a chicken.*

NOUN
3 an act of sacrificing something
EG *He was willing to make any sacrifice for peace.*

sad /sæd/
sadder saddest

ADJECTIVE
1 If you are sad, you feel unhappy.
EG *I will be sad to leave this house.*

2 Something sad makes you feel unhappy.
EG *... a sad story*

sadness /'sædnɪs/
NOUN
Sadness is the state of feeling sad.
EG *... with a mixture of sadness and joy*

safe /seɪf/
safer safest; safes

ADJECTIVE
1 Something that is safe does not cause harm or danger.
EG *The doll is safe for children.*

2 If you are safe, you are not in any danger.
EG *Where is Sophie? Is she safe?*

NOUN
3 a strong metal box with special locks, in which you can keep valuable things
EG *It's best to keep your valuables in a safe.*

safety /'seɪftɪ/
NOUN
Safety is the state of being free from harm or danger.
EG *Wear a seat belt for your own safety.*
EG *... fears about the safety of nuclear power*

said /sɛd/
past participle and past tense of **say**

sail /seɪl/
sails sailing sailed

VERB
1 When a ship sails, it moves across water.
EG *The boat will sail from Zeebrugge.*

2 If you sail somewhere, you go there by ship.
EG *She sailed from Hong Kong to Singapore.*

NOUN
3 Sails are large pieces of material attached to a boat so that it can be moved by the wind.
EG *... every time they lowered the sails*

saint /seɪnt/
saints

NOUN
a dead person who is officially honoured by the Christian Church because they lived a very holy life
EG *... Saint John*

sake /seɪk/

NOUN
1 If you do something **for** someone's **sake**, you do it in order to help or please them.
EG *Do it for my sake!*

2 If you do something **for the sake of** a particular thing, you do it for that purpose or reason.
EG *He gave up smoking for the sake of his health.*

salad /'sæləd/
salads

NOUN
a mixture of raw vegetables
EG *... a green salad*

salary /'sælərɪ/
salaries

NOUN
a regular monthly payment to an employee
EG *She earns a huge salary.*

sale /seɪl/
sales

NOUN
1 The sale of goods is the selling of them.

EG *... limits on the sale of alcohol*

2 an occasion when a shop sells things at a reduced price
EG *I bought these jeans in a sale.*

3 If something is **for sale**, it is available to buy.
EG *The company is not for sale.*

PLURAL NOUN
4 The **sales** of a product are the quantity that are sold.
EG *Sales have increased this year.*

salt /sɔːlt/

NOUN
Salt is a white substance that is used to flavour and preserve food.
EG *... salt and pepper*

same /seɪm/

ADJECTIVE
1 If two or more things are **the same**, they are very similar or exactly alike.
EG *The houses were all the same.*
EG *She was wearing the same dress as me.*

2 You use **the same** to indicate that you are referring to only one thing or person and not to different ones.
EG *They were born in the same town.*

3 Someone or something that remains **the same** has not changed.
EG *Does he still look the same?*

sample /'sɑːmpl/
samples

NOUN
A sample of something is a small amount of it that you can try or test.
EG *We're giving away 2000 free samples.*
EG *They took a sample of my blood.*

sand /sænd/

NOUN
Sand is a powder that consists of very small pieces of stone.
EG ... the sand on the beach

sandal /'sændl/
sandals

NOUN
Sandals are light shoes with straps, usually worn in warm weather.
EG ... a pair of sandals

sandwich /'sændwɪtʃ/
sandwiches

NOUN
A sandwich is two slices of bread with a layer of food between them.
EG ... a cheese sandwich

sang /sæŋ/
past tense of sing

sanitary towel sanitary towels

NOUN
Sanitary towels are pads of thick, soft material which women wear during their periods.
EG ... a box of sanitary towels

sank /sæŋk/
past tense of sink

sat /sæt/
past participle and past tense of sit

satellite /'sætəlaɪt/
satellites

NOUN
an object which has been sent into space in order to collect information or as part of a communications system
EG ... a communications satellite
EG ... satellite TV

satisfaction /sætɪs'fækʃən/

NOUN
Satisfaction is the pleasure you feel when you do something that you wanted or needed to do.

EG Both sides expressed satisfaction with the results.

satisfactory /sætɪs'fæktərɪ/

ADJECTIVE
acceptable or adequate
EG I never got a satisfactory answer.

satisfied /'sætɪsfaɪd/

ADJECTIVE
If you are **satisfied with** something, you are happy because you have got what you wanted or needed.
EG We were not satisfied with the results.

Saturday /'sætədɪ/
Saturdays

NOUN
Saturday is the day between Friday and Sunday.
EG ... the big match on Saturday

sauce /sɔːs/
sauces

NOUN
a thick liquid which is served with other food
EG ... pasta with tomato sauce

saucepan /'sɔːspən/
saucepans

NOUN
a deep metal cooking pot with a handle and a lid
EG Place the rice in a saucepan of water.

saucer /'sɔːsər/
saucers

NOUN
a small curved plate on which you put a cup
EG ... a set of cups and saucers

sausage /'sɒsɪdʒ/
sausages

NOUN
a mixture of chopped meat and

herbs inside a long, thin skin

EG ... *pork sausages*

save /seɪv/

saves saving saved

VERB

1 If you save someone or something, you rescue them or help to keep them safe.

EG *He saved my life.*

EG ... *a final attempt to save 4,000 jobs*

2 If you save something, you keep it so that you can use it later.

EG *She saved the paper and used it to wrap Christmas presents.*

3 If you save or **save up**, you collect money, usually in order to buy something.

EG *He's saving up for a new car.*

4 If you save time, money, or effort, you prevent it from being wasted.

EG *You'll save time if you take a bus home.*

5 If a goalkeeper saves a shot, they prevent it from going into the goal.

EG *Wright's shot was saved by Walsh.*

savings /'seɪvɪŋz/

PLURAL NOUN

Your savings are the money that you have saved.

EG *I keep my savings in a bank account.*

saw /sɔː/

saws

1 Saw is the past tense of **see**

NOUN

2 a tool for cutting wood, which has a blade with sharp teeth along one edge

EG *He cut off the branch with a saw.*

say /seɪ/

says saying said

VERB

1 When you **say** something **to** someone, you speak words to them.

EG *What did he say to you?*

EG *"I'm sorry," he said.*

EG *Did he say where he was going?*

2 If a piece of writing says something, that is what is written there.

EG *It says here you must be over 18.*

3 You can use 'say' when you imagine a situation that might be true or when you give an example of something.

EG *Say you weren't married, what would you do then?*

EG ... *someone with, say, a few thousand pounds*

NOUN

4 If you **have a say** in something, you have the right to give your opinion and influence decisions.

EG *It's time we had a say in our own future.*

scale /skeɪl/

scales

NOUN

1 The scale of something is its size or extent.

EG *The scale of the programme is quite limited.*

EG ... *killing on a massive scale*

2 a set of levels or numbers that is used for measuring things

EG ... *an earthquake measuring 5.5 on the Richter scale*

PLURAL NOUN

3 scales are a piece of equipment for weighing things or people

EG ... *a set of bathroom scales*

scan /skæn/

scans scanning scanned

VERB

1 If you scan something, you look at it carefully.
EG *I scanned the advertisements in the newspaper.*

2 If a machine scans something, it examines it with a ray of light or X-rays.
EG *Our luggage was scanned at the airport.*

NOUN

3 an examination of part of the body with X-ray or laser equipment
EG *... a brain scan*

scandal /'skændl/
scandals

NOUN

a situation or event that people think is shocking and immoral
EG *... a financial scandal*

scar /skɑː/
scars scarring scarred

NOUN

1 a mark that is left on your skin after a wound has healed
EG *He had a scar on his forehead.*

VERB

2 If you **are scarred**, your skin is badly marked as a result of a wound.
EG *He was scarred for life after a fight.*

scarce /skeəs/
scarcer scarcest

ADJECTIVE

If something is scarce, there is not very much of it.
EG *Jobs are very scarce now.*

scarcely /'skeəslɪ/

ADVERB

1 almost not or not quite
EG *I could scarcely hear her.*
EG *I scarcely ever see him.*

2 certainly not
EG *It's scarcely surprising that she*

was upset.

scare /skeər/
scares scaring scared

VERB

If someone or something scares you, they frighten you.
EG *I didn't mean to scare you.*

scared /'skeəd/

ADJECTIVE

1 If you are **scared of** someone or something, you are frightened of them.
EG *I'm scared of dogs.*
EG *I was too scared to move.*

2 If you are scared that something might happen, you are worried that it might happen.
EG *I was scared that I might be sick.*

scarf /skɑːf/
scarfs or **scarves**

NOUN

a piece of cloth that you wear round your neck or head
EG *... a long woollen scarf*

scatter /'skætər/
scatters scattering scattered

VERB

If you scatter things somewhere, you throw or drop them all over an area.
EG *She scattered the petals over the grave.*

scene /siːn/
scenes

NOUN

1 a part of a play, film, or book in which a series of events happen in one place
EG *... the opening scenes of the film*

2 The scene of an event is the place where it happened.
EG *The gang left the scene soon afterwards.*

scent /sɛnt/
scents

NOUN
a smell, especially a pleasant one
EG *These flowers have a lovely scent.*

sceptical /ˈskɛptɪkl/
US **skeptical**

ADJECTIVE
If you are **sceptical about** something, you have doubts about it.
EG *John remained sceptical about his chances.*

schedule /ˈʃɛdjuːl/
schedules scheduling scheduled

NOUN
1 a plan that gives a list of events or tasks, together with the times at which each thing should be done
EG *He was forced to change his schedule.*

VERB
2 If something **is scheduled** to happen at a particular time, it is planned to happen at that time.
EG *New talks are scheduled for next month.*

scheme /skiːm/
schemes

NOUN
a plan or arrangement
EG *... a private pension scheme*

school /skuːl/
schools

NOUN
1 a place where children are educated
EG *... a school built in the 1960s*
EG *Where does your daughter go to school?*
2 the pupils or staff at a school
EG *The competition is open to all schools.*

3 Some colleges and university departments are referred to as schools.
EG *Stella is at art school.*

science /ˈsaɪəns/
sciences

NOUN
1 Science is the study of the nature and behaviour of natural things.
EG *... the importance of science and technology*
2 a branch of science, for example physics or biology
EG *She's studying the sciences.*

scientific /saɪənˈtɪfɪk/

ADJECTIVE
1 relating to science or to a particular science
EG *... scientific research*
2 Something that is scientific is done in a careful and thorough way, using experiments or tests.
EG *The test wasn't very scientific.*

scientist /ˈsaɪəntɪst/
scientists

NOUN
a person who has studied science and who does work connected with it
EG *... a team of American scientists*

scissors /ˈsɪzəz/

PLURAL NOUN
Scissors are a tool for cutting paper or cloth with two sharp blades which are screwed together.
EG *... a pair of scissors*

score /skɔːʳ/
scores scoring scored

VERB
1 If you score in a game, you get a goal or a point.
EG *He almost scored in the opening minute.*

EG *... after Owen scored the winning goal*

NOUN

2 The score in a game is the number of goals or points obtained by the players or teams.
EG *The final score was 4-1.*

Scottish /'skɒtɪʃ/

ADJECTIVE

belonging or relating to Scotland
EG *Both her parents are Scottish.*

scrap /skræp/
scraps

NOUN

A scrap of something is a very small piece or amount of it.
EG *... a scrap of paper*
EG *There wasn't a scrap of evidence.*

scrape /skreɪp/
scrapes scraping scraped

VERB

1 If you scrape something off a surface, you remove it by pulling a sharp object over the surface.
EG *I scraped the frost off the windows.*

2 If something scrapes against something else, it rubs against it, making a noise.
EG *... as the chair scraped against the floor*

scratch /skrætʃ/
scratches scratching scratched

VERB

1 If you scratch or **scratch yourself**, you rub your skin with your fingernails because it is itching.
EG *He scratched himself under his arm.*

2 If a sharp object scratches someone or something, it makes small cuts on their surface or skin.

EG *Knives will scratch the worktop.*

NOUN

3 a small cut
EG *There were scratches on the table.*

scream /skri:m/
screams screaming screamed

VERB

1 If you scream, you make a loud, high-pitched cry.
EG *He staggered around, screaming in agony.*
EG *I screamed at them to get out of my house.*

NOUN

2 a loud, high-pitched cry
EG *Hilda let out a scream.*

screen /skri:n/
screens screening screened

NOUN

1 a flat vertical surface on which a picture is shown
EG *... a television screen*

2 a panel that is used to separate different parts of a room
EG *There was a screen around his bed.*

VERB

3 When a film or a television programme is screened, it is shown in the cinema or broadcast on television.
EG *The series is to be screened in January.*

screw /skru:/
screws screwing screwed

NOUN

1 a small, sharp piece of metal that is used for fixing things together
EG *... a box of nails and screws*

VERB

2 If you screw something somewhere, you fix it there using

A
B
C
D
E
F
G
H
I
J
K
L
M
N
O
P
Q
R
S
T
U
V
W
X
Y
Z

screws.

EG *I had screwed the shelf on the wall.*

3 If you screw something onto something else, you fix it there by twisting it round and round.

EG *He screwed the top on the bottle.*

screw up

VERB

If you screw up a piece of paper, you twist or squeeze it so that it no longer has its proper shape.

EG *She screwed up the letter and threw it in the bin.*

scrub /skrʌb/

scrubs scrubbing scrubbed

VERB

If you scrub something, you clean it with a stiff brush and water.

EG *... the hours she had spent scrubbing the floor*

sculpture /ˈskʌlptʃəʳ/

sculptures

NOUN

1 a work of art produced by carving materials such as stone

EG *... a sculpture of a fish*

2 Sculpture is the art of making sculptures.

EG *He studied sculpture in Vienna.*

sea /siː/

seas

NOUN

The sea is the salt water that covers much of the earth's surface; also a particular area of salt water.

EG *Many city children have never seen the sea.*

EG *... the North Sea*

seal /siːl/

seals sealing sealed

1 a covering over the opening of a container that prevents air or

liquid from getting in or out

EG *The seal of the carton was broken.*

VERB

2 When you seal an envelope, you stick down the flap.

EG *... a sealed envelope*

3 If you seal an opening or a container, you cover it tightly so that air or liquid cannot get in or out.

EG *She filled each bottle and sealed it with a cork.*

search /sɜːtʃ/

searches searching searched

VERB

1 If you **search for** something or someone, you look carefully for them.

EG *Police are searching for a missing child.*

2 If someone such as a policeman searches you, they examine your clothing for hidden objects.

EG *You may be searched at the airport.*

NOUN

3 an attempt to find something

EG *I found my purse after a long search.*

season /ˈsiːzn/

seasons

NOUN

1 The seasons are the periods into which a year is divided: spring, summer, autumn, and winter.

EG *Autumn is my favourite season.*

2 a period of the year when a particular thing usually happens

EG *... the football season*

seat /siːt/

seats

NOUN

an object that you can sit on

EG *I found an empty seat near the*

back.

seat belt seat belts

NOUN

a strap that you fasten across your body for safety when travelling in a car or an aircraft
EG ... as the 'Fasten your seat belt' sign came on

second /'sɛkənd/
seconds

ADJECTIVE

1 The second item in a series is the one counted as number two.
EG This is the second time I have heard the name.
EG ... Cambodia's second biggest city

NOUN

2 one of the sixty parts that a minute is divided into
EG She broke the world record by over two seconds.
EG Seconds later, he was dead.

secondary school
secondary schools

NOUN

a school for pupils between the ages of eleven and eighteen
EG He is in his fourth year at secondary school.

second-class /'sɛkənd'klɑːs/

ADJECTIVE

1 Second-class people or things are regarded as less important than other people or things of the same kind.
EG He has been treated as a second-class citizen.

2 Second-class postage is a slower and cheaper kind of postage.
EG ... a second-class stamp

second-hand /'sɛkənd'hænd/

ADJECTIVE OR ADVERB

Something that is second-hand

has already been owned by someone else.
EG ... a second-hand car
EG He bought his boat second-hand.

secret /'siːkrɪt/
secrets

ADJECTIVE

1 Something that is secret is known about by only a small number of people.
EG ... at a secret location
EG He tried to keep the information secret.

NOUN

2 a fact that is known by only a small number of people
EG She was hopeless at keeping secrets.

secretary /'sɛkrətərɪ/
secretaries

NOUN

a person who is employed to do office work, such as typing letters and answering phone calls
EG Ask the secretary to arrange an appointment.

section /'sɛkʃən/
sections

NOUN

A section of something is one of the parts that it is divided into.
EG ... certain sections of the motorway

secure /sɪ'kjuəʳ/

ADJECTIVE

1 If a place is secure, it is tightly locked or well protected.
EG We will make our house as secure as possible.

2 If an object is secure, it is firmly fixed in place.
EG These shelves seem quite secure.

3 If someone's job or future is secure, it is safe.

A B C D E F G H I J K L M N O P Q R S T U V W X Y Z

EG *The industry's future looks secure.*

security /sɪˈkjuərɪtɪ/

NOUN

Security refers to all the measures that are taken to protect a place.

EG *Airport security was increased.*

EG *... a security guard*

see /siː/

sees seeing saw seen

VERB

1 When you see something, you notice it with your eyes.

EG *Did you see that car?*

EG *I saw him leave.*

2 If you see something such as a film or a sports game, you watch it.

EG *... the best film I've ever seen*

3 If you see someone, you visit them or meet them.

EG *I went to see my doctor.*

EG *We haven't seen each other for years.*

4 If you see something, you realize or understand it.

EG *I see what you mean.*

EG *"He came home in my car." — "I see."*

5 If you see someone or something in a particular way, you think of them in that way.

EG *He saw me as his enemy.*

6 If you say that you **will see** if something is happening, you mean that you will find out.

EG *I'll see if she can help.*

EG *Let's see who's playing before we buy tickets.*

seed /siːd/

seeds

NOUN

The seeds of a plant are the small, hard parts from which new plants grow.

EG *... sunflower seeds*

seek /siːk/

seeks seeking sought

VERB

A FORMAL WORD

If you seek something, you try to find it or obtain it.

EG *... people seeking work*

EG *... after she sought professional advice*

seem /siːm/

seems seeming seemed

VERB

If something seems to be the case, it appears to be the case or you think that it is the case.

EG *Everyone seems busy.*

EG *Audiences seem to love it.*

EG *He seemed such a quiet man.*

seen /siːn/

past participle of **see**

seize /siːz/

seizes seizing seized

VERB

If you seize something, you take hold of it quickly and firmly.

EG *He seized my arm.*

seldom /ˈsɛldəm/

ADVERB

not often

EG *They seldom speak to each other.*

select /sɪˈlɛkt/

selects selecting selected

VERB

If you select someone or something, you choose them.

EG *A panel of judges is now selecting the finalists.*

selection /sɪˈlɛkʃən/

selections

NOUN

1 Selection is the act of selecting people or things.

EG *... rules governing the selection of candidates*

2 A selection of people or things is a set of them chosen from a larger group.
EG ... this selection of popular songs

self /sɛlf/
selves

NOUN
Your self is your basic personality or nature.
EG You're looking more like your usual self.

self- /sɛlf/

PREFIX
Self- is used to form words which indicate that you do something to yourself or by yourself.
EG ... a self-addressed envelope
EG ... a self-employed builder

selfish /'sɛlfɪʃ/

ADJECTIVE
People who are selfish care only about themselves and not about other people.
EG I'm afraid I've been very selfish.

sell /sɛl/
sells selling sold

VERB
1 If you sell someone something or if you **sell** it **to** them, you let them have it in return for money.
EG I sold my car to my neighbour.
EG We're trying to sell our house.
2 If a shop sells something, people can buy it from that shop.
EG ... a newsagent that sells stamps

sell out

VERB
If a shop has **sold out of** something, it has sold it all.
EG The bookshops sold out of her new novel.

semi- /'sɛmɪ/

PREFIX

Semi- is used to form words that mean 'half' or 'partly'.
EG ... a semi-detached house
EG ... semi-skilled workers

semi-final /sɛmɪ'faɪnl/
semi-finals

NOUN
one of the two matches or races in a competition that are held to decide who will compete in the final
EG They were beaten in the semi-finals.

send /sɛnd/
sends sending sent

VERB
1 If you send someone something or if you **send** it **to** them, you arrange for them to receive it, for example by post.
EG She sent me flowers on my birthday.
EG I sent a copy to the manager.
2 If you send someone somewhere, you tell them to go there or arrange for them to go there.
EG Tom came to see her, but she sent him away.
EG Troops were sent to the region.

send off for

VERB
If you send off for something, you write and ask for it to be sent to you.
EG I sent off for their new catalogue.

senior /'siːnɪər/

ADJECTIVE
The senior people in an organization have the most important jobs in it.
EG ... senior government officials

sensation /sɛn'seɪʃən/
sensations

NOUN
a feeling, especially a physical feeling
EG *She felt a burning sensation in her leg.*

sense /sɛns/
senses sensing sensed

NOUN
1 Your senses are the physical abilities of sight, hearing, smell, touch, and taste.
EG *... a good sense of smell*
2 a feeling
EG *... a sense of guilt*
3 Sense is the ability to think and behave sensibly.
EG *... because he was older and had more sense*
4 If something **makes sense**, you can understand it or it seems sensible.
EG *His words just didn't make sense.*

VERB
5 If you sense something, you become aware of it.
EG *I sensed that he wasn't being honest.*

sensible /'sɛnsɪbl/

ADJECTIVE
A sensible person makes good decisions based on reason.
EG *It would be sensible to get advice.*

sensitive /'sɛnsɪtɪv/

ADJECTIVE
1 If you are **sensitive to** other people's feelings, you show that you understand them.
EG *... universities which are sensitive to students' needs*
EG *She was always so sensitive and caring.*
2 If you are **sensitive about** something, you are easily upset when people talk about it.

EG *He's sensitive about his weight.*
EG *Don't be so sensitive!*

sent /sɛnt/
past participle and past tense of **send**

sentence /'sɛntns/
sentences sentencing sentenced

NOUN
1 a group of words which begins with a capital letter and makes a statement, question, or command
EG *The note consisted of a single sentence.*
2 a punishment that is given to a person found guilty in a law court
EG *He had served a prison sentence for robbery.*

VERB
3 When a guilty person is sentenced, they are told officially what their punishment will be.
EG *She was sentenced to three months in prison.*

separate /'sɛprɪt/
separates separating separated

ADJECTIVE
1 If something is separate from something else, the two things are not connected.
EG *My brother and I have separate rooms.*
EG *I've always kept my private and professional life separate.*

VERB : /'sɛpəreɪt/
☑ Note that you pronounce the verb differently from the adjective.
2 If you separate people or things that are together, or if they separate, they move apart.
EG *Police moved in to separate the two groups.*
EG *The front end separated from the rest of the car.*

3 If something separates two people or things, it exists between them.

EG ... *the fence that separated the garden from the road*

4 If a couple who are married or living together separate, they decide to live apart.

EG *They separated the following month.*

September /sɛp'tɛmbər/

NOUN

September is the ninth month of the year.

EG ... *the meeting he had in September*

sequence /'si:kwəns/
sequences

NOUN

1 A sequence of things is a number of them that come one after another.

EG ... *the sequence of events which led to the murder*

2 The sequence in which things are arranged is the order in which they are arranged.

EG ... *to do things in the right sequence*

series /'sɪəriz/

☑ The plural is *series*.

NOUN

1 A series of things is a number of them that come one after another.

EG ... *a series of explosions*

2 A radio or television series is a set of related programmes with the same title.

EG ... *a new drama series*

serious /'sɪəriəs/

ADJECTIVE

1 A serious problem or situation is very bad and worrying.

EG *Crime is a serious problem here.*

EG ... *a serious accident*

2 Serious matters are important and should be thought about carefully.

EG ... *a question which deserved serious consideration*

3 If you are **serious about** something, you are sincere about it and not joking.

EG *Are you serious about leaving?*

4 People who are serious think carefully about things and do not laugh much.

EG ... *a very serious man*

servant /'sɜːvənt/
servants

NOUN

someone who is employed to work in another person's house, especially in former times

EG ... *the cook, the gardener and most of the servants*

serve /sɜːv/
serves serving served

VERB

1 If you serve a country, organization, or person, you do useful work for them.

EG *These soldiers have served their country for years.*

2 If one thing **serves as** another thing, it is used as that thing.

EG *The room serves as their office.*

3 If something serves people in a particular place, it provides them with something they need.

EG ... *a hospital which serves the whole of the county*

4 If you serve food or drink to people, you give them food or drink.

EG ... *before you serve the main course*

5 Someone who serves customers in a shop or bar provides them

with what they want.
EG *I waited ten minutes before I was served.*

service /'sɜːvɪs/
services

NOUN

1 an organization or system that provides something for the public
EG *... a regular bus service*

2 Service is the activity of working for a company or organization.
EG *Pat is leaving the company after 12 years service.*

3 The standard of service provided by an organization is the quality of the work it does for people.
EG *... the need for improved customer service*

4 a religious ceremony
EG *... the wedding service*

session /'seʃən/
sessions

NOUN

A session of a particular activity is a period of that activity.
EG *... an emergency session of parliament*
EG *... a photo session*

set /set/
sets setting set

NOUN

1 A set of things is a number of things that form a group.
EG *... a spare set of keys*

2 A set or a **television set** is a television.
EG *... an old black-and-white set*

VERB

3 If you set something somewhere, you put it there carefully.
EG *He set the glass on the counter.*

4 You can use 'set' to say that someone causes something to be in a particular condition.

EG *... after the hostages were set free*
EG *Many vehicles were set on fire.*

5 If you set a date, price, level, or target for something, you decide what it will be.
EG *He hasn't set a date for his wedding yet.*

6 If you set a clock or a control, you adjust it to a particular position.
EG *Set the volume as high as possible.*

7 If you set a record or an example, you create it for other people to copy.
EG *... after he had set a new world record*
EG *Smoking in front of children sets a bad example.*

8 If someone sets you a task, you have to do that task.
EG *... teachers who set too much homework*

9 When the sun sets, it goes below the horizon.
EG *... as the sun was setting*

10 When something such as glue or cement sets, it becomes hard.
EG *I stood on the cement before it had set.*

ADJECTIVE

11 If something is set somewhere, that is where it is or where it happens.
EG *The castle is set in beautiful grounds.*
EG *The play is set in a small American town.*

12 Something that is set does not change.
EG *... a set menu*

set off

VERB

1 When you set off, you start a journey.

EG *He set off for the station.*
2 If something sets off an alarm or a bomb, it causes it to start operating.
EG *The slightest noise sets off the alarm.*

set out

VERB
1 When you set out, you start a journey.
EG *I set out for the cottage.*
2 If you **set out to do** something, you start trying to do it.
EG *We set out to find the truth.*

set up

VERB
If you set something up, you make all the necessary preparations for it.
EG *... in order to set up his own business*

settle /'sɛtl/
settles settling settled

VERB
1 If two people settle an argument, they resolve it.
EG *We are trying to settle our differences.*
2 If you settle a bill, you pay it.
EG *He barely had enough to settle his bill.*
3 If something **is settled**, it has been decided and arranged.
EG *It's all settled, we're leaving tomorrow.*
4 If you settle somewhere, you make it your permanent home.
EG *He eventually settled in Paris.*
5 If something settles, it sinks slowly and becomes still.
EG *... after the dust had settled*

seven /'sɛvn/
sevens
the number 7
EG *... seven years*

seventeen /sɛvn'tiːn/
the number 17
EG *... seventeen years*

seventeenth /sɛvn'tiːnθ/

ADJECTIVE
The seventeenth item in a series is the one counted as number seventeen.
EG *... the seventeenth day*

seventh /'sɛvnθ/
sevenths

ADJECTIVE
1 The seventh item in a series is the one counted as number seven.
EG *... on the seventh day*

NOUN
2 one of seven equal parts
EG *... one seventh of the people*

seventieth /'sɛvntɪɪθ/

ADJECTIVE
The seventieth item in a series is the one counted as number seventy.
EG *... the seventieth year*

seventy /'sɛvntɪ/
seventies
the number 70
EG *... seventy degrees*
EG *... temperatures in the seventies*

several /'sɛvərl/

ADJECTIVE OR PRONOUN
Several people or things means a small number of them but more than two.
EG *She spent several years in Africa.*
EG *Several of my friends are doctors.*

severe /sɪ'vɪər/

ADJECTIVE
extremely bad or unpleasant
EG *... severe delays*
EG *... severe stomach pains*

sew /səu/
sews sewing sewed sewn

VERB

When you sew things, you use a needle and thread to make or mend them.

EG *She sewed the dresses on her sewing machine.*

sex /sɛks/
sexes

NOUN

1 The sexes are the two groups, male and female, into which people and animals are divided.

EG *... differences between the sexes*

2 The sex of a person or animal is their characteristic of being either male or female.

EG *She did not get the job because of her sex.*

3 Sex is the physical activity by which people and animals produce young.

EG *The film contains a lot of sex and violence.*

EG *She's too young to be having sex.*

sexual /'sɛksjuəl/

ADJECTIVE

1 connected with the act of sex

EG *... his first sexual relationship*

2 relating to the differences between men and women

EG *... sexual equality*

sexy /'sɛksɪ/
sexier sexiest

ADJECTIVE

sexually attractive or exciting

EG *... those sexy blue eyes*

shade /ʃeɪd/
shades shading shaded

NOUN

1 Shade is an area of darkness where the sun does not reach.

EG *The table was in the shade.*

2 The shades of a colour are its different forms.

EG *... a lovely shade of pink*

VERB

3 If a place **is shaded** by something, that thing prevents light from falling on it.

EG *The street was shaded by buildings.*

shadow /'ʃædəʊ/
shadows

NOUN

the dark shape that is made when an object prevents light from reaching a surface

EG *All I could see was his shadow.*

EG *... the shadows cast by the trees*

shake /ʃeɪk/
shakes shaking shook shaken

VERB

1 If you shake someone or something, you move them quickly from side to side or up and down.

EG *... as she shook the bottle*

EG *The dog shook itself.*

2 If someone or something shakes, they move from side to side or up and down with small, quick movements.

EG *His hand was shaking badly.*

EG *The ground beneath us was shaking.*

3 If an event shakes you, it shocks and upsets you.

EG *She was badly shaken by the accident.*

4 If you **shake** someone's **hand** or **shake hands with** them, you grasp their hand as a way of greeting them.

EG *The Prince shook hands with half the town.*

5 If you **shake** your **head**, you move it from side to side in order to say 'no'.

EG *I asked her to come but she shook her head.*

NOUN

6 A shake is the act of shaking something.

EG *... with a shake of his fist*

shall /ʃæl/

☑ 'Shall' is a modal verb. It has only one form. There are no forms ending in -s, -ing, or -ed. Shall not is often shortened to *shan't: I shan't miss him.*

VERB

1 You use 'shall' in questions when you are asking what to do or making a suggestion.

EG *Shall I go and check for you?*

EG *Let's take a walk, shall we?*

2 You can use 'shall' when you are saying what you intend to do or what you are sure will happen.

EG *We shall be landing shortly.*

EG *I shall miss you very much.*

shallow /ˈʃæləʊ/
shallower shallowest

ADJECTIVE

not deep

EG *The water is quite shallow.*

shame /ʃeɪm/

NOUN

1 Shame is the feeling of guilt or embarrassment that you get when you know you have done something wrong or foolish.

EG *She felt a deep sense of shame.*

2 If you say that something is **a shame**, you mean that you are disappointed about it and you wish it had happened differently.

EG *It's a shame you can't come.*

shampoo /ʃæmˈpuː/

NOUN

Shampoo is a soapy liquid that you use for washing your hair.

EG *... a bottle of shampoo*

shape /ʃeɪp/
shapes

NOUN

1 The shape of something is the form of its outline.

EG *... a box in the shape of a heart*

2 A shape is something with a definite form, for example a circle.

EG *... a kidney shape*

shaped /ʃeɪpt/

ADJECTIVE

Something that is shaped in a particular way has that shape.

EG *... biscuits shaped like hearts*

share /ʃeəʳ/
shares sharing shared

VERB

1 If two people share something, they both use it, do it, or have it.

EG *We shared a bottle of champagne.*

EG *... the house he shares with his sister*

NOUN

2 A share of something is a portion of it.

EG *I want a fair share of the money.*

3 The shares of a company are the equal parts into which its ownership is divided and which people can buy.

EG *The shares had doubled in value.*

sharp /ʃɑːp/
sharper sharpest

ADJECTIVE

1 A sharp object has a fine edge or point that is good for cutting or piercing things.

EG *... a sharp knife*

2 A sharp bend is one that changes direction suddenly.

EG *I was approaching a fairly sharp bend.*

A B C D E F G H I J K L M N O P Q R S T U V W X Y Z

A B C D E F G H I J K L M N O P Q R S T U V W X Y Z

3 A sharp change is sudden and great.
EG *... a sharp rise in prices*

shatter /ˈʃætəʳ/
shatters shattering shattered

VERB

If something shatters, or if someone or something shatters it, it breaks into a lot of small pieces.
EG *The windows shattered in the explosion.*
EG *One bullet shattered his skull.*

shave /ʃeɪv/
shaves shaving shaved

VERB

1 If you shave, you remove hair from your face or body with a razor.
EG *He washed and shaved before breakfast.*
EG *... women who never shave their legs*

NOUN

2 When a man has a shave, he shaves the hair from his face.
EG *You need a shave!*

she /ʃiː/

PRONOUN

You use 'she' to refer to a woman, girl, or female animal.
EG *She was seventeen.*

shed /ʃɛd/
sheds

NOUN

a small building that is used for storing things
EG *... the garden shed*

sheep /ʃiːp/
☑ The plural is *sheep*.

NOUN

a farm animal with a thick woolly coat
EG *... a flock of sheep*

sheet /ʃiːt/
sheets

NOUN

1 a large rectangular piece of cloth that is used to cover a bed
EG *The maid changes the sheets every morning.*

2 A sheet of paper is a rectangular piece of paper.
EG *I was able to fit the letter on one sheet.*

shelf /ʃɛlf/
shelves

NOUN

a flat piece of wood, metal, or glass that is attached to a wall and used for putting things on
EG *He took a book from the shelf.*

shell /ʃɛl/
shells

NOUN

1 The shell of an egg or nut is its hard outer layer.
EG *They cracked the nuts and removed the shells.*

2 The shell of an animal such as a snail or crab is the hard cover that protects its back.
EG *The tortoise came out of its shell.*

3 Shells are the coloured objects found on beaches which surround, or used to surround, small sea creatures.
EG *... a collection of sea shells*

4 a type of ammunition that can be fired over long distances from a large gun
EG *... an unexploded shell*

shelter /ˈʃɛltəʳ/
shelters sheltering sheltered

NOUN

1 a small building that is designed to protect people from bad weather or danger
EG *... a bus shelter*

2 Shelter is protection from bad weather or danger.
EG *The refugees were given food and shelter.*

VERB
3 If you shelter somewhere, you stay there to protect yourself from bad weather or danger.
EG *I saw a man sheltering in a doorway.*

shelves /ʃɛlvz/
the plural of **shelf**

shield /ʃiːld/
shields shielding shielded

NOUN
1 a large piece of metal or other material which soldiers used to carry to protect themselves in battle
EG *... a display of old swords and shields*

VERB
2 If someone or something **shields** you **from** something, they protect you from it.
EG *She was shielded from the blast by a low wall.*

shift /ʃɪft/
shifts shifting shifted

VERB
1 If you shift something, or if it shifts, it moves slightly.
EG *She shifted the glass to her left hand.*
EG *He shifted from foot to foot.*

NOUN
2 a set period of work in a place like a factory or hospital
EG *... the night shift*

shin /ʃɪn/
shins

NOUN
Your shins are the front parts of your legs between your knees and your ankles.

EG *She kicked him in the shins.*

shine /ʃaɪn/
shines shining shone

VERB
1 When the sun or a light shines, it gives out bright light.
EG *The sun was shining.*
2 If you shine a torch or lamp somewhere, you point it there.
EG *A man shone a torch in his face.*

shiny /ʃaɪnɪ/
shinier shiniest

ADJECTIVE
Shiny things are bright and reflect light.
EG *... a shiny brass plate*

ship /ʃɪp/
ships shipping shipped

NOUN
1 a large boat which carries passengers or goods
EG *... a passenger ship*

VERB
2 If people or things **are shipped** somewhere, they are sent there by ship.
EG *Food is being shipped to the worst-affected areas.*

shirt /ʃəːt/
shirts

NOUN
a piece of clothing that you wear on the upper part of your body, with a collar, sleeves, and buttons down the front
EG *I think you should wear a shirt and tie.*

shiver /ʃɪvəʳ/
shivers shivering shivered

VERB
When you shiver, your body shakes slightly because you are cold or frightened.
EG *He shivered in the cold.*

A
B
C
D
E
F
G
H
I
J
K
L
M
N
O
P
Q
R
S
T
U
V
W
X
Y
Z

shock /ʃɒk/
shocks shocking shocked

NOUN

1 a sudden experience that upsets or surprises you

EG *The news was a terrible shock to us all.*

EG *I got quite a shock when I saw him again.*

2 Shock is a person's emotional and physical condition when something frightening or upsetting has happened to them.

EG *She's still in a state of shock.*

VERB

3 If something shocks you, it upsets you because it is unpleasant and unexpected.

EG *I was shocked by his appearance.*

4 If something shocks you, it offends you because you think it is rude or immoral.

EG *People were easily shocked in those days.*

shoe /ʃuː/
shoes

NOUN

Shoes are objects that you wear on your feet. They cover most of your feet, but not your ankles.

EG *... a new pair of shoes*

shone /ʃɒn/
past participle and past tense of **shine**

shook /ʃuk/
past tense of **shake**

shoot /ʃuːt/
shoots shooting shot

VERB

1 If someone shoots a person or animal, they kill or injure them by firing a gun at them.

EG *He shot himself in the head.*

EG *They started shooting at us.*

2 If something shoots somewhere, it moves there suddenly and quickly.

EG *Another car shot past them.*

3 In sports such as football, when someone shoots, they try to score a goal.

EG *... after Young had shot wide*

4 When people shoot a film, they make a film.

EG *The film was shot in California.*

shop /ʃɒp/
shops shopping shopped

NOUN

1 a place where things are sold

EG *... a clothes shop*

EG *It's not available in the shops.*

VERB

2 When you shop, you go to shops and buy things.

EG *He always shopped at the Co-op.*

shopping /'ʃɒpɪŋ/

NOUN

1 Your shopping is the things that you have just bought from shops, especially food.

EG *... before we put the shopping away*

2 When you **do the shopping**, you go to shops and buy things, especially food.

EG *It was my turn to do the shopping.*

shore /ʃɔːʳ/
shores

NOUN

The shore of a sea, lake, or wide river is the land along the edge of it.

EG *They walked down to the shore.*

short /ʃɔːt/
shorter shortest; shorts

ADJECTIVE

1 If something is short, it is not

very long or does not last very long.
EG *... a short time ago*
EG *... a short holiday*

2 Someone or something that is short is small in length, distance, or height.
EG *... a short piece of string*
EG *I came by the shortest road.*
EG *... a rather short man*

3 If you are **short of** something, you do not have enough of it.
EG *The family is short of money.*

4 If a name is **short for** another name, it is a short version of it.
EG *... her friend Kes (short for Kesewa)*

ADVERB
5 If something is **cut short** or **stops short of** something, it stops before it is supposed to or expected to.
EG *He cut short his trip to Africa.*
EG *The ball stoped a few inches short of the hole.*

PLURAL NOUN
6 **shorts** are trousers with very short legs
EG *... a pair of shorts*

shortage /ˈʃɔːtɪdʒ/
shortages

NOUN
If there is a shortage of something, there is not enough of it.
EG *... food shortages*

shortcut /ˈʃɔːtkʌt/
shortcuts

NOUN
a quicker way of getting somewhere than the usual route
EG *I tried to take a shortcut and got lost.*

shortly /ˈʃɔːtlɪ/

ADVERB
1 a short time

EG *He called shortly after she had left.*

2 soon
EG *I'll be back shortly.*

shot /ʃɒt/
shots

1 Shot is the past tense and past participle of **shoot**
EG *Someone has been shot.*

NOUN
2 the act of firing a gun
EG *My first two shots missed the target.*

3 In sport, a shot is the act of kicking or hitting a ball, especially in an attempt to score.
EG *He had only one shot at goal.*

4 a photograph or a sequence of pictures in a film
EG *A video crew was taking shots of the lane.*

should /ʃʊd/
☑ 'Should' is a modal verb. It has only one form. There are no forms ending in -s, -ing, or -ed.

VERB
1 You use 'should' to say that something ought to happen.
EG *I should exercise more.*
EG *She should have done better.*

2 You use 'should' to say that you expect something to happen.
EG *I should be there on time.*
EG *He should have arrived by now.*

3 You use 'should' in questions when you are asking for advice.
EG *Should we tell her about it?*

shoulder /ˈʃəʊldər/
shoulders

NOUN
Your shoulders are the parts of your body between your neck and the tops of your arms.
EG *He looked back over his shoulder.*

A B C D E F G H I J K L M N O P Q R S T U V W X Y Z

shout /ʃaʊt/
shouts shouting shouted

NOUN
1 a loud call or cry
EG *I heard a distant shout.*

VERB
2 If you shout something, you say it very loudly.
EG *He shouted something to his brother.*
EG *She was shouting for help.*

show /ʃəʊ/
shows showing showed shown

VERB
1 To show that something exists or is true means to prove it or to make it clear.
EG *The survey shows that more people are going on holiday.*

2 If you show someone something or **show** it **to** them, you let them see it.
EG *He showed them his passport.*
EG *… before showing it to the police*

3 If a picture or film shows something, it represents it.
EG *The picture shows how the dress should look.*

4 If you show someone somewhere, you lead them there or point it out to them.
EG *I was shown to my room at the hotel.*
EG *He showed me where the gun was.*

5 If you show someone how to do something, you demonstrate it to them.
EG *Jane showed me how to make a chocolate cake.*

6 If something shows, it is visible.
EG *Daylight was beginning to show through the trees.*
EG *She was unhappy and it showed.*

NOUN
7 a form of entertainment at the theatre or on television
EG *… a West End show*
EG *… a talk show*

8 an exhibition
EG *… a flower show*

show off

VERB
If someone shows off, they try to impress people.
EG *There's no need to show off.*

shower /ˈʃaʊər/
showers showering showered

NOUN
1 a device which sprays you with water so that you can wash yourself
EG *She heard him turn on the shower.*

2 If you **have** or **take a shower**, you wash yourself by standing under a shower.
EG *She took two showers a day.*
EG *I need a shower.*

3 a short period of rain
EG *The weather forecast was for scattered showers.*

VERB
4 If you shower, you have a shower.
EG *There wasn't time to shower.*

shown /ʃəʊn/
past participle of **show**

shrink /ʃrɪŋk/
shrinks shrinking shrank shrunk

VERB
If something shrinks, it becomes smaller.
EG *… jumpers that shrink in the wash*

shrug /ʃrʌg/
shrugs shrugging shrugged

VERB

If you shrug or **shrug your shoulders**, you raise your shoulders in order to show that you do not know or care about something.
EG *I asked Anne but she just shrugged her shoulders.*

shrunk /ʃrʌŋk/
past participle of **shrink**

shut /ʃʌt/
shuts shutting shut

VERB

1 If you shut something or if it shuts, it closes.
EG *I shut the door gently.*
EG *His mouth opened and then shut again.*

2 When a shop shuts, it closes and you cannot go into it.
EG *What time do the shops shut?*

ADJECTIVE

3 If something is shut, it is closed.
EG *The windows are all shut.*
EG *His eyes were shut.*

4 If a shop is shut, it is closed and you cannot go into it.
EG *The local shop may be shut.*

shut up

VERB

AN INFORMAL EXPRESSION

If you tell someone to shut up, you want them to stop talking.
EG *Tell him to shut up!*

shuttle /ʃʌtl/
shuttles

NOUN

A shuttle is a plane, bus, or train which makes frequent journeys between two places.
EG *... the BA shuttle to Glasgow*

shy /ʃaɪ/
shyer shyest

ADJECTIVE

A shy person is nervous and uncomfortable in the company of other people.
EG *She was a shy, quiet girl.*

sick /sɪk/
sicker sickest

ADJECTIVE

1 If you are sick, you are ill.
EG *He is sick and needs to see a doctor.*

2 If you are sick, you vomit.
EG *She was sick on the carpet.*

3 If you feel sick, you feel as if you are going to vomit.
EG *The thought of food made him feel sick.*

4 If you are **sick of** something, you are annoyed or bored by it and want it to stop.
EG *I'm so sick of hearing him complain.*

side /saɪd/
sides

NOUN

1 The side of something is a position to the left or right of it.
EG *Park at the side of the road.*
EG *... both sides of the border*

2 The sides of an object are its outside surfaces which are not the top or bottom.
EG *The carton lay on its side.*
EG *... a label on the side of the box*

3 The two sides of an area, surface, or object are its two surfaces or halves.
EG *Write on one side of the paper only.*
EG *... both sides of your face*

4 Your sides are the parts of your body from the inside of your shoulders down to your hips.
EG *I lay down on my side.*

5 The two sides in a war, argument, or game are the two

A
B
C
D
E
F
G
H
I
J
K
L
M
N
O
P
Q
R
S
T
U
V
W
X
Y
Z

people or groups involved.
EG *Whose side are you on?*
EG *Italy were definitely the best side.*

ADJECTIVE

6 situated on one side of a
building, vehicle, or road
EG *... the side door*
EG *... a side street*

sidewalk /'saɪdwɔːk/
sidewalks

NOUN

In American English, a sidewalk is a
pavement.
EG *... the amount of trash on the
sidewalk*

sideways /'saɪdweɪz/

ADVERB OR ADJECTIVE

from or towards the side of
something or someone
EG *I took a step sideways.*
EG *... a sideways glance*

sigh /saɪ/
sighs sighing sighed

VERB

1 When you sigh, you let out a
deep breath.
EG *She sighed loudly.*

NOUN

2 a deep breath
EG *... with a sigh of relief*

sight /saɪt/
sights

NOUN

1 Sight is the ability to see.
EG *His sight was so poor that he
couldn't watch TV.*

2 A sight is something you see or
the act of seeing it.
EG *It was a terrible sight.*
EG *I faint at the sight of blood.*

3 If something is **in sight**, you
can see it. If it is **out of sight**,
you cannot see it.
EG *The beach was in sight.*

EG *I parked the car out of sight of
the main road.*

PLURAL NOUN

4 The **sights** are interesting
places which tourists visit.
EG *We toured the sights of Paris.*

sightseeing /'saɪtsiːɪŋ/

NOUN

Sightseeing is the activity of
visiting interesting places as a
tourist.
EG *... a sightseeing tour*

sign /saɪn/
signs signing signed

NOUN

1 a mark or symbol with a
particular meaning, for example in
mathematics or music
EG *... a plus sign*

2 a movement or gesture with a
particular meaning
EG *He gave us the thumbs-up sign.*

3 a board with words or pictures
on it that gives information or
instructions
EG *Follow the road signs.*

4 If there is a **sign of** something,
there is evidence that it exists.
EG *We are now seeing the first signs
of recovery.*

VERB

5 If you sign something, you put
your signature on it.
EG *He hurriedly signed the death
certificate.*

signal /'sɪgnl/
signals

NOUN

a sound or action that is intended
to send a particular message
EG *You musn't fire without my
signal.*

signature /'sɪgnətʃər/
signatures

NOUN
Your signature is your name,
written in the way that you usually
write it.
EG *I wrote my signature at the
bottom of the page.*

significant /sɪgˈnɪfɪkənt/
ADJECTIVE
1 A significant amount of
something is quite a large amount
of it.
EG *A significant number of people
can't read.*
2 important and fundamental
EG *He has made a significant
contribution to the project.*

silence /ˈsaɪləns/
silences silencing silenced
NOUN
1 If there is silence, it is completely
quiet.
EG *They stood in silence.*
EG *... a long silence*
VERB
2 To silence someone or
something means to stop them
speaking or making a noise.
EG *A ringing phone silenced her.*

silent /ˈsaɪlənt/
ADJECTIVE
Someone or something that is
silent makes no sound.
EG *He remained silent throughout
the meeting.*
EG *The guns finally fell silent.*

silk /sɪlk/
NOUN
Silk is a fine, soft cloth.
EG *... a silk dress*

silly /ˈsɪlɪ/
sillier silliest
ADJECTIVE
foolish or childish
EG *That was a silly thing to do.*

EG *You silly boy!*

silver /ˈsɪlvər/
NOUN
Silver is a valuable greyish-white
metal that is used for making
jewellery and ornaments.
EG *... a brooch made from silver*

similar /ˈsɪmɪlər/
ADJECTIVE
If one thing is **similar to** another,
or if they are similar, they are like
each other.
EG *The accident was similar to one
that happened in 1973.*
EG *... a group of similar pictures*

similarity /sɪmɪˈlærɪtɪ/
similarities
NOUN
If there is a similarity between
things, they are similar in some
way.
EG *... the astonishing similarities
between my brother and my son*

simple /ˈsɪmpl/
simpler simplest
ADJECTIVE
1 Something that is simple is not
complicated and is easy to
understand or do.
EG *The questions were quite simple.*
2 plain in style
EG *... a simple dinner of rice and
beans*

simply /ˈsɪmplɪ/
ADVERB
1 merely
EG *It's simply a question of
remaining calm.*
EG *Most of the damage was simply
due to fallen trees.*
2 If you do something simply, you
do it in a way that is not
complicated.
EG *State your reasons simply and*

A
B
C
D
E
F
G
H
I
J
K
L
M
N
O
P
Q
R
S
T
U
V
W
X
Y
Z

clearly.

3 You can use 'simply' to emphasize what you are saying.
EG *It's simply not true.*

sin /sɪn/
sins

NOUN

an action or type of behaviour which is believed to break the laws of God
EG *… the idea that abortion is a sin*

since /sɪns/

PREPOSITION, CONJUNCTION, OR ADVERB

1 from a particular time in the past until now
EG *I've been waiting since 2 o'clock.*
EG *So much has changed since I was young.*
EG *We quarrelled once but have been friends ever since.*

☑ Note the tense of 'have' in the above examples: I *have been* waiting since 2 o'clock; so much *has changed* since I was young.

ADVERB

2 at some time after a particular time in the past
EG *They split up and he has since married again.*

CONJUNCTION

3 A FORMAL USE
because
EG *Since you never listen, I'll repeat it.*

sincere /sɪnˈsɪəʳ/

ADJECTIVE

If you are sincere, you say things that you really mean.
EG *He's sincere in his views.*

sing /sɪŋ/
sings singing sang sung

VERB

1 If you sing, you make musical

sounds with your voice, usually producing words that fit a tune.
EG *She sang an old song.*
EG *He sings very well.*

2 When birds sing, they make pleasant sounds.
EG *It was early morning and the birds were singing.*

single /ˈsɪŋgl/
singles

ADJECTIVE

1 Single means only one and not more.
EG *A single shot was fired.*

2 People who are single are not married.
EG *When I was single I had no worries.*

3 You use 'single' to emphasize that something applies to all the things or people you are talking about.
EG *Every single house was damaged.*
EG *Not a single guest arrived.*

NOUN

4 A single or a **single room** is a room that is intended to be used by one person.
EG *I reserved a single room at the hotel.*

5 A single or a **single ticket** is a ticket for a journey to a place but not back again.
EG *A single to Birmingham, please.*

6 a record or CD which has one short song on each side
EG *… their latest hit single*

singular /ˈsɪŋgjʊləʳ/

ADJECTIVE

The **singular** form of a noun is the form that is used to refer to only one example of a person or thing, for example 'one **man**' or 'a **book**'.

sink /sɪŋk/
sinks sinking sank sunk

NOUN
1 a large bowl fixed to a wall with taps that supply water
EG *There were dirty dishes in the sink.*

VERB
2 If something that is in water sinks, it disappears below the surface.
EG *... a ship that sank in icy seas*

3 If something sinks, it moves slowly downwards.
EG *... as the sun was sinking in the west*

sip /sɪp/
sips sipping sipped

VERB
1 If you sip a drink, you drink a small amount of it at a time.
EG *She sipped her coffee.*

NOUN
2 a small amount of drink that you take into your mouth
EG *Harry took a sip of whisky.*

sir /sər/

NOUN
'Sir' is a polite way of addressing a man.
EG *Good afternoon, sir.*

siren /ˈsaɪərn/
sirens

NOUN
a warning device, for example on a fire engine or an ambulance, which makes a long, loud noise
EG *... an ambulance siren*

sister /ˈsɪstər/
sisters

NOUN
Your sister is a girl or woman who has the same parents as you.
EG *I didn't know you had a sister.*

sister-in-law /ˈsɪstərɪnlɔː/
sisters-in-law

NOUN
Your sister-in-law is the sister of your husband or wife, or the woman who is married to your brother.
EG *... her sister-in-law, Sarah*

sit /sɪt/
sits sitting sat

VERB
1 If you are sitting, your weight is supported by your bottom rather than your feet.
EG *He was sitting on the chair beside me.*

2 When you sit or **sit down**, you lower your body until you are sitting.
EG *She told me to sit on the sofa.*
EG *I sat down on the wall.*

3 If you sit someone somewhere, you place them there in a sitting position.
EG *He used to sit me on his lap.*

4 If you sit an examination, you take it.
EG *I am sitting exams in June.*

site /saɪt/
sites

NOUN
a piece of ground where a particular thing happens or is situated
EG *... a building site*
EG *... the site of an old Roman villa*

situated /ˈsɪtjueɪtɪd/

ADJECTIVE
If something is situated somewhere, that is where it is.
EG *... a town situated 45 minutes from Geneva*

situation /sɪtjuˈeɪʃən/
situations

NOUN
You use 'situation' to refer in general terms to what is happening at a particular place and time.
EG *The situation is now under control.*
EG *What would you do in my situation?*

six /sɪks/
sixes
the number 6
EG *... six people*

sixteen /sɪks'tiːn/
the number 16
EG *... sixteen days*

sixteenth /sɪks'tiːnθ/
ADJECTIVE
The sixteenth item in a series is the one counted as number sixteen.
EG *... the sixteenth day*

sixth /sɪksθ/
sixths
ADJECTIVE
1 The sixth item in a series is the one counted as number six.
EG *... the sixth month*
NOUN
2 one of six equal parts
EG *... a sixth of the land*

sixtieth /'sɪkstɪɪθ/
ADJECTIVE
The sixtieth item in a series is the one counted as number sixty.
EG *... the sixtieth time*

sixty /'sɪkstɪ/
sixties
the number 60
EG *... sixty days*
EG *... the nineteen-sixties*

size /saɪz/
sizes
NOUN

1 The size of something is how big or small it is.
EG *... the size of the audience*
EG *... an area half the size of Britain*
2 The size of something is the fact that it is very large.
EG *I was impressed by the size of the rooms.*
3 one of the standard measurements of clothes and shoes
EG *Have you got it in a bigger size?*

skate /skeɪt/
skates skating skated
NOUN
1 Skates are ice-skates.
EG *Bring your skates with you.*
VERB
2 If you skate, you move about wearing ice-skates.
EG *Dan skated up to them.*

skeleton /'skelɪtn/
skeletons
NOUN
Your skeleton is the framework of bones in your body.
EG *Police found a human skeleton.*

skeptical /'skeptɪkl/
see **sceptical**

sketch /sketʃ/
sketches sketching sketched
NOUN
1 a quick, rough drawing
EG *Make a sketch of the area.*
VERB
2 If you sketch something, you draw it quickly and roughly.
EG *He sketched a map for us.*

ski /skiː/
skis skiing skied
NOUN
1 Skis are long pieces of wood, metal, or plastic that you fasten to special boots so that you can move easily over snow.

EG *I hired a pair of skis.*
VERB
2 When you ski, you move over snow wearing skis.
EG *They skied down the mountain.*

skid /skɪd/
skids skidding skidded
VERB
If a vehicle skids, it slides in an uncontrolled way, for example because the road is wet or covered in ice.
EG *The plane skidded off the runway.*

skilful /'skɪlful/
US **skillful**
ADJECTIVE
If you are skilful at something, you can do it very well.
EG *... a skilful politician*

skill /skɪl/
skills
NOUN
1 Skill is the knowledge and ability that allows you to do something well.
EG *... his lack of skill at sports*
2 a type of work or technique which requires special training or knowledge
EG *... someone who is always learning new skills*

skilled /skɪld/
ADJECTIVE
Someone who is skilled has the knowledge and ability to do something well.
EG *Most doctors are highly skilled in treating patients.*

skillful /'skɪlful/
see **skilful**

skin /skɪn/
skins
NOUN

1 Your skin is the natural covering of your body.
EG *His skin is clear and smooth.*
2 An animal skin is skin which has been removed from a dead animal.
EG *... a bag made of real crocodile skin*
3 The skin of a fruit or vegetable is its outer layer.
EG *... a banana skin*

skinny /'skɪnɪ/
skinnier skinniest
ADJECTIVE
AN INFORMAL WORD
very thin
EG *... skinny legs*

skip /skɪp/
skips skipping skipped
VERB
1 If you skip somewhere, you move there by jumping from one foot to the other.
EG *They skipped down the street.*
2 When someone skips, they swing a rope up and down and jump over it.
EG *... a little girl skipping and singing*
3 If you skip something, you decide not to do it.
EG *It is important not to skip meals.*

skirt /skɜːt/
skirts
NOUN
a piece of clothing worn by women and girls, which fastens at the waist and hangs down over the legs
EG *... a short skirt*

skull /skʌl/
skulls
NOUN
Your skull is the top part of your head which surrounds your brain.

EG *He has a fractured skull.*

sky /skaɪ/
skies

NOUN

The sky is the space around the earth which you can see when you look upwards.

EG *The sun was high in the sky.*

EG *... warm sunshine and blue skies*

slam /slæm/
slams slamming slammed

VERB

1 If you slam a door, or if it slams, it shuts noisily and with great force.

EG *He slammed the gate behind him.*

2 If you slam something down, you put it there quickly and with great force.

EG *She slammed the phone down.*

slap /slæp/
slaps slapping slapped

VERB

1 If you slap someone, you hit them with the flat, open part of your hand.

EG *I slapped him on the face.*

NOUN

2 If you give someone a slap, you slap them.

EG *She gave her sister a hard slap.*

slash /slæʃ/
slashes slashing slashed

VERB

If you slash something, you make a long, deep cut in it.

EG *Four cars had their tyres slashed.*

slaughter /ˈslɔːtər/
slaughters slaughtering slaughtered

VERB

1 If people or animals are slaughtered, they are killed in an unjust or cruel way.

EG *Most of the villagers had been slaughtered.*

2 When farm animals are slaughtered, they are killed for their meat.

EG *... causing farmers to slaughter their stock*

slave /sleɪv/
slaves

NOUN

a person who is owned by another person and must work for them

EG *The state was founded by freed slaves from the USA.*

sleep /sliːp/
sleeps sleeping slept

NOUN

1 Sleep is the natural state of rest in which your eyes are closed, your body is inactive, and you do not think.

EG *Try to get some sleep.*

EG *Be quiet and go to sleep.*

2 a period of sleep

EG *... after a long sleep*

VERB

3 When you sleep, you rest in a state of sleep.

EG *She slept till noon.*

sleeve /sliːv/
sleeves

NOUN

The sleeves of a piece of clothing are the parts that cover your arms.

EG *... a shirt with long sleeves*

slept /slept/
past participle and past tense of **sleep**

slice /slaɪs/
slices slicing sliced

NOUN

1 A slice of cake, bread, or other food is a piece of it cut from a larger piece.

EG *... a small slice of cake*

VERB
2 If you slice food, you cut it into thin pieces.
EG *... sliced bread*

slide /slaɪd/
slides sliding slid

VERB
1 When something slides, or when you slide it, it moves smoothly over or against something else.
EG *Tears were sliding down his cheeks.*
EG *She slid the door open.*

NOUN
2 a small piece of photographic film which you project onto a screen
EG *... a slide show*

slight /slaɪt/
slighter slightest

ADJECTIVE
small in amount or degree
EG *... a slight dent in the car*
EG *It doesn't make the slightest difference.*

slightly /ˈslaɪtlɪ/

ADVERB
Slightly means to some degree but not to a very large degree.
EG *They moved to a slightly larger house.*
EG *You can adjust it slightly.*

slim /slɪm/
slimmer slimmest; slims slimming slimmed

ADJECTIVE
1 A slim person has a thin and well-shaped body.
EG *She looked slimmer after her holiday.*

2 A slim object is thinner than usual.
EG *... a slim book*

3 A slim chance or possibility is a very small one.
EG *There is a slim chance we will meet later.*

VERB
4 If you **are slimming**, you are trying to become thinner by eating less.
EG *... to refuse foods because I was slimming*

slip /slɪp/
slips slipping slipped

VERB
1 If you slip, you accidentally slide and lose your balance.
EG *She slipped on the ice.*

2 If something slips, it slides out of place.
EG *One of the knives slipped from her hand.*

3 If you slip somewhere, you go there quickly and quietly.
EG *She slipped out of the house.*

4 If you slip something somewhere, you put it there quickly and quietly.
EG *He slipped a ten-pound note into my pocket.*

NOUN
5 a small or unimportant mistake
EG *There must be no slips.*

6 A slip of paper is a small piece of paper.
EG *... little slips of paper torn from a notebook*

slipper /ˈslɪpəʳ/
slippers

NOUN
Slippers are loose, soft shoes that you wear indoors.
EG *... a pair of comfortable slippers*

slippery /ˈslɪpərɪ/

ADJECTIVE
smooth, wet, or greasy, and difficult to walk on or to hold

A
B
C
D
E
F
G
H
I
J
K
L
M
N
O
P
Q
R
S
T
U
V
W
X
Y
Z

EG *The floor was wet and slippery.*

slope /sləup/
slopes sloping sloped

NOUN
1 a flat surface that is at an angle, so that one end is higher than the other
EG *The street is on a slope.*

VERB
2 If a surface slopes, it is at an angle.
EG *The hill slopes down to the river.*

slot /slɒt/
slots slotting slotted

NOUN
1 a narrow opening in a machine or container, for example for putting coins in
EG *I dropped a coin in the slot and dialled the number.*

VERB
2 If you **slot** something **into** something else, you put it into a space where it fits.
EG *He was slotting a CD into the CD player.*

slow /sləu/
slower slowest; slows slowing slowed

ADJECTIVE
1 Something that is slow moves or happens with very little speed.
EG *His progress was slow.*
EG *... a slow process*
2 If a clock or watch is slow, it shows a time earlier than the correct one.
EG *My watch was 15 minutes slow.*

VERB
3 If something slows, or if you slow it, it moves or happens more slowly.
EG *Traffic has slowed in the city.*
EG *She slowed the car and turned the corner.*

slow down
VERB
If someone or something slows down, or if something slows them down, they move more slowly.
EG *The car slowed down.*
EG *His injury slowed him down.*

slowly /'sləuli/
ADVERB
moving or happening with very little speed
EG *She walked slowly away.*
EG *He speaks very slowly.*

smack /smæk/
smacks smacking smacked

VERB
1 If you smack someone, you hit them with your open hand.
EG *... parents who smack their children*

NOUN
2 an act of smacking someone
EG *... a smack on the hand*

small /smɔːl/
smaller smallest

ADJECTIVE
1 not large in size, number, or amount
EG *She is small for her age.*
EG *... a small group of students*
EG *... a small amount of money*
2 not important or significant
EG *It needs a few small changes.*
3 A small child is a very young child.
EG *I have a wife and two small children.*

smart /smɑːt/
smarter smartest

ADJECTIVE
1 neat and clean in appearance
EG *She wore a black dress and looked very smart.*
EG *... smart new offices*

A
B
C
D
E
F
G
H
I
J
K
L
M
N
O
P
Q
R
S
T
U
V
W
X
Y
Z

2 clever

EG *He thinks he's so smart.*

smash /smæʃ/
smashes smashing smashed

VERB

1 If something smashes, or if you smash it, it breaks into many pieces.

EG *The glass fell and smashed on the floor.*

EG *Someone smashed a bottle.*

2 If you **smash through** something such as a wall, you go through it by breaking it.

EG *Demonstrators used trucks to smash through the gates.*

3 If something **smashes against** or **into** something else, it hits it with great force.

EG *A huge wave smashed against the boat.*

smell /smɛl/
smells smelling smelled or **smelt**

NOUN

1 The smell of something is a quality it has which you become aware of through your nose.

EG *... the smell of freshly baked bread*

EG *There was a funny smell in the kitchen.*

2 Your **sense of smell** is your ability to smell things.

EG *She has lost her sense of smell.*

VERB

3 If you smell something, you become aware of it through your nose.

EG *As soon as we came in, we could smell gas.*

EG *I picked up a rose and smelled it.*

4 If someone or something **smells of** a particular thing, they have a particular quality which you

become aware of through your nose.

EG *He smelled of tobacco.*

EG *It smells delicious!*

5 If something smells, it has an unpleasant smell.

EG *Do my feet smell?*

smile /smaɪl/
smiles smiling smiled

VERB

1 When you smile, the corners of your mouth curve outwards, usually because you are pleased or find something funny.

EG *We both smiled at the picture.*

NOUN

2 the expression that you have on your face when you smile

EG *She's got a lovely smile.*

smoke /sməuk/
smokes smoking smoked

NOUN

1 Smoke is a mixture of gas and other material that is sent into the air when something burns.

EG *... cigarette smoke*

VERB

2 When someone smokes a cigarette, cigar, or pipe, they suck smoke from it into their mouth and blow it out again.

EG *He sat in the corner and smoked a cigarette.*

3 If you smoke, you regularly smoke cigarettes, cigars, or a pipe.

EG *When did you start smoking?*

4 If something is smoking, smoke is coming from it.

EG *... a pile of smoking wood*

smooth /smuːð/
smoother smoothest; smooths smoothing smoothed

ADJECTIVE

1 A smooth surface or mixture has

no rough parts or lumps in it.
EG *... a smooth surface such as glass*

2 A smooth movement or process happens evenly and with no sudden changes.
EG *She turned round in a smooth movement.*

3 successful and without problems
EG *... the smooth transition from communism to capitalism*

VERB

4 If you **smooth** something **down** or **smooth** it **out**, you move your hands over it to make it smooth and flat.
EG *She stood up and smoothed down her dress.*

smuggle /'smʌgl/
smuggles smuggling smuggled

VERB

If someone smuggles things or people into a place or out of a place, they take them there illegally or secretly.
EG *If you try to smuggle drugs, you are stupid.*
EG *... an attempt to smuggle a bomb into the airport*

snack /snæk/
snacks

NOUN

a simple, quick meal
EG *I only had time for a snack.*

snail /sneɪl/
snails

NOUN

a small, slow-moving creature with a long, shiny body and a shell on its back
EG *... a restaurant that served snails*

snake /sneɪk/
snakes

NOUN

a long, thin reptile with no legs
EG *She was afraid of snakes.*

snap /snæp/
snaps snapping snapped

VERB

1 If something snaps, or if you snap it, it breaks with a sharp cracking noise.
EG *The rope snapped.*
EG *She gripped the pipe, trying to snap it in half.*

2 If someone **snaps** at you, they speak to you in a sharp, unfriendly way.
EG *I was upset because Linda snapped at me.*

NOUN

3 the sound of something snapping
EG *The branch broke with a snap.*

snatch /snætʃ/
snatches snatching snatched

VERB

1 If you snatch something, you reach out for it and take it quickly.
EG *Mick snatched the letter from her hand.*

NOUN

2 A snatch of a conversation or song is a very small piece of it.
EG *I only heard snatches of the conversation.*

sneak /sniːk/
sneaks sneaking sneaked

VERB

If you sneak somewhere, you go there quietly, trying to be seen or heard.
EG *He used to sneak out of the house late at night.*

sneeze /sniːz/
sneezes sneezing sneezed

VERB

1 When you sneeze, you suddenly take in breath and blow it down your nose suddenly, because you have a cold or because something has irritated your nose.
EG *I couldn't stop sneezing.*

NOUN
2 an act of sneezing
EG *Coughs and sneezes spread colds.*

sniff /snɪf/
sniffs sniffing sniffed

VERB
1 When you sniff, you breathe in air noisily through your nose, for example because you are trying not to cry.
EG *She wiped her eyes and sniffed loudly.*

2 If you sniff something, you smell it by sniffing.
EG *He sniffed the perfume she wore.*

NOUN
3 an act of sniffing
EG *Her tears gave way to sniffs.*

snooker /'snuːkər/

NOUN
Snooker is a game played on a large table. Players score points by knocking coloured balls into pockets using a long stick called a cue.
EG *... a game of snooker*

snore /snɔːr/
snores snoring snored

VERB
1 When someone who is asleep snores, they make a loud noise each time they breathe.
EG *His mouth was open and he was snoring loudly.*

NOUN
2 an act of snoring
EG *His snores kept me awake.*

snow /snəʊ/
snows snowing snowed

NOUN
1 Snow is the soft white bits of ice which fall from the sky in cold weather.
EG *The ground was covered in snow.*

VERB
2 When snow falls, you can say that **it is snowing**.
EG *It has been snowing all night.*
EG *It hardly snowed at all last winter.*

snuck /snʌk/
In American English, snuck is the past participle and past tense of **sneak**

so /səʊ/

ADVERB
1 You use 'so' to refer back to something that has just been mentioned.
EG *Had he locked the car? If so, where were the keys?*
EG *"Was it worth it?" — "I think so."*

2 You use 'so' to say that something that has just been said about one person or thing is also true of another one.
EG *He laughed, and so did I.*

3 You use 'so' to emphasize the degree or extent of something.
EG *He was so tired that he slept for 15 hours.*
EG *Why are you so cruel?*

4 You use 'so' before 'much' and 'many' to emphasize the degree or extent of something.
EG *It hurt so much that I could hardly breathe.*
EG *So many children cannot read or write.*

5 AN INFORMAL EXPRESSION
You can say **So what?** to indicate

that something is not important.
EG *"It's a bit expensive." — "So what? It's worth it."*

6 You use **and so on** at the end of a list to indicate that there are other items that you could also mention.
EG *... health, education, tax and so on*

CONJUNCTION
7 You use 'so' to talk about the result of something.
EG *I was an only child, so I had no experience of large families.*

8 You use 'so', **so that** and **so as** to talk about the reason for something.
EG *Come here so I can see you.*
EG *He hurried her upstairs so that they wouldn't be seen.*
EG *I said nothing so as not to worry them.*

soak /səuk/
soaks soaking soaked
VERB
1 If you soak something, you put it into a liquid and leave it there.
EG *Soak the beans for 2 hours.*
2 If a liquid soaks something, it makes it very wet.
EG *Heavy rain had soaked the road.*
soak up
VERB
If something soaks up a liquid, the liquid goes up into it.
EG *Stir until the wheat has soaked up all the water.*

soap /səup/
NOUN
Soap is a substance that you use with water when you wash yourself.
EG *... a bar of soap*

soar /sɔːr/
soars soaring soared
VERB
1 If something soars into the air, it goes quickly up into the air.
EG *... as the jet soared away*
2 If an amount soars, it quickly increases by a great deal.
EG *Property prices soared.*

sober /ˈsəubər/
ADJECTIVE
If someone is sober, they are not drunk.
EG *He was seldom sober.*

so-called /ˈsəuˈkɔːld/
ADJECTIVE
You use 'so-called' to indicate that something is generally referred to by a particular word or name, especially when you think that word or name is misleading.
EG *She was one of the so-called Gang of Four.*
EG *... so-called experts*

soccer /ˈsɒkər/
NOUN
Soccer is a game played by two teams of eleven players who kick a ball in an attempt to score goals.
EG *... a soccer team*
☑ 'Soccer' is the usual name for the game in American English. In Britain it is usually referred to as *football*.

social /ˈsəuʃl/
ADJECTIVE
1 relating to society
EG *... crime and other social problems*
2 relating to leisure activities that involve meeting other people
EG *She has a busy social life.*

socialism /ˈsəuʃəlɪzəm/
NOUN
Socialism is a political philosophy which aims to create a fair and

equal society and which believes
that the state should own the
country's main industries.
EG ... *the decline of socialism*

socialist /'səʊʃəlɪst/
socialists

NOUN

1 a person who believes in
socialism
EG *He's a committed socialist.*

ADJECTIVE

2 relating to socialism
EG ... *her socialist views*

society /sə'saɪətɪ/
societies

NOUN

1 Society is all the people in a
particular country or region.
EG ... *people in Western society*
EG *We live in a capitalist society.*

2 an organization for people who
have the same interest or aim
EG ... *the local art appreciation
society*

sock /sɒk/
socks

NOUN

Socks are pieces of clothing that
cover your feet and ankles and are
worn inside shoes.
EG ... *a pair of dirty socks*

socket /'sɒkɪt/
sockets

NOUN

a device on a wall or on a piece of
electrical equipment into which
you can put a plug or bulb
EG *Remember to take the plug out
of the socket.*

sofa /'səʊfə/
sofas

NOUN

a long, comfortable seat for two or
three people with a back and arms

EG *We sat down on the sofa.*

soft /sɒft/
softer softest

ADJECTIVE

1 not hard or rough
EG ... *a soft bed*
EG *Her skin is so soft.*

2 gentle and without force
EG ... *a soft breeze*
EG *Her voice grew softer.*

3 If you are **soft on** someone,
you do not treat them as severely
as you should.
EG *You're far too soft on those kids.*

4 Soft drugs are illegal drugs
which some people do not
consider to be harmful.
EG ... *experimenting with soft drugs*

soft drink soft drinks

NOUN

a cold, non-alcoholic drink
EG ... *a wide selection of soft drinks*

software /'sɒftweəʳ/

NOUN

Computer programs are referred
to as software.
EG *There was a problem with the
software.*

soil /sɔɪl/

NOUN

Soil is the substance on the surface
of the Earth in which plants grow.
EG ... *an area with very good soil*

sold /səʊld/
past participle and past tense of
sell

soldier /'səʊldʒəʳ/
soldiers

NOUN

a person in an army
EG *Both his brothers are soldiers.*

sole /səʊl/
soles

A
B
C
D
E
F
G
H
I
J
K
L
M
N
O
P
Q
R
S
T
U
V
W
X
Y
Z

ADJECTIVE

1 The sole thing or person of a particular type is the only one of that type.
EG *Their sole aim is to make money.*
EG *He was the sole survivor.*

NOUN

2 The sole of your foot or shoe is the underneath part of it.
EG *They were beaten on the soles of their feet.*
EG *... shoes with rubber soles*

solicitor /sə'lɪsɪtəʳ/
solicitors

NOUN

a lawyer who gives legal advice and prepares legal documents and cases
EG *If you are arrested, you can phone a solicitor.*

solid /'sɒlɪd/
solids

ADJECTIVE

1 A solid substance or object is hard or firm, and not a liquid or gas.
EG *The cement will quickly turn solid.*
EG *He was not allowed to eat solid foods.*

2 A solid object does not have any holes or gaps in it.
EG *... a wall of solid rock*
EG *The car park is packed solid.*

NOUN

3 a substance or object that is solid
EG *Solids turn to liquids at certain temperatures.*

solution /sə'lu:ʃən/
solutions

NOUN

1 a way of dealing with a problem or difficult situation
EG *... a peaceful solution to the conflict*

2 The solution to a puzzle is the answer.
EG *The solution can be found on page 8.*

solve /sɒlv/
solves solving solved

VERB

If you solve a problem or a question, you find a solution or answer to it.
EG *Sarah solved their financial problems by taking lodgers.*
EG *Henry solved the puzzle in fifteen minutes.*

some /sʌm/

ADJECTIVE OR PRONOUN

1 You use 'some' to refer to a quantity or number when you are not stating the quantity or number exactly.
EG *There's some money on the table.*
EG *Some of the members are very old.*

☑ You do not use 'some' in negative sentences. Instead you use 'not any': *there isn't any money*. You only use 'some' in questions when you expect the answer yes: *did you buy some wine?*. Otherwise you say 'any': *did you buy any wine?*

ADJECTIVE

2 You use 'some' to emphasize that a quantity or number is fairly large.
EG *She had been there for some time.*

somebody /'sʌmbədɪ/

PRONOUN

Somebody means the same as someone.
EG *Somebody must know his address.*

☑ You do not use 'somebody' in

negative sentences. Instead you use 'not anybody': *there isn't anybody here*. You only use 'somebody' in questions when you expect the answer yes: *is somebody there?* Otherwise you say 'anybody': *is anybody there?*

somehow /'sʌmhaʊ/

ADVERB

1 You use 'somehow' to say that you do not know how something was done or will be done.
EG *You'll find a way of doing it somehow.*

2 You use 'somehow' to say that you do not know the reason for something.
EG *Somehow it didn't feel quite right.*

someone /'sʌmwʌn/

PRONOUN

You use 'someone' to refer to a person without saying exactly who you mean.
EG *I need someone to help me.*
☑ You do not use 'someone' in negative sentences. Instead you use 'not anyone': *there isn't anyone here*. You only use 'someone' in questions when you expect the answer yes: *is someone there?* Otherwise you say 'anyone': *is anyone there?*

something /'sʌmθɪŋ/

PRONOUN

You use 'something' to refer to a thing, idea, or event without saying exactly what it is.
EG *He had something in his hand.*
EG *Something was wrong.*
EG *He was busy doing something in the garden.*
☑ You do not use 'something' in negative sentences. Instead you use 'not anything': *there isn't*

anything here. You only use 'something' in questions when you expect the answer yes: *is something wrong?* Otherwise you say 'anything': *is anything wrong?*

sometimes /'sʌmtaɪmz/

ADVERB

You use 'sometimes' to say that something happens on some occasions.
EG *We sometimes play cards together.*

somewhat /'sʌmwɒt/

ADVERB

to some extent or degree
EG *He said conditions had improved somewhat.*

somewhere /'sʌmweəʳ/

ADVERB

1 You use 'somewhere' to refer to a place without saying exactly where it is.
EG *... a flat somewhere in London*
☑ You do not use 'somewhere' in negative sentences. Instead you use 'not anywhere': *he isn't going anywhere*. You only use 'somewhere' in questions when you expect the answer yes: *are you going somewhere tonight?* Otherwise you say 'anywhere': *are you going anywhere tonight?*

2 You use 'somewhere' when giving an amount, number, or time that is approximately correct.
EG *He is somewhere between 73 and 80 years of age.*

son /sʌn/
sons

NOUN

Your son is your male child.
EG *They have two sons and a daughter.*

A B C D E F G H I J K L M N O P Q R S T U V W X Y Z

song /sɒŋ/
songs

NOUN

a piece of music with words that are sung to the music

EG ... *a pop song*

son-in-law /'sʌnɪnlɔː/
sons-in-law

NOUN

Your son-in-law is the husband of your daughter.

EG ... *her son-in-law, Mark*

soon /suːn/
sooner soonest

ADVERB

1 If something is going to happen **soon**, it will happen after a short time.

EG *It will soon be Christmas.*

EG *The sooner we find him the better.*

2 If something happened **soon after** something else, it happened a short time after it.

EG *He qualified soon after leaving school.*

3 If something happens **as soon as** something else happens, it happens immediately after it.

EG *I'll let you know as soon as I hear anything.*

soothe /suːð/
soothes soothing soothed

VERB

1 If you **soothe** someone who is angry or upset, you make them calmer.

EG *She needed to be soothed and reassured.*

2 Something that **soothes** a part of your body makes it more relaxed or less painful.

EG ... *a bowl of water to soothe her tired feet*

sophisticated /səˈfɪstɪkeɪtɪd/

ADJECTIVE

1 A **sophisticated** person knows about culture, fashion, and other matters that are considered socially important.

EG ... *a very beautiful and sophisticated young woman*

2 A **sophisticated** machine or device is more advanced than others.

EG ... *a sophisticated new telescope*

sore /sɔːʳ/
sorer sorest; sores

ADJECTIVE

1 If part of your body is **sore**, it causes you pain and discomfort.

EG ... *a sore throat*

NOUN

2 a painful area of skin where the skin has become infected

EG ... *the sore on her lip*

sorry /'sɒrɪ/
sorrier sorriest

ADJECTIVE

1 If you say that you are **sorry about** something, you are expressing the sadness, regret, or sympathy that you feel because of it.

EG *She was very sorry about all the trouble she'd caused.*

EG *Sorry I'm late.*

EG *I'm sorry to bother you.*

2 If you **feel sorry for** someone, you feel sympathy and sadness for the situation that they are in.

EG *It's the children I feel sorry for.*

3 You say **Sorry?** when you want someone to repeat what they have just said.

EG *"It's in the fridge." — "Sorry?" — "I said it's in the fridge."*

sort /sɔːt/
sorts sorting sorted

NOUN

1 The different sorts of something are the different kinds or types of it.
EG *What sort of school did you go to?*
EG *... mushrooms of various sorts*

VERB
2 If you sort things, you arrange them into different groups.
EG *He sorted the papers into neat piles.*

sort out
VERB
If you sort out a problem, you solve it.
EG *We sorted out the problem about the tickets.*

sought /sɔːt/
past participle and past tense of **seek**.

soul /səʊl/
souls
NOUN
A person's soul is the spiritual part of them which some people think continues to exist after their body dies.
EG *They prayed for the souls of the dead.*

sound /saʊnd/
sounds sounding sounded; sounder soundest
NOUN
1 A sound is something that you hear.
EG *... the sound of a door opening*
2 Sound is what you hear when you hear something.
EG *... the speed of sound*

VERB
3 The way that someone or something sounds is the impression that you have of them when they speak or make a noise.
EG *She sounded angry.*
EG *It sounded like an explosion.*

4 If something such as a bell sounds, it makes a noise.
EG *The buzzer sounded in Daniel's office.*

ADJECTIVE
5 in good condition
EG *... a guarantee that the house is sound.*

6 reliable and sensible
EG *The logic behind the argument seems sound.*

soup /suːp/
soups
NOUN
Soup is a liquid food made by boiling meat, fish, or vegetables in water.
EG *... a bowl of chicken soup*

sour /ˈsaʊər/
ADJECTIVE
If something is sour, it has a sharp taste like the taste of a lemon.
EG *... sweet and sour sauce*

source /sɔːs/
sources
NOUN
The source of something is the person, place, or thing that it comes from.
EG *... new sources of energy*
EG *... a major source of income*

south /saʊθ/
NOUN
1 The south is the direction on your right when you are looking towards where the sun rises.
EG *... a warm breeze from the south*
2 The south of a place is the part which is towards the south.
EG *... a hotel in the south of France*

ADJECTIVE OR ADVERB
3 in or towards the south
EG *... the south coast of England*
EG *We were driving south.*

A B C D E F G H I J K L M N O P Q R S T U V W X Y Z

South America
NOUN
South America is the continent that lies to the south of North America.
EG ... a holiday in South America

south-east /sauθˈiːst/
NOUN, ADVERB, OR ADJECTIVE
South-east is halfway between south and east.
EG ... a city in the south-east
EG They moved south-east.
EG ... an area of south-east Ireland

southern /ˈsʌðən/
ADJECTIVE
in or from the south
EG ... the southern shores of the lake

south-west /sauθˈwɛst/
NOUN, ADVERB, OR ADJECTIVE
South-west is halfway between south and west.
EG ... a city in the south-west of America
EG We turned south-west.
EG ... the south-west tip of the island

souvenir /suːvəˈnɪəʳ/
souvenirs
NOUN
something that you keep to remind you of a holiday, place, or event
EG ... a souvenir of their holiday in Portugal

space /speɪs/
spaces
NOUN
1 Space is any area that is empty or available in a place.
EG There was plenty of space for the luggage.
2 Space is the area beyond the Earth's atmosphere.

EG ... launching satellites into space
3 a gap between two things
EG ... the space between the tables

span /spæn/
a past tense of spin

Spanish /ˈspænɪʃ/
ADJECTIVE
1 belonging or relating to Spain
EG ... a Spanish town
NOUN
2 Spanish is the main language spoken in Spain.
EG ... a degree in Spanish

spare /spɛəʳ/
spares sparing spared
ADJECTIVE
1 extra to what is needed
EG Don't forget to take some spare batteries.
EG ... the spare bedroom
NOUN
2 a thing that is extra to what is needed
EG ... two discs, with one as a spare
VERB
3 If you spare something such as time or money for a particular purpose, you make it available.
EG I simply can't spare the time.
4 If you have something to spare, you have more of it than you need.
EG She arrived with a few minutes to spare.
5 If someone is spared an unpleasant experience, they are prevented from having it.
EG I'll spare you the details.

spark /spɑːk/
sparks
NOUN
1 a tiny, bright piece of burning material that is thrown up by a fire
EG ... the sparks from the fire

2 a flash of light caused by electricity

EG *... a spark from the plug*

sparkle /'spɑːkl/
sparkles sparkling sparkled

VERB

If something sparkles, it shines with a lot of small, bright points of light.

EG *The waves sparkled in the starlight.*

spat /spæt/

past participle and past tense of **spit**

speak /spiːk/
speaks speaking spoke spoken

VERB

1 When you speak, you use your voice to say something.

EG *She was speaking about some of her experiences in India.*

EG *... as I spoke these words*

2 If you speak a foreign language, you know it and can use it.

EG *He doesn't speak English.*

speaker /'spiːkər/
speakers

NOUN

1 a person who is speaking, especially someone making a speech

EG *One speaker launched an attack on the government.*

2 a part of a radio or stereo through which sound comes out

EG *... a pair of speakers fixed to the wall*

special /'speʃl/

ADJECTIVE

Someone or something that is special is different from normal, often in a way that makes it more important or better than other people or things.

EG *You're very special to me, darling.*

EG *... special occasions such as weddings and birthdays*

EG *Karen had to get special permission to go there.*

specialise /'speʃəlaɪz/

another spelling of **specialize**

specialist /'speʃəlɪst/
specialists

NOUN

a person who has a particular skill or who knows a lot about a particular subject

EG *... a skin specialist*

specialize /'speʃəlaɪz/
specializes specializing specialized; also spelt **specialise**

VERB

If you **specialize in** something, you know a lot about it and spend a lot of time on it.

EG *... a shop specializing in pottery*

species /'spiːʃiːz/

☑ The plural is *species*.

NOUN

a class of plants or animals whose members have the same characteristics and are able to breed with each other

EG *... an endangered species*

specific /spə'sɪfɪk/

ADJECTIVE

1 You use 'specific' to emphasize that you are talking about a particular thing.

EG *There are several specific problems to be dealt with.*

2 precise and exact

EG *I asked him to be more specific.*

spectacle /'spektəkl/
spectacles

A
B
C
D
E
F
G
H
I
J
K
L
M
N
O
P
Q
R
S
T
U
V
W
X
Y
Z

NOUN

1 an interesting or impressive sight or event

EG … *an astonishing spectacle*

PLURAL NOUN

2 A FORMAL USE

Someone's **spectacles** are their glasses.

EG … *a pair of spectacles on a gold chain*

spectacular /spɛkˈtækjələʳ/

ADJECTIVE

very impressive or dramatic

EG *a spectacular success*

EG *The view was spectacular.*

speculate /ˈspɛkjuleɪt/

speculates speculating speculated

VERB

If you speculate about something, you guess about its nature or about what might happen.

EG *He refused to speculate about the reasons for the decision.*

sped /spɛd/

past participle and past tense of **speed**

speech /spiːtʃ/

speeches

NOUN

1 Speech is the ability to speak or the act of speaking.

EG … *the development of speech in children*

EG *She liked to imitate his speech.*

2 a formal talk that is given to an audience

EG … *a long speech about farming*

speed /spiːd/

speeds speeding sped or **speeded**

NOUN

1 The speed of something is the rate at which it moves or happens.

EG … *the speed of light*

EG *Each learner can proceed at his own speed.*

2 Speed is very fast movement.

EG *Speed is what motor racing is all about.*

VERB

3 If you speed somewhere, you move or travel there quickly.

EG *He sped through the empty streets.*

4 Someone who **is speeding** is driving a vehicle faster than the legal speed limit.

EG *He was not insured and he was speeding.*

speed up

VERB

If something speeds up, or if you speed it up, it moves or happens more quickly.

EG *Her breathing had speeded up.*

☑ The past tense and past participle for 'speed up' are *speeded*, but for the other senses they are *sped*.

spell /spɛl/

spells spelling spelt or **spelled**

VERB

1 When you spell a word, you say or write its letters in the correct order.

EG *She spelt her name for him and he wrote it down.*

NOUN

2 A spell of something is a short period of it.

EG … *a spell of fine weather*

3 a word or sequence of words that is used to perform magic

EG … *after a witch cast a spell on her*

spend /spɛnd/

spends spending spent

VERB

1 When you spend money, you buy things with it.
EG *I spent a hundred pounds on clothes.*

2 If you spend time or energy doing something, you use time or energy doing it.
EG *He spent ten minutes studying the diagrams.*

3 If you spend time somewhere, you stay there for that time.
EG *We spent the night in a hotel.*

spice /spaɪs/
spices

NOUN
a powder or seeds from a plant that you add to food to give it flavour
EG *... herbs and spices*

spider /'spaɪdər/
spiders

NOUN
a small creature with eight legs that spins webs to catch insects for food
EG *He is frightened of spiders.*

spill /spɪl/
spills spilling spilled or **spilt**

VERB
If you spill a liquid, or if it spills, it accidentally flows out of its container.
EG *I almost spilled my drink.*
EG *Petrol spilled onto the ground.*

spin /spɪn/
spins spinning span spun
☑ The past tense can be either 'spun' or 'span', but 'spun' is more common.

VERB
1 If someone or something spins, or if you spin them, they turn quickly around a central point.
EG *He spun round and fired.*

EG *Ella spun the wheel and turned onto Main Street.*

NOUN
2 a rapid turn around a central point
EG *... a spin of the wheel*

spine /spaɪn/
spines

NOUN
Your spine is the row of bones down your back.
EG *... an operation on her spine*

spirit /'spɪrɪt/
spirits

NOUN
1 Your spirit is the part of you that is not physical and that is connected with your deepest thoughts and feelings.
EG *Marian still has a youthful spirit.*

2 A person's spirit is the part of them that is believed to remain alive after they die.
EG *... the spirits of the dead*

3 a ghost or non-physical being
EG *... woods haunted by evil spirits*

4 Spirit is courage and determination.
EG *I admired her spirit.*

PLURAL NOUN
5 You can refer to your **spirits** when you are saying how happy or unhappy you are.
EG *He is in very good spirits.*

6 spirits are strong alcoholic drinks such as whisky and gin
EG *He never drinks spirits.*

spiritual /'spɪrɪtjuəl/

ADJECTIVE
relating to people's religious beliefs
EG *... spiritual guidance*

spit /spɪt/
spits spitting spat
☑ In American English, the past

A B C D E F G H I J K L M N O P Q R S T U V W X Y Z

tense and past participle is 'spit'.

VERB
If you spit, or if you spit
something **out**, you force liquid or
food out of your mouth.
EG *One of the soldiers spat at her.*
EG *Sinclair took one sip and spat
the wine out.*

spite /spaɪt/
NOUN
1 You use **in spite of** to
introduce a statement which
makes the rest of what you are
saying seem surprising.
EG *In spite of all the gossip, Virginia
stayed behind.*
2 If you do something **out of
spite**, you do it in order to hurt or
upset someone.
EG *I refused her a divorce, out of
spite I suppose.*

splash /splæʃ/
splashes splashing splashed
VERB
1 If you splash around in water,
you disturb the water in a noisy
way.
EG *... the sound of children
splashing about in the waves*
2 If you splash a liquid
somewhere, or if it splashes, it
scatters in a lot of small drops.
EG *He splashed some water on his
face.*
EG *... the beer that had splashed
onto the carpet*
NOUN
3 A splash is the sound made
when something hits or falls into
water.
EG *She hit the water with a huge
splash.*

splendid /'splendɪd/
ADJECTIVE
very good or impressive

EG *Maree is a splendid cook.*

split /splɪt/
splits splitting split
VERB
1 If something splits, or if you split
it, it divides into two or more parts.
EG *The ship split in two.*
EG *The children were split into three
groups.*
2 If people split something, they
share it between them.
EG *They split the money equally.*
NOUN
3 a crack or tear
EG *... a big split in his jeans*

spoil /spɔɪl/
spoils spoiling spoiled or
spoilt
VERB
1 If someone or something spoils
something, they prevent it from
being successful or satisfactory.
EG *My holiday was spoiled by rain.*
EG *He spoiled everything by getting
drunk.*
2 If someone spoils their children,
they give their children everything
they want.
EG *She was spoiled as a child.*

spoke /spəʊk/
past tense of **speak**

spoken /'spəʊkn/
past participle of **speak**

spokesman /'spəʊksmən/
spokesmen
NOUN
a man who speaks as the
representative of a group or
organization
EG *... a spokesman for the
government*
☑ If the person is a woman, you
can refer to her as a
'spokeswoman'. A 'spokesperson'

can be either a man or a woman.

sponsor /'spɒnsər/
sponsors sponsoring sponsored

VERB

1 If an organization sponsors something, it gives money to pay for it.
EG *The exhibition was sponsored by The Independent.*

2 If you sponsor someone who is doing something for charity, you give them money for the charity if they succeed in doing it.
EG *I sponsored Andrew to run the London marathon.*

NOUN

3 a person or organization that sponsors something or someone
EG *... a shirt with the name of the club's sponsors on it*

spoon /spu:n/
spoons

NOUN

an object shaped like a small shallow bowl with a long handle, used for eating, stirring, and serving food
EG *... a wooden spoon*

sport /spɔːt/
sports

NOUN

Sports are games such as football and tennis which require physical effort and skill.
EG *Her favourite sport is tennis.*
EG *He's not interested in sport.*

spot /spɒt/
spots spotting spotted

NOUN

1 Spots are small, round, coloured areas on a surface.
EG *... a white skirt with blue spots*
EG *... spots of blood*

2 a place
EG *... the most beautiful spot in the garden*

3 a small lump on a person's skin
EG *... a cream for removing spots*

VERB

4 If you spot someone or something, you notice them.
EG *I spotted him going into a shop.*

sprang /spræŋ/
past tense of **spring**

spray /spreɪ/
sprays spraying sprayed

NOUN

1 Spray consists of many small drops of liquid which are splashed or forced into the air.
EG *... the spray from the waterfall*

VERB

2 If you spray a liquid somewhere, or if it sprays somewhere, it covers a place with drops of the liquid.
EG *She sprayed perfume on her wrists.*
EG *Drops of blood sprayed across the room.*

spread /spred/
spreads spreading spread

VERB

1 If you spread something somewhere or **spread** it **out**, you open or arrange it so that all of it can be seen or used.
EG *He spread out the map on the floor.*

2 If you **spread** a substance **on** a surface, you put a thin layer of it on the surface.
EG *... as she spread butter on her toast*

3 If something spreads or is spread, it gradually reaches a larger area or affects more people.
EG *The news spread quickly.*
EG *... the lies that were being*

spread about him

4 If something **is spread over** a period of time, it is distributed evenly over that period.
EG *The course was spread over five weeks.*

NOUN

5 The spread of something is its increasing presence or growth.
EG *... the spread of modern technology*

spring /sprɪŋ/
springs springing sprang sprung

NOUN

1 Spring is the season between winter and summer.
EG *The weather in spring can be very changeable.*
EG *... in the spring of 1999*

2 a piece of wire formed into loops which returns to its original shape after it is pressed or pulled
EG *... an old chair with the springs sticking out*

3 a place where water comes up through the ground
EG *... a hot spring*

VERB

4 If someone or something springs somewhere, they move there suddenly and quickly.
EG *Martha sprang to her feet.*
EG *The car boot sprang open.*

sprinkle /'sprɪŋkl/
sprinkles sprinkling sprinkled

VERB

If you sprinkle a liquid or powder over something, you scatter it over it.
EG *She sprinkled sand on the fire.*

sprint /sprɪnt/
sprints sprinting sprinted

NOUN

1 a short, fast race
EG *... the 100-metres sprint*

VERB

2 If you sprint somewhere, you run there very quickly.
EG *... as she sprinted up the steps*

sprung /sprʌŋ/
past participle of **spring**

spun /spʌn/
past participle and past tense of **spin**

spur /spɜːr/
spurs spurring spurred

VERB

1 If something **spurs** you **to do** something or **spurs** you **on**, it encourages you to do it.
EG *The complaint spurred the government to change the law.*

NOUN

2 If you do something **on the spur of the moment**, you do it suddenly, without planning it.
EG *They decided to go fishing on the spur of the moment.*

spy /spaɪ/
spies spying spied

NOUN

1 a person whose job is to find out secret information about a country or organization
EG *He was arrested as a spy.*

VERB

2 Someone who spies tries to find out secret information about another country or organization.
EG *... four men spying for the United States*

3 If you **spy on** someone, you watch them secretly.
EG *His bosses spied on him for months.*

squad /skwɒd/
squads

NOUN

a small group of people that is chosen to do a particular activity

EG ... *the Dutch football squad*

EG ... *a firing squad*

square /skweə^r/

squares

NOUN

1 a shape with four sides of the same length and four ninety-degree angles

EG *She drew a square on the envelope.*

2 a flat, open place in a town or city, bordered by buildings or streets

EG ... *Trafalgar Square*

ADJECTIVE

3 shaped like a square

EG ... *a big square desk*

squash /skwɒʃ/

squashes squashing squashed

VERB

1 If you squash something, you press it so that it becomes flat or loses its shape.

EG *She squashed the wasp with her foot.*

NOUN

2 Squash is a game in which two players hit a rubber ball against the walls of a court using special bats.

EG ... *a game of squash*

squeak /skwiːk/

squeaks squeaking squeaked

VERB

1 If something squeaks, it makes a short, high-pitched sound.

EG *My boots squeaked as I walked.*

NOUN

2 a short, high-pitched sound

EG ... *the squeak of the garden gate*

squeeze /skwiːz/

squeezes squeezing squeezed

VERB

1 When you squeeze something, you press it firmly from two sides.

EG *She paused to squeeze my hand.*

EG ... *freshly squeezed oranges*

2 If you squeeze somewhere, you manage to get into or through a small space.

EG ... *youngsters who can squeeze through tiny windows*

NOUN

3 an act of squeezing something

EG *She gave my hand a squeeze.*

stab /stæb/

stabs stabbing stabbed

VERB

If someone stabs another person, they push a knife into their body.

EG *George was stabbed in the chest.*

stable /'steɪbl/

stables

ADJECTIVE

1 Something that is stable is not likely to change or move.

EG *The price of oil remained stable.*

EG ... *a stable platform*

NOUN

2 A stable or **a stables** is a building in which horses are kept.

EG *The horses were led back to the stables.*

stack /stæk/

stacks

NOUN

A stack of things is a pile of them, one on top of the other.

EG ... *a stack of books*

stadium /'steɪdɪəm/

stadiums or **stadia**

NOUN

a sports ground with rows of seats

528

around it
EG ... the new football stadium

staff /stɑːf/

NOUN
The staff of an organization are the people who work for it.
EG ... the lack of staff
☑ You can use either a singular or a plural verb after: *the staff was helpful*; *the staff were helpful*.

stage /steɪdʒ/
stages staging staged

NOUN
1 A stage of a process or activity is one part of it.
EG ... the final stage of their world tour
2 In a theatre, the stage is the area where the actors or entertainers perform.
EG ... the lights above the stage

VERB
3 If someone stages a play or other event, they organize and present it.
EG The group planned to stage a concert in Berlin.

stain /steɪn/
stains staining stained

NOUN
1 a mark on something that is difficult to remove
EG She had a dark stain on her dress.

VERB
2 If a liquid stains something, the thing becomes coloured or marked by the liquid.
EG Tea and coffee can stain your teeth.

stair /steər/
stairs

PLURAL NOUN
1 stairs are a set of steps inside a

building which go from one floor to another
EG We walked up a flight of stairs.

NOUN
2 one of the steps in a flight of stairs
EG Terry was sitting on the bottom stair.

stake /steɪk/
stakes staking staked

NOUN
1 If something is **at stake**, it might be lost or damaged if something else is not successful.
EG The whole future of the company was at stake.

PLURAL NOUN
2 The **stakes** involved in something are the things that can be gained or lost.
EG ... a game of poker for high stakes

VERB
3 If you **stake** your career or reputation **on** the result of something, you risk harming your career or reputation if the result is unfavourable.
EG He is prepared to stake his career on this.

stalk /stɔːk/
stalks stalking stalked

NOUN
1 The stalk of a flower, leaf, or fruit is the thin part that joins it to the plant or tree.
EG ... a single flower on a long stalk

VERB
2 If someone stalks a person or wild animal, they follow them quietly in order to observe them or catch them.
EG ... like a hunter stalking his prey

stall /stɔːl/
stalls

NOUN
a large table containing information or goods for sale
EG ... *a market stall selling local fruit*

stamp /stæmp/
stamps stamping stamped

NOUN
1 a small piece of paper which you stick on a letter or parcel to show that you have paid the cost of posting it
EG ... *a first-class stamp*

2 a mark made by stamping something
EG *You need a special stamp in your passport.*

VERB
3 If you stamp a piece of paper, you make a mark on it using a small block with words or a design on it.
EG *He examined her ticket and stamped it.*

4 If you stamp or **stamp** your **foot**, you lift your foot and put it down hard on the ground.
EG ... *the woman who had stamped on my toe*
EG *She was stamping her feet to keep out the cold.*

stamp out

VERB
If you stamp something out, you put an end to it.
EG ... *the battle to stamp out bullying in schools*

stand /stænd/
stands standing stood

VERB
1 When you are standing, you are upright, your legs are straight, and your weight is supported by your feet.
EG ... *a young man who was standing outside the hotel*

EG *They told me to stand still.*

2 When someone who is sitting stands or **stands up**, they change position so that they are standing.
EG *When I walked in, they all stood up.*

3 If something stands somewhere, that is where it is.
EG *The house stands on top of a small hill.*

4 If you stand something somewhere, you put it there in an upright position.
EG *I stood the ladder against the wall.*

5 If a decision or offer stands, it it still exists and has not been cancelled.
EG *My offer stands until Wednesday.*

6 If you stand in an election, you are a candidate in it.
EG *She was invited to stand as the Labour candidate.*

7 If something can stand a situation or test, it is good enough or strong enough not to be damaged by it.
EG ... *books that have stood the test of time*

8 If you **cannot stand** someone or something, you hate them.
EG *I can't stand that woman.*

9 When someone **stands trial**, they are tried in a law court.
EG *Five people are to stand trial for the murder.*

NOUN
10 a small shop or stall, usually outdoors
EG ... *a hot dog stand*

11 an object that is designed for supporting or holding something
EG ... *an umbrella stand*

stand for

VERB

1 If a letter **stands for** a particular word, it is an abbreviation for that word.

EG *DVD stands for Digital Versatile Disc.*

2 The ideas that someone or something **stands for** are the ones that they support or represent.

EG *He hates us and everything we stand for.*

standard /ˈstændəd/
standards

NOUN

1 a level of quality or achievement, especially one that is considered acceptable

EG *The standard of professional cricket has never been lower.*

EG *... work of a very high standard*

ADJECTIVE

2 usual and normal

EG *Everyone wore suits, which is standard practice.*

star /staːʳ/
stars

NOUN

1 a large ball of burning gas in space that appears to us as a point of light in the sky at night

EG *... the stars in the sky*

2 a shape with four or more points sticking out in a regular pattern

EG *... a list of names with gold stars next to them*

3 Famous actors, sports players, and musicians are referred to as stars.

EG *... a pop star*

stare /steəʳ/
stares staring stared

VERB

If you **stare at** someone or something, you look at them for a long time.

EG *He kept staring at the photograph.*

start /staːt/
starts starting started

VERB

1 If you **start doing** something or **start to do** it, you do something that you were not doing before.

EG *Suzy started crying.*

EG *He started to walk away.*

2 When something **starts**, or when someone **starts** it, it begins to exist or happen.

EG *The meeting starts at 10.30.*

EG *He wants to start his own restaurant.*

NOUN

3 The **start** of something is the point or time at which it begins.

EG *... at the start of the summer*

startle /ˈstaːtl/
startles startling startled

VERB

If something sudden and unexpected **startles** you, it surprises you and frightens you slightly.

EG *The sound of his voice startled her.*

starve /staːv/
starves starving starved

VERB

If people **are starving**, they are suffering from a serious lack of food and may die.

EG *Millions were starving in Africa.*

state /steɪt/
states stating stated

NOUN

1 The **state** of something is its condition or what it is like at a particular time.

EG *He complained about the terrible state of the room.*

EG *... a report on the state of the British economy*

2 Countries are sometimes referred to as states.
EG *... a small European state*

3 Some countries are divided into regions called states which make some of their own laws.
EG *... the State of Vermont*

4 You can refer to the government of a country as **the state**.
EG *Carmen received a pension from the state.*

VERB

5 If you state something, you say it or write it, especially in a formal way.
EG *Please state your name and address.*

statement /'steɪtmənt/
statements

NOUN
something that you say or write which gives information in a formal way
EG *Her husband made a statement to the police.*

station /'steɪʃən/
stations stationing stationed

NOUN
1 a building by a railway line where trains stop for passengers
EG *... Euston Station*

2 A **bus station** or **coach station** is a place where buses or coaches start a journey.
EG *You can consult timetables at any bus station.*

3 A radio or television station is a particular radio or television company.
EG *... a local radio station*

VERB
4 Someone who **is stationed** somewhere is sent there to work

or do a particular job.
EG *Her husband was stationed in Vienna.*

statistics /stə'tɪstɪks/

PLURAL NOUN
Statistics are facts that are expressed in numbers.
EG *... official statistics about wage increases*

statue /'stætjuː/
statues

NOUN
a large model of a person or animal, made of stone, bronze, or some other hard material
EG *... a statue of Queen Victoria*

status /'steɪtəs/

NOUN
1 A person's status is their social or professional position.
EG *He was promoted to the status of foreman.*

2 Status is the importance and respect that people give to something.
EG *... in order to give the job more status*

stay /steɪ/
stays staying stayed

VERB
1 If you stay in a place or position, you continue to be there and do not leave.
EG *She stayed at home all day.*
EG *Stay away from the rocks.*

2 If you stay in a town or hotel, you live there for a short time.
EG *We stayed at a lovely hotel.*

3 If someone or something stays in a particular condition, they continue to be in it.
EG *Nothing stays the same for long.*
EG *She struggled to stay awake.*

NOUN

4 a period of time spent somewhere
EG *... after a short stay in hospital*

steady /'stɛdɪ/
steadier steadiest
ADJECTIVE
1 Something that is steady continues or develops gradually without sudden changes.
EG *... a steady rise in profits*
2 If an object is steady, it is firm and does not move about.
EG *Hold the camera steady.*

steak /steɪk/
steaks
NOUN
a large flat piece of beef without much fat on it
EG *... a T-bone steak*

steal /stiːl/
steals stealing stole stolen
VERB
If you steal something, you take it without permission and without intending to return it.
EG *He was accused of stealing a bicycle from the club.*

steam /stiːm/
NOUN
Steam is the hot mist that forms when water boils.
EG *The kettle sent out clouds of steam.*

steel /stiːl/
NOUN
Steel is a very strong metal made mainly from iron.
EG *... a steel blade*

steep /stiːp/
steeper steepest
ADJECTIVE
A steep slope rises sharply and is difficult to go up.
EG *The town stands on a steep hill.*

steer /stɪər/
steers steering steered
VERB
When you steer a vehicle, you control it so that it goes in the direction you want.
EG *What is it like to steer a ship this size?*

stem /stɛm/
stems stemming stemmed
VERB
1 If you stem something, you stop it from spreading or continuing.
EG *... trying to stem the flow of blood*
2 If a problem **stems from** something, that is what caused it.
EG *All my problems stem from drink.*
NOUN
3 The stem of a plant is the thin upright part on which the leaves and flowers grow.
EG *... a large plant with a red stem*

step /stɛp/
steps stepping stepped
NOUN
1 A step is the movement made by lifting your foot and putting it down somewhere else.
EG *I took another step back.*
EG *He heard steps behind him.*
2 one of a series of actions that you take in order to achieve something
EG *... the first step towards peace*
3 a raised flat surface, usually one of a series that you can walk up or down
EG *Ann walked down the stone steps.*
VERB
4 If you **step on** something, you put your foot on it.
EG *He stepped on some glass and cut his foot.*

5 If you step in a particular direction, you move your foot in that direction.

EG *Doug stepped sideways.*

step- /stɛp/

PREFIX

If a word like 'father' or 'sister' has 'step-' in front of it, it shows that the family relationship has come about because a parent has married again.

EG ... *her stepfather*

EG ... *his stepsister*

stereo /'stɛrɪəʊ/
stereos

NOUN

a piece of equipment that reproduces sound from records, tapes, or CDs by sending the sound through two speakers

EG ... *the music from the stereo*

stern /stɜːn/
sterner sternest

ADJECTIVE

very serious and strict

EG ... *a stern warning*

stick /stɪk/
sticks sticking stuck

NOUN

1 a long, thin piece of wood

EG *I gathered some sticks for the fire.*

EG ... *a walking stick*

VERB

2 If you stick a pointed object into something, you push it in.

EG *The doctor stuck the needle in Joe's arm.*

3 If you stick one thing to another, you attach it with glue or tape.

EG *Do you want me to stick a notice on the window?*

4 If something sticks somewhere, it becomes attached there.

EG *It stops the rice sticking to the pan.*

5 AN INFORMAL USE

If you stick something somewhere, you put it there.

EG *I stuck the letter back on the shelf.*

stick out

VERB

If something sticks out, or if you stick it out, it extends beyond something else.

EG ... *with a needle sticking out of his arm*

EG *She stuck out her tongue at him.*

stiff /stɪf/
stiffer stiffest

ADJECTIVE

1 Something that is stiff is firm and not easily bent or moved.

EG ... *a stiff brown envelope*

EG *The drawers are a bit stiff.*

2 If you are stiff, your muscles or joints ache when you move.

EG *Harry was stiff and tired after the long drive.*

still /stɪl/
stiller stillest

ADVERB

1 If a situation still exists, it continues to exist.

EG *I'm still in love with her.*

2 If something could still happen, it might happen although it has not happened yet.

EG *We could still get there if we rush.*

3 You use 'still' to emphasize that something remains the case in spite of other things.

EG *Despite the lack of evidence, he was still found guilty.*

ADJECTIVE

4 If someone or something is still, they stay in the same position without moving.

A
B
C
D
E
F
G
H
I
J
K
L
M
N
O
P
Q
R
S
T
U
V
W
X
Y
Z

EG *Sit still.*
EG *The air was still.*

stimulate /'stɪmjuleɪt/
**stimulates stimulating
stimulated**

VERB
To stimulate something means to
encourage it to begin or develop.
EG *... using pictures to stimulate
discussion*

sting /stɪŋ/
stings stinging stung

VERB
1 If a creature or plant stings you,
it pricks your skin so that you feel
pain.
EG *She was stung by a wasp.*
2 If a part of your body stings, you
feel a sharp pain there.
EG *His cheeks were stinging from
the icy wind.*

stir /stɜːr/
stirs stirring stirred

VERB
1 When you stir a liquid, you
move it around using a spoon or
stick.
EG *Mrs Plant was stirring sugar into
her tea.*
2 A FORMAL USE
If someone or something stirs,
they move slightly.
EG *She shook him, but he did not
stir.*
EG *A slight wind stirred the curtains.*

stitch /stɪtʃ/
stitches stitching stitched

VERB
1 If you stitch cloth, you use a
needle and thread to sew two
pieces together or to make a
decoration.
EG *... finely stitched collars*

NOUN

2 one of the pieces of thread that
has been sewn in a piece of cloth
EG *... a cushion cover embroidered
in tiny stitches*
3 one of the pieces of thread that
has been used to heal a wound
EG *He needed six stitches in his lip.*

stock /stɒk/
stocks stocking stocked

NOUN
1 A shop's stock is the total
amount of goods that it has for
sale.
EG *The entire stock was destroyed
in the flood.*
2 A stock of things is a supply of
them.
EG *Stocks of ammunition were
running low.*
3 Stocks are shares in the
ownership of a company which
people can buy as an investment.
EG *... the stock market*
EG *... stocks and shares*

VERB
4 A shop that stocks particular
goods keeps a supply of them to
sell.
EG *The shop stocks everything from
cigarettes to toilet paper.*

stocking /'stɒkɪŋ/
stockings

NOUN
Stockings are items of women's
clothing that fit closely over their
legs and feet.
EG *... a pair of silk stockings*

stole /stəʊl/
past tense of **steal**

stolen /'stəʊln/
past participle of **steal**

stomach /'stʌmək/
stomachs

NOUN

1 Your stomach is the organ inside your body that processes the food you eat.
EG *I woke up with a pain in my stomach.*

2 You can refer to the front part of your body below your waist as your stomach.
EG *Gordon punched him in the stomach.*

tone /stəun/
stones

NOUN

1 Stone is a hard, solid substance found in the ground and used for building.
EG *... a statue carved out of stone*
EG *... stone walls*

2 a small piece of rock
EG *He removed a stone from his shoe.*

3 a unit of weight equal to 14 pounds or about 6.35 kilograms
EG *He weighed only nine stone.*
☑ When 'stone' refers to a unit of weight, the plural is 'stone'.

tood /stud/
past participle and past tense of **stand**

tool /stu:l/
stools

NOUN

a seat with legs but no back or arms
EG *... a bar stool*

top /stɔp/
stops stopping stopped

VERB

1 If you **stop doing** something, you no longer do it.
EG *She decided to stop smoking.*

2 If an activity or process stops, it comes to an end or no longer happens.

EG *The rain had stopped.*

3 If people or things that are moving stop, or if something stops them, they no longer move.
EG *The car stopped to let them out.*
EG *A guard stopped them at the border.*

4 If you stop something, you prevent it from happening or continuing.
EG *He tried to stop them seeing each other.*

NOUN

5 a place where a bus, train, or other vehicle stops during a journey
EG *He got off at the next stop.*

6 If something that is moving **comes to a stop**, it no longer moves.
EG *The traffic came to a complete stop.*

store /stɔːʳ/
stores storing stored

NOUN

1 a shop
EG *... a record store*

2 A store of something is a supply of it that you keep until it is needed.
EG *... her secret store of cigarettes*

3 If something is **in store** for you, it is going to happen to you.
EG *We had no idea what lay in store.*

VERB

4 If you store something, you keep it somewhere until it is needed.
EG *The computer stores information about each name.*

storey /'stɔːrɪ/
storeys
US **story**

NOUN

one of the floors or levels of a

building

EG *Houses must not be more than two storeys high.*

storm /stɔːm/

storms

NOUN

A storm is very bad weather, with heavy rain, strong winds, and often thunder and lightning.

EG *Their boat sank during a storm.*

story /'stɔːri/

stories

NOUN

1 a description of imaginary people and events that is written or told in order to entertain people

EG *... a story about a rabbit*

2 an account of things that have happened

EG *He told us his life story.*

see **storey**

straight /streit/

straighter straightest

ADJECTIVE OR ADVERB

1 Something that is straight continues in one direction without curving or bending.

EG *... a straight line*

EG *He couldn't walk straight.*

ADVERB

2 immediately and directly

EG *We will go straight to the hotel.*

straightforward

/streit'fɔːwəd/

ADJECTIVE

easy to do or understand

EG *It's quite straightforward.*

EG *... a straightforward question*

strain /strein/

strains straining strained

NOUN

1 If strain is put on a person or organization, they have to do more than is reasonable or normal.

EG *The police were put under considerable strain.*

2 Strain is a force that pulls or pushes something in a way that may damage it.

EG *Spread your feet to ease the strain on your back.*

VERB

3 If you strain something, you make it do more than is reasonable or normal.

EG *He strained his ears to hear better.*

4 If you strain food, you separate the liquid part from the solid part.

EG *Strain the vegetables and serve.*

strange /streindʒ/

stranger strangest

ADJECTIVE

1 unusual or unexpected

EG *... a strange dream*

2 A strange person or place is one that you do not know.

EG *She was all alone in a strange country.*

stranger /'streindʒər/

strangers

NOUN

someone you have never met before

EG *She often talked to strangers on the bus.*

strap /stræp/

straps strapping strapped

NOUN

1 a narrow piece of leather or cloth, used to fasten things or to hold them together

EG *... a watch strap*

VERB

2 If you strap something somewhere, you fasten it there with a strap.

EG *We strapped the skis onto the roof of the car.*

straw /strɔː/
straws

NOUN

1 Straw is the dry, yellowish stalks from some crops.
EG ... *a straw hat*

2 a hollow tube of paper or plastic which you use to suck a drink into your mouth
EG ... *sucking orange juice through a straw*

strawberry /'strɔːbəri/
strawberries

NOUN

a small red fruit with tiny seeds in its skin
EG ... *strawberries and cream*

streak /striːk/
streaks

NOUN

a long narrow mark or stain
EG ... *a streak of dried blood*

stream /striːm/
streams streaming streamed

NOUN

1 a small river
EG ... *a mountain stream*

2 A **stream of** people or things is a large number of them occurring one after another.
EG ... *a constant stream of visitors*

VERB

3 If people or things stream somewhere, large numbers or amounts of them move there.
EG *Rain streamed down the windscreen.*

street /striːt/
streets

NOUN

a road in a town or village, usually with buildings along it
EG *Children were playing in the street.*

strength /strɛŋθ/
strengths

NOUN

1 Your strength is your physical energy and the power of your muscles.
EG *He pulled with all his strength.*

2 Someone's strength is their courage and determination.
EG *She has great mental strength.*

3 Someone's strengths are their good qualities and abilities.
EG ... *the strengths and weaknesses of the team*

4 The strength of an object is its ability to be treated roughly or to support heavy weights.
EG *He checked the strength of the rope.*

strengthen /'strɛŋθn/
strengthens strengthening strengthened

VERB

To strengthen something means to make it stronger.
EG ... *exercises which strengthen the spine*
EG *The accident strengthened their friendship.*

stress /strɛs/
stresses stressing stressed

NOUN

1 Stress is worry and nervous tension.
EG *She was suffering from stress.*

2 Stress is emphasis on a word or part of a word when it is pronounced.
EG *The stress should be on the first syllable.*

VERB

3 If you stress something, you emphasize it and draw attention to its importance.
EG *Nathan stressed how difficult*

A B C D E F G H I J K L M N O P Q R S T U V W X Y Z

their task was.

stretch /stretʃ/
stretches stretching stretched

VERB

1 Something that stretches over an area covers the whole of that area.

EG *The procession stretched for several miles.*

2 When you stretch, you hold out part of your body as far as you can.

EG *He yawned and stretched.*

EG *She stretched out a hand.*

3 If something stretches, or if you stretch it, it becomes longer and thinner, usually because it is pulled.

EG *The cables are designed not to stretch.*

EG *Sticking plaster was stretched across his mouth.*

NOUN

4 A stretch of land or water is a length or area of it.

EG *... a dangerous stretch of road*

strict /strɪkt/
stricter strictest

ADJECTIVE

1 Someone who is strict demands that rules and instructions are obeyed.

EG *My parents were very strict.*

2 A strict rule is one that must be obeyed absolutely.

EG *She gave me strict instructions not to say anything.*

strike /straɪk/
strikes striking struck

NOUN

1 If there is a strike, or if people **go on strike**, people stop working as a protest.

EG *... a three-day strike over pay and conditions*

EG *... after the miners went on strike*

VERB

2 If someone or something strikes another person or thing, they hit them.

EG *She struck him across the mouth*

EG *His head struck the bottom of the pool.*

3 If something unpleasant strikes, it suddenly affects or attacks someone.

EG *A powerful earthquake struck Sicily.*

EG *The killer says he will strike again.*

4 If an idea or impression strikes you, you become aware of it.

EG *It suddenly struck me that I might be wrong.*

EG *He struck me as a very friendly man.*

5 If you **are struck by** something, it impresses you.

EG *She was struck by his energy.*

6 When a clock strikes, it makes a sound to indicate the time.

EG *The clock struck nine.*

7 If you strike a match, you rub it against something to make it burn

EG *... the sound of someone striking matches in the dark*

string /strɪŋ/
strings

NOUN

1 String is thin rope made of twisted threads.

EG *... a parcel tied with string*

2 You can refer to a row or series of similar things as a **string of** them.

EG *... a string of islands*

EG *... a string of injuries*

strip /strɪp/
strips stripping stripped

NOUN

1 A strip of something is a long,

narrow piece of it.
EG *They fastened a strip of cloth around his eyes.*
EG *... a narrow strip of land*

VERB
2 If you strip, you take off all your clothes.
EG *She stripped and bathed in the cool water.*

stripe /straɪp/
stripes

NOUN
a long line which is a different colour from the areas next to it
EG *... a pattern of blue and white stripes*

stroke /strəʊk/
strokes stroking stroked

VERB
1 If you stroke something, you move your hand smoothly and gently over it.
EG *... a cat that loved to be stroked*

NOUN
2 a medical condition which affects the brain and which may kill or paralyse a person
EG *Their mother died of a stroke.*

strong /strɒŋ/
stronger strongest

ADJECTIVE
1 Someone who is strong has powerful muscles.
EG *... the world's strongest man*
2 Strong objects are not easily broken.
EG *... a strong rope*
3 confident and determined
EG *Isabel was the strong one in our family.*
4 great in degree or intensity
EG *... a strong wind*
EG *... a strong smell of soap*

struck /strʌk/

past participle and past tense of **strike**

structure /'strʌktʃər/
structures

NOUN
1 The structure of something is the way it is made, built, or organized.
EG *... the structure of the brain*
2 something that has been built or constructed
EG *... a four-storey brick structure*

struggle /'strʌgl/
struggles struggling struggled

VERB
1 If you **struggle to do** something difficult, you try hard to do it.
EG *Bernard struggled to explain.*
2 If you struggle when you are being held, you twist and turn in an attempt to get free.
EG *I struggled, but could not get free.*

NOUN
3 a fight
EG *... after a struggle with prison officers*
4 something which is difficult to achieve and which takes a lot of effort
EG *Losing weight was a terrible struggle.*

stubborn /'stʌbən/

ADJECTIVE
Someone who is stubborn is determined to do what they want and refuses to change their mind.
EG *... a stubborn old fool who refused to try anything new*

stuck /stʌk/
1 Stuck is the past participle and past tense of **stick**

ADJECTIVE

2 If someone or something is stuck somewhere, they are unable to move or leave.
EG *His car was stuck in the snow.*
EG *... after being stuck in a lift for an hour*

student /'stju:dənt/
students

NOUN
a person who is studying at a university, college, or school
EG *... a music student*

studio /'stju:dɪəu/
studios

NOUN
1 a room where an artist or photographer works
EG *... a photographic studio*
2 a room where records, films, or radio or television programmes are made
EG *... a television studio*

study /'stʌdɪ/
studies studying studied

VERB
1 If you study a particular subject, you spend time learning about it.
EG *She studied History and Politics.*
2 If you study something, you look at it carefully.
EG *He studied the map in silence.*

NOUN
3 Study is the activity of studying.
EG *... study aids*
4 a piece of research
EG *... the first serious study of the problem*

stuff /stʌf/
stuffs stuffing stuffed

NOUN
1 You can use 'stuff' to refer to things in a general way.
EG *She spread out her stuff on the table.*
EG *... creams and lotions and stuff like that*

VERB
2 If you stuff something somewhere, you push it there quickly and roughly.
EG *A woman stuffed a piece of paper into his hand.*
3 If you **stuff** something **with** a substance or objects, you fill it with the substance or objects.
EG *... wallets stuffed with dollars*

stumble /'stʌmbl/
stumbles stumbling stumbled

VERB
If you stumble while you are walking or running, you trip and nearly fall.
EG *He stumbled as he climbed the stairs.*

stun /stʌn/
stuns stunning stunned

VERB
If you **are stunned by** something, you are very shocked by it.
EG *I was stunned by the news.*

stung /stʌŋ/
past participle and past tense of **sting**

stupid /'stju:pɪd/
stupider stupidest

ADJECTIVE
Someone or something that is stupid shows a lack of judgment or intelligence and is not at all sensible.
EG *How could I have been so stupid*
EG *... a stupid mistake*

style /staɪl/
styles

NOUN

1 The style of something is the general way in which it is done or presented.
EG *... an aggressive style of management*
EG *The food was cooked in genuine Chinese style.*

2 A person or place that has style is smart and elegant.
EG *... a building with style and grace*

3 The style of something is its design.
EG *The new windows fit in with the style of the house.*

subject /'sʌbdʒɪkt/
subjects subjecting subjected

NOUN

1 The subject of a piece of writing or a conversation is the thing or person that is being discussed.
EG *His struggle is the subject of a new book.*
EG *We got on to the subject of relationships.*

2 an area of study
EG *Biology was my favourite subject at school.*

3 The subjects of a country are the people who live there.
EG *The victims were all British subjects.*

When people talk about the **subject** of a verb or of a sentence, they mean the person or thing that does the action, rather than the person or thing that is affected by it.
EG ***The cat*** *chased a mouse.*

ADJECTIVE

4 Someone or something that is **subject to** something is affected by it.

EG *Prices may be subject to alteration.*

VERB : /səb'dʒɛkt/
☑ Note that you pronounce the verb differently from the noun and the adjective.

5 If you **subject** someone **to** something unpleasant, you make them experience it.
EG *He was subjected to constant interruption.*

submarine /sʌbmə'riːn/
submarines

NOUN
a ship that can travel beneath the surface of the sea
EG *... a nuclear submarine*

submit /səb'mɪt/
submits submitting submitted

VERB
If you **submit to** something, you accept it because you are not powerful enough to resist it.
EG *... if I submitted to their demands*

subsequently /'sʌbsɪkwəntlɪ/

ADVERB
If something subsequently happens, it happens after something else that you have just mentioned.
EG *She left her job and subsequently moved abroad.*

substance /'sʌbstəns/
substances

NOUN
any solid, powder, liquid, or gas
EG *... a sticky black substance*

substantial /səb'stænʃl/

ADJECTIVE
very large in degree or amount
EG *... a substantial pay rise*

substitute /'sʌbstɪtjuːt/
substitutes substituting substituted

VERB

1 If you **substitute** one thing **for** another thing, you use it instead of the other thing.
EG *We substituted margarine for butter.*

NOUN

2 If one thing is a **substitute for** another, it is used instead of the other thing.
EG *A book is not a substitute for professional treatment.*

subtle /'sʌtl/
subtler subtlest

ADJECTIVE

Something subtle is not immediately obvious.
EG *... a subtle change*

subtract /səb'trækt/
subtracts subtracting subtracted

VERB

If you **subtract** one number **from** another, you take away the first number from the second.
EG *Mandy subtracted the date of birth from the date of death.*

suburb /'sʌbəːb/
suburbs

NOUN

an area of a town or city that is away from its centre
EG *... a fashionable suburb of Monte Carlo*

subway /'sʌbweɪ/
subways

NOUN

In American English, a subway is an underground railway.
EG *... the New York subway*
☑ The usual British word is *underground*.

succeed /sək'siːd/
succeeds succeeding succeeded

VERB

1 If someone or something succeeds, they achieve the result that was intended.
EG *The plan is unlikely to succeed.*
EG *Sarah had succeeded in winning his trust.*

2 If you succeed another person, you take over their job when they leave.
EG *He felt that Dobson should succeed him as chairman.*

success /sək'ses/
successes

NOUN

1 Success is the achievement of something that you have been trying to do.
EG *The cast were amazed at the play's success.*

2 Someone or something that is a success is successful.
EG *The book was a great success.*

successful /sək'sesful/

ADJECTIVE

Someone or something that is successful achieves the result that was intended.
EG *... a successful lawyer*
EG *The treatment was not successful.*

such /sʌtʃ/

ADJECTIVE OR PRONOUN

1 You use 'such' to refer to the person or thing you have just mentioned, or to someone or something similar.
EG *Such were the fashions in those days.*
EG *... Naples or Palermo or some such place*

ADJECTIVE

A
B
C
D
E
F
G
H
I
J
K
L
M
N
O
P
Q
R
S
T
U
V
W
X
Y
Z

2 You use 'such' to emphasize the degree or extent of something.
EG *It was such a pleasant surprise.*
EG *How did he acquire such power?*
☑ 'Such' is followed by 'a' when the noun is something that can be counted: *such a pleasant surprise.* It is not followed by 'a' when the noun is plural or something that cannot be counted: *such beautiful women; such power.*
3 You use such as to introduce an example of something.
EG *... serious offences such as assault*
EG *... such professions as law or medicine*

suck /sʌk/
sucks sucking sucked
VERB
If you suck something, you hold it in your mouth and pull at it with your cheeks and tongue, usually in order to get liquid out of it.
EG *... a child sucking a sweet*

sudden /'sʌdn/
ADJECTIVE
happening quickly and unexpectedly
EG *... the sudden death of her father*

suddenly /'sʌdnlɪ/
ADVERB
quickly and unexpectedly
EG *The door opened suddenly.*
EG *Suddenly she felt cold.*

suffer /'sʌfəʳ/
suffers suffering suffered
VERB
If you **suffer from** an illness or from some other unpleasant condition, you are badly affected by it.
EG *They were suffering from shock.*
EG *The poor have suffered most from the shortages.*

EG *... if you suffer any ill effects*

suffering /'sʌfərɪŋ/
NOUN
Suffering is great physical or mental pain.
EG *Few of the survivors could talk about their suffering.*

sufficient /sə'fɪʃənt/
ADJECTIVE
If something is sufficient for a particular purpose, there is enough of it available.
EG *His savings were not sufficient to cover the cost.*

sugar /'ʃʊgəʳ/
NOUN
Sugar is a sweet substance that is used to flavour food and drinks.
EG *... a bag of sugar*

suggest /sə'dʒɛst/
suggests suggesting suggested
VERB
1 If you suggest a plan or idea to someone, you ask them to consider doing it.
EG *I suggested we walk to the park.*
EG *John first suggested this idea to me in 1986.*
2 If one thing suggests another, it implies it or makes you think that it is true.
EG *This suggests that he may have been lying.*

suggestion /sə'dʒɛstʃən/
suggestions
NOUN
a plan or idea for someone to consider
EG *Jim made some suggestions for improvements.*

suicide /'suːɪsaɪd/
NOUN
People who commit suicide

A B C D E F G H I J K L M N O P Q R S T U V W X Y Z

deliberately kill themselves.
EG ... *the number of young men committing suicide*

suit /suːt/
suits suiting suited

NOUN
1 a matching jacket and trousers, or a matching jacket and skirt
EG ... *men in grey suits*

VERB
2 If an arrangement suits you, it is convenient or acceptable.
EG *Would 9 o'clock suit you?*
EG *They devised a scheme which would suit them both.*

3 If a piece of clothing or a style suits you, you look good when you are wearing it.
EG *I couldn't find a hat that suited me.*

suitable /ˈsuːtəbl/

ADJECTIVE
right or acceptable for a particular purpose or occasion
EG *Many roads are not suitable for cycling.*
EG ... *a suitable dress for a wedding*

suitcase /ˈsuːtkeɪs/
suitcases

NOUN
a case in which you carry your clothes when you are travelling
EG *Her suitcase had somehow been diverted to Rome.*

sum /sʌm/
sums

NOUN
an amount of money
EG *The company spent a vast sum on advertising.*
EG *Large sums of money were lost.*

summary /ˈsʌməri/
summaries

NOUN
a short account of something that gives the main points but not the details
EG ... *a summary of the report*

summer /ˈsʌmər/
summers

NOUN
Summer is the warm season between spring and autumn.
EG *Every summer the family goes on holiday.*
EG ... *the summer of 1967*

sun /sʌn/

NOUN
1 The sun is the ball of fire in the sky that the Earth goes around.
EG *The sun was low in the sky.*

2 You use **the sun** to refer to the heat and light that reaches us from the sun.
EG *How pleasant to sit in the sun.*

sunbathe /ˈsʌnbeɪð/
sunbathes sunbathing sunbathed

VERB
If you sunbathe, you sit or lie in the sunshine in order to get a suntan.
EG ... *people who sunbathe at every opportunity*

Sunday /ˈsʌndɪ/
Sundays

NOUN
Sunday is the day between Saturday and Monday.
EG ... *people who go to church on Sundays*

sung /sʌŋ/
past participle of **sing**

sunglasses /ˈsʌnglɑːsɪz/

PLURAL NOUN
Sunglasses are spectacles with dark lenses that you wear to protect your eyes from the sun.

545

EG ... *a pair of sunglasses*

sunk /sʌŋk/
past participle of **sink**

sunlight /'sʌnlaɪt/
NOUN
Sunlight is the light that comes from the sun.
EG *I awoke to bright sunlight.*

sunny /'sʌnɪ/
sunnier sunniest
ADJECTIVE
When it is sunny, the sun is shining brightly.
EG ... *a warm, sunny day*

sunrise /'sʌnraɪz/
sunrises
NOUN
Sunrise is the time in the morning when the sun first appears in the sky.
EG *We leave at sunrise.*
EG ... *a spectacular sunrise*

sunset /'sʌnset/
sunsets
NOUN
Sunset is the time in the evening when the sun disappears from the sky.
EG *We returned at sunset.*
EG ... *a beautiful sunset*

sunshine /'sʌnʃaɪn/
NOUN
Sunshine is the light and heat that comes from the sun.
EG *The water glittered in the sunshine.*

suntan /'sʌntæn/
suntans
NOUN
If you have a suntan, the sun has turned your skin brown.
EG ... *suntan lotion*

super /'suːpər/

ADJECTIVE
AN INFORMAL WORD
very nice or very good
EG ... *a super party*

super- /'suːpə/
PREFIX
Super- is added to some words to describe something that is larger or better than other similar things.
EG ... *a new superweapon*
EG ... *super-fast computers*

superb /suːˈpəːb/
ADJECTIVE
very good
EG ... *a superb selection of local cheeses*

superior /suːˈpɪərɪər/
ADJECTIVE
1 People or things that are superior are better than other similar people or things.
EG ... *which produces superior results*
EG ... *an education greatly superior to my own*
2 A superior person in an organization is in a more important position than another person.
EG ... *his superior officers*

superlative /suːˈpəːlətɪv/
superlatives
NOUN OR ADJECTIVE
Many adjectives have a basic form and two other forms. The **comparative** and **superlative** forms are used when you make comparisons.
The superlative form is usually made by adding the ending -est to the basic form of the adjective. It shows that someone or something has the most of something compared with

A B C D E F G H I J K L M N O P Q R S T U V W X Y Z

all other people or things of the same kind.

EG *Matthew is the **tallest** boy in his class.*

You can also make superlatives by using the words *most* or *least* with the basic form of the adjective.

EG *She's the **most beautiful** woman I've ever seen.*

EG *I have the **least important** job in the office.*

See also **comparative**.

supermarket /'suːpəmɑːkɪt/
supermarkets

NOUN

a large shop which sells many kinds of food, toiletries, and kitchen goods

EG *... a new chain of supermarkets*

supervise /'suːpəvaɪz/
supervises supervising supervised

VERB

If you supervise an activity or a person, you make sure that the activity is done correctly or that the person behaves correctly.

EG *I supervise the packing of all orders.*

EG *He trained and supervised more than 400 volunteers.*

supper /'sʌpəʳ/
suppers

NOUN

Supper is a meal eaten in the evening or a snack eaten before you go to bed.

EG *Some guests like to dress for supper.*

EG *... after she had given the children their supper*

supply /sə'plaɪ/
supplies supplying supplied

VERB

1 If you **supply** someone **with** something or **supply** it **to** them, you provide them with it.

EG *... the farm which supplied them with their vegetables*

EG *He was accused of supplying arms to terrorists.*

NOUN

2 A supply of something is an amount of it that is available.

EG *... the world's supply of precious metals*

PLURAL NOUN

3 supplies are food or equipment that is used for a particular purpose

EG *His medical supplies were running low.*

support /sə'pɔːt/
supports supporting supported

VERB

1 If you support someone, you agree with their aims and want them to succeed.

EG *He thanked everyone who had supported him during the campaign.*

2 If something supports an object, it is underneath the object and holding it up.

EG *Thick wooden posts support the ceiling.*

NOUN

3 If you give support to someone during a difficult time, you are kind to them and help them.

EG *He praised his wife for her constant support.*

supporter /sə'pɔːtəʳ/
supporters

NOUN

someone who supports a person or activity

EG *... supporters of the President*

EG *... football supporters*

A
B
C
D
E
F
G
H
I
J
K
L
M
N
O
P
Q
R
S
T
U
V
W
X
Y
Z

suppose /sə'pəʊz/
supposes supposing
supposed

VERB

1 You can say **I suppose** when you are not enthusiastic or completely certain about something.
EG *I suppose I'd better go home.*
EG *"Will John be there?" — "I suppose so."*

2 You can use 'suppose' or 'supposing' when you are asking someone to consider a possible situation.
EG *Supposing he's right, what shall I do then?*

3 If you suppose that something is true, you believe that it is probably true.
EG *The problem was more complex than he supposed.*

supposed /sə'pəʊzd/

ADJECTIVE

1 If something **is supposed to** be done, it should be done.
EG *You are supposed to report it to the police.*

2 If something **is supposed to** happen, it is planned or expected to happen.
EG *It's supposed to rain today.*
☑ If you say that something *was supposed to* happen, you mean that it was planned to happen, but it did not in fact happen: *she was supposed to meet me at midday.*

3 If something **is supposed to** be true, it is generally believed to be true.
EG *It's supposed to be a terrific film.*

sure /ʃʊəʳ/
surer surest

ADJECTIVE

1 If you are sure that something is

true, you have no doubt that it is true.
EG *I have always been sure that he was innocent.*
EG *I'm not even sure of his name.*

2 If someone is **sure of** getting something, they will definitely get it.
EG *Neither can be sure of success.*

3 If something is **sure to** happen, it will definitely happen.
EG *I'm sure to forget.*

4 If you **make sure** that something is done, you take action so that it is done or you check that it is done.
EG *We need to make sure this never happens again.*
EG *She looked in on the children to make sure they were still asleep.*

surely /'ʃʊəlɪ/

ADVERB

You use 'surely' when you think that something should be true but you are not certain that it is true.
EG *Surely you remember, it was last week.*

surface /'səːfɪs/
surfaces

NOUN

The surface of something is the top or outside area of it.
EG *... the reflections in the surface of the water*
EG *... ten miles above the Earth's surface*

surgeon /'səːdʒən/
surgeons

NOUN

a doctor who performs operations
EG *... a heart surgeon*

surgery /'səːdʒərɪ/
surgeries

NOUN

A
B
C
D
E
F
G
H
I
J
K
L
M
N
O
P
Q
R
S
T
U
V
W
X
Y
Z

1 Surgery is medical treatment that involves cutting open part of a person's body in order to repair or remove a damaged part.
EG *She required immediate surgery.*

2 a room or building where a doctor or dentist works
EG *The surgery doesn't open until 9 o'clock.*

surname /ˈsɜːneɪm/
surnames

NOUN
Your surname is the name that you share with other members of your family, usually your last name.
EG *She'd never known his surname.*

surplus /ˈsɜːpləs/
surpluses

NOUN
1 If there is a surplus of something, there is more of it than is needed.
EG *Germany suffers from a surplus of teachers.*

ADJECTIVE
2 Surplus things are extra or more than is needed.
EG *... large sums of surplus cash*

surprise /səˈpraɪz/
surprises surprising surprised

NOUN
1 an unexpected event
EG *His success came as a great surprise.*

2 Surprise is the feeling that you have when something unexpected happens.
EG *They all looked at her in surprise.*

VERB
3 If something surprises you, it gives you a feeling of surprise.
EG *The way they reacted to the news surprised me.*

surrender /səˈrɛndər/
surrenders surrendering surrendered

VERB
1 If you surrender, you stop fighting or resisting and agree that you have been beaten.
EG *He surrendered to the authorities after three weeks.*

NOUN
2 Surrender is the act of surrendering.
EG *... after the Japanese surrender in 1945*

surround /səˈraʊnd/
surrounds surrounding surrounded

VERB
If someone or something is surrounded by something, that thing is situated all around them.
EG *The house is surrounded by a high fence.*
EG *A squad of police cars has surrounded the area.*

surroundings /səˈraʊndɪŋz/

PLURAL NOUN
You can refer to the area around a place or person as their surroundings.
EG *... a holiday home in beautiful surroundings*

survey /ˈsɜːveɪ/
surveys surveying surveyed

NOUN
1 A survey of something is a detailed examination of it, often in the form of a series of questions.
EG *... a survey of people's eating habits*

VERB : /səˈveɪ/
☑ Note the change in stress.
2 If people are surveyed about their opinions or behaviour, they are asked a series of questions

about them.
EG *Only 18 percent of those surveyed opposed the idea.*
3 If you survey something, you look carefully at the whole of it.
EG *They stood back and surveyed the scene.*

survive /sə'vaɪv/
survives surviving survived
VERB
If someone survives a dangerous situation, they do not die.
EG *Three people survived the crash.*
EG *He is not expected to survive.*

suspect /səs'pɛkt/
suspects suspecting suspected
VERB
1 If you suspect that something is true, you believe it is probably true.
EG *I suspect you're right.*
EG *He suspected that the woman upstairs was using heroin.*
2 If you suspect someone **of doing** something wrong, you think that they have probably done it.
EG *He suspected Tom of being a thief.*
NOUN : /'sʌspɛkt/
☑ Note the change in stress.
3 a person who the police think may be guilty of a crime
EG *The most obvious suspect was her boyfriend.*

suspend /səs'pɛnd/
suspends suspending suspended
VERB
1 If you suspend something, you delay it or stop it for a while.
EG *Lessons were suspended for the day.*
2 If something is suspended from a high place, it is hanging from

that place.
EG *... a map suspended from the ceiling*

suspicion /səs'pɪʃən/
suspicions
NOUN
1 Suspicion is the feeling of not trusting someone or the feeling that someone has done something wrong.
EG *He regarded his fellow workers with extreme suspicion.*
EG *He was arrested on suspicion of drunk driving.*
2 a feeling that something is probably true or likely to happen
EG *I had a sneaking suspicion that she was enjoying herself.*

suspicious /səs'pɪʃəs/
ADJECTIVE
1 If you are **suspicious of** someone or something, you do not trust them.
EG *He was suspicious of all journalists.*
EG *She has a suspicious mind.*
2 Someone or something that is suspicious is believed to be involved in a crime or a dishonest activity.
EG *Police last night found a suspicious package.*

swallow /'swɒləʊ/
swallows swallowing swallowed
VERB
When you swallow something, you cause it to go down your throat and into your stomach.
EG *Simon swallowed the remains of his coffee.*

swam /swæm/
past tense of **swim**

A
B
C
D
E
F
G
H
I
J
K
L
M
N
O
P
Q
R
S
T
U
V
W
X
Y
Z

swap /swɒp/
swaps swapping swapped

VERB

If you **swap** one thing **for** another, you replace the first thing with the second, often by making an exchange with another person.

EG *Karen swapped her empty glass for a full one.*

EG *I'd gladly swap places with you.*

sway /sweɪ/
sways swaying swayed

VERB

If people or things sway, they lean or swing slowly from side to side.

EG *The crowd swayed back and forth.*

swear /sweər/
swears swearing swore sworn

VERB

1 If you swear, you use very rude or obscene words.

EG *... the sort of driver my father always swore at*

2 If you **swear to do** something or swear that something is true, you say very firmly that you will do it or that it is true.

EG *They swore to fight cruelty wherever they found it.*

EG *I swear I didn't know.*

sweat /swɛt/
sweats sweating sweated

NOUN

1 Sweat is the salty liquid which comes through your skin when you are hot or afraid.

EG *Danny wiped the sweat off his face.*

VERB

2 When you sweat, sweat comes through your skin.

EG *The man in the suit was sweating heavily.*

sweater /ˈswɛtər/
sweaters

NOUN

a warm, knitted piece of clothing which covers your upper body and your arms

EG *He was wearing a bright red sweater.*

sweep /swiːp/
sweeps sweeping swept

VERB

1 If you sweep an area of ground, you push dust or rubbish off it with a brush or broom.

EG *He got a job sweeping the streets.*

2 If you sweep things somewhere, you push them there with a quick, smooth movement.

EG *She swept the cards from the table.*

EG *... a storm that swept cars into the sea*

3 If events or ideas sweep a place or **sweep through** it, they spread quickly through it.

EG *A flu epidemic is sweeping through Moscow.*

sweet /swiːt/
sweeter sweetest; sweets

ADJECTIVE

1 Sweet food or drink contains a lot of sugar.

EG *... a cup of sweet tea*

2 pleasant and kind

EG *How sweet of you to think of me!*

3 pleasant and satisfying

EG *Few things are quite as sweet as revenge.*

4 attractive in a simple or child-like way

EG *... a sweet little baby*

NOUN

5 a sweet thing such as a chocolate

EG *... a packet of sweets*

6 something sweet, such as fruit or

a pudding, that you eat at the end of a meal
EG *... a delicious selection of sweets*

swell /swɛl/
swells swelling swelled swollen

VERB
1 If a part of your body swells, it becomes larger and rounder.
EG *Do your ankles swell at night?*
2 If the amount or size of something swells, it increases.
EG *The population swelled during the 1980s.*

swept /swɛpt/
past participle and past tense of **sweep**

swerve /swɜːv/
swerves swerving swerved

VERB
If a moving object swerves, it suddenly changes direction, usually in order to avoid colliding with something else.
EG *Her car swerved off the road.*

swim /swɪm/
swims swimming swam swum

VERB
When you swim, you move through water by making movements with your arms and legs.
EG *He never learned to swim.*
EG *I swim a mile every day.*

swimming pool swimming pools

NOUN
a place that has been built for people to swim in
EG *They took lessons at the local swimming pool.*

swing /swɪŋ/
swings swinging swung

VERB
1 If something swings, or if you swing it, it moves from side to side from a fixed point.
EG *A large key swung from his belt.*
EG *Sam was swinging a golf club.*
EG *Roy swung his legs off the couch.*
NOUN
2 a seat hanging from a frame or branch, which can be made to move backwards and forwards when you sit on it
EG *... a garden swing*

switch /swɪtʃ/
switches switching switched

NOUN
1 a small control for an electrical device or machine
EG *... a light switch*
2 a change
EG *... following a switch in the paper's policy*
VERB
3 If you **switch from** one thing **to** another thing, you stop doing the first thing and begin doing the second thing.
EG *Jack switched from maths to biology.*
EG *... after he decided to switch jobs*

switch off

VERB
If you switch off a light or a machine, you stop it working by pressing a switch.
EG *The driver switched off the headlights.*

switch on

VERB
If you switch on a light or a machine, you start it working by pressing a switch.
EG *I had forgotten to switch on the heater.*

A
B
C
D
E
F
G
H
I
J
K
L
M
N
O
P
Q
R
S
T
U
V
W
X
Y
Z

swollen /'swəʊlən/
past participle of **swell**

sword /sɔːd/
swords

NOUN
a weapon with a long blade and a handle
EG … a sword fight

swore /swɔːr/
past tense of **swear**

sworn /swɔːn/
past participle of **swear**

swum /swʌm/
past participle of **swim**

swung /swʌŋ/
past participle and past tense of **swing**

symbol /'sɪmbl/
symbols

NOUN
a shape, design, or idea that is used to represent something
EG … a red circle as a symbol of the Revolution

sympathetic /sɪmpə'θɛtɪk/
ADJECTIVE
If you are **sympathetic to** someone who is in a difficult situation, you show that you understand how they feel.
EG She was sympathetic to their problems.
EG … a sympathetic friend

sympathy /'sɪmpəθɪ/
NOUN
Sympathy is the kindness and understanding that someone shows towards a person who is in a difficult situation.
EG She received no sympathy from her parents.

symptom /'sɪmptəm/
symptoms

NOUN
The symptoms of an illness or problem are the things which show that the illness or problem exists.
EG … patients with flu symptoms
EG This is just a symptom of a larger problem.

system /'sɪstəm/
systems

NOUN
an organized way of doing something which follows a fixed plan or set of rules
EG … a system for dealing with complaints
EG … the British legal system

A
B
C
D
E
F
G
H
I
J
K
L
M
N
O
P
Q
R
S
T
U
V
W
X
Y
Z

table /'teɪbl/
tables

NOUN

1 a piece of furniture with a flat top supported by one or more legs
EG … the kitchen table

2 a set of facts or figures arranged in rows or columns
EG … a table of exam results

tablecloth /'teɪblklɔθ/
tablecloths

NOUN

a cloth used to cover a table and keep it clean
EG … a check tablecloth

tablespoon /'teɪblspuːn/
tablespoons

NOUN

a large spoon used for serving food; also the amount that a tablespoon contains
EG Pass me a tablespoon.
EG … two tablespoons of vegetable oil

tablet /'tæblɪt/
tablets

NOUN

a small, round pill of medicine
EG … sleeping tablets

tabloid /'tæblɔɪd/
tabloids

NOUN

a newspaper with small pages, short news stories, and lots of photographs
EG … a story in the tabloids

tackle /'tækl/
tackles tackling tackled

VERB

1 If you tackle a difficult task, you start dealing with it in a determined way.
EG We need to tackle this crisis.

2 If you tackle someone in a game such as soccer, you try to get the ball away from them.
EG He was tackled before he had a chance to shoot.

NOUN

3 an attempt to get the ball away from your opponent in a game such as soccer
EG … a bad tackle on the goalkeeper

tactic /'tæktɪk/
tactics

NOUN

Tactics are the methods that you use to achieve something.
EG They used delaying tactics.

tail /teɪl/
tails

NOUN

1 The tail of an animal is the part that extends beyond the end of its body.
EG The dog wagged its tail.

2 You can use 'tail' to refer to the end part of something.
EG … the tail of the plane

ADVERB

3 When you toss a coin, the side called **tails** is the one without a picture of a head on it.
EG Heads or tails?

tail off

VERB

If something tails off, it becomes gradually less.
EG The rain tails off in September.

tailor /'teɪləʳ/
tailors tailoring tailored

NOUN

A
B
C
D
E
F
G
H
I
J
K
L
M
N
O
P
Q
R
S
T
U
V
W
X
Y
Z

1 a person who makes clothes, especially for men
EG *... a tailor's shop*
VERB
2 If something **is tailored to** a particular purpose, it is specially designed for it.
EG *... products tailored to your needs*

take /teɪk/
takes taking took taken
VERB
1 You use 'take' to show what action or activity is being done.
EG *Amy took a bath.*
EG *She took her driving test.*
EG *He was taking an interest in life again.*
2 If you take something, you put your hand round it and hold it or carry it.
EG *Here, let me take your coat.*
EG *You'd better take an umbrella.*
3 If you take something that does not belong to you, you steal it.
EG *Someone has taken my pen.*
4 If you take someone somewhere, you drive them there by car or lead them there.
EG *He offered to take her home in a taxi.*
5 If you take a bus or train, or a road or route, you use it to go from one place to another.
EG *She took the train to New York.*
6 If you take something that is offered to you, you accept it.
EG *He had to take the job.*
EG *Take my advice and get out now.*
7 If something takes a certain amount of time or a particular quality or ability, it requires it.
EG *It takes him three hours to get ready.*
EG *Walking upstairs took all her*

strength.
8 If you take a piece of news or information in a particular way, you react to it in that way.
EG *No-one took the warning seriously.*
9 If you take a particular size in shoes or clothes, that size fits you.
EG *What size shoes do you take?*
10 If you take pills or medicine, you swallow them.
EG *I took a couple of pills for my headache.*
11 If you cannot take something unpleasant, you cannot bear it.
EG *We can't take much more of this.*

take after
VERB
If you take after someone in your family, you look or behave like them.
EG *He takes after his dad.*

take off
VERB
1 When an aircraft takes off, it leaves the ground and begins to fly.
EG *By the time we took off, it was dark.*
2 If you take off something that you are wearing, you remove it from your body.
EG *She took off her glasses.*

take over
VERB
To take something over means to start controlling it.
EG *He is trying to take over the company.*

takeaway /ˈteɪkəweɪ/
takeaways
NOUN
1 a shop or restaurant that sells hot cooked food to be eaten

elsewhere
EG ... a Chinese takeaway
2 a hot cooked meal bought from
a takeaway
EG Let's get a takeaway tonight.

taken /'teɪkən/
past participle of **take**

tale /teɪl/
tales

NOUN
a story
EG ... tales of magic and adventure

talent /'tælnt/
talents

NOUN
Talent is the natural ability to do
something well.
EG ... a player with lots of talent
EG ... among my many talents

talk /tɔːk/
talks talking talked

VERB
1 When you talk, you say things to
someone.
EG They were talking about
American food.

2 If you **talk on** or **about**
something, you make an informal
speech about it.
EG He talks to young people about
the dangers of AIDS.

NOUN
3 a conversation or discussion
EG We had a long talk about her
father.
EG ... peace talks
4 an informal speech about
something
EG He gave a talk on working
abroad.

tall /tɔːl/
taller tallest

ADJECTIVE
1 Someone or something that is

tall is above average height.
EG He's very tall for his age.

2 You use 'tall' to talk about the
height of someone or something.
EG I'm only 5 ft. tall.
EG How tall is the new office block?
☑ You use 'tall' to describe things
that are much higher than they are
wide. Otherwise you use 'high': a
wall 3 foot high.

tame /teɪm/
**tamer tamest; tames
taming tamed**

ADJECTIVE
1 A tame animal or bird is not
afraid of people.
EG Some of the cats weren't even
tame.

2 Something that is tame is weak
or uninteresting.
EG The report was pretty tame.

VERB
3 If you tame a wild animal or
bird, you train it not to be afraid of
people.
EG ... the first people to tame horses

tan /tæn/
tans

NOUN
If you have a tan, your skin is
darker than usual because you
have been in the sun.
EG I came back from holiday with a
deep tan.

tangle /'tæŋgl/
tangles tangling tangled

NOUN
1 a mass of things such as hair or
string that is twisted together and
difficult to separate
EG ... a tangle of wires

VERB
2 If you **are tangled in**
something, you are trapped in it
so that it is difficult to get free.

A B C D E F G H I J K L M N O P Q R S T U V W X Y Z

A B C D E F G H I J K L M N O P Q R S T U V W X Y Z

EG *Animals can get tangled in fishing nets.*

tank /tæŋk/
tanks

NOUN

1 a large container for storing liquid or gas
EG *... a petrol tank.*

2 a military vehicle equipped with large guns which moves on tracks
EG *The army sent in its tanks.*

tap /tæp/
taps tapping tapped

NOUN

1 a device that you turn to control the flow of liquid or gas from a pipe or container
EG *Someone left the tap running.*

2 the action of hitting something lightly; also the sound that this action makes
EG *She gave him a little tap on the arm.*
EG *I heard a tap on the door.*

VERB

3 If you tap something or **tap on** it, you hit it lightly.
EG *I tapped him on the shoulder.*

4 If a telephone is tapped, a device is fitted to it so that someone can listen secretly to the calls.
EG *I think my phone has been tapped.*

tape /teɪp/
tapes taping taped

NOUN

1 Tape is plastic ribbon covered with a magnetic substance and used to record sounds, pictures, and computer information.
EG *Many students were interviewed on tape.*

2 a cassette with magnetic tape wound round it
EG *We listened to an old Beatles'*

tape.

3 a long, thin strip of cloth or plastic that is used to fasten things together
EG *Use the tapes to tie the curtains back.*
EG *... a piece of sticky tape*

VERB

4 If you tape sounds or television pictures, you record them using a tape recorder or a video recorder.
EG *I want to tape this programme.*

5 If you **tape** one thing to another, you fasten them together using tape.
EG *... a list taped to the fridge door*

target /'tɑːgɪt/
targets targeting targeted

NOUN

1 something which you aim at with a weapon or other object
EG *... an easy target for an air attack*

2 The target of an action or remark is the person or thing at which it is directed.
EG *He became a target for our hatred.*

3 Your target is a result that you are trying to achieve.
EG *... the park's target of 11 million visitors*

VERB

4 If someone targets a person or thing, they decide to criticize or attack them.
EG *The terrorists targeted military bases.*

tart /tɑːt/
tarts

NOUN

a pastry case, usually with a sweet filling
EG *... jam tarts*

task /tɑːsk/

tasks

NOUN

a piece of work which has to be done

EG *My task was to collect the wood.*

taste /teɪst/

tastes tasting tasted

NOUN

1 The taste of something is its flavour.

EG *I don't like the taste of fish.*

EG *It's got a strange taste.*

2 Your **sense of taste** is your ability to recognize the flavour of things in your mouth.

EG *I lost my sense of taste when I was ill.*

3 If you have a **taste for** something, you enjoy it.

EG *She has a taste for publicity.*

4 If you have a **taste of** something, you experience it.

EG *... my first taste of defeat*

5 A person's **taste in** something is their choice in the things they like to buy or have around them.

EG *His taste in music is great.*

VERB

6 When you can taste something in your mouth, you are aware of its flavour.

EG *I could hardly taste the meat.*

7 If food or drink **tastes of** something, it has that flavour.

EG *... a cup of tea that tasted of petrol*

EG *This pizza tastes delicious.*

taught /tɔːt/

past participle and past tense of **teach**

tax /tæks/

taxes taxing taxed

NOUN

1 Tax is an amount of money that the people in a country have to

pay to the government so that it can provide public services such as health care and education.

EG *... the rate of income tax*

VERB

2 If a sum of money is taxed, a certain amount of it has to be paid to the government.

EG *Everything you earn is taxed.*

3 If goods are taxed, a certain amount of their price has to be paid to the government.

EG *Biscuits are taxed at 11 per cent.*

4 If a person or company is taxed, they have to pay a certain amount of their income to the government.

EG *The government intends to tax the rich more.*

taxi /'tæksɪ/

taxis

NOUN

a car driven by a person whose job is to take people where they want to go in return for money

EG *Take a taxi to the city centre.*

tea /tiː/

teas

NOUN

1 Tea is the dried leaves of a plant found in Asia.

EG *... a packet of tea*

2 Tea is a drink made by pouring boiling water on the leaves of the tea plant; also a cup of this drink.

EG *... a cup of tea*

EG *Two teas, please.*

3 Tea is a meal eaten in the late afternoon or early evening.

EG *I'm going home for my tea.*

teach /tiːtʃ/

teaches teaching taught

VERB

1 If you teach someone something, you give them information so that they know about it or know how to do it.

EG *My mother taught me how to cook.*

2 If you teach a subject, you help students learn about that subject at school, college, or university.

EG *I taught history for many years.*

teacher /'tiːtʃəʳ/
teachers

NOUN

someone who teaches at a school, college, or university

EG *... her chemistry teacher*

team /tiːm/
teams

NOUN

a group of people who play together against another group in a sport or game

EG *... the New Zealand rugby team*

☑ You can use either a singular or a plural verb after 'team': *the team was delighted*; *the team were delighted*.

teapot /'tiːpɒt/
teapots

NOUN

a round pot with a handle and a lid, used for making and serving tea

EG *... a china teapot*

tear /tɪəʳ/
tears

NOUN

Tears are the drops of liquid that come out of your eyes when you cry.

EG *Tears ran down his face.*

tear /tɛəʳ/
tears tearing tore torn

VERB

1 If you tear something, you pull it into two pieces or you pull it so that a hole appears in it.

EG *He tore a page out of the book.*

EG *She tore her dress on a nail.*

2 If you tear something from somewhere, you remove it roughly and violently.

EG *He tore the tie from his neck.*

NOUN

3 a hole that has been made in a piece of paper or cloth

EG *There was a tear in the curtain.*

tear up

VERB

If you tear something up, you tear it into two or more pieces.

EG *She tore the letter up without reading it.*

tease /tiːz/
teases teasing teased

VERB

If someone teases you, they deliberately make fun of you or embarrass you.

EG *He gets teased a lot because of his size.*

teaspoon /'tiːspuːn/
teaspoons

NOUN

a small spoon used for stirring drinks; also the amount that a teaspoon holds

EG *... a plastic teaspoon*

EG *Add two teaspoons of sugar.*

technical /'tɛknɪkl/

ADJECTIVE

1 involving machines, processes, and materials used in industry, transport, and communications

EG *A number of technical problems have to be solved.*

2 Technical language involves words which are only used in a certain activity.

EG *It sounds a bit technical.*

technique /tɛk'niːk/

techniques

NOUN

1 a particular method of doing something

EG *... modern manufacturing techniques*

2 Technique is skill and ability in an activity that is developed through training and practice.

EG *... the band's lack of technique*

technology /tɛk'nɔlədʒɪ/

NOUN

Technology refers to practical things that are the result of scientific knowledge.

EG *... new technology such as faster computers*

teenager /'tiːneɪdʒəʳ/
teenagers

NOUN

someone who is between thirteen and nineteen years old

EG *As a teenager he went to the local high school.*

teens /tiːnz/

PLURAL NOUN

Your teens are the period of your life when you are between thirteen and nineteen years old.

EG *I first met John in my late teens.*

tee-shirt /'tiːʃəːt/

another spelling of **T-shirt**

teeth /tiːθ/

the plural of **tooth**

telephone /'tɛlɪfəʊn/
telephones telephoning telephoned

NOUN

1 a piece of electrical equipment for talking directly to someone who is in a different place

EG *He answered the telephone.*

VERB

2 If you telephone someone, you

speak to them using a telephone.

EG *Peter telephoned his sister to thank her.*

teletext /'tɛlɪtɛkst/

NOUN

Teletext is an electronic system that broadcasts pages of information onto a television set.

EG *Check teletext to see what the weather will be like.*

television /'tɛlɪvɪʒən/
televisions

NOUN

1 a piece of electrical equipment which receives pictures and sounds by electrical signals and displays them on a screen

EG *I turned on the television.*

2 Television is the system of sending pictures and sounds by electrical signals.

EG *It was advertised on television.*

EG *... a television programme*

tell /tɛl/
tells telling told

VERB

1 If you tell someone something, you give them information about it.

EG *He told me that he was a farmer.*

2 If you **tell** someone **to do** something, you order or advise them to do it.

EG *A policeman told the driver to move his car.*

3 If you **can tell** something, you are able to judge correctly what is happening.

EG *I could tell he was scared.*

temper /'tɛmpəʳ/
tempers

NOUN

1 A person's temper is their tendency to become angry very

A B C D E F G H I J K L M N O P Q R S T U V W X Y Z

easily.
EG *I hope he can control his temper.*

2 If you are **in a** particular kind of **temper**, that is the way you are feeling.
EG *I started the day in a bad temper.*

3 If you **lose** your **temper**, you become very angry.
EG *He lost his temper and smashed a window.*

temperature /'tɛmprətʃəʳ/
temperatures

NOUN

1 The temperature of something is how hot or cold it is.
EG *... a sudden drop in temperature*

2 Your temperature is the temperature of your body.
EG *His temperature continued to rise.*

temporary /'tɛmpərərɪ/

ADJECTIVE

lasting for only a short time
EG *His job here is only temporary.*

tempt /tɛmpt/
tempts tempting tempted

VERB

1 If you tempt someone, you try to persuade them to do something by offering them something they want.
EG *He tempted her to stay by offering her a higher salary.*

2 If you **are tempted to** do something, you want to do it.
EG *I'm tempted to sell my house.*

ten /tɛn/
tens

the number 10
EG *... ten cars*
EG *... tens of thousands of people*

tend /tɛnd/
tends tending tended

VERB

1 If something **tends to** happen, it happens usually or often.
EG *I tend to wake up early.*

2 If you tend someone or something, you look after them.
EG *He tends the flower beds.*

tendency /'tɛndənsɪ/
tendencies

NOUN

a trend or type of behaviour that happens very often
EG *He has a tendency to be critical.*

tender /'tɛndəʳ/
tenderest

ADJECTIVE

1 Someone or something that is tender is gentle and caring.
EG *... tender, loving care*

2 Tender food is easy to cut or chew.
EG *Cook until the meat is tender.*

3 If a part of your body is tender, it is painful and sore.
EG *My neck felt very tender.*

tennis /'tɛnɪs/

NOUN

Tennis is a game played by two or four players on a rectangular court in which the players hit a ball over a net.
EG *... a tennis match*

tense /tɛns/
tenser tensest; tenses tensing tensed

ADJECTIVE

1 If you are tense, you are nervous and cannot relax.
EG *I have never seen him so tense.*

2 If your body is tense, your muscles are tight.
EG *A bath can relax tense muscles.*

VERB

3 If you tense your muscles, or if

they tense, your muscles become tight and stiff.
EG *He tensed his stomach muscles.*

NOUN
The **tense** of a verb is the form which shows whether you are talking about the past, present, or future.
EG *The captain **asked** Matthew for advice.*
EG *I **hear** a noise.*
EG *They **will go** to Fiji in September.*

---

tension /ˈtɛnʃən/
tensions

NOUN
Tension is a feeling of nervousness or worry.
EG *Laughing can actually relieve tension.*
EG *... the tension between the two countries*

tent /tɛnt/
tents

NOUN
a shelter made of fabric and held up by poles and ropes
EG *We put up our tent in a field.*

tenth /tɛnθ/
tenths

ADJECTIVE
1 The tenth item in a series is the one counted as number ten.
EG *... the tenth man*

NOUN
2 one of ten equal parts
EG *... a tenth of a second*

term /tɜːm/
terms

NOUN
1 a name or word for a particular thing
EG *... the medical term for a heart*

attack
2 a fixed period of time
EG *... a seven year term in prison*
3 one of the periods of time that each year is divided into at a school or college
EG *... the last day of term*

PLURAL NOUN
4 The **terms** of an agreement are the conditions that have been accepted by the people involved in it.
EG *They would not surrender on any terms.*
5 If you express something **in** particular **terms**, you express it using a particular type of language or in a way that shows what you think of it.
EG *The young priest spoke of her in glowing terms.*
6 If you **come to terms with** something difficult or unpleasant, you learn to accept it.
EG *It was hard to come to terms with her death.*

terminal /ˈtɜːmɪnl/
terminals

ADJECTIVE
1 A terminal illness or disease cannot be cured and causes death.
EG *... terminal cancer*

NOUN
2 a place where vehicles, passengers, or goods begin or end a journey
EG *... a new terminal at the airport*

terrible /ˈtɛrɪbl/

ADJECTIVE
1 serious and unpleasant
EG *... a terrible illness*
2 very bad or of poor quality
EG *... a terrible haircut*

terrific /təˈrɪfɪk/

A
B
C
D
E
F
G
H
I
J
K
L
M
N
O
P
Q
R
S
T
U
V
W
X
Y
Z

ADJECTIVE

1 very pleasing or impressive

EG *... a terrific film*

2 very great or strong

EG *... a terrific explosion*

terrify /ˈtɛrɪfaɪ/

terrifies terrifying terrified

VERB

If something terrifies you, it makes you feel extremely frightened.

EG *The idea of death terrifies me.*

territory /ˈtɛrɪtərɪ/

territories

NOUN

1 The territory of a country is the land that it controls.

EG *... Russian territory*

2 an area of knowledge

EG *Football is familiar territory to him.*

terror /ˈtɛrəʳ/

terrors

NOUN

Terror is great fear or panic.

EG *I was shaking with terror.*

EG *He had a real terror of facing people.*

terrorism /ˈtɛrərɪzəm/

NOUN

Terrorism is the use of violence for political reasons.

EG *... acts of terrorism*

test /tɛst/

tests testing tested

VERB

1 When you test something, you try to find out what it is, what condition it is in, or how well it works.

EG *The drug was tested on rats.*

2 If you test someone, you ask them questions to find out how much they know.

EG *I'll test you on your knowledge of*

French.

NOUN

3 a deliberate action or experiment to find out whether something works or how well it works

EG *... a ban on nuclear tests*

4 a set of questions or tasks given to someone to find out what they know or can do

EG *... an intelligence test*

text /tɛkst/

texts

NOUN

1 Text is any written material.

EG *The disc stores thousands of pages of text.*

2 a book or other piece of writing used at a school or college

EG *I studied many texts in my English class.*

than /ðæn, ðən/

PREPOSITION OR CONJUNCTION

1 You use 'than' to link two parts of a comparison.

EG *She was older than me.*

EG *He earns more than I do.*

2 You use 'than' to link two parts of a contrast.

EG *This tastes more like coffee than tea.*

EG *Players would rather play than train.*

thank /θæŋk/

thanks thanking thanked

VERB

1 When you **thank** someone **for** something, you show that you are grateful for something, usually by saying 'thank you'.

EG *He thanked me for bringing the books.*

EG *I forgot to thank him.*

2 You say **thank you** to show that you are grateful for

something.
EG *Thank you very much for coming to see me.*
EG *"Would you like a drink?" — "No thank you."*

thanks /θæŋks/

PLURAL NOUN

1 When you express your thanks to someone, you tell them or show them how grateful you are for something.
EG *... a letter of thanks*

2 If something happened **thanks to** someone or something, it happened because of them.
EG *I'm as prepared as I can be, thanks to you.*

INTERJECTION

3 You say 'thanks' to show that you are grateful for something.
EG *Thanks for the gift.*
EG *"Would you like a coffee?" — "No thanks."*

that /ðæt/
those

ADJECTIVE OR PRONOUN

1 You use 'that' to talk about something which you have already referred to.
EG *She returned to work later that week.*
EG *You say you're sad. Why is that?*

2 You use 'that' to refer to someone or something which is a distance away from you, especially when you are pointing to them.
EG *That man was waving at us.*
EG *That looks heavy.*

CONJUNCTION

3 You use 'that' to introduce a clause saying what a person says, thinks, or feels.
EG *I said that I was coming home.*
EG *He thought that I was ill.*

PRONOUN

4 You use 'that' after a noun to introduce a clause which gives more information about the noun.
EG *... a car that won't start*
EG *... a man that I have known for twenty years*
☑ You only use 'that' when it helps you to identify the person or thing you are talking about: *a man that I met*. If people already know which person or thing you are talking about, you should use 'who' or 'which': *my father, who is a builder; the train, which was late.*

the /ðiː, ðə/

ARTICLE

1 The word 'the' is called the 'definite article'. You use it when you are talking about something that is known about, or when it is clear what you are talking about.
EG *Amy sat outside in the sun.*
EG *I patted him on the head.*
EG *The waiter brought the bill.*

2 You use 'the' in front of numbers that refer to days and dates.
EG *... the fifth of May*
EG *... in the 1930s*

3 You can use 'the' to refer to all people of a particular type.
EG *... help for the unemployed*
EG *The Germans use a different system.*
EG *... dinner with the McCormacks*

4 You can use 'the' to make a general statement about things or people of a particular type.
EG *... the rise of the computer*

5 You use 'the' in front of superlative adjectives.
EG *... the best film this year*

theatre /ˈθɪətəʳ/
theatres
US **theater**

NOUN

A B C D E F G H I J K L M N O P Q R S T U V W X Y Z

1 a building where plays and other forms of entertainment are performed on a stage
EG *We went to the theatre.*
EG *... a movie theater*
2 Theatre is the entertainment performed in a theatre.
EG *... his love of theatre*

their /ðeəʳ/

ADJECTIVE
You use 'their' to refer to something that belongs or relates to the people, animals, or things that you are talking about.
EG *It was their fault.*
EG *Trees lose their leaves in autumn.*

theirs /ðeəz/

PRONOUN
You use 'theirs' to refer to something that belongs or relates to the people, animals, or things that you are talking about.
EG *Amy is my friend, not theirs.*
EG *... the table next to theirs*

them /ðem, ðəm/

PRONOUN
You use 'them' to refer to a group of people, animals, or things that have already been mentioned.
EG *I like the Beatles. I often listen to them.*
EG *His socks had stripes on them.*

theme /θiːm/
themes

NOUN
a central idea in a piece of writing or work of art
EG *The main theme of the book is money.*

themselves /ðəm'selvz/

PRONOUN
1 You use 'themselves' to refer to people, animals, or things that have already been mentioned.

EG *They were talking amongst themselves.*
2 You use 'themselves' to emphasize 'they'.
EG *He was as excited as they were themselves.*
EG *The islands themselves are very small.*
3 If people do something themselves, they do it without any help.
EG *They developed the system themselves.*

then /ðen/

ADVERB
1 You use 'then' to refer to a particular time in the past or future.
EG *I'd left home by then.*
EG *I'll be there on Saturday, so I'll speak to you then.*
2 You use 'then' to indicate that one thing happens after another thing.
EG *She phoned him and then regretted it.*
EG *Pour in the milk, then add the sugar.*
3 You use 'then' to introduce a summary or conclusion to what you have just said.
EG *That's settled, then.*

theory /ˈθɪərɪ/
theories

NOUN
1 an idea or set of ideas that is intended to explain something
EG *... the theory of evolution*
2 You use **in theory** to say that, although something is supposed to happen, it may not actually happen.
EG *In theory, prices should rise.*

there /ðeəʳ/

PRONOUN
1 You use 'there' to say that

something exists or does not exist, or to draw attention to something.
EG *There's a letter for you in my office.*
EG *There is nothing to do here.*
EG *There must be a cheaper way.*

ADVERB
2 You use 'there' to refer to a place that has already been mentioned.
EG *The house is still there today.*

3 You use 'there' to indicate a place that you are pointing to or looking at.
EG *He's sitting over there.*
EG *Where did I put it? Oh, there it is.*

therefore /'ðεəfɔːʳ/
ADVERB
as a result
EG *This bottle is bigger and therefore more expensive.*

these /ðiːz/
the plural of **this**

they /ðeɪ/
PRONOUN
1 You use 'they' to refer to people, animals, or things that have already been mentioned.
EG *They married two years later.*

2 You can use 'they' instead of 'he' or 'she' when you want to refer to a person without saying whether the person is male or female. Some people think this is incorrect.
EG *Ask your teacher and they will help you.*

thick /θɪk/
thicker thickest
ADJECTIVE
1 Something that is thick has a large distance between its two sides.
EG *... a thick stone wall*
2 You can use 'thick' to talk about

how wide or deep something is.
EG *... a folder two centimetres thick*
EG *How thick are these walls?*
3 dense or close together
EG *... thick dark hair*
EG *... thick bushes*
4 Thick liquids are quite solid and do not flow easily.
EG *... thick mud*

thief /θiːf/
thieves
NOUN
a person who steals
EG *... a car thief*

thigh /θaɪ/
thighs
NOUN
Your thighs are the top parts of your legs, between your knees and your hips.
EG *I hate my fat thighs.*

thin /θɪn/
thinner thinnest
ADJECTIVE
1 Something that is thin is much narrower than it is long.
EG *... a thin wire*
2 A thin person or animal has very little fat on their body.
EG *... a tall, thin man*
3 Thin liquids contain a lot of water and flow easily.
EG *The soup was thin and clear.*

thing /θɪŋ/
things
NOUN
1 You use 'thing' instead of another word when you are not able to be more exact or do not need to be more exact.
EG *Trees and flowers and things like that.*
EG *A strange thing happened today.*
2 an object, rather than a plant, an

A
B
C
D
E
F
G
H
I
J
K
L
M
N
O
P
Q
R
S
T
U
V
W
X
Y
Z

animal, or a person
EG *Babies are people, not things!*

PLURAL NOUN
3 Your **things** are your clothes or possessions.
EG *I'll get my things and we'll go.*

think /θɪŋk/
thinks thinking thought

VERB
1 If you think that something is the case, you believe that it is the case.
EG *I think she's got a boyfriend.*
2 When you **think about** ideas or problems, you use your mind to consider them or solve them.
EG *I'll need to think about that.*
3 If you **think of** something, you remember it or it comes into your mind.
EG *Nobody could think of anything to say.*
4 If you **are thinking of doing** something, you are considering doing it.
EG *I'm thinking of moving to London.*

third /θɜːd/
thirds

ADJECTIVE
1 The third item in a series is the one counted as number three.
EG *... the third floor*

NOUN
2 one of three equal parts
EG *... a third of the people*

thirsty /'θɜːstɪ/
thirstier thirstiest

ADJECTIVE
If you are thirsty, you feel a need to drink something.
EG *If a baby is thirsty, it feeds more often.*

thirteen /θɜː'tiːn/

the number 13
EG *... thirteen days*

thirteenth /θɜː'tiːnθ/

ADJECTIVE
The thirteenth item in a series is the one counted as number thirteen.
EG *... the thirteenth day*

thirtieth /'θɜːtɪɪθ/

ADJECTIVE
The thirtieth item in a series is the one counted as number thirty.
EG *... the thirtieth day*

thirty /'θɜːtɪ/
thirties

the number 30
EG *... thirty people*
EG *... a man in his thirties*

this /ðɪs/
these

ADJECTIVE OR PRONOUN
1 You use 'this' to talk about things or people that you have already referred to.
EG *We've been preparing for this match for weeks.*
EG *I'd been on many holidays but never one like this.*
2 You use 'this' to refer to a person or thing that is near you.
EG *This place is run like a hotel.*
EG *Is this what you were looking for?*
3 You use 'this' to refer to the present time.
EG *I've been on holiday this week.*
EG *We'll sell the house next year, not this.*

PRONOUN
4 You use 'this' to refer to something you are going to talk about.
EG *This is what we'll do: we'll buy a car and leave.*
5 You use 'this' in order to say

who someone is.
EG *This is my colleague, Mr Marshall.*

thorough /'θʌrə/

ADJECTIVE

done very carefully and completely
EG *... a thorough examination*

those /ðəuz/

the plural of **that**

though /ðəu/

CONJUNCTION

1 You use 'though' when you are saying something which contrasts with something else that has been said.
EG *I climbed the hill, though not very far.*

2 You use **as though** to say what seems to be happening or to compare two situations.
EG *It looks as though you were right.*
EG *He fell down as though he had been hit.*

thought /θɔːt/

thoughts

1 Thought is the past tense and past participle of **think**

NOUN

2 an idea or opinion that you have
EG *What are your thoughts on the subject?*

3 Thought is the activity of thinking.
EG *She was lost in thought.*

thousand /'θauzənd/

thousands

the number 1000
EG *... a thousand pounds*
EG *... thousands of people*

thousandth /'θauzəntθ/

thousandths

ADJECTIVE

1 The thousandth item in a series is the one counted as number one

thousand.
EG *... the thousandth person*

NOUN

2 one of a thousand equal parts
EG *... a thousandth of a second*

thread /θrɛd/

threads

NOUN

a long, fine piece of cotton, silk, nylon, or wool
EG *... a needle and thread*

threat /θrɛt/

threats

NOUN

1 something or someone that seems likely to harm you
EG *... the threat of illegal drugs*

2 a statement by someone that they will harm you, especially if you do not do what they want
EG *He received death threats.*

threaten /'θrɛtn/

threatens threatening threatened

VERB

1 If someone threatens you, or if they **threaten to do** something unpleasant to you, they say or imply that they will do something unpleasant to you.
EG *He threatened me with a knife.*
EG *The army threatened to destroy the town.*

2 If something threatens a person or thing, it is likely to harm them.
EG *... criminals threatened with prison*

three /θriː/

threes

the number 3
EG *... three children*

threw /θruː/

past tense of **throw**

A
B
C
D
E
F
G
H
I
J
K
L
M
N
O
P
Q
R
S
T
U
V
W
X
Y
Z

thrill /θrɪl/
thrills

NOUN

a feeling of great pleasure or excitement

EG ... *the thrill of waking up on Christmas morning*

thriller /'θrɪlər/
thrillers

NOUN

a book, film, or play that tells an exciting story about dangerous or mysterious events

EG ... *a writer of thrillers*

throat /θrəut/
throats

NOUN

1 the back of your mouth and the top part of the tubes inside your neck

EG *I have a sore throat.*

2 the front part of your neck

EG *He cut his throat.*

through /θruː/

PREPOSITION OR ADVERB

1 moving or passing from one side of something to the other

EG ... *a path through the woods*

EG *He could hear them arguing through the ceiling.*

EG *She went through to the kitchen.*

2 during the whole of a period of time

EG *He has to work through the summer.*

EG ... *right through till the evening*

PREPOSITION

3 because of

EG *He was exhausted through lack of sleep.*

throughout /θruː'aut/

PREPOSITION OR ADVERB

1 during the whole of a period of time

EG *I stayed awake throughout the night.*

EG *I enjoyed the film, but the guy behind me was talking throughout.*

2 in all parts of a place

EG ... *projects throughout Africa*

EG *The house was painted brown throughout.*

throw /θrəu/
throws throwing threw thrown

VERB

1 When you throw something that you are holding, you move your hand quickly and let it go, so that it moves through the air.

EG *He was throwing a ball against a wall.*

2 If you **throw yourself** somewhere, you move there suddenly and with force.

EG *We threw ourselves on the ground.*

throw away

VERB

If you throw away something that you do not want, you get rid of it.

EG *I never throw anything away.*

thrust /θrʌst/
thrusts thrusting thrust

VERB

If you thrust something somewhere, you move or push it there quickly with a lot of force.

EG *They thrust him into the back of a truck.*

thumb /θʌm/
thumbs

NOUN

the short, thick finger on the side of your hand

EG ... *a baby sucking its thumb*

thunder /'θʌndər/

NOUN

Thunder is the loud noise that you

hear from the sky after a flash of lightning.
EG *... a clap of thunder*

Thursday /'θɜːzdɪ/
Thursdays

NOUN
Thursday is the day between Wednesday and Friday.
EG *We usually meet on Thursdays.*

thus /ðʌs/
ADVERB
A FORMAL WORD
1 therefore
EG *Some people will be more capable and thus better paid than others.*
2 in this way
EG *I sat thus for half an hour.*

tick /tɪk/
ticks ticking ticked

NOUN
1 a written mark which shows that something is correct or has been dealt with
EG *Place a tick in the appropriate box.*

VERB
2 If you tick something that is written on a piece of paper, you put a tick next to it.
EG *Tick the correct box on the form.*
3 When a clock ticks, it makes a regular series of short sounds as it works.
EG *The clock was ticking in the corner.*

ticket /'tɪkɪt/
tickets

NOUN
a piece of paper or card which shows that you have paid for a journey or have paid to enter a place of entertainment
EG *... a bus ticket*

EG *... a ticket for the match*

tickle /'tɪkl/
tickles tickling tickled

VERB
When you tickle someone, you move your fingers lightly over their body in order to make them laugh.
EG *She tickled him until he begged her to stop.*

tide /taɪd/
tides

NOUN
The tide is the regular change in the level of the sea on the shore.
EG *The tide is coming in.*

tidy /'taɪdɪ/
tidier tidiest; tidies tidying tidied

ADJECTIVE
1 Something that is tidy is neat and arranged in a careful way.
EG *... a tidy desk*
2 Someone who is tidy always keeps their things neat.
EG *She has always been tidy.*

VERB
3 If you tidy a place, you make it neat by putting things in their proper place.
EG *Tidy your room.*

tie /taɪ/
ties tying tied

VERB
1 If you tie something or **tie** it **up**, you fasten it with a knot.
EG *He tied up the bag and took it outside.*
2 If you tie something in a particular position, you fasten it in that position using rope or string.
EG *She tied the dog to a tree.*
EG *He tied her hands behind her back.*
3 If you tie a knot or bow in

A B C D E F G H I J K L M N O P Q R S T U V W X Y Z

something, you fasten its ends together to make a knot or bow.
EG *He tied a knot in his handkerchief.*

NOUN
4 a long, narrow piece of cloth that is worn round the neck under a shirt collar and tied in a knot at the front
EG *He wears a tie to work.*

tight /taɪt/
tighter tightest

ADJECTIVE
1 Tight clothes or shoes fit very closely.
EG *... her tight black jeans*
2 Cloth or string that is tight is stretched so that it is straight.
EG *Pull the elastic tight.*

ADVERB
3 firmly and securely
EG *He held me tight.*

tights /taɪts/

PLURAL NOUN
Tights are a piece of clothing made of thin material that fits closely round your hips, legs, and feet.
EG *... a pair of tights*

tile /taɪl/
tiles

NOUN
Tiles are flat, square pieces of material that are used to cover a floor, wall, or roof.
EG *... floor tiles*

till /tɪl/
tills

PREPOSITION OR CONJUNCTION
1 Till means the same as until.
EG *They had to wait till Monday.*
EG *She slept till the alarm woke her.*
☑ 'Till' is usually used in spoken and informal English. 'Until' is

used in formal writing.

NOUN
2 a drawer or box in a shop where money is kept, usually in a cash register
EG *... long queues at the tills in Harrods*

time /taɪm/
times timing timed

NOUN
1 Time is what is measured in minutes, hours, days, and years.
EG *You have plenty of time to get here.*
2 You use 'time' to talk about a particular point in the day.
EG *"What time is it?" — "Eight o'clock."*
EG *He asked me the time.*
3 You use 'time' to mean a particular period or occasion when something happens.
EG *I enjoyed my time in Mexico.*
EG *Did you have a nice time?*
EG *... the last time I saw her*
4 If you say it is **time for** something or it is **time to do** it, you mean that it ought to happen or be done now.
EG *It's time for a change.*
EG *It was time to go home.*
5 If you are **in time** for a particular event, or if you are **on time**, you are not late.
EG *I arrived just in time for my flight.*
EG *Their planes usually arrive on time.*
6 If something will happen, for example, **in a week's time**, it will happen a week from now.
EG *He's due to arrive in a week's time.*

PLURAL NOUN
7 You use **times** after numbers to indicate how often something

happens.
EG *I saw my father four times a year.*

✓ You do not say *one time a year* or *two times a year*; you say *once a year* or *twice a year.*

8 You use **times** after numbers when you are saying how much bigger, smaller, better, or worse one thing is compared to another.
EG *The Belgians drink three times as much beer as the French.*

✓ You do not say *two times as much*; you say *twice as much.*

VERB

9 If you time something for a particular time, you plan that it should happen then.
EG *We could not have timed our arrival better.*

10 If you time an activity or action, you measure how long it lasts.
EG *She timed me as I ran.*

11 You use **times** in mathematics to link numbers that are multiplied together.
EG *Two times three is six.*

timetable /ˈtaɪmteɪbl/
timetables

NOUN

1 a plan of the times when particular activities or jobs should be done
EG *... a timetable of events*

2 a list of the times when particular trains, boats, buses, or aircraft arrive and depart
EG *Consult the timetable for departures.*

tin /tɪn/
tins

NOUN

1 Tin is a soft silvery-white metal.
EG *... a tin roof*

2 a metal container which is filled with food and then sealed in order to preserve the food
EG *... a tin of baked beans*

3 a small metal container which may have a lid
EG *... a cake tin*

tiny /ˈtaɪnɪ/
tinier tiniest

ADJECTIVE
extremely small
EG *The bedroom is tiny.*

tip /tɪp/
tips tipping tipped

NOUN

1 the end of something long and thin
EG *... the tips of her fingers*

2 If you give someone such as a waiter a tip, you give them money to thank them for their services.
EG *The waitress earned a lot from tips.*

VERB

3 If you tip an object, you move it so that it is no longer horizontal or upright.
EG *She tipped her head back and laughed.*

tire /ˈtaɪər/
see **tyre**

tired /ˈtaɪəd/

ADJECTIVE

1 If you are tired, you feel like you want to rest or sleep.
EG *I'm too tired to go out.*

2 If you are **tired of** something, you are bored with it and do not want it to continue.
EG *I was tired of having no money.*

tissue /ˈtɪʃuː/
tissues

NOUN
a small piece of soft paper that you

A
B
C
D
E
F
G
H
I
J
K
L
M
N
O
P
Q
R
S
T
U
V
W
X
Y
Z

use as a handkerchief
EG ... a box of tissues

title /'taɪtl/
titles

NOUN

1 the name of a book, play, or piece of music
EG ... the title of his book

2 a word that describes someone's rank or job
EG My official title is Design Manager.

to /tuː, tə/

1 You use 'to' when forming an infinitive.
EG I want to go home.

2 You use 'to' when indicating why something is done.
EG I said it to annoy him.

PREPOSITION

3 You use 'to' when indicating the place that someone or something is visiting, moving towards, or pointing at.
EG ... a trip to China
EG She went to the window and looked out.

4 When you give something to someone, they receive it.
EG He picked up the knife and gave it to me.

5 You use 'to' when indicating who or what a feeling or action is directed towards.
EG He was kind to her.
EG It was clear to me that she was wrong.

6 You use 'to' when stating a time.
EG ... a quarter to eight

7 You use 'to' when indicating the last item in a range of things.
EG I read everything from fiction to science.

8 You use 'to' in ratios and rates.
EG I only get 30 kilometres to the gallon from it.

toast /təʊst/
toasts toasting toasted

NOUN

1 Toast is slices of bread heated until they are brown and crisp.
EG ... a piece of toast

2 If you drink a toast to someone, you wish them success and then drink something.
EG We drank a toast to the bride and groom.

VERB

3 When you toast bread, you heat it so that it becomes brown and crisp.
EG ... a toasted sandwich

tobacco /tə'bækəʊ/

NOUN

Tobacco is the dried leaves of the tobacco plant which people smoke in pipes, cigarettes, and cigars.
EG ... a tin of tobacco

today /tə'deɪ/

ADVERB OR NOUN

1 Today means the day on which you are speaking or writing.
EG How are you today?
EG Today is Friday.

2 Today means the present time.
EG ... the problems we face today
EG ... teaching in today's schools

toe /təʊ/
toes

NOUN

1 Your toes are the five moveable parts at the end of your foot.
EG I've broken my toe.

2 The toe of a shoe or sock is the part that covers the end of your foot.
EG ... a hole in the toe of my tights

together /tə'gɛðər/

ADVERB

1 If people do something together, they do it with each other.

EG *They all live together in a flat.*

2 If two things happen together, they happen at the same time.

EG *"Yes," they said together.*

3 If things are joined or fixed together, they are joined or fixed to each other.

EG *Mix the flour and water together.*

4 If things or people are together, they are very near to each other.

EG *The trees are close together.*

toilet /'tɔɪlət/
toilets

NOUN

1 a large bowl, connected to the drains, which you use to get rid of waste from your body

EG *She flushed the toilet.*

2 a small room containing a toilet

EG *Where are the toilets?*

EG *... the ladies' toilet*

toiletries /'tɔɪlətrɪz/

PLURAL NOUN

Toiletries are things that you use when cleaning and taking care of your body, such as soap and toothpaste.

EG *Remember to pack your toiletries.*

token /'təukən/
tokens

NOUN

a piece of paper, plastic, or metal which can be used instead of money

EG *... a gift token*

EG *Some of the telephones only take tokens.*

told /təuld/

past participle and past tense of **tell**

tolerate /'tɒləreɪt/

tolerates tolerating tolerated

VERB

1 If you tolerate things that you do not approve of or agree with, you allow them.

EG *We will not tolerate this behaviour.*

2 If you can tolerate something, you accept it, even though it is unsatisfactory or unpleasant.

EG *Women tolerate pain better than men.*

toll /təul/
tolls

NOUN

1 The death toll in an accident is the number of people who have died in it.

EG *There are fears that the death toll may be higher.*

2 a sum of money that you have to pay in order to use a particular bridge or road

EG *They've recently introduced a toll on the bridge.*

tomato /tə'mɑːtəu/
tomatoes

NOUN

a small, round, red fruit, used as a vegetable and eaten cooked or raw

EG *... tomato sauce*

tomorrow /tə'mɒrəu/

ADVERB OR NOUN

1 the day after today

EG *The results will be announced tomorrow.*

EG *Tomorrow is her birthday.*

2 You can refer to the future, especially the near future, as tomorrow.

EG *What will education be like tomorrow?*

EG *... the car of tomorrow*

A B C D E F G H I J K L M N O P Q R S T U V W X Y Z

ton /tʌn/
tons

NOUN

a unit of weight equal to 2240 pounds in Britain or 2000 pounds in America

EG *Hundreds of tons of oil have spilled.*

☑ In America, a ton is equal to 2000 pounds.

tone /təʊn/
tones

NOUN

1 The tone of a sound is the kind of sound it has.

EG *... the clear tone of the bell*

2 Someone's tone is a quality in their voice or words which shows what they are thinking or feeling.

EG *Her tone implied that she was getting impatient.*

EG *I was shocked at the tone of your article.*

tongue /tʌŋ/
tongues

NOUN

Your tongue is the soft part inside your mouth that you use for tasting, licking, and speaking.

EG *I've bitten my tongue.*

tonight /təˈnaɪt/

ADVERB OR NOUN

Tonight is the evening or night that will come at the end of today.

EG *What are you doing tonight?*

EG *Tonight is the opening night of the play.*

too /tuː/

ADVERB

1 also or as well

EG *She was there too.*

EG *I, too, have wondered such things.*

☑ 'Too' and 'also' are similar in meaning. 'Also' never comes at the end of a clause, whereas 'too' usually comes at the end: *He's a singer and an actor too.*

2 You use 'too' to indicate that there is more of something than is desirable or acceptable.

EG *The tea was too hot to drink.*

EG *She was drinking too much.*

took /tʊk/

past tense of **take**

tool /tuːl/
tools

NOUN

any piece of equipment, such as a hammer or knife, that you hold in your hand and use to do a particular kind of work

EG *... a tool for cutting wood*

tooth /tuːθ/
teeth

NOUN

Your teeth are the hard, white objects in your mouth that you use for biting and chewing food.

EG *I had to have a tooth taken out.*

EG *She has very bad teeth.*

toothbrush /ˈtuːθbrʌʃ/
toothbrushes

NOUN

a small brush that you use for cleaning your teeth

EG *He'd forgotten his toothbrush.*

toothpaste /ˈtuːθpeɪst/

NOUN

Toothpaste is a substance which you use to clean your teeth.

EG *... a tube of toothpaste*

top /tɒp/
tops

NOUN

1 The top of something is its highest point, part, or surface.

EG *... the top of the stairs*

EG *Fill it to the top.*

2 The top of a bottle, jar, or tube is its cap or lid.
EG *Put the top back on the toothpaste.*

3 a piece of clothing worn on the upper half of your body
EG *She bought a new top.*

4 If one thing is **on top of** another thing, it is on its highest part.
EG *... hot chocolate with whipped cream on top*

ADJECTIVE

5 The top thing in a series of things is the highest or best one.
EG *... the top floor of the building*
EG *She came top in French.*

topic /'tɒpɪk/
topics

NOUN

a particular subject that you write about or discuss
EG *... his favourite topic of conversation*

torch /tɔːtʃ/
torches

NOUN

a small electric light, powered by batteries, which you carry in your hand
EG *He shone a torch into the room.*

tore /tɔːr/
past tense of **tear**

torn /tɔːn/
past participle of **tear**

torture /'tɔːtʃər/
tortures torturing tortured

NOUN

1 Torture is great pain that is deliberately caused to someone in order to punish them or get information from them.
EG *... victims of torture*

VERB

2 If someone tortures another person, they deliberately cause that person great pain in order to punish them or get information.
EG *The prisoner was tortured to death.*

Tory /'tɔːrɪ/
Tories

NOUN OR ADJECTIVE

In Britain, a Tory is a member or supporter of the Conservative Party.
EG *... the defeat of the Tories*
EG *... the last Tory government*

toss /tɒs/
tosses tossing tossed

VERB

1 If you toss something somewhere, you throw it there lightly and carelessly.
EG *She tossed her case onto the bed.*

2 If you toss a coin, you throw it into the air and guess which side will face upwards when it lands.
EG *We'll toss a coin to see who goes first.*

total /'təʊtl/
totals totalling totalled

NOUN

1 the number you get when you add several numbers together
EG *The meal cost a total of twenty pounds.*

VERB

If several numbers total a certain figure, that is the figure you get when all the numbers are added together.
EG *Their debts totalled over 300,000 dollars.*

ADJECTIVE

2 complete
EG *... a total failure*

touch /tʌtʃ/
touches touching touched

A B C D E F G H I J K L M N O P Q R S T U V W X Y Z

VERB
1 If you touch something, you put your fingers or hand on it.
EG *I touched his arm.*

2 When two things touch, they come into contact.
EG *Their knees were touching.*

3 If an experience touches you, it affects you emotionally, usually because someone is suffering or being very kind.
EG *I was deeply touched by his words.*

NOUN
4 the act of touching something
EG *... doors that open at the touch of a button*

5 Your sense of touch is your ability to tell what something is like by touching it.
EG *The water was cold to the touch.*

6 a detail which is added to improve something
EG *She added a few finishing touches to the sketch.*

7 If you are **in touch** with someone, you are in contact with them.
EG *I'll be in touch soon.*
EG *Where can I get in touch with you?*

tough /tʌf/
tougher toughest

ADJECTIVE
1 A tough person is strong and able to tolerate difficult situations.
EG *He is tough enough to do the job.*

2 Something that is tough is strong and difficult to break.
EG *... tough plastic*

3 A tough task or way of life is difficult or full of problems.
EG *She had a tough childhood.*

4 Tough actions are strict and firm.
EG *... tough measures against crime*

tour /'tuər/
tours touring toured

NOUN
1 a long journey during which you visit several places
EG *... a tour of Spain*

2 a short trip round a place such as a city or famous building
EG *There are daily tours of the castle.*

VERB
3 If you tour a place, you go on a journey or trip round it.
EG *He toured Europe for three months.*

tourist /'tuərist/
tourists

NOUN
a person who visits places for pleasure or interest
EG *... foreign tourists*
EG *... the tourist season*

towards /təˈwɔːdz/
US **toward**

PREPOSITION
1 in the direction of
EG *He turned towards the door.*

2 about or involving
EG *My feelings towards Susan have changed.*

towel /'tauəl/
towels

NOUN
a piece of thick, soft cloth that you use to dry yourself with
EG *... a bath towel*

tower /'tauər/
towers

NOUN
a tall, narrow building, sometimes attached to a larger building such as a castle or church
EG *... the Tower of London*

town /taun/

towns

NOUN

1 a place with many streets and buildings where people live and work

EG *... a small town in America*

2 Town is the central part of a town where the shops and offices are.

EG *She has gone into town.*

toy /tɔɪ/
toys

NOUN

an object that children play with

EG *He is too old for toys now.*

EG *... a toy telephone*

trace /treɪs/
traces tracing traced

VERB

1 If you trace someone or something, you find them after looking for them.

EG *Police are trying to trace the owner of the car.*

NOUN

2 a sign which shows that someone or something has been in a place

EG *No trace of his father had been found.*

track /træk/
tracks tracking tracked

NOUN

1 a narrow road or path

EG *... a mountain track*

2 a strip of ground with rails on it that a train travels along

EG *Someone fell on to the tracks.*

3 a piece of ground that is used for races

EG *We watched the horses go round the track.*

track down

VERB

If you track someone or something down, you find them after a long and difficult search.

EG *It took two years to track him down.*

trade /treɪd/
trades trading traded

NOUN

1 Trade is the activity of buying, selling, or exchanging goods or services.

EG *... international trade*

VERB

2 When people or countries trade, they buy, sell, or exchange goods or services.

EG *The two countries have stopped trading with each other.*

trade union trade unions

NOUN

an organization of workers who meet with their employers to protect the workers' interests

EG *Talks are taking place between the managers and the trade union.*

tradition /trəˈdɪʃən/
traditions

NOUN

a custom or belief that has existed for a long time

EG *... our family tradition of growing flowers*

traditional /trəˈdɪʃənəl/

ADJECTIVE

Traditional customs or beliefs have existed for a long time.

EG *... traditional teaching methods*

traffic /ˈtræfɪk/

NOUN

Traffic refers to all the vehicles that are moving along the roads in an area.

EG *There was a lot of traffic on the road.*

traffic light traffic lights

NOUN

Traffic lights are the coloured lights which control the flow of traffic on roads.

EG *Turn left at the traffic lights.*

tragedy /'trædʒədɪ/ tragedies

NOUN

1 an extremely sad event or situation

EG *They have suffered a personal tragedy.*

2 a serious story or play that usually ends with the death of the main character

EG *... Shakespeare's tragedies*

tragic /'trædʒɪk/

ADJECTIVE

Something tragic is very sad because it involves death, suffering, or disaster.

EG *... a tragic accident*

trail /treɪl/ trails trailing trailed

NOUN

1 a rough path across open country or through forests

EG *We set out on the trail again.*

2 a series of marks or other signs left by someone or something as they move along

EG *He left a trail of mud behind him.*

VERB

3 If you trail something or if it trails, it drags along behind you as you move, or it hangs down loosely.

EG *She trailed her fingers through the water.*

train /treɪn/ trains training trained

NOUN

1 a number of carriages or trucks pulled by a railway engine

EG *... a high-speed train*

EG *He is going by train.*

VERB

2 If you train or if someone trains you, you learn how to do a particular job.

EG *She trained as a serious actress.*

3 If you **train for** a sports match or a race, you prepare for it by doing exercises.

EG *I'm training for the London marathon.*

trainers /'treɪnəz/

PLURAL NOUN

Trainers are special shoes designed for running.

EG *... a pair of old trainers*

tram /træm/ trams

NOUN

a vehicle which runs on rails along the street and is powered by electricity from an overhead wire

EG *You can get a tram to the beach.*

transfer /træns'fɜːr/ transfers transferring transferred

VERB

If you transfer someone or something from one place to another, you move them there.

EG *They transferred the money to a Swiss bank.*

translate /trænz'leɪt/ translates translating translated

VERB

If you translate something that someone has said or written, you say it or write it in a different language.

EG *Translate these sentences into English.*

transport /'trænspɔːt/
**transports transporting
transported**

NOUN

1 Transport refers to any type of vehicle that you can travel in.
EG *Have you got your own transport?*
EG *... public transport*

2 Transport is the moving of goods or people from one place to another.
EG *The transport of equipment is now complete.*

VERB : /træns'pɔːt/
☑ Note the change in stress.

3 When goods or people are transported from one place to another, they are moved there.
EG *They use tankers to transport the oil to Los Angeles.*

trap /træp/
traps trapping trapped

NOUN

1 a device for catching animals
EG *... a rabbit trap*

2 a trick that is intended to catch or deceive someone
EG *The thief was caught in a police trap.*

VERB

3 If you trap animals, you catch them using a trap.
EG *The locals were encouraged to trap and kill the birds.*

4 If you are trapped somewhere, you cannot move or escape.
EG *People were trapped in the building by the locked doors.*

trash /træʃ/

NOUN

In American English, trash is unwanted things or waste material such as old food.
EG *The trash is collected on*

Mondays.
☑ The usual British word is rubbish.

travel /'trævl/
travels travelling travelled

VERB

1 If you travel, you go from one place to another.
EG *Students travel hundreds of miles to get here.*

NOUN

2 Travel is the act of travelling.
EG *... air travel*

PLURAL NOUN

3 Someone's **travels** are the journeys that they make to places a long way from their home.
EG *... my travels in the Himalayas*

traveller's cheque
traveller's cheques
US **traveler's check**

NOUN

Traveller's cheques are cheques that you can exchange for foreign currency when you are abroad.
EG *... fifty dollars worth of traveller's cheques*

tray /treɪ/
trays

NOUN

a flat object with raised edges, used for carrying food or drinks
EG *The waiter brought a tray of drinks.*

tread /trɛd/
**treads treading trod
trodden**

VERB

If you **tread on** something, you walk on it or step on it.
EG *... the man who trod on my foot*

treasure /'trɛʒəʳ/
**treasures treasuring
treasured**

A
B
C
D
E
F
G
H
I
J
K
L
M
N
O
P
Q
R
S
T
U
V
W
X
Y
Z

NOUN
1 Treasure is a collection of precious objects, especially one that has been hidden.
EG ... *buried treasure*

VERB
2 If you treasure something, you think it is very special.
EG *She treasures her memories of those days.*

treat /triːt/
treats treating treated

VERB
1 If you treat someone or something in a particular way, you behave that way towards them.
EG *Stop treating me like a child.*
2 When a doctor treats a patient or an illness, he or she gives them medical care and attention.
EG *The boy was treated for a leg injury.*

NOUN
3 If you give someone a treat, you buy or arrange something special for them which they will enjoy.
EG *For my birthday treat he took me to the theatre.*

treatment /ˈtriːtmənt/
treatments

NOUN
1 Treatment is medical attention given to a sick or injured person or animal.
EG *She is receiving treatment for cuts.*
EG *There are two possible treatments for this disease.*
2 Your treatment of someone is the way you behave towards them.
EG *We don't want any special treatment.*

treble /ˈtrɛbl/
trebles trebling trebled
VERB

If something trebles or if you treble it, it becomes three times greater in number or amount.
EG *The price of houses has trebled.*

tree /triː/
trees

NOUN
a large plant with a hard trunk, branches, and leaves
EG ... *a palm tree*
EG *Something moved in the trees.*

tremble /ˈtrɛmbl/
trembles trembling trembled

VERB
If you tremble, you shake slightly, usually because you are frightened or cold.
EG *I was trembling with fear.*

tremendous /trɪˈmɛndəs/

ADJECTIVE
1 very large or great
EG ... *a tremendous amount of information*
2 very good or pleasing
EG *The game was tremendous fun.*

trend /trɛnd/
trends

NOUN
a change towards something different
EG ... *the trend towards healthier living*

trial /ˈtraɪəl/
trials

NOUN
1 a legal process in which a judge and jury decide whether a person is guilty of a crime
EG ... *a murder trial*
2 an experiment in which something is tested
EG *Trials of the drug start next month.*

A
B
C
D
E
F
G
H
I
J
K
L
M
N
O
P
Q
R
S
T
U
V
W
X
Y
Z

trick /trɪk/
tricks tricking tricked

VERB
1 If someone tricks you, they deceive you.
EG *His family tricked him into leaving home.*

NOUN
2 an action that is done in order to deceive someone
EG *He will use any trick to get what he wants.*

3 a clever or skilful action that is done in order to entertain people
EG *... a card trick*

trigger /'trɪgəʳ/
triggers

NOUN
the small device on a gun which you pull in order to fire it
EG *Don't pull the trigger!*

trim /trɪm/
trimmer trimmest; trims trimming trimmed

ADJECTIVE
1 neat and attractive
EG *The gardens are tidy and trim.*

VERB
2 If you trim something, you cut small amounts off it.
EG *Trim the edges off the card.*

NOUN
3 If you give something a trim, you cut small amounts off it.
EG *I need to give my hair a trim.*

trip /trɪp/
trips tripping tripped

NOUN
1 a journey that you make to a place and back again
EG *... during a trip to Africa*

VERB
2 If you trip or **trip up**, you knock your foot against something and fall over.

EG *I tripped on the stairs.*

3 If you trip someone or **trip** them **up**, you make them fall over by making them knock their foot against something.
EG *He tripped Susan up as she passed.*

triple /'trɪpl/
triples tripling tripled

ADJECTIVE
1 consisting of three things or three parts
EG *... a triple ice cream*

VERB
2 If you triple something or if it triples, it becomes three times greater in number or size.
EG *The school has tripled in size since last year.*

trod /trɒd/
past tense of **tread**

trodden /'trɒdn/
past participle of **tread**

trolley /'trɒlɪ/
trolleys

NOUN
a small cart on wheels used for carrying heavy objects
EG *... a supermarket trolley*

troops /truːps/

PLURAL NOUN
Troops are soldiers.
EG *... more than 35,000 troops from twelve countries*

trophy /'trəʊfɪ/
trophies

NOUN
a cup or shield given as a prize to the winner of a competition
EG *The Queen will present the trophy.*

trouble /'trʌbl/
troubles troubling troubled

A B C D E F G H I J K L M N O P Q R S T U V W X Y Z

NOUN

1 Trouble is difficulties or problems.

EG *Try to forget your troubles.*

EG *I had trouble parking.*

2 If there is trouble, people are arguing or fighting.

EG *There was more trouble after the match.*

3 If you are **in trouble**, you are likely to be punished because you have done something wrong.

EG *He was in trouble with his teachers.*

VERB

4 If something troubles you, it makes you feel worried or anxious.

EG *He was troubled by the change in his son.*

trousers /'traʊzəz/

PLURAL NOUN

Trousers are a piece of clothing that covers the body from the waist down, fitting round each leg separately.

EG *... a pair of trousers*

truck /trʌk/
trucks

NOUN

a large vehicle that is used to transport goods by road

EG *The job involved driving a truck.*

true /truː/
truer truest

ADJECTIVE

1 A true story or statement is based on facts and is not invented.

EG *It's true that I don't like him.*

EG *The film is based on a true story.*

2 real or genuine

EG *She was a true friend.*

3 If something **comes true**, it happens.

EG *I hope your wish comes true.*

trunk /trʌŋk/
trunks

NOUN

1 the main stem of a tree from which the branches and roots grow

EG *She leaned against a tree trunk.*

2 the long flexible nose of an elephant

EG *The elephant blew water through its trunk.*

3 a large, strong case or box with a lid, used for storing things

EG *He put all his things in a trunk.*

4 In American English, the trunk of a car is a covered space at the back or front that is used for luggage.

EG *Put your stuff in the trunk.*

☑ The British word is *boot.*

PLURAL NOUN

5 A man's **trunks** are shorts worn for swimming.

EG *... a pair of baggy swimming trunks*

trust /trʌst/
trusts trusting trusted

VERB

1 If you trust someone, you believe that they are honest and will not harm you.

EG *I simply don't trust him.*

2 If you **trust** someone **to do** something, you believe they will do it.

EG *I could trust him to meet the deadline.*

NOUN

3 Trust is the responsibility that someone gives you for important or secret things.

EG *He was in a position of trust.*

EG *You've betrayed their trust.*

truth /truːθ/
truths

NOUN

The truth is the facts about

something, rather than things that are imagined or invented.
EG *I know she was telling the truth.*
EG *There is some truth in what she says.*
EG *... universal truths*

try /traɪ/
tries trying tried

VERB

1 If you **try to do** something, you make an effort to do it.
EG *I must try to see him.*

☑ 'Try and' is often used instead of 'try to' in spoken English, but you should avoid it in writing: *just try and stop me!*

2 If you **try** something, you use it or do it to test how useful or enjoyable it is.
EG *Howard wanted me to try the wine.*

3 When a person **is tried**, they appear in court and a judge and jury decide if they are guilty.
EG *He was tried for murder.*

NOUN

4 an attempt to do something
EG *After a few tries, he gave up.*

try on

VERB

If you **try on** a piece of clothing, you wear it to see if it fits you or if it looks nice.
EG *Could I try it on, please?*

T-shirt /'tiːʃəːt/
T-shirts; also spelt **tee-shirt**

NOUN

a simple, short-sleeved, cotton shirt with no collar
EG *... my red T-shirt*

tube /tjuːb/
tubes

NOUN

1 a long, hollow object like a pipe
EG *He is fed by a tube that enters*

his nose.
2 a long, thin container
EG *... a tube of toothpaste*
3 the tube is the underground railway system in London
EG *I took the tube to Euston.*

tuck /tʌk/
tucks tucking tucked

VERB

If you **tuck** something somewhere, you put it there so that it is safe, comfortable, or neat.
EG *She tucked the letter into her handbag.*
EG *He tucked his shirt into his trousers.*

tucker /'tʌkər/

NOUN

AN INFORMAL WORD

In Australian and New Zealand English, tucker is food.
EG *... his ancestors' traditional tucker*

Tuesday /'tjuːzdɪ/
Tuesdays

NOUN

Tuesday is the day between Monday and Wednesday.
EG *The results will be announced on Tuesday.*

tug /tʌg/
tugs tugging tugged

VERB

1 If you **tug** something, you give it a quick, hard pull.
EG *He tugged at the handle.*

NOUN

2 a quick, hard pull
EG *He felt a tug at his arm.*

tune /tjuːn/
tunes

NOUN

a series of musical notes arranged in a particular way

EG *That's a nice tune.*

tunnel /'tʌnl/
tunnels

NOUN
a long underground passage
EG *... a railway tunnel*

turkey /'tɜːkɪ/
turkeys

NOUN
a large bird that is kept on farms;
also the meat of this bird
EG *... a turkey for Christmas*
EG *... a plate of turkey*

turn /tɜːn/
turns turning turned

VERB
1 When you turn, you move so
that you are facing or moving in a
different direction.
EG *Turn right at the end of the road.*
2 When you turn something or
when it turns, it moves so that it
faces in a different direction or is in
a different position.
EG *She turned the chair to face the
door.*
3 If you **turn to** someone or
something, or if you turn your
attention to them, you start
thinking about or discussing
them.
EG *We'll turn now to the British
news.*
4 When something **turns into** or
is turned into something else, it
becomes something different.
EG *A hobby can be turned into a
career.*

NOUN
5 a change of direction
EG *Take a right turn at the lights.*
6 If it is your **turn to do**
something, you have the right or
duty to do it.
EG *It's my turn to cook tonight.*

7 You use **in turn** to refer to
things that are done in sequence
one after the other.
EG *She spoke to each student in
turn.*

turn down

VERB
1 If you turn down a request or
offer, you refuse or reject it.
EG *This job is too good to turn
down.*
2 If you turn down something
such as a radio or heater, you
reduce the amount of sound or
heat being produced.
EG *She told him to turn the music
down.*

turn off

VERB
If you turn off a piece of
equipment, you cause it to stop
operating.
EG *Turn the light off after you.*

turn on

VERB
When you turn on a piece of
equipment, you cause it to start
operating.
EG *They turned the lights on.*

turn over

VERB
If you turn something over, you
move it so that the top part faces
downwards.
EG *Could you turn over the tape,
please?*

turn up

VERB
1 If someone or something turns
up, they arrive or appear
somewhere.
EG *I waited for the bus but it didn't
turn up.*
2 If you turn up something such as
a radio or heater, you increase the

amount of sound or heat being produced.
EG *I turned the volume up.*

TV TVs

NOUN
1 TV is television.
EG *What's on TV tonight?*

2 a television set
EG *I have a small TV in my room.*

twelfth /twɛlfθ/

ADJECTIVE
The twelfth item in a series is the one counted as number twelve.
EG *... the twelfth man*

twelve /twɛlv/
the number 12
EG *... twelve houses*

twentieth /'twɛntɪɪθ/

ADJECTIVE
The twentieth item in a series is the one counted as number twenty.
EG *... the twentieth year*

twenty /'twɛntɪ/
twenties
the number 20
EG *... twenty people*
EG *... when I was in my twenties*

twice /twaɪs/

ADVERB
Twice means two times.
EG *I've been to New York twice.*
EG *He exercises twice a day.*
EG *The journey back took almost twice as long.*

twin /twɪn/
twins

NOUN
1 If two people are twins, they have the same mother and were born on the same day.
EG *Are you two twins?*

ADJECTIVE
2 You can use 'twin' to describe two similar things.
EG *... a building with twin towers*

twist /twɪst/
twists twisting twisted

VERB
1 When you twist something, you turn its two ends in opposite directions.
EG *She twisted the lid off the bottle.*

2 When something twists or is twisted, it moves or bends into a strange shape.
EG *... the twisted wreckage of the train*

NOUN
3 an unexpected development
EG *There's a great twist at the end of the film.*

two /tuː/
twos
the number 2
EG *... two cats*

type /taɪp/
types typing typed

NOUN
1 A type of something is a group of those things that have the same qualities.
EG *What type of dog should we get?*
EG *Have you done this type of work before?*

VERB
2 If you type something, you use a typewriter or computer keyboard to write it.
EG *I'll type the letter so it's neater.*

typewriter /'taɪpraɪtər/
typewriters

NOUN
a machine with keys which you press in order to produce letters

A
B
C
D
E
F
G
H
I
J
K
L
M
N
O
P
Q
R
S
T
U
V
W
X
Y
Z

and numbers on a page

EG *... an electric typewriter*

typical /'tɪpɪkl/

ADJECTIVE

You use 'typical' to describe
someone or something that shows
the usual characteristics of a
particular type of person or thing.

EG *... a typical American child*

EG *It's typical of him to be late.*

tyre /'taɪəʳ/
tyres
US **tire**

NOUN

a thick ring of rubber fitted round
each wheel of a vehicle and filled
with air

EG *... a flat tyre*

ugly /ˈʌglɪ/
uglier ugliest

ADJECTIVE

not attractive or pleasant to look at
EG *He's so ugly.*
EG *... an ugly building*

UK an abbreviation for **United Kingdom**

ultimate /ˈʌltɪmət/

ADJECTIVE

1 You use 'ultimate' to describe the final result or the original cause of a long series of events.
EG *The ultimate aim is to expand the network further.*
EG *Plants are the ultimate source of all foods.*

2 most important or powerful
EG *... the ultimate challenge in mountaineering*

ultimately /ˈʌltɪmətlɪ/

ADVERB

finally
EG *The struggle will ultimately succeed.*

umbrella /ʌmˈbrɛlə/
umbrellas

NOUN

a device that you use to protect yourself from the rain. It consists of a folding frame covered in cloth attached to a long stick.
EG *The wind broke my umbrella.*

umpire /ˈʌmpaɪəʳ/
umpires

NOUN

The umpire in cricket or tennis is the person who makes sure that the game is played fairly and the rules of the game are not broken.
EG *You must accept the umpire's decision.*

UN

an abbreviation for **United Nations**

un- /ʌn/

PREFIX

'Un-' is added to the beginning of many words to form a word with the opposite meaning
EG *He unlocked the door.*
EG *She was feeling unwell.*

unable /ʌnˈeɪbl/

ADJECTIVE

If you are **unable to do** something, you cannot do it.
EG *I was unable to go to the party.*

unbearable /ʌnˈbɛərəbl/

ADJECTIVE

Something unbearable is so unpleasant or upsetting that you feel unable to accept it.
EG *The pain was unbearable.*

unbelievable /ˌʌnbɪˈliːvəbl/

ADJECTIVE

1 extremely great or surprising
EG *... unbelievable courage*

2 difficult to believe
EG *It sounds unbelievable but I didn't mean to cheat.*

uncertain /ʌnˈsɜːtn/

ADJECTIVE

1 If you are uncertain about something, you do not know what to do.
EG *For a minute he looked uncertain.*

2 If something is uncertain, it is doubtful or not known.
EG *The outcome of the war was uncertain.*

uncle /'ʌŋkl/
uncles

NOUN

Your uncle is the brother of your mother or father or the husband of your aunt.

EG ... my uncle Pat

unclear /ʌn'klɪəʳ/

ADJECTIVE

If something is unclear, it is not known or not certain.

EG It is unclear why this attack took place.

uncomfortable /ʌn'kʌmfətəbl/

ADJECTIVE

1 If you are uncomfortable, you are not physically relaxed and feel slight pain or discomfort.

EG I felt uncomfortable on the floor.

2 Something that is uncomfortable makes you feel slight pain or discomfort.

EG ... an uncomfortable chair

3 If you are uncomfortable, you are slightly worried or embarrassed.

EG I would feel uncomfortable doing that.

unconscious /ʌn'kɔnfəs/

ADJECTIVE

Someone who is unconscious is in a state similar to sleep as a result of a shock, accident, or injury.

EG She was unconscious when the ambulance arrived.

under /'ʌndəʳ/

PREPOSITION

1 below or beneath

EG ... tunnels under the ground

EG A boat passed under the bridge.

2 less than

EG ... under five kilometres

EG ... children under the age of 14

3 If something happens under particular circumstances, it happens when those circumstances exist.

EG Under normal circumstances, we would never have met.

EG Under current laws, this is not possible.

under- /'ʌndə/

PREFIX

'Under-' is used to form words that describe something which has not been provided to a sufficient extent or which has not happened to a sufficient extent.

EG He looked rather underfed.

EG ... underdeveloped countries

underestimate /'ʌndər'estɪmeɪt/
**underestimates
underestimating
underestimated**

VERB

If you underestimate something or someone, you do not realize how large or effective they are.

EG They had underestimated how much money they owed.

EG His opponents often underestimate him.

undergo /ʌndə'gəʊ/
**undergoes undergoing
underwent undergone**

VERB

If you undergo something necessary or unpleasant, it happens to you.

EG I have to undergo training for the job.

EG He recently underwent brain surgery.

underground /'ʌndəgraʊnd/

ADJECTIVE OR ADVERB

1 below the surface of the ground

EG ... an underground car park

EG The waste will be buried deep

underground.

ADJECTIVE

2 secret and usually illegal
EG *... an underground political party*

NOUN

3 the underground is a railway system in which trains travel in tunnels below the ground
EG *... a woman alone in the underground*

underline /ʌndə'laɪn/
underlines underlining underlined

VERB

1 If something underlines a feeling or a problem, it emphasizes it.
EG *The report underlines the dangers of smoking.*

2 If you underline a word or sentence, you draw a line under it.
EG *I underlined the most important sentences in the letter.*

underneath /ʌndə'ni:θ/

ADVERB OR PREPOSITION

1 below or beneath
EG *Take off the lid to see what's underneath.*
EG *We all dived underneath the tables.*

NOUN

2 The underneath of something is the part that touches or faces the ground.
EG *I know what the underneath of a car looks like.*

understand /ʌndə'stænd/
understands understanding understood

VERB

1 If you understand someone or understand what they are saying, you know what they mean.
EG *He spoke so fast I couldn't understand him.*
EG *I don't understand what you are*

talking about.

2 If you understand a situation, you know what is happening and why.
EG *You're too young to understand what's going on.*

3 If you understand that something is the case, you have heard that it is the case.
EG *I understand she's a lot better now.*

understanding /ʌndə'stændɪŋ/
understandings

NOUN

1 If you have an **understanding of** something, you have some knowledge about it.
EG *I have a basic understanding of computers.*

2 an informal agreement between people
EG *We had an understanding that we'd talk in the summer.*

ADJECTIVE

3 kind and sympathetic
EG *They will need to be patient and understanding.*

understood /ʌndə'stud/
past tense and past participle of **understand**

undertake /ʌndə'teɪk/
undertakes undertaking undertook undertaken

VERB

1 When you undertake a task or job, you start doing it.
EG *... whatever job they undertake*

2 When you **undertake to do** something, you promise that you will do it.
EG *He undertook to write the report himself.*

A B C D E F G H I J K L M N O P Q R S T U V W X Y Z

undertaker /ˈʌndəteɪkəʳ/
undertakers

NOUN

a person whose job is to take care of the bodies of people who have died and arrange funerals
EG *Make arrangements with the local undertaker.*

undertook /ʌndəˈtuk/
past tense of **undertake**

underwater /ˈʌndəˈwɔːtəʳ/

ADVERB OR ADJECTIVE

beneath the surface of the sea, a river, or a lake
EG *Some parts of the beach are completely underwater.*
EG *... underwater photography*

underway /ʌndəˈweɪ/

ADJECTIVE

If something is underway, it has already started.
EG *An investigation is underway.*

underwear /ˈʌndəweəʳ/

NOUN

Your underwear is the clothing that you wear under your other clothes, next to your skin.
EG *... items of underwear*

underwent /ʌndəˈwent/
past tense of **undergo**

undo /ʌnˈduː/
undoes undoing undid undone

VERB

1 If you undo a piece of clothing, you unfasten it, for example by opening the buttons.
EG *She undid her jacket.*

2 If you undo something that has been done, you reverse the effect of it.
EG *It will be difficult to undo the damage that has been caused.*

undress /ʌnˈdres/
undresses undressing undressed

VERB

When you undress or **get undressed**, you take off your clothes.
EG *He undressed in the bathroom.*

uneasy /ʌnˈiːzɪ/

ADJECTIVE

If you are uneasy, you feel worried that something may be wrong.
EG *He looked uneasy and would not answer my questions.*

unemployed /ʌnɪmˈplɔɪd/

ADJECTIVE

without a job
EG *... an unemployed mechanic*

unemployment
/ʌnɪmˈplɔɪmənt/

NOUN

Unemployment is the state of being without a job.
EG *... the highest rate of unemployment for five years*

unexpected /ʌnɪksˈpektɪd/

ADJECTIVE

Something unexpected is surprising because it was not thought likely to happen.
EG *His death was totally unexpected.*

unfair /ʌnˈfeəʳ/

ADJECTIVE

not right or just
EG *It was unfair that he was punished.*

unfamiliar /ʌnfəˈmɪlɪəʳ/

ADJECTIVE

If something is **unfamiliar** to you, or if you are **unfamiliar with** it, you have not seen, heard, or done it before.
EG *... plants that were unfamiliar to me*

EG *She is unfamiliar with Japanese culture.*

unfit /ʌn'fɪt/

ADJECTIVE

1 If you are unfit, your body is not in good condition because you have not been taking enough exercise.

EG *I am too unfit to run fast.*

2 Something that is **unfit for** a particular purpose is not suitable for that purpose.

EG *Most of the wine was unfit for drinking.*

unfold /ʌn'fəʊld/
unfolds unfolding unfolded

VERB

1 If you unfold something that has been folded, you open it out so that it is flat.

EG *He quickly unfolded the blankets.*

2 When a situation unfolds, it develops and becomes known.

EG *The facts started to unfold later.*

unforgettable /ʌnfə'gɛtəbl/

ADJECTIVE

Something unforgettable is so good or so bad that you are unlikely to forget it.

EG *A visit to the museum is an unforgettable experience.*

unfortunate /ʌn'fɔːtʃənət/

ADJECTIVE

1 Someone who is unfortunate is unlucky.

EG *... one of those unfortunate people who put on weight very easily*

2 If you describe an event as unfortunate, you mean that it is a pity that it happened.

EG *... an unfortunate accident*

unfortunately /ʌn'fɔːtʃənətlɪ/

ADVERB

You can use 'unfortunately' to show that you are sorry about something.

EG *Unfortunately, I can't stay for long.*

unhappy /ʌn'hæpɪ/
unhappier unhappiest

ADJECTIVE

1 sad and depressed

EG *She is desperately unhappy.*

2 not pleased or satisfied

EG *They are unhappy that the government isn't doing more.*

unhealthy /ʌn'hɛlθɪ/

ADJECTIVE

1 Something that is unhealthy is likely to cause illness.

EG *... unhealthy foods*

2 An unhealthy person is not very fit or well.

EG *I'm quite unhealthy really.*

unidentified /ʌnaɪ'dɛntɪfaɪd/

ADJECTIVE

You say that someone or something is unidentified when nobody knows who or what they are.

EG *... an unidentified flying object*

uniform /'juːnɪfɔːm/
uniforms

NOUN

1 a special set of clothes worn by people at work or school

EG *... a policeman's uniform*

ADJECTIVE

2 even and regular throughout

EG *Chips should be cut into uniform size.*

union /'juːnjən/
unions

NOUN

1 an organization of workers that aims to improve the working conditions, pay, and benefits of its members

A B C D E F G H I J K L M N O P Q R S T U V W X Y Z

EG *She is thinking of joining a union.*
2 When the union of two things takes place, they are joined together to become one thing.
EG *... closer union with our partners in Europe*

unique /juːˈniːk/
ADJECTIVE
1 Something that is unique is the only one of its kind.
EG *Each person's fingerprint is unique.*
2 If something is **unique to** one person or thing, it concerns or belongs only to that person or thing.
EG *... trees unique to the Canary Islands*

unit /ˈjuːnɪt/
units
NOUN
If you consider something as a unit, you consider it as a single complete thing.
EG *... the family unit*

unite /juːˈnaɪt/
unites uniting united
VERB
If a number of people unite, they join together and act as a group.
EG *The other parties united to defeat the government.*

United Kingdom
NOUN
The United Kingdom is the official name for the country consisting of Great Britain and Northern Ireland.
EG *... residents of the United Kingdom*

United Nations
NOUN
The United Nations is an international organization which tries to encourage peace,

cooperation, and friendship between countries.
EG *... a spokesman from the United Nations*

United States of America
or **United States**
NOUN
The United States of America is a republic in North America consisting of 50 states.
EG *... the national anthem of the United States of America*

unity /ˈjuːnɪti/
NOUN
1 Unity is the state of different areas or groups being joined together to form a single country or organization.
EG *... European economic unity*
2 When there is unity, people are in agreement and act together for a particular purpose.
EG *The idea was to create an impression of unity.*

universal /juːnɪˈvəːsl/
ADJECTIVE
Something that is universal relates to everyone in the world or to every part of the world.
EG *Music and sport have a universal appeal.*

universe /ˈjuːnɪvəːs/
NOUN
The universe is the whole of space, including all the stars and planets.
EG *... all the stars in the universe*

university /juːnɪˈvəːsɪti/
universities
NOUN
a place where students study for degrees
EG *He spent three years at university.*

unknown /ʌnˈnəʊn/

ADJECTIVE
If someone or something is unknown, people do not know about them or have not heard of them.
EG ... an unknown actor
EG The motive for the killing is unknown.

unless /ʌnˈlɛs/
CONJUNCTION
You use 'unless' to introduce the only circumstances in which something will not take place or is not true.
EG They played in the garden unless it was raining.
EG I'm not happy unless I ride every day.

unlike /ʌnˈlaɪk/
PREPOSITION
1 If one person or thing is unlike another, they are different.
EG She was unlike him in every way.
2 You can use 'unlike' to contrast two people or things.
EG Unlike cycling, walking does not need expensive equipment.

unlikely /ʌnˈlaɪklɪ/
ADJECTIVE
1 If something is unlikely, it is probably not true or probably will not happen.
EG It is unlikely that he'll arrive today.
EG You're unlikely to notice any difference.
2 strange or surprising
EG It was an unlikely place to meet one's future wife.

unlucky /ʌnˈlʌkɪ/
ADJECTIVE
1 Someone who is unlucky has bad luck.
EG He was unlucky not to qualify for the final.

2 If something is unlucky, it is believed to cause bad luck.
EG Some people think it's unlucky to break a mirror.

unnecessary /ʌnˈnɛsəsərɪ/
ADJECTIVE
Something that is unnecessary is not needed or does not have to be done.
EG Tom was causing unnecessary problems.

unpack /ʌnˈpæk/
unpacks unpacking unpacked
VERB
When you unpack, you take everything out of a suitcase or bag.
EG After I'd unpacked, I went out.

unpleasant /ʌnˈplɛznt/
ADJECTIVE
1 Something unpleasant causes you to have bad feelings, for example by making you uncomfortable or upset.
EG The fish has an unpleasant smell.
2 An unpleasant person is unfriendly or rude.
EG She was very unpleasant to me.

unplug /ʌnˈplʌg/
unplugs unplugging unplugged
VERB
If you unplug an electrical device, you take the plug out of the socket.
EG I had to unplug the telephone.

unpopular /ʌnˈpɒpjʊləʳ/
ADJECTIVE
disliked by most people
EG He had been unpopular at school.
EG ... an unpopular idea

unpredictable /ʌnprɪˈdɪktəbl/
ADJECTIVE
If someone or something is

A
B
C
D
E
F
G
H
I
J
K
L
M
N
O
P
Q
R
S
T
U
V
W
X
Y
Z

unpredictable, you cannot tell
how they will behave or what they
will do.
EG *The weather has been
unpredictable recently.*

unreasonable /ʌn'riːznəbl/

ADJECTIVE

not fair or sensible
EG *... an unreasonable request*
EG *It's unreasonable to expect
everyone to like you.*

unreliable /ʌnrɪ'laɪəbl/

ADJECTIVE

If people, machines, or methods
are unreliable, you cannot trust
them to do what you want.
EG *The car was slow and unreliable.*

unrest /ʌn'rɛst/

NOUN

If there is unrest, people are angry
and dissatisfied.
EG *There was unrest among
students in many cities.*

unsatisfactory
/ʌnsætɪs'fæktərɪ/

ADJECTIVE

not good enough
EG *... unsatisfactory answers to my
questions*

unskilled /ʌn'skɪld/

ADJECTIVE

Unskilled work does not require
any special training.
EG *... unskilled jobs with low pay*

unstable /ʌn'steɪbl/

ADJECTIVE

1 An unstable situation is likely to
change suddenly and create
difficulty or danger.
EG *The political situation in Moscow
is unstable.*
2 Unstable objects are likely to
move or fall.
EG *The boat was unstable in the*

wind.

unsteady /ʌn'stɛdɪ/

ADJECTIVE

1 If you are unsteady, you have
difficulty in controlling the
movement of your body.
EG *She's still unsteady on her feet.*
2 not held or fixed securely and
likely to fall over
EG *... a slightly unsteady item of
furniture*

unsuccessful /ʌnsək'sɛsful/

ADJECTIVE

Someone or something that is
unsuccessful does not achieve
what it was intended to achieve.
EG *He was unsuccessful in finding a
job.*
EG *... an unsuccessful operation*

unsuitable /ʌn'suːtəbl/

ADJECTIVE

not right for a particular purpose
EG *Jane's shoes were unsuitable for
walking.*
EG *He's quite unsuitable for the job.*

untidy /ʌn'taɪdɪ/
untidier untidiest

ADJECTIVE

1 Something that is untidy is not
neat and not arranged in a careful
way.
EG *The place quickly became untidy.*
2 Someone who is untidy does not
care about whether things are
neat and well arranged.
EG *I'm untidy in most ways.*

untie /ʌn'taɪ/
unties untying untied

VERB

1 If you untie something that is
tied to another thing, you remove
the string or rope that holds it.
EG *Just untie my hands.*
2 If you untie something such as

string or rope, you undo the knot in it.

EG *Then she untied her scarf.*

until /ən'tɪl/

PREPOSITION OR CONJUNCTION

1 If something happens until a particular time, it happens before that time and stops at that time.

EG *The shop stayed open until midnight.*

EG *She waited until her husband was asleep.*

2 If something does not happen until a particular time, it does not happen before that time and only starts happening at that time.

EG *School doesn't begin again until September.*

EG *It was not until they arrived that they found out who he was.*

☑ 'Until' is used in formal writing. 'Till' is usually used in spoken and informal English.

unusual /ʌn'juːʒuəl/

ADJECTIVE

Something that is unusual does not happen very often or you do not experience it very often.

EG *It's very unusual for him to make a mistake.*

EG *... an unusual sight*

unwilling /ʌn'wɪlɪŋ/

ADJECTIVE

If you are **unwilling to do** something, you do not want to do it.

EG *He's unwilling to discuss the matter.*

unwise /ʌn'waɪz/

ADJECTIVE

foolish or not sensible

EG *It would be unwise to expect too much.*

unwrap /ʌn'ræp/

unwraps unwrapping unwrapped

VERB

When you unwrap something, you take off the paper or covering around it.

EG *I unwrapped the box.*

up /ʌp/

PREPOSITION OR ADVERB

1 towards or in a higher place

EG *I ran up the stairs.*

EG *He put his hand up.*

PREPOSITION

2 If you go up a road or river, you go along it.

EG *I saw him walking up the street.*

ADVERB

3 If you **get up** or **stand up**, you move so that you are standing.

EG *He got up and went outside.*

4 If an amount **goes up**, it increases.

EG *The price of fish has gone up.*

5 towards or in the north

EG *I'm flying up to Darwin.*

6 If you go **up to** someone or something, you move to the place where they are and stop there.

EG *The girl ran up to the car.*

7 You use **up to** to say how large something can be or what level it has reached.

EG *... traffic jams up to 15 kilometres long*

8 If it is **up to** someone to do something, it is their responsibility.

EG *It's up to you to make a choice.*

9 AN INFORMAL USE

If someone is **up to** something, they are secretly doing something they should not be doing.

EG *They must have seen what their friend was up to.*

ADJECTIVE

10 If you are up, you are not in

A
B
C
D
E
F
G
H
I
J
K
L
M
N
O
P
Q
R
S
T
U
V
W
X
Y
Z

bed.
EG *Are you up yet?*

11 If a period of time is up, it has come to an end.
EG *When the two weeks were up, I was sad to leave.*

uphill /ˈʌpˈhɪl/

ADVERB OR ADJECTIVE
If you go uphill, you go up a slope.
EG *He had been running uphill and was tired.*
EG *... a long uphill journey*

upon /əˈpɒn/

PREPOSITION
A FORMAL WORD
Upon means on.
EG *I stood upon the stair.*

upper /ˈʌpəʳ/

ADJECTIVE
Upper refers to something that is above something else.
EG *... a restaurant on the upper floor*

upright /ˈʌpraɪt/

ADJECTIVE OR ADVERB
If you are upright, you are standing or sitting up straight, rather than bending or lying down.
EG *He moved into an upright position.*
EG *The wind was so strong I couldn't stand upright.*

upset /ʌpˈsɛt/

upsets upsetting upset

ADJECTIVE
1 unhappy and disappointed
EG *She sounded very upset.*

VERB
2 If something upsets you, it makes you feel worried or unhappy.
EG *I'm sorry if I've upset you.*

3 If events upset a procedure or state of affairs, they cause it to go wrong.
EG *The weather upset our plans.*
NOUN : /ˈʌpsɛt/
☑ Note the change in stress.

4 A **stomach upset** is a slight stomach illness caused by an infection or by something you have eaten.
EG *Paul was unwell last night with a stomach upset.*

upside down

ADVERB OR ADJECTIVE
If something is upside down, the part that is usually lowest is above the part that is usually highest.
EG *The painting was hung upside down.*
EG *... an upside-down map of Britain*

upstairs /ʌpˈstɛəz/

ADVERB OR ADJECTIVE
If you go upstairs in a building, you go to a higher floor.
EG *Maureen ran upstairs to her bedroom.*
EG *... the upstairs flat*

up-to-date /ˈʌptəˈdeɪt/

ADJECTIVE
If something is up-to-date, it is the newest thing of its kind.
EG *... Germany's most up-to-date electric power station*

upwards /ˈʌpwədz/

ADVERB
towards a higher place or level
EG *People stared upwards and pointed.*
EG *Lie face upwards with a cushion under your head.*

urban /ˈɜːbən/

ADJECTIVE
relating to a town or city
EG *... densely populated urban areas*

A
B
C
D
E
F
G
H
I
J
K
L
M
N
O
P
Q
R
S
T
U
V
W
X
Y
Z

urge /ˈəːdʒ/
urges urging urged

NOUN

1 If you have an **urge to do** something, you have a strong wish to do it.
EG ... the urge to have children

VERB

2 If you **urge** someone **to do** something, you try hard to persuade them to do it.
EG He urged her to come to Ireland.

urgent /ˈəːdʒənt/

ADJECTIVE

If something is urgent, it needs to be dealt with as soon as possible.
EG He had urgent business in New York.

urine /ˈjuərɪn/

NOUN

Urine is the waste liquid that you get rid of from your body when you go to the toilet.
EG ... a urine sample

US an abbreviation for **United States**

us /ʌs/

PRONOUN

You use 'us' to refer a group of people that includes yourself.
EG Why don't you tell us?
EG Neither of us forgot about it.

USA an abbreviation for **United States of America**

use /juːz/
uses using used

VERB

1 If you use something, you do something with it in order to do a job or achieve something.
EG May I use your phone?

2 If you use someone, you take advantage of them by making them do things for you.

EG Be careful she's not just using you.

3 Something that **used to** be done or used to be true was done or was true in the past.
EG People used to come and visit him every day.
EG I didn't use to like pasta.

4 If you are **used to** something, you are familiar with it and have often experienced it.
EG I'm used to having very little sleep.
EG You'll soon get used to it.

NOUN : /juːs/

☑ Note that you pronounce the noun differently from the verb.

5 The use of something is the act of using it.
EG ... without the use of drugs

6 The use that something has is the purpose it has.
EG The land has many uses.
EG I loved the fabric but couldn't find a use for it.

7 If you have **the use of** something, you have the ability or permission to use it.
EG He lost the use of his legs.
EG John gave me the use of his car.

8 If you say **it's no use** doing something, you are saying that it is pointless and will not succeed.
EG It's no use arguing with him, he won't listen.

use up

VERB

If you use up a supply of something, you use it until it is finished.
EG Don't use up all the toothpaste.

used /juːzd/

ADJECTIVE

A used car has had a previous owner.

EG *... a garage selling used cars*

useful /ˈjuːsful/
ADJECTIVE
If something is useful, you can use it to do something or to help you.
EG *... useful information*

useless /ˈjuːslɪs/
ADJECTIVE
1 If something is useless, you cannot use it because it is not suitable or helpful.
EG *Their money was useless in this country.*
EG *... a useless piece of advice*
2 If a course of action is useless, it will not achieve what is wanted.
EG *She knew it was useless to complain.*

usual /ˈjuːʒəl/
ADJECTIVE
1 Usual refers to what happens or what is done most often in a particular situation.
EG *An officer was asking the usual questions.*

EG *The winter has been colder than usual.*
2 If something happens as usual, it normally happens or happens in the way that it normally does.
EG *As usual when he was nervous, he started to yawn.*
EG *Life is going on as usual.*

usually /ˈjuːʒuəlɪ/
ADVERB
If something usually happens, that is the thing that most often happens in a particular situation.
EG *We usually eat in the kitchen.*

utter /ˈʌtəʳ/
utters uttering uttered
VERB
1 If someone utters sounds or words, they say them.
EG *They departed without uttering a word.*
ADJECTIVE
2 complete or total
EG *This is utter nonsense.*

vacant /'veɪkənt/

ADJECTIVE
If something is vacant, it is not being used.
EG ... a vacant seat

vacation /və'keɪʃən/
vacations

NOUN
1 In American English, a vacation is a holiday.
EG We went on vacation to Puerto Rico.
2 a period at a university or college when no teaching takes place
EG ... the summer vacation

vague /veɪg/
vaguer vaguest

ADJECTIVE
If something is vague, it is not clear or distinct.
EG The description was pretty vague.
EG They have only a vague idea of what's required.

vain /veɪn/
vainer vainest

ADJECTIVE
1 A vain action or attempt is one which is not successful.
EG He made a vain effort to cheer her up.
2 A vain person is very proud of their appearance, intelligence, or other qualities.
EG He is very vain about his hair.

NOUN
3 If you do something **in vain**, what you do has no effect.
EG All her complaints were in vain.

valid /'vælɪd/

ADJECTIVE

1 A valid ticket or document is one which is accepted by people in authority and can be used.
EG You must have a valid passport.
2 A valid argument is logical and reasonable.
EG She made a lot of valid points.

valley /'vælɪ/
valleys

NOUN
a long stretch of land between hills, often with a river flowing through it
EG ... the Loire Valley

valuable /'væljuəbl/
valuables

ADJECTIVE
1 Something that is valuable is worth a lot of money or is very useful.
EG ... a valuable watch
EG ... valuable information

PLURAL NOUN
2 valuables are things that you own that are worth a lot of money
EG Leave your valuables in the hotel safe.

value /'væljuː/
values valuing valued

NOUN
1 The value of something is its importance or usefulness.
EG ... information of great value
2 The value of something is the amount of money that it is worth.
EG The value of the company rose to £5 million.

PLURAL NOUN
3 Someone's **values** are their moral principles and beliefs.
EG ... traditional family values

VERB

4 If you value someone or something, you think that they are important and you appreciate them.
EG *I value my free time.*

5 If something is valued at a particular price, that is how much it is worth.
EG *... cocaine valued at $53 million*

van /væn/
vans

NOUN
a covered vehicle larger than a car but smaller than a lorry, used for carrying goods
EG *... a baker's van*

vanish /'vænɪʃ/
vanishes vanishing vanished

VERB
If someone or something vanishes, they disappear or stop existing.
EG *Anne vanished from outside her home last Wednesday.*
EG *... species which have now vanished*

variety /və'raɪətɪ/
varieties

NOUN
1 If something has variety, it consists of things which are different from each other.
EG *I like to have variety in my life.*

2 A variety of things is a number of different kinds of them.
EG *... a wide variety of shops*

3 A variety of something is a particular type of it.
EG *... a new variety of rose*

various /'veərɪəs/

ADJECTIVE
of several different types
EG *... trees of various sorts*

vary /'veərɪ/
varies varying varied

VERB
1 If things vary, they are different.
EG *The amount of sleep we need varies from person to person.*

2 If you vary something, you change it.
EG *Vary your route as much as possible.*

vast /vɑːst/

ADJECTIVE
extremely large
EG *... vast amounts of money*
EG *... in the vast majority of cases*

vegetable /'vedʒtəbl/
vegetables

NOUN
Vegetables are plants which can be eaten, such as potatoes and onions.
EG *Eat plenty of fresh vegetables.*

vegetarian /vedʒɪ'teərɪən/
vegetarians

NOUN
someone who does not eat meat or fish
EG *She's a strict vegetarian.*

vehicle /'viːɪkl/
vehicles

NOUN
a machine with an engine, such as a car or bus
EG *... army vehicles*

vein /veɪn/
veins

NOUN
Your veins are the tubes in your body through which your blood flows to your heart.
EG *Many veins are just under the skin.*

velvet /'velvɪt/

NOUN
Velvet is a very soft material which has a thick layer of short threads

on one side.
EG ... *a velvet dress*

venue /'venju:/
venues

NOUN
The venue for an event is the place where it will happen.
EG ... *the venue for the conference*

verb /vɜːb/
verbs

NOUN
A **verb** is a word that describes what someone or something does or what happens.
EG *Rosie **visited** the dentist.*
EG *It **rained** for three hours.*
See also **auxiliary** and **modal**.

verdict /'vɜːdɪkt/
verdicts

NOUN
the decision given by a jury or judge at the end of a trial
EG *The jury returned a verdict of not guilty.*

verge /vɜːdʒ/
verges verging verged

NOUN
1 If you are **on the verge of** something, you are going to do it soon or it is likely to happen soon.
EG *Carol was on the verge of tears.*

VERB
2 Something that **verges on** something else is almost the same as it.
EG ... *a fury verging on madness*

verse /vɜːs/
verses

NOUN
1 Verse is poetry.
EG ... *a book of verse*

2 one part of a poem, song, or

chapter of the Bible
EG ... *a poem with ten verses*

version /'vɜːʃən/
versions

NOUN
A version of something is a form of it in which some details are different from other forms.
EG ... *an earlier version of the song*

vertical /'vɜːtɪkl/

ADJECTIVE
Something that is vertical points straight up.
EG ... *a vertical line*

very /'veri/

ADVERB
1 You use 'very' to emphasize what you are saying.
EG ... *a very bad dream*
EG *Thank you very much.*

2 You use **not very** to mean that something is not true or is true only to a small degree.
EG *I'm not very good at tennis.*

ADJECTIVE
3 You use 'very' to refer to an extreme position in space or time.
EG *I turned to the very end of the book.*
EG ... *from the very beginning*

vet /vet/
vets

NOUN
a doctor for animals
EG *I must take the dog to the vet.*

veteran /'vetərn/
veterans

NOUN
1 someone who has served in the armed forces, particularly during a war
EG ... *a Gulf War veteran*

2 someone who has been involved in a particular activity for a long

A

time

EG ... a veteran of British politics

B **via** /'vaɪə/

C   PREPOSITION

If you go to one place via another,

D you travel through that other

place on the way to your

E destination.

EG He drove to Bonn via Paris.

F **vibrate** /vaɪ'breɪt/

G **vibrates vibrating vibrated**

VERB

H If something vibrates, it shakes

with repeated, small, quick

I movements.

EG The table vibrated as the train

J passed.

K **vicar** /'vɪkər/

vicars

L   NOUN

a priest in the Church of England

M EG ... the vicar of St Mary's Church

N **vice** /vaɪs/

vices

O   NOUN

1 a habit which is regarded as a

P weakness in someone's character

EG Smoking is his only vice.

Q **2** Vice is criminal activities

connected with sex.

R EG ... crimes involving vice and

drugs

S **vicious** /'vɪʃəs/

T   ADJECTIVE

cruel and violent

U EG ... a vicious attack

V **victim** /'vɪktɪm/

victims

W   NOUN

someone who has been hurt or

X killed by someone or something

EG ... victims of violent crime

Y

victory /'vɪktəri/

Z

victories

NOUN

a success in a war or competition

EG ... Spain's victory over France

video /'vɪdɪəʊ/

videos videoing videoed

NOUN

1 A video is a sound and picture

recording which can be played

back on a television set.

EG ... the makers of films and videos

2 A video or a **video recorder** is

a machine for recording television

programmes.

EG Set the video for 8.00.

3 Video is the recording and

showing of films and events using

a video recorder.

EG She watched the race on video.

VERB

4 If you video something, you

record it by using a video recorder

or a video camera.

EG I'll video that programme for

you.

view /vjuː/

views viewing viewed

NOUN

1 Your views are your beliefs or

opinions.

EG ... his political views

EG In my view, things won't change.

2 The view from a particular place

is everything you can see from that

place.

EG The new building spoiled the

view from my window.

VERB

3 If you view something in a

particular way, you think of it in

that way.

EG They viewed the USA as a land

of opportunity.

village /'vɪlɪdʒ/

villages

NOUN
a small town in the countryside
EG ... *a village in Kent*

vinegar /'vɪnɪgər/

NOUN
Vinegar is a liquid made from sour
wine and used in things like salad
dressing.
EG ... *a bottle of vinegar*

violence /'vaɪələns/

NOUN
Violence is behaviour which is
meant to hurt or kill people.
EG *He threatened her with violence.*

violent /'vaɪələnt/

ADJECTIVE
1 If someone is violent, they use
physical force or weapons to hurt
or kill people.
EG ... *a violent criminal*
2 A violent event happens with
great force.
EG ... *a violent storm*

violin /vaɪə'lɪn/
violins

NOUN
a musical instrument with four
strings that is held under the chin
and played with a bow
EG *Liz used to play the violin.*

virgin /'və:dʒɪn/
virgins

NOUN
someone who has never had sex
EG *She was a virgin until she was
thirty years old.*

virtual /'və:tjuəl/

ADJECTIVE
You use 'virtual' to mean that
something is so nearly true that it
can be regarded as completely
true.
EG *The train came to a virtual halt.*

virtually /'və:tjuəlɪ/

ADVERB
You use 'virtually' to mean that
something is so nearly true that it
can be regarded as completely
true.
EG *It is virtually impossible to see
everything in one day.*

virus /'vaɪərəs/
viruses

NOUN
1 a kind of germ that can cause
disease
EG ... *a flu virus*
2 a program that damages the
information stored in a computer
system
EG *Check the disk for viruses.*

visa /'vi:zə/
visas

NOUN
an official document or a stamp
put in your passport, that allows
you to visit or leave a particular
country
EG *A visa is not required.*

visible /'vɪzəbl/

ADJECTIVE
If something is visible, it can be
seen.
EG *The island is visible from the
beach.*

vision /'vɪʒən/
visions

NOUN
1 Vision is the ability to see clearly.
EG *The illness can cause loss of
vision.*
2 Your vision of something is what
you imagine it might be like.
EG ... *my vision of the future*

visit /'vɪzɪt/
visits visiting visited

VERB

1 If you visit someone, you go to see them.

EG *He was visited by an old friend.*

2 If you visit a place, you go there.

EG *I have visited many cities.*

NOUN

3 a trip to see a person or place

EG *Helen had recently paid him a visit.*

EG *... the Pope's visit to Canada*

visitor /ˈvɪzɪtər/
visitors

NOUN

someone who is visiting a person or place

EG *I have some visitors from Switzerland.*

EG *... visitors to this country*

visual /ˈvɪzjuəl/

ADJECTIVE

relating to sight

EG *... the visual arts*

vital /ˈvaɪtl/

ADJECTIVE

necessary or very important

EG *It is vital that action is taken quickly.*

EG *... vital information*

vitamin /ˈvɪtəmɪn/
vitamins

NOUN

Vitamins are substances in food which you need in order to remain healthy.

EG *... vitamin C*

EG *... vitamin tablets*

vivid /ˈvɪvɪd/

ADJECTIVE

clear and detailed

EG *... a very vivid dream*

vodka /ˈvɒdkə/
vodkas

NOUN

a strong clear alcoholic drink

EG *... a vodka and lime*

voice /vɔɪs/
voices voicing voiced

NOUN

1 Your voice is what you hear when you speak or sing.

EG *She has a lovely voice.*

VERB

2 If you voice an opinion or an emotion, you say what you think or feel.

EG *Many different opinions were voiced.*

EG *Scientists have voiced concern over the results.*

volcano /vɒlˈkeɪnəʊ/
volcanoes

NOUN

a mountain from which melted rock, gas, and ash sometimes burst

EG *The volcano erupted again last year.*

volume /ˈvɒljuːm/
volumes

NOUN

1 The volume of something is the amount of it that exists.

EG *... the sheer volume of traffic*

2 The volume of an object is the amount of space that it contains or occupies.

EG *They can rise to several times their original volume.*

3 The volume of a radio, TV, or stereo is how loud it is.

EG *He turned down the volume.*

4 one of a series of books

EG *... the first volume of his diaries*

voluntary /ˈvɒləntərɪ/

ADJECTIVE

1 Voluntary refers to actions that you do because you choose them rather than because you have to

do them.
EG *These classes are voluntary.*
2 Voluntary work is work done by people who are not paid for what they do.
EG *She does voluntary work for a number of charities.*

volunteer /ˌvɒlənˈtɪəʳ/
volunteers volunteering volunteered

NOUN
1 someone who offers to do a task without being asked or without being paid
EG *I want two volunteers to help me with the experiment.*
EG *She helps out in a local school as a volunteer.*

VERB
2 If you **volunteer to do** something, you offer to do it without being asked.
EG *James volunteered to clean the kitchen.*

vomit /ˈvɒmɪt/
vomits vomiting vomited

VERB
1 If you vomit, food and drink comes back up from your stomach and out through your mouth.
EG *The smell made me want to vomit.*

NOUN
2 Vomit is food and drink that has come back up from someone's stomach and out through their mouth.
EG *... a pool of vomit*

vote /vəʊt/
votes voting voted

NOUN
1 a choice made by a person or group in a meeting or election
EG *They took a vote and decided*

not to do it.
EG *Mr Brown was elected by 102 votes to 60.*

VERB
2 When you vote, you indicate your choice at a meeting or election, for example by writing on a piece of paper or by raising your hand.
EG *Who are you going to vote for?*
EG *The residents voted to restore the city's original name.*

voucher /ˈvaʊtʃəʳ/
vouchers

NOUN
a piece of paper that can be used instead of money to pay for something
EG *... a voucher for two cinema tickets*

vow /vaʊ/
vows vowing vowed

VERB
1 If you **vow to do** something, you promise or decide to do it.
EG *He vowed to do better in future.*
EG *I vowed that one day I would return.*

NOUN
2 a promise
EG *I made a silent vow to be more careful in future.*

voyage /ˈvɔɪɪdʒ/
voyages

NOUN
a long journey at sea or in space
EG *... Columbus's voyage to the West Indies*

vulnerable /ˈvʌlnərəbl/

ADJECTIVE
weak and without protection
EG *... vulnerable members of society*
EG *... people who are particularly vulnerable to the disease*

A
B
C
D
E
F
G
H
I
J
K
L
M
N
O
P
Q
R
S
T
U
V
W
X
Y
Z

Ww

wage /weɪdʒ/
wages waging waged

PLURAL NOUN
1 Someone's **wages** are the regular payment they receive each week for the work they do.
EG *His wages have gone up.*

VERB
2 If a person or country wages a campaign or war, they start it and carry it on over a period of time.
EG *Rebels have been waging a campaign against the government.*

waist /weɪst/
waists

NOUN
the middle part of your body where it narrows slightly above your hips
EG *She has a very slim waist.*

wait /weɪt/
waits waiting waited

VERB
1 If you wait, you spend time, usually doing very little, before something happens.
EG *I waited for her to get ready.*
EG *I had to wait a week for the results.*
2 If something can wait, it can be dealt with later.
EG *I want to talk to you, but it can wait.*
3 If you **can't wait to do** something, you are very excited and eager to do it.
EG *We can't wait to get started.*

NOUN
4 a period of time before something happens
EG *You'll have a long wait for a bus.*

waiter /'weɪtəʳ/
waiters

NOUN
a man who serves food and drink in a restaurant
EG *The waiter brought the bill.*

waitress /'weɪtrɪs/
waitresses

NOUN
a woman who serves food and drink in a restaurant
EG *She's working as a waitress.*

wake /weɪk/
wakes waking woke woken

VERB
1 When you wake or when you **wake up**, you become conscious again after being asleep.
EG *She woke to find her mother in her room.*
EG *I woke up early.*
2 If someone or something wakes you or **wakes** you **up**, they cause you to become conscious again after you have been asleep.
EG *He was woken by the sound of thunder.*
EG *I woke him up to tell him we were leaving.*

walk /wɔːk/
walks walking walked

VERB
1 When you walk, you move along by putting one foot in front of the other on the ground.
EG *The baby had just learnt to walk.*
EG *i have to walk two miles to school.*
2 If you walk your dog, you take it for a walk in order to keep it healthy.
EG *I walk my dog every morning.*

NOUN

3 a journey made by walking

EG *He often took long walks in the hills.*

EG *The hotel is a short walk from the station.*

wall /wɔːl/
walls

NOUN

1 one of the vertical sides of a building or room

EG *… the bedroom walls*

2 a long, narrow, vertical structure made of stone or brick that surrounds or divides an area of land

EG *… the garden wall*

wallet /'wɒlɪt/
wallets

NOUN

a small, flat case where you can keep paper money and credit cards

EG *… a leather wallet*

wander /'wɒndər/
wanders wandering wandered

VERB

1 If you wander around a place, you walk around it in a casual way.

EG *I like to wander around the shops.*

2 If a person or animal wanders somewhere, they move away from the place where they are supposed to stay.

EG *He has wandered off somewhere.*

want /wɒnt/
wants wanting wanted

VERB

1 If you want something or **want to do** something, you feel a desire or need for it.

EG *Do you want a drink?*

EG *People wanted to know who he was.*

2 If someone **is wanted** by the police, the police are searching for them.

EG *John was wanted for fraud.*

war /wɔːr/
wars

NOUN

1 a period of fighting between countries

EG *They've been at war for the last ten years.*

EG *… the Second World War*

2 a competition between groups of people, or a campaign against something

EG *… a trade war*

EG *… the war against drugs*

ward /wɔːd/
wards

NOUN

a room in a hospital which has beds for several people

EG *… the emergency ward*

warden /'wɔːdn/
wardens

NOUN

1 an official who makes sure that certain laws or rules are obeyed in a particular place

EG *… a traffic warden*

2 someone who works in a prison supervising the prisoners

EG *… a prison warden*

wardrobe /'wɔːdrəub/
wardrobes

NOUN

1 a tall cupboard in which you hang your clothes

EG *… a fitted wardrobe*

2 Someone's wardrobe is their collection of clothes.

EG *His wardrobe consists mainly of t-shirts and jeans.*

warehouse /'wɛəhaus/
warehouses

A
B
C

NOUN
a large building where raw materials or manufactured goods are stored
EG ... *a furniture warehouse*

D **warm** /wɔːm/
warmer warmest; warms
warming warmed

E
F ADJECTIVE
1 Something that is warm has some heat, but not enough to be hot.

G EG *It's not very warm today, is it?*
EG ... *warm water*

H
I **2** Warm clothes and blankets are made of a material which protects you from the cold.

J EG *You will need warm clothes for the winter.*

K **3** friendly and showing affection
EG ... *a warm smile*

L
M VERB
4 If you warm a part of your body, you heat it gently so that it stops being cold.

N
O EG *He warmed his hands by the fire.*

warmth /wɔːmθ/

P NOUN
Warmth is a moderate amount of heat.

Q
R EG *I could feel the warmth of the fire.*

warn /wɔːn/
S **warns warning warned**

T VERB
1 If you warn someone about a problem or danger, you tell them about it.

U
V EG *They warned him of the dangers of sailing alone.*
EG *My friends warned me that children were expensive.*

W **2** If you **warn** someone **not to do** something, you advise them not to do it, in order to avoid

X
Y
Z

possible danger or punishment.
EG *Mrs Blount warned me not to interfere.*

warning /'wɔːnɪŋ/
warnings

NOUN
something which is said or written to tell people of a possible problem or danger
EG *Police have issued a warning about the gang.*
EG *The soldiers opened fire without warning.*

wary /'weərɪ/
warier wariest

ADJECTIVE
cautious
EG *Michelle is wary of marriage.*
EG *They were very wary about giving him a contract.*

was /wɒz/
a past tense of **be**

wash /wɒʃ/
washes washing washed

VERB
1 If you wash something, you clean it with water and soap.
EG *It took a long time to wash the mud out of his hair.*

2 If you wash or **get washed**, you clean yourself using soap and water.
EG *Is there somewhere I can wash?*
EG *You can get washed and go to bed.*

NOUN
3 If you have a wash, you clean yourself using soap and water.
EG *She had a wash and changed her clothes.*

wash up

VERB
1 If you wash up, you wash the dishes, pans, and other things

used in cooking and eating a meal.
EG *I made breakfast and washed up.*

2 If something **is washed up** on land, it is carried there by a river or the sea and left there.
EG *A body had been washed up on the beach.*

washing /'wɔʃɪŋ/

NOUN

Washing is clothes, sheets, and other things which need to be washed or have been washed.
EG *... a pile of dirty washing*
EG *Bring in the washing before it rains.*

washing machine washing machines

NOUN

a machine for washing clothes in
EG *Put your things in the washing machine.*

wasp /wɔsp/ wasps

NOUN

an insect with yellow and black stripes across its body, which can sting like a bee
EG *... a wasp's nest*

waste /weɪst/ wastes wasting wasted

VERB

1 If you waste time, money, or energy, you use too much of it on something that is not important or necessary.
EG *He wasn't going to waste time speculating on the reasons.*
EG *I don't want to waste money on a hotel.*

2 If you waste an opportunity, you do not take advantage of it.
EG *When he had the chance to score, he wasted it.*

NOUN

3 If an activity is a waste of time, money, or energy, it is not important or necessary.
EG *It's a waste of time complaining about it.*
EG *Those sweets are a waste of money.*

4 Waste is material that has been used and is no longer wanted.
EG *... nuclear waste*

ADJECTIVE

5 unwanted or unused
EG *... waste paper*
EG *... waste land*

watch /wɔtʃ/ watches watching watched

NOUN

1 a small clock which you usually wear on a strap on your wrist
EG *... a gold watch*

VERB

2 If you watch something, you look at it or pay attention to it.
EG *They were sitting watching television.*
EG *I had watched Jimmy's progress with interest.*

watch out

VERB

If you watch out for something, you pay attention so that you notice it.
EG *Watch out for more special offers next week.*

water /'wɔːtər/ waters watering watered

NOUN

1 Water is the liquid that falls from clouds as rain.
EG *... a glass of water*
EG *Children were splashing about in the water.*

PLURAL NOUN

2 You use **waters** to refer to a large area of sea.

A B C D E F G H I J K L M N O P Q R S T U V W X Y Z

EG *... the calm waters of the harbour*

VERB

3 If you water a plant, you pour water into the soil around it.
EG *He forgot to water the plants.*

4 If your eyes water, you have tears in them, for example because they are sore.
EG *His eyes were watering from all the smoke.*

5 If your mouth waters, it produces a watery liquid because you can smell or see some food that you would like.
EG *The smell of frying bacon made his mouth water.*

wave /weɪv/
waves waving waved

VERB

1 If you wave, or if you wave your hand, you move your hand from side to side, usually to say hello or goodbye.
EG *He smiled and waved to journalists.*

2 If you wave someone somewhere, you make a movement with your hand to tell them which way to go.
EG *He waited for a policeman to wave him on.*

3 If you wave something, you hold it up and move it from side to side.
EG *... people waving flags*

NOUN

4 the action of waving your hand
EG *She gave them a wave from the window.*

5 a raised mass of water on the surface of the sea, caused by winds or tides
EG *The waves broke on the shore.*

6 the form in which some types of energy such as heat, light, or

sound travel
EG *... radio waves*

7 a sudden increase in a feeling or activity
EG *She felt a wave of panic.*
EG *... a crime wave*

wax /wæks/

NOUN

Wax is a solid, shiny substance made of fat or oil and used to make candles and polish.
EG *... a pool of melted wax from the candles*

way /weɪ/
ways

NOUN

1 A way of doing something is the method that you use in order to do it.
EG *... an excellent way of cooking meat*

2 The way in which you do something is the manner in which you do it.
EG *She smiled in a friendly way.*
EG *I hate the way he speaks.*

3 You use 'way' to indicate the degree to which a statement is true.
EG *In some ways, I still love her.*
EG *He helped me in several ways.*
EG *In a way, that's true.*

4 The way to a particular place is the route that you take in order to get there.
EG *Does anyone know the way to the bathroom?*
EG *Is this the way in?*

5 You use 'way' to refer to the direction or position of something.
EG *As I left, I met Martin coming the other way.*
EG *Turn the cake the right way up.*

6 The way you feel about something is your attitude to it or your opinion about it.

EG *I didn't know you felt that way.*

7 You use 'way' to indicate movement or progress, especially when this is difficult or slow.

EG *He made his way to the bar.*

EG *She started at the bottom and worked her way up.*

8 You use 'way' in expressions such as **a little way** or **a long way** to say how far away something is.

EG *It's only a little way to the shops.*

EG *Christmas is still a long way away.*

EG *He had to walk all the way home.*

9 If someone or something is **in the way**, they prevent you from moving freely or seeing clearly.

EG *We couldn't get out because a truck was in the way.*

10 You say **by the way** to add something to what you have said, especially something that you have just thought of.

EG *By the way, how's your back?*

we /wiː/

PRONOUN

You use 'we' to refer to a group of people that includes yourself.

EG *We ordered another bottle of wine.*

weak /wiːk/
weaker weakest

ADJECTIVE

1 If someone is weak, they do not have much strength or energy.

EG *He was weak from lack of sleep.*

2 If something is weak, it is likely to break or fail.

EG *Ron has weak eyesight.*

3 If someone is weak, they are not very determined and they are easily influenced by other people.

EG *He was a weak man who wouldn't speak out.*

4 A weak drink or drug contains very little of a particular substance.

EG *... a cup of weak tea*

weaken /'wiːkn/
weakens weakening weakened

VERB

To weaken something means to make it less strong.

EG *Tom has been weakened by his illness.*

EG *Family structures are weakening and breaking up.*

weakness /'wiːknɪs/
weaknesses

NOUN

1 Weakness is a lack of physical or moral strength.

EG *Symptoms include weakness and nausea.*

EG *They felt that admitting to stress was a sign of weakness.*

2 A weakness in an argument is something which fails to convince people.

EG *... the strengths and weaknesses of the government's case*

wealth /wɛlθ/

NOUN

1 Wealth is a large amount of money or property which someone owns.

EG *His own wealth grew.*

2 a wealth of something is a lot of it

EG *... a wealth of opportunities*

wealthy /'wɛlθɪ/
wealthier wealthiest

ADJECTIVE

Wealthy people have a large amount of money or property.

EG *... a wealthy businessman*

A B C D E F G H I J K L M N O P Q R S T U V W X Y Z

weapon /ˈwɛpən/
weapons

NOUN

an object that is used to kill or hurt people, such as a gun, knife, or missile

EG ... *nuclear weapons*

wear /wɛəʳ/
wears wearing wore worn

VERB

1 When you wear clothes, jewellery, or make-up, you have them on your body or face.

EG *He was wearing a brown uniform.*

EG *She wasn't wearing any lipstick.*

NOUN

2 You can use 'wear' to refer to clothes that are suitable for a particular time or occasion.

EG ... *a wide range of beach wear*

wear off

VERB

If a feeling wears off, it gradually disappears.

EG *After an hour the pain wore off.*

wear out

VERB

1 When something wears out or when you wear it out, it is used so much that it becomes thin or weak.

EG *He wore out his shoes walking around the city.*

2 If someone or something wears you out, they make you very tired.

EG *The kids wore him out.*

weather /ˈwɛðəʳ/

NOUN

The weather is the condition of the atmosphere at a particular time, for example whether it is raining, hot, or windy.

EG *The weather was bad.*

EG ... *cold weather*

web /wɛb/

webs

NOUN

1 a fine net of threads produced by a spider from a substance in its body

EG ... *a spider's web*

2 something that has a complicated structure or pattern

EG ... *a web of lies*

3 the Web is the same as the Internet

EG ... *the funniest site on the Web*

website /ˈwɛbsaɪt/
websites

NOUN

a collection of information on the Internet relating to a particular subject

EG ... *visitors to our website*

wedding /ˈwɛdɪŋ/
weddings

NOUN

a marriage ceremony

EG *I would like a traditional wedding.*

EG ... *a wedding present*

Wednesday /ˈwɛnzdɪ/
Wednesdays

NOUN

Wednesday is the day between Tuesday and Thursday.

EG ... *the party on Wednesday nigh*

weed /wiːd/
weeds weeding weeded

NOUN

1 a wild plant growing where it is not wanted

EG *The garden is full of weeds.*

VERB

2 If you weed a place, you remove the weeds from it.

EG *Can you help me weed the garden?*

week /wiːk/

weeks

NOUN

1 a period of seven days, especially one beginning on a Sunday and ending on a Saturday
EG *I had a letter from my mother last week.*
EG *Her cousin stayed for another two weeks.*
2 A week is the number of hours you spend at work during a week.
EG *He works a 35-hour week.*
3 the week is the part of the week that does not include Saturday and Sunday
EG *… looking after the children during the week*

weekday /ˈwiːkdeɪ/
weekdays

NOUN

any day except Saturday and Sunday
EG *The shop is only open on weekdays.*

weekend /wiːkˈɛnd/
weekends

NOUN

A weekend is Saturday and Sunday.
EG *I'll see you at the weekend.*

weekly /ˈwiːklɪ/

ADJECTIVE OR ADVERB

Weekly refers to something that happens or appears once a week.
EG *… a weekly magazine*
EG *The group meets weekly.*

weigh /weɪ/
weighs weighing weighed

VERB

1 If someone or something weighs a particular amount, that is how heavy they are.
EG *He weighs 60 kilograms.*
EG *How much do you weigh?*
2 If you weigh something, you

measure how heavy it is using scales.
EG *Weigh your parcels before you post them.*

weigh down

VERB

If a load weighs you down, it stops you moving easily.
EG *He was weighed down by his heavy bag.*

weight /weɪt/
weights

NOUN

1 The weight of someone or something is how heavy they are.
EG *What is your height and weight?*
EG *This adds to the weight of the load.*
2 any heavy object
EG *… straining to lift heavy weights*

weird /wɪəd/
weirder weirdest

ADJECTIVE

strange or odd
EG *It must be weird to be rich.*

welcome /ˈwɛlkəm/
welcomes welcoming welcomed

VERB

1 If you welcome someone, you greet them in a friendly way when they arrive.
EG *She was there to welcome him home from the war.*
EG *Welcome to Washington.*
2 If you welcome something, you approve of it and support it.
EG *He welcomed the decision.*

NOUN

3 a greeting to a visitor
EG *He's sure to receive a warm welcome.*

ADJECTIVE

4 If someone is welcome somewhere, they will be accepted

there in a friendly way.
EG *New members are always welcome.*

5 A welcome action or decision is one that you approve of and support.
EG *This was certainly a welcome change.*

6 If you tell someone they are **welcome to do** something, you are encouraging them to do it.
EG *... a room which guests are welcome to use*

7 You can acknowledge someone's thanks by saying **You're welcome**.
EG *"Thanks for your help." — "You're welcome."*

welfare /ˈwɛlfɛəʳ/
NOUN
1 The welfare of a person or group is their general state of health and comfort.
EG *I am concerned for his welfare.*

2 In American English, welfare is money paid by the government to people who are unemployed, poor, or ill.
EG *She's on welfare.*

ADJECTIVE
3 Welfare services are provided to help with people's living conditions and financial problems.
EG *... changes to the welfare system*

well /wɛl/
better best; wells
ADVERB
1 in a good, skilful, or pleasing way
EG *We treat our employees well.*
EG *He played well.*
EG *The interview went well.*

2 thoroughly and completely
EG *Mix the ingredients well.*
EG *I don't know her very well.*

3 If something **may well** be true

or **could well** be true, it is likely to be true.
EG *The murderer may well come from this town.*

4 You use 'well' to emphasize what you are saying.
EG *He was well aware of that.*
EG *The show is well worth a visit.*

5 You can say 'well' when you are hesitating, correcting a statement, or changing the topic.
EG *There was a note. Well, not really a note.*
EG *Well, I'd better be going.*

6 **as well** means also
EG *It's usually women who are affected, but sometimes men as well.*

7 **as well as** means in addition to
EG *Jim Morrison was a poet as well as a singer.*

8 If you say that you **may as well** or **might as well** do something, you mean that you will do it although you do not have a strong desire to do it.
EG *Now I've started the course, I may as well complete it.*

9 You say **Well done** to show that you are pleased that someone has done something right or good.
EG *"Daddy! I came second in history." — "Well done, sweetheart."*

ADJECTIVE
10 If you are well, you are healthy.
EG *I'm not very well today.*

NOUN
11 a hole drilled in the ground from which water, oil, or gas is obtained
EG *... to fetch some water from the well*
EG *... an oil well*

well-known /ˈwɛlˈnəʊn/
ADJECTIVE

famous or familiar to many people
EG ... *a well-known writer*

well-off /'wɛlˈɔf/
ADJECTIVE
quite rich but not very rich
EG *My grandparents were quite well-off.*

Welsh /wɛlʃ/
ADJECTIVE
1 belonging or relating to Wales
EG *Her mother is Welsh.*
NOUN
2 a language spoken in some parts of Wales
EG ... *speakers of Welsh*

went /wɛnt/
past tense of **go**

were /wəːʳ/
a past tense of **be**

west /wɛst/
NOUN
1 The west is the direction in which you look to see the sun set.
EG *The road runs from east to west.*
2 The west of a place is the part which is towards the west.
EG ... *a house in the west of the city*
ADJECTIVE OR ADVERB
3 in or towards the west
EG ... *the west coast of America*
EG *We will drive west to Paris.*

western /'wɛstən/
westerns
ADJECTIVE
in or from the west
EG ... *the western suburbs*
NOUN
a book or film about life in the west of America in the nineteenth century
EG *He played a cowboy in a western.*

wet /wɛt/
wetter wettest; wets

wetting wet or **wetted**
ADJECTIVE
1 If something is wet, it is covered in water or another liquid.
EG *My hair was still wet.*
2 If the weather is wet, it is raining.
EG *It was very wet and windy that day.*
3 If something such as paint or cement is wet, it is not yet dry.
EG ... *the wet paint on the walls*
VERB
4 If you wet something, you put water or some other liquid on it.
EG *For the best results, wet the hair first.*

whale /weɪl/
whales
NOUN
a very large sea creature
EG ... *the campaign to save the whale*

what /wɔt/
PRONOUN
1 You use 'what' in questions when you are asking for information.
EG *What do you want?*
EG *What's the time?*
2 You use 'what' to refer to something that is unknown or that has not been described.
EG *I don't know what you mean.*
EG ... *once she realized what had happened*
3 You use **what about** when you are making a suggestion or offer.
EG *What about a cup of tea?*
4 You use **what if** in questions about the consequences of something.
EG *What if it doesn't work?*
ADJECTIVE
5 You use 'what' to show that you are talking about the whole of an

A
B
C
D
E
F
G
H
I
J
K
L
M
N
O
P
Q
R
S
T
U
V
W
X
Y
Z

amount.

EG *They had to use what money they had.*

6 You use 'what' to express your opinion of something.

EG *What a terrible thing to do!*

INTERJECTION

7 You say **What?** when you want someone to repeat something.

EG *"Was that the phone?" — "What?"*

☑ It is more polite to say "Pardon?" or "Sorry?" rather than "What?" when you want someone to repeat something.

8 You say **What!** to express surprise.

EG *"It only cost a few thousand." — "What!"*

whatever /wɒtˈɛvəʳ/

PRONOUN

1 You use 'whatever' to refer to anything or everything of a particular type.

EG *He said he would do whatever he could.*

CONJUNCTION

2 You use 'whatever' when you do not know precisely what something is.

EG *Whatever it is, I don't like it.*

3 You use 'whatever' to say that something is the case in all circumstances.

EG *Whatever happens, you have to behave properly.*

ADVERB

4 You use 'whatever' to emphasize a negative statement or a question.

EG *You have no proof whatever.*

EG *Whatever is wrong with you?*

whatsoever /wɒtsəʊˈɛvəʳ/

ADVERB

You use 'whatsoever' to emphasize a negative statement.

EG *I have no memory of it whatsoever.*

wheat /wiːt/

NOUN

Wheat is a cereal plant grown for its grain which is used to make flour.

EG *… farmers growing wheat and corn*

wheel /wiːl/
wheels wheeling wheeled

NOUN

1 a circular object which turns on a rod attached to its centre.

EG *The car's wheels spun.*

2 The wheel of a car is the wheel that the driver holds to steer the car.

EG *My dad was at the wheel of his van.*

VERB

3 If you wheel something somewhere, you push it along on its wheels.

EG *He wheeled his bike into the alley.*

wheelchair /ˈwiːltʃeəʳ/
wheelchairs

NOUN

a chair with wheels in which sick or disabled people can move around

EG *He has been in a wheelchair since he was six.*

when /wɛn/

ADVERB

1 You use 'when' to ask what time something happened or will happen.

EG *When are you leaving?*

CONJUNCTION

2 You use 'when' to refer to the time at which something happens.

EG *I met him when I was sixteen.*

EG *I asked him when he'd be back.*

3 You use 'when' to introduce the reason for an opinion or question.
EG *How did you pass the exam when you hadn't studied for it?*

whenever /wɛnˈɛvəʳ/

CONJUNCTION

at any time, or every time that something happens
EG *Avoid fried food whenever possible.*
EG *I still go on courses whenever I can.*

where /weəʳ/

ADVERB

1 You use 'where' to ask about the place something is in, or the place it is coming from or going to.
EG *Where is Philip?*
EG *Where are you going?*

CONJUNCTION OR PRONOUN

2 You use 'where' to refer to the place in which something is situated or happening.
EG *I don't know where we are.*
EG *... at the travel agent's where you booked your holiday*

CONJUNCTION

3 You use 'where' to introduce a clause that contrasts with another part of the sentence.
EG *A teacher will be listened to, where a parent might not.*

whereas /weərˈæz/

CONJUNCTION

You use 'whereas' to introduce a comment that contrasts with the other part of the sentence.
EG *Her eyes are blue, whereas mine are brown.*

wherever /weərˈɛvəʳ/

CONJUNCTION

1 in every place or situation
EG *Alex heard the same thing*

wherever he went.

2 You use 'wherever' when you do not know precisely where a place or person is.
EG *... the nearest police station, wherever that is*

whether /ˈwɛðəʳ/

CONJUNCTION

You use 'whether' when you are talking about a choice between two or more alternatives.
EG *They have two weeks to decide whether or not to buy it.*
EG *Did she say whether she's coming?*

which /wɪtʃ/

ADJECTIVE OR PRONOUN

1 You use 'which' to ask about two or more alternatives or to refer to a choice between alternatives.
EG *Which room are you in?*
EG *There are so many diets available, how do you know which to choose?*

PRONOUN

2 You use 'which' at the beginning of a clause in order to identify the thing you are talking about or to give more information about it.
EG *Soldiers opened fire on a car which failed to stop.*
EG *He's based in Katowice, which is the largest city in the region.*

while /waɪl/

CONJUNCTION

1 If something happens while something else is happening, the two things happen at the same time.
EG *I look after the children while she works.*

2 You use 'while' to introduce something which contrasts with another part of the sentence.

EG *The first two services are free, while the third costs £35.*

NOUN

3 a period of time

EG *They walked on in silence for a while.*

EG *He was married a little while ago.*

whip /wɪp/
whips whipping whipped

NOUN

1 a thin piece of leather or rope attached to a handle, which is used for hitting people or animals

EG *... a leather whip*

VERB

2 If you whip a person or animal, you hit them with a whip.

EG *He was whipping the horse too hard.*

whisky /'wɪskɪ/
whiskies
us **whiskey**

NOUN

Whisky is a strong alcoholic drink made from grain.

EG *... a glass of whisky*

whisper /'wɪspəʳ/
whispers whispering whispered

VERB

1 If you whisper something, you say it very quietly, using your breath and not your throat.

EG *He whispered the message to David.*

NOUN

2 If you talk in a whisper, you whisper.

EG *They spoke in whispers.*

whistle /'wɪsl/
whistles whistling whistled

VERB

1 When you whistle, you produce a sound by forcing your breath out between your lips or teeth.

EG *She had never learned to whistle.*

EG *He whistled a tune.*

2 If something whistles, it makes a loud, high sound.

EG *Somewhere a train whistled.*

NOUN

3 a small metal tube which you blow in order to produce a whistling sound

EG *The referee blew his whistle.*

white /waɪt/
whiter whitest; whites

ADJECTIVE OR NOUN

1 White is the lightest possible colour, like snow.

EG *He had nice white teeth.*

EG *She was dressed in white.*

2 Someone who is white has a pale skin and is of European origin.

EG *He was white, with short brown hair.*

ADJECTIVE

3 White coffee contains milk or cream.

EG *I take my coffee white.*

4 White wine is wine that is pale yellow in colour.

EG *... a bottle of white wine*

who /huː/

PRONOUN OR CONJUNCTION

1 You use 'who' when you are asking or talking about someone's identity.

EG *Who's there?*

EG *Who do you work for?*

EG *I asked who she was.*

PRONOUN

2 You use 'who' at the beginning of a clause in order to identify the person or people you are talking about or to give more information about them.

EG *... a factory worker who wants to be a postman*

EG *… my brother, who is three years older than me*

☑ See the note at 'whom'.

whoever /huːˈɛvəʳ/

PRONOUN
1 You use 'whoever' to refer to someone whose identity you do not know.
EG *Whoever wins is going to be very famous.*

CONJUNCTION
2 You use 'whoever' to show that the actual identity of the person you are talking about is not important.
EG *I pity him, whoever he is.*

whole /həʊl/

NOUN OR ADJECTIVE
1 The whole of something is all of it.
EG *… throughout the whole of Africa*
EG *We spent the whole summer there.*

NOUN
2 You say **on the whole** to show that what you are saying is true only in a general sense.
EG *On the whole, I'm in favour of it.*

ADJECTIVE
3 in one piece and not broken or damaged
EG *He swallowed it whole.*

whom /huːm/

PRONOUN OR CONJUNCTION
1 You use 'whom' when you are asking or talking about someone's identity.
EG *Whom did he expect to answer his phone?*
EG *They are free to appoint whom they like.*

PRONOUN
2 You use 'whom' at the beginning of a clause in order to identify the person or people you

are talking about or to give more information about them.
EG *… the girl whom Albert would marry*
EG *… the local residents, whom I knew were angry*

☑ 'Whom' is used instead of 'who' in very formal English. In less formal English, 'who' is used: *the girl who Albert would marry; a man who I work with.*

whose /huːz/

ADJECTIVE, PRONOUN, OR CONJUNCTION
1 You use 'whose' to talk about the person that something belongs to or is associated with.
EG *Whose daughter is she?*
EG *Whose is this?*
EG *I can't remember whose idea it was.*

PRONOUN
2 You use 'whose' at the beginning of a clause in order to give information about something relating or belonging to the thing or person you are talking about.
EG *… a driver whose car was blocking the street*

why /waɪ/

ADVERB OR CONJUNCTION
1 You use 'why' when you are talking about the reason for something.
EG *Why did you do it?*
EG *He wondered why she suddenly looked happy.*

ADVERB
2 You use 'why' with 'not' when you are making a suggestion.
EG *Why don't you come with us?*

wicked /ˈwɪkɪd/

ADJECTIVE
very bad in a harmful way
EG *It was a wicked thing to do.*

A
B
C
D
E
F
G
H
I
J
K
L
M
N
O
P
Q
R
S
T
U
V
W
X
Y
Z

wide /waɪd/
wider widest

ADJECTIVE

1 Something that is wide measures a large distance from one side to the other.
EG *Wreckage was scattered over a wide area.*

2 You use 'wide' to talk about how much something measures from one side to the other.
EG *... a desk as wide as the room*

3 If there is a wide range or selection of things, there are many different kinds of them.
EG *... available in a wide range of colours*

ADVERB

4 If you open or spread something wide, you open it as far as you can.
EG *Open your mouth wide.*

widen /waɪdn/
widens widening widened

VERB

If something widens or if you widen it, it becomes bigger from one side to the other.
EG *The river widens as it flows east.*
EG *... the need to widen the road*

widespread /waɪdspred/

ADJECTIVE

Something that is widespread exists or happens over a large area or to a great extent.
EG *... the widespread use of chemicals*
EG *Food shortages are widespread.*

width /wɪdθ/
widths

NOUN

The width of something is the distance from one side to the other.
EG *Measure the width of the window.*

wife /waɪf/
wives

NOUN

A man's wife is the woman he is married to.
EG *His wife is a teacher.*

wig /wɪg/
wigs

NOUN

a mass of false hair which can be worn on the head
EG *She was wearing a blonde wig.*

wild /waɪld/
wilder wildest

ADJECTIVE

1 Wild animals and plants live or grow in natural surroundings and are not looked after by people.
EG *... wild flowers*

2 Wild land is natural and not used for agriculture.
EG *... forests and other wild areas*

3 Wild behaviour is excited or uncontrolled.
EG *As George came on stage, they went wild.*

will /wɪl/

☑ 'Will' is a modal verb. It has only one form. There are no forms ending in -s, -ing, or -ed. Will is often shortened to 'll: he'll arrive soon. Will not is often shortened to won't: she won't bother.

VERB

1 You use 'will' to form the future tense.
EG *Robin will be quite annoyed.*

2 You use 'will' to say that you intend to do something.
EG *I will not lie to you.*

3 You use 'will' when making offers or requests.
EG *Will you stay for dinner?*
EG *Won't you sit down?*
EG *Will you do me a favour?*

4 You use 'will' to say that you are willing to do something.
EG *All right, I'll forgive you.*

will /wɪl/
wills willing willed

VERB
1 If you will something to happen, you try to make it happen using mental effort.
EG *I looked at the phone, willing it to ring.*

NOUN
2 Will is the determination to do something.
EG *He lost his will to live.*

3 If something is the will of a person or group, they want it to happen.
EG *... the will of the people*

4 a legal document stating what you want to happen to your money and property when you die
EG *He left the house to his grandson in his will.*

willing /'wɪlɪŋ/

ADJECTIVE
If you are **willing to do** something, you will do it if someone wants you to.
EG *They are now willing to hold talks.*
EG *That's a question I am not willing to answer.*

win /wɪn/
wins winning won

VERB
1 If you win a fight, contest, or argument, you defeat your opponent.
EG *I don't think they'll win the election.*

2 If you win a prize, you get it because you have been successful at something.
EG *He won a gold medal at the last*

Olympics.
3 If you win something that you want or need, you succeed in getting it.
EG *The government tried to win the support of the poor.*

NOUN
4 a victory in a game or contest
EG *... eight games without a win*

wind /wɪnd/
winds

NOUN
1 a current of air moving across the earth's surface
EG *There was a strong wind blowing.*

2 Wind is gas in your stomach, which produces discomfort.
EG *... people who suffer from wind*

wind /waɪnd/
winds winding wound

VERB
1 If a road or river winds somewhere, it twists and turns in that direction.
EG *The road winds uphill for another mile.*

2 When you wind something round something else, you wrap it round it several times.
EG *She wound the bandage round his knee.*

3 When you wind a device such as a watch, you turn a key or handle several times in order to make it work.
EG *I'd forgotten to wind my watch.*

window /'wɪndəʊ/
windows

NOUN
a space in the wall of a building or in the side of a vehicle, with glass in it so that people can see in or out
EG *I looked out of the window.*

windscreen /'wɪndskriːn/
windscreens

NOUN

the glass at the front of a vehicle through which the driver looks
EG *The windscreen was shattered by a stone.*

windy /'wɪndɪ/
windier windiest

ADJECTIVE

If it is windy, the wind is blowing a lot.
EG *It was so windy yesterday.*

wine /waɪn/
wines

NOUN

Wine is an alcoholic drink, usually made from grapes.
EG *... a glass of wine*
EG *... fine wines*

wing /wɪŋ/
wings

NOUN

1 The wings of a bird or insect are the two parts of its body that it uses for flying.
EG *The bird flapped its wings furiously.*

2 The wings of an aircraft are the long, flat parts on each side that support it while it is flying.
EG *... a seat beside the wing*

wink /wɪŋk/
winks winking winked

VERB

When you **wink at** someone, you look at them and close one eye briefly, often to show that something is a joke or a secret.
EG *He smiled and winked at her.*

winner /'wɪnər/
winners

NOUN

The winner of a prize, race, or competition is the person or thing that wins it.
EG *The winner was a horse called Last Town.*

winter /'wɪntər/
winters

NOUN

Winter is the cold season between autumn and spring.
EG *In winter the nights are long and cold.*
EG *... the winter of 1941*

wipe /waɪp/
wipes wiping wiped

VERB

1 If you wipe something, you rub its surface to remove dirt or liquid from it.
EG *She wiped her hands on a towel.*

2 If you wipe dirt or liquid from something, you remove it using a cloth or your hands.
EG *Anne wiped the tears from her eyes.*

wire /'waɪər/
wires

NOUN

a long, thin piece of metal that is used to fasten things or to carry electric current
EG *... a bundle of wires*
EG *... thin copper wire*

wise /waɪz/
wiser wisest

ADJECTIVE

Someone who is wise uses their experience and knowledge to make sensible decisions.
EG *He was wise not to go out.*
EG *... a wise choice*

wish /wɪʃ/
wishes wishing wished

VERB

1 If you **wish to do** something,

you want to do it.
EG *... if you wish to leave a message*

2 If you wish that something were the case, you would like it to be the case, even though it is unlikely.
EG *I wish I could paint.*

3 If you wish someone luck or happiness, you express the hope that they will be lucky or happy.
EG *I wished them luck.*

NOUN

4 a desire for something
EG *It was her wish to be in films.*

PLURAL NOUN

5 If you express your **best wishes** to someone, you are expressing your hope that they will be happy or successful.
EG *Please give him my best wishes.*

witch /wɪtʃ/
witches

NOUN

a woman who claims to have magic powers
EG *... a fairy tale about an evil witch*

with /wɪð, wɪθ/

PREPOSITION

1 If one thing or person is with another, they are together in one place.
EG *He was at home with me.*
EG *He walked with her to the car.*

2 If you fight, compete, or discuss something with someone, you are both involved in a fight, competition, or discussion.
EG *... the war with Spain*
EG *I didn't discuss it with him.*

3 If you do something with a tool or object, you use that tool or object to do it.
EG *Wipe the mushrooms with a damp cloth.*

4 You use 'with' to indicate the way something is done.

EG *He listened with great care.*

5 having or carrying
EG *... a man with a moustache*
EG *... a waiter with a tray of drinks*

6 concerning
EG *She has a problem with her phone bill.*

within /wɪð'ɪn/

PREPOSITION OR ADVERB

1 in or inside
EG *... communication within the organization*
EG *A man appeared from within.*

PREPOSITION

2 If something is within a particular distance, you are less than that distance from it.
EG *... a restaurant within easy walking distance of the hotel*

3 If something happens within a particular time, it happens before that period of time has passed.
EG *You must write back within fourteen days.*

without /wɪð'aut/

PREPOSITION

1 You use 'without' to say that someone or something does not have or do the thing mentioned.
EG *He looked younger without his glasses.*
EG *Alex had done this without consulting her.*
EG *... five hours without a break*

2 If you do something without someone else, they are not with you when you do it.
EG *He went without me.*

witness /'wɪtnɪs/
witnesses witnessing
witnessed

NOUN

1 A witness to an accident or crime is someone who saw it.
EG *There were no witnesses to the*

A
B
C
D
E
F
G
H
I
J
K
L
M
N
O
P
Q
R
S
T
U
V
W
X
Y
Z

assault.

2 someone who appears in a law court to say what they know about a crime or other event

EG *Ten witnesses will be called to testify.*

VERB

3 If you witness something, you see it happen.

EG *Anyone who witnessed the attack should call the police.*

witty /'wɪtɪ/
wittier wittiest

ADJECTIVE

amusing in a clever way

EG *... a witty novel*

EG *He can be very witty.*

wives /waɪvz/
the plural of **wife**

woke /wəʊk/
past tense of **wake**

woken /'wəʊkn/
past participle of **wake**

wolf /wʊlf/
wolves

NOUN

a wild animal that looks like a large dog

EG *... a pack of wolves*

woman /'wʊmən/
women

NOUN

an adult female human being

EG *... a young woman from Kenya*

EG *... a woman doctor*

won /wʌn/
past participle and past tense of **win**

wonder /'wʌndəʳ/
wonders wondering wondered

VERB

1 If you wonder about something,

you think about it and try to guess or understand more about it.

EG *He wondered if she would join him.*

EG *I wonder what that noise was.*

NOUN

2 Wonder is a feeling of great surprise and admiration.

EG *I still feel a sense of wonder when I think back on it.*

3 something or someone remarkable that people admire

EG *... the wonders of science*

wonderful /'wʌndəful/

ADJECTIVE

very good

EG *It's wonderful to see you.*

EG *... a wonderful film*

won't /wəʊnt/

VERB

Won't means the same as will not.

EG *I won't tell anyone.*

wood /wʊd/
woods

NOUN

1 Wood is the material which forms the trunks and branches of trees.

EG *... dishes made of wood*

2 a large area of trees

EG *... a path through a wood*

☑ People sometimes refer to a very large wood as 'the woods': *they got lost in the woods.*

wooden /'wʊdn/

ADJECTIVE

made of wood

EG *... a wooden box*

wool /wʊl/

NOUN

1 Wool is the hair that grows on sheep and some other animals.

EG *... sheep bred for their wool*

2 Wool is a material made from

the wool of animals which is used to make clothes, blankets, and carpets.

EG ... a ball of wool

word /wɜːd/
words wording worded

NOUN

1 a single unit of language in speech or writing

EG ... a word like 'alphabet'

2 If you **have a word** with someone, you have a short conversation with them.

EG Could I have a word with you?

3 If you **give** someone your **word**, you promise to do something.

EG He gave me his word that he would come.

VERB

4 If something is worded in a particular way, it is expressed in that way.

EG I would have worded it differently.

wore /wɔːr/
past tense of **wear**

work /wɜːk/
works working worked

VERB

1 People who work have a job, usually one which they are paid to do.

EG My husband works for a national newspaper.

2 When you work, you do the tasks that your job involves.

EG She's been working really hard.

3 If a machine works, it operates and performs its function.

EG The radio doesn't work.

4 If something such as an idea or a system works, it is successful.

EG The system is not working.

NOUN

5 People who have work have a job, usually one which they are paid to do.

EG What kind of work do you do?

EG She's still trying to find work.

6 Work is the tasks which your job involves.

EG I've got a lot of work to do.

7 Work is the place where you do your job.

EG He travels to work by train.

EG She was at work when he called.

8 A work is something such as a painting, book, or piece of music.

EG ... a work of art

EG ... the complete works of Shakespeare

work out

VERB

1 If you work out a solution to a problem, you find the solution.

EG We haven't worked out how to do it yet.

2 If something works out at a particular amount, it is calculated to be that amount.

EG It will work out cheaper to hire a van.

3 If a situation works out in a particular way, it happens in that way.

EG The plan isn't working out as well as we'd hoped.

4 If you work out, you perform a physical exercise routine.

EG He works out at the gym twice a week.

worker /'wɜːkər/
workers

NOUN

a person who is employed in industry or business and who is not a manager

EG ... office workers

A
B
C
D
E
F
G
H
I
J
K
L
M
N
O
P
Q
R
S
T
U
V
W
X
Y
Z

world /wɜːld/
worlds

NOUN
1 The world is the planet that we live on, or any planet.
EG *I'd like to travel around the world.*
EG *... life on other worlds*
2 Someone's world is the life they lead and the things they experience.
EG *I lost my job and my whole world collapsed.*
3 A particular world is a field of activity and the people involved in it.
EG *... the world of football*
EG *... the ancient world*

ADJECTIVE
4 You can use 'world' to describe someone or something that is one of the best or most important of its kind.
EG *... the world champion*

worldwide /ˈwɜːldˈwaɪd/

ADJECTIVE OR ADVERB
happening throughout the world
EG *... a worldwide epidemic*
EG *Millions of her books have been sold worldwide.*

worm /wɜːm/
worms

NOUN
a small, thin animal without bones or legs, which lives in the soil
EG *... using worms to catch fish*

worn /wɔːn/
past participle of **wear**

worried /ˈwʌrɪd/

ADJECTIVE
If you are worried, you are anxious about a problem or about something unpleasant that might happen.

EG *I'm worried about losing my passport.*
EG *She was worried that she might get lost.*

worry /ˈwʌrɪ/
worries worrying worried

VERB
1 If you worry about something, you feel anxious about a problem or about something unpleasant that might happen.
EG *I worry about her constantly.*
EG *Don't worry, your luggage will arrive soon.*
2 If someone or something worries you, they cause you to feel anxious.
EG *I didn't want to worry you.*

NOUN
3 Worry is a feeling of anxiety caused by a problem or by thinking about something unpleasant that might happen.
EG *Money was a great cause of worry.*
4 a problem that makes you feel anxious
EG *Rain is the least of our worries.*

worse /wɜːs/

ADJECTIVE OR ADVERB
Worse is the comparative of 'bad' and 'badly'.
EG *His new book is worse than his last.*
EG *Billy was feeling worse.*

worst /wɜːst/

ADJECTIVE OR ADVERB
1 Worst is the superlative of 'bad' and 'badly'.
EG *... the worst film I have ever seen*
EG *... the worst possible result*

NOUN
2 the worst is the most unpleasant or unfavourable thing that can happen
EG *The worst is over.*

worth /wə:θ/

PREPOSITION

1 If something is worth a sum of money, it has that value.
EG *... a house worth £200,000*

2 You use 'worth' to say that something is so good or enjoyable that it deserves to be done.
EG *It cost a lot but it was worth it.*
EG *... to see if the car was worth buying*

NOUN

3 A particular amount of money's **worth of** something is the quantity of it that you can buy for that money.
EG *... five pound's worth of petrol*

worthwhile /'wə:θ'waɪl/

ADJECTIVE

If something is worthwhile, it is worth the time, money, or effort spent on it.
EG *... a worthwhile career*

would /wʊd/

☑ 'Would' is a modal verb. It has only one form. There are no forms ending in -s, -ing, or -ed. Would is often shortened to 'd: I'd like to.

VERB

1 You use 'would' when you are saying what someone thought was going to happen.
EG *We were sure it would be a success.*

2 You use 'would' when you are referring to the result of a possible situation.
EG *It would be fun to try.*

3 You use 'would' to say that someone was willing to do something.
EG *She said she would help me.*

4 You use 'would' when you are saying what someone wants.
EG *She asked me what I would like*

to do.

5 You use 'would' in polite questions.
EG *Would you like a drink?*

wound /waʊnd/
Wound is the past participle and past tense of **wind**

wound /wu:nd/
wounds wounding wounded

NOUN

1 an injury to your body, especially a cut or hole caused by a weapon
EG *The soldier died from his wounds.*

VERB

2 If a weapon wounds you, it injures your body.
EG *Six people were wounded in the blast.*

wrap /ræp/
wraps wrapping wrapped

VERB

1 If you wrap something or **wrap** it **up**, you fold paper or cloth around it to cover it.
EG *Carrie was wrapping up the family's presents.*

2 If you **wrap** paper or cloth **around** something, you put paper or cloth around it.
EG *She wrapped a handkerchief around her bleeding finger.*

wreck /rɛk/
wrecks wrecking wrecked

VERB

1 To wreck something means to completely destroy or ruin it.
EG *Fifty houses were wrecked in the storm.*
EG *... the scandal which wrecked his career*

NOUN

2 a vehicle which has been badly damaged in an accident

EG *The car was a total wreck.*

wrist /rɪst/
wrists

NOUN

the part of your body between your hand and your arm which bends when you move your hand
EG *She was pulling the child along by the wrist.*

write /raɪt/
writes writing wrote written

VERB

1 When you write or when you write something, you use a pen or pencil to form letters, words, or numbers.
EG *Write your name and address on a postcard.*
EG *She cannot read or write.*

2 If you write something such as a poem, a book, or a piece of music, you create it and record it.
EG *I have written a lot of music in the past year.*

3 When you **write to** someone or write them a letter, you ask or tell them something in a letter.
EG *She had written to her aunt in Holland.*
EG *I wrote him a letter asking for advice.*

write down

VERB

If you write something down, you record it on a piece of paper.
EG *He wrote down everything I said.*

writer /ˈraɪtər/
writers

NOUN

a person who writes books, stories, or articles as a job
EG *... an American writer*

written /ˈrɪtn/
past participle of **write**

wrong /rɒŋ/

ADJECTIVE

1 unsatisfactory or not working properly
EG *Is anything wrong?*
EG *There was something wrong with the car.*

2 bad or immoral
EG *I didn't do anything wrong.*
EG *She was wrong to leave her child alone.*

ADJECTIVE OR ADVERB

3 not correct
EG *... the wrong answer*
EG *I was wrong about him.*
EG *You've done it wrong.*

NOUN

4 'Wrong' refers to actions that are bad or immoral.
EG *... the difference between right and wrong*

wrote /rəʊt/
past tense of **write**

Xx

A B C D E F G H I J K L M N O P Q R S T U V W X Y Z

Xmas /'ɛksməs/

NOUN

AN INFORMAL WORD

Xmas means the same as
Christmas.

EG *I'll be home for Xmas.*

X-ray /'ɛksreɪ/
X-rays X-raying X-rayed

NOUN

1 a type of radiation that can pass
through most solid materials.
X-rays are used to examine

people's bones or organs and to
see inside people's luggage at
airports.

EG *... the use of X-rays in medicine*

2 a picture made by sending
X-rays through something

EG *The doctor took an X-ray of my
stomach.*

VERB

3 If someone or something is
X-rayed, an X-ray is taken of them.

EG *All bags are X-rayed.*

Yy

yacht /jɒt/
yachts

NOUN

a boat with sails or an engine, used for racing or for pleasure trips

EG … *a round-the-world yacht race*

yard /jɑːd/
yards

NOUN

1 a unit of length equal to 36 inches or about 91.4 centimetres

EG … *200 yards away*

EG … *a few yards from my house*

2 an area next to a building, often with a wall around it

EG *I saw him standing in the yard.*

3 In American English, a yard is a garden.

EG *He dug a hole in the yard.*

yawn /jɔːn/
yawns yawning yawned

VERB

When you yawn, you open your mouth wide and take in more air than usual, often because you are tired.

EG *I couldn't stop yawning.*

yeah /jɛə/

INTERJECTION

AN INFORMAL WORD

yes

EG *Yeah, I'd love to come.*

year /jɪəʳ/
years

NOUN

1 a period of twelve months, beginning on the first of January and ending on the thirty-first of December

EG *I am going to America next year.*

2 any period of twelve months

EG *The museum attracts a million visitors a year.*

EG … *the current financial year*

yellow /'jɛləʊ/
yellower yellowest; yellows

ADJECTIVE OR NOUN

Yellow is the colour of lemons or butter.

EG *I painted the room bright yellow.*

EG … *a mix of yellows and greens*

yes /jɛs/

INTERJECTION

1 You say 'yes' as a positive answer to a question.

EG *"Are you a friend of Nick's?" — "Yes."*

2 You say 'yes' when accepting something.

EG *"Would you like more wine?" — "Yes, please."*

3 You say 'yes' when agreeing that something is true or when giving permission.

EG *"It's a shame, isn't it?" — "Yes, it is."*

EG *"Can I ask you something?" — "Yes, of course."*

4 You can say 'yes' when contradicting someone.

EG *"Anyway, it's not far." — "Yes, it is."*

yesterday /'jɛstədɪ/

ADVERB OR NOUN

Yesterday is the day before today.

EG *What did you do yesterday?*

EG … *yesterday's newspaper*

yet /jɛt/

ADVERB

1 If something has not happened yet, it has not happened up to the present time.

EG *I haven't decided yet.*

EG *Have you got satellite TV yet?*

2 If something should not be done yet, it should not be done now, but later.

EG *Don't go yet, I've more to say.*

3 You use 'yet' to say that there is still a possibility that something will happen.

EG *An agreement might yet be possible.*

4 You use 'yet' to say how much longer a situation will continue.

EG *The film doesn't start for an hour yet.*

5 You use 'yet' to emphasize that something is a further case of something that has happened before.

EG *We were late yet again.*

EG *I saw yet another doctor.*

CONJUNCTION

6 You use 'yet' to introduce a fact which is surprising.

EG *He isn't a smoker, yet he always carries a lighter.*

you /juː/

PRONOUN

1 'You' refers to the person or people that someone is speaking or writing to.

EG *When I saw you I knew I'd met you before.*

EG *You can all come along.*

☑ 'You' is used whether one person or many people are being spoken to, and in both formal and informal situations.

2 'You' refers to people in general.

EG *In those days you did what you were told.*

young /jʌŋ/
younger youngest

ADJECTIVE

1 A young person or animal has not lived very long and is not yet mature.

EG *You were quite young when she died.*

EG *… his younger brother*

PLURAL NOUN

2 The young of an animal are its babies.

EG *The hen may not be able to feed its young.*

your /jɔːr/

ADJECTIVE

1 You use 'yours' to refer to something that belongs or relates to the person or people that you are speaking or writing to.

EG *I put them on your desk.*

EG *I value your opinion.*

☑ 'Your' is used whether one person or many people are being spoken to.

2 'Your' indicates that something belongs or relates to people in general.

EG *Cigarettes can damage your health.*

yours /jɔːz/

PRONOUN

1 You use 'yours' to refer to something that belongs or relates to the person or people that you are speaking or writing to.

EG *His hair is longer than yours.*

EG *Is she a friend of yours?*

☑ 'Yours' is used whether one person or many people are being spoken to.

2 People write **Yours sincerely** or **Yours faithfully** at the end of a letter before they sign their name.

EG *Yours sincerely, Ray Peacock.*

EG *Yours faithfully, P. Garrett, University of Bangor.*

A
B
C
D
E
F
G
H
I
J
K
L
M
N
O
P
Q
R
S
T
U
V
W
X
Y
Z

yourself /jɔː'sɛlf/
yourselves

PRONOUN

1 You use 'yourself' to refer to the person that you are speaking or writing to.

EG *You need to be honest with yourself.*

EG *Help yourselves to food.*

2 You use 'yourself' to emphasize 'you'.

EG *You yourself once said the same thing.*

3 If you do something yourself, you do it without any help.

EG *Why can't you do it yourself?*

youth /juːθ/
youths

NOUN

1 Someone's youth is the period of their life before they are fully adult.

EG *In my youth I wanted to be a pilot.*

2 Youth is the quality or condition of being young.

EG *The team is a mixture of experience and youth.*

3 a young man

EG *... a gang of youths*

Zz

zero /'zɪərəu/
zeroes
1 the number 0
EG *He scored zero.*
EG *... one followed by twelve zeroes*

NOUN
2 Zero is freezing point, 0°
Centigrade.
EG *... thirty degrees below zero*

zip /zɪp/
zips zipping zipped

NOUN
1 a device for fastening clothes
and bags, with two rows of teeth
which separate or close as you pull
the zip up or down
EG *He pulled the zip of his jacket
down.*
☑ 'Zip' is used in British English.

The usual American word is
'zipper'.

VERB
2 When you zip something or **zip**
it **up**, you fasten it using a zip.
EG *He zipped up his jeans.*

zone /zəun/
zones

NOUN
an area that has particular features
or characteristics
EG *... a war zone*
EG *... different time zones*

zoo /zu:/
zoos

NOUN
a place where live animals are kept
so that people can look at them
EG *He took his son to the zoo.*

A
B
C
D
E
F
G
H
I
J
K
L
M
N
O
P
Q
R
S
T
U
V
W
X
Y
Z

1	one	first	1st
2	two	second	2nd
3	three	third	3rd
4	four	fourth	4th
5	five	fifth	5th
6	six	sixth	6th
7	seven	seventh	7th
8	eight	eighth	8th
9	nine	ninth	9th
10	ten	tenth	10th
11	eleven	eleventh	11th
12	twelve	twelfth	12th
13	thirteen	thirteenth	13th
14	fourteen	fourteenth	14th
15	fifteen	fifteenth	15th
16	sixteen	sixteenth	16th
17	seventeen	seventeenth	17th
18	eighteen	eighteenth	18th
19	nineteen	nineteenth	19th
20	twenty	twentieth	20th
21	twenty-one	twenty-first	21st
30	thirty	thirtieth	30th
40	forty	fortieth	40th
50	fifty	fiftieth	50th
60	sixty	sixtieth	60th
70	seventy	seventieth	70th
80	eighty	eightieth	80th
90	ninety	ninetieth	90th
100	hundred	hundredth	100th
101	hundred and one	hundred-and-first	101st
1,000	thousand	thousandth	1,000th
1,000,000	million	millionth	1,000,000th

EG *Turn to Chapter Seven*   *he lives on the fifth floor*
    a hundred pounds   *on his thirtieth birthday*
    on page two hundred and one   *the millionth copy to be sold*

PRESENT	PAST TENSE	PAST PARTICIPLE
be (am, is, are)	was, were	been
bear	bore	borne
beat	beat	beaten
become	became	become
begin	began	begun
bend	bent	bent
bet	bet	bet
bid	bid	bid
bind	bound	bound
bite	bit	bitten
bleed	bled	bled
blow	blew	blown
break	broke	broken
breed	bred	bred
bring	brought	brought
build	built	built
burn	burned, burnt	burned, burnt
burst	burst	burst
bust	bust, busted	bust, busted
buy	bought	bought
can	could	(been able)
cast	cast	cast
catch	caught	caught
choose	chose	chosen
cling	clung	clung
come	came	come
cost	cost	cost
creep	crept	crept
cut	cut	cut
deal	dealt	dealt
dig	dug	dug
do (does)	did	done
draw	drew	drawn

PRESENT	PAST TENSE	PAST PARTICIPLE
dream	dreamed, dreamt	dreamed, dreamt
drink	drank	drunk
drive	drove	driven
eat	ate	eaten
fail	fell	fallen
feed	fed	fed
feel	felt	felt
fight	fought	fought
find	found	found
fling	flung	flung
fly	flew	flown
forbid	forbade	forbidden
forecast	forecast, forecasted	forecast, forecasted
forget	forgot	forgotten
forgive	forgave	forgiven
freeze	froze	frozen
get	got	got (*US* gotten)
give	gave	given
go (goes)	went	gone
grind	ground	ground
grow	grew	grown
hang (= *suspend*)	hung	hung
hang (= *execute*)	hanged	hanged
have (has)	had	had
hear	heard	heard
hide	hid	hidden
hit	hit	hit
hold	held	held
hurt	hurt	hurt
keep	kept	kept
kneel	kneeled, knelt	kneeled, knelt
know	knew	known
lay	laid	laid

PRESENT	PAST TENSE	PAST PARTICIPLE
lead	led	led
lean	leant, leaned	leant, leaned
leap	leapt, leaped	leapt, leaped
learn	learnt, learned	learnt, learned
leave	left	left
lend	lent	lent
let	let	let
lie	lay	lain
light	lighted, lit	lighted, lit
lose	lost	lost
make	made	made
may	might	-
mean	meant	meant
meet	met	met
mistake	mistook	mistaken
must	(had to)	(had to)
overcome	overcame	overcome
overtake	overtook	overtaken
pay	paid	paid
put	put	put
quit	quit	quit
read	read	read
rid	rid	rid
ride	rode	ridden
ring	rang	rung
rise	rose	risen
run	ran	run
say	said	said
see	saw	seen
sell	sold	sold
send	sent	sent
set	set	set
sew	sewed	sewn

PRESENT	PAST TENSE	PAST PARTICIPLE
shake	shook	shaken
shine	shone	shone
shoot	shot	shot
show	showed	shown
shrink	shrank	shrunk
shut	shut	shut
sing	sang	sung
sink	sank	sunk
sit	sat	sat
sleep	slept	slept
slide	slid	slid
smell	smelled, smelt	smelled, smelt
speak	spoke	spoken
speed	sped, speeded	sped, speeded
spell	spelt, spelled	spelt, spelled
spend	spent	spent
spill	spilled, spilt	spilled, spilt
spin	spun, span	spun
spit	spat (*US spit*)	spat (*US spit*)
spoil	spoiled, spoilt	spoiled, spoilt
spread	spread	spread
spring	sprang	sprung
stand	stood	stood
steal	stole	stolen
stick	stuck	stuck
sting	stung	stung
strike	struck	struck
swear	swore	sworn
sweep	swept	swept
swell	swelled	swollen
swim	swam	swum
swing	swung	swung
take	took	taken

PRESENT	PAST TENSE	PAST PARTICIPLE
teach	taught	taught
tear	tore	torn
tell	told	told
think	thought	thought
throw	threw	thrown
thrust	thrust	thrust
tread	trod	trod
undergo (undergoes)	underwent	undergone
understand	understood	understood
undertake	undertook	undertaken
undo (undoes)	undid	undone
upset	upset	upset
wake	woke	woken
wear	wore	worn
win	won	won
wind	wound	wound
write	wrote	written